New International Reader's Version

Chris Tracy

David Greene

On:

May God give peace to all of you

HOLY BIBLE

NIrV

New International Reader's Version

New Testament

Zondervan Publishing House
Grand Rapids, Michigan

You will be pleased to know that a portion of the purchase price of your new NIrV Bible has been provided to International Bible Society to help spread the gospel of Jesus Christ around the world!

Contents

A WORD ABOUT THE NEW INTERNATIONAL READER'S VERSION

God has always spoken so people would know what he meant. When God first gave the Bible to his people, he used their languages. They could understand what they read. God wants us to understand the Bible today too. So we have worked hard to make the *New International Reader's Version* easy to read and understand.

What is the New International Reader's Version?

The *New International Reader's Version* (NIrV) is a new Bible version based on the *New International Version* (NIV). The NIV is easy to understand and very clear. More people read the NIV than any other English Bible. We made the NIrV even easier to read and understand. We used the words of the NIV when we could. Sometimes we used shorter words. We explained words that might be hard to understand. We made the sentences shorter.

We also did some other things to make the NIrV a helpful Bible version for you. For example, sometimes a Bible verse quotes from another place in the Bible. When that happens, we put the other Bible book's name, chapter and verse right there.

We separated each chapter into shorter sections. We gave a title to almost every chapter. Sometimes we even gave a title to the shorter sections. That will help you understand what each chapter or section is all about.

Is the NIrV an accurate Bible?

At the time the Bible was written, God's people used the Hebrew and Greek languages. So the first writers of the Bible used those languages. We wanted the NIrV to say just what the first writers of the Bible said. So we kept checking what the Hebrew and Greek said.

We used the best and oldest copies of the Hebrew and Greek. Some of the first English Bibles could not use those copies because they had not yet been found. But today we can check copies that are closer in time to the ones the first Bible writers wrote. We wanted to make sure we were giving you the actual Word of God.

There are two places in the NIrV where some verses are marked with long lines. We don't know whether the first writers of the Bible wrote those verses. They may have been added later on. You will find the long lines at Mark 16:9–20 and John 7:53—8:11.

What is our prayer for you?

The Lord has blessed the *New International Version* in a wonderful way. He has used it to help millions of its readers. Many have put their faith in Jesus after reading it. Many others have become stronger believers because they have read it.

We hope and pray that the *New International Reader's Version* will help you in the same way. If that happens, we will give God all of the glory.

Verses That Were Not Found in Earliest Greek New Testaments

Later copies of the Greek New Testament added several verses that the earlier ones don't have. An example is Mark 9:44. That verse is not in the oldest Greek New Testaments. So we put the number 43/44 right before Mark 9:43. The verse for Mark 9:44 is listed below.

Matthew 17:21	But that kind does not go out except by prayer and fasting.
Matthew 18:11	The Son of Man came to save what was lost.
Matthew 23:14	How terrible for you, teachers of the law and Pharisees! You pretenders! You take over the houses of widows. You say long prayers to show off. So God will punish you much more.
Mark 7:16	Everyone who has ears to hear should listen.
Mark 9:44	In hell, "'their worms do not die, and the fire does not go out.'
Mark 9:46	In hell, "'their worms do not die, and the fire does not go out.'

Mark 11:26	But if you do not forgive, your Father who is in heaven will not forgive your sins either.
Mark 15:28	Scripture came true. It says, "And he was counted among those who disobey the law."
Luke 17:36	Two men will be in the field. One will be taken and the other left.
Luke 23:17	It was Pilate's duty to let one prisoner go free for them at the Feast.
John 5:4	From time to time an angel of the Lord would come down. The angel would stir up the waters. The first disabled person to go into the pool after it was stirred would be healed.
Acts 8:37	Philip said, "If you believe with all your heart, you can." The official answered, "I believe that Jesus Christ is the Son of God."
Acts 15:34	But Silas decided to remain there.
Acts 24:7	But Lysias, the commander, came. By using a lot of force, he took Paul from our hands.
Acts 28:29	After he said that, the Jews left. They were arguing strongly among themselves.
Romans 16:24	May the grace of our Lord Jesus Christ be with all of you. Amen.

THE ABC'S OF SALVATION

A

All people are sinners.
Romans 3:23

Everyone has sinned. No one measures up to God's glory.

B

*The **Bible** is God's word of love and salvation.*
John 20:31

But these are written down so that you may believe that Jesus is the Christ, the Son of God. If you believe this, you will have life because you belong to him.

C

*The **condition** of sinners is serious.*
2 Thessalonians 2:12

Many will not believe the truth. They will take pleasure in evil. They will be judged.

D

*Christ **died** to save sinners.*
Romans 5:8

While we were still sinners, Christ died for us.

E

*Everyone who believes will have **eternal** life.*
John 3:16

Anyone who believes in [Jesus] will not die but will have eternal life.

F

*You are saved through **faith**.*
Romans 1:17

The good news shows how God makes people right with himself.

From beginning to end, becoming right with God depends on a person's faith.

G

***Good works** will not save you.*
Ephesians 2:8–9

God's grace has saved you because of your faith in Christ. Your salvation doesn't come from anything you do. It is God's gift. It is not based on anything you have done.

H

***Hell** and punishment are waiting for those who don't believe.*
2 Thessalonians 1:8–9

He will punish those who don't know God. He will punish those who don't obey the good news about our Lord Jesus. They will be destroyed forever. They will be shut out of heaven. They will never see the glory of the Lord's power.

I

*Nothing is **impossible** for God.*
Luke 1:37

Nothing is impossible with God.

J

*There is **joy** in heaven over one sinner who repents.*
Luke 15:10

There is joy in heaven over one sinner who turns away from sin.

K

*If you trust God, he will **keep** you from sin.*
Jude 24

Give praise to the One who is able to keep you from falling into sin.

L

*God **loves** sinners and wants to save them.*
John 3:16

God loved the world so much that he gave his one and only Son. Anyone who believes in him will not die but will have eternal life.

M

*God has **mercy** on unbelievers.*
Romans 11:32

God has found everyone guilty of not obeying him. So now he can have mercy on everyone.

N

*Jesus is the only **name** by which you can be saved.*
Acts 4:12

You can't be saved by believing in anyone else. God has given us no other name under heaven that will save us.

O

*You show God you love him by **obeying** his commandments.*
1 John 5:3

Here is what it means to love God. It means that we obey his commands. And his commands are not hard to obey.

P

*God is **patient** with unbelievers.*
2 Peter 3:9

The Lord is not slow to keep his promise. He is not slow in the way some people understand it. He is patient with you. He doesn't want anyone to be destroyed. Instead, he wants all people to turn away from their sins.

Q

*Those who don't believe should **quickly** decide to follow Jesus.*
2 Corinthians 6:2

I tell you, now is the time God shows his favor. Now is the day he saves.

R

*Christians have a reason to **rejoice**.*
Luke 10:20

Be glad that your names are written in heaven.

S

*The Bible, the **Scriptures**, can teach you how to be saved.*
2 Timothy 3:15

You have known the Holy Scriptures ever since you were a little child. They are able to teach you how to be saved by believing in Christ Jesus.

T

*You should give **thanks** to God for the wonderful gift of salvation.*
2 Corinthians 9:15

Let us give thanks to God for his gift. It is so great that no one can tell how wonderful it really is!

U

*The Holy Spirit helps us **understand** God's Word.*
1 Corinthians 2:12

We have not received the spirit of the world. We have received the Spirit who is from God. The Spirit helps us understand what God has freely given us.

V

*Jesus has gained **victory** over death for you.*
1 Corinthians 15:54

What does not last will be dressed with what lasts forever. What dies will be dressed with what does not die. Then what is written will come true. It says, "Death has been swallowed up. It has lost the battle."

W

***Whoever** calls on Jesus will be saved.*
Acts 2:21

Everyone who calls on the name of the Lord will be saved.

Y

*God loves **you** so much he calls you his child.*
1 John 3:1

How great is the love the Father has given us so freely! Now we can be called children of God. And that's what we really are!

5 Ways to Read the New Testament

Why should you read the New Testament?

An angel visits a young girl, a young couple and their baby escape an evil ruler, a man walks on water, disabled people walk again, blind people see, a man chooses to die for his people—all these exciting stories and more are in the New Testament. The New Testament also tells about Peter and Paul and how the church began. There are also letters in the New Testament that give directions on how to live as God's people. You'll find all this right within the pages of the book you are holding.

But the New Testament is more than just a collection of good stories. It is God's message of love to you. God wants you to answer his love letter by loving him back. As you spend time reading the New Testament, you will get to know God better. As you get to know him, you will see how much he loves and cares for you. And your love for him will grow.

How should you begin?

Set aside a time every day. Choose a time that is best for you, but make it the same every day, if you can. Choose a quiet and comfortable place.

As you begin, pray for the Holy Spirit to guide you. The Holy Spirit gave you the desire to read the New Testament. He will also help you understand it.

Don't worry if you don't understand everything you read the first time. You may have to read a passage several times before the meaning becomes clear. Look up words you don't know in the dictionary at the back of this Bible.

Also, you can write down what you learn from your reading in a small notebook. Looking back at what you've read will help you remember and grow. Suggestions are given with each reading plan for what you could write in your notebook.

Finally, have a plan. A plan will help you stay on track in your daily reading. Following are five ways to read the New Testament. They are in order from easiest to hardest, but you should choose the way that seems best for you. As you finish one way, try another. As you read you will see the New Testament from different points of view and your reading time will be exciting and interesting.

1 READ A STORY AT A TIME.

You can read the New Testament story by story. When you read a story from the New Testament, ask yourself these questions:

Who are the main people in the story?
What are the main things that happen in the story?
What is this story talking about?
What can I learn from this story?

Write down the name of the story and your answers to one or more of these questions in your notebook. Here are some stories from the New Testament to help you get started.

2 READ A SUBJECT AT A TIME.

You can read the New Testament subject by subject. After you read a passage, write down your thoughts in a notebook. If you want to know more about a subject, look it up in a Bible dictionary. Here are some subjects to help you get started.

3 READ ABOUT A PERSON AT A TIME.

You can read the New Testament by reading about and getting to know the people you'll find there. In your notebook, write down the name of the person and one thing you learned from him or her. Following is a list of some of the main people in the New Testament and where to find them.

You can find other characters to study in "Who's Who in the New Testament" on page 585 at the back of this Bible.

4 READ A BOOK AT A TIME.

Another way to read the New Testament is to read through one book at a time. Begin by reading the introduction to each book. Then read one section of the text at a time. Ask yourself these questions:

What are the main things that happen in the story?
What are the main words in the story?
What is this story talking about?
What can I learn from this Bible story?

In your notebook, write down what you have read and a sentence or two telling what you learned from reading it. Look up the meaning of hard words in the dictionary at the back of this Bible or in a regular dictionary. Use the list below to mark off each book as you complete it.

5 READ THE ENTIRE NEW TESTAMENT.

You can use the following plan to read through the entire New Testament in one year. Be sure to write down in your notebook all your thoughts and the things that you learn as you read.

JANUARY

DAY	READ
☐ 1	Matthew 1
☐ 2	Matthew 2
☐ 3	Matthew 3
☐ 4	Matthew 4
☐ 5	Matthew 5
☐ 6	Matthew 6
☐ 7	Matthew 7
☐ 8	Matthew 8
☐ 9	Matthew 9
☐ 10	Matthew 10
☐ 11	Matthew 11
☐ 12	Matthew 12
☐ 13	Matthew 13:1–52
☐ 14	Matthew 13:53—14:36
☐ 15	Matthew 15
☐ 16	Matthew 16
☐ 17	Matthew 17
☐ 18	Matthew 18
☐ 19	Matthew 19:1—20:16
☐ 20	Matthew 20:17—21:17
☐ 21	Matthew 21:18–46
☐ 22	Matthew 22:1–40
☐ 23	Matthew 22:41—23:38
☐ 24	Matthew 24:1–44
☐ 25	Matthew 24:45—25:30
☐ 26	Matthew 25:31—26:16
☐ 27	Matthew 26:17–56
☐ 28	Matthew 26:57–75
☐ 29	Matthew 27:1–31
☐ 30	Matthew 27:32–66
☐ 31	Matthew 28

FEBRUARY

DAY	READ
☐ 1	Mark 1:1–20
☐ 2	Mark 1:21–45
☐ 3	Mark 2
☐ 4	Mark 3:1–19
☐ 5	Mark 3:20–35
☐ 6	Mark 4:1–34
☐ 7	Mark 4:35—5:20
☐ 8	Mark 5:21–43
☐ 9	Mark 6:1–13
☐ 10	Mark 6:14–29
☐ 11	Mark 6:30–56
☐ 12	Mark 7:1–23
☐ 13	Mark 7:24–37
☐ 14	Mark 8:1–21
☐ 15	Mark 8:22—9:13
☐ 16	Mark 9:14–50
☐ 17	Mark 10:1–31
☐ 18	Mark 10:32–52
☐ 19	Mark 11:1–19
☐ 20	Mark 11:20—12:12
☐ 21	Mark 12:13–44
☐ 22	Mark 13
☐ 23	Mark 14:1–26
☐ 24	Mark 14:27–52
☐ 25	Mark 14:53–72
☐ 26	Mark 15:1–20
☐ 27	Mark 15:21–47
☐ 28	Mark 16

MARCH

DAY	READ
☐ 1	Luke 1:1–38
☐ 2	Luke 1:39–56
☐ 3	Luke 1:57–80
☐ 4	Luke 2
☐ 5	Luke 3
☐ 6	Luke 4
☐ 7	Luke 5

☐ **8**   Luke 6:1–16

☐ **9**   Luke 6:17–49

☐ **10**   Luke 7:1–35

☐ **11**   Luke 7:36–50

☐ **12**   Luke 8

☐ **13**   Luke 9:1–36

☐ **14**   Luke 9:37–62

☐ **15**   Luke 10

☐ **16**   Luke 11

☐ **17**   Luke 12

☐ **18**   Luke 13

☐ **19**   Luke 14

☐ **20**   Luke 15

☐ **21**   Luke 16

☐ **22**   Luke 17

☐ **23**   Luke 18

☐ **24**   Luke 19

☐ **25**   Luke 20

☐ **26**   Luke 21:1–36

☐ **27**   Luke 21:37—22:23

☐ **28**   Luke 22:24–53

☐ **29**   Luke 22:54—23:25

☐ **30**   Luke 23:26–56

☐ **31**   Luke 24

APRIL

DAY   READ

☐ **1**   John 1:1–28

☐ **2**   John 1:29–51

☐ **3**   John 2

☐ **4**   John 3

☐ **5**   John 4:1–42

☐ **6**   John 4:43–54

☐ **7**   John 5

☐ **8**   John 6:1–21

☐ **9**   John 6:22–65

☐ **10**   John 6:66—7:13

☐ **11**   John 7:14–44

☐ **12**   John 7:45—8:11

☐ **13**   John 8:12–30

☐ **14**   John 8:31–59

☐ **15**   John 9

☐ **16**   John 10:1–21

☐ **17**   John 10:22–42

☐ **18**   John 11

☐ **19**   John 12:1–36

☐ **20**   John 12:37–50

☐ **21**   John 13:1–30

☐ **22**   John 13:31—14:31

☐ **23**   John 15

☐ **24**   John 16

☐ **25**   John 17

☐ **26**   John 18

☐ **27**   John 19:1–27

☐ **28**   John 19:28–42

☐ **29**   John 20

☐ **30**   John 21

MAY

DAY   READ

☐ **1**   Acts 1

☐ **2**   Acts 2

☐ **3**   Acts 3:1—4:4

☐ **4**   Acts 4:5–37

☐ **5**   Acts 5:1–11

☐ **6**   Acts 5:12—6:7

☐ **7**   Acts 6:8—7:60

☐ **8**   Acts 8

☐ **9**   Acts 9

☐ **10**   Acts 10

☐ **11**   Acts 11

☐ **12**   Acts 12

☐ **13**   Acts 13

☐ **14**   Acts 14

☐ **15**   Acts 15:1–21

☐ **16**   Acts 15:22–41

☐ **17**   Acts 16:1–15

☐ **18**   Acts 16:16–40

☐ **19**   Acts 17

☐ **20**   Acts 18

☐ **21**   Acts 19:1–22

☐ **22**   Acts 19:23–41

☐ **23**   Acts 20

☐ **24**   Acts 21:1–36

- ☐ **25** Acts 21:37—22:29
- ☐ **26** Acts 22:30—23:35
- ☐ **27** Acts 24
- ☐ **28** Acts 25:1–22
- ☐ **29** Acts 25:23—26:32
- ☐ **30** Acts 27
- ☐ **31** Acts 28

JUNE

DAY	READ
☐ **1**	Romans 1:1–17
☐ **2**	Romans 1:18–32
☐ **3**	Romans 2:1–16
☐ **4**	Romans 2:17–29
☐ **5**	Romans 3:1–20
☐ **6**	Romans 3:21–31
☐ **7**	Romans 4:1–12
☐ **8**	Romans 4:13–25
☐ **9**	Romans 5:1–11
☐ **10**	Romans 5:12–21
☐ **11**	Romans 6:1–14
☐ **12**	Romans 6:15–23
☐ **13**	Romans 7:1–6
☐ **14**	Romans 7:7–25
☐ **15**	Romans 8:1–17
☐ **16**	Romans 8:18–39
☐ **17**	Romans 9:1–29
☐ **18**	Romans 9:30—10:21
☐ **19**	Romans 11:1–10
☐ **20**	Romans 11:11–24
☐ **21**	Romans 11:25–36
☐ **22**	Romans 12:1–8
☐ **23**	Romans 12:9–21
☐ **24**	Romans 13:1–7
☐ **25**	Romans 13:8–14
☐ **26**	Romans 14:1–12
☐ **27**	Romans 14:13–23
☐ **28**	Romans 15:1–13
☐ **29**	Romans 15:14–33
☐ **30**	Romans 16

JULY

DAY	READ
☐ **1**	1 Corinthians 1:1—2:5
☐ **2**	1 Corinthians 2:5–16
☐ **3**	1 Corinthians 3
☐ **4**	1 Corinthians 4
☐ **5**	1 Corinthians 5
☐ **6**	1 Corinthians 6
☐ **7**	1 Corinthians 7
☐ **8**	1 Corinthians 8
☐ **9**	1 Corinthians 9
☐ **10**	1 Corinthians 10:1—11:1
☐ **11**	1 Corinthians 11:2–34
☐ **12**	1 Corinthians 12:1–31
☐ **13**	1 Corinthians 13:1–13
☐ **14**	1 Corinthians 14:1–25
☐ **15**	1 Corinthians 14:26–40
☐ **16**	1 Corinthians 15:1–34
☐ **17**	1 Corinthians 15:35–58
☐ **18**	1 Corinthians 16
☐ **19**	2 Corinthians 1:1—2:11
☐ **20**	2 Corinthians 2:12—3:18
☐ **21**	2 Corinthians 4
☐ **22**	2 Corinthians 5:1–10
☐ **23**	2 Corinthians 5:11—6:2
☐ **24**	2 Corinthians 6:3—7:1
☐ **25**	2 Corinthians 7:2–16
☐ **26**	2 Corinthians 8:1–15
☐ **27**	2 Corinthians 8:16—9:15
☐ **28**	2 Corinthians 10
☐ **29**	2 Corinthians 11:1–15
☐ **30**	2 Corinthians 11:16—12:10
☐ **31**	2 Corinthians 12:11—13:14

AUGUST

DAY	READ
☐ **1**	Galatians 1
☐ **2**	Galatians 2
☐ **3**	Galatians 3:1–14
☐ **4**	Galatians 3:15–25
☐ **5**	Galatians 3:26—4:20
☐ **6**	Galatians 4:21—5:15

SEPTEMBER

OCTOBER

- ☐ **24** James 2:1–13
- ☐ **25** James 2:14–26
- ☐ **26** James 3:1–12
- ☐ **27** James 3:13—4:3
- ☐ **28** James 4:4–12
- ☐ **29** James 4:13—5:6
- ☐ **30** James 5:7–12
- ☐ **31** James 5:13–20

NOVEMBER

DAY   READ

- ☐ **1** 1 Peter 1:1–12
- ☐ **2** 1 Peter 1:13—2:3
- ☐ **3** 1 Peter 2:4–12
- ☐ **4** 1 Peter 2:13–25
- ☐ **5** 1 Peter 3:1–7
- ☐ **6** 1 Peter 3:8–22
- ☐ **7** 1 Peter 4:1–11
- ☐ **8** 1 Peter 4:12–19
- ☐ **9** 1 Peter 5
- ☐ **10** 2 Peter 1:1–11
- ☐ **11** 2 Peter 1:12–21
- ☐ **12** 2 Peter 2:1–9
- ☐ **13** 2 Peter 2:10–22
- ☐ **14** 2 Peter 3:1–9
- ☐ **15** 2 Peter 3:10–18
- ☐ **16** 1 John 1:1–4
- ☐ **17** 1 John 1:5—2:2
- ☐ **18** 1 John 2:3–11
- ☐ **19** 1 John 2:12–17
- ☐ **20** 1 John 2:18–27
- ☐ **21** 1 John 2:28—3:10
- ☐ **22** 1 John 3:11–24
- ☐ **23** 1 John 4:1–6
- ☐ **24** 1 John 4:7–21
- ☐ **25** 1 John 5:1–12
- ☐ **26** 1 John 5:13–21
- ☐ **27** 2 John

- ☐ **28** 3 John
- ☐ **29** Jude 1–16
- ☐ **30** Jude 17–25

DECEMBER

DAY   READ

- ☐ **1** Revelation 1:1–8
- ☐ **2** Revelation 1:9–20
- ☐ **3** Revelation 2:1–11
- ☐ **4** Revelation 2:12–29
- ☐ **5** Revelation 3:1–6
- ☐ **6** Revelation 3:7–13
- ☐ **7** Revelation 3:14–22
- ☐ **8** Revelation 4
- ☐ **9** Revelation 5
- ☐ **10** Revelation 6
- ☐ **11** Revelation 7
- ☐ **12** Revelation 8
- ☐ **13** Revelation 9
- ☐ **14** Revelation 10
- ☐ **15** Revelation 11:1–14
- ☐ **16** Revelation 11:15–19
- ☐ **17** Revelation 12:1–17
- ☐ **18** Revelation 13:1–10
- ☐ **19** Revelation 13:11–18
- ☐ **20** Revelation 14
- ☐ **21** Revelation 15
- ☐ **22** Revelation 16
- ☐ **23** Revelation 17
- ☐ **24** Revelation 18
- ☐ **25** Revelation 19:1–10
- ☐ **26** Revelation 19:11–21
- ☐ **27** Revelation 20:1–6
- ☐ **28** Revelation 20:7–15
- ☐ **29** Revelation 21:1–8
- ☐ **30** Revelation 21:9–27
- ☐ **31** Revelation 22

THE NEW TESTAMENT

Matthew

Why Was This Book Written? Matthew is one of the Gospels. *Gospel* means good news. Matthew tells us good news. Jesus loves us and died for our sins. Matthew was one of Jesus' twelve disciples. He wrote this book before Jerusalem was destroyed.

What Is This Book About? There are four Gospels—Matthew, Mark, Luke and John. Early Christians thought Matthew was the most important Gospel. Each writer tells us something different. Matthew wrote to the Jews. He taught that Jesus is the Messiah. He quoted many Old Testament verses. He said they came true in Jesus' life. He wrote down Jesus' words about heaven too.

What Is in This Book?

The Family Line of Jesus

1 This is a record of the family line of Jesus Christ. He is the son of David. He is also the son of Abraham.

2 Abraham was the father of Isaac.
Isaac was the father of Jacob.
Jacob was the father of Judah and his brothers.
3 Judah was the father of Perez and Zerah. Tamar was their mother.
Perez was the father of Hezron.
Hezron was the father of Ram.
4 Ram was the father of Amminadab.
Amminadab was the father of Nahshon.
Nahshon was the father of Salmon.
5 Salmon was the father of Boaz. Rahab was Boaz's mother.
Boaz was the father of Obed. Ruth was Obed's mother.
Obed was the father of Jesse.
6 And Jesse was the father of King David.

David was the father of Solomon. Solomon's mother had been Uriah's wife.
7 Solomon was the father of Rehoboam.
Rehoboam was the father of Abijah.
Abijah was the father of Asa.
8 Asa was the father of Jehoshaphat.
Jehoshaphat was the father of Jehoram.
Jehoram was the father of Uzziah.
9 Uzziah was the father of Jotham.
Jotham was the father of Ahaz.
Ahaz was the father of Hezekiah.
10 Hezekiah was the father of Manasseh.
Manasseh was the father of Amon.
Amon was the father of Josiah.
11 And Josiah was the father of Jeconiah and his brothers. At that time, the Jewish people were forced to go away to Babylon.

12 After this, the family line continued.
Jeconiah was the father of Shealtiel.
Shealtiel was the father of Zerubbabel.
13 Zerubbabel was the father of Abiud.
Abiud was the father of Eliakim.
Eliakim was the father of Azor.
14 Azor was the father of Zadok.

Zadok was the father of Akim.
Akim was the father of Eliud.
[15] Eliud was the father of Eleazar.
Eleazar was the father of Matthan.
Matthan was the father of Jacob.
[16] Jacob was the father of Joseph. Joseph was the husband of Mary. And Mary gave birth to Jesus, who is called Christ.

[17] So there were 14 generations from Abraham to David. There were 14 from David until the Jewish people were forced to go away to Babylon. And there were 14 from that time to the Christ.

Jesus Christ Is Born

[18] This is how the birth of Jesus Christ came about. His mother Mary and Joseph had promised to get married. But before they started to live together, it became clear that she was going to have a baby. She became pregnant by the power of the Holy Spirit. [19] Her husband Joseph was a godly man. He did not want to put her to shame in public. So he planned to divorce her quietly.

[20] But as Joseph was thinking about this, an angel of the Lord appeared to him in a dream. The angel said, "Joseph, son of David, don't be afraid to take Mary home as your wife. The baby inside her is from the Holy Spirit. [21] She is going to have a son. You must give him the name Jesus. That is because he will save his people from their sins."

[22] All of this took place to bring about what the Lord had said would happen. He had said through the prophet, [23] "The virgin is going to have a baby. She will give birth to a son. And they will call him Immanuel." *(Isaiah 7:14)* The name Immanuel means "God with us."

[24] Joseph woke up. He did what the angel of the Lord commanded him to do. He took Mary home as his wife. [25] But he did not have sex with her until after she gave birth to a son. And Joseph gave him the name Jesus.

GREAT VERSE — TO — REMEMBER **1:23** They will call him Immanuel.

The Wise Men Visit Jesus

2 Jesus was born in Bethlehem in Judea. This happened while Herod was king of Judea.

After Jesus' birth, Wise Men from the east came to Jerusalem. [2]They asked, "Where is the child who has been born to be king of the Jews? When we were in the east, we saw his star. Now we have come to worship him."

[3]When King Herod heard about it, he was very upset. Everyone in Jerusalem was troubled too. [4]So Herod called together all the chief priests of the people. He also called the teachers of the law. He asked them where the Christ was going to be born.

[5]"In Bethlehem in Judea," they replied. "This is what the prophet has written. He said,

[6]"'But you, Bethlehem, in the land of Judah,
    are certainly not the least important among the
        rulers of Judah.
A ruler will come from you.
    He will be the shepherd of my people Israel.'"   *(Micah 5:2)*

[7]Then Herod called for the Wise Men secretly. He found out from them exactly when the star had appeared. [8]He sent them to Bethlehem. He said, "Go! Make a careful search for the child. As soon as you find him, bring me a report. Then I can go and worship him too."

[9]After the Wise Men had listened to the king, they went on their way. The star they had seen when they were in the east went ahead of them. It finally stopped over the place where the child was. [10]When they saw the star, they were filled with joy.

[11]The Wise Men went to the house. There they saw the child with his mother Mary. They bowed down and worshiped him. Then they opened their treasures. They gave him gold, incense and myrrh.

[12]But they were warned in a dream not to go back to Herod. So they returned to their country on a different road.

Jesus' Family Escapes to Egypt

[13]When the Wise Men had left, Joseph had a dream. In the dream an angel of the Lord appeared to him. "Get up!" the angel said. "Take the child and his mother and escape to Egypt. Stay there until I tell you to come back. Herod is going to search for the child. He wants to kill him."

¹⁴Joseph got up. During the night, he left for Egypt with the child and his mother Mary. ¹⁵They stayed there until King Herod died. So the words the Lord had spoken through the prophet came true. He had said, "Out of Egypt I called my son." *(Hosea 11:1)*

¹⁶Herod realized that the Wise Men had tricked him. So he became very angry. He gave orders concerning Bethlehem and the area around it. All the boys two years old and under were to be killed. This agreed with the time when the Wise Men had seen the star.

¹⁷In this way, the words the prophet Jeremiah spoke came true. He had said,

¹⁸ "A voice is heard in Ramah.
   It is the sound of crying and deep sadness.
   Rachel is crying over her children.
   She refuses to be comforted,
because they are gone." *(Jeremiah 31:15)*

Jesus' Family Returns to Nazareth

¹⁹After Herod died, Joseph had a dream while he was still in Egypt. In the dream an angel of the Lord appeared to him. ²⁰The angel said, "Get up! Take the child and his mother. Go to the land of Israel. Those who were trying to kill the child are dead."

²¹So Joseph got up. He took the child and his mother Mary back to the land of Israel. ²²But then he heard that Archelaus was king of Judea. Archelaus was ruling in place of his father Herod. This made Joseph afraid to go there.

Warned in a dream, Joseph went back to the land of Galilee instead. ²³There he lived in a town called Nazareth. So what the prophets had said about Jesus came true. They had said, "He will be called a Nazarene."

John the Baptist Prepares the Way

3 In those days John the Baptist came and preached in the Desert of Judea. ²He said, "Turn away from your sins! The kingdom of heaven is near."

³John is the one the prophet Isaiah had spoken about. He had said,

"A voice calls out in the desert,
'Prepare the way for the Lord.
   Make straight paths for him.'" *(Isaiah 40:3)*

⁴John's clothes were made out of camel's hair. He had a leather

belt around his waist. His food was locusts and wild honey.
⁵People went out to him from Jerusalem and all of Judea. They
also came from the whole area around the Jordan River. ⁶When
they admitted they had sinned, John baptized them in the Jordan.

⁷John saw many Pharisees and Sadducees coming to where he
was baptizing. He said to them, "You nest of poisonous snakes!
Who warned you to escape the coming of God's anger? ⁸Produce
fruit that shows you have turned away from your sins. ⁹Don't
think you can say to yourselves, 'Abraham is our father.' I tell
you, God can raise up children for Abraham even from these
stones. ¹⁰The ax is already lying at the roots of the trees. All the
trees that don't produce good fruit will be cut down. They will be
thrown into the fire.

¹¹"I baptize you with water, calling you to turn away from your
sins. But after me, one will come who is more powerful than I
am. And I'm not fit to carry his sandals. He will baptize you with
the Holy Spirit and with fire. ¹²His pitchfork is in his hand to clear
the straw from his threshing floor. He will gather his wheat into
the storeroom. But he will burn up the husks with fire that can't
be put out."

Jesus Is Baptized

¹³Jesus came from Galilee to the Jordan River. He wanted to be
baptized by John. ¹⁴But John tried to stop him. He told Jesus, "I
need to be baptized by you. So why do you come to me?"

¹⁵Jesus replied, "Let it be this way for now. It is right for us to
do this. It carries out God's holy plan." Then John agreed.

¹⁶As soon as Jesus was baptized, he came up out of the water. At
that moment heaven was opened. Jesus saw the Spirit of God
coming down on him like a dove.

¹⁷A voice from heaven said, "This is my Son, and I love him. I
am very pleased with him."

Jesus Is Tempted

4 The Holy Spirit led Jesus into the desert. There the devil
tempted him. ²After 40 days and 40 nights of going without
eating, Jesus was hungry.

3:17 This is my Son, and I love
him. I am very pleased with him.

³The tempter came to him. He said, "If you are the Son of God, tell these stones to become bread."

⁴Jesus answered, "It is written: 'People don't live only on bread. They live on every word that comes from the mouth of God.'" *(Deuteronomy 8:3)*

⁵Then the devil took Jesus to the holy city. He had him stand on the highest point of the temple. ⁶"If you are the Son of God," he said, "throw yourself down. It is written:

"'The Lord will command his angels to take good care
of you.
They will lift you up in their hands.
Then you won't trip over a stone.'" *(Psalm 91:11,12)*

⁷Jesus answered him, "It is also written: 'Do not put the Lord your God to the test.'" *(Deuteronomy 6:16)*

⁸Finally, the devil took Jesus to a very high mountain. He showed him all the kingdoms of the world and their glory. ⁹"If you bow down and worship me," he said, "I will give you all of this."

¹⁰Jesus said to him, "Get away from me, Satan! It is written: 'Worship the Lord your God. Serve only him.'" *(Deuteronomy 6:13)*

¹¹Then the devil left Jesus. Angels came and took care of him.

Jesus Begins to Preach

¹²John had been put in prison. When Jesus heard about this, he returned to Galilee.

¹³Jesus left Nazareth. He went to live in the city of Capernaum. It was by the lake in the area of Zebulun and Naphtali. ¹⁴In that way, what the prophet Isaiah had said came true. He had said,

¹⁵"Land of Zebulun! Land of Naphtali!
Galilee, where non-Jewish people live,
by the way of the sea, along the Jordan River!
¹⁶The people who live in darkness
have seen a great light.
They live in the land of the shadow of death.
But on them a light now shines." *(Isaiah 9:1,2)*

¹⁷From that time on Jesus began to preach. "Turn away from your sins!" he said. "The kingdom of heaven is near."

Jesus Chooses the First Disciples

¹⁸One day Jesus was walking beside the Sea of Galilee. There he

saw two brothers. They were Simon Peter and his brother
Andrew. They were throwing a net into the lake. They were fishermen. ¹⁹"Come. Follow me," Jesus said. "I will make you fishers
of people."
²⁰At once they left their nets and followed him.
²¹Going on from there, he saw two other brothers. They were
James, son of Zebedee, and his brother John. They were in a boat
with their father Zebedee. As they were preparing their nets, Jesus
called out to them.
²²Right away they left the boat and their father and followed
Jesus.

Jesus Heals Sick People

²³Jesus went all over Galilee. There he taught in the synagogues.
He preached the good news of God's kingdom. He healed every
illness and sickness the people had.
²⁴News about him spread all over Syria. People brought to him
all who were ill with different kinds of sicknesses. Some were suffering great pain. Others were controlled by demons. Some were
shaking wildly. Others couldn't move at all. And Jesus healed all
of them.
²⁵Large crowds followed him. Some people came from Galilee,
from the area known as the Ten Cities, and from Jerusalem and
Judea. Others came from the area across the Jordan River.

Jesus Gives Blessings

5 Jesus saw the crowds. So he went up on a mountainside and
sat down. His disciples came to him. ²Then he began to teach
them.
He said,

> ³ "Blessed are those who are spiritually needy.
>   The kingdom of heaven belongs to them.
> ⁴ Blessed are those who are sad.
>   They will be comforted.
> ⁵ Blessed are those who are free of pride.
>   They will be given the earth.
> ⁶ Blessed are those who are hungry and thirsty
>   for what is right.
>   They will be filled.
> ⁷ Blessed are those who show mercy.
>   They will be shown mercy.

[8]Blessed are those whose hearts are pure.
    They will see God.
[9]Blessed are those who make peace.
    They will be called children of God.
[10]Blessed are those who suffer for doing what
      is right.
    The kingdom of heaven belongs to them.

[11]"Blessed are you when people make fun of you and hurt you because of me. You are also blessed when they tell all kinds of evil lies about you because of me. [12]Be joyful and glad. Your reward in heaven is great. In the same way, people hurt the prophets who lived long ago.

Salt and Light

[13]"You are the salt of the earth. But suppose the salt loses its saltiness. How can it be made salty again? It is no longer good for anything. It will be thrown out. People will walk all over it.

[14]"You are the light of the world. A city on a hill can't be hidden. [15]Also, people do not light a lamp and put it under a bowl. Instead, they put it on its stand. Then it gives light to everyone in the house.

[16]"In the same way, let your light shine in front of others. Then they will see the good things you do. And they will praise your Father who is in heaven.

Jesus Gives Full Meaning to the Law

[17]"Do not think I have come to get rid of what is written in the Law or in the Prophets. I have not come to do that. Instead, I have come to give full meaning to what is written. [18]What I'm about to tell you is true. Heaven and earth will disappear before the smallest letter disappears from the Law. Not even the small-

GREAT VERSE — TO — REMEMBER

5:14-15 You are the light of the world ... people do not light a lamp and put it under a bowl. Instead, they put it on its stand. Then it gives light to everyone in the house.

est stroke of a pen will disappear from the Law until everything is completed.

[19]"Do not break even one of the least important commandments. And do not teach others to break them. If you do, you will be called the least important person in the kingdom of heaven. Instead, practice and teach these commands. Then you will be called important in the kingdom of heaven.

[20]"Here is what I tell you. You must be more godly than the Pharisees and the teachers of the law. If you are not, you will certainly not enter the kingdom of heaven.

Murder

[21]"You have heard what was said to people who lived long ago. They were told, 'Do not commit murder. *(Exodus 20:13)* Anyone who murders will be judged for it.' [22]But here is what I tell you. Do not be angry with your brother or sister. Anyone who is angry with a brother or sister will be judged. Again, anyone who says to a brother or sister, 'Raca,' must stand trial in the Sanhedrin. But anyone who says, 'You fool!' will be in danger of the fire in hell.

[23]"Suppose you are offering your gift at the altar. And suppose you remember that your brother or sister has something against you. [24]Leave your gift in front of the altar. First go and make peace with your brother or sister. Then come back and offer your gift.

[25]"Suppose someone has a claim against you and is taking you to court. Settle the matter quickly. Do it while you are both still together on your way. If you don't, you may be handed over to the judge. The judge may hand you over to the officer. And you may be thrown into prison. [26]What I'm about to tell you is true. You will not get out until you have paid the very last penny!

Adultery

[27]"You have heard that it was said, 'Do not commit adultery.' *(Exodus 20:14)* [28]But here is what I tell you. Do not even look at a woman in the wrong way. Anyone who does has already committed adultery with her in his heart.

[29]"If your right eye causes you to sin, dig it out and throw it away. Your eye is only one part of your body. It is better to lose it than for your whole body to be thrown into hell.

[30]"If your right hand causes you to sin, cut it off and throw it away. Your hand is only one part of your body. It is better to lose it than for your whole body to go into hell.

Divorce

[31]"It has been said, 'Suppose a man divorces his wife. If he does, he must give her a letter of divorce.' *(Deuteronomy 24:1)* [32]But here is what I tell you. Anyone who divorces his wife causes her to commit adultery. And anyone who gets married to the divorced woman commits adultery. A man may divorce his wife only if she has not been faithful to him.

Oaths

[33]"Again, you have heard what was said to your people long ago. They were told, 'Do not break the promises you make to the Lord. Keep the oaths you have made to him.' [34]But here is what I tell you. Do not make any promises like that at all. Do not make them in the name of heaven. That is God's throne. [35]Do not make them in the name of the earth. That is the stool for God's feet. Do not make them in the name of Jerusalem. That is the city of the Great King. [36]And do not take an oath in the name of your head. You can't make even one hair white or black.

[37]"Just let your 'Yes' mean 'Yes.' Let your 'No' mean 'No.' Anything more than this comes from the evil one.

Be Kind to Others

[38]"You have heard that it was said, 'An eye must be put out for an eye. A tooth must be knocked out for a tooth.' *(Exodus 21:24; Leviticus 24:20; Deuteronomy 19:21)* [39]But here is what I tell you. Do not fight against an evil person.

"Suppose someone hits you on your right cheek. Turn your other cheek also. [40]Suppose someone takes you to court to get your shirt. Give up your coat also. [41]Suppose someone forces you to go one mile. Go two miles.

[42]"Give to the one who asks you for something. Don't turn away from the one who wants to borrow something from you.

Love Your Enemies

[43]"You have heard that it was said, 'Love your neighbor. *(Leviticus 19:18)* Hate your enemy.' [44]But here is what I tell you. Love your

GREAT VERSE —TO— REMEMBER   **5:44** Love your enemies. Pray for those who hurt you.

enemies. Pray for those who hurt you. ⁴⁵Then you will be children of your Father who is in heaven.

"He causes his sun to shine on evil people and good people. He sends rain on those who do right and those who don't.

⁴⁶"If you love those who love you, what reward will you get? Even the tax collectors do that. ⁴⁷If you greet only your own people, what more are you doing than others? Even people who are ungodly do that. ⁴⁸So be perfect, just as your Father in heaven is perfect.

Giving to Needy People

6 "Be careful not to do 'good works' in front of others. Don't do them to be seen by others. If you do, your Father in heaven will not reward you.

²"When you give to needy people, do not announce it by having trumpets blown. Do not be like those who only pretend to be holy. They announce what they do in the synagogues and on the streets. They want to be honored by others. What I'm about to tell you is true. They have received their complete reward.

³"When you give to the needy, don't let your left hand know what your right hand is doing. ⁴Then your giving will be done secretly. Your Father will reward you. He sees what you do secretly.

Prayer

⁵"When you pray, do not be like those who only pretend to be holy. They love to stand and pray in the synagogues and on the street corners. They want to be seen by others. What I'm about to tell you is true. They have received their complete reward.

⁶"When you pray, go into your room. Close the door and pray to your Father, who can't be seen. He will reward you. Your Father sees what is done secretly.

⁷"When you pray, do not keep talking on and on the way ungodly people do. They think they will be heard because they talk a lot. ⁸Do not be like them. Your Father knows what you need even before you ask him.

⁹"This is how you should pray.

"'Our Father in heaven,
    may your name be honored.
¹⁰May your kingdom come.
    May what you want to happen be done
        on earth as it is done in heaven.

¹¹Give us today our daily bread.
¹²Forgive us our sins,
  just as we also have forgiven those who sin
    against us.
¹³Keep us from falling into sin when we are
    tempted.
  Save us from the evil one.'

¹⁴"Forgive people when they sin against you. If you do, your Father who is in heaven will also forgive you. ¹⁵But if you do not forgive people their sins, your Father will not forgive your sins.

Fasting

¹⁶"When you go without eating, do not look gloomy like those who only pretend to be holy. They make their faces very sad. They want to show people they are fasting. What I'm about to tell you is true. They have received their complete reward. ¹⁷"But when you go without eating, put olive oil on your head. Wash your face. ¹⁸Then others will not know that you are fasting. Only your Father, who can't be seen, will know it. He will reward you. Your Father sees what is done secretly.

Put Away Riches in Heaven

¹⁹"Do not put away riches for yourselves on earth. Moths and rust can destroy them. Thieves can break in and steal them. ²⁰Instead, put away riches for yourselves in heaven. There, moths and rust do not destroy them. There, thieves do not break in and steal them. ²¹Your heart will be where your riches are.

²²"The eye is like a lamp for the body. Suppose your eyes are good. Then your whole body will be full of light. ²³But suppose your eyes are bad. Then your whole body will be full of darkness. If the light inside you is darkness, then it is very dark!

²⁴"You can't serve two masters at the same time. You will hate one of them and love the other. Or you will be faithful to one and dislike the other. You can't serve God and Money at the same time.

Do Not Worry

²⁵"I tell you, do not worry. Don't worry about your life and what you will eat or drink. And don't worry about your body and what you will wear. Isn't there more to life than eating? Aren't there more important things for the body than clothes?

²⁶"Look at the birds of the air. They don't plant or gather crops. They don't put away crops in storerooms. But your Father who is in heaven feeds them. Aren't you worth much more than they are?

²⁷"Can you add even one hour to your life by worrying?

²⁸"And why do you worry about clothes? See how the wild flowers grow. They don't work or make clothing. ²⁹But here is what I tell you. Not even Solomon in all of his glory was dressed like one of these.

³⁰"If that is how God dresses the wild grass, won't he dress you even better? After all, the grass is here only today. Tomorrow it is thrown into the fire. Your faith is so small!

³¹"So don't worry. Don't say, 'What will we eat?' Or, 'What will we drink?' Or, 'What will we wear?' ³²People who are ungodly run after all of those things. Your Father who is in heaven knows that you need them.

³³"But seek God's kingdom first of all. Do what he wants you to do. Then all of those things will also be given to you.

³⁴"So don't worry about tomorrow. Tomorrow will worry about itself. Each day has enough trouble of its own.

Be Fair When You Judge Others

7 "Do not judge others. Then you will not be judged. ²You will be judged in the same way you judge others. You will be measured in the same way you measure others.

³"You look at the bit of sawdust in your friend's eye. But you pay no attention to the piece of wood in your own eye. ⁴How can you say to your friend, 'Let me take the bit of sawdust out of your eye'? How can you say this while there is a piece of wood in your own eye?

⁵"You pretender! First take the piece of wood out of your own eye. Then you will be able to see clearly to take the bit of sawdust out of your friend's eye.

⁶"Do not give holy things to dogs. Do not throw your pearls to

6:33 But seek God's kingdom first of all. Do what he wants you to do. Then all of those things will also be given to you.

pigs. If you do, they might walk all over them. Then they might turn around and tear you to pieces.

Ask, Search, Knock

[7]"Ask, and it will be given to you. Search, and you will find. Knock, and the door will be opened to you. [8]All who ask will receive. All who search will find. The door will be opened to all who knock.

[9]"Suppose your children ask for bread. Which of you will give them a stone? [10]Or suppose your children ask for a fish. Which of you will give them a snake? [11]Even though you are evil, you know how to give good gifts to your children. How much more will your Father who is in heaven give good gifts to those who ask him!

[12]"In everything, do to others what you would want them to do to you. This is what is written in the Law and in the Prophets.

The Large and Small Gates

[13]"Enter through the narrow gate. The gate is large and the road is wide that lead to death and hell. Many people go that way. [14]But the gate is small and the road is narrow that lead to life. Only a few people find it.

A Tree and Its Fruit

[15]"Watch out for false prophets. They come to you pretending to be sheep. But on the inside they are hungry wolves. [16]You can tell what they really are by what they do.

"Do people pick grapes from bushes? Do they pick figs from thorns? [17]In the same way, every good tree bears good fruit. But a bad tree bears bad fruit. [18]A good tree can't bear bad fruit. And a bad tree can't bear good fruit. [19]Every tree that does not bear

---

GREAT VERSE — TO — REMEMBER

7:13-14 The gate is large and the road is wide that lead to death and hell. Many people go that way. But the gate is small and the road is narrow that lead to life. Only a few people find it.

good fruit is cut down. It is thrown into the fire. ²⁰You can tell each tree by its fruit.

²¹"Not everyone who says to me, 'Lord, Lord,' will enter the kingdom of heaven. Only those who do what my Father in heaven wants will enter.

²²"Many will say to me on that day, 'Lord! Lord! Didn't we prophesy in your name? Didn't we drive out demons in your name? Didn't we do many miracles in your name?' ²³Then I will tell them clearly, 'I never knew you. Get away from me, you who do evil!'

The Wise and Foolish Builders

²⁴"So then, everyone who hears my words and puts them into practice is like a wise man. He builds his house on the rock. ²⁵The rain comes down. The water rises. The winds blow and beat against that house. But it does not fall. It is built on the rock.

²⁶"But everyone who hears my words and does not put them into practice is like a foolish man. He builds his house on sand. ²⁷The rain comes down. The water rises. The winds blow and beat against that house. And it falls with a loud crash."

²⁸Jesus finished saying all these things. The crowds were amazed at his teaching. ²⁹He taught like one who had authority. He did not speak like their teachers of the law.

Jesus Heals a Man With a Skin Disease

8 Jesus came down from the mountainside. Large crowds followed him.

²A man who had a skin disease came and got down on his knees in front of Jesus. He said, "Lord, if you are willing to make me 'clean,' you can do it."

³Jesus reached out his hand and touched the man. "I am willing to do it," he said. "Be 'clean'!"

Right away the man was healed of his skin disease.

⁴Then Jesus said to him, "Don't tell anyone. Go and show yourself to the priest. Offer the gift Moses commanded. It will be a witness to them."

A Roman Commander Has Faith

⁵When Jesus entered Capernaum, a Roman commander came to him. He asked Jesus for help. ⁶"Lord," he said, "my servant lies at home and can't move. He is suffering terribly."

⁷Jesus said, "I will go and heal him."

⁸The commander replied, "Lord, I am not good enough to have you come into my house. But just say the word, and my servant will be healed. ⁹I myself am a man under authority. And I have soldiers who obey my orders. I tell this one, 'Go,' and he goes. I tell that one, 'Come,' and he comes. I say to my servant, 'Do this,' and he does it."

¹⁰When Jesus heard this, he was amazed. He said to those following him, "What I'm about to tell you is true. In Israel I have not found anyone whose faith is so strong.

¹¹"I say to you that many will come from the east and the west. They will take their places at the feast in the kingdom of heaven. They will sit with Abraham, Isaac and Jacob. ¹²But those who think they belong to the kingdom will be thrown outside, into the darkness. There they will sob and grind their teeth."

¹³Then Jesus said to the Roman commander, "Go! It will be done just as you believed it would."

And his servant was healed at that very hour.

Jesus Heals Many People

¹⁴When Jesus came into Peter's house, he saw Peter's mother-in-law. She was lying in bed. She had a fever.

¹⁵Jesus touched her hand, and the fever left her. She got up and began to wait on him.

¹⁶When evening came, many people controlled by demons were brought to Jesus. He drove out the spirits with a word. He healed all who were sick.

¹⁷He did it to make what the prophet Isaiah had said come true. He had said,

> "He took on himself our weaknesses.
> He placed on himself our illnesses." *(Isaiah 53:4)*

It Costs to Follow Jesus

¹⁸Jesus saw the crowd around him. So he gave orders to go to the other side of the lake.

¹⁹Then a teacher of the law came to him. He said, "Teacher, I will follow you no matter where you go."

²⁰Jesus replied, "Foxes have holes. Birds of the air have nests. But the Son of Man has no place to lay his head."

²¹Another follower said to him, "Lord, first let me go and bury my father."

²²But Jesus told him, "Follow me. Let the dead bury their own dead."

Jesus Calms the Storm

²³Jesus got into a boat. His disciples followed him. ²⁴Suddenly a terrible storm came up on the lake. The waves crashed over the boat. But Jesus was sleeping.

²⁵The disciples went and woke him up. They said, "Lord! Save us! We're going to drown!"

²⁶He replied, "Your faith is so small! Why are you so afraid?"

Then Jesus got up and ordered the winds and the waves to stop. It became completely calm.

²⁷The disciples were amazed. They asked, "What kind of man is this? Even the winds and the waves obey him!"

Jesus Heals Two Men Controlled by Demons

²⁸Jesus arrived at the other side of the lake in the area of the Gadarenes. Two men controlled by demons met him. They came from the tombs. The men were so wild that no one could pass that way.

²⁹"Son of God, what do you want with us?" they shouted. "Have you come here to punish us before the time for us to be judged?"

³⁰Not very far away, a large herd of pigs was feeding. ³¹The demons begged Jesus, "If you drive us out, send us into the herd of pigs."

³²Jesus said to them, "Go!"

So they came out of the men and went into the pigs. The whole herd rushed down the steep bank. They ran into the lake and drowned in the water.

³³Those who were tending the pigs ran off. They went into the town and reported all this. They told the people what had happened to the men who had been controlled by demons.

³⁴Then the whole town went out to meet Jesus. When they saw him, they begged him to leave their area.

8:20 Foxes have holes. Birds of the air have nests. But the Son of Man has no place to lay his head.

Jesus Heals a Man Who Could Not Walk

9 Jesus stepped into a boat. He went over to the other side of the lake and came to his own town. ²Some people brought to him a man who could not walk. He was lying on a mat. Jesus saw that they had faith. So he said to the man, "Don't lose hope, son. Your sins are forgiven."

³Then some teachers of the law said to themselves, "This fellow is saying a very evil thing!"

⁴Jesus knew what they were thinking. So he said, "Why do you have evil thoughts in your hearts? ⁵Is it easier to say, 'Your sins are forgiven'? Or to say, 'Get up and walk'? ⁶I want you to know that the Son of Man has authority on earth to forgive sins."

Then he spoke to the man who could not walk. "Get up," he said. "Take your mat and go home." ⁷The man got up and went home.

⁸When the crowd saw this, they were filled with wonder. They praised God for giving that kind of authority to people.

Jesus Chooses Matthew

⁹As Jesus went on from there, he saw a man named Matthew. He was sitting at the tax collector's booth.

"Follow me," Jesus told him. Matthew got up and followed him.

¹⁰Later Jesus was having dinner at Matthew's house. Many tax collectors and "sinners" came. They ate with Jesus and his disciples.

¹¹The Pharisees saw this. So they asked the disciples, "Why does your teacher eat with tax collectors and 'sinners'?"

¹²Jesus heard that. So he said, "Those who are healthy don't need a doctor. Sick people do. ¹³Go and learn what this means: 'I want mercy and not sacrifice.' *(Hosea 6:6)* I have not come to get those who think they are right with God to follow me. I have come to get sinners to follow me."

Jesus Is Asked About Fasting

¹⁴One day John's disciples came. They said to Jesus, "We and the Pharisees go without eating. Why don't your disciples go without eating?"

¹⁵Jesus answered, "How can the guests of the groom be sad while he is with them? The time will come when the groom will be taken away from them. Then they will fast.

¹⁶"People don't sew a patch of new cloth on old clothes. The new piece will pull away from the old. That will make the tear worse. ¹⁷People don't pour new wine into old wineskins. If they do, the skins will burst. The wine will run out, and the wineskins will be destroyed. No, everyone pours new wine into new wineskins. Then both are saved."

A Dead Girl and a Suffering Woman

¹⁸While Jesus was saying this, a ruler came. He got down on his knees in front of Jesus. He said, "My daughter has just died. But come and place your hand on her. Then she will live again."

¹⁹Jesus got up and went with him. So did his disciples.

²⁰Just then a woman who had an illness that made her bleed came up behind Jesus. Her illness had lasted 12 years. She touched the edge of his clothes. ²¹She thought, "I only need to touch his clothes. Then I will be healed."

²²Jesus turned and saw her. "Dear woman, don't give up hope," he said. "Your faith has healed you." The woman was healed at that very moment.

²³When Jesus entered the ruler's house, he saw the flute players there. And he saw the noisy crowd. ²⁴He said, "Go away. The girl is not dead. She is sleeping." But they laughed at him.

²⁵After the crowd had been sent outside, Jesus went in. He took the girl by the hand, and she got up. ²⁶News about what Jesus had done spread all over that area.

Jesus Heals Two Blind Men

²⁷As Jesus went on from there, two blind men followed him. They called out, "Have mercy on us, Son of David!"

²⁸When Jesus went indoors, the blind men came to him. He asked them, "Do you believe that I can do this?"

"Yes, Lord," they replied.

²⁹Then he touched their eyes. He said, "It will happen to you just as you believed." ³⁰They could now see again. Jesus strongly warned them, "Be sure that no one knows about this." ³¹But they went out and spread the news. They talked about him all over that area.

³²While they were going out, another man was brought to Jesus. A demon controlled him, and he could not speak. ³³When the demon was driven out, the man spoke.

The crowd was amazed. They said, "Nothing like this has ever been seen in Israel." [34]But the Pharisees said, "He drives out demons by the power of the prince of demons."

There Are Only a Few Workers

[35]Jesus went through all the towns and villages. He taught in their synagogues. He preached the good news of the kingdom. And he healed every illness and sickness. [36]When he saw the crowds, he felt deep concern for them. They were beaten down and helpless, like sheep without a shepherd.

[37]Then Jesus said to his disciples, "The harvest is huge. But there are only a few workers. [38]So ask the Lord of the harvest to send workers out into his harvest field."

Jesus Sends Out the Twelve Disciples

10 Jesus called for his 12 disciples to come to him. He gave them authority to drive out evil spirits and to heal every illness and sickness.

[2]Here are the names of the 12 apostles. First are Simon Peter and his brother Andrew. Then come James, son of Zebedee, and his brother John. [3]Next are Philip and Bartholomew, and also Thomas and Matthew the tax collector. Two more are James, son of Alphaeus, and Thaddaeus. [4]The last are Simon the Zealot and Judas Iscariot. Judas is the one who was later going to hand Jesus over to his enemies.

[5]Jesus sent these 12 out with the following orders. "Do not go among those who aren't Jews," he said. "Do not enter any town of the Samaritans. [6]Instead, go to the lost sheep of Israel. [7]As you go, preach this message: 'The kingdom of heaven is near.' [8]Heal those who are sick. Bring those who are dead back to life. Make those who have skin diseases clean again. Drive out demons. You have received freely, so give freely.

[9]"Do not take along any gold, silver or copper in your belts. [10]Do not take a bag for the journey. Do not take extra clothes or san-

---

GREAT VERSE —TO— REMEMBER **9:37-38** The harvest is huge. But there are only a few workers. So ask the Lord of the harvest to send workers out into his harvest field.

dals or walking sticks. Workers should be given what they need.

¹¹"When you enter a town or village, look for someone who is willing to welcome you. Stay at that person's house until you leave. ¹²As you enter the home, greet those who live there. ¹³If that home welcomes you, give it your blessing of peace. If it does not, don't bless it.

¹⁴"Some people may not welcome you or listen to your words. If they don't, shake the dust off your feet when you leave that home or town. ¹⁵What I'm about to tell you is true. On judgment day it will be easier for Sodom and Gomorrah than for that town.

¹⁶"I am sending you out like sheep among wolves. So be as wise as snakes and as harmless as doves.

¹⁷"Watch out! People will hand you over to the local courts. They will whip you in their synagogues. ¹⁸You will be brought to governors and kings because of me. You will be witnesses to them and to those who aren't Jews.

¹⁹"But when they arrest you, don't worry about what you will say or how you will say it. At that time you will be given the right words to say. ²⁰It will not be you speaking. The Spirit of your Father will be speaking through you.

²¹"Brothers will hand over brothers to be killed. Fathers will hand over their children. Children will rise up against their parents and have them put to death. ²²Everyone will hate you because of me. But the one who stands firm to the end will be saved.

²³"When people attack you in one place, escape to another. What I'm about to tell you is true. You will not finish going through the cities of Israel before the Son of Man comes.

²⁴"Students are not better than their teachers. Servants are not better than their masters. ²⁵It is enough for students to be like their teachers. And it is enough for servants to be like their masters. If the head of the house has been called Beelzebub, what can the others who live there expect?

²⁶"So don't be afraid of them. Everything that is secret will be brought out into the open. Everything that is hidden will be uncovered. ²⁷What I tell you in the dark, speak in the daylight. What is whispered in your ear, shout from the rooftops. ²⁸Do not

GREAT VERSE —TO— REMEMBER

10:31 Don't be afraid. You are worth more than many sparrows.

be afraid of those who kill the body but can't kill the soul. Instead, be afraid of the One who can destroy both soul and body in hell.

[29]"Aren't two sparrows sold for only a penny? But not one of them falls to the ground without your Father knowing it. [30]He even counts the very hairs of your head! [31]So don't be afraid. You are worth more than many sparrows.

[32]"What about those who say in front of others that they know me? I will also say in front of my Father who is in heaven that I know them. [33]But what about those who say in front of others that they don't know me? I will say in front of my Father who is in heaven that I don't know them.

[34]"Do not think that I came to bring peace to the earth. I didn't come to bring peace. I came to bring a sword. [35]I have come to turn

> "'a son against his father.
>   I have come to turn a daughter against her mother.
> I have come to turn a daughter-in-law against her
>   mother-in-law.
> [36]   Your enemies will be members of your own
>   family.'   *(Micah 7:6)*

[37]"Do you love your father or mother more than me? If you do, you are not worthy of me. Do you love your son or daughter more than me? If you do, you are not worthy of me. [38]If you do not take your cross and follow me, you are not worthy of me. [39]If you find your life, you will lose it. If you lose your life because of me, you will find it.

[40]"Anyone who welcomes you welcomes me. And anyone who welcomes me welcomes the One who sent me. [41]Suppose someone welcomes a prophet as a prophet. That one will receive a prophet's reward. And suppose someone welcomes a godly person as a godly person. That one will receive a godly person's reward. [42]Suppose someone gives even a cup of cold water to a little one who follows me. What I'm about to tell you is true. That one will certainly be rewarded."

Jesus and John the Baptist

11 Jesus finished teaching his 12 disciples. Then he went on to teach and preach in the towns of Galilee.

[2]John was in prison. When he heard what Christ was doing, he sent his disciples to him. [3]They asked Jesus, "Are you the one who

was supposed to come? Or should we look for someone else?"
⁴Jesus replied, "Go back to John. Report to him what you hear
and see. ⁵Blind people receive sight. Disabled people walk. Those
who have skin diseases are healed. Deaf people hear. Those who
are dead are raised to life. And the good news is preached to those
who are poor. ⁶Blessed are those who do not give up their faith
because of me."

⁷As John's disciples were leaving, Jesus began to speak to the
crowd about John. He said, "What did you go out into the desert
to see? Tall grass waving in the wind? ⁸If not, what did you go out
to see? A man dressed in fine clothes? No. People who wear fine
clothes are in kings' palaces. ⁹Then what did you go out to see?
A prophet? Yes, I tell you, and more than a prophet. ¹⁰He is the
one written about in Scripture. It says,

> "'I will send my messenger ahead of you.
>   He will prepare your way for you.'   *(Malachi 3:1)*

¹¹"What I'm about to tell you is true. No one more important
than John the Baptist has ever been born. But the least important
person in the kingdom of heaven is more important than he is.
¹²Since the days of John the Baptist, the kingdom of heaven has
been advancing with force. And forceful people are taking hold
of it. ¹³All the Prophets and the Law prophesied until John came.
¹⁴If you are willing to accept it, John is the Elijah who was supposed to come. ¹⁵Those who have ears should listen.

¹⁶"What can I compare today's people to? They are like children
sitting in the market places and calling out to others. They say,

> ¹⁷ "'We played the flute for you.
>   But you didn't dance.
> We sang a funeral song.
>   But you didn't become sad.'

¹⁸When John came, he didn't eat or drink as you do. And people
say, 'He has a demon.' ¹⁹But when the Son of Man came, he ate
and drank as you do. And people say, 'This fellow is always eating and drinking far too much. He's a friend of tax collectors and
"sinners."' Those who act wisely prove that wisdom is right."

Cities That Do Not Turn Away From Sin

²⁰Jesus began to speak against the cities where he had done most
of his miracles. The people there had not turned away from their
sins. So he said, ²¹"How terrible it will be for you, Korazin! How

terrible for you, Bethsaida! Suppose the miracles done in you had been done in Tyre and Sidon. They would have turned away from their sins long ago. They would have put on black clothes. They would have sat down in ashes. ²²But I tell you this. On judgment day it will be easier for Tyre and Sidon than for you.

²³"And what about you, Capernaum? Will you be lifted up to heaven? No! You will go down to the place of the dead. Suppose the miracles done in you had been done in Sodom. It would still be here today. ²⁴But I tell you this. On judgment day it will be easier for Sodom than for you."

Rest for All Who Are Tired

²⁵At that time Jesus said, "I praise you, Father. You are Lord of heaven and earth. You have hidden these things from the wise and educated. But you have shown them to little children. ²⁶Yes, Father. This is what you wanted.

²⁷"My Father has given all things to me. The Father is the only one who knows the Son. And the only ones who know the Father are the Son and those to whom the Son chooses to make him known.

²⁸"Come to me, all of you who are tired and are carrying heavy loads. I will give you rest. ²⁹Become my servants and learn from me. I am gentle and free of pride. You will find rest for your souls. ³⁰Serving me is easy, and my load is light."

Jesus Is Lord of the Sabbath Day

12 One Sabbath day Jesus walked through the grainfields. His disciples were hungry. So they began to break off some heads of grain and eat them. ²The Pharisees saw this. They

---

GREAT VERSE –TO– REMEMBER **11:28-29** Come to me, all of you who are tired and are carrying heavy loads. I will give you rest. Become my servants and learn from me. I am gentle and free of pride. You will find rest for your souls.

said to him, "Look! It is against the Law to do this on the Sabbath. But your disciples are doing it anyway!"

³Jesus answered, "Haven't you read about what David did? He and his men were hungry. ⁴So he entered the house of God. He and his men ate the holy bread. Only priests were allowed to eat it. ⁵Haven't you read the Law? It tells how every Sabbath day the priests in the temple have to do their work on that day. But they are not considered guilty.

⁶"I tell you that one who is more important than the temple is here. ⁷Scripture says, 'I want mercy and not sacrifice.' *(Hosea 6:6)* You don't know what those words mean. If you did, you would not bring charges against those who are not guilty. ⁸The Son of Man is Lord of the Sabbath day."

⁹Going on from that place, Jesus went into their synagogue. ¹⁰A man with a weak and twisted hand was there. The Pharisees were trying to find fault with Jesus. So they asked him, "Does the Law allow us to heal on the Sabbath day?"

¹¹He said to them, "What if one of your sheep falls into a pit on the Sabbath? Won't you take hold of it and lift it out? ¹²People are worth more than sheep! So the Law allows us to do good on the Sabbath day."

¹³Then Jesus said to the man, "Stretch out your hand." So he stretched it out. It was as good as new, just as good as the other hand. ¹⁴But the Pharisees went out and planned how to kill Jesus.

God's Chosen Servant

¹⁵Jesus knew all about the Pharisees' plans. So he left that place. Many followed him, and he healed all their sick people. ¹⁶But he warned them not to tell who he was. ¹⁷This was to make what was spoken through the prophet Isaiah come true. It says,

¹⁸ "Here is my servant. I have chosen him.
    He is the one I love. I am very pleased with him.
  I will put my Spirit on him.
    He will announce to the nations that everything will
        be made right.
¹⁹ He will not argue or cry out.
    No one will hear his voice in the streets.
²⁰ He will not break a bent twig.
    He will not put out a dimly burning flame.
  He will make everything right.
²¹   The nations will put their hope in his name." *(Isaiah 42:1–4)*

Jesus and Beelzebub

[22]A man controlled by demons was brought to Jesus. The man was blind and could not speak. Jesus healed him. Then the man could speak and see. [23]All the people were amazed. They said, "Could this be the Son of David?"

[24]The Pharisees heard this. So they said, "This fellow drives out demons by the power of Beelzebub, the prince of demons."

[25]Jesus knew what they were thinking. So he said to them, "Every kingdom that fights against itself will be destroyed. Every city or family that is divided against itself will not stand. [26]If Satan drives out Satan, he fights against himself. Then how can his kingdom stand? [27]You say I drive out demons by the power of Beelzebub. Then by whose power do your people drive them out? So then, they will be your judges. [28]But suppose I drive out demons by the Spirit of God. Then God's kingdom has come to you.

[29]"Or think about this. How can you enter a strong man's house and just take what the man owns? You must first tie him up. Then you can rob his house.

[30]"Anyone who is not with me is against me. Anyone who does not gather sheep with me scatters them. [31]So here is what I tell you. Every sin and every evil word spoken against God will be forgiven. But speaking evil things against the Holy Spirit will not be forgiven. [32]Anyone who speaks a word against the Son of Man will be forgiven. But anyone who speaks against the Holy Spirit will not be forgiven. A person like that won't be forgiven either now or in days to come.

[33]"If you make a tree good, its fruit will be good. If you make a tree bad, its fruit will be bad. You can tell a tree by its fruit.

[34]"You nest of poisonous snakes! How can you who are evil say anything good? Your mouths say everything that is in your hearts. [35]Good people say good things. These come from the good that is put away inside them. Evil people say evil things. These come from the evil that is put away inside them. [36]But here is

GREAT VERSE — TO — REMEMBER   **12:35** Good people say good things. These come from the good that is put away inside them.

what I tell you. On judgment day, people will have to account for every careless word they have spoken. [37]By your words you will be found guilty or not guilty."

The Miraculous Sign of Jonah

[38]Some of the Pharisees and the teachers of the law came to Jesus. They said, "Teacher, we want to see a miraculous sign from you."

[39]He answered, "Evil and unfaithful people ask for a miraculous sign! But none will be given except the sign of the prophet Jonah. [40]Jonah was in the stomach of a huge fish for three days and three nights. Something like that will happen to the Son of Man. He will spend three days and three nights in the grave.

[41]"The people of Nineveh will stand up on judgment day with the people now living. And the Ninevites will prove that those people are guilty. The people of Nineveh turned away from their sins when Jonah preached to them. And now one who is more important than Jonah is here. [42]The Queen of the South will stand up on judgment day with the people now living. And she will prove that those people are guilty. She came from very far away to listen to Solomon's wisdom. And now one who is more important than Solomon is here.

[43]"What happens when an evil spirit comes out of someone? It goes through dry areas looking for a place to rest. But it doesn't find it. [44]Then it says, 'I will return to the house I left.' When it arrives there, it finds the house empty. The house has been swept clean and put in order. [45]Then the evil spirit goes and takes with it seven other spirits more evil than itself. They go in and live there. That person is worse off than before. That is how it will be with the evil people of today."

Jesus' Mother and Brothers

[46]While Jesus was still talking to the crowd, his mother and brothers stood outside. They wanted to speak to him. [47]Someone told him, "Your mother and brothers are standing outside. They want to speak to you."

[48]Jesus replied to him, "Who is my mother? And who are my brothers?" [49]Jesus pointed to his disciples. He said, "Here is my mother! Here are my brothers! [50]Anyone who does what my Father in heaven wants is my brother and sister and mother."

The Story of the Farmer

13 That same day Jesus left the house and sat by the lake. [2]Large crowds gathered around him. So he got into a boat. He sat down in it. All the people stood on the shore. [3]Then he told them many things by using stories.

He said, "A farmer went out to plant his seed. [4]He scattered the seed on the ground. Some fell on a path. Birds came and ate it up. [5]Some seed fell on rocky places, where there wasn't much soil. The plants came up quickly, because the soil wasn't deep. [6]When the sun came up, it burned the plants. They dried up because they had no roots. [7]Other seed fell among thorns. The thorns grew up and crowded out the plants. [8]Still other seed fell on good soil. It produced a crop 100, 60 or 30 times more than what was planted. [9]Those who have ears should listen."

[10]The disciples came to him. They asked, "Why do you use stories when you speak to the people?"

[11]He replied, "You have been given the chance to understand the secrets of the kingdom of heaven. It has not been given to outsiders. [12]Those who have that kind of knowledge will be given more. In fact, they will have very much. If people do not have that kind of knowledge, even what little they have will be taken away from them. [13]Here is why I use stories when I speak to the people. I say,

"They look, but they don't really see.
They listen, but they don't really hear or understand.

[14]In them the words of the prophet Isaiah come true. He said,

"'You will hear but never understand.
You will see but never know what you are
seeing.
[15]These people's hearts have become stubborn.
They can barely hear with their ears.
They have closed their eyes.
Otherwise they might see with their eyes.
They might hear with their ears.
They might understand with their hearts.
They might turn, and then I would heal
them.'   *(Isaiah 6:9,10)*

[16]"But blessed are your eyes because they see. And blessed are your ears because they hear. [17]What I'm about to tell you is true. Many prophets and godly people wanted to see what you see.

But they didn't see it. They wanted to hear what you hear. But they didn't hear it.

[18]"Listen! Here is the meaning of the story of the farmer. [19]People hear the message about the kingdom but do not understand it. Then the evil one comes. He steals what was planted in their hearts. Those people are like the seed planted on a path. [20]Others received the seed that fell on rocky places. They are those who hear the message and at once receive it with joy. [21]But they have no roots. So they last only a short time. They quickly fall away from the faith when trouble or suffering comes because of the message. [22]Others received the seed that fell among the thorns. They are those who hear the message. But then the worries of this life and the false promises of wealth crowd it out. They keep it from producing fruit. [23]But still others received the seed that fell on good soil. They are those who hear the message and understand it. They produce a crop 100, 60 or 30 times more than the farmer planted."

The Story of the Weeds

[24]Jesus told the crowd another story. "Here is what the kingdom of heaven is like," he said. "A man planted good seed in his field. [25]But while everyone was sleeping, his enemy came. The enemy planted weeds among the wheat and then went away. [26]The wheat began to grow and form grain. At the same time, weeds appeared.

[27]"The owner's servants came to him. They said, 'Sir, didn't you plant good seed in your field? Then where did the weeds come from?'

[28]" 'An enemy did this,' he replied.

"The servants asked him, 'Do you want us to go and pull the weeds up?'

[29]" 'No,' the owner answered. 'While you are pulling up the weeds, you might pull up the wheat with them. [30]Let both grow together until the harvest. At that time I will tell the workers what to do. Here is what I will say to them. First collect the weeds. Tie them in bundles to be burned. Then gather the wheat. Bring it into my storeroom.' "

The Stories of the Mustard Seed and the Yeast

[31]Jesus told the crowd another story. He said, "The kingdom of heaven is like a mustard seed. Someone took the seed and

planted it in a field. ³²It is the smallest of all your seeds. But when it grows, it is the largest of all garden plants. It becomes a tree. Birds come and rest in its branches."

³³Jesus told them still another story. "The kingdom of heaven is like yeast," he said. "A woman mixed it into a large amount of flour. The yeast worked its way all through the dough."

³⁴Jesus spoke all these things to the crowd by using stories. He did not say anything to them without using a story. ³⁵So the words spoken by the prophet came true. He had said,

> "I will open my mouth and use stories.
> I will speak about things that were hidden since the
> world was made." *(Psalm 78:2)*

Jesus Explains the Story of the Weeds

³⁶Then Jesus left the crowd and went into the house. His disciples came to him. They said, "Explain to us the story of the weeds in the field."

³⁷He answered, "The one who planted the good seed is the Son of Man. ³⁸The field is the world. The good seed stands for the people who belong to the kingdom. The weeds are the people who belong to the evil one. ³⁹The enemy who plants them is the devil. The harvest is judgment day. And the workers are angels.

⁴⁰"The weeds are pulled up and burned in the fire. That is how it will be on judgment day. ⁴¹The Son of Man will send out his angels. They will weed out of his kingdom everything that causes sin. They will also get rid of all who do evil. ⁴²They will throw them into the blazing furnace. There people will sob and grind their teeth. ⁴³Then God's people will shine like the sun in their Father's kingdom. Those who have ears should listen.

The Stories of the Hidden Treasure and the Pearl

⁴⁴"The kingdom of heaven is like treasure that was hidden in a field. When a man found it, he hid it again. He was very happy. So he went and sold everything he had. And he bought that field.

13:43 God's people will shine like the sun in their Father's kingdom.

⁴⁵"Again, the kingdom of heaven is like a businessman looking for fine pearls. ⁴⁶He found one that was very valuable. So he went away and sold everything he had. And he bought that pearl.

The Story of the Net

⁴⁷"Again, the kingdom of heaven is like a net. It was let down into the lake. It caught all kinds of fish. ⁴⁸When it was full, the fishermen pulled it up on the shore. Then they sat down and gathered the good fish in baskets. But they threw the bad fish away. ⁴⁹This is how it will be on judgment day. The angels will come. They will separate the people who did what is wrong from those who did what is right. ⁵⁰They will throw the evil people into the blazing furnace. There the evil ones will sob and grind their teeth.

⁵¹"Do you understand all these things?" Jesus asked.

"Yes," they replied.

⁵²He said to them, "Every teacher of the law who has been taught about the kingdom of heaven is like the owner of a house. He brings new treasures out of his storeroom as well as old ones."

A Prophet Without Honor

⁵³Jesus finished telling these stories. Then he moved on from there. ⁵⁴He came to his hometown. There he began teaching the people in their synagogue. They were amazed.

"Where did this man get this wisdom? Where did he get this power to do miracles?" they asked. ⁵⁵"Isn't this the carpenter's son? Isn't his mother's name Mary? Aren't his brothers James, Joseph, Simon and Judas? ⁵⁶Aren't all his sisters with us? Then where did this man get all these things?" ⁵⁷They were not pleased with him at all.

But Jesus said to them, "Prophets are not honored in their hometowns. They don't receive any honor in their own homes."

⁵⁸He did only a few miracles there because they had no faith.

John the Baptist's Head Is Cut Off

14 At that time Herod, the ruler of Galilee and Perea, heard reports about Jesus. ²He said to his attendants, "This is John the Baptist. He has risen from the dead! That is why he has the power to do miracles."

³Herod had arrested John. He had tied him up and put him in prison because of Herodias. She was the wife of Herod's brother

Philip. [4]John had been saying to Herod, "It is against the Law for you to have her." [5]Herod wanted to kill John. But he was afraid of the people, because they thought John was a prophet.

[6]On Herod's birthday the daughter of Herodias danced for Herod and his guests. She pleased Herod very much. [7]So he promised with an oath to give her anything she asked for. [8]Her mother told her what to say. So the girl said to Herod, "Give me the head of John the Baptist on a big plate."

[9]The king was very upset. But he thought of his promise and his dinner guests. So he told one of his men to give her what she asked for. [10]Herod had John's head cut off in the prison. [11]His head was brought in on a big plate and given to the girl. She then carried it to her mother.

[12]John's disciples came and took his body and buried it. Then they went and told Jesus.

Jesus Feeds the Five Thousand

[13]Jesus heard what had happened to John. He wanted to be alone. So he went in a boat to a quiet place. The crowds heard about this. They followed him on foot from the towns. [14]When Jesus came ashore, he saw a large crowd. He felt deep concern for them. He healed their sick people.

[15]When it was almost evening, the disciples came to him. "There is nothing here," they said. "It's already getting late. Send the crowds away. They can go and buy some food in the villages."

[16]Jesus replied, "They don't need to go away. You give them something to eat."

[17]"We have only five loaves of bread and two fish," they answered.

[18]"Bring them here to me," he said. [19]Then Jesus directed the people to sit down on the grass. He took the five loaves and the two fish. He looked up to heaven and gave thanks. He broke the loaves into pieces. Then he gave them to the disciples. And the disciples gave them to the people.

[20]All of them ate and were satisfied. The disciples picked up 12 baskets of leftover pieces. [21]The number of men who ate was about 5,000. Women and children also ate.

Jesus Walks on the Water

[22]Right away Jesus made the disciples get into the boat. He had them go on ahead of him to the other side of the lake. Then he sent the crowd away. [23]After he had sent them away, he went up

on a mountainside by himself to pray. When evening came, he was there alone. ²⁴The boat was already a long way from land. It was being pounded by the waves because the wind was blowing against it.

²⁵Early in the morning, Jesus went out to the disciples. He walked on the lake. ²⁶They saw him walking on the lake and were terrified. "It's a ghost!" they said. And they cried out in fear.

²⁷Right away Jesus called out to them, "Be brave! It is I. Don't be afraid."

²⁸"Lord, is it you?" Peter asked. "If it is, tell me to come to you on the water."

²⁹"Come," Jesus said.

So Peter got out of the boat. He walked on the water toward Jesus. ³⁰But when Peter saw the wind, he was afraid. He began to sink. He cried out, "Lord! Save me!"

³¹Right away Jesus reached out his hand and caught him. "Your faith is so small!" he said. "Why did you doubt me?"

³²When they climbed into the boat, the wind died down. ³³Then those in the boat worshiped Jesus. They said, "You really are the Son of God!"

³⁴They crossed over the lake and landed at Gennesaret. ³⁵The people who lived there recognized Jesus. So they sent a message all over the nearby countryside. People brought all their sick to Jesus. ³⁶They begged him to let those who were sick just touch the edge of his clothes. And all who touched him were healed.

What Makes People "Unclean"?

15 Some Pharisees and some teachers of the law came from Jerusalem to see Jesus. They asked, ²"Why don't your disciples obey the teachings of the elders? Your disciples don't wash their hands before they eat!"

³Jesus replied, "And why don't you obey God's command? You would rather follow your own teachings! ⁴God said, 'Honor your father and mother.' *(Exodus 20:12; Deuteronomy 5:16)* He also said, 'If you call down a curse on your father or mother, you will be put to death.' *(Exodus 21:17; Leviticus 20:9)* ⁵But you allow people to say to their parents,

---

GREAT VERSE —TO— REMEMBER   **14:27** Jesus called out to them, "Be brave! It is I. Don't be afraid."

'Any help you might have received from us is a gift set apart for God.' [6]So they do not need to honor their parents with their gift. You make the word of God useless in order to follow your own teachings.

[7]"You pretenders! Isaiah was right when he prophesied about you. He said,

[8]"'These people honor me by what they say.
But their hearts are far away from me.
[9]Their worship means nothing to me.
Their teachings are only human
rules.'"

(Isaiah 29:13)

[10]Jesus called the crowd to him. He said, "Listen and understand. [11]What goes into your mouth does not make you 'unclean.' It's what comes out of your mouth that makes you 'unclean.'"

[12]Then the disciples came to him. They asked, "Do you know that the Pharisees were angry when they heard this?"

[13]Jesus replied, "There are plants that my Father in heaven has not planted. They will be pulled up by the roots. [14]Leave them. The Pharisees are blind guides. If a blind person leads another who is blind, both of them will fall into a pit."

[15]Peter said, "Explain this to us."

[16]"Don't you understand yet?" Jesus asked them. [17]"Don't you see? Everything that enters the mouth goes into the stomach. Then it goes out of the body. [18]But the things that come out of the mouth come from the heart. Those are the things that make you 'unclean.' [19]Evil thoughts come out of the heart. So do murder, adultery, and other sexual sins. And so do stealing, false witness, and telling lies about others. [20]Those are the things that make you 'unclean.' But eating without washing your hands does not make you 'unclean.'"

The Faith of a Woman From Canaan

[21]Leaving that place, Jesus went to the area of Tyre and Sidon. [22]A woman from Canaan lived near Tyre and Sidon. She came to him and cried out, "Lord! Son of David! Have mercy on me! A demon controls my daughter. She is suffering terribly."

[23]Jesus did not say a word. So his disciples came to him. They begged him, "Send her away. She keeps crying out after us."

[24]Jesus answered, "I was sent only to the lost sheep of Israel."

[25]Then the woman fell to her knees in front of him. "Lord! Help me!" she said.

²⁶He replied, "It is not right to take the children's bread and throw it to their dogs."

²⁷"Yes, Lord," she said. "But even the dogs eat the crumbs that fall from their owners' table."

²⁸Then Jesus answered, "Woman, you have great faith! You will be given what you are asking for." And her daughter was healed at that very moment.

Jesus Feeds the Four Thousand

²⁹Jesus left there. He walked along the Sea of Galilee. Then he went up on a mountainside and sat down. ³⁰Large crowds came to him. They brought the blind and those who could not walk. They also brought the disabled, those who could not speak, and many others. They laid them at his feet, and he healed them.

³¹The people were amazed. Those who could not speak were speaking. The disabled were made well. Those not able to walk were walking. Those who were blind could see. So the people praised the God of Israel.

³²Then Jesus called for his disciples to come to him. He said, "I feel deep concern for these people. They have already been with me three days. They don't have anything to eat. I don't want to send them away hungry. If I do, they will become too weak on their way home."

³³His disciples answered him. "There is nothing here," they said. "Where could we get enough bread to feed this large crowd?"

³⁴"How many loaves do you have?" Jesus asked.

"Seven," they replied, "and a few small fish."

³⁵Jesus told the crowd to sit down on the ground. ³⁶He took the seven loaves and the fish and gave thanks. Then he broke them and gave them to the disciples. And the disciples passed them out to the people. ³⁷All of them ate and were satisfied. After that, the disciples picked up seven baskets of leftover pieces. ³⁸The number of men who ate was 4,000. Women and children also ate.

³⁹After Jesus had sent the crowd away, he got into the boat. He went to the area near Magadan.

Jesus Is Asked for a Miraculous Sign

16 The Pharisees and Sadducees came to put Jesus to the test. They asked him to show them a miraculous sign from heaven.

²He replied, "In the evening you look at the sky. You say, 'It will

be good weather. The sky is red.' ³And in the morning you say, 'Today it will be stormy. The sky is red and cloudy.' You know the meaning of what you see in the sky. But you can't understand the signs of what is happening right now. ⁴An evil and unfaithful people look for a miraculous sign. But none will be given to them except the sign of Jonah."

Then Jesus left them and went away.

The Yeast of the Pharisees and Sadducees

⁵The disciples crossed over to the other side of the lake. They had forgotten to take bread. ⁶"Be careful," Jesus said to them. "Watch out for the yeast of the Pharisees and Sadducees."

⁷The disciples talked about this among themselves. They said, "He must be saying this because we didn't bring any bread."

⁸Jesus knew what they were saying. So he said, "Your faith is so small! Why are you talking to each other about having no bread? ⁹Don't you understand yet? Don't you remember the five loaves for the 5,000? Don't you remember how many baskets of pieces you gathered? ¹⁰Don't you remember the seven loaves for the 4,000? Don't you remember how many baskets of pieces you gathered? ¹¹How can you possibly not understand? I wasn't talking to you about bread. But watch out for the yeast of the Pharisees and Sadducees."

¹²Then the disciples understood that Jesus was not telling them to watch out for the yeast used in bread. He was warning them against what the Pharisees and Sadducees taught.

Peter Says That Jesus Is the Christ

¹³Jesus went to the area of Caesarea Philippi. There he asked his disciples, "Who do people say the Son of Man is?"

¹⁴They replied, "Some say John the Baptist. Others say Elijah. Still others say Jeremiah, or one of the prophets."

¹⁵"But what about you?" he asked. "Who do you say I am?"

¹⁶Simon Peter answered, "You are the Christ. You are the Son of the living God."

¹⁷Jesus replied, "Blessed are you, Simon, son of Jonah! No human being showed this to you. My Father in heaven showed it to you. ¹⁸Here is what I tell you. You are Peter. On this rock I will build my church. The gates of hell will not be strong enough to destroy it. ¹⁹I will give you the keys to the kingdom of heaven. What you lock on earth will be locked in heaven. What you unlock on earth will be unlocked in heaven."

²⁰Then Jesus warned his disciples not to tell anyone that he was the Christ.

Jesus Tells About His Coming Death

²¹From that time on Jesus began to explain to his disciples what would happen to him. He told them he must go to Jerusalem. There he must suffer many things from the elders, the chief priests and the teachers of the law. He must be killed and on the third day rise to life again.

²²Peter took Jesus to one side and began to scold him. "Never, Lord!" he said. "This will never happen to you!"

²³Jesus turned and said to Peter, "Get behind me, Satan! You are standing in my way. You do not have in mind the things of God. Instead, you are thinking about human things."

²⁴Then Jesus spoke to his disciples. "If you want to come after me," he said, "you must say no to yourself. You must take your cross and follow me. ²⁵If you want to save your life, you will lose it. But if you lose your life for me, you will find it.

²⁶"What good is it for you to gain the whole world but lose your soul? Or what can you trade for your soul? ²⁷The Son of Man is going to come in his Father's glory. His angels will come with him. And he will reward everyone in keeping with what they have done.

²⁸"What I'm about to tell you is true. Some who are standing here will not die before they see the Son of Man coming in his kingdom."

Jesus' Appearance Is Changed

17 After six days Jesus took Peter, James, and John the brother of James with him. He led them up a high mountain. They were all alone. ²There in front of them his appearance was changed. His face shone like the sun. His clothes became as white as the light. ³Just then Moses and Elijah appeared in front of them. Moses and Elijah were talking with Jesus.

GREAT VERSE —TO— REMEMBER   **16:24** "If you want to come after me," he said, "you must say no to yourself. You must take your cross and follow me."

⁴Peter said to Jesus, "Lord, it is good for us to be here. If you wish, I will put up three shelters. One will be for you, one for Moses, and one for Elijah."

⁵While Peter was still speaking, a bright cloud surrounded them. A voice from the cloud said, "This is my Son, and I love him. I am very pleased with him. Listen to him!"

⁶When the disciples heard this, they were terrified. They fell with their faces to the ground. ⁷But Jesus came and touched them. "Get up," he said. "Don't be afraid." ⁸When they looked up, they saw no one except Jesus.

⁹They came down the mountain. On the way down, Jesus told them what to do. "Don't tell anyone what you have seen," he said. "Wait until the Son of Man has been raised from the dead."

¹⁰The disciples asked him, "Why do the teachers of the law say that Elijah has to come first?"

¹¹Jesus replied, "That's right. Elijah is supposed to come and make all things new again. ¹²But I tell you, Elijah has already come. They did not recognize him. They have done to him everything they wanted to do. In the same way, they are going to make the Son of Man suffer."

¹³Then the disciples understood that Jesus was talking to them about John the Baptist.

Jesus Heals a Boy Who Had a Demon

¹⁴When they came near the crowd, a man approached Jesus. He got on his knees in front of him. ¹⁵"Lord," he said, "have mercy on my son. He shakes wildly and suffers a great deal. He often falls into the fire or into the water. ¹⁶I brought him to your disciples. But they couldn't heal him."

¹⁷"You unbelieving and evil people!" Jesus replied. "How long do I have to stay with you? How long do I have to put up with you? Bring the boy here to me."

¹⁸Jesus ordered the demon to leave the boy, and it came out of him. He was healed at that very moment.

¹⁹Then the disciples came to Jesus in private. They asked, "Why couldn't we drive out the demon?"

²⁰/²¹He replied, "Because your faith is much too small. What I'm about to tell you is true. If you have faith as small as a mustard seed, it is enough. You can say to this mountain, 'Move from here to there.' And it will move. Nothing will be impossible for you."

²²They came together in Galilee. Then Jesus said to them, "The

Son of Man is going to be handed over to human authorities. [23]They will kill him. On the third day he will rise from the dead." Then the disciples were filled with deep sadness.

Jesus Pays the Temple Tax

[24]Jesus and his disciples arrived in Capernaum. There the tax collectors came to Peter. They asked him, "Doesn't your teacher pay the temple tax?"

[25]"Yes, he does," he replied.

When Peter came into the house, Jesus spoke first. "What do you think, Simon?" he asked. "Who do the kings of the earth collect taxes and fees from? Do they collect from their own children or from others?"

[26]"From others," Peter answered.

"Then the children don't have to pay," Jesus said to him. [27]"But we don't want to make them angry. So go to the lake and throw out your fishing line. Take the first fish you catch. Open its mouth. There you will find the exact coin you need. Take it and give it to them for my tax and yours."

Who Is the Most Important Person in the Kingdom?

18 At that time the disciples came to Jesus. They asked him, "Who is the most important person in the kingdom of heaven?"

[2]Jesus called a little child over to him. He had the child stand among them. [3]Jesus said, "What I'm about to tell you is true. You need to change and become like little children. If you don't, you will never enter the kingdom of heaven. [4]Anyone who becomes as free of pride as this child is the most important in the kingdom of heaven.

[5]"Anyone who welcomes a little child like this in my name welcomes me.

[6]"But what if people lead one of these little ones who believe in me to sin? If they do, it would be better for them to have a large

---

GREAT
VERSE
— TO —
REMEMBER

18:4 Anyone who becomes as free of pride as this child is the most important in the kingdom of heaven.

millstone hung around their neck and be drowned at the bottom of the sea.

⁷"How terrible it will be for the world because of the things that lead people to sin! Things like that must come. But how terrible for those who cause them!

⁸"If your hand or foot causes you to sin, cut it off and throw it away. It would be better for you to enter the kingdom of heaven with only one hand or one foot than to go into hell with two hands and two feet. In hell the fire burns forever. ⁹If your eye causes you to sin, dig it out and throw it away. It would be better for you to enter the kingdom of heaven with one eye than to have two eyes and be thrown into the fire of hell.

The Story of the Lost Sheep

¹⁰/¹¹"See that you don't look down on one of these little ones. Here is what I tell you. Their angels in heaven can go at any time to see my Father who is in heaven.

¹²"What do you think? Suppose a man owns 100 sheep and one of them wanders away. Won't he leave the 99 sheep on the hills? Won't he go and look for the one that wandered off? ¹³What I'm about to tell you is true. If he finds that sheep, he is happier about the one than about the 99 that didn't wander off. ¹⁴It is the same with your Father in heaven. He does not want any of these little ones to be lost.

When Someone Sins Against You

¹⁵"If your brother or sister sins against you, go to them. Tell them what they did wrong. Keep it among yourselves. If they listen to you, you have won them back.

¹⁶"But what if they won't listen to you? Then take one or two others with you. Scripture says, 'Every matter must be proved by the words of two or three witnesses.' *(Deuteronomy 19:15)* ¹⁷But what if they also refuse to listen to the witnesses? Then tell it to the church. And what if they refuse to listen even to the church? Then don't treat them as your brother or sister. Treat them as you would treat an ungodly person or a tax collector.

¹⁸"What I'm about to tell you is true. What you lock on earth will be locked in heaven. What you unlock on earth will be unlocked in heaven.

¹⁹"Again, here is what I tell you. Suppose two of you on earth agree about anything you ask for. My Father in heaven will do it

for you. [20]Where two or three meet together in my name, I am there with them."

The Servant Who Had No Mercy

[21]Peter came to Jesus. He asked, "Lord, how many times should I forgive my brother or sister when they sin against me? Up to seven times?"

[22]Jesus answered, "I tell you, not seven times, but 77 times.

[23]"The kingdom of heaven is like a king who wanted to collect all the money his servants owed him. [24]As the king began to do it, a man who owed him millions of dollars was brought to him. [25]The man was not able to pay. So his master gave an order. The man, his wife, his children, and all he owned had to be sold to pay back what he owed.

[26]"The servant fell on his knees in front of him. 'Give me time,' he begged. 'I'll pay everything back.'

[27]"His master felt sorry for him. He forgave him what he owed and let him go.

[28]"But then that servant went out and found one of the other servants who owed him a few dollars. He grabbed him and began to choke him. 'Pay back what you owe me!' he said.

[29]"The other servant fell on his knees. 'Give me time,' he begged him. 'I'll pay you back.'

[30]"But the first servant refused. Instead, he went and had the man thrown into prison. He would be held there until he could pay back what he owed. [31]The other servants saw what had happened. It troubled them greatly. They went and told their master everything that had happened.

[32]"Then the master called the first servant in. 'You evil servant,' he said. 'I forgave all that you owed me because you begged me to. [33]Shouldn't you have had mercy on the other servant just as I had mercy on you?' [34]In anger his master turned him over to the jailers. He would be punished until he paid back everything he owed.

[35]"This is how my Father in heaven will treat each of you unless you forgive one another from your heart."

Jesus Teaches About Divorce

19 When Jesus finished saying these things, he left Galilee. He went into the area of Judea on the other side of the Jordan River. [2]Large crowds followed him. He healed them there.

³Some Pharisees came to put him to the test. They asked, "Does the Law allow a man to divorce his wife for any reason at all?"

⁴Jesus replied, "Haven't you read that in the beginning the Creator 'made them male and female'?" *(Genesis 1:27)* ⁵He said, 'That's why a man will leave his father and mother and be joined to his wife. The two will become one.' *(Genesis 2:24)* ⁶They are no longer two, but one. So let no one separate what God has joined together."

⁷They asked, "Then why did Moses command that a man can give his wife a letter of divorce and send her away?"

⁸Jesus replied, "Moses let you divorce your wives because you were stubborn. But it was not this way from the beginning. ⁹Here is what I tell you. Anyone who divorces his wife and gets married to another woman commits adultery. A man may divorce his wife only if she has not been faithful to him."

¹⁰The disciples said to him, "If that's the way it is between a husband and wife, it is better not to get married."

¹¹Jesus replied, "Not everyone can accept the idea of staying single. Only those who have been helped to live without getting married can accept it. ¹²Some men are not able to have children because they were born that way. Some have been made that way by other people. Others have made themselves that way in order to serve the kingdom of heaven. The one who can accept living that way should do it."

Little Children Are Brought to Jesus

¹³Some people brought little children to Jesus. They wanted him to place his hands on the children and pray for them. But the disciples told the people to stop.

¹⁴Jesus said, "Let the little children come to me. Don't keep them away. The kingdom of heaven belongs to people like them." ¹⁵Jesus placed his hands on them. Then he went on from there.

GREAT VERSE —TO— REMEMBER

19:14 Jesus said, "Let the little children come to me. Don't keep them away. The kingdom of heaven belongs to people like them."

Jesus and the Rich Young Man

¹⁶A man came up to Jesus. He asked, "Teacher, what good thing must I do to receive eternal life?"

¹⁷"Why do you ask me about what is good?" Jesus replied. "There is only One who is good. If you want to enter the kingdom, obey the commandments."

¹⁸"Which ones?" the man asked.

Jesus said, "'Do not commit murder. Do not commit adultery. Do not steal. Do not give false witness. ¹⁹Honor your father and mother.' *(Exodus 20:12–16; Deuteronomy 5:16–20)* And 'love your neighbor as you love yourself.'" *(Leviticus 19:18)*

²⁰"I have obeyed all those commandments," the young man said. "What else do I need to do?"

²¹Jesus answered, "If you want to be perfect, go and sell everything you have. Give the money to those who are poor. You will have treasure in heaven. Then come and follow me."

²²When the young man heard this, he went away sad. He was very rich.

²³Then Jesus said to his disciples, "What I'm about to tell you is true. It is hard for rich people to enter the kingdom of heaven. ²⁴Again I tell you, it is hard for a camel to go through the eye of a needle. But it is even harder for the rich to enter God's kingdom."

²⁵When the disciples heard this, they were really amazed. They asked, "Then who can be saved?"

²⁶Jesus looked at them and said, "With people, that is impossible. But with God, all things are possible."

²⁷Peter answered him, "We have left everything to follow you! What reward will be given to us?"

²⁸"What I'm about to tell you is true," Jesus said to them. "When all things are made new, the Son of Man will sit on his glorious throne. Then you who have followed me will also sit on 12 thrones. You will judge the 12 tribes of Israel. ²⁹Everyone who has left houses or families or fields because of me will receive 100 times as much. They will also receive eternal life. ³⁰But many who are first will be last. And many who are last will be first.

The Story of the Workers in the Vineyard

20 "The kingdom of heaven is like a man who owned land. He went out early in the morning to hire people to work in his vineyard. ²He agreed to give them the usual pay for a day's work. Then he sent them into his vineyard.

³"About nine o'clock in the morning he went out again. He saw others standing in the market place doing nothing. ⁴He told them, 'You also go and work in my vineyard. I'll pay you what is right.' ⁵So they went.

"He went out again about noon and at three o'clock and did the same thing. ⁶About five o'clock he went out and found still others standing around. He asked them, 'Why have you been standing here all day long doing nothing?'

⁷"'Because no one has hired us,' they answered.

"He said to them, 'You also go and work in my vineyard.'

⁸"When evening came, the owner of the vineyard spoke to the person who was in charge of the workers. He said, 'Call the workers and give them their pay. Begin with the last ones I hired. Then go on to the first ones.'

⁹"The workers who were hired about five o'clock came. Each received the usual day's pay. ¹⁰So when those who were hired first came, they expected to receive more. But each of them also received the usual day's pay.

¹¹"When they received it, they began to complain about the owner. ¹²'These people who were hired last worked only one hour,' they said. 'You have paid them the same as us. We have done most of the work and have been in the hot sun all day.'

¹³"The owner answered one of them. 'Friend,' he said, 'I'm being fair to you. Didn't you agree to work for the usual day's pay? ¹⁴Take your money and go. I want to give the ones I hired last the same pay I gave you. ¹⁵Don't I have the right to do what I want with my own money? Do you feel cheated because I gave so freely to the others?'

¹⁶"So the last will be first. And the first will be last."

Jesus Again Tells About His Coming Death

¹⁷Jesus was going up to Jerusalem. On the way, he took the 12 disciples to one side to talk to them.

¹⁸"We are going up to Jerusalem," he said. "The Son of Man will be handed over to the chief priests and the teachers of the law. They will sentence him to death. ¹⁹Then they will turn him over

20:16 The last will be first. And the first will be last.

to people who are not Jews. The people will make fun of him and whip him. They will nail him to a cross. On the third day, he will rise from the dead!"

A Mother Asks a Favor of Jesus

²⁰The mother of Zebedee's sons came to Jesus. Her sons came with her. Getting on her knees, she asked a favor of him.

²¹"What do you want?" Jesus asked.

She said, "Promise me that one of my two sons may sit at your right hand in your kingdom. Promise that the other one may sit at your left hand."

²²"You don't know what you're asking for," Jesus said to them. "Can you drink the cup of suffering I am going to drink?"

"We can," they answered.

²³Jesus said to them, "You will certainly drink from my cup. But it is not for me to say who will sit at my right or left hand. These places belong to those my Father has prepared them for."

²⁴The other ten disciples heard about this. They became angry at the two brothers.

²⁵Jesus called them together. He said, "You know about the rulers of the nations. They hold power over their people. Their high officials order them around. ²⁶Don't be like that. Instead, anyone who wants to be important among you must be your servant. ²⁷And anyone who wants to be first must be your slave.

²⁸"Be like the Son of Man. He did not come to be served. Instead, he came to serve others. He came to give his life as the price for setting many people free."

Two Blind Men Receive Their Sight

²⁹Jesus and his disciples were leaving Jericho. A large crowd followed him. ³⁰Two blind men were sitting by the side of the road. They heard that Jesus was going by. So they shouted, "Lord! Son of David! Have mercy on us!"

³¹The crowd commanded them to stop. They told them to be quiet. But the two men shouted even louder, "Lord! Son of David! Have mercy on us!"

³²Jesus stopped and called out to them. "What do you want me to do for you?" he asked.

³³"Lord," they answered, "we want to be able to see."

³⁴Jesus felt deep concern for them. He touched their eyes. Right away they could see. And they followed him.

Jesus Enters Jerusalem

21 As they all approached Jerusalem, they came to Bethphage. It was on the Mount of Olives. Jesus sent out two disciples. ²He said to them, "Go to the village ahead of you. At once you will find a donkey tied there. Her colt will be with her. Untie them and bring them to me. ³If anyone says anything to you, say that the Lord needs them. The owner will send them right away."

⁴This took place so that what was spoken through the prophet would come true. It says,

⁵ "Say to the Daughter of Zion,
  'See, your king comes to you.
He is gentle and riding on a donkey.
  He is riding on a colt, a young donkey.'" *(Zechariah 9:9)*

⁶The disciples went and did what Jesus told them to do. ⁷They brought the donkey and the colt. They placed their coats on them. Then Jesus sat on the coats. ⁸A very large crowd spread their coats on the road. Others cut branches from the trees and spread them on the road. ⁹Some of the people went ahead of him, and some followed. They all shouted,

"Hosanna to the Son of David!"

"Blessed is the one who comes in the name of the
  Lord!" *(Psalm 118:26)*

"Hosanna in the highest heaven!"

¹⁰When Jesus entered Jerusalem, the whole city was stirred up. The people asked, "Who is this?"

¹¹The crowds answered, "This is Jesus. He is the prophet from Nazareth in Galilee."

GREAT VERSE — TO — REMEMBER

21:9 Some of the people went ahead of him, and some followed. They all shouted, "Hosanna to the Son of David! Blessed is the one who comes in the name of the Lord!"

Jesus Clears Out the Temple

¹²Jesus entered the temple area. He began chasing out all those who were buying and selling there. He turned over the tables of the people who were exchanging money. He also turned over the benches of those who were selling doves. ¹³He said to them, "It is written: 'My house will be called a house of prayer.' *(Isaiah 56:7)* But you are making it a 'den for robbers.'" *(Jeremiah 7:11)*

¹⁴The blind and the disabled came to Jesus at the temple. There he healed them. ¹⁵The chief priests and the teachers of the law saw the wonderful things he did. They also saw the children in the temple area shouting, "Hosanna to the Son of David!" But when they saw all of this, they became angry.

¹⁶"Do you hear what these children are saying?" they asked him.

"Yes," replied Jesus. "Haven't you ever read about it in Scripture? It says,

> "'You have made sure that children and infants
> speak your praises.'"   *(Psalm 8:2)*

¹⁷Then Jesus left the people and went out of the city to Bethany. He spent the night there.

The Fig Tree Dries Up

¹⁸Early in the morning, Jesus was on his way back to Jerusalem. He was hungry. ¹⁹He saw a fig tree by the road. He went up to it but found nothing on it except leaves. Then he said to it, "May you never bear fruit again!" Right away the tree dried up.

²⁰When the disciples saw this, they were amazed. "How did the fig tree dry up so quickly?" they asked.

²¹Jesus replied, "What I'm about to tell you is true. You must have faith and not doubt. Then you can do what was done to the fig tree. And you can say to this mountain, 'Go and throw yourself into the sea.' It will be done. ²²If you believe, you will receive what you ask for when you pray."

The Authority of Jesus Is Questioned

²³Jesus entered the temple courtyard. While he was teaching there, the chief priests and the elders of the people came to him. "By what authority are you doing these things?" they asked. "Who gave you this authority?"

²⁴Jesus replied, "I will also ask you one question. If you answer

me, I will tell you by what authority I am doing these things. ²⁵Where did John's baptism come from? Was it from heaven? Or did it come from human authority?"

They talked to each other about it. They said, "If we say, 'From heaven,' he will ask, 'Then why didn't you believe him?' ²⁶But what if we say, 'From human authority'? We are afraid of the people. Everyone believes that John was a prophet."

²⁷So they answered Jesus, "We don't know."

Jesus said, "Then I won't tell you by what authority I am doing these things either.

The Story of the Two Sons

²⁸"What do you think about this? A man had two sons. He went to the first and said, 'Son, go and work today in the vineyard.'

²⁹"'I will not,' the son answered. But later he changed his mind and went.

³⁰"Then the father went to the other son. He said the same thing. The son answered, 'I will, sir.' But he did not go.

³¹"Which of the two sons did what his father wanted?"

"The first," they answered.

Jesus said to them, "What I'm about to tell you is true. Tax collectors and prostitutes will enter the kingdom of God ahead of you. ³²John came to show you the right way to live. And you did not believe him. But the tax collectors and the prostitutes did. You saw this. But even then you did not turn away from your sins and believe him.

The Story of the Renters

³³"Listen to another story. A man who owned some land planted a vineyard. He put a wall around it. He dug a pit for a winepress in it. He also built a lookout tower. He rented the vineyard out to some farmers. Then he went away on a journey. ³⁴When harvest time approached, he sent his servants to the renters. He told the servants to collect his share of the fruit.

³⁵"But the renters grabbed his servants. They beat one of them. They killed another. They threw stones at the third to kill him. ³⁶Then the man sent other servants to the renters. He sent more than he did the first time. The renters treated them the same way.

³⁷"Last of all, he sent his son to them. 'They will respect my son,' he said.

³⁸"But the renters saw the son coming. They said to each other, 'This is the one who will receive all the owner's property some-

day. Come, let's kill him. Then everything will be ours.' ³⁹So they took him and threw him out of the vineyard. Then they killed him.

⁴⁰"When the owner of the vineyard comes back, what will he do to those renters?"

⁴¹"He will destroy those evil people," they replied. "Then he will rent the vineyard out to other renters. They will give him his share of the crop at harvest time."

⁴²Jesus said to them, "Haven't you ever read what the Scriptures say,

"'The stone the builders did not accept
    has become the most important stone.
The Lord has done this.
    It is wonderful in our eyes'?   *(Psalm 118:22,23)*

⁴³"So here is what I tell you. The kingdom of God will be taken away from you. It will be given to people who will produce its fruit. ⁴⁴Everyone who falls on that stone will be broken to pieces. But the stone will crush anyone it falls on."

⁴⁵The chief priests and the Pharisees heard Jesus' stories. They knew he was talking about them. ⁴⁶So they looked for a way to arrest him. But they were afraid of the crowd. The people believed that Jesus was a prophet.

The Story of the Wedding Dinner

22 Jesus told them more stories. He said, ²"Here is what the kingdom of heaven is like. A king prepared a wedding dinner for his son. ³He sent his servants to those who had been invited to the dinner. The servants told them to come. But they refused.

⁴"Then he sent some more servants. He said, 'Tell those who were invited that I have prepared my dinner. I have killed my oxen and my best-fed cattle. Everything is ready. Come to the wedding dinner.'

⁵"But the people paid no attention. One went away to his field. Another went away to his business. ⁶The rest grabbed his servants. They treated them badly and then killed them.

⁷"The king became very angry. He sent his army to destroy them. They killed those murderers and burned their city.

⁸"Then the king said to his servants, 'The wedding dinner is ready. But those I invited were not fit to come. ⁹Go to the street corners. Invite to the dinner anyone you can find.' ¹⁰So the ser-

vants went out into the streets. They gathered all the people they could find, both good and bad. Soon the wedding hall was filled with guests.

[11]"The king came in to see the guests. He noticed a man there who was not wearing wedding clothes. [12]'Friend,' he asked, 'how did you get in here without wedding clothes?' The man was left without anything to say.

[13]"Then the king told his servants, 'Tie him up, hand and foot. Throw him outside into the darkness. Out there people will sob and grind their teeth.'

[14]"Many are invited, but few are chosen."

Is It Right to Pay Taxes to Caesar?

[15]The Pharisees went out. They made plans to trap Jesus with his own words. [16]They sent their followers to him. They sent the Herodians with them.

"Teacher," they said, "we know you are a man of honor. You teach the way of God truthfully. You don't let others tell you what to do or say. You don't care how important they are. [17]Tell us then, what do you think? Is it right to pay taxes to Caesar or not?"

[18]But Jesus knew their evil plans. He said, "You pretenders! Why are you trying to trap me? [19]Show me the coin used for paying the tax."

They brought him a silver coin.

[20]He asked them, "Whose picture is this? And whose words?"

[21]"Caesar's," they replied.

Then he said to them, "Give to Caesar what belongs to Caesar. And give to God what belongs to God."

[22]When they heard this, they were amazed. So they left him and went away.

Marriage When the Dead Rise

[23]That same day the Sadducees came to Jesus with a question. They do not believe that people rise from the dead.

[24]"Teacher," they said, "here is what Moses told us. If a man dies without having children, his brother must get married to the

GREAT VERSE — TO — REMEMBER

22:14 Many are invited, but few are chosen.

widow. He must have children for his brother. ²⁵There were seven brothers among us. The first one got married and died. Since he had no children, he left his wife to his brother. ²⁶The same thing happened to the second and third brothers. It happened right on down to the seventh brother. ²⁷Finally, the woman died. ²⁸Now then, when the dead rise, whose wife will she be? All seven of them were married to her."

²⁹Jesus replied, "You are mistaken, because you do not know the Scriptures. And you do not know the power of God. ³⁰When the dead rise, they won't get married. And their parents won't give them to be married. They will be like the angels in heaven.

³¹"What about the dead rising? Haven't you read what God said to you? ³²He said, 'I am the God of Abraham. I am the God of Isaac. And I am the God of Jacob.' *(Exodus 3:6)* He is not the God of the dead. He is the God of the living."

³³When the crowds heard this, they were amazed by what he taught.

The Most Important Commandment

³⁴The Pharisees heard that the Sadducees weren't able to answer Jesus. So the Pharisees got together. ³⁵One of them was an authority on the law. So he tested Jesus with a question. ³⁶"Teacher," he asked, "which is the most important commandment in the Law?"

³⁷Jesus replied, "'Love the Lord your God with all your heart and with all your soul. Love him with all your mind.' *(Deuteronomy 6:5)* ³⁸This is the first and most important commandment. ³⁹And the second is like it. 'Love your neighbor as you love yourself.' *(Leviticus 19:18)* ⁴⁰Everything that is written in the Law and the Prophets is based on these two commandments."

Whose Son Is the Christ?

⁴¹The Pharisees were gathered together. Jesus asked them, ⁴²"What do you think about the Christ? Whose son is he?"

GREAT VERSE —TO— REMEMBER

22:37-39 Love the Lord your God with all your heart and with all your soul ... Love your neighbor as you love yourself.

"The son of David," they replied.

⁴³He said to them, "Then how is it that David calls him 'Lord'? David himself spoke by the Holy Spirit. He said,

⁴⁴ " 'The Lord said to my Lord,
    "Sit at my right hand
    until I put your enemies
    under your control." '   *(Psalm 110:1)*

⁴⁵So if David calls him 'Lord,' how can he be David's son?"

⁴⁶No one could answer him with a single word. From that day on, no one dared to ask him any more questions.

Jesus Judges the Pharisees and the Teachers of the Law

23 Jesus spoke to the crowds and to his disciples. ²"The teachers of the law and the Pharisees sit in Moses' seat," he said. ³"So you must obey them. Do everything they tell you. But don't do what they do. They don't practice what they preach. ⁴They tie up heavy loads and put them on other people's shoulders. But they themselves aren't willing to lift a finger to move them.

⁵"Everything they do is done for others to see. On their foreheads and arms they wear little boxes that hold Scripture verses. They make the boxes very wide. And they make the tassels on their coats very long.

⁶"They love to sit down in the place of honor at dinners. They also love to have the most important seats in the synagogues. ⁷They love to be greeted in the market places. They love it when people call them 'Rabbi.'

⁸"But you shouldn't be called 'Rabbi.' You have only one Master, and you are all brothers and sisters. ⁹Do not call anyone on earth 'father.' You have one Father, and he is in heaven. ¹⁰You shouldn't be called 'teacher.' You have one Teacher, and he is the Christ. ¹¹The most important person among you will be your servant. ¹²Those who lift themselves up will be brought down. And those who are brought down will be lifted up.

¹³/¹⁴"How terrible it will be for you, teachers of the law and Pharisees! You pretenders! You shut the kingdom of heaven in people's faces. You yourselves do not enter. And you will not let those enter who are trying to.

¹⁵"How terrible for you, teachers of the law and Pharisees! You pretenders! You travel everywhere to win one person to your

faith. Then you make that person twice as much a child of hell as you are.

¹⁶"How terrible for you, blind guides! You say, 'If anyone takes an oath in the name of the temple, it means nothing. But anyone who takes an oath in the name of the gold of the temple must keep the oath.' ¹⁷You blind fools! Which is more important? Is it the gold? Or is it the temple that makes the gold holy?

¹⁸"You also say, 'If anyone takes an oath in the name of the altar, it means nothing. But anyone who takes an oath in the name of the gift on it must keep the oath.' ¹⁹You blind men! Which is more important? Is it the gift? Or is it the altar that makes the gift holy?

²⁰"So anyone who takes an oath in the name of the altar takes an oath in the name of it and of everything on it. ²¹And anyone who takes an oath in the name of the temple takes an oath in the name of it and of the One who lives in it. ²²And anyone who takes an oath in the name of heaven takes an oath in the name of God's throne and of the One who sits on it.

²³"How terrible for you, teachers of the law and Pharisees! You pretenders! You give God a tenth of your spices, like mint, dill and cummin. But you have not practiced the more important things of the law, like fairness, mercy and faithfulness. You should have practiced the last things without failing to do the first. ²⁴You blind guides! You remove the smallest insect from your food. But you swallow a whole camel!

²⁵"How terrible for you, teachers of the law and Pharisees! You pretenders! You clean the outside of the cup and dish. But on the inside you are full of greed. You only want to satisfy yourselves. ²⁶Blind Pharisee! First clean the inside of the cup and dish. Then the outside will also be clean.

²⁷"How terrible for you, teachers of the law and Pharisees! You pretenders! You are like tombs painted white. They look beautiful on the outside. But on the inside they are full of the bones of the dead. They are also full of other things that are not pure and clean. ²⁸It is the same with you. On the outside you seem to be doing what is right. But on the inside you are full of what is wrong. You pretend to be what you are not.

²⁹"How terrible for you, teachers of the law and Pharisees! You pretenders! You build tombs for the prophets. You decorate the graves of the godly. ³⁰And you say, 'If we had lived in the days of those who lived before us, we wouldn't have done what they did. We wouldn't have helped to kill the prophets.' ³¹So you give wit-

ness against yourselves. You admit that you are the children of those who murdered the prophets. ³²So finish the sins that those who lived before you started!

³³"You nest of poisonous snakes! How will you escape from being sentenced to hell? ³⁴So I am sending you prophets, people who are wise, and teachers. You will kill some of them. You will nail some to a cross. Others you will whip in your synagogues. You will chase them from town to town.

³⁵"So you will pay for all the godly people's blood spilled on earth. I mean from the blood of godly Abel to the blood of Zechariah, the son of Berekiah. Zechariah was the one you murdered between the temple and the altar. ³⁶What I'm about to tell you is true. All this will happen to those who are now living.

³⁷"Jerusalem! Jerusalem! You kill the prophets and throw stones in order to kill those who are sent to you. Many times I have wanted to gather your people together. I have wanted to be like a hen who gathers her chicks under her wings. But you would not let me! ³⁸Look, your house is left empty. ³⁹I tell you, you will not see me again until you say, 'Blessed is the one who comes in the name of the Lord.'" *(Psalm 118:26)*

Signs of the End

24 Jesus left the temple. He was walking away when his disciples came up to him. They wanted to call his attention to the temple buildings.

²"Do you see all these things?" Jesus asked. "What I'm about to tell you is true. Not one stone here will be left on top of another. Every stone will be thrown down."

³Jesus was sitting on the Mount of Olives. There the disciples came to him in private. "Tell us," they said. "When will this happen? And what will be the sign of your coming? What will be the sign of the end?"

⁴Jesus answered, "Keep watch! Be careful that no one fools you.

GREAT VERSE —TO— REMEMBER

24:4-5 Jesus answered, "Keep watch! Be careful that no one fools you. Many will come in my name. They will claim, 'I am the Christ!' They will fool many people."

⁵Many will come in my name. They will claim, 'I am the Christ!' They will fool many people.

⁶"You will hear about wars. You will also hear people talking about future wars. Don't be alarmed. Those things must happen. But the end still isn't here. ⁷Nation will fight against nation. Kingdom will fight against kingdom. People will go hungry. There will be earthquakes in many places. ⁸All these are the beginning of birth pains.

⁹"Then people will hand you over to be treated badly and killed. All nations will hate you because of me. ¹⁰At that time, many will turn away from their faith. They will hate each other. They will hand each other over to their enemies. ¹¹Many false prophets will appear. They will fool many people. ¹²Because evil will grow, most people's love will grow cold. ¹³But the one who stands firm to the end will be saved. ¹⁴This good news of the kingdom will be preached in the whole world. It will be a witness to all nations. Then the end will come.

¹⁵"The prophet Daniel spoke about 'the hated thing that destroys.' *(Daniel 9:27; 11:31; 12:11)* Someday you will see it standing in the holy place. The reader should understand this. ¹⁶Then those who are in Judea should escape to the mountains. ¹⁷No one on the roof should go down into the house to take anything out. ¹⁸No one in the field should go back to get a coat. ¹⁹How awful it will be in those days for pregnant women! How awful for nursing mothers! ²⁰Pray that you will not have to escape in winter or on the Sabbath day. ²¹There will be terrible suffering in those days. It will be worse than any other from the beginning of the world until now. And there will never be any like them again. ²²If the time had not been cut short, no one would live. But because of God's chosen people, it will be shortened.

²³"At that time someone may say to you, 'Look! Here is the Christ!' Or, 'There he is!' Do not believe it. ²⁴False Christs and false prophets will appear. They will do great signs and miracles. They will try to fool God's chosen people if possible. ²⁵See, I have told you ahead of time.

²⁶"So if anyone tells you, 'He is far out in the desert,' do not go out there. Or if anyone says, 'He is deep inside the house,' do not believe it. ²⁷Lightning that comes from the east can be seen in the west. It will be the same when the Son of Man comes. ²⁸The vultures will gather wherever there is a dead animal.

²⁹"Right after the terrible suffering of those days,

"'the sun will be darkened.

> The moon will not shine.
> The stars will fall from the sky.
> The heavenly bodies will be shaken.' *(Isaiah 13:10; 34:4)*

[30]"At that time the sign of the Son of Man will appear in the sky. All the nations on earth will be sad. They will see the Son of Man coming on the clouds of the sky. He will come with power and great glory. [31]He will send his angels with a loud trumpet call. They will gather his chosen people from all four directions. They will bring them from one end of the heavens to the other.

[32]"Learn a lesson from the fig tree. As soon as its twigs get tender and its leaves come out, you know that summer is near. [33]In the same way, when you see all those things happening, you know that the end is near. It is right at the door. [34]What I'm about to tell you is true. The people living at that time will certainly not pass away until all those things have happened. [35]Heaven and earth will pass away. But my words will never pass away.

The Day and Hour Are Not Known

[36]"No one knows about that day or hour. Not even the angels in heaven know. The Son does not know. Only the Father knows.

[37]"Remember how it was in the days of Noah. It will be the same when the Son of Man comes. [38]In the days before the flood, people were eating and drinking. They were getting married. They were giving their daughters to be married. They did all those things right up to the day Noah entered the ark. [39]They knew nothing about what would happen until the flood came and took them all away. That is how it will be when the Son of Man comes.

[40]"Two men will be in the field. One will be taken and the other left. [41]Two women will be grinding with a hand mill. One will be taken and the other left.

[42]"So keep watch. You do not know on what day your Lord will come. [43]You must understand something. Suppose the owner of the house knew what time of night the robber was coming. Then

GREAT VERSE —TO— REMEMBER **24:35** Heaven and earth will pass away. But my words will never pass away.

he would have kept watch. He would not have let his house be broken into. [44]So you also must be ready. The Son of Man will come at an hour when you don't expect him.

[45]"Suppose a master puts one of his servants in charge of the other servants in his house. The servant's job is to give them their food at the right time. The master wants a faithful and wise servant for this. [46]It will be good for the servant if the master finds him doing his job when the master returns. [47]What I'm about to tell you is true. The master will put that servant in charge of everything he owns.

[48]"But suppose that servant is evil. Suppose he says to himself, 'My master is staying away a long time.' [49]Suppose he begins to beat the other servants. And suppose he eats and drinks with those who drink too much. [50]The master of that servant will come back on a day the servant doesn't expect him. He will return at an hour the servant does not know. [51]Then the master will cut him to pieces. He will send him to the place where pretenders go. There people will sob and grind their teeth.

The Story of Ten Bridesmaids

25 "Here is what the kingdom of heaven will be like at that time. Ten bridesmaids took their lamps and went out to meet the groom. [2]Five of them were foolish. Five were wise. [3]The foolish ones took their lamps but didn't take any olive oil with them. [4]The wise ones took oil in jars along with their lamps. [5]The groom did not come for a long time. So the bridesmaids all grew tired and fell asleep.

[6]"At midnight someone cried out, 'Here's the groom! Come out to meet him!'

[7]"Then all the bridesmaids woke up and got their lamps ready. [8]The foolish ones said to the wise ones, 'Give us some of your oil. Our lamps are going out.'

[9]"'No,' they replied. 'There may not be enough for all of us. Instead, go to those who sell oil. Buy some for yourselves.'

[10]"So they went to buy the oil. But while they were on their way, the groom arrived. The bridesmaids who were ready went in with him to the wedding dinner. Then the door was shut.

[11]"Later, the other bridesmaids also came. 'Sir! Sir!' they said. 'Open the door for us!'

[12]"But he replied, 'What I'm about to tell you is true. I don't know you.'

¹³"So keep watch. You do not know the day or the hour that the groom will come.

The Story of Three Servants

¹⁴"Again, here is what the kingdom of heaven will be like. A man was going on a journey. He sent for his servants and put them in charge of his property. ¹⁵He gave $10,000 to one. He gave $4,000 to another. And he gave $2,000 to the third. The man gave each servant the amount of money he knew the servant could take care of. Then he went on his journey.

¹⁶"The servant who had received the $10,000 went at once and put his money to work. He earned $10,000 more. ¹⁷The one with the $4,000 earned $4,000 more. ¹⁸But the man who had received $2,000 went and dug a hole in the ground. He hid his master's money in it.

¹⁹"After a long time the master of those servants returned. He wanted to collect all the money they had earned. ²⁰The man who had received $10,000 brought the other $10,000. 'Master,' he said, 'you trusted me with $10,000. See, I have earned $10,000 more.'

²¹"His master replied, 'You have done well, good and faithful servant! You have been faithful with a few things. I will put you in charge of many things. Come and share your master's happiness!'

²²"The man with $4,000 also came. 'Master,' he said, 'you trusted me with $4,000. See, I have earned $4,000 more.'

²³"His master replied, 'You have done well, good and faithful servant! You have been faithful with a few things. I will put you in charge of many things. Come and share your master's happiness!'

²⁴"Then the man who had received $2,000 came. 'Master,' he said, 'I knew that you are a hard man. You harvest where you have not planted. You gather crops where you have not scattered seed. ²⁵So I was afraid. I went out and hid your $2,000 in the ground. See, here is what belongs to you.'

²⁶"His master replied, 'You evil, lazy servant! So you knew that I harvest where I have not planted? You knew that I gather crops where I have not scattered seed? ²⁷Well then, you should have put my money in the bank. When I returned, I would have received it back with interest.

²⁸"'Take the $2,000 from him. Give it to the one who has $20,000. ²⁹Those who have will be given more. They will have

more than enough. And what about those who do not have? Even what they have will be taken away from them. ³⁰Throw that worthless servant outside. There in the darkness, people will sob and grind their teeth.'

The Sheep and the Goats

³¹"The Son of Man will come in all his glory. All the angels will come with him. Then he will sit on his throne in the glory of heaven. ³²All the nations will be gathered in front of him. He will separate the people into two groups. He will be like a shepherd who separates the sheep from the goats. ³³He will put the sheep to his right and the goats to his left.

³⁴"Then the King will speak to those on his right. He will say, 'You are blessed by my Father. Come and take what is yours. It is the kingdom prepared for you since the world was created. ³⁵I was hungry. And you gave me something to eat. I was thirsty. And you gave me something to drink. I was a stranger. And you invited me in. ³⁶I needed clothes. And you gave them to me. I was sick. And you took care of me. I was in prison. And you came to visit me.'

³⁷"Then the people who have done what is right will answer him. 'Lord,' they will ask, 'when did we see you hungry and feed you? When did we see you thirsty and give you something to drink? ³⁸When did we see you as a stranger and invite you in? When did we see you needing clothes and give them to you? ³⁹When did we see you sick or in prison and go to visit you?'

⁴⁰"The King will reply, 'What I'm about to tell you is true. Anything you did for one of the least important of these brothers and sisters of mine, you did for me.'

⁴¹"Then he will say to those on his left, 'You are cursed! Go away from me into the fire that burns forever. It has been prepared for the devil and his angels. ⁴²I was hungry. But you gave me nothing to eat. I was thirsty. But you gave me nothing to

GREAT VERSE — TO — REMEMBER

25:40 Anything you did for one of the least important of these brothers and sisters of mine, you did for me.

drink. ⁴³I was a stranger. But you did not invite me in. I needed clothes. But you did not give me any. I was sick and in prison. But you did not take care of me.'

⁴⁴"They also will answer, 'Lord, when did we see you hungry or thirsty and not help you? When did we see you as a stranger or needing clothes or sick or in prison and not help you?'

⁴⁵"He will reply, 'What I'm about to tell you is true. Anything you didn't do for one of the least important of these, you didn't do for me.'

⁴⁶"Then they will go away to be punished forever. But those who have done what is right will receive eternal life."

The Plan to Kill Jesus

26 Jesus finished saying all these things. Then he said to his disciples, ²"As you know, the Passover Feast is two days away. The Son of Man will be handed over to be nailed to a cross."

³Then the chief priests met with the elders of the people. They met in the palace of Caiaphas, the high priest. ⁴They made plans to arrest Jesus in a clever way. They wanted to kill him. ⁵"But not during the Feast," they said. "The people may stir up trouble."

A Woman Pours Perfume on Jesus

⁶Jesus was in Bethany. He was in the home of a man named Simon, who had a skin disease. ⁷A woman came to Jesus with a special sealed jar of very expensive perfume. She poured the perfume on his head while he was at the table.

⁸When the disciples saw this, they became angry. "Why this waste?" they asked. ⁹"The perfume could have been sold at a high price. The money could have been given to poor people."

¹⁰Jesus was aware of this. So he said to them, "Why are you bothering this woman? She has done a beautiful thing to me. ¹¹You will always have poor people with you. But you will not always have me. ¹²She poured the perfume on my body to prepare me to be buried. ¹³What I'm about to tell you is true. What she has done will be told anywhere this good news is preached all over the world. It will be told in memory of her."

Judas Agrees to Hand Jesus Over

¹⁴One of the Twelve went to the chief priests. His name was Judas Iscariot. ¹⁵He asked, "What will you give me if I hand Jesus over to

you?" So they counted out 30 silver coins for him. ¹⁶From then on, Judas watched for the right time to hand Jesus over to them.

The Lord's Supper

¹⁷It was the first day of the Feast of Unleavened Bread. The disciples came to Jesus. They asked, "Where do you want us to prepare for you to eat the Passover meal?"

¹⁸He replied, "Go into the city to a certain man. Tell him, 'The Teacher says: My time is near. I am going to celebrate the Passover at your house with my disciples.'"

¹⁹So the disciples did what Jesus had told them to do. They prepared the Passover meal.

²⁰When evening came, Jesus was at the table with the Twelve. ²¹While they were eating, he said, "What I'm about to tell you is true. One of you will hand me over to my enemies."

²²The disciples became very sad. One after the other, they began to say to him, "It's not I, Lord, is it?"

²³Jesus replied, "The one who has dipped his hand into the bowl with me will hand me over. ²⁴The Son of Man will go just as it is written about him. But how terrible it will be for the one who hands over the Son of Man! It would be better for him if he had not been born."

²⁵Judas was the one who was going to hand him over. He said, "It's not I, Rabbi, is it?"

Jesus answered, "Yes. It is you."

²⁶While they were eating, Jesus took bread. He gave thanks and broke it. He handed it to his disciples and said, "Take this and eat it. This is my body."

²⁷Then he took the cup. He gave thanks and handed it to them. He said, "All of you drink from it. ²⁸This is my blood of the new covenant. It is poured out to forgive the sins of many. ²⁹Here is what I tell you. From now on, I will not drink from the fruit of the vine until the day I drink it again with you in my Father's kingdom."

³⁰Then they sang a hymn and went out to the Mount of Olives.

Jesus Says That Peter Will Fail

³¹Jesus told them, "This very night you will all turn away because of me. It is written:

"'I will strike the shepherd.
    The sheep of the flock will be scattered.' *(Zechariah 13:7)*

³²But after I rise from the dead, I will go ahead of you into Galilee."

³³Peter replied, "All the others may turn away because of you. But I never will."

³⁴"What I'm about to tell you is true," Jesus answered. "It will happen this very night. Before the rooster crows, you will say three times that you don't know me."

³⁵But Peter said, "I may have to die with you. But I will never say I don't know you." And all the other disciples said the same thing.

Jesus Prays in Gethsemane

³⁶Then Jesus went with his disciples to a place called Gethsemane. He said to them, "Sit here while I go over there and pray."

³⁷He took Peter and the two sons of Zebedee along with him. He began to be sad and troubled. ³⁸Then he said to them, "My soul is very sad. I feel close to death. Stay here. Keep watch with me."

³⁹He went a little farther. Then he fell with his face to the ground. He prayed, "My Father, if it is possible, take this cup of suffering from me. But let what you want be done, not what I want."

⁴⁰Then he returned to his disciples and found them sleeping. "Couldn't you men keep watch with me for one hour?" he asked Peter. ⁴¹"Watch and pray. Then you won't fall into sin when you are tempted. The spirit is willing. But the body is weak."

⁴²Jesus went away a second time. He prayed, "My Father, is it possible for this cup to be taken away? But if I must drink it, may what you want be done."

⁴³Then he came back. Again he found them sleeping. They couldn't keep their eyes open. ⁴⁴So he left them and went away once more. For the third time he prayed the same thing.

⁴⁵Then he returned to the disciples. He said to them, "Are you still sleeping and resting? Look! The hour is near. The Son of Man

GREAT VERSE — TO — REMEMBER

26:39 [Jesus] prayed, "My Father, if it is possible, take this cup of suffering from me. But let what you want be done, not what I want."

is about to be handed over to sinners. ⁴⁶Get up! Let us go! Here comes the one who is handing me over to them!"

Jesus Is Arrested

⁴⁷While Jesus was still speaking, Judas arrived. He was one of the Twelve. A large crowd was with him. They were carrying swords and clubs. The chief priests and the elders of the people had sent them. ⁴⁸Judas, who was going to hand Jesus over, had arranged a signal with them. "The one I kiss is the man," he said. "Arrest him." ⁴⁹So Judas went to Jesus at once. He said, "Greetings, Rabbi!" And he kissed him.

⁵⁰Jesus replied, "Friend, do what you came to do."

Then the men stepped forward. They grabbed Jesus and arrested him. ⁵¹At that moment, one of Jesus' companions reached for his sword. He pulled it out and struck the servant of the high priest with it. He cut off the servant's ear.

⁵²"Put your sword back in its place," Jesus said to him. "All who use the sword will die by the sword. ⁵³Do you think I can't ask my Father for help? He would send an army of more than 70,000 angels right away. ⁵⁴But then how would the Scriptures come true? They say it must happen in this way."

⁵⁵At that time Jesus spoke to the crowd. "Am I leading a band of armed men against you?" he asked. "Do you have to come out with swords and clubs to capture me? Every day I sat in the temple courtyard teaching. And you didn't arrest me. ⁵⁶But all this has happened so that the words of the prophets would come true."

Then all the disciples left him and ran away.

Jesus Is Taken to the Sanhedrin

⁵⁷Those who had arrested Jesus took him to Caiaphas, the high priest. The teachers of the law and the elders had come together there. ⁵⁸Not too far away, Peter followed Jesus. He went right up to the courtyard of the high priest. He entered and sat down with the guards to see what would happen.

⁵⁹The chief priests and the whole Sanhedrin were looking for something to use against Jesus. They wanted to put him to death. ⁶⁰But they did not find any proof, even though many false witnesses came forward.

Finally, two other witnesses came forward. ⁶¹They said, "This fellow claimed, 'I am able to destroy the temple of God. I can build it again in three days.'"

⁶²Then the high priest stood up. He asked Jesus, "Aren't you going to answer? What are these charges that these men are bringing against you?"

⁶³But Jesus remained silent.

The high priest said to him, "I command you under oath by the living God. Tell us if you are the Christ, the Son of God."

⁶⁴"Yes. It is just as you say," Jesus replied. "But here is what I say to all of you. In days to come, you will see the Son of Man sitting at the right hand of the Mighty One. You will see the Son of Man coming on the clouds of heaven."

⁶⁵Then the high priest tore his clothes. He said, "He has spoken a very evil thing against God! Why do we need any more witnesses? You have heard him say this evil thing. ⁶⁶What do you think?"

"He must die!" they answered.

⁶⁷Then they spit in his face. They hit him with their fists. Others slapped him. ⁶⁸They said, "Prophesy to us, Christ! Who hit you?"

Peter Says He Does Not Know Jesus

⁶⁹Peter was sitting out in the courtyard. A woman servant came to him. "You also were with Jesus of Galilee," she said.

⁷⁰But in front of all of them, Peter said he was not. "I don't know what you're talking about," he said.

⁷¹Then he went out to the gate leading into the courtyard. There another woman saw him. She said to the people, "This fellow was with Jesus of Nazareth."

⁷²Again he said he was not. With an oath he said, "I don't know the man!"

⁷³After a little while, those standing there went up to Peter. "You must be one of them," they said. "The way you talk gives you away."

⁷⁴Then Peter began to call down curses on himself. He took an oath and said to them, "I don't know the man!"

Right away a rooster crowed. ⁷⁵Then Peter remembered what Jesus had spoken. "The rooster will crow," he had said. "Before it does, you will say three times that you don't know me." Peter went outside. He broke down and sobbed.

Judas Hangs Himself

27 It was early in the morning. All the chief priests and the elders of the people decided to put Jesus to death. ²They tied him up and led him away. Then they handed him over to Pilate, who was the governor.

³Judas, who had handed him over, saw that Jesus had been sentenced to die. He felt deep shame and sadness for what he had done. So he returned the 30 silver coins to the chief priests and the elders. ⁴"I have sinned," he said. "I handed over a man who is not guilty."

"What do we care?" they replied. "That's your problem."

⁵So Judas threw the money into the temple and left. Then he went away and hanged himself.

⁶The chief priests picked up the coins. They said, "It's against the law to put this money into the temple fund. It is blood money. It has paid for a man's death." ⁷So they decided to use the money to buy the potter's field. People from other countries would be buried there. ⁸That is why it has been called The Field of Blood to this very day. ⁹Then the words spoken by Jeremiah the prophet came true. He had said, "They took the 30 silver coins. This was the price set for him by the people of Israel. ¹⁰They used the coins to buy the potter's field, just as the Lord commanded me." *(Zechariah 11:12,13; Jeremiah 19:1–13; 32:6–9)*

Jesus Is Brought to Pilate

¹¹Jesus was standing in front of the governor. The governor asked him, "Are you the king of the Jews?"

"Yes. It is just as you say," Jesus replied.

¹²But when the chief priests and the elders brought charges against him, he did not answer. ¹³Then Pilate asked him, "Don't you hear the charges they are bringing against you?"

¹⁴But Jesus made no reply, not even to a single charge. The governor was really amazed.

¹⁵It was the governor's practice at the Passover Feast to let one prisoner go free. The people could choose the one they wanted. ¹⁶At that time they had a well-known prisoner named Barabbas. ¹⁷So when the crowd gathered, Pilate asked them, "Which one do you want me to set free? Barabbas? Or Jesus who is called Christ?" ¹⁸Pilate knew that the leaders were jealous. He knew this was why they had handed Jesus over to him.

¹⁹While Pilate was sitting on the judge's seat, his wife sent him a message. It said, "Don't have anything to do with that man. He is not guilty. I have suffered a great deal in a dream today because of him."

²⁰But the chief priests and the elders talked the crowd in-

to asking for Barabbas and having Jesus put to death.
²¹"Which of the two do you want me to set free?" asked the
governor.

"Barabbas," they answered.

²²"Then what should I do with Jesus who is called Christ?"
Pilate asked.

They all answered, "Crucify him!"

²³"Why? What wrong has he done?" asked Pilate.

But they shouted even louder, "Crucify him!"

²⁴Pilate saw that he wasn't getting anywhere. Instead, the crowd
was starting to get angry. So he took water and washed his hands
in front of them. "I am not guilty of this man's death," he said.
"You are accountable for that!"

²⁵All the people answered, "We and our children will accept the
guilt for his death!"

²⁶Pilate let Barabbas go free. But he had Jesus whipped. Then
he handed him over to be nailed to a cross.

The Soldiers Make Fun of Jesus

²⁷The governor's soldiers took Jesus into the palace, which was
called the Praetorium. All the rest of the soldiers gathered around
him. ²⁸They took off his clothes and put a purple robe on him.
²⁹Then they twisted thorns together to make a crown. They
placed it on his head. They put a stick in his right hand. Then
they fell on their knees in front of him and made fun of him.
"We honor you, king of the Jews!" they said. ³⁰They spit on him.
They hit him on the head with the stick again and again. ³¹After
they had made fun of him, they took off the robe. They put his
own clothes back on him. Then they led him away to nail him
to a cross.

Jesus Is Nailed to a Cross

³²On their way out of the city, they met a man from Cyrene.
His name was Simon. They forced him to carry the cross.

³³They came to a place called Golgotha. The word Golgotha
means The Place of the Skull. ³⁴There they mixed wine with bitter spices and gave it to Jesus to drink. After tasting it, he refused
to drink it. ³⁵When they had nailed him to the cross, they divided
up his clothes by casting lots. ³⁶They sat down and kept watch
over him there.

³⁷Above his head they placed the written charge against him. It
read, THIS IS JESUS, THE KING OF THE JEWS.

³⁸Two robbers were crucified with him. One was on his right and one was on his left. ³⁹Those who passed by shouted at Jesus and made fun of him. They shook their heads ⁴⁰and said, "So you are going to destroy the temple and build it again in three days? Then save yourself! Come down from the cross, if you are the Son of God!"

⁴¹In the same way the chief priests, the teachers of the law and the elders made fun of him. ⁴²"He saved others," they said. "But he can't save himself! He's the King of Israel! Let him come down now from the cross! Then we will believe in him. ⁴³He trusts in God. Let God rescue him now if he wants him. He's the one who said, 'I am the Son of God.'" ⁴⁴In the same way the robbers who were being crucified with Jesus also made fun of him.

Jesus Dies

⁴⁵From noon until three o'clock, the whole land was covered with darkness. ⁴⁶About three o'clock, Jesus cried out in a loud voice. He said, *"Eloi, Eloi, lama sabachthani?"* This means "My God, my God, why have you deserted me?" *(Psalm 22:1)*

⁴⁷Some of those standing there heard Jesus cry out. They said, "He's calling for Elijah."

⁴⁸Right away one of them ran and got a sponge. He filled it with wine vinegar and put it on a stick. He offered it to Jesus to drink. ⁴⁹The rest said, "Leave him alone. Let's see if Elijah comes to save him."

⁵⁰After Jesus cried out again in a loud voice, he died.

⁵¹At that moment the temple curtain was torn in two from top to bottom. The earth shook. The rocks split. ⁵²Tombs broke open. The bodies of many holy people who had died were raised to life. ⁵³They came out of the tombs. After Jesus was raised to life, they went into the holy city. There they appeared to many people.

⁵⁴The Roman commander and those guarding Jesus saw the earthquake and all that had happened. They were terrified. They exclaimed, "He was surely the Son of God!"

⁵⁵Not very far away, many women were watching. They had followed Jesus from Galilee to take care of his needs. ⁵⁶Mary Magdalene was among them. Mary, the mother of James and Joses, was also there. So was the mother of Zebedee's sons.

Jesus Is Buried

⁵⁷As evening approached, a rich man came from the town of Arimathea. His name was Joseph. He had become a follower of

Jesus. [58]He went to Pilate and asked for Jesus' body. Pilate ordered that it be given to him. [59]Joseph took the body and wrapped it in a clean linen cloth. [60]He placed it in his own new tomb that he had cut out of the rock. He rolled a big stone in front of the entrance to the tomb. Then he went away.

[61]Mary Magdalene and the other Mary were sitting there across from the tomb.

The Guard at the Tomb

[62]The next day was the day after Preparation Day. The chief priests and the Pharisees went to Pilate. [63]"Sir," they said, "we remember something that liar said while he was still alive. He claimed, 'After three days I will rise again.' [64]So give the order to make the tomb secure until the third day. If you don't, his disciples may come and steal the body. Then they will tell the people that he has been raised from the dead. This last lie will be worse than the first."

[65]"Take a guard," Pilate answered. "Go. Make the tomb as secure as you can." [66]So they went and made the tomb secure. They put a seal on the stone and placed a guard on duty.

Jesus Rises From the Dead

28 The Sabbath day was now over. It was dawn on the first day of the week. Mary Magdalene and the other Mary went to look at the tomb.

[2]There was a powerful earthquake. An angel of the Lord came down from heaven. The angel went to the tomb, rolled back the stone and sat on it. [3]His appearance was like lightning. His clothes were as white as snow. [4]The guards were so afraid of him that they shook and became like dead men.

[5]The angel said to the women, "Don't be afraid. I know that you are looking for Jesus, who was crucified. [6]He is not here! He has risen, just as he said he would! Come and see the place where he was lying. [7]Go quickly! Tell his disciples, 'He has risen from the dead. He is going ahead of you into Galilee. There you will see him.' Now I have told you."

[8]So the women hurried away from the tomb. They were afraid, but they were filled with joy. They ran to tell the disciples.

[9]Suddenly Jesus met them. "Greetings!" he said.

They came to him, took hold of his feet and worshiped him.

[10]Then Jesus said to them, "Don't be afraid. Go and tell my brothers to go to Galilee. There they will see me."

The Guards Report to the Chief Priests

¹¹While the women were on their way, some of the guards went into the city. They reported to the chief priests all that had happened. ¹²When the chief priests met with the elders, they came up with a plan. They gave the soldiers a large amount of money. ¹³They told the soldiers, "We want you to say, 'His disciples came during the night. They stole his body while we were sleeping.' ¹⁴If the governor hears this report, we will pay him off. That will keep you out of trouble."

¹⁵So the soldiers took the money and did as they were told. This story has spread all around among the Jews to this very day.

Jesus' Final Orders to His Disciples

¹⁶Then the 11 disciples went to Galilee. They went to the mountain where Jesus had told them to go. ¹⁷When they saw him, they worshiped him. But some still had their doubts.

¹⁸Then Jesus came to them. He said, "All authority in heaven and on earth has been given to me. ¹⁹So you must go and make disciples of all nations. Baptize them in the name of the Father and of the Son and of the Holy Spirit. ²⁰Teach them to obey everything I have commanded you. And you can be sure that I am always with you, to the very end."

GREAT VERSE —TO— REMEMBER

28:19-20 Go and make disciples of all nations. Baptize them in the name of the Father and of the Son and of the Holy Spirit. Teach them to obey everything I have commanded you. And you can be sure that I am always with you, to the very end.

Mark

Why Was This Book Written?

John Mark wrote this Gospel. He was a follower of Jesus. He was the first person to write about Jesus' life. John Mark worked with Paul and Barnabas on their missionary trips. He worked with Peter too. He learned Jesus' stories from Peter. He wrote these stories in the book of Mark.

What Is This Book About?

The book of Mark told believers about Jesus. It told why he had to die. John Mark wrote an exciting book. Jesus was a man of action. He was always busy. Jesus did many things to prove he is the son of God.

What Is in This Book?

John the Baptist Prepares the Way

1 This is the beginning of the good news about Jesus Christ, the Son of God.

²Long ago Isaiah the prophet wrote,

"I will send my messenger ahead of you.
  He will prepare your way."   *(Malachi 3:1)*
³"A voice calls out in the desert,
'Prepare the way for the Lord.
  Make straight paths for him.'"   *(Isaiah 40:3)*

⁴And so John came. He baptized people in the desert. He also preached that people should be baptized and turn away from their sins. Then God would forgive them. ⁵All the people from the countryside of Judea went out to him. All the people from Jerusalem went too. When they admitted they had sinned, John baptized them in the Jordan River. ⁶John wore clothes made out of camel's hair. He had a leather belt around his waist. And he ate locusts and wild honey.

⁷Here is what John was preaching. "After me, one will come who is more powerful than I am. I'm not good enough to bend down and untie his sandals. ⁸I baptize you with water. But he will baptize you with the Holy Spirit."

Jesus Is Baptized and Tempted

⁹At that time Jesus came from Nazareth in Galilee. John baptized him in the Jordan River. ¹⁰Jesus was coming up out of the water. Just then he saw heaven being torn open. He saw the Holy Spirit coming down on him like a dove. ¹¹A voice came from heaven. It said, "You are my Son, and I love you. I am very pleased with you."

¹²At once the Holy Spirit sent Jesus out into the desert. ¹³He was in the desert 40 days. There Satan tempted him. Jesus was with the wild animals. And angels took care of him.

Jesus Chooses the First Disciples

¹⁴After John was put in prison, Jesus went into Galilee. He preached God's good news. ¹⁵"The time has come," he said. "The kingdom of God is near. Turn away from your sins and believe the good news!"

¹⁶One day Jesus was walking beside the Sea of Galilee. There he saw Simon and his brother Andrew. They were throwing a net

into the lake. They were fishermen. [17]"Come. Follow me," Jesus said. "I will make you fishers of people." [18]At once they left their nets and followed him.

[19]Then Jesus walked a little farther. As he did, he saw James, son of Zebedee, and his brother John. They were in a boat preparing their nets. [20]Right away he called out to them. They left their father Zebedee in the boat with the hired men. Then they followed Jesus.

Jesus Drives Out an Evil Spirit

[21]Jesus and those with him went to Capernaum. When the Sabbath day came, he went into the synagogue. There he began to teach. [22]The people were amazed at his teaching. He taught them like one who had authority. He did not talk like the teachers of the law.

[23]Just then a man in their synagogue cried out. He was controlled by an evil spirit. He said, [24]"What do you want with us, Jesus of Nazareth? Have you come to destroy us? I know who you are. You are the Holy One of God!"

[25]"Be quiet!" said Jesus firmly. "Come out of him!"

[26]The evil spirit shook the man wildly. Then it came out of him with a scream.

[27]All the people were amazed. So they asked each other, "What is this? A new teaching! And with so much authority! He even gives orders to evil spirits, and they obey him." [28]News about Jesus spread quickly all over Galilee.

Jesus Heals Many People

[29]Jesus and those with him left the synagogue. Right away they went with James and John to the home of Simon and Andrew. [30]Simon's mother-in-law was lying in bed. She had a fever. They told Jesus about her. [31]So he went to her. He took her hand and helped her up. The fever left her. Then she began to wait on them.

[32]That evening after sunset, the people brought to Jesus all who

GREAT VERSE —TO— REMEMBER

1:17 "Come. Follow me," Jesus said. "I will make you fishers of people."

were sick. They also brought all who were controlled by demons. ³³All the people in town gathered at the door. ³⁴Jesus healed many who had sicknesses of all kinds. He also drove out many demons. But he would not let the demons speak, because they knew who he was.

Jesus Prays in a Quiet Place

³⁵It was very early in the morning and still dark. Jesus got up and left the house. He went to a place where he could be alone. There he prayed. ³⁶Simon and his friends went to look for Jesus. ³⁷When they found him, they called out, "Everyone is looking for you!"

³⁸Jesus replied, "Let's go somewhere else. I want to go to the nearby towns. I must preach there also. That is why I have come." ³⁹So he traveled all around Galilee. He preached in their synagogues. He also drove out demons.

Jesus Heals a Man With a Skin Disease

⁴⁰A man who had a skin disease came to Jesus. On his knees he begged Jesus. He said, "If you are willing to make me 'clean,' you can do it."

⁴¹Jesus was filled with deep concern. He reached out his hand and touched the man. "I am willing to do it," he said. "Be 'clean'!" ⁴²Right away the disease left him. He was healed.

⁴³Jesus sent him away at once. He gave the man a strong warning. ⁴⁴"Don't tell this to anyone," he said. "Go and show yourself to the priest. Offer the sacrifices that Moses commanded. It will be a witness to the priest and the people that you are 'clean.'"

⁴⁵But the man went out and started talking right away. He spread the news to everyone. So Jesus could no longer enter a town openly. He stayed outside in lonely places. But people still came to him from everywhere.

Jesus Heals a Man Who Could Not Walk

2 A few days later, Jesus entered Capernaum again. The people heard that he had come home. ²So many people gathered that there was no room left. There was not even room outside the door. And Jesus preached the word to them.

³Four of those who came were carrying a man who could not walk. ⁴But they could not get him to Jesus because of the crowd. So they made a hole in the roof above Jesus. Then they lowered the man through it on a mat.

⁵Jesus saw their faith. So he said to the man, "Son, your sins are forgiven."

⁶Some teachers of the law were sitting there. They were thinking, ⁷"Why is this fellow talking like that? He's saying a very evil thing! Only God can forgive sins!"

⁸Right away Jesus knew what they were thinking. So he said to them, "Why are you thinking these things? ⁹Is it easier to say to this man, 'Your sins are forgiven'? Or to say, 'Get up, take your mat and walk'? ¹⁰I want you to know that the Son of Man has authority on earth to forgive sins."

Then Jesus spoke to the man who could not walk. ¹¹"I tell you," he said, "get up. Take your mat and go home."

¹²The man got up and took his mat. Then he walked away while everyone watched. All the people were amazed. They praised God and said, "We have never seen anything like this!"

Jesus Chooses Levi

¹³Once again Jesus went out beside the lake. A large crowd came to him. He began to teach them. ¹⁴As he walked along he saw Levi, son of Alphaeus. Levi was sitting at the tax collector's booth. "Follow me," Jesus told him. Levi got up and followed him.

¹⁵Later Jesus was having dinner at Levi's house. Many tax collectors and "sinners" were eating with him and his disciples. They were part of the large crowd following Jesus.

¹⁶Some teachers of the law who were Pharisees were there. They saw Jesus eating with "sinners" and tax collectors. So they asked his disciples, "Why does he eat with tax collectors and 'sinners'?"

¹⁷Jesus heard that. So he said to them, "Those who are healthy don't need a doctor. Sick people do. I have not come to get those who think they are right with God to follow me. I have come to get sinners to follow me."

Jesus Is Asked About Fasting

¹⁸John's disciples and the Pharisees were going without eating. Some people came to Jesus. They said to him, "John's disciples are fasting. The disciples of the Pharisees are also fasting. But your disciples are not. Why aren't they?"

¹⁹Jesus answered, "How can the guests of the groom go without eating while he is with them? They will not fast as long as he is with them. ²⁰But the time will come when the groom will be taken away from them. On that day they will go without eating.

²¹"People don't sew a patch of new cloth on old clothes. If they

do, the new piece will pull away from the old. That will make the tear worse. ²²People don't pour new wine into old wineskins. If they do, the wine will burst the skins. Then the wine and the wineskins will both be destroyed. No, everyone pours new wine into new wineskins."

Jesus Is Lord of the Sabbath Day

²³One Sabbath day Jesus was walking with his disciples through the grainfields. The disciples began to break off some heads of grain. ²⁴The Pharisees said to Jesus, "Look! It is against the Law to do this on the Sabbath. Why are your disciples doing it?"

²⁵He answered, "Haven't you ever read about what David did? He and his men were hungry and in need. ²⁶It was when Abiathar was high priest. David entered the house of God and ate the holy bread. Only priests were allowed to eat it. David also gave some to his men."

²⁷Then Jesus said to them, "The Sabbath day was made for people. People were not made for the Sabbath day. ²⁸So the Son of Man is Lord even of the Sabbath day."

3 Another time Jesus went into the synagogue. A man with a weak and twisted hand was there. ²Some Pharisees were trying to find fault with Jesus. They watched him closely. They wanted to see if he would heal the man on the Sabbath day.

³Jesus spoke to the man with the weak and twisted hand. "Stand up in front of everyone," he said.

⁴Then Jesus asked them, "What does the Law say we should do on the Sabbath day? Should we do good? Or should we do evil? Should we save life? Or should we kill?" But no one answered.

⁵Jesus looked around at them in anger. He was very upset because their hearts were stubborn. Then he said to the man, "Stretch out your hand." He stretched it out, and his hand was as good as new.

⁶Then the Pharisees went out and began to make plans with the Herodians. They wanted to kill Jesus.

GREAT VERSE — TO — REMEMBER

2:27-28 The Sabbath day was made for people. People were not made for the Sabbath day. So the Son of Man is Lord even of the Sabbath day.

Crowds Follow Jesus

⁷Jesus went off to the lake with his disciples. A large crowd from Galilee followed. ⁸People heard about all that Jesus was doing. And many came to him. They came from Judea, Jerusalem, and Idumea. They came from the lands on the other side of the Jordan River. And they came from the area around Tyre and Sidon.

⁹Because of the crowd, Jesus told his disciples to get a small boat ready for him. This would keep the people from crowding him. ¹⁰Jesus had healed many people. So those who were sick were pushing forward to touch him.

¹¹When people with evil spirits saw him, they fell down in front of him. The spirits shouted, "You are the Son of God!" ¹²But Jesus ordered them not to tell who he was.

Jesus Appoints the Twelve Apostles

¹³Jesus went up on a mountainside. He called for certain people to come to him, and they came. ¹⁴He appointed 12 of them and called them apostles. From that time on they would be with him. He would also send them out to preach. ¹⁵They would have authority to drive out demons.

¹⁶So Jesus appointed the Twelve. Simon was one of them. Jesus gave him the name Peter. ¹⁷There were James, son of Zebedee, and his brother John. Jesus gave them the name Boanerges. Boanerges means Sons of Thunder. ¹⁸There were also Andrew, Philip, Bartholomew, Matthew, Thomas, and James, son of Alphaeus. And there were Thaddaeus and Simon the Zealot. ¹⁹Judas Iscariot was one of them too. He was the one who was later going to hand Jesus over to his enemies.

Jesus and Beelzebub

²⁰Jesus entered a house. Again a crowd gathered. It was so large that Jesus and his disciples were not even able to eat. ²¹His family heard about this. So they went to take charge of him. They said, "He is out of his mind."

²²Some teachers of the law were there. They had come down from Jerusalem. They said, "He is controlled by Beelzebub! He is driving out demons by the power of the prince of demons."

²³So Jesus called them over and spoke to them by using stories. He said, "How can Satan drive out Satan? ²⁴If a kingdom fights against itself, it can't stand. ²⁵If a family is divided, it can't stand.

²⁶And if Satan fights against himself, and his helpers are divided, he can't stand. That is the end of him. ²⁷In fact, none of you can enter a strong man's house and just take what the man owns. You must first tie him up. Then you can rob his house.

²⁸"What I'm about to tell you is true. Everyone's sins and evil words against God will be forgiven. ²⁹But those who speak evil things against the Holy Spirit will never be forgiven. Their guilt will last forever."

³⁰Jesus said this because the teachers of the law were saying, "He has an evil spirit."

Jesus' Mother and Brothers

³¹Jesus' mother and brothers came and stood outside. They sent someone in to get him. ³²A crowd was sitting around Jesus. They told him, "Your mother and your brothers are outside. They are looking for you."

³³"Who is my mother? Who are my brothers?" he asked.

³⁴Then Jesus looked at the people sitting in a circle around him. He said, "Here is my mother! Here are my brothers! ³⁵Anyone who does what God wants is my brother and sister and mother."

The Story of the Farmer

4 Again Jesus began to teach by the lake. The crowd that gathered around him was very large. So he got into a boat. He sat down in it out on the lake. All the people were along the shore at the water's edge. ²He taught them many things by using stories.

In his teaching he said, ³"Listen! A farmer went out to plant his seed. ⁴He scattered the seed on the ground. Some fell on a path. Birds came and ate it up. ⁵Some seed fell on rocky places, where

---

3:28-29 What I'm about to tell you is true. Everyone's sins and evil words against God will be forgiven. But those who speak evil things against the Holy Spirit will never be forgiven. Their guilt will last forever.

there wasn't much soil. The plants came up quickly, because the soil wasn't deep. ⁶When the sun came up, it burned the plants. They dried up because they had no roots. ⁷Other seed fell among thorns. The thorns grew up and crowded out the plants. So the plants did not bear grain. ⁸Still other seed fell on good soil. It grew up and produced a crop 30, 60, or even 100 times more than the farmer planted."

⁹Then Jesus said, "Those who have ears to hear should listen." ¹⁰Later Jesus was alone. The Twelve asked him about the stories. So did the others around him. ¹¹He told them, "The secret of God's kingdom has been given to you. But to outsiders everything is told by using stories. ¹²In that way,

"'They will see but never know what they are seeing.
They will hear but never understand.
Otherwise they might turn and be forgiven!'" *(Isaiah 6:9,10)*

¹³Then Jesus said to them, "Don't you understand this story? Then how will you understand any stories of this kind? ¹⁴The seed the farmer plants is God's message. ¹⁵What is seed scattered on a path like? The message is planted. The people hear the message. Then Satan comes. He takes away the message that was planted in them. ¹⁶And what is seed scattered on rocky places like? The people hear the message. At once they receive it with joy. ¹⁷But they have no roots. So they last only a short time. They quickly fall away from the faith when trouble or suffering comes because of the message. ¹⁸And what is seed scattered among thorns like? The people hear the message. ¹⁹But then the worries of this life come to them. Wealth comes with its false promises. The people also long for other things. All of those are the kinds of things that crowd out the message. They keep it from producing fruit. ²⁰And what is seed scattered on good soil like? The people hear the message. They accept it. They produce a good crop 30, 60, or even 100 times more than the farmer planted."

A Lamp on a Stand

²¹Jesus said to them, "Do you bring in a lamp to put it under a large bowl or a bed? Don't you put it on its stand? ²²What is hidden is meant to be seen. And what is put out of sight is meant to be brought out into the open. ²³Everyone who has ears to hear should listen."

²⁴"Think carefully about what you hear," he said. "As you give, so you will receive. In fact, you will receive even more. ²⁵If you

have something, you will be given more. If you have nothing, even what you have will be taken away from you."

The Story of the Growing Seed

²⁶Jesus also said, "Here is what God's kingdom is like. A farmer scatters seed on the ground. ²⁷Night and day the seed comes up and grows. It happens whether the farmer sleeps or gets up. He doesn't know how it happens. ²⁸All by itself the soil produces grain. First the stalk comes up. Then the head appears. Finally, the full grain appears in the head. ²⁹Before long the grain ripens. So the farmer cuts it down, because the harvest is ready."

The Story of the Mustard Seed

³⁰Again Jesus said, "What can we say God's kingdom is like? What story can we use to explain it? ³¹It is like a mustard seed, which is the smallest seed planted in the ground. ³²But when you plant the seed, it grows. It becomes the largest of all garden plants. Its branches are so big that birds can rest in its shade."

³³With many stories like those, Jesus spoke the word to them. He told them as much as they could understand. ³⁴He did not say anything to them without using a story. But when he was alone with his disciples, he explained everything.

Jesus Calms the Storm

³⁵When evening came, Jesus said to his disciples, "Let's go over to the other side of the lake." ³⁶They left the crowd behind. And they took him along in a boat, just as he was. There were also other boats with him.

³⁷A wild storm came up. Waves crashed over the boat. It was about to sink. ³⁸Jesus was in the back, sleeping on a cushion. The disciples woke him up. They said, "Teacher! Don't you care if we drown?"

³⁹He got up and ordered the wind to stop. He said to the waves, "Quiet! Be still!" Then the wind died down. And it was completely calm.

4:41 They were terrified. They asked each other, "Who is this? Even the wind and the waves obey him!

⁴⁰He said to his disciples, "Why are you so afraid? Don't you have any faith at all yet?"

⁴¹They were terrified. They asked each other, "Who is this? Even the wind and the waves obey him!"

Jesus Heals a Man Controlled by Demons

5 They went across the lake to the area of the Gerasenes. ²Jesus got out of the boat. A man with an evil spirit came from the tombs to meet him. ³The man lived in the tombs. No one could keep him tied up anymore. Not even a chain could hold him. ⁴His hands and feet had often been chained. But he tore the chains apart. And he broke the iron cuffs on his ankles. No one was strong enough to control him. ⁵Night and day he screamed among the tombs and in the hills. He cut himself with stones.

⁶When he saw Jesus a long way off, he ran to him. He fell on his knees in front of him. ⁷He shouted at the top of his voice, "Jesus, Son of the Most High God, what do you want with me? Promise before God that you won't hurt me!" ⁸This was because Jesus had said to him, "Come out of this man, you evil spirit!"

⁹Then Jesus asked him, "What is your name?"

"My name is Legion," he replied. "There are many of us." ¹⁰And he begged Jesus again and again not to send them out of the area.

¹¹A large herd of pigs was feeding on the nearby hillside. ¹²The demons begged Jesus, "Send us among the pigs. Let us go into them." ¹³Jesus allowed it. The evil spirits came out of the man and went into the pigs. There were about 2,000 pigs in the herd. The whole herd rushed down the steep bank. They ran into the lake and drowned.

¹⁴Those who were tending the pigs ran off. They told the people in the town and countryside what had happened. The people went out to see for themselves. ¹⁵Then they came to Jesus. They saw the man who had been controlled by many demons. He was sitting there. He was now dressed and thinking clearly. All this made the people afraid. ¹⁶Those who had seen it told them what had happened to the man. They told about the pigs as well. ¹⁷Then the people began to beg Jesus to leave their area.

¹⁸Jesus was getting into the boat. The man who had been controlled by demons begged to go with him. ¹⁹Jesus did not let him. He said, "Go home to your family. Tell them how much the Lord has done for you. Tell them how he has been kind to you."

²⁰So the man went away. In the area known as the Ten Cities he

began to tell how much Jesus had done for him. And all the people were amazed.

A Dying Girl and a Suffering Woman

²¹Jesus again crossed over by boat to the other side of the lake. There a large crowd gathered around him. ²²Then a man named Jairus came. He was a synagogue ruler. Seeing Jesus, he fell at his feet. ²³He begged Jesus, "Please come. My little daughter is dying. Place your hands on her to heal her. Then she will live." ²⁴So Jesus went with him.

A large group of people followed. They crowded around him. ²⁵A woman was there who had an illness that made her bleed. Her illness had lasted 12 years. ²⁶She had suffered a great deal, even though she had gone to many doctors. She had spent all the money she had. But she was getting worse, not better. ²⁷Then she heard about Jesus. She came up behind him in the crowd and touched his clothes. ²⁸She thought, "I just need to touch his clothes. Then I will be healed." ²⁹Right away her bleeding stopped. She felt in her body that her suffering was over.

³⁰At once Jesus knew that power had gone out from him. He turned around in the crowd. He asked, "Who touched my clothes?"

³¹"You see the people," his disciples answered. "They are crowding against you. And you still ask, 'Who touched me?'"

³²But Jesus kept looking around. He wanted to see who had touched him.

³³Then the woman came and fell at his feet. She knew what had happened to her. She was shaking with fear. But she told him the whole truth.

³⁴He said to her, "Dear woman, your faith has healed you. Go in peace. You are free from your suffering."

³⁵While Jesus was still speaking, some people came from the

GREAT VERSE — TO — REMEMBER

5:19 [Jesus] said, "Go home to your family. Tell them how much the Lord has done for you. Tell them how he has been kind to you."

house of Jairus. He was the synagogue ruler. "Your daughter is dead," they said. "Why bother the teacher anymore?"

³⁶But Jesus didn't listen to them. He told the synagogue ruler, "Don't be afraid. Just believe."

³⁷He let only Peter, James, and John, the brother of James, follow him. ³⁸They came to the home of the synagogue ruler. There Jesus saw a lot of confusion. People were crying and sobbing loudly. ³⁹He went inside. Then he said to them, "Why all this confusion and sobbing? The child is not dead. She is only sleeping." ⁴⁰But they laughed at him.

He made them all go outside. He took only the child's father and mother and the disciples who were with him. And he went in where the child was. ⁴¹He took her by the hand. Then he said to her, *"Talitha koum!"* This means, "Little girl, I say to you, get up!" ⁴²The girl was 12 years old. Right away she stood up and walked around. They were totally amazed at this. ⁴³Jesus gave strict orders not to let anyone know what had happened. And he told them to give her something to eat.

A Prophet Without Honor

6 Jesus left there and went to his hometown. His disciples went with him. ²When the Sabbath day came, he began to teach in the synagogue. Many who heard him were amazed.

"Where did this man get these things?" they asked. "What's this wisdom that has been given to him? He even does miracles! ³Isn't this the carpenter? Isn't this Mary's son? Isn't this the brother of James, Joseph, Judas and Simon? Aren't his sisters here with us?" They were not pleased with him at all.

⁴Jesus said to them, "Prophets are not honored in their hometowns. They don't receive any honor among their relatives. And they don't receive any in their own homes."

⁵Jesus laid his hands on a few sick people and healed them. But he could not do any other miracles there. ⁶He was amazed because they had no faith.

Jesus Sends Out the Twelve Disciples

Jesus went around teaching from village to village. ⁷He called the Twelve to him. Then he sent them out two by two. He gave them authority over evil spirits.

⁸Here were his orders. "Take only a walking stick for your trip. Do not take bread or a bag. Take no money in your belts. ⁹Wear sandals. But do not take extra clothes. ¹⁰When you are invited

into a house, stay there until you leave town. [11]Some places may not welcome you or listen to you. If they don't, shake the dust off your feet when you leave. That will be a witness against the people living there."

[12]They went out. And they preached that people should turn away from their sins. [13]They drove out many demons. They poured olive oil on many sick people and healed them.

John the Baptist's Head Is Cut Off

[14]King Herod heard about this. Jesus' name had become well known. Some were saying, "John the Baptist has been raised from the dead! That is why he has the power to do miracles."

[15]Others said, "He is Elijah."

Still others claimed, "He is a prophet. He is like one of the prophets of long ago."

[16]But when Herod heard this, he said, "I had John's head cut off. And now he has been raised from the dead!"

[17]In fact, it was Herod himself who had given orders to arrest John. He had him tied up and put in prison. He did this because of Herodias. She was the wife of Herod's brother Philip. But now Herod was married to her. [18]John had been saying to Herod, "It is against the Law for you to have your brother's wife." [19]Herodias held that against John. She wanted to kill him. But she could not, [20]because Herod was afraid of John. So he kept John safe. Herod knew John was a holy man who did what was right. When Herod heard him, he was very puzzled. But he liked to listen to him.

[21]Finally the right time came. Herod gave a big dinner on his birthday. He invited his high officials and military leaders. He also invited the most important men in Galilee. [22]Then the daughter of Herodias came in and danced. She pleased Herod and his dinner guests.

The king said to the girl, "Ask me for anything you want. I'll give it to you." [23]And he promised her with an oath, "Anything you ask for I will give you. I'll give you up to half of my kingdom."

[24]She went out and said to her mother, "What should I ask for?"

"The head of John the Baptist," she answered.

[25]At once the girl hurried to ask the king. She said, "I want you to give me the head of John the Baptist on a big plate right now."

[26]The king was very upset. But he thought of his promise and his dinner guests. So he did not want to say no to her. [27]He sent a man right away to bring John's head. The man went to the

prison and cut off John's head. [28]He brought it back on a big plate. He gave it to the girl, and she gave it to her mother.

[29]John's disciples heard about this. So they came and took his body. Then they placed it in a tomb.

Jesus Feeds the Five Thousand

[30]The apostles gathered around Jesus. They told him all they had done and taught. [31]But many people were coming and going. So they did not even have a chance to eat.

Then Jesus said to his apostles, "Come with me by yourselves to a quiet place. You need to get some rest." [32]So they went away by themselves in a boat to a quiet place.

[33]But many who saw them leaving recognized them. They ran from all the towns and got there ahead of them. [34]When Jesus came ashore, he saw a large crowd. He felt deep concern for them. They were like sheep without a shepherd. So he began teaching them many things.

[35]By that time it was late in the day. His disciples came to him. "There is nothing here," they said. "It's already very late. [36]Send the people away. They can go and buy something to eat in the nearby countryside and villages."

[37]But Jesus answered, "You give them something to eat."

They said to him, "That would take eight months of a person's pay! Should we go and spend that much on bread? Are we supposed to feed them?"

[38]"How many loaves do you have?" Jesus asked. "Go and see."

When they found out, they said, "Five loaves and two fish."

[39]Then Jesus directed them to have all the people sit down in groups on the green grass. [40]So they sat down in groups of 100s and 50s.

[41]Jesus took the five loaves and the two fish. He looked up to heaven and gave thanks. He broke the loaves into pieces. Then he gave them to his disciples to set in front of the people. He also divided the two fish among them all.

[42]All of them ate and were satisfied. [43]The disciples picked up 12 baskets of broken pieces of bread and fish. [44]The number of men who had eaten was 5,000.

Jesus Walks on the Water

[45]Right away Jesus made his disciples get into the boat. He had them go on ahead of him to Bethsaida. Then he sent the crowd

away. [46]After leaving them, he went up on a mountainside to pray.

[47]When evening came, the boat was in the middle of the lake. Jesus was alone on land. [48]He saw the disciples pulling hard on the oars. The wind was blowing against them.

Early in the morning, he went out to them. He walked on the lake. When he was about to pass by them, [49]they saw him walking on the lake. They thought he was a ghost. They cried out. [50]They all saw him and were terrified.

Right away he said to them, "Be brave! It is I. Don't be afraid."

[51]Then he climbed into the boat with them. The wind died down. And they were completely amazed. [52]They had not understood about the loaves. They were stubborn.

[53]They crossed over the lake and landed at Gennesaret. There they tied up the boat. [54]As soon as Jesus and his disciples got out, people recognized him. [55]They ran through that whole area to bring to him those who were sick. They carried them on mats to where they heard he was.

[56]He went into the villages, the towns and the countryside. Everywhere he went, the people brought the sick to the market places. Those who were sick begged him to let them touch just the edge of his clothes. And all who touched him were healed.

What Makes People "Unclean"?

7 The Pharisees gathered around Jesus. So did some of the teachers of the law. All of them had come from Jerusalem. [2]They saw some of his disciples eating food with "unclean" hands. That means they were not washed.

[3]The Pharisees and all the Jews do not eat unless they wash

---

GREAT VERSE —TO— REMEMBER

6:56 He went into the villages, the towns and the countryside. Everywhere he went, the people brought the sick to the market places. Those who were sick begged him to let them touch just the edge of his clothes. And all who touched him were healed.

their hands to make them pure. This is in keeping with the teachings of the elders. [4]When they come from the market place, they do not eat unless they wash. And they follow many other teachings. For example, they wash cups, pitchers, and kettles in a special way.

[5]So the Pharisees and the teachers of the law questioned Jesus. "Why don't your disciples live by the teachings of the elders?" they asked. "Why do they eat their food with 'unclean' hands?"

[6]He replied, "Isaiah was right. He prophesied about you people who pretend to be good. He said,

> "'These people honor me by what they say.
>   But their hearts are far away from me.
> [7]Their worship means nothing to me.
>   Their teachings are only human rules.' *(Isaiah 29:13)*

[8]You have let go of God's commands. And you are holding on to the teachings that people have made up."

[9]Jesus then said to them, "You have a fine way of setting aside God's commands! You do this so you can follow your own teachings. [10]Moses said, 'Honor your father and your mother.' *(Exodus 20:12; Deuteronomy 5:16)* He also said, 'Those who ask for evil things to happen to their father or mother must be put to death.' *(Exodus 21:17; Leviticus 20:9)* [11]But you allow people to say to their parents, 'Any help you might have received from us is Corban.' (Corban means 'a gift set apart for God.') [12]So you no longer let them do anything for their parents. [13]You make the word of God useless by putting your own teachings in its place. And you do many things like that."

[14]Again Jesus called the crowd to him. He said, "Listen to me, everyone. Understand this. [15/16]Nothing outside of you can make you 'unclean' by going into you. It is what comes out of you that makes you 'unclean.'"

[17]Then he left the crowd and entered the house. His disciples asked him about this teaching.

[18]"Don't you understand?" Jesus asked. "Don't you see?

7:15 Nothing outside of you can make you "unclean" by going into you. It is what comes out of you that makes you "unclean."

Nothing that enters people from the outside can make them 'unclean.' ¹⁹It doesn't go into the heart. It goes into the stomach. Then it goes out of the body." In saying this, Jesus was calling all foods "clean."

²⁰He went on to say, "What comes out of people makes them 'unclean.' ²¹Evil thoughts come from the inside, from people's hearts. So do sexual sins, stealing and murder. Adultery, ²²greed, hate and cheating come from people's hearts too. So do desires that are not pure, and wanting what belongs to others. And so do telling lies about others and being proud and being foolish. ²³All those evil things come from inside a person. They make that person 'unclean.'"

The Faith of a Greek Woman

²⁴Jesus went from there to a place near Tyre. He entered a house. He did not want anyone to know where he was. But he could not keep it a secret.

²⁵Soon a woman heard about him. An evil spirit controlled her little daughter. The woman came to Jesus and fell at his feet. ²⁶She was a Greek, born in Syrian Phoenicia. She begged Jesus to drive the demon out of her daughter.

²⁷"First let the children eat all they want," he told her. "It is not right to take the children's bread and throw it to their dogs."

²⁸"Yes, Lord," she replied. "But even the dogs under the table eat the children's crumbs."

²⁹Then he told her, "That was a good reply. You may go. The demon has left your daughter."

³⁰So she went home and found her child lying on the bed. And the demon was gone.

Jesus Heals a Man Who Could Not Hear or Speak

³¹Then Jesus left the area of Tyre and went through Sidon. He went down to the Sea of Galilee and into the area known as the Ten Cities.

³²There some people brought a man to him. The man was deaf and could hardly speak. They begged Jesus to place his hand on him.

³³Jesus took the man to one side, away from the crowd. He put his fingers into the man's ears. Then he spit and touched the man's tongue. ³⁴Jesus looked up to heaven. With a deep sigh, he said to the man, *"Ephphatha!"* That means "Be opened!" ³⁵The

man's ears were opened. His tongue was freed up, and he began to speak clearly.

³⁶Jesus ordered the people not to tell anyone. But the more he did so, the more they kept talking about it.

³⁷People were really amazed. "He has done everything well," they said. "He even makes the deaf hear. And he makes those who can't speak able to talk."

Jesus Feeds the Four Thousand

8 During those days another large crowd gathered. They had nothing to eat. So Jesus called for his disciples to come to him. He said, ²"I feel deep concern for these people. They have already been with me three days. They don't have anything to eat. ³If I send them away hungry, they will become too weak on their way home. Some of them have come from far away."

⁴His disciples answered him. "There is nothing here," they said. "Where can anyone get enough bread to feed them?"

⁵"How many loaves do you have?" Jesus asked.

"Seven," they replied.

⁶He told the crowd to sit down on the ground. He took the seven loaves and gave thanks to God. Then he broke them and gave them to his disciples. They set the loaves down in front of the people. ⁷They also had a few small fish. Jesus gave thanks for them too. He told the disciples to pass them around. ⁸The people ate and were satisfied.

After that, the disciples picked up seven baskets of leftover pieces. ⁹About 4,000 men were there. Jesus sent them away. ¹⁰Then he got into a boat with his disciples. He went to the area of Dalmanutha.

¹¹The Pharisees came and began to ask Jesus questions. They wanted to put him to the test. So they asked him for a miraculous sign from heaven. ¹²He sighed deeply. He said, "Why do you people ask for a sign? What I'm about to tell you is true. No sign will be given to you."

¹³Then he left them. He got back into the boat and crossed to the other side of the lake.

The Yeast of the Pharisees and Herod

¹⁴The disciples had forgotten to bring bread. They had only one loaf with them in the boat.

¹⁵"Be careful," Jesus warned them. "Watch out for the yeast of the Pharisees. And watch out for the yeast of Herod."

¹⁶They talked about this with each other. They said, "He must be saying this because we don't have any bread."

¹⁷Jesus knew what they were saying. So he asked them, "Why are you talking about having no bread? Why can't you see or understand? Are you stubborn? ¹⁸Do you have eyes and still don't see? Do you have ears and still don't hear? And don't you remember? ¹⁹Earlier I broke five loaves for the 5,000. How many baskets of pieces did you pick up?"

"Twelve," they replied.

²⁰"Later I broke seven loaves for the 4,000. How many baskets of pieces did you pick up?"

"Seven," they answered.

²¹He said to them, "Can't you understand yet?"

Jesus Heals a Blind Man

²²Jesus and his disciples came to Bethsaida. Some people brought a blind man. They begged Jesus to touch him.

²³He took the blind man by the hand. Then he led him outside the village. He spit on the man's eyes and put his hands on him.

"Do you see anything?" Jesus asked.

²⁴The man looked up. He said, "I see people. They look like trees walking around."

²⁵Once more Jesus put his hands on the man's eyes. Then his eyes were opened so that he could see again. He saw everything clearly.

²⁶Jesus sent him home. He told him, "Don't go into the village."

Peter Says That Jesus Is the Christ

²⁷Jesus and his disciples went on to the villages around Caesarea Philippi. On the way he asked them, "Who do people say I am?"

²⁸They replied, "Some say John the Baptist. Others say Elijah. Still others say one of the prophets."

²⁹"But what about you?" he asked. "Who do you say I am?"

Peter answered, "You are the Christ."

³⁰Jesus warned them not to tell anyone about him.

Jesus Tells About His Coming Death

³¹Jesus then began to teach his disciples. He taught them that the Son of Man must suffer many things. He taught them that the elders would not accept him. The chief priests and the teachers of the law would not accept him either. He must be killed and after three days rise again. ³²He spoke clearly about this.

Peter took Jesus to one side and began to scold him.

³³Jesus turned and looked at his disciples. He scolded Peter. "Get behind me, Satan!" he said. "You are not thinking about the things of God. Instead, you are thinking about human things."

³⁴Jesus called the crowd to him along with his disciples. He said, "If you want to come after me, you must say no to yourself. You must take your cross and follow me. ³⁵If you want to save your life, you will lose it. But if you lose your life for me and for the good news, you will save it. ³⁶What good is it for you to gain the whole world but lose your soul? ³⁷Or what can you trade for your soul?

³⁸"Suppose you are ashamed of me and my words among these adulterous and sinful people. Then the Son of Man will be ashamed of you when he comes in his Father's glory with the holy angels."

9 Jesus said to them, "What I'm about to tell you is true. Some who are standing here will not die before they see God's kingdom coming with power."

Jesus' Appearance Is Changed

²After six days Jesus took Peter, James and John with him. He led them up a high mountain. They were all alone. There in front of them his appearance was changed. ³His clothes became so white they shone. They were whiter than anyone in the world could bleach them. ⁴Elijah and Moses appeared in front of them. The two of them were talking with Jesus.

⁵Peter said to Jesus, "Rabbi, it is good for us to be here. Let us put up three shelters. One will be for you, one for Moses, and one for Elijah." ⁶Peter didn't really know what to say, because they were so afraid.

⁷Then a cloud appeared and surrounded them. A voice came from the cloud. It said, "This is my Son, and I love him. Listen to him!"

⁸They looked around. Suddenly they no longer saw anyone with them except Jesus.

GREAT VERSE —TO— REMEMBER

8:36 What good is it for you to gain the whole world but lose your soul?

⁹They came down the mountain. On the way down, Jesus ordered them not to tell anyone what they had seen. He told them to wait until the Son of Man had risen from the dead. ¹⁰So they kept the matter to themselves. But they asked each other what "rising from the dead" meant.

¹¹Then they asked Jesus, "Why do the teachers of the law say that Elijah has to come first?"

¹²Jesus replied, "That's right. Elijah does come first. He makes all things new again. So why is it written that the Son of Man must suffer much and not be accepted? ¹³I tell you, Elijah has come. They have done to him everything they wanted to do. They did it just as it is written about him."

Jesus Heals a Boy Who Had an Evil Spirit

¹⁴When Jesus and those who were with him came to the other disciples, they saw a large crowd around them. The teachers of the law were arguing with them. ¹⁵When all the people saw Jesus, they were filled with wonder. And they ran to greet him.

¹⁶"What are you arguing with them about?" Jesus asked.

¹⁷A man in the crowd answered. "Teacher," he said, "I brought you my son. He is controlled by a spirit. Because of this, my son can't speak anymore. ¹⁸When the spirit takes hold of him, it throws him to the ground. He foams at the mouth. He grinds his teeth. And his body becomes stiff. I asked your disciples to drive out the spirit. But they couldn't do it."

¹⁹"You unbelieving people!" Jesus replied. "How long do I have to stay with you? How long do I have to put up with you? Bring the boy to me."

²⁰So they brought him. As soon as the spirit saw Jesus, it threw the boy into a fit. He fell to the ground. He rolled around and foamed at the mouth.

²¹Jesus asked the boy's father, "How long has he been like this?"

"Since he was a child," he answered. ²²"The spirit has often

9:7 Then a cloud appeared and surrounded them. A voice came from the cloud. It said, "This is my Son, and I love him. Listen to him!"

thrown him into fire or water to kill him. But if you can do anything, take pity on us. Please help us."

²³"'If you can'?" said Jesus. "Everything is possible for the one who believes."

²⁴Right away the boy's father cried out, "I do believe! Help me overcome my unbelief!"

²⁵Jesus saw that a crowd was running over to see what was happening. Then he ordered the evil spirit to leave the boy. "You spirit that makes him unable to hear and speak!" he said. "I command you, come out of him. Never enter him again."

²⁶The spirit screamed. It shook the boy wildly. Then it came out of him. The boy looked so lifeless that many said, "He's dead." ²⁷But Jesus took him by the hand. He lifted the boy to his feet, and the boy stood up.

²⁸Jesus went indoors. Then his disciples asked him in private, "Why couldn't we drive out the evil spirit?"

²⁹He replied, "This kind can come out only by prayer."

³⁰They left that place and passed through Galilee. Jesus did not want anyone to know where they were. ³¹That was because he was teaching his disciples.

He said to them, "The Son of Man is going to be handed over to human authorities. They will kill him. After three days he will rise from the dead." ³²But they didn't understand what he meant. And they were afraid to ask him about it.

Who Is the Most Important Person?

³³Jesus and his disciples came to a house in Capernaum. There he asked them, "What were you arguing about on the road?" ³⁴But they kept quiet. On the way, they had argued about who was the most important person.

³⁵Jesus sat down and called for the Twelve to come to him. Then he said, "If you want to be first, you must be the very last. You must be the servant of everyone."

³⁶Jesus took a little child and had the child stand among them. Then he took the child in his arms. He said to them, ³⁷"Anyone who welcomes one of these little children in my name welcomes me. And anyone who welcomes me doesn't welcome only me but also the One who sent me."

Anyone Who Is Not Against Us Is for Us

³⁸"Teacher," said John, "we saw a man driving out demons in your name. We told him to stop, because he was not one of us."

[39]"Do not stop him," Jesus said. "No one who does a miracle in my name can in the next moment say anything bad about me. [40]Anyone who is not against us is for us.

[41]"What I'm about to tell you is true. Suppose someone gives you a cup of water in my name because you belong to Christ. That one will certainly not go without a reward.

Leading People to Sin

[42]"What if people lead one of these little ones who believe in me to sin? If they do, it would be better for them to be thrown into the sea with a large millstone tied around their neck.

[43/44]"If your hand causes you to sin, cut it off. It would be better for you to enter God's kingdom with only one hand than to go into hell with two hands. In hell the fire never goes out.

[45/46]"If your foot causes you to sin, cut it off. It would be better for you to enter God's kingdom with only one foot than to have two feet and be thrown into hell.

[47]"If your eye causes you to sin, poke it out. It would be better for you to enter God's kingdom with only one eye than to have two eyes and be thrown into hell. [48]In hell,

> "'Their worms do not die,
>   and the fire does not go out.'   *(Isaiah 66:24)*

[49]Everyone will be salted with fire.

[50]"Salt is good. But suppose it loses its saltiness. How can you make it salty again? Have salt in yourselves. And be at peace with each other."

Jesus Teaches About Divorce

10 Jesus left that place and went into the area of Judea and across the Jordan River. Again crowds of people came to him. As usual, he taught them.

[2]Some Pharisees came to put him to the test. They asked, "Does the Law allow a man to divorce his wife?"

GREAT VERSE — TO — REMEMBER

9:41 Suppose someone gives you a cup of water in my name because you belong to Christ. That one will certainly not go without a reward.

³"What did Moses command you?" he replied.

⁴They said, "Moses allowed a man to write a letter of divorce and send her away."

⁵"You were stubborn. That's why Moses wrote you this law," Jesus replied. ⁶"But at the beginning of creation, God 'made them male and female.' *(Genesis 1:27)* ⁷"That's why a man will leave his father and mother and be joined to his wife. ⁸The two will become one.' *(Genesis 2:24)* They are no longer two, but one. ⁹So let no one separate what God has joined together."

¹⁰When they were in the house again, the disciples asked Jesus about this.

¹¹He answered, "What if a man divorces his wife and gets married to another woman? He commits adultery against her. ¹²And what if she divorces her husband and gets married to another man? She commits adultery."

Little Children Are Brought to Jesus

¹³People were bringing little children to Jesus. They wanted him to touch them. But the disciples told the people to stop.

¹⁴When Jesus saw this, he was angry. He said to his disciples, "Let the little children come to me. Don't keep them away. God's kingdom belongs to people like them. ¹⁵What I'm about to tell you is true. Anyone who will not receive God's kingdom like a little child will never enter it."

¹⁶Then he took the children in his arms. He put his hands on them and blessed them.

Jesus and the Rich Young Man

¹⁷As Jesus started on his way, a man ran up to him. He fell on his knees before Jesus. "Good teacher," he said, "what must I do to receive eternal life?"

¹⁸"Why do you call me good?" Jesus answered. "No one is good except God. ¹⁹You know what the commandments say. 'Do not commit murder. Do not commit adultery. Do not steal. Do not give false witness. Do not cheat. Honor your father and mother.'"

(Exodus 20:12–16; Deuteronomy 5:16–20)

²⁰"Teacher," he said, "I have obeyed all those commandments since I was a boy."

²¹Jesus looked at him and loved him. "You are missing one thing," he said. "Go and sell everything you have. Give the money to those who are poor. You will have treasure in heaven. Then come and follow me."

²²The man's face fell. He went away sad, because he was very rich.

²³Jesus looked around. He said to his disciples, "How hard it is for rich people to enter God's kingdom!"

²⁴The disciples were amazed at his words. But Jesus said again, "Children, how hard it is to enter God's kingdom! ²⁵Is it hard for a camel to go through the eye of a needle? It is even harder for the rich to enter God's kingdom!"

²⁶The disciples were even more amazed. They said to each other, "Then who can be saved?"

²⁷Jesus looked at them and said, "With people, that is impossible. But not with God. All things are possible with God."

²⁸Peter said to him, "We have left everything to follow you!"

²⁹"What I'm about to tell you is true," Jesus replied. "Has anyone left home or family or fields for me and the good news? ³⁰They will receive 100 times as much in this world. They will have homes and families and fields. But they will also be treated badly by others. In the world to come they will live forever. ³¹But many who are first will be last. And the last will be first."

Jesus Again Tells About His Coming Death

³²They were on their way up to Jerusalem, with Jesus leading the way. The disciples were amazed. Those who followed were afraid.

Again Jesus took the Twelve to one side. He told them what was going to happen to him. ³³"We are going up to Jerusalem," he said. "The Son of Man will be handed over to the chief priests and the teachers of the law. They will sentence him to death. Then they will hand him over to people who are not Jews. ³⁴The people will make fun of him and spit on him. They will whip him and kill him. Three days later he will rise from the dead!"

James and John Ask a Favor of Jesus

³⁵James and John came to Jesus. They were the sons of Zebedee. "Teacher," they said, "we would like to ask a favor of you."

GREAT VERSE —TO— REMEMBER

10:27 Jesus looked at them and said, "With people, that is impossible. But not with God. All things are possible with God."

³⁶"What do you want me to do for you?" he asked.

³⁷They replied, "Let one of us sit at your right hand in your glorious kingdom. Let the other one sit at your left hand."

³⁸"You don't know what you're asking for," Jesus said. "Can you drink the cup of suffering I drink? Or can you go through the baptism of suffering I must go through?"

³⁹"We can," they answered.

Jesus said to them, "You will drink the cup I drink. And you will go through the baptism I go through. ⁴⁰But it is not for me to say who will sit at my right or left hand. These places belong to those they are prepared for."

⁴¹The other ten disciples heard about it. They became angry at James and John.

⁴²Jesus called them together. He said, "You know about those who are rulers of the nations. They hold power over their people. Their high officials order them around. ⁴³Don't be like that. Instead, anyone who wants to be important among you must be your servant. ⁴⁴And anyone who wants to be first must be the slave of everyone. ⁴⁵Even the Son of Man did not come to be served. Instead, he came to serve others. He came to give his life as the price for setting many people free."

Blind Bartimaeus Receives His Sight

⁴⁶Jesus and his disciples came to Jericho. They were leaving the city. A large crowd was with them.

A blind man was sitting by the side of the road begging. His name was Bartimaeus. Bartimaeus means Son of Timaeus. ⁴⁷He heard that Jesus of Nazareth was passing by. So he began to shout, "Jesus! Son of David! Have mercy on me!"

⁴⁸Many people commanded him to stop. They told him to be quiet. But he shouted even louder, "Son of David! Have mercy on me!"

⁴⁹Jesus stopped and said, "Call for him."

GREAT VERSE — TO — REMEMBER

10:45 Even the Son of Man did not come to be served. Instead, he came to serve others. He came to give his life as the price for setting many people free.

So they called out to the blind man, "Cheer up! On your feet! Jesus is calling for you."

⁵⁰He threw his coat to one side. Then he jumped to his feet and came to Jesus.

⁵¹"What do you want me to do for you?" Jesus asked him.

The blind man said, "Rabbi, I want to be able to see."

⁵²"Go," said Jesus. "Your faith has healed you."

Right away he could see. And he followed Jesus along the road.

Jesus Enters Jerusalem

11 As they all approached Jerusalem, they came to Bethphage and Bethany at the Mount of Olives. Jesus sent out two of his disciples. ²He said to them, "Go to the village ahead of you. Just as you enter it, you will find a young donkey tied there. No one has ever ridden it. Untie it and bring it here. ³Someone may ask you, 'Why are you doing this?' If so, say, 'The Lord needs it. But he will send it back here soon.'"

⁴So they left. They found a young donkey out in the street. It was tied at a doorway. They untied it. ⁵Some people standing there asked, "What are you doing? Why are you untying that donkey?" ⁶They answered as Jesus had told them to. So the people let them go.

⁷They brought the donkey to Jesus. They threw their coats over it. Then he sat on it.

⁸Many people spread their coats on the road. Others spread branches they had cut in the fields. ⁹Those in front and those in back shouted,

> "Hosanna!"

> "Blessed is the one who comes in the name of the Lord!"   *(Psalm 118:25,26)*

> ¹⁰"Blessed is the coming kingdom of our father David!"

> "Hosanna in the highest heaven!"

¹¹Jesus entered Jerusalem and went to the temple. He looked around at everything. But it was already late. So he went out to Bethany with the Twelve.

Jesus Clears the Temple

¹²The next day as Jesus and his disciples were leaving Bethany, they were hungry. ¹³Not too far away, he saw a fig tree. It was cov-

ered with leaves. He went to find out if it had any fruit. When he reached it, he found nothing but leaves. It was not the season for figs.

¹⁴Then Jesus said to the tree, "May no one ever eat fruit from you again!" And his disciples heard him say it.

¹⁵When Jesus reached Jerusalem, he entered the temple area. He began chasing out those who were buying and selling there. He turned over the tables of the people who were exchanging money. He also turned over the benches of those who were selling doves. ¹⁶He would not allow anyone to carry items for sale through the temple courtyards.

¹⁷Then he taught them. He said, "Is it not written:

"'My house will be called
    a house of prayer for all nations'?   *(Isaiah 56:7)*

But you have made it a 'den for robbers.'" *(Jeremiah 7:11)*

¹⁸The chief priests and the teachers of the law heard about this. They began looking for a way to kill Jesus. They were afraid of him, because the whole crowd was amazed at his teaching.

¹⁹When evening came, they went out of the city.

The Dried-up Fig Tree

²⁰In the morning as Jesus and his disciples walked along, they saw the fig tree. It was dried up all the way down to the roots.

²¹Peter remembered. He said to Jesus, "Rabbi, look! The fig tree you put a curse on has dried up!"

²²"Have faith in God," Jesus said. ²³"What I'm about to tell you is true. Suppose one of you says to this mountain, 'Go and throw yourself into the sea.' You must not doubt in your heart. You must believe that what you say will happen. Then it will be done for you.

²⁴"So I tell you, when you pray for something, believe that you have already received it. Then it will be yours. ²⁵/²⁶And when you stand praying, forgive anyone you have anything against. Then your Father in heaven will forgive your sins."

GREAT VERSE –TO– REMEMBER

11:24 So I tell you, when you pray for something, believe that you have already received it. Then it will be yours.

The Authority of Jesus Is Questioned

[27]Jesus and his disciples arrived again in Jerusalem. He was walking in the temple courtyards. Then the chief priests came to him. The teachers of the law and the elders came too.

[28]"By what authority are you doing these things?" they asked. "Who gave you authority to do this?"

[29]Jesus replied, "I will ask you one question. Answer me, and I will tell you by what authority I am doing these things. [30]Was John's baptism from heaven? Or did it come from human authority? Tell me!"

[31]They talked to each other about it. They said, "If we say, 'From heaven,' he will ask, 'Then why didn't you believe him?' [32]But what if we say, 'From human authority'?" They were afraid of the people. Everyone believed that John really was a prophet.

[33]So they answered Jesus, "We don't know."

Jesus said, "Then I won't tell you by what authority I am doing these things either."

The Story of the Renters

12 Jesus began to speak to the people by using stories. He said, "A man planted a vineyard. He put a wall around it. He dug a pit for a winepress. He also built a lookout tower. He rented the vineyard out to some farmers. Then he went away on a journey.

[2]"At harvest time he sent a servant to the renters. He told the servant to collect from them some of the fruit of the vineyard. [3]But they grabbed the servant and beat him up. Then they sent him away with nothing. [4]So the man sent another servant to the renters. They hit this one on the head and treated him badly. [5]The man sent still another servant. The renters killed him. The man sent many others. The renters beat up some of them. Others they killed.

[6]"The man had one person left to send. It was his son, and he loved him. He sent him last of all. He said, 'They will respect my son.'

[7]"But the renters said to each other, 'This is the one who will receive all the owner's property someday. Come, let's kill him. Then everything will be ours.' [8]So they took him and killed him. They threw him out of the vineyard.

[9]"What will the owner of the vineyard do then? He will come and kill those renters. He will give the vineyard to others.

[10]"Haven't you read what Scripture says,

" 'The stone the builders did not accept
   has become the most important stone.
[11]The Lord has done this.
   It is wonderful in our eyes'?"   *(Psalm 118:22,23)*

[12]Then the religious leaders looked for a way to arrest Jesus. They knew he had told the story against them. But they were afraid of the crowd. So they left him and went away.

Is It Right to Pay Taxes to Caesar?

[13]Later the religious leaders sent some of the Pharisees and Herodians to Jesus. They wanted to trap him with his own words.

[14]They came to him and said, "Teacher, we know you are a man of honor. You don't let others tell you what to do or say. You don't care how important they are. But you teach the way of God truthfully. Is it right to pay taxes to Caesar or not? [15]Should we pay or shouldn't we?"

But Jesus knew what they were trying to do. So he asked, "Why are you trying to trap me? Bring me a silver coin. Let me look at it."

[16]They brought the coin.

He asked them, "Whose picture is this? And whose words?"

"Caesar's," they replied.

[17]Then Jesus said to them, "Give to Caesar what belongs to Caesar. And give to God what belongs to God."

They were amazed at him.

Marriage When the Dead Rise

[18]The Sadducees came to Jesus with a question. They do not believe that people rise from the dead. [19]"Teacher," they said, "Moses wrote for us about a man's brother who dies. Suppose the brother leaves a wife but has no children. Then the man must get married to the widow. He must have children for his brother.

[20]"There were seven brothers. The first one got married. He died

GREAT VERSE —TO— REMEMBER

12:17 Give to Caesar what belongs to Caesar. And give to God what belongs to God.

without leaving any children. ²¹The second one got married to the widow. He also died and left no child. It was the same with the third one. ²²In fact, none of the seven left any children. Last of all, the woman died too. ²³When the dead rise, whose wife will she be? All seven of them were married to her."

²⁴Jesus replied, "You are mistaken because you do not know the Scriptures. And you do not know the power of God. ²⁵When the dead rise, they won't get married. And their parents won't give them to be married. They will be like the angels in heaven.

²⁶"What about the dead rising? Haven't you read in the book of Moses the story of the bush? God said to Moses, 'I am the God of Abraham. I am the God of Isaac. And I am the God of Jacob.' *(Exodus 3:6)* ²⁷He is not the God of the dead. He is the God of the living. You have made a big mistake!"

The Most Important Commandment

²⁸One of the teachers of the law came and heard the Sadducees arguing. He noticed that Jesus had given the Sadducees a good answer. So he asked him, "Which is the most important of all the commandments?"

²⁹Jesus answered, "Here is the most important one. 'Israel, listen to me. The Lord is our God. The Lord is one. ³⁰Love the Lord your God with all your heart and with all your soul. Love him with all your mind and with all your strength.' *(Deuteronomy 6:4,5)* ³¹And here is the second one. 'Love your neighbor as you love yourself.' *(Leviticus 19:18)* There is no commandment more important than these."

³²"You have spoken well, teacher," the man replied. "You are right in saying that God is one. There is no other God but him. ³³To love God with all your heart and mind and strength is very important. So is loving your neighbor as you love yourself. These things are more important than all burnt offerings and sacrifices."

³⁴Jesus saw that the man had answered wisely. He said to him, "You are not far from God's kingdom."

From then on, no one dared to ask Jesus any more questions.

Whose Son Is the Christ?

³⁵Jesus was teaching in the temple courtyard. He asked, "Why do the teachers of the law say that the Christ is the son of David? ³⁶David himself spoke by the Holy Spirit. He said,

" 'The Lord said to my Lord,
  "Sit at my right hand
until I put your enemies
  under your control." '   *(Psalm 110:1)*

³⁷David himself calls him 'Lord.' So how can he be David's son?"
The large crowd listened to Jesus with delight.

³⁸As he taught, he said, "Watch out for the teachers of the law.
They like to walk around in long robes. They like to be greeted in
the market places. ³⁹They love to have the most important seats
in the synagogues. They also love to have the places of honor at
dinners. ⁴⁰They take over the houses of widows. They say long
prayers to show off. God will punish those people very much."

The Widow's Offering

⁴¹Jesus sat down across from the place where people put their
temple offerings. He watched the crowd putting their money into
the offering boxes. Many rich people threw large amounts into
them.

⁴²But a poor widow came and put in two very small copper
coins. They were worth much less than a penny.

⁴³Jesus asked his disciples to come to him. He said, "What I'm
about to tell you is true. That poor widow has put more into the
offering box than all the others. ⁴⁴They all gave out of their
wealth. But she gave even though she was poor. She put in everything she had. She gave all she had to live on."

Signs of the End

13 Jesus was leaving the temple. One of his disciples said to
him, "Look, Teacher! What huge stones! What wonderful
buildings!"

²"Do you see these huge buildings?" Jesus asked. "Not one
stone here will be left on top of another. Every stone will be
thrown down."

³Jesus was sitting on the Mount of Olives, across from the temple. Peter, James, John and Andrew asked him a question in
private. ⁴"Tell us," they said. "When will these things happen?
And what will be the sign that they are all about to come true?"

⁵Jesus said to them, "Keep watch! Be careful that no one fools
you. ⁶Many will come in my name. They will claim, 'I am he.'
They will fool many people. ⁷You will hear about wars. You will
also hear people talking about future wars. Don't be alarmed.

Those things must happen. But the end still isn't here. ⁸Nation will fight against nation. Kingdom will fight against kingdom. There will be earthquakes in many places. People will go hungry. All of those things are the beginning of birth pains.

⁹"Watch out! You will be handed over to the local courts. You will be whipped in the synagogues. You will stand in front of governors and kings because of me. In that way you will be witnesses to them. ¹⁰The good news has to be preached to all nations before the end comes. ¹¹You will be arrested and brought to trial. But don't worry ahead of time about what you will say. Just say what God brings to your mind at the time. It is not you speaking, but the Holy Spirit.

¹²"Brothers will hand over brothers to be killed. Fathers will hand over their children. Children will rise up against their parents and have them put to death. ¹³Everyone will hate you because of me. But the one who stands firm to the end will be saved.

¹⁴"You will see 'the hated thing that destroys.' *(Daniel 9:27; 11:31; 12:11)* It will stand where it does not belong. The reader should understand this. Then those who are in Judea should escape to the mountains. ¹⁵No one on the roof should go down into the house to take anything out. ¹⁶No one in the field should go back to get a coat. ¹⁷How awful it will be in those days for pregnant women! How awful for nursing mothers! ¹⁸Pray that this will not happen in winter.

¹⁹"Those days will be worse than any others from the time God created the world until now. And there will never be any like them again. ²⁰If the Lord had not cut the time short, no one would live. But because of God's chosen people, he has shortened it.

²¹"At that time someone may say to you, 'Look! Here is the Christ!' Or, 'Look! There he is!' Do not believe it. ²²False Christs and false prophets will appear. They will do signs and miracles. They will try to fool God's chosen people if possible. ²³Keep watch! I have told you everything ahead of time.

²⁴"But in those days, after that terrible suffering, Scripture says,

> "'The sun will be darkened.
>   The moon will not shine.
> ²⁵ The stars will fall from the sky.
>   The heavenly bodies will be shaken.'   *(Isaiah 13:10; 34:4)*

²⁶"At that time people will see the Son of Man coming in

clouds. He will come with great power and glory. [27]He will send his angels. He will gather his chosen people from all four directions. He will bring them from the ends of the earth to the ends of the heavens.

[28]"Learn a lesson from the fig tree. As soon as its twigs get tender and its leaves come out, you know that summer is near. [29]In the same way, when you see those things happening, you know that the end is near. It is right at the door. [30]What I'm about to tell you is true. The people living at that time will certainly not pass away until all those things have happened. [31]Heaven and earth will pass away. But my words will never pass away.

The Day and Hour Are Not Known

[32]"No one knows about that day or hour. Not even the angels in heaven know. The Son does not know. Only the Father knows.

[33]"Keep watch! Stay awake! You do not know when that time will come. [34]It's like a man going away. He leaves his house and puts his servants in charge. Each one is given a task to do. He tells the one at the door to keep watch.

[35]"So keep watch! You do not know when the owner of the house will come back. It may be in the evening or at midnight. It may be when the rooster crows or at dawn. [36]He may come suddenly. So do not let him find you sleeping.

[37]"What I say to you, I say to everyone. 'Watch!'"

A Woman Pours Perfume on Jesus

14 The Passover and the Feast of Unleavened Bread were only two days away. The chief priests and the teachers of the law were looking for a clever way to arrest Jesus. They wanted to kill him. [2]"But not during the Feast," they said. "The people may stir up trouble."

[3]Jesus was in Bethany. He was at the table in the home of a man named Simon, who had a skin disease. A woman came with a special sealed jar of very expensive perfume. It was made out of pure nard. She broke the jar open and poured the perfume on Jesus' head.

GREAT VERSE — TO — REMEMBER **13:31** Heaven and earth will pass away. But my words will never pass away.

⁴Some of the people there became angry. They said to one another, "Why waste this perfume? ⁵It could have been sold for more than a year's pay. The money could have been given to poor people." So they told the woman off.

⁶"Leave her alone," Jesus said. "Why are you bothering her? She has done a beautiful thing to me. ⁷You will always have poor people with you. You can help them any time you want to. But you will not always have me. ⁸She did what she could. She poured perfume on my body to prepare me to be buried. ⁹What I'm about to tell you is true. What she has done will be told anywhere the good news is preached all over the world. It will be told in memory of her."

¹⁰Judas Iscariot was one of the Twelve. He went to the chief priests to hand Jesus over to them. ¹¹They were delighted to hear that he would do this. They promised to give Judas money. So he watched for the right time to hand Jesus over to them.

The Lord's Supper

¹²It was the first day of the Feast of Unleavened Bread. That was the time to sacrifice the Passover lamb.

Jesus' disciples asked him, "Where do you want us to go and prepare for you to eat the Passover meal?"

¹³So he sent out two of his disciples. He told them, "Go into the city. A man carrying a jar of water will meet you. Follow him. ¹⁴He will enter a house. Say to its owner, 'The Teacher asks: Where is my guest room? Where can I eat the Passover meal with my disciples?' ¹⁵He will show you a large upstairs room. It will have furniture and will be ready. Prepare for us to eat there."

¹⁶The disciples left and went into the city. They found things just as Jesus had told them. So they prepared the Passover meal.

¹⁷When evening came, Jesus arrived with the Twelve. ¹⁸While they were at the table eating, Jesus said, "What I'm about to tell you is true. One of you who is eating with me will hand me over to my enemies."

¹⁹The disciples became sad. One by one they said to him, "It's not I, is it?"

²⁰"It is one of the Twelve," Jesus replied. "It is the one who dips bread into the bowl with me. ²¹The Son of Man will go just as it is written about him. But how terrible it will be for the one who hands over the Son of Man! It would be better for him if he had not been born."

²²While they were eating, Jesus took bread. He gave thanks and

broke it. He handed it to his disciples and said, "Take it. This is my body."

²³Then he took the cup. He gave thanks and handed it to them. All of them drank from it.

²⁴"This is my blood of the new covenant," he said to them. "It is poured out for many. ²⁵What I'm about to tell you is true. I will not drink from the fruit of the vine until the day I drink it again in God's kingdom."

²⁶Then they sang a hymn and went out to the Mount of Olives.

Jesus Says That Peter Will Fail

²⁷"You will all turn away," Jesus told the disciples. "It is written:

> "'I will strike the shepherd.
>   The sheep will be scattered.' *(Zechariah 13:7)*

²⁸But after I rise from the dead, I will go ahead of you into Galilee."

²⁹Peter said, "All the others may turn away. But I will not."

³⁰"What I'm about to tell you is true," Jesus answered. "It will happen today, this very night. Before the rooster crows twice, you yourself will say three times that you don't know me."

³¹But Peter would not give in. He said, "I may have to die with you. But I will never say I don't know you." And all the others said the same thing.

Jesus Prays in Gethsemane

³²Jesus and his disciples went to a place called Gethsemane. Jesus said to them, "Sit here while I pray."

³³He took Peter, James and John along with him. He began to be very upset and troubled. ³⁴"My soul is very sad. I feel close to death," he said to them. "Stay here. Keep watch."

³⁵He went a little farther. Then he fell to the ground. He prayed

GREAT VERSE —TO— REMEMBER

14:36 *"Abba,"* he said, "everything is possible for you. Take this cup of suffering from me. But let what you want be done, not what I want."

that, if possible, the hour might pass by him. [36]"*Abba*," he said, "everything is possible for you. Take this cup of suffering from me. But let what you want be done, not what I want." *Abba* means Father.

[37]Then he returned to his disciples and found them sleeping. "Simon," he said to Peter, "are you asleep? Couldn't you keep watch for one hour? [38]Watch and pray. Then you won't fall into sin when you are tempted. The spirit is willing. But the body is weak."

[39]Once more Jesus went away and prayed the same thing. [40]Then he came back. Again he found them sleeping. They couldn't keep their eyes open. They did not know what to say to him.

[41]Jesus returned the third time. He said to them, "Are you still sleeping and resting? Enough! The hour has come. Look! The Son of Man is about to be handed over to sinners. [42]Get up! Let us go! Here comes the one who is handing me over to them!"

Jesus Is Arrested

[43]Just as Jesus was speaking, Judas appeared. He was one of the Twelve. A crowd was with him. They were carrying swords and clubs. The chief priests, the teachers of the law, and the elders had sent them.

[44]Judas, who was going to hand Jesus over, had arranged a signal with them. "The one I kiss is the man," he said. "Arrest him and have the guards lead him away."

[45]So Judas went to Jesus at once. He said, "Rabbi!" And he kissed him.

[46]The men grabbed Jesus and arrested him.

[47]Then one of those standing nearby pulled his sword out. He struck the servant of the high priest and cut off his ear.

[48]"Am I leading a band of armed men against you?" asked Jesus. "Do you have to come out with swords and clubs to capture me? [49]Every day I was with you. I taught in the temple courtyard, and you didn't arrest me. But the Scriptures must come true."

[50]Then everyone left him and ran away.

[51]A young man was following Jesus. The man was wearing nothing but a piece of linen cloth. When the crowd grabbed him, [52]he ran away naked. He left his clothing behind.

Jesus Is Taken to the Sanhedrin

[53]The crowd took Jesus to the high priest. All of the chief priests, the elders, and the teachers of the law came together.

⁵⁴Not too far away, Peter followed Jesus. He went right into the courtyard of the high priest. There he sat with the guards. He warmed himself at the fire.

⁵⁵The chief priests and the whole Sanhedrin were looking for something to use against Jesus. They wanted to put him to death. But they did not find any proof. ⁵⁶Many witnesses lied about him. But their stories did not agree.

⁵⁷Then some stood up. They gave false witness about him. ⁵⁸"We heard him say, 'I will destroy this temple made by human hands. In three days I will build another temple, not made by human hands.'" ⁵⁹But what they said did not agree.

⁶⁰Then the high priest stood up in front of them. He asked Jesus, "Aren't you going to answer? What are these charges these men are bringing against you?"

⁶¹But Jesus remained silent. He gave no answer.

Again the high priest asked him, "Are you the Christ? Are you the Son of the Blessed One?"

⁶²"I am," said Jesus. "And you will see the Son of Man sitting at the right hand of the Mighty One. You will see the Son of Man coming on the clouds of heaven."

⁶³The high priest tore his clothes. "Why do we need any more witnesses?" he asked. ⁶⁴"You have heard him say a very evil thing against God. What do you think?"

They all found him guilty and said he must die.

⁶⁵Then some began to spit at him. They blindfolded him. They hit him with their fists. They said, "Prophesy!" And the guards took him and beat him.

Peter Says He Does Not Know Jesus

⁶⁶Peter was below in the courtyard. One of the high priest's women servants came by. ⁶⁷When she saw Peter warming himself, she looked closely at him.

"You also were with Jesus, that Nazarene," she said.

⁶⁸But Peter said he had not been with him. "I don't know or understand what you're talking about," he said. He went out to the entrance to the courtyard.

⁶⁹The servant saw him there. She said again to those standing around, "This fellow is one of them."

⁷⁰Again he said he was not.

After a little while, those standing nearby said to Peter, "You must be one of them. You are from Galilee."

⁷¹He began to call down curses on himself. He took an oath and

said to them, "I don't know this man you're talking about!"

⁷²Right away the rooster crowed the second time. Then Peter remembered what Jesus had spoken to him. "The rooster will crow twice," he had said. "Before it does, you will say three times that you don't know me." Peter broke down and sobbed.

Jesus Is Brought to Pilate

15 It was very early in the morning. The chief priests, with the elders, the teachers of the law, and the whole Sanhedrin, made a decision. They tied Jesus up and led him away. Then they handed him over to Pilate.

²"Are you the king of the Jews?" asked Pilate.

"Yes. It is just as you say," Jesus replied.

³The chief priests brought many charges against him. ⁴So Pilate asked him again, "Aren't you going to answer? See how many things they charge you with."

⁵But Jesus still did not reply. Pilate was amazed.

⁶It was the usual practice at the Passover Feast to let one prisoner go free. The people could choose the one they wanted. ⁷A man named Barabbas was in prison. He was there with some other people who had fought against the country's rulers. They had committed murder while they were fighting against the rulers. ⁸The crowd came up and asked Pilate to do for them what he usually did.

⁹"Do you want me to let the king of the Jews go free?" asked Pilate. ¹⁰He knew that the chief priests had handed Jesus over to him because they were jealous. ¹¹But the chief priests stirred up the crowd. So the crowd asked Pilate to let Barabbas go free instead.

¹²"Then what should I do with the one you call the king of the Jews?" Pilate asked them.

¹³"Crucify him!" the crowd shouted.

¹⁴"Why? What wrong has he done?" asked Pilate.

But they shouted even louder, "Crucify him!"

¹⁵Pilate wanted to satisfy the crowd. So he let Barabbas go free. He ordered that Jesus be whipped. Then he handed him over to be nailed to a cross.

The Soldiers Make Fun of Jesus

¹⁶The soldiers led Jesus away into the palace. It was called the Praetorium. They called together the whole company of soldiers.

[17]They put a purple robe on Jesus. Then they twisted thorns together to make a crown. They placed it on his head. [18]They began to call out to him, "We honor you, king of the Jews!" [19]Again and again they hit him on the head with a stick. They spit on him. They fell on their knees and pretended to honor him.

[20]After they had made fun of him, they took off the purple robe. They put his own clothes back on him. Then they led him out to nail him to a cross.

Jesus Is Nailed to a Cross

[21]A man named Simon from Cyrene was passing by. He was the father of Alexander and Rufus. Simon was on his way in from the country. The soldiers forced him to carry the cross.

[22]They brought Jesus to the place called Golgotha. The word Golgotha means The Place of the Skull. [23]Then they gave him wine mixed with spices. But he did not take it.

[24]They nailed him to the cross. Then they divided up his clothes. They cast lots to see what each of them would get.

[25]It was nine o'clock in the morning when they crucified him. [26]They wrote out the charge against him. It read, THE KING OF THE JEWS.

[27/28]They crucified two robbers with him. One was on his right and one was on his left.

[29]Those who passed by shouted at Jesus and made fun of him. They shook their heads and said, "So you are going to destroy the temple and build it again in three days? [30]Then come down from the cross! Save yourself!"

[31]In the same way the chief priests and the teachers of the law made fun of him among themselves. "He saved others," they said. "But he can't save himself! [32]Let this Christ, this King of Israel, come down now from the cross! When we see that, we will believe."

Those who were being crucified with Jesus also made fun of him.

Jesus Dies

[33]At noon, the whole land was covered with darkness. It lasted three hours. [34]At three o'clock Jesus cried out in a loud voice, *"Eloi, Eloi, lama sabachthani?"* This means "My God, my God, why have you deserted me?" *(Psalm 22:1)*

³⁵Some of those standing nearby heard Jesus cry out. They said, "Listen! He's calling for Elijah."

³⁶One of them ran and filled a sponge with wine vinegar. He put it on a stick. He offered it to Jesus to drink. "Leave him alone," he said. "Let's see if Elijah comes to take him down."

³⁷With a loud cry, Jesus took his last breath.

³⁸The temple curtain was torn in two from top to bottom.

³⁹A Roman commander was standing there in front of Jesus. He heard his cry and saw how Jesus died. Then he said, "This man was surely the Son of God!"

⁴⁰Not very far away, some women were watching. Mary Magdalene was among them. Mary, the mother of the younger James and of Joses, was also there. So was Salome. ⁴¹In Galilee those women had followed Jesus. They had taken care of his needs.

Many other women were also there. They had come up with him to Jerusalem.

Jesus Is Buried

⁴²It was Preparation Day, the day before the Sabbath. As evening approached, ⁴³Joseph went boldly to Pilate and asked for Jesus' body. Joseph was from the town of Arimathea. He was a leading member of the Council. He was waiting for God's kingdom.

⁴⁴Pilate was surprised to hear that Jesus was already dead. So he called for the Roman commander. He asked him if Jesus had already died. ⁴⁵The commander said it was true. So Pilate gave the body to Joseph.

⁴⁶Then Joseph bought some linen cloth. He took the body down and wrapped it in the linen. He put it in a tomb cut out of rock. Then he rolled a stone against the entrance to the tomb.

⁴⁷Mary Magdalene and Mary the mother of Joses saw where Jesus had been placed.

GREAT VERSE –TO– REMEMBER

15:39 A Roman commander was standing there in front of Jesus. He heard his cry and saw how Jesus died. Then he said, "This man was surely the Son of God!"

Jesus Rises From the Dead

16 The Sabbath day ended. Mary Magdalene, Mary the mother of James, and Salome bought spices. They were going to apply them to Jesus' body.

²Very early on the first day of the week, they were on their way to the tomb. It was just after sunrise. ³They asked each other, "Who will roll the stone away from the entrance to the tomb?"

⁴Then they looked up and saw that the stone had been rolled away. The stone was very large.

⁵They entered the tomb. As they did, they saw a young man dressed in a white robe. He was sitting on the right side. They were alarmed.

⁶"Don't be alarmed," he said. "You are looking for Jesus the Nazarene, who was crucified. But he has risen! He is not here! See the place where they had put him. ⁷Go! Tell his disciples and Peter, 'He is going ahead of you into Galilee. There you will see him. It will be just as he told you.'"

⁸The women were shaking and confused. They went out and ran away from the tomb. They said nothing to anyone, because they were afraid.

---

⁹Jesus rose from the dead early on the first day of the week. He appeared first to Mary Magdalene. He had driven seven demons out of her. ¹⁰She went and told those who had been with him. She found them crying. They were very sad. ¹¹They heard that Jesus was alive and that she had seen him. But they did not believe it.

¹²After that, Jesus appeared in a different form to two of them. This happened while they were walking out in the country. ¹³The two returned and told the others about it. But the others did not believe them either.

¹⁴Later Jesus appeared to the Eleven as they were eating. He spoke firmly to them because they had no faith. They would not believe those who had seen him after he rose from the dead.

¹⁵He said to them, "Go into all the world. Preach the good news to everyone. ¹⁶Anyone who believes and is baptized will be saved. But anyone who does not believe will be punished. ¹⁷Here are the miraculous signs that those who believe will do. In my name they will drive out demons. They will speak in languages they had not known before. ¹⁸They will pick up snakes with their hands. And when they drink deadly poison, it will not hurt them

at all. They will place their hands on sick people. And the people will get well."

¹⁹When the Lord Jesus finished speaking to them, he was taken up into heaven. He sat down at the right hand of God.

²⁰Then the disciples went out and preached everywhere. The Lord worked with them. And he backed up his word by the signs that went with it.

16:15-16 Go into all the world. Preach the good news to everyone. Anyone who believes and is baptized will be saved. But anyone who does not believe will be punished.

Luke

Why Was This Book Written? Luke wrote the third Gospel. He was a doctor who traveled with Paul. He wrote his book to tell us the true story of Jesus' life. He learned many of the stories about Jesus from talking to Paul. Other friends told Luke stories about Jesus too.

What Is This Book About? The book of Luke has many stories. One story is about a lost son. Another story is about a good man from Samaria. These stories are called parables. These stories show us that Jesus loves all people. Someone said the book of Luke is "the most beautiful book ever written."

What Is in This Book?

Luke Writes an Orderly Report

1 Many people have attempted to write about the things that have taken place among us. [2]Reports of these things were handed down to us. There were people who saw these things for themselves from the beginning and then passed the word on.

[3]I myself have carefully looked into everything from the beginning. So it seemed good also to me to write down an orderly report of exactly what happened. I am doing this for you, most excellent Theophilus. [4]I want you to know that the things you have been taught are true.

The Coming Birth of John the Baptist

[5]In the time of Herod, the king of Judea, there was a priest named Zechariah. He belonged to a group of priests named after Abijah. His wife Elizabeth also came from the family line of Aaron. [6]Both of them did what was right in God's eyes. They obeyed all the Lord's commandments and rules faithfully. [7]But they had no children, because Elizabeth was not able to have any. And they were both very old.

[8]One day Zechariah's group was on duty. He was serving as a priest in God's temple. [9]He happened to be chosen, in the usual way, to go into the temple of the Lord. There he was supposed to burn incense. [10]The time came for this to be done. All who had gathered to worship were praying outside.

[11]Then an angel of the Lord appeared to Zechariah. The angel was standing at the right side of the incense altar. [12]When Zechariah saw him, he was amazed and terrified.

[13]But the angel said to him, "Do not be afraid, Zechariah. Your prayer has been heard. Your wife Elizabeth will have a child. It will be a boy, and you must name him John. [14]He will be a joy and delight to you. His birth will make many people very glad. [15]He will be important in the Lord's eyes.

"He must never use wine or other such drinks. He will be filled with the Holy Spirit from the time he is born. [16]He will bring many of Israel's people back to the Lord their God. [17]And he will prepare the way for the Lord. He will have the same spirit and power that Elijah had. He will turn the hearts of parents to their children. He will also turn people who disobey to the wisdom of those who do right. In this way, he will prepare a people who are ready for the Lord."

[18]Zechariah asked the angel, "How can I be sure of this? I am an old man, and my wife is old too."

¹⁹The angel answered, "I am Gabriel. I serve God. I have been sent to speak to you and to tell you this good news. ²⁰And now you will have to be silent. You will not be able to speak until the day this happens. That's because you did not believe my words. They will come true when the time is right."

²¹During that time, the people were waiting for Zechariah. They wondered why he stayed in the temple so long. ²²When he came out, he could not speak to them. They realized he had seen a vision in the temple. They knew this because he kept motioning to them. He still could not speak.

²³When his time of service was over, he returned home. ²⁴After that, his wife Elizabeth became pregnant. She stayed at home for five months. ²⁵"The Lord has done this for me," she said. "In these days, he has been kind to me. He has taken away my shame among the people."

The Coming Birth of Jesus

²⁶In the sixth month, God sent the angel Gabriel to Nazareth, a town in Galilee. ²⁷He was sent to a virgin. The girl was engaged to a man named Joseph. He came from the family line of David. The virgin's name was Mary. ²⁸The angel greeted her and said, "The Lord has given you special favor. He is with you."

²⁹Mary was very upset because of his words. She wondered what kind of greeting this could be. ³⁰But the angel said to her, "Do not be afraid, Mary. God is very pleased with you. ³¹You will become pregnant and give birth to a son. You must name him Jesus. ³²He will be great and will be called the Son of the Most High. The Lord God will make him a king like his father David of long ago. ³³He will rule forever over his people, who came from Jacob's family. His kingdom will never end."

³⁴"How can this happen?" Mary asked the angel. "I am a virgin."

³⁵The angel answered, "The Holy Spirit will come to you. The

GREAT VERSE —TO— REMEMBER

1:30-31 But the angel said to her, "Do not be afraid, Mary. God is very pleased with you. You will become pregnant and give birth to a son. You must name him Jesus."

power of the Most High God will cover you. So the holy one that is born will be called the Son of God. [36]Your relative Elizabeth is old. And even she is going to have a child. People thought she could not have children. But she has been pregnant for six months now. [37]Nothing is impossible with God."

[38]"I serve the Lord," Mary answered. "May it happen to me just as you said it would." Then the angel left her.

Mary Visits Elizabeth

[39]At that time Mary got ready and hurried to a town in Judea's hill country. [40]There she entered Zechariah's home and greeted Elizabeth. [41]When Elizabeth heard Mary's greeting, the baby inside her jumped. And Elizabeth was filled with the Holy Spirit. [42]In a loud voice she called out, "God has blessed you more than other women. And blessed is the child you will have! [43]But why is God so kind to me? Why has the mother of my Lord come to me? [44]As soon as I heard the sound of your voice, the baby inside me jumped for joy. [45]You are a woman God has blessed. You have believed that what the Lord has said to you will be done!"

Mary's Song

[46]Mary said,

> "My soul gives glory to the Lord.
> [47]   My spirit delights in God my Savior.
> [48]He has taken note of me
>   even though I am not important.
> From now on all people will call me blessed.
> [49]   The Mighty One has done great things for me.
>   His name is holy.
> [50]His mercy goes out to those who have respect for him,
>   from parent to child down through the years.
> [51]He has done mighty things with his arm.
>   He has scattered those who are proud in their
>   deepest thoughts.
> [52]He has brought down rulers from their thrones.
>   But he has lifted up people who are not important.
> [53]He has filled those who are hungry with good things.
>   But he has sent those who are rich away empty.
> [54]He has helped the people of Israel, who serve him.
>   He has always remembered to be kind
> [55]to Abraham and his children down through the years.

He has done it just as he said to our people of long
ago."

⁵⁶Mary stayed with Elizabeth about three months. Then she returned home.

John the Baptist Is Born

⁵⁷The time came for Elizabeth to have her baby. She gave birth to a son. ⁵⁸Her neighbors and relatives heard that the Lord had been very kind to her. They shared her joy.

⁵⁹On the eighth day, they came to circumcise the child. They were going to name him Zechariah, like his father. ⁶⁰But his mother spoke up. "No!" she said. "He must be called John."

⁶¹They said to her, "No one among your relatives has that name."

⁶²Then they motioned to his father. They wanted to find out what he would like to name the child. ⁶³He asked for something to write on. Then he wrote, "His name is John." Everyone was amazed.

⁶⁴Right away Zechariah could speak again. His first words gave praise to God. ⁶⁵The neighbors were all filled with fear and wonder. All through Judea's hill country, people were talking about all these things. ⁶⁶Everyone who heard this wondered about it. And because the Lord was with John, they asked, "What is this child going to be?"

Zechariah's Song

⁶⁷His father Zechariah was filled with the Holy Spirit. He prophesied,

⁶⁸"Give praise to the Lord, the God of Israel!
   He has come and set his people free.
⁶⁹He has acted with great power and has saved us.
   He did it for those who are in the family line of his
      servant David.
⁷⁰Long ago holy prophets said he would do it.
⁷¹He has saved us from our enemies.
   We are rescued from all who hate us.
⁷²He has been kind to our people.
   He has remembered his holy covenant.
⁷³   He made an oath to our father Abraham.
⁷⁴He promised to save us from our enemies,
   so that we could serve him without fear.

⁷⁵   He wants us to be holy and godly as long as we live.

⁷⁶"And you, my child, will be called a prophet of the
            Most High.
      You will go ahead of the Lord to prepare the way for
            him.
⁷⁷ You will tell his people how they can be saved.
      You will tell them that their sins can be forgiven.
⁷⁸ All of that will happen because our God is tender and
            caring.
      His kindness will bring the rising sun to us from
            heaven.
⁷⁹ It will shine on those living in darkness
      and in the shadow of death.
      It will guide our feet on the path of peace."

⁸⁰The child grew up, and his spirit became strong. He lived in
the desert until he appeared openly to Israel.

Jesus Is Born

2 In those days, Caesar Augustus made a law. It required that
a list be made of everyone in the whole Roman world. ²It
was the first time a list was made of the people while Quirinius
was governor of Syria. ³All went to their own towns to be listed.

⁴So Joseph went also. He went from the town of Nazareth in
Galilee to Judea. That is where Bethlehem, the town of David,
was. Joseph went there because he belonged to the family line of
David. ⁵He went there with Mary to be listed. Mary was engaged
to him. She was expecting a baby.

⁶While they were there, the time came for the child to be born.
⁷She gave birth to her first baby. It was a boy. She wrapped him
in large strips of cloth. Then she placed him in a manger. There
was no room for them in the inn.

Angels Appear to the Shepherds

⁸There were shepherds living out in the fields nearby. It was
night, and they were looking after their sheep. ⁹An angel of the
Lord appeared to them. And the glory of the Lord shone around
them. They were terrified.

¹⁰But the angel said to them, "Do not be afraid. I bring you
good news of great joy. It is for all the people. ¹¹Today in the town
of David a Savior has been born to you. He is Christ the Lord.

¹²Here is how you will know I am telling you the truth. You will find a baby wrapped in strips of cloth and lying in a manger." ¹³Suddenly a large group of angels from heaven also appeared. They were praising God. They said,

¹⁴"May glory be given to God in the highest heaven!
   And may peace be given to those he is pleased with
      on earth!"

¹⁵The angels left and went into heaven. Then the shepherds said to one another, "Let's go to Bethlehem. Let's see this thing that has happened, which the Lord has told us about."

¹⁶So they hurried off and found Mary and Joseph and the baby. The baby was lying in the manger. ¹⁷After seeing him, they told everyone. They reported what the angel had said about this child. ¹⁸All who heard it were amazed at what the shepherds said to them.

¹⁹But Mary kept all these things like a secret treasure in her heart. She thought about them over and over.

²⁰The shepherds returned. They gave glory and praise to God. Everything they had seen and heard was just as they had been told.

Joseph and Mary Take Jesus to the Temple

²¹When the child was eight days old, he was circumcised. At the same time he was named Jesus. This was the name the angel had given him before his mother became pregnant.

²²The time for making them pure came as it is written in the Law of Moses. So Joseph and Mary took Jesus to Jerusalem. There they presented him to the Lord. ²³In the Law of the Lord it says, "The first boy born in every family must be set apart for the Lord." *(Exodus 13:2,12)* ²⁴They also offered a sacrifice. They did it in keeping with the Law, which says, "a pair of doves or two young pigeons." *(Leviticus 12:8)*

GREAT VERSE — TO — REMEMBER

2:10-11 Do not be afraid. I bring you good news of great joy. It is for all the people. Today in the town of David a Savior has been born to you. He is Christ the Lord.

²⁵In Jerusalem there was a man named Simeon. He was a good and godly man. He was waiting for God's promise to Israel to happen. The Holy Spirit was with him. ²⁶The Spirit had told Simeon that he would not die before he had seen the Lord's Christ. ²⁷The Spirit led him into the temple courtyard.

Then Jesus' parents brought the child in. They came to do for him what the Law required.

²⁸Simeon took Jesus in his arms and praised God. He said,

²⁹"Lord, you are the King over all.
    Now let me, your servant, go in peace.
    That is what you promised.
³⁰My eyes have seen your salvation.
³¹   You have prepared it in the sight of all people.
³²It is a light to be given to those who aren't Jews.
    It will bring glory to your people Israel."

³³The child's father and mother were amazed at what was said about him. ³⁴Then Simeon blessed them. He said to Mary, Jesus' mother, "This child is going to cause many in Israel to fall and to rise. He is a sign that will be spoken against. ³⁵The thoughts of many hearts will be known. A sword will wound your own soul too."

³⁶There was also a prophet named Anna. She was the daughter of Phanuel from the tribe of Asher. Anna was very old. After getting married, she lived with her husband seven years. ³⁷Then she was a widow until she was 84. She never left the temple. She worshiped night and day, praying and going without eating.

³⁸Anna came up to Jesus' family at that very moment. She gave thanks to God. And she spoke about the child to all who were looking forward to the time when Jerusalem would be set free.

³⁹Joseph and Mary did everything the Law of the Lord required. Then they returned to Galilee. They went to their own town of Nazareth. ⁴⁰And the child grew and became strong. He was very wise. He was blessed by God's grace.

GREAT VERSE — TO — REMEMBER

2:40 And the child grew and became strong. He was very wise. He was blessed by God's grace.

The Boy Jesus at the Temple

⁴¹Every year Jesus' parents went to Jerusalem for the Passover Feast. ⁴²When he was 12 years old, they went up to the Feast as usual.

⁴³After the Feast was over, his parents left to go back home. The boy Jesus stayed behind in Jerusalem. But they were not aware of it. ⁴⁴They thought he was somewhere in their group. So they traveled on for a day.

Then they began to look for him among their relatives and friends. ⁴⁵They did not find him. So they went back to Jerusalem to look for him. ⁴⁶After three days they found him in the temple courtyard. He was sitting with the teachers. He was listening to them and asking them questions. ⁴⁷Everyone who heard him was amazed at how much he understood. They also were amazed at his answers.

⁴⁸When his parents saw him, they were amazed. His mother said to him, "Son, why have you treated us like this? Your father and I have been worried about you. We have been looking for you everywhere."

⁴⁹"Why were you looking for me?" he asked. "Didn't you know I had to be in my Father's house?" ⁵⁰But they did not understand what he meant by that.

⁵¹Then he went back to Nazareth with them, and he obeyed them. But his mother kept all these things like a secret treasure in her heart. ⁵²Jesus became wiser and stronger. He also became more and more pleasing to God and to people.

John the Baptist Prepares the Way

3 Tiberius Caesar had been ruling for 15 years. Pontius Pilate was governor of Judea. Herod was the ruler of Galilee. His brother Philip was the ruler of Iturea and Traconitis. Lysanias was ruler of Abilene. ²Annas and Caiaphas were high priests. At that time God's word came to John, son of Zechariah, in the desert. ³He went into all the countryside around the Jordan River. There he preached that people should be baptized and turn away from their sins. Then God would forgive them.

⁴In the book of Isaiah the prophet it is written:

"A voice calls out in the desert,
'Prepare the way for the Lord.
      Make straight paths for him.
⁵ Every valley will be filled in.

Every mountain and hill will be made low.
The crooked roads will become straight.
The rough ways will become smooth.
⁶And all people will see God's salvation.'" *(Isaiah 40:3–5)*

⁷John spoke to the crowds coming to be baptized by him. He said, "You nest of poisonous snakes! Who warned you to escape the coming of God's anger? ⁸Produce fruit that shows you have turned away from your sins. And don't start saying to yourselves, 'Abraham is our father.' I tell you, God can raise up children for Abraham even from these stones. ⁹The ax is already lying at the roots of the trees. All the trees that don't produce good fruit will be cut down. They will be thrown into the fire."

¹⁰"Then what should we do?" the crowd asked.

¹¹John answered, "If you have extra clothes, you should share with those who have none. And if you have food, you should do the same."

¹²Tax collectors also came to be baptized. "Teacher," they asked, "what should we do?"

¹³"Don't collect any more than you are required to," John told them.

¹⁴Then some soldiers asked him, "And what should we do?"

John replied, "Don't force people to give you money. Don't bring false charges against people. Be happy with your pay."

¹⁵The people were waiting. They were expecting something. They were all wondering in their hearts if John might be the Christ.

¹⁶John answered them all, "I baptize you with water. But one who is more powerful than I am will come. I'm not good enough to untie the straps of his sandals. He will baptize you with the

---

GREAT VERSE —TO— REMEMBER

3:16 John answered them all, "I baptize you with water. But one who is more powerful than I am will come. I'm not good enough to untie the straps of his sandals. He will baptize you with the Holy Spirit and with fire."

Holy Spirit and with fire. ¹⁷His pitchfork is in his hand to toss the straw away from his threshing floor. He will gather the wheat into his storeroom. But he will burn up the husks with fire that can't be put out."

¹⁸John said many other things to warn the people. He also preached the good news to them.

¹⁹But John found fault with Herod, the ruler or Galilee, because of Herodias. She was the wife of Herod's brother. John also spoke strongly to Herod about all the other evil things he had done. ²⁰So Herod locked him up in prison. He added this sin to all his others.

The Baptism and Family Line of Jesus

²¹When all the people were being baptized, Jesus was baptized too. And as he was praying, heaven was opened. ²²The Holy Spirit came down on him in the form of a dove. A voice came from heaven. It said, "You are my Son, and I love you. I am very pleased with you."

²³Jesus was about 30 years old when he began his special work for God and others. It was thought that he was the son of Joseph.

Joseph was the son of Heli. ²⁴Heli was the son of Matthat.

Matthat was the son of Levi. Levi was the son of Melki.

Melki was the son of Jannai. Jannai was the son of Joseph.

²⁵Joseph was the son of Mattathias. Mattathias was the son of Amos.

Amos was the son of Nahum. Nahum was the son of Esli.

Esli was the son of Naggai. ²⁶Naggai was the son of Maath.

Maath was the son of Mattathias. Mattathias was the son of Semein.

Semein was the son of Josech. Josech was the son of Joda.

²⁷Joda was the son of Joanan. Joanan was the son of Rhesa.

Rhesa was the son of Zerubbabel. Zerubbabel was the son of Shealtiel.

Shealtiel was the son of Neri. ²⁸Neri was the son of Melki.

Melki was the son of Addi. Addi was the son of Cosam.

Cosam was the son of Elmadam. Elmadam was the son of Er.

²⁹ Er was the son of Joshua. Joshua was the son of Eliezer. Eliezer was the son of Jorim. Jorim was the son of Matthat.

Matthat was the son of Levi. ³⁰Levi was the son of Simeon.

Simeon was the son of Judah. Judah was the son of Joseph.

Joseph was the son of Jonam. Jonam was the son of Eliakim.

³¹ Eliakim was the son of Melea. Melea was the son of Menna.

Menna was the son of Mattatha. Mattatha was the son of Nathan.

Nathan was the son of David. ³²David was the son of Jesse.

Jesse was the son of Obed. Obed was the son of Boaz.

Boaz was the son of Salmon. Salmon was the son of Nahshon.

³³ Nahshon was the son of Amminadab. Amminadab was the son of Ram.

Ram was the son of Hezron. Hezron was the son of Perez.

Perez was the son of Judah. ³⁴Judah was the son of Jacob.

Jacob was the son of Isaac. Isaac was the son of Abraham.

Abraham was the son of Terah. Terah was the son of Nahor.

³⁵ Nahor was the son of Serug. Serug was the son of Reu.

Reu was the son of Peleg. Peleg was the son of Eber.

Eber was the son of Shelah. ³⁶Shelah was the son of Cainan.

Cainan was the son of Arphaxad. Arphaxad was the son of Shem.

Shem was the son of Noah. Noah was the son of Lamech.

³⁷ Lamech was the son of Methuselah. Methuselah was the son of Enoch.

Enoch was the son of Jared. Jared was the son of Mahalalel.

Mahalalel was the son of Kenan. ³⁸Kenan was the son of
    Enosh.
Enosh was the son of Seth. Seth was the son of Adam.
Adam was the son of God.

Jesus Is Tempted

4 Jesus, full of the Holy Spirit, returned from the Jordan River. The Spirit led him into the desert. ²There the devil tempted him for 40 days.

Jesus ate nothing during that time. At the end of the 40 days, he was hungry.

³The devil said to him, "If you are the Son of God, tell this stone to become bread."

⁴Jesus answered, "It is written: 'People don't live only on bread.'" *(Deuteronomy 8:3)*

⁵Then the devil led Jesus up to a high place. In an instant, he showed Jesus all the kingdoms of the world. ⁶He said to him, "I will give you all their authority and glory. It has been given to me, and I can give it to anyone I want to. ⁷So if you worship me, it will all be yours."

⁸Jesus answered, "It is written: 'Worship the Lord your God. Serve only him.'" *(Deuteronomy 6:13)*

⁹Then the devil led Jesus to Jerusalem. He had him stand on the highest point of the temple. "If you are the Son of God," he said, "throw yourself down from here. ¹⁰It is written:

> "'The Lord will command his angels to take good care
>   of you.
> ¹¹They will lift you up in their hands.
>   Then you won't trip over a stone.'"   *(Psalm 91:11,12)*

¹²Jesus answered, "Scripture says, 'Do not put the Lord your God to the test.'" *(Deuteronomy 6:16)*

¹³When the devil finished all this tempting, he left Jesus until a better time.

GREAT VERSE — TO — REMEMBER

4:8 It is written: "Worship the Lord your God. Serve only him."

Jesus Is Not Accepted in Nazareth

[14]Jesus returned to Galilee in the power of the Holy Spirit. News about him spread through the whole countryside. [15]He taught in their synagogues, and everyone praised him.

[16]Jesus went to Nazareth, where he had been brought up. On the Sabbath day he went into the synagogue as he usually did. And he stood up to read.

[17]The scroll of the prophet Isaiah was handed to him. He unrolled it and found the right place. There it is written:

[18] "The Spirit of the Lord is on me.
  He has anointed me
    to tell the good news to poor people.
  He has sent me to announce freedom for the prisoners.
  He has sent me so that the blind will see again.
  He has sent me to free those who are beaten down.
[19]   And he has sent me to announce the year of the
    Lord's favor."   *(Isaiah 61:1,2)*

[20]Then Jesus rolled up the scroll. He gave it back to the attendant and sat down. The eyes of everyone in the synagogue were staring at him.

[21]He began by saying to them, "Today this passage of Scripture is coming true as you listen."

[22]Everyone said good things about him. They were amazed at the gracious words they heard from his lips. "Isn't this Joseph's son?" they asked.

[23]Jesus said, "Here is a saying you will certainly apply to me. 'Doctor, heal yourself! Do the things here in your hometown that we heard you did in Capernaum.'"

[24]"What I'm about to tell you is true," he continued. "Prophets are not accepted in their hometowns. [25]I tell you for sure that there were many widows in Israel in the days of Elijah. And there had been no rain for three and a half years. There wasn't enough food to eat anywhere in the land. [26]But Elijah was not sent to any of those widows. Instead, he was sent to a widow in Zarephath near Sidon. [27]And there were many in Israel who had skin diseases in the days of Elisha the prophet. But not one of them was healed except Naaman the Syrian."

[28]All the people in the synagogue were very angry when they heard that. [29]They got up and ran him out of town. They took him to the edge of the hill on which the town was built. They

planned to throw him down the cliff. ³⁰But Jesus walked right through the crowd and went on his way.

Jesus Drives Out an Evil Spirit

³¹Then Jesus went to Capernaum, a town in Galilee. On the Sabbath day he began to teach the people. ³²They were amazed at his teaching, because his message had authority.

³³In the synagogue there was a man controlled by a demon, an evil spirit. He cried out at the top of his voice. ³⁴"Ha!" he said. "What do you want with us, Jesus of Nazareth? Have you come to destroy us? I know who you are. You are the Holy One of God!"

³⁵"Be quiet!" Jesus said firmly. "Come out of him!"

Then the demon threw the man down in front of everybody. And it came out without hurting him.

³⁶All the people were amazed. They said to each other, "What is this teaching? With authority and power he gives orders to evil spirits. And they come out!"

³⁷The news about Jesus spread throughout the whole area.

Jesus Heals Many People

³⁸Jesus left the synagogue and went to the home of Simon. At that time, Simon's mother-in-law was suffering from a high fever. So they asked Jesus to help her. ³⁹He bent over her and commanded the fever to leave, and it left her. She got up at once and began to wait on them.

⁴⁰At sunset, people brought to Jesus all who were sick. He placed his hands on each one and healed them. ⁴¹Also, demons came out of many people. They shouted, "You are the Son of God!" But he commanded them to be quiet. He would not allow them to speak, because they knew he was the Christ.

⁴²At dawn, Jesus went out to a place where he could be by himself. The people went to look for him. When they found him, they tried to keep him from leaving them. ⁴³But he said, "I must announce the good news of God's kingdom to the other towns also. That is why I was sent." ⁴⁴And he kept on preaching in the synagogues of Judea.

Jesus Chooses the First Disciples

5 One day Jesus was standing by the Sea of Galilee. The people crowded around him and listened to the word of God.

²Jesus saw two boats at the edge of the water. They had been left there by the fishermen, who were washing their nets. ³He got into the boat that belonged to Simon. Jesus asked him to go out a little way from shore. Then he sat down in the boat and taught the people.

⁴When he finished speaking, he turned to Simon. He said, "Go out into deep water. Let down the nets for a catch of fish."

⁵Simon answered, "Master, we've worked hard all night and haven't caught anything. But because you say so, I will let down the nets."

⁶When they had done so, they caught a large number of fish. There were so many that their nets began to break. ⁷So they motioned to their partners in the other boat to come and help them. They came and filled both boats so full that they began to sink.

⁸When Simon Peter saw this, he fell at Jesus' knees. "Go away from me, Lord!" he said. "I am a sinful man!"

⁹He and everyone with him were amazed at the number of fish they had caught. ¹⁰So were James and John, the sons of Zebedee, who worked with Simon.

Then Jesus said to Simon, "Don't be afraid. From now on you will catch people."

¹¹So they pulled their boats up on shore. Then they left everything and followed him.

Jesus Heals a Man With a Skin Disease

¹²While Jesus was in one of the towns, a man came along. He had a skin disease all over his body. When he saw Jesus, he fell with his face to the ground. He begged him, "Lord, if you are willing to make me 'clean,' you can do it."

¹³Jesus reached out his hand and touched the man. "I am willing to do it," he said. "Be 'clean'!" Right away the disease left him.

¹⁴Then Jesus ordered him, "Don't tell anyone. Go and show yourself to the priest. Offer the sacrifices that Moses commanded. It will be a witness to the priest and the people that you are 'clean.'"

¹⁵But the news about Jesus spread even more. So crowds of people came to hear him. They also came to be healed of their sicknesses. ¹⁶But Jesus often went away to be by himself and pray.

Jesus Heals a Man Who Could Not Walk

¹⁷One day Jesus was teaching. Pharisees and teachers of the law

were sitting there. They had come from every village of Galilee and from Judea and Jerusalem. The power of the Lord was present for Jesus to heal the sick.

[18]Some people came carrying a man who could not walk. He was lying on a mat. They tried to take him into the house to place him in front of Jesus. [19]They could not find a way to do this because of the crowd. So they went up on the roof. Then they lowered the man on his mat through the opening in the roof tiles. They lowered him into the middle of the crowd, right in front of Jesus.

[20]When Jesus saw that they had faith, he said, "Friend, your sins are forgiven."

[21]The Pharisees and the teachers of the law began to think, "Who is this fellow who says such an evil thing? Who can forgive sins but God alone?"

[22]Jesus knew what they were thinking. So he asked, "Why are you thinking these things in your hearts? [23]Is it easier to say, 'Your sins are forgiven'? Or to say, 'Get up and walk'? [24]I want you to know that the Son of Man has authority on earth to forgive sins." So he spoke to the man who could not walk. "I tell you," he said, "get up. Take your mat and go home."

[25]Right away, the man stood up in front of them. He took his mat and went home praising God. [26]Everyone was amazed and gave praise to God. They were filled with wonder. They said, "We have seen unusual things today."

Jesus Chooses Levi

[27]After this, Jesus left the house. He saw a tax collector sitting at the tax booth. The man's name was Levi.

"Follow me," Jesus said to him.

[28]Levi got up, left everything and followed him.

[29]Then Levi gave a huge dinner for Jesus at his house. A large crowd of tax collectors and others were eating with them. [30]But the Pharisees and their teachers of the law complained to Jesus' disciples. They said, "Why do you eat and drink with tax collectors and 'sinners'?"

GREAT VERSE – TO – REMEMBER

5:16 But Jesus often went away to be by himself and pray.

³¹Jesus answered them, "Those who are healthy don't need a doctor. Sick people do. ³²I have not come to get those who think they are right with God to follow me. I have come to get sinners to turn away from their sins."

Jesus Is Asked About Fasting

³³Some of the people who were there said to Jesus, "John's disciples often pray and go without eating. So do the disciples of the Pharisees. But yours go on eating and drinking."

³⁴Jesus answered, "Can you make the guests of the groom go without eating while he is with them? ³⁵But the time will come when the groom will be taken away from them. In those days they will fast."

³⁶Then Jesus gave them an example. He said, "People don't tear a patch from new clothes and sew it on old clothes. If they do, they will tear the new clothes. Also, the patch from the new clothes will not match the old. ³⁷People don't pour new wine into old wineskins. If they do, the new wine will burst the skins. The wine will run out, and the wineskins will be destroyed. ³⁸No, new wine must be poured into new wineskins. ³⁹After people drink old wine, they don't want the new. They say, 'The old is better.'"

Jesus Is Lord of the Sabbath Day

6 One Sabbath day Jesus was walking through the grainfields. His disciples began to break off some heads of grain. They rubbed them in their hands and ate them.

²Some of the Pharisees said, "It is against the Law to do this on the Sabbath. Why are you doing it?"

³Jesus answered them, "Haven't you ever read about what David did? He and his men were hungry. ⁴He entered the house of God and took the holy bread. He ate the bread that only priests were allowed to eat. David also gave some to his men."

⁵Then Jesus said to them, "The Son of Man is Lord of the Sabbath day."

⁶On another Sabbath day, Jesus went into the synagogue and was teaching. A man whose right hand was weak and twisted was there. ⁷The Pharisees and the teachers of the law were trying to find fault with Jesus. So they watched him closely. They wanted to see if he would heal on the Sabbath.

⁸But Jesus knew what they were thinking. He spoke to the man with the weak and twisted hand. "Get up and stand in front of everyone," he said. So the man got up and stood there.

⁹Then Jesus said to them, "What does the Law say we should do on the Sabbath day? Should we do good? Or should we do evil? Should we save life? Or should we destroy it?"

¹⁰He looked around at all of them.

Then he said to the man, "Stretch out your hand."

He did, and his hand was as good as new.

¹¹But the Pharisees and the teachers of the law were very angry. They began to talk to each other about what they might do to Jesus.

Jesus Chooses the Twelve Apostles

¹²One of those days, Jesus went out to a mountainside to pray. He spent the night praying to God. ¹³When morning came, he called for his disciples to come to him. He chose 12 of them and made them apostles.

¹⁴Simon was one of them. Jesus gave him the name Peter. There were also Simon's brother Andrew, James, John, Philip and Bartholomew. ¹⁵And there were Matthew, Thomas, and James, son of Alphaeus. There were also Simon who was called the Zealot ¹⁶and Judas, son of James. Judas Iscariot was one of them too. He was the one who would later hand Jesus over to his enemies.

Jesus Gives Blessings and Warnings

¹⁷Jesus went down with them and stood on a level place. A large crowd of his disciples was there. A large number of other people were there too. They came from all over Judea, including Jerusalem. They also came from the coast of Tyre and Sidon.

¹⁸They had all come to hear Jesus and to be healed of their sicknesses. People troubled by evil spirits were made well. ¹⁹Everyone tried to touch Jesus. Power was coming from him and healing them all.

²⁰Jesus looked at his disciples. He said to them,

"Blessed are you who are needy.
    God's kingdom belongs to you.
²¹Blessed are you who are hungry now.
    You will be satisfied.
Blessed are you who are sad now.
    You will laugh.
²²Blessed are you when people hate you,
    when they have nothing to do with you
    and say bad things about you,

and when they treat your name as something evil.
They do all this because you are followers of the
Son of Man.

²³"Their people treated the prophets the same way long ago. When these things happen to you, be glad and jump for joy. You will receive many blessings in heaven.

²⁴"But how terrible it will be for you who are rich!
You have already had your easy life.
²⁵How terrible for you who are well fed now!
You will go hungry.
How terrible for you who laugh now!
You will cry and be sad.
²⁶How terrible for you when everyone says good things
about you!
Their people treated the false prophets the same way
long ago.

Love Your Enemies

²⁷"But here is what I tell you who hear me. Love your enemies. Do good to those who hate you. ²⁸Bless those who call down curses on you. And pray for those who treat you badly.

²⁹"Suppose someone hits you on one cheek. Turn your other cheek to that person also. Suppose someone takes your coat. Don't stop that person from taking your shirt.

³⁰"Give to everyone who asks you. And if anyone takes what belongs to you, don't ask to get it back. ³¹Do to others as you want them to do to you.

³²"Suppose you love those who love you. Should anyone praise you for that? Even 'sinners' love those who love them. ³³And suppose you do good to those who are good to you. Should anyone praise you for that? Even 'sinners' do that. ³⁴And suppose you

---

GREAT VERSE —TO— REMEMBER

6:27-28 Love your enemies. Do good to those who hate you. Bless those who call down curses on you. And pray for those who treat you badly.

lend money to those who can pay you back. Should anyone praise you for that? Even a 'sinner' lends to 'sinners,' expecting them to pay everything back. ³⁵"But love your enemies. Do good to them. Lend to them without expecting to get anything back. Then you will receive a lot in return. And you will be children of the Most High God. He is kind to people who are evil and are not thankful. ³⁶So have mercy, just as your Father has mercy.

Be Fair When You Judge Others

³⁷"If you do not judge others, then you will not be judged. If you do not find others guilty, then you will not be found guilty. Forgive, and you will be forgiven. ³⁸Give, and it will be given to you. A good amount will be poured into your lap. It will be pressed down, shaken together, and running over. The same amount you use will be used to measure out to you."

³⁹Jesus also gave them another example. He asked, "Can a blind person lead another blind person? Won't they both fall into a pit? ⁴⁰Students are not better than their teachers. But all who are completely trained will be like their teachers.

⁴¹"You look at the bit of sawdust in your friend's eye. But you pay no attention to the piece of wood in your own eye. ⁴²How can you say to your friend, 'Let me take the bit of sawdust out of your eye'? How can you say this while there is a piece of wood in your own eye? You pretender! First take the piece of wood out of your own eye. Then you will be able to see clearly to take the bit of sawdust out of your friend's eye.

A Tree and Its Fruit

⁴³"No good tree bears bad fruit. And a bad tree doesn't bear good fruit. ⁴⁴You can tell each tree by its fruit. People do not pick figs from thorns. And they don't pick grapes from bushes.

⁴⁵"Good people say good things. These come from the good that is put away in their hearts. Evil people say evil things. These come from the evil that is put away in their hearts. Their mouths say everything that is in their hearts.

The Wise and Foolish Builders

⁴⁶"Why do you call me, 'Lord, Lord,' and still don't do what I say? ⁴⁷Some people come to me and listen to me and do what I say. I will show you what they are like. ⁴⁸They are like someone who builds a house. He digs down deep and sets it on solid rock.

When a flood comes, the river rushes against the house. But the water can't shake it. The house is well built.

⁴⁹"But here is what happens when people listen to my words and do not obey them. They are like someone who builds a house on the ground and not on solid rock. The moment the river rushes against that house, it falls down. It is completely destroyed."

A Roman Commander Has Faith

7 Jesus finished saying all those things to the people. Then he entered Capernaum.

²There the servant of a Roman commander was sick and about to die. His master thought highly of him. ³The commander heard about Jesus. So he sent some elders of the Jews to him. He told them to ask Jesus to come and heal his servant.

⁴They came to Jesus and begged him, "This man deserves to have you do this. ⁵He loves our nation and has built our synagogue." ⁶So Jesus went with them.

When Jesus came near the house, the Roman commander sent friends to him. He told them to say, "Lord, don't trouble yourself. I am not good enough to have you come into my house. ⁷That is why I did not even think I was fit to come to you. But just say the word, and my servant will be healed. ⁸I myself am a man who is under authority. And I have soldiers who obey my orders. I tell this one, 'Go,' and he goes. I tell that one, 'Come,' and he comes. I say to my servant, 'Do this,' and he does it."

⁹When Jesus heard this, he was amazed at him. He turned to the crowd that was following him. He said, "I tell you, even in Israel I have not found anyone whose faith is so strong."

¹⁰Then the men who had been sent to Jesus returned to the house. They found that the servant was healed.

Jesus Raises a Widow's Son From the Dead

¹¹Some time later, Jesus went to a town called Nain. His disciples and a large crowd went along with him. ¹²He approached the town gate. Just then, a dead person was being carried out. He was the only son of his mother. She was a widow. A large crowd from the town was with her.

¹³When the Lord saw her, he felt sorry for her. So he said, "Don't cry."

¹⁴Then he went up and touched the coffin. Those carrying it stood still.

Jesus said, "Young man, I say to you, get up!"

¹⁵The dead man sat up and began to talk. Then Jesus gave him back to his mother.

¹⁶The people were all filled with wonder and praised God. "A great prophet has appeared among us," they said. "God has come to help his people." ¹⁷This news about Jesus spread all through Judea and the whole country.

Jesus and John the Baptist

¹⁸John's disciples told him about all these things. So he chose two of them. ¹⁹He sent them to the Lord. They were to ask Jesus, "Are you the one who was supposed to come? Or should we look for someone else?"

²⁰The men came to Jesus. They said, "John the Baptist sent us to ask you, 'Are you the one who was supposed to come? Or should we look for someone else?'"

²¹At that very time Jesus healed many people. They had illnesses, sicknesses and evil spirits. He also gave sight to many who were blind. ²²So Jesus replied to the messengers, "Go back to John. Tell him what you have seen and heard. Blind people receive sight. Disabled people walk. Those who have skin diseases are healed. Deaf people hear. Those who are dead are raised to life. And the good news is preached to those who are poor. ²³Blessed are those who do not give up their faith because of me."

²⁴So John's messengers left. Then Jesus began to speak to the crowd about John. He said, "What did you go out into the desert to see? Tall grass waving in the wind? ²⁵If not, what did you go out to see? A man dressed in fine clothes? No. Those who wear fine clothes and have many expensive things are in palaces. ²⁶Then what did you go out to see? A prophet? Yes, I tell you, and more than a prophet.

²⁷He is the one written about in Scripture. It says,

GREAT VERSE —TO— REMEMBER

7:16 The people were all filled with wonder and praised God. "A great prophet has appeared among us," they said. "God has come to help his people."

"'I will send my messenger ahead of you.
He will prepare your way for you.'   *(Malachi 3:1)*

[28]I tell you, no one more important than John has ever been born. But the least important person in God's kingdom is more important than he is."

[29]All the people who heard Jesus' words agreed that God's way was right. Even the tax collectors agreed. These people had all been baptized by John. [30]But the Pharisees and the authorities on the law did not accept God's purpose for themselves. They had not been baptized by John.

[31]"What can I compare today's people to?" Jesus asked. "What are they like? [32]They are like children sitting in the market place and calling out to each other. They say,

"'We played a flute for you.
But you didn't dance.
We sang a funeral song.
But you didn't cry.'

[33]"That is how it has been with John the Baptist. When he came to you, he didn't eat bread or drink wine. And you say, 'He has a demon.' [34]But when the Son of Man came, he ate and drank as you do. And you say, 'This fellow is always eating and drinking far too much. He's a friend of tax collectors and "sinners."' [35]All who follow wisdom prove that wisdom is right."

A Sinful Woman Pours Perfume on Jesus

[36]One of the Pharisees invited Jesus to have dinner with him. So he went to the Pharisee's house. He took his place at the table.

[37]There was a woman in that town who had lived a sinful life. She learned that Jesus was eating at the Pharisee's house. So she came with a special sealed jar of perfume. [38]She stood behind Jesus and cried at his feet. She began to wet his feet with her tears. Then she wiped them with her hair. She kissed them and poured perfume on them.

[39]The Pharisee who had invited Jesus saw this. He said to himself, "If this man were a prophet, he would know who is touching him. He would know what kind of woman she is. She is a sinner!"

[40]Jesus answered him, "Simon, I have something to tell you."

"Tell me, teacher," he said.

[41]"Two people owed money to a certain lender. One owed him

500 silver coins. The other owed him 50 silver coins. [42]Neither of them had the money to pay him back. So he let them go without paying. Which of them will love him more?"

[43]Simon replied, "I suppose the one who owed the most money."

"You are right," Jesus said.

[44]Then he turned toward the woman. He said to Simon, "Do you see this woman? I came into your house. You did not give me any water to wash my feet. But she wet my feet with her tears and wiped them with her hair. [45]You did not give me a kiss. But this woman has not stopped kissing my feet since I came in. [46]You did not put any olive oil on my head. But she has poured perfume on my feet. [47]So I tell you this. Her many sins have been forgiven. She has loved a lot. But the one who has been forgiven little loves only a little."

[48]Then Jesus said to her, "Your sins are forgiven."

[49]The other guests began to talk about this among themselves. They said, "Who is this who even forgives sins?"

[50]Jesus said to the woman, "Your faith has saved you. Go in peace."

The Story of the Farmer

8 After this, Jesus traveled around from one town and village to another. He announced the good news of God's kingdom. The Twelve were with him. [2]So were some women who had been healed of evil spirits and sicknesses. One was Mary Magdalene. Seven demons had come out of her. [3]Another was Joanna, the wife of Cuza. He was the manager of Herod's household. Susanna and many others were there also. These women were helping to support Jesus and the Twelve with their own money.

[4]A large crowd was gathering. People were coming to Jesus from town after town. As they did, he told a story. He said, [5]"A farmer went out to plant his seed. He scattered the seed on the ground. Some fell on a path. People walked on it, and the birds of the air ate it up. [6]Some seed fell on rocky places. When it grew, the plants dried up because they had no water. [7]Other seed fell among thorns. The thorns grew up with it and crowded out the plants. [8]Still other seed fell on good soil. It grew up and produced a crop 100 times more than the farmer planted."

When Jesus said this, he called out, "Those who have ears to hear should listen."

[9]His disciples asked him what the story meant.

[10]He said, "You have been given the chance to understand the secrets of God's kingdom. But to outsiders I speak by using stories. In that way,

> "'They see, but they may not know what they are
> seeing.
> They hear, but they may not understand.'   *(Isaiah 6:9)*

[11]"Here is what the story means. The seed is God's message. [12]People on the path are those who hear. But then the devil comes. He takes away the message from their hearts. He does it so they won't believe. Then they can't be saved. [13]Those on the rock are the ones who hear the message and receive it with joy. But they have no roots. They believe for a while. But when they are put to the test, they fall away from the faith. [14]The seed that fell among thorns stands for those who hear the message. But as they go on their way, they are choked by life's worries, riches and pleasures. So they do not reach full growth.

[15]"But the seed on good soil stands for those with an honest and good heart. They hear the message. They hold on to it. By staying with it, they produce a good crop.

A Lamp on a Stand

[16]"People do not light a lamp and then hide it in a jar or put it under a bed. Instead, they put it on a stand. Then those who come in can see its light. [17]What is hidden will be seen. And what is out of sight will be brought into the open and made known.

[18]"So think carefully how you listen. If you have something, you will be given more. If you have nothing, even what you think you have will be taken away from you."

Jesus' Mother and Brothers

[19]Jesus' mother and brothers came to see him. But they could not get near him because of the crowd. [20]Someone told him, "Your mother and brothers are standing outside. They want to see you."

GREAT VERSE — TO — REMEMBER

8:21 My mother and brothers are those who hear God's word and do what it says.

²¹He replied, "My mother and brothers are those who hear God's word and do what it says."

Jesus Calms the Storm

²²One day Jesus said to his disciples, "Let's go over to the other side of the lake." So they got into a boat and left.

²³As they sailed, Jesus fell asleep. A storm came down on the lake. It was so bad that the boat was about to sink. They were in great danger.

²⁴The disciples went and woke Jesus up. They said, "Master! Master! We're going to drown!"

He got up and ordered the wind and the huge waves to stop. The storm quieted down. It was completely calm.

²⁵"Where is your faith?" he asked his disciples.

They were amazed and full of fear. They asked one another, "Who is this? He commands even the winds and the water, and they obey him."

Jesus Heals a Man Controlled by Demons

²⁶Jesus and his disciples sailed to the area of the Gerasenes across the lake from Galilee. ²⁷When Jesus stepped on shore, he was met by a man from the town. The man was controlled by demons. For a long time he had not worn clothes or lived in a house. He lived in the tombs.

²⁸When he saw Jesus, he cried out and fell at his feet. He shouted at the top of his voice, "Jesus, Son of the Most High God, what do you want with me? I beg you, don't hurt me!"

²⁹This was because Jesus had commanded the evil spirit to come out of the man. Many times the spirit had taken hold of him. His hands and feet were chained, and he was kept under guard. But he had broken his chains. And then the demon had forced him to go out into lonely places in the countryside.

³⁰Jesus asked him, "What is your name?"

"Legion," he replied, because many demons had gone into him. ³¹And they begged Jesus again and again not to order them to go into the Abyss.

³²A large herd of pigs was feeding there on the hillside. The demons begged Jesus to let them go into the pigs. And he allowed it.

³³When the demons came out of the man, they went into pigs. Then the herd rushed down the steep bank. They ran into the lake and drowned.

³⁴Those who were tending the pigs saw what had happened. They ran off and reported it in the town and countryside. ³⁵The people went out to see what had happened.

Then they came to Jesus. They found the man who was now free of the demons. He was sitting at Jesus' feet. He was dressed and thinking clearly. All this made the people afraid.

³⁶Those who had seen it told the others how the man who had been controlled by demons was now healed. ³⁷Then all the people who lived in the area of the Gerasenes asked Jesus to leave them. They were filled with fear. So he got into the boat and left.

³⁸The man who was now free of the demons begged to go with him. But Jesus sent him away. He said to him, ³⁹"Return home and tell how much God has done for you."

So the man went away. He told people all over town how much Jesus had done for him.

A Dying Girl and a Suffering Woman

⁴⁰When Jesus returned, a crowd welcomed him. They were all expecting him.

⁴¹Then a man named Jairus came. He was a synagogue ruler. He fell at Jesus' feet. He begged Jesus to come to his house. ⁴²His only daughter was dying. She was about 12 years old.

As Jesus was on his way, the crowds almost crushed him.

⁴³A woman was there who had an illness that made her bleed. Her illness had lasted 12 years. No one could heal her. ⁴⁴She came up behind Jesus and touched the edge of his clothes. Right away her bleeding stopped.

⁴⁵"Who touched me?" Jesus asked.

They all said they didn't do it. Then Peter said, "Master, the people are crowding and pushing against you."

⁴⁶But Jesus said, "Someone touched me. I know that power has gone out from me."

⁴⁷The woman realized that people would notice her. Shaking with fear, she came and fell at his feet. In front of everyone, she told why she had touched him. She also told how she had been healed in an instant.

⁴⁸Then he said to her, "Dear woman, your faith has healed you. Go in peace."

⁴⁹While Jesus was still speaking, someone came from the house of Jairus. Jairus was the synagogue ruler. "Your daughter is dead," the messenger said. "Don't bother the teacher anymore."

⁵⁰Hearing this, Jesus said to Jairus, "Don't be afraid. Just believe. She will be healed."

⁵¹When he arrived at the house of Jairus, he did not let everyone go in with him. He took only Peter, John and James, and the child's father and mother.

⁵²During this time, all the people were crying and sobbing loudly over the child. "Stop crying!" Jesus said. "She is not dead. She is sleeping."

⁵³They laughed at him. They knew she was dead.

⁵⁴But he took her by the hand and said, "My child, get up!"

⁵⁵Her spirit returned, and right away she stood up. Then Jesus told them to give her something to eat. ⁵⁶Her parents were amazed. But Jesus ordered them not to tell anyone what had happened.

Jesus Sends Out the Twelve Disciples

9 Jesus called the Twelve together. He gave them power and authority to drive out all demons and to heal sicknesses. ²Then he sent them out to preach about God's kingdom and to heal those who are sick.

³He told them, "Don't take anything for the journey. Do not take a walking stick or a bag. Do not take any bread, money or extra clothes. ⁴When you are invited into a house, stay there until you leave town. ⁵Some people may not welcome you. If they don't, shake the dust off your feet when you leave their town. This will be a witness against the people living there."

⁶So the Twelve left. They went from village to village. They preached the good news and healed people everywhere.

⁷Now Herod, the ruler of Galilee, heard about everything that was going on. He was bewildered, because some were saying that John had been raised from the dead. ⁸Others were saying that Elijah had appeared. Still others were saying that a prophet of long ago had come back to life. ⁹But Herod said, "I had John's head cut off. So who is it that I hear such things about?" And he tried to see Jesus.

Jesus Feeds the Five Thousand

¹⁰The apostles returned. They told Jesus what they had done. Then he took them with him. They went off by themselves to a town called Bethsaida. ¹¹But the crowds learned about it and followed Jesus. He welcomed them and spoke to them about God's kingdom. He also healed those who needed to be healed.

¹²Late in the afternoon the Twelve came to him. They said, "Send the crowd away. They can go to the nearby villages and countryside. There they can find food and a place to stay. There is nothing here."

¹³Jesus replied, "You give them something to eat."

The disciples answered, "We have only five loaves of bread and two fish. We would have to go and buy food for all this crowd." ¹⁴About 5,000 men were there.

But Jesus said to his disciples, "Have them sit down in groups of about 50 each." ¹⁵The disciples did so, and everyone sat down.

¹⁶Jesus took the five loaves and the two fish. He looked up to heaven and gave thanks. He broke them into pieces. Then he gave them to the disciples to set in front of the people. ¹⁷All of them ate and were satisfied. The disciples picked up 12 baskets of leftover pieces.

Peter Says That Jesus Is the Christ

¹⁸One day Jesus was praying alone. Only his disciples were with him. He asked them, "Who do the crowds say I am?"

¹⁹They replied, "Some say John the Baptist. Others say Elijah. Still others say that one of the prophets of long ago has come back to life."

²⁰"But what about you?" he asked. "Who do you say I am?"

Peter answered, "The Christ of God."

²¹Jesus strongly warned them not to tell this to anyone. ²²He said, "The Son of Man must suffer many things. The elders will not accept him. The chief priests and teachers of the law will not accept him either. He must be killed and on the third day rise from the dead."

²³Then he said to all of them, "If you want to come after me, you must say no to yourself. You must take your cross every day and follow me. ²⁴If you want to save your life, you will lose it. But

GREAT VERSE — TO — REMEMBER

9:24-25 If you want to save your life, you will lose it. But if you lose your life for me, you will save it. What good is it for you to gain the whole world but lose or give up your very self?

if you lose your life for me, you will save it. [25]What good is it for you to gain the whole world but lose or give up your very self?

[26]"Suppose you are ashamed of me and my words. The Son of Man will come in his glory and in the glory of the Father and the holy angels. Then he will be ashamed of you.

[27]"What I'm about to tell you is true. Some who are standing here will not die before they see God's kingdom."

Jesus' Appearance Is Changed

[28]About eight days after Jesus said this, he went up on a mountain to pray. He took Peter, John and James with him.

[29]As he was praying, the appearance of his face changed. His clothes became as bright as a flash of lightning. [30]Two men, Moses and Elijah, [31]appeared in shining glory. Jesus and the two of them talked together. They spoke about his coming death. He was going to bring it about in Jerusalem.

[32]Peter and his companions had been very sleepy. But then they became completely awake. They saw Jesus' glory and the two men standing with him.

[33]As the men were leaving Jesus, Peter spoke up. "Master," he said to him, "it is good for us to be here. Let us put up three shelters. One will be for you, one for Moses, and one for Elijah." He didn't really know what he was saying.

[34]While Jesus was speaking, a cloud appeared. It surrounded them. They were afraid as they entered the cloud. [35]A voice came from the cloud. It said, "This is my Son, and I have chosen him. Listen to him." [36]When the voice had spoken, they found that Jesus was alone.

The disciples kept quiet about this. They didn't tell anyone at that time what they had seen.

Jesus Heals a Boy Who Had an Evil Spirit

[37]The next day Jesus and those who were with him came down from the mountain. A large crowd met Jesus.

[38]A man in the crowd called out. "Teacher," he said, "I beg you to look at my son. He is my only child. [39]A spirit takes hold of him, and he suddenly screams. It throws him into fits so that he foams at the mouth. It hardly ever leaves him. It is destroying him. [40]I begged your disciples to drive it out. But they couldn't do it."

[41]"You unbelieving and evil people!" Jesus replied. "How long

do I have to stay with you? How long do I have to put up with you?"

Then he said to the man, "Bring your son here."

⁴²Even while the boy was coming, the demon threw him into a fit. The boy fell to the ground. But Jesus ordered the evil spirit to leave the boy. Then Jesus healed him and gave him back to his father. ⁴³They were all amazed at God's greatness.

Everyone was wondering about all that Jesus did. Then Jesus said to his disciples, ⁴⁴"Listen carefully to what I am about to tell you. The Son of Man is going to be handed over to human authorities." ⁴⁵But they didn't understand what this meant. That was because it was hidden from them. And they were afraid to ask Jesus about it.

Who Is the Most Important Person?

⁴⁶The disciples began to argue about which of them would be the most important person. ⁴⁷Jesus knew what they were thinking. So he took a little child and had the child stand beside him. ⁴⁸Then he spoke to them. "Anyone who welcomes this little child in my name welcomes me," he said. "And anyone who welcomes me welcomes the One who sent me. The least important person among all of you is the most important."

⁴⁹"Master," said John, "we saw a man driving out demons in your name. We tried to stop him, because he is not one of us."

⁵⁰"Do not stop him," Jesus said. "Anyone who is not against you is for you."

The Samaritans Do Not Welcome Jesus

⁵¹The time grew near for Jesus to be taken up to heaven. So he committed himself to go to Jerusalem. ⁵²He sent messengers on ahead. They went into a Samaritan village to get things ready for him. ⁵³But the people there did not welcome Jesus. That was because he was heading for Jerusalem.

⁵⁴The disciples James and John saw this. They asked, "Lord, do you want us to call down fire from heaven to destroy them?"

⁵⁵But Jesus turned and commanded them not to do it. ⁵⁶They went on to another village.

It Costs to Follow Jesus

⁵⁷Once Jesus and those who were with him were walking along the road. A man said to Jesus, "I will follow you no matter where you go."

⁵⁸Jesus replied, "Foxes have holes. Birds of the air have nests. But the Son of Man has no place to lay his head."

⁵⁹He said to another man, "Follow me."

But the man replied, "Lord, first let me go and bury my father."

⁶⁰Jesus said to him, "Let the dead bury their own dead. You go and tell others about God's kingdom."

⁶¹Still another man said, "I will follow you, Lord. But first let me go back and say good-by to my family."

⁶²Jesus replied, "Suppose you start to plow and then look back. If you do, you are not fit for service in God's kingdom."

Jesus Sends Out the Seventy-two

10 After this the Lord appointed 72 others. He sent them out two by two ahead of him. They went to every town and place where he was about to go.

²He told them, "The harvest is huge, but the workers are few. So ask the Lord of the harvest to send out workers into his harvest field.

³"Go! I am sending you out like lambs among wolves. ⁴Do not take a purse or bag or sandals. And don't greet anyone on the road.

⁵"When you enter a house, first say, 'May this house be blessed with peace.' ⁶If someone there loves peace, your blessing of peace will rest on that person. If not, it will return to you. ⁷Stay in that house. Eat and drink anything they give you. Workers are worthy of their pay. Do not move around from house to house.

⁸"When you enter a town and are welcomed, eat what is set down in front of you. ⁹Heal the sick people who are there. Tell them, 'God's kingdom is near you.'

¹⁰"But what if you enter a town and are not welcomed? Then go into its streets and say, ¹¹'We wipe off even the dust of your town that sticks to our feet. We do it against you. But here is what you can be sure of. God's kingdom is near.'

10:2 The harvest is huge, but the workers are few. So ask the Lord of the harvest to send out workers into his harvest field.

¹²"I tell you this. On judgment day it will be easier for Sodom than for that town.

¹³"How terrible it will be for you, Korazin! How terrible for you, Bethsaida! Suppose the miracles done in you had been done in Tyre and Sidon. They would have turned away from their sins long ago. They would have put on black clothes. They would have sat down in ashes. ¹⁴On judgment day it will be easier for Tyre and Sidon than for you.

¹⁵"And what about you, Capernaum? Will you be lifted up to heaven? No! You will go down to the place of the dead."

¹⁶"Anyone who listens to you listens to me. Anyone who does not accept you does not accept me. And anyone who does not accept me does not accept the One who sent me."

¹⁷The 72 returned with joy. They said, "Lord, even the demons obey us when we speak in your name."

¹⁸Jesus replied, "I saw Satan fall like lightning from heaven. ¹⁹I have given you authority to walk all over snakes and scorpions. You will be able to destroy all the power of the enemy. Nothing will harm you. ²⁰But do not be glad when the evil spirits obey you. Instead, be glad that your names are written in heaven."

²¹At that time Jesus was full of joy through the Holy Spirit. He said, "I praise you, Father. You are Lord of heaven and earth. You have hidden these things from the wise and educated. But you have shown them to little children. Yes, Father. This is what you wanted.

²²"My Father has given all things to me. The Father is the only one who knows who the Son is. And the only ones who know the Father are the Son and those to whom the Son chooses to make the Father known."

²³Then Jesus turned to his disciples. He said to them in private, "Blessed are the eyes that see what you see. ²⁴I tell you, many prophets and kings wanted to see what you see. But they didn't see it. They wanted to hear what you hear. But they didn't hear it."

The Story of the Good Samaritan

²⁵One day an authority on the law stood up to put Jesus to the test. "Teacher," he asked, "what must I do to receive eternal life?"

²⁶"What is written in the Law?" Jesus replied. "How do you understand it?"

²⁷He answered, "'Love the Lord your God with all your heart and with all your soul. Love him with all your strength and with

all your mind.' *(Deuteronomy 6:5)* And, 'Love your neighbor as you love yourself.'" *(Leviticus 19:18)*

²⁸"You have answered correctly," Jesus replied. "Do that, and you will live."

²⁹But the man wanted to make himself look good. So he asked Jesus, "And who is my neighbor?"

³⁰Jesus replied, "A man was going down from Jerusalem to Jericho. He was attacked by robbers. They stripped off his clothes and beat him. Then they went away, leaving him almost dead. ³¹A priest happened to be going down that same road. When he saw the man, he passed by on the other side. ³²A Levite also came by. When he saw the man, he passed by on the other side too.

³³But a Samaritan came to the place where the man was. When he saw the man, he felt sorry for him. ³⁴He went to him, poured olive oil and wine on his wounds and bandaged them. Then he put the man on his own donkey. He took him to an inn and took care of him. ³⁵The next day he took out two silver coins. He gave them to the owner of the inn. 'Take care of him,' he said. 'When I return, I will pay you back for any extra expense you may have.'

³⁶"Which of the three do you think was a neighbor to the man who was attacked by robbers?"

³⁷The authority on the law replied, "The one who felt sorry for him."

Jesus told him, "Go and do as he did."

Jesus at the Home of Martha and Mary

³⁸Jesus and his disciples went on their way. Jesus came to a village where a woman named Martha lived. She welcomed him into her home. ³⁹She had a sister named Mary.

Mary sat at the Lord's feet listening to what he said. ⁴⁰But Martha was busy with all the things that had to be done. She came to Jesus and said, "Lord, my sister has left me to do the work by myself. Don't you care? Tell her to help me!"

⁴¹"Martha, Martha," the Lord answered. "You are worried and upset about many things. ⁴²But only one thing is needed. Mary has chosen what is better. And it will not be taken away from her."

Jesus Teaches About Prayer

11 One day Jesus was praying in a certain place. When he finished, one of his disciples spoke to him. "Lord," he said, "teach us to pray, just as John taught his disciples."

²Jesus said to them, "When you pray, this is what you should say.

> "'Father,
> may your name be honored.
> May your kingdom come.
> ³Give us each day our daily bread.
> ⁴Forgive us our sins,
>   as we also forgive everyone who sins against us.
> Keep us from falling into sin when we are tempted.'"

⁵Then Jesus said to them, "Suppose someone has a friend. He goes to him at midnight. He says, 'Friend, lend me three loaves of bread. ⁶A friend of mine on a journey has come to stay with me. I have nothing for him to eat.'

⁷"Then the one inside answers, 'Don't bother me. The door is already locked. My children are with me in bed. I can't get up and give you anything.'

⁸"I tell you, that person will not get up. And he won't give the man bread just because he is his friend. But because the man keeps on asking, he will get up. He will give him as much as he needs.

⁹"So here is what I say to you. Ask, and it will be given to you. Search, and you will find. Knock, and the door will be opened to you. ¹⁰All who ask will receive. All who search will find. And the door will be opened to all who knock.

¹¹"Fathers, suppose your children ask for a fish. Which of you will give them a snake instead? ¹²Or suppose they ask for an egg. Which of you will give them a scorpion? ¹³Even though you are evil, you know how to give good gifts to your children. How much more will your Father who is in heaven give the Holy Spirit to those who ask him!"

Jesus and Beelzebub

¹⁴Jesus was driving out a demon. The man who had the demon

11:9 Ask, and it will be given to you. Search, and you will find. Knock, and the door will be opened to you.

could not speak. When the demon left, the man began to speak. The crowd was amazed.

[15]But some of them said, "Jesus is driving out demons by the power of Beelzebub, the prince of demons." [16]Others put Jesus to the test by asking for a miraculous sign from heaven.

[17]Jesus knew what they were thinking. So he said to them, "Any kingdom that fights against itself will be destroyed. A family that is divided against itself will fall. [18]If Satan fights against himself, how can his kingdom stand?

"I say this because of what you claim. You say I drive out demons by the power of Beelzebub. [19]Suppose I do drive out demons with Beelzebub's help. With whose help do your followers drive them out? So then, they will be your judges. [20]But suppose I drive out demons with the help of God's powerful finger. Then God's kingdom has come to you.

[21]"When a strong man is completely armed and guards his house, what he owns is safe. [22]But when someone stronger attacks, he is overpowered. The attacker takes away the armor the man had trusted in. Then he divides up what he has stolen.

[23]"Anyone who is not with me is against me. Anyone who does not gather sheep with me scatters them.

[24]"What happens when an evil spirit comes out of someone? It goes through dry areas looking for a place to rest. But it doesn't find it. Then it says, 'I will return to the house I left.' [25]When it arrives there, it finds the house swept clean and put in order. [26]Then the evil spirit goes and takes seven other spirits more evil than itself. They go in and live there. That person is worse off than before."

[27]As Jesus was saying these things, a woman in the crowd called out. She shouted, "Blessed is the mother who gave you birth and nursed you."

[28]He replied, "Instead, blessed are those who hear God's word and obey it."

The Miraculous Sign of Jonah

[29]As the crowds grew larger, Jesus spoke to them. "The people of today are evil," he said. "They ask for a miraculous sign from God. But none will be given except the sign of Jonah. [30]He was a sign from God to the people of Nineveh. In the same way, the Son of Man will be a sign from God to the people of today.

[31]"The Queen of the South will stand up on judgment day with the people now living. And she will prove that those people are

guilty. She came from very far away to listen to Solomon's wisdom. And now one who is more important than Solomon is here.

³²"The people of Nineveh will stand up on judgment day with the people now living. And the Ninevites will prove that those people are guilty. The people of Nineveh turned away from their sins when Jonah preached to them. And now one who is more important than Jonah is here.

The Eye Is the Lamp of the Body

³³"No one lights a lamp and hides it. No one puts it under a bowl. Instead, people put a lamp on its stand. Then those who come in can see the light.

³⁴"Your eye is like a lamp for your body. Suppose your eyes are good. Then your whole body also is full of light. But suppose your eyes are bad. Then your body also is full of darkness. ³⁵So make sure that the light inside you is not darkness.

³⁶"Suppose your whole body is full of light. And suppose no part of it is dark. Then your body will be completely lit up. It will be as when the light of a lamp shines on you."

Six Warnings

³⁷Jesus finished speaking. Then a Pharisee invited him to eat with him. So Jesus went in and took his place at the table. ³⁸But the Pharisee noticed that Jesus did not wash before the meal. He was surprised.

³⁹Then the Lord spoke to him. "You Pharisees clean the outside of the cup and dish," he said. "But inside you are full of greed and evil. ⁴⁰You foolish people! Didn't the one who made the outside make the inside also? ⁴¹Give to poor people what is inside the dish. Then everything will be clean for you.

⁴²"How terrible it will be for you Pharisees! You give God a tenth of your garden plants, such as mint and rue. But you have forgotten to be fair and to love God. You should have practiced the last things without failing to do the first.

⁴³"How terrible for you Pharisees! You love the most important seats in the synagogues. You love having people greet you in the market places.

⁴⁴"How terrible for you! You are like graves that are not marked. People walk over them without knowing it."

⁴⁵An authority on the law spoke to Jesus. He said, "Teacher, when you say things like that, you say bad things about us too."

⁴⁶Jesus replied, "How terrible for you authorities on the law!

You put such heavy loads on people that they can hardly carry them. But you yourselves will not lift one finger to help them.

[47] "How terrible for you! You build tombs for the prophets. It was your people of long ago who killed them. [48] So you give witness that you agree with what your people before you did. They killed the prophets, and now you build the prophets' tombs.

[49] "So God in his wisdom said, 'I will send prophets and apostles to them. They will kill some. And they will try to hurt others.' [50] So the people of this time will be punished. They will pay for all the prophets' blood spilled since the world began. [51] I mean from the blood of Abel to the blood of Zechariah, who was killed between the altar and the temple. Yes, I tell you, the people of today will be punished for all these things.

[52] "How terrible for you authorities on the law! You have taken away the key to the door of knowledge. You yourselves have not entered. And you have stood in the way of those who were entering."

[53] When Jesus left there, the Pharisees and the teachers of the law strongly opposed him. They threw a lot of questions at him. [54] They were setting traps to catch him in something he might say.

Jesus Gives Words of Warning and Hope

12 During that time a crowd of many thousands had gathered. There were so many people that they were stepping on one another.

Jesus spoke first to his disciples. "Be on your guard against the yeast of the Pharisees," he said. "They just pretend to be godly. [2] Everything that is secret will be brought out into the open. Everything that is hidden will be uncovered. [3] What you have said in the dark will be heard in the daylight. What you have whispered to someone behind closed doors will be shouted from the rooftops.

[4] "My friends, listen to me. Don't be afraid of those who kill the body and can't do any more than that. [5] But I will show you whom you should be afraid of. Be afraid of the One who can kill the body and also has the power to throw you into hell. Yes, I tell you, be afraid of him.

[6] "Aren't five sparrows sold for two pennies? But God does not forget even one of them. [7] In fact, he even counts the very hairs of your head! So don't be afraid. You are worth more than many sparrows.

⁸"What about those who say in front of others that they know me? I tell you, the Son of Man will say that he knows them in front of God's angels. ⁹But what about those who say in front of others that they don't know me? I, the Son of Man, will say that I don't know them in front of God's angels.

¹⁰"Everyone who speaks a word against the Son of Man will be forgiven. But anyone who speaks evil things against the Holy Spirit will not be forgiven.

¹¹"You will be brought before synagogues, rulers and authorities. But do not worry about how to stand up for yourselves or what to say. ¹²The Holy Spirit will teach you at that time what you should say."

The Story of the Rich Fool

¹³Someone in the crowd spoke to Jesus. "Teacher," he said, "tell my brother to divide the family property with me."

¹⁴Jesus replied, "Friend, who made me a judge or umpire between you?"

¹⁵Then he said to them, "Watch out! Be on your guard against wanting to have more and more things. Life is not made up of how much a person has."

¹⁶Then Jesus told them a story. He said, "A certain rich man's land produced a good crop. ¹⁷He thought to himself, 'What should I do? I don't have any place to store my crops.'

¹⁸"Then he said, 'This is what I'll do. I will tear down my storerooms and build bigger ones. I will store all my grain and my other things in them. ¹⁹I'll say to myself, "You have plenty of good things stored away for many years. Take life easy. Eat, drink and have a good time."'

²⁰"But God said to him, 'You fool! This very night your life will be taken from you. Then who will get what you have prepared for yourself?'

GREAT VERSE —TO— REMEMBER

12:8 What about those who say in front of others that they know me? I tell you, the Son of Man will say that he knows them in front of God's angels.

²¹"That is how it will be for those who store things away for themselves but are not rich in God's eyes."

Do Not Worry

²²Then Jesus spoke to his disciples. He said, "I tell you, do not worry. Don't worry about your life and what you will eat. And don't worry about your body and what you will wear. ²³There is more to life than eating. There are more important things for the body than clothes.

²⁴"Think about the ravens. They don't plant or gather crops. They don't have any storerooms at all. But God feeds them. You are worth much more than birds!

²⁵"Can you add even one hour to your life by worrying? ²⁶You can't do that very little thing. So why worry about the rest?

²⁷"Think about how the lilies grow. They don't work or make clothing. But here is what I tell you. Not even Solomon in all of his glory was dressed like one of these. ²⁸If that is how God dresses the wild grass, how much better will he dress you! After all, the grass is here only today. Tomorrow it is thrown into the fire. Your faith is so small!

²⁹"Don't spend time thinking about what you will eat or drink. Don't worry about it. ³⁰People who are ungodly run after all of those things. Your Father knows that you need them.

³¹"But seek God's kingdom. Then those other things will also be given to you.

³²"Little flock, do not be afraid. Your Father has been pleased to give you the kingdom. ³³Sell what you own. Give to those who are poor. Provide purses for yourselves that will not wear out. Put away riches in heaven that will not be used up. There, no thief can come near it. There, no moth can destroy it. ³⁴Your heart will be where your riches are.

Be Ready

³⁵"Be dressed and ready to serve. Keep your lamps burning. ³⁶Be like servants waiting for their master to return from a wedding

---

GREAT VERSE —TO— REMEMBER

12:31 Seek God's kingdom. Then those other things will also be given to you.

dinner. When he comes and knocks, they can open the door for him at once.

[37]"It will be good for those servants whose master finds them ready when he comes. What I'm about to tell you is true. The master will then dress himself so he can serve them. He will have them take their places at the table. And he will come and wait on them. [38]It will be good for those servants whose master finds them ready. It will even be good if he comes very late at night.

[39]"But here is what you must understand. Suppose the owner of the house knew at what hour the robber was coming. He would not have let his house be broken into. [40]You also must be ready. The Son of Man will come at an hour when you don't expect him."

[41]Peter asked, "Lord, are you telling this story to us, or to everyone?"

[42]The Lord answered, "Suppose a master puts one of his servants in charge of his other servants. The servant's job is to give them the food they are to receive at the right time. The master wants a faithful and wise manager for this. [43]It will be good for the servant if the master finds him doing his job when the master returns. [44]What I'm about to tell you is true. The master will put that servant in charge of everything he owns.

[45]"But suppose the servant says to himself, 'My master is taking a long time to come back.' Suppose he begins to beat the other servants. Suppose he feeds himself. And suppose he drinks until he gets drunk. [46]The master of that servant will come back on a day the servant doesn't expect him. He will return at an hour the servant doesn't know. Then the master will cut him to pieces. He will send him to the place where unbelievers go.

[47]"Suppose a servant knows his master's wishes. But he doesn't get ready. And he doesn't do what his master wants. That servant will be beaten with many blows.

[48]"But suppose the servant does not know his master's wishes. And suppose he does things for which he should be punished. He will be beaten with only a few blows.

"Much will be required of everyone who has been given much. Even more will be asked of the person who is supposed to take care of much.

Jesus Comes to Separate People

[49]"I have come to bring fire on the earth. How I wish the fire had already started! [50]But I have a baptism of suffering to go

through. And I will be very troubled until it is completed.

⁵¹"Do you think I came to bring peace on earth? No, I tell you. I have come to separate people. ⁵²From now on there will be five members in a family, each one against the other. There will be three against two and two against three. ⁵³They will be separated. Father will turn against son and son against father. Mother will turn against daughter and daughter against mother. Mother-in-law will turn against daughter-in-law and daughter-in-law against mother-in-law."

Understanding What Is Happening

⁵⁴Jesus spoke to the crowd. He said, "You see a cloud rising in the west. Right away you say, 'It's going to rain.' And it does. ⁵⁵The south wind blows. So you say, 'It's going to be hot.' And it is. ⁵⁶You pretenders! You know how to understand the appearance of the earth and the sky. Why can't you understand the meaning of what is happening right now?

⁵⁷"Why don't you judge for yourselves what is right? ⁵⁸Suppose someone has a claim against you, and you are on your way to court. Try hard to settle the matter on the way. If you don't, that person may drag you off to the judge. The judge may turn you over to the officer. And the officer may throw you into prison. ⁵⁹I tell you, you will not get out until you have paid the very last penny!"

Jesus Gives a Warning

13 Some people who were there at that time told Jesus about certain Galileans. Pilate had mixed their blood with their sacrifices.

²Jesus said, "These people from Galilee suffered greatly. Do you think they were worse sinners than all the other Galileans? ³I tell you, no! But unless you turn away from your sins, you will all die too. ⁴Or what about the 18 people in Siloam? They died when the tower fell on them. Do you think they were more guilty than all the others living in Jerusalem? ⁵I tell you, no! But unless you turn away from your sins, you will all die too."

⁶Then Jesus told a story. "A man had a fig tree," he said. "It had been planted in his vineyard. When he went to look for fruit on it, he didn't find any. ⁷So he went to the man who took care of the vineyard. He said, 'For three years now I've been coming to look for fruit on this fig tree. But I haven't found any. Cut it down! Why should it use up the soil?'

[8]"'Sir,' the man replied, 'leave it alone for one more year. I'll dig around it and feed it. [9]If it bears fruit next year, fine! If not, then cut it down.'"

Jesus Heals a Disabled Woman on the Sabbath Day

[10]Jesus was teaching in one of the synagogues on a Sabbath day. [11]A woman there had been disabled by an evil spirit for 18 years. She was bent over and could not stand up straight.

[12]Jesus saw her. He asked her to come to him. He said to her, "Woman, you will no longer be disabled. I am about to set you free." [13]Then he put his hands on her.

Right away, she stood up straight and praised God.

[14]Jesus had healed the woman on the Sabbath day. This made the synagogue ruler angry. He told the people, "There are six days for work. So come and be healed on those days. But do not come on the Sabbath."

[15]The Lord answered him, "You pretenders! Doesn't each of you go to the barn and untie his ox or donkey on the Sabbath day? Then don't you lead it out to give it water? [16]This woman is a daughter of Abraham. But Satan has kept her disabled for 18 long years. Shouldn't she be set free on the Sabbath day from what was keeping her disabled?"

[17]When Jesus said this, all those who opposed him were put to shame. But the people were delighted. They loved all the wonderful things he was doing.

The Stories of the Mustard Seed and the Yeast

[18]Then Jesus asked, "What is God's kingdom like? What can I compare it to? [19]It is like a mustard seed. Someone took the seed and planted it in a garden. It grew and became a tree. The birds sat in its branches."

[20]Again he asked, "What can I compare God's kingdom to? [21]It is like yeast that a woman used. She mixed it into a large amount of flour. The yeast worked its way all through the dough."

The Narrow Door

[22]Then Jesus went through the towns and villages, teaching the people. He was on his way to Jerusalem. [23]Someone asked him, "Lord, are only a few people going to be saved?"

He said to them, [24]"Try very hard to enter through the narrow door. I tell you, many will try to enter and will not be able to. [25]The owner of the house will get up and close the door. Then you will stand outside knocking and begging. You will say, 'Sir, open the door for us.'

"But he will answer, 'I don't know you. And I don't know where you come from.'

²⁶"Then you will say, 'We ate and drank with you. You taught in our streets.'

²⁷"But he will reply, 'I don't know you. And I don't know where you come from. Get away from me, all you who do evil!'

²⁸"You will sob and grind your teeth when you see those who are in God's kingdom. You will see Abraham, Isaac and Jacob and all the prophets there. But you yourselves will be thrown out. ²⁹People will come from east and west and north and south. They will take their places at the feast in God's kingdom. ³⁰Then the last will be first. And the first will be last."

Jesus' Sadness Over Jerusalem

³¹At that time some Pharisees came to Jesus. They said to him, "Leave this place. Go somewhere else. Herod wants to kill you."

³²He replied, "Go and tell that fox, 'I will drive out demons. I will heal people today and tomorrow. And on the third day I will reach my goal.' ³³In any case, I must keep going today and tomorrow and the next day. Certainly no prophet can die outside Jerusalem!

³⁴"Jerusalem! Jerusalem! You kill the prophets and throw stones in order to kill those who are sent to you. Many times I have wanted to gather your people together. I have wanted to be like a hen who gathers her chicks under her wings. But you would not let me!

³⁵"Look, your house is left empty. I tell you, you will not see me again until you say, 'Blessed is the one who comes in the name of the Lord.'" *(Psalm 118:26)*

13:29-30 People will come from east and west and north and south. They will take their places at the feast in God's kingdom. Then the last will be first. And the first will be last.

Jesus Eats at a Pharisee's House

14 One Sabbath day, Jesus went to eat in the house of a well-known Pharisee. While he was there, he was being carefully watched. ²In front of him was a man whose body was badly swollen.

³Jesus turned to the Pharisees and the authorities on the law. He asked them, "Is it breaking the Law to heal on the Sabbath?"

⁴But they remained silent.

So Jesus took hold of the man and healed him. Then he sent him away.

⁵He asked them another question. He said, "Suppose one of you has a child or an ox that falls into a well on the Sabbath day. Wouldn't you pull it out right away?" ⁶And they had nothing to say.

⁷Jesus noticed how the guests picked the places of honor at the table. So he told them a story. ⁸He said, "Suppose someone invites you to a wedding feast. Do not take the place of honor. A person more important than you may have been invited. ⁹If so, the host who invited both of you will come to you. He will say, 'Give this person your seat.' Then you will be filled with shame. You will have to take the least important place.

¹⁰"But when you are invited, take the lowest place. Then your host will come over to you. He will say, 'Friend, move up to a better place.' Then you will be honored in front of all the other guests. ¹¹All who lift themselves up will be brought down. And those who are brought down will be lifted up."

¹²Then Jesus spoke to his host. "Suppose you give a lunch or a dinner," he said. "Do not invite your friends, your brothers or sisters, or your relatives, or your rich neighbors. If you do, they may invite you to eat with them. So you will be paid back.

¹³"But when you give a big dinner, invite those who are poor. Also invite those who can't walk, the disabled and the blind. ¹⁴Then you will be blessed. Your guests can't pay you back. But you will be paid back when those who are right with God rise from the dead."

The Story of the Big Dinner

¹⁵One of the people at the table with Jesus heard him say those things. So he said to Jesus, "Blessed is the one who will eat at the feast in God's kingdom."

¹⁶Jesus replied, "A certain man was preparing a big dinner. He invited many guests. ¹⁷Then the day of the dinner arrived. He

sent his servant to those who had been invited. The servant told them, 'Come. Everything is ready now.'

¹⁸"But they all had the same idea. They began to make excuses. The first one said, 'I have just bought a field. I have to go and see it. Please excuse me.'

¹⁹"Another said, 'I have just bought five pairs of oxen. I'm on my way to try them out. Please excuse me.'

²⁰"Still another said, 'I just got married, so I can't come.'

²¹"The servant came back and reported this to his master.

"Then the owner of the house became angry. He ordered his servant, 'Go out quickly into the streets and lanes of the town. Bring in those who are poor. Also bring those who can't walk, the blind and the disabled.'

²²"'Sir,' the servant said, 'what you ordered has been done. But there is still room.'

²³"Then the master told his servant, 'Go out to the roads. Go out to the country lanes. Make the people come in. I want my house to be full. ²⁴I tell you, not one of those who were invited will get a taste of my dinner.'"

It Costs to Be a Disciple

²⁵Large crowds were traveling with Jesus. He turned and spoke to them. He said, ²⁶"Those who come to me must hate their father and mother. They must hate their wife and children, their brothers and sisters. And they must hate even their own lives. Unless they do, they can't be my disciples. ²⁷Those who don't carry their cross and follow me can't be my disciples.

²⁸"Suppose someone wants to build a tower. Won't he sit down first and figure out how much it will cost? Then he will see whether he has enough money to finish it. ²⁹Suppose he starts building and is not able to finish. Then everyone who sees what he has done will laugh at him. ³⁰They will say, 'This fellow started to build. But he wasn't able to finish.'

³¹"Or suppose a king is about to go to war against another king. And suppose he has 10,000 men, while the other has 20,000

GREAT VERSE —TO— REMEMBER   **14:27** Those who don't carry their cross and follow me can't be my disciples.

coming against him. Won't he first sit down and think about whether he can win?

³²"And suppose he decides he can't win. Then he will send some men to ask how peace can be made. He will do this while the other king is still far away.

³³"In the same way, you must give up everything you have. If you don't, you can't be my disciple.

³⁴"Salt is good. But suppose it loses its saltiness. How can it be made salty again? ³⁵It is not good for the soil. And it is not good for the trash pile. It will be thrown out.

"Those who have ears to hear should listen."

The Story of the Lost Sheep

15 The tax collectors and "sinners" were all gathering around to hear Jesus. ²But the Pharisees and the teachers of the law were whispering among themselves. They said, "This man welcomes sinners and eats with them."

³Then Jesus told them a story. ⁴He said, "Suppose one of you has 100 sheep and loses one of them. Won't he leave the 99 in the open country? Won't he go after the one lost sheep until he finds it? ⁵When he finds it, he will joyfully put it on his shoulders ⁶and go home. Then he will call his friends and neighbors together. He will say, 'Be joyful with me. I have found my lost sheep.'

⁷"I tell you, it will be the same in heaven. There will be great joy when one sinner turns away from sin. Yes, there will be more joy than for 99 godly people who do not need to turn away from their sins.

The Story of the Lost Coin

⁸"Or suppose a woman has ten silver coins and loses one. She will light a lamp and sweep the house. She will search carefully until she finds it. ⁹And when she finds it, she will call her friends and neighbors together. She will say, 'Be joyful with me. I have found my lost coin.'

GREAT VERSE — TO — REMEMBER

15:10 There is joy in heaven over one sinner who turns away from sin.

[10]"I tell you, it is the same in heaven. There is joy in heaven over one sinner who turns away from sin."

The Story of the Lost Son

[11]Jesus continued, "There was a man who had two sons. [12]The younger son spoke to his father. He said, 'Father, give me my share of the family property.' So the father divided his property between his two sons.

[13]"Not long after that, the younger son packed up all he had. Then he left for a country far away. There he wasted his money on wild living. [14]He spent everything he had.

"Then the whole country ran low on food. So the son didn't have what he needed. [15]He went to work for someone who lived in that country, who sent him to the fields to feed the pigs. [16]The son wanted to fill his stomach with the food the pigs were eating. But no one gave him anything.

[17]"Then he began to think clearly again. He said, 'How many of my father's hired workers have more than enough food! But here I am dying from hunger! [18]I will get up and go back to my father. I will say to him, "Father, I have sinned against heaven. And I have sinned against you. [19]I am no longer fit to be called your son. Make me like one of your hired workers."' [20]So he got up and went to his father.

"While the son was still a long way off, his father saw him. He was filled with tender love for his son. He ran to him. He threw his arms around him and kissed him.

[21]"The son said to him, 'Father, I have sinned against heaven and against you. I am no longer fit to be called your son.'

[22]"But the father said to his servants, 'Quick! Bring the best robe and put it on him. Put a ring on his finger and sandals on his feet. [23]Bring the best-fed calf and kill it. Let's have a big dinner and celebrate. [24]This son of mine was dead. And now he is alive again. He was lost. And now he is found.'

"So they began to celebrate.

[25]"The older son was in the field. When he came near the house, he heard music and dancing. [26]So he called one of the servants. He asked him what was going on.

[27]"'Your brother has come home,' the servant replied. 'Your father has killed the best-fed calf. He has done this because your brother is back safe and sound.'

[28]"The older brother became angry. He refused to go in. So his father went out and begged him.

²⁹"But he answered his father, 'Look! All these years I've worked like a slave for you. I have always obeyed your orders. You never gave me even a young goat so I could celebrate with my friends. ³⁰But this son of yours wasted your money with some prostitutes. Now he comes home. And for him you kill the best-fed calf!'

³¹"'My son,' the father said, 'you are always with me. Everything I have is yours. ³²But we had to celebrate and be glad. This brother of yours was dead. And now he is alive again. He was lost. And now he is found.'"

The Story of the Clever Manager

16 Jesus told his disciples another story. He said, "There was a rich man who had a manager. Some said that the manager was wasting what the rich man owned. ²So the rich man told him to come in. He asked him, 'What is this I hear about you? Tell me exactly how you have handled what I own. You can't be my manager any longer.'

³"The manager said to himself, 'What will I do now? My master is taking away my job. I'm not strong enough to dig. And I'm too ashamed to beg. ⁴I know what I'm going to do. I'll do something so that when I lose my job here, people will welcome me into their houses.'

⁵"So he called in each person who owed his master something. He asked the first one, 'How much do you owe my master?'

⁶"'I owe 800 gallons of olive oil,' he replied.

"The manager told him, 'Take your bill. Sit down quickly and make it 400.'

⁷"Then he asked the second one, 'And how much do you owe?'

"'I owe 1,000 bushels of wheat,' he replied.

"The manager told him, 'Take your bill and make it 800.'

⁸"The manager had not been honest. But the master praised him for being clever. The people of this world are clever in dealing with those who are like themselves. They are more clever than God's people.

⁹"I tell you, use the riches of this world to help others. In that way, you will make friends for yourselves. Then when your riches are gone, you will be welcomed into your eternal home in heaven.

¹⁰"Suppose you can be trusted with very little. Then you can be trusted with a lot. But suppose you are not honest with very little. Then you will not be honest with a lot.

¹¹"Suppose you have not been worthy of trust in handling

worldly wealth. Then who will trust you with true riches? [12]Suppose you have not been worthy of trust in handling someone else's property. Then who will give you property of your own?

[13]"No servant can serve two masters at the same time. You will hate one of them and love the other. Or you will be faithful to one and dislike the other. You can't serve God and Money at the same time."

[14]The Pharisees loved money. They heard all that Jesus said and made fun of him. [15]Jesus said to them, "You try to make yourselves look good in the eyes of other people. But God knows your hearts. What is worth a great deal among people is hated by God.

More Teachings

[16]"The teachings of the Law and the Prophets were preached until John came. Since then, the good news of God's kingdom is being preached. And everyone is trying very hard to enter it. [17]It is easier for heaven and earth to disappear than for the smallest part of a letter to drop out of the Law.

[18]"Anyone who divorces his wife and gets married to another woman commits adultery. Also, the man who gets married to a divorced woman commits adultery.

The Rich Man and Lazarus

[19]"Once there was a rich man. He was dressed in purple cloth and fine linen. He lived an easy life every day. [20]A man named Lazarus was placed at his gate. Lazarus was a beggar. His body was covered with sores. [21]Even dogs came and licked his sores. All he wanted was to eat what fell from the rich man's table.

[22]"The time came when the beggar died. The angels carried him to Abraham's side. The rich man also died and was buried. [23]In hell, the rich man was suffering terribly. He looked up and saw

---

16:13 No servant can serve two masters at the same time. You will hate one of them and love the other . . . You can't serve God and Money at the same time.

Abraham far away. Lazarus was by his side. ²⁴So the rich man called out, 'Father Abraham! Have pity on me! Send Lazarus to dip the tip of his finger in water. Then he can cool my tongue. I am in terrible pain in this fire.'

²⁵"But Abraham replied, 'Son, remember what happened in your lifetime. You received your good things. Lazarus received bad things. Now he is comforted here, and you are in terrible pain. ²⁶Besides, a wide space has been placed between us and you. So those who want to go from here to you can't go. And no one can cross over from there to us.'

²⁷"The rich man answered, 'Then I beg you, father. Send Lazarus to my family. ²⁸I have five brothers. Let Lazarus warn them. Then they will not come to this place of terrible suffering.'

²⁹"Abraham replied, 'They have the teachings of Moses and the Prophets. Let your brothers listen to them.'

³⁰"'No, father Abraham,' he said. 'But if someone from the dead goes to them, they will turn away from their sins.'

³¹"Abraham said to him, 'They do not listen to Moses and the Prophets. So they will not be convinced even if someone rises from the dead.'"

Sin, Faith and Duty

17 Jesus spoke to his disciples. "Things that make people sin are sure to come," he said. "But how terrible it will be for the person who brings them! ²Suppose people lead one of these little ones to sin. It would be better for those people to be thrown into the sea with a millstone tied around their neck. ³So watch what you do.

"If your brother or sister sins, tell them they are wrong. Then if they turn away from their sins, forgive them. ⁴Suppose they sin against you seven times in one day. And suppose they come back to you each time and say, 'We're sorry.' Forgive them."

⁵The apostles said to the Lord, "Give us more faith!"

⁶He replied, "Suppose you have faith as small as a mustard seed. Then you can say to this mulberry tree, 'Be pulled up. Be planted in the sea.' And it will obey you.

⁷"Suppose one of you had a servant plowing or looking after the sheep. And suppose the servant came in from the field. Would you say to him, 'Come along now and sit down to eat'? ⁸No. Instead, you would say, 'Prepare my supper. Get yourself ready. Wait on me while I eat and drink. Then after that you can

eat and drink.' ⁹Would you thank the servant because he did what he was told to do?

¹⁰"It's the same with you. Suppose you have done everything you were told to do. Then you should say, 'We are not worthy to serve you. We have only done our duty.'"

Jesus Heals Ten Men

¹¹Jesus was on his way to Jerusalem. He traveled along the border between Samaria and Galilee. ¹²As he was going into a village, ten men met him. They had a skin disease. They stood not very far away. ¹³And they called out in a loud voice, "Jesus! Master! Have pity on us!"

¹⁴Jesus saw them and said, "Go. Show yourselves to the priests." While they were on the way, they were healed.

¹⁵When one of them saw that he was healed, he came back. He praised God in a loud voice. ¹⁶He threw himself at Jesus' feet and thanked him. The man was a Samaritan.

¹⁷Jesus asked, "Weren't all ten healed? Where are the other nine? ¹⁸Didn't anyone else return and give praise to God except this outsider?"

¹⁹Then Jesus said to him, "Get up and go. Your faith has healed you."

The Coming of God's Kingdom

²⁰Once the Pharisees asked Jesus when God's kingdom would come. He replied, "The coming of God's kingdom is not something you can see just by watching for it carefully. ²¹People will not say, 'Here it is.' Or, 'There it is.' God's kingdom is among you."

²²Then Jesus spoke to his disciples. "The time is coming," he said, "when you will long to see one of the days of the Son of Man. But you won't see it. ²³People will tell you, 'There he is!' Or, 'Here he is!' Don't go running off after them.

²⁴"When the Son of Man comes, he will be like the lightning. It flashes and lights up the sky from one end to the other. ²⁵But first the Son of Man must suffer many things. He will not be accepted by the people of today.

²⁶"Remember how it was in the days of Noah. It will be the same in the days of the Son of Man. ²⁷People were eating and drinking. They were getting married. They were giving their daughters to be married. They did all those things right up to the day Noah entered the ark. Then the flood came and destroyed them all.

²⁸"It was the same in the days of Lot. People were eating and drinking. They were buying and selling. They were planting and building. ²⁹But on the day Lot left Sodom, fire and sulfur rained down from heaven. And all the people were destroyed.

³⁰"It will be just like that on the day the Son of Man is shown to the world. ³¹Suppose people are on the roof of the house on that day. And suppose their goods are inside the house. They should not go down to get them. No one in the field should go back for anything either. ³²Remember Lot's wife! ³³Those who try to keep their life will lose it. Those who lose their life will keep it.

³⁴"I tell you, on that night two people will be in one bed. One person will be taken and the other left. ³⁵/³⁶Two women will be grinding grain together. One will be taken and the other left."

³⁷"Where, Lord?" his disciples asked.

He replied, "The vultures will gather where there is a dead body."

The Story of the Widow Who Would Not Give Up

18 Jesus told his disciples a story. He wanted to show them that they should always pray and not give up. ²He said, "In a certain town there was a judge. He didn't have any respect for God or care about people. ³A widow lived in that town. She came to the judge again and again. She kept begging him, 'Make things right for me. Someone is doing me wrong.'

⁴"For some time the judge refused. But finally he said to himself, 'I don't have any respect for God. I don't care about people. ⁵But this widow keeps bothering me. So I will see that things are made right for her. If I don't, she will wear me out by coming again and again!'"

⁶The Lord said, "Listen to what the unfair judge says.

⁷God's chosen ones cry out to him day and night. Won't he make things right for them? Will he keep putting them off? ⁸I tell you, God will see that things are made right for them. He will make sure it happens quickly.

17:33 Those who try to keep their life will lose it. Those who lose their life will keep it.

"But when the Son of Man comes, will he find people who have faith on the earth?"

The Story of the Pharisee and the Tax Collector

⁹Jesus told a story to some people who were sure they were right with God. They looked down on everybody else. ¹⁰He said to them, "Two men went up to the temple to pray. One was a Pharisee. The other was a tax collector.

¹¹"The Pharisee stood up and prayed about himself. 'God, I thank you that I am not like other people,' he said. 'I am not like robbers or those who do other evil things. I am not like those who commit adultery. I am not even like this tax collector. ¹²I fast twice a week. And I give a tenth of all I get.'

¹³"But the tax collector stood not very far away. He would not even look up to heaven. He beat his chest and said, 'God, have mercy on me. I am a sinner.'

¹⁴"I tell you, the tax collector went home accepted by God. But not the Pharisee. All who lift themselves up will be brought down. And those who are brought down will be lifted up."

Little Children Are Brought to Jesus

¹⁵People were also bringing babies to Jesus. They wanted him to touch them. When the disciples saw this, they told the people to stop.

¹⁶But Jesus asked the children to come to him. "Let the little children come to me," he said. "Don't keep them away. God's kingdom belongs to people like them. ¹⁷What I'm about to tell you is true. Anyone who will not receive God's kingdom like a little child will never enter it."

Jesus and the Rich Ruler

¹⁸A certain ruler asked Jesus a question. "Good teacher," he said, "what must I do to receive eternal life?"

GREAT VERSE — TO — REMEMBER

18:17 What I'm about to tell you is true. Anyone who will not receive God's kingdom like a little child will never enter it.

¹⁹"Why do you call me good?" Jesus answered. "No one is good except God. ²⁰You know what the commandments say. 'Do not commit adultery. Do not commit murder. Do not steal. Do not give false witness. Honor your father and mother.'" *(Exodus 20:12–16; Deuteronomy 5:16–20)*

²¹"I have obeyed all those commandments since I was a boy," the ruler said.

²²When Jesus heard this, he said to him, "You are still missing one thing. Sell everything you have. Give the money to those who are poor. You will have treasure in heaven. Then come and follow me."

²³When the ruler heard this, he became very sad. He was very rich.

²⁴Jesus looked at him. Then he said, "How hard it is for rich people to enter God's kingdom! ²⁵Is it hard for a camel to go through the eye of a needle? It is even harder for the rich to enter God's kingdom!"

²⁶Those who heard this asked, "Then who can be saved?"

²⁷Jesus replied, "Things that are impossible with people are possible with God."

²⁸Peter said to him, "We have left everything we had in order to follow you!"

²⁹"What I'm about to tell you is true," Jesus said to them. "Has anyone left home or family for God's kingdom? ³⁰They will receive many times as much in this world. In the world to come they will live forever."

Jesus Again Tells About His Coming Death

³¹Jesus took the Twelve to one side. He told them, "We are going up to Jerusalem. Everything that the prophets wrote about the Son of Man will come true. ³²He will be handed over to people who are not Jews. They will make fun of him. They will laugh at him and spit on him. They will whip him and kill him. ³³On the third day, he will rise from the dead!"

³⁴The disciples did not understand any of this. Its meaning was hidden from them. So they didn't know what Jesus was talking about.

A Blind Beggar Receives His Sight

³⁵Jesus was approaching Jericho. A blind man was sitting by the side of the road begging. ³⁶The blind man heard the crowd going

by. He asked what was happening. ³⁷They told him, "Jesus of Nazareth is passing by."

³⁸So the blind man called out, "Jesus! Son of David! Have mercy on me!"

³⁹Those who led the way commanded him to stop. They told him to be quiet. But he shouted even louder, "Son of David! Have mercy on me!"

⁴⁰Jesus stopped and ordered the man to be brought to him. When the man came near, Jesus spoke to him. ⁴¹"What do you want me to do for you?" he asked.

"Lord, I want to be able to see," the blind man replied.

⁴²Jesus said to him, "Receive your sight. Your faith has healed you."

⁴³Right away he could see. He followed Jesus, praising God. When all the people saw it, they also praised God.

Zacchaeus the Tax Collector

19 Jesus entered Jericho and was passing through. ²A man named Zacchaeus was there. He was a chief tax collector and was very rich.

³Zacchaeus wanted to see who Jesus was. But he was a short man. He could not see Jesus because of the crowd. ⁴So he ran ahead and climbed a sycamore-fig tree. He wanted to see Jesus, who was coming that way.

⁵Jesus reached the spot where Zacchaeus was. He looked up and said, "Zacchaeus, come down at once. I must stay at your house today." ⁶So Zacchaeus came down at once and welcomed him gladly.

⁷All the people saw this. They began to whisper among themselves. They said, "Jesus has gone to be the guest of a 'sinner.'"

⁸But Zacchaeus stood up. He said, "Look, Lord! Here and now I give half of what I own to those who are poor. And if I have cheated anybody out of anything, I will pay it back. I will pay back four times the amount I took."

⁹Jesus spoke to Zacchaeus. "Today salvation has come to this house," he said. "This man also is a son of Abraham. ¹⁰The Son of Man came to look for the lost and save them."

The Story of Three Servants

¹¹While the people were listening to these things, Jesus told them a story. He was near Jerusalem. The people thought that God's kingdom was going to appear right away.

¹²Jesus said, "A man from an important family went to a country far away. He went there to be made king and then return home. ¹³So he sent for ten of his servants. He gave them each about three months' pay. 'Put this money to work until I come back,' he said.

¹⁴"But those he ruled over hated him. They sent a group of people after him. They were sent to say, 'We don't want this man to be our king.'

¹⁵"But he was made king and returned home. Then he sent for the servants he had given the money to. He wanted to find out what they had earned with it.

¹⁶"The first one came to him. He said, 'Sir, your money has earned ten times as much.'

¹⁷"'You have done well, my good servant!' his master replied. 'You have been faithful in a very small matter. So I will put you in charge of ten towns.'

¹⁸"The second servant came to his master. He said, 'Sir, your money has earned five times as much.'

¹⁹"His master answered, 'I will put you in charge of five towns.'

²⁰"Then another servant came. He said, 'Sir, here is your money. I have kept it hidden in a piece of cloth. ²¹I was afraid of you. You are a hard man. You take out what you did not put in. You harvest what you did not plant.'

²²"His master replied, 'I will judge you by your own words, you evil servant! So you knew that I am a hard man? You knew that I take out what I did not put in? You knew that I harvest what I did not plant? ²³Then why didn't you put my money in the bank? When I came back, I could have collected it with interest.'

²⁴"Then he said to those standing by, 'Take his money away from him. Give it to the one who has ten times as much.'

²⁵"'Sir,' they said, 'he already has ten times as much!'

²⁶"He replied, 'I tell you that those who have will be given more. But here is what will happen to those who have nothing. Even what they have will be taken away from them. ²⁷And what about my enemies who did not want me to be king over them? Bring them here! Kill them in front of me!'"

Jesus Enters Jerusalem

²⁸After Jesus had said this, he went on ahead. He was going up to Jerusalem.

²⁹He approached Bethphage and Bethany. The hill there was called the Mount of Olives. Jesus sent out two of his disciples. He

said to them, ³⁰"Go to the village ahead of you. As you enter it, you will find a young donkey tied there. No one has ever ridden it. Untie it and bring it here. ³¹Someone may ask you, 'Why are you untying it?' If so, say, 'The Lord needs it.'"

³²Those who were sent ahead went and found the young donkey. It was there just as Jesus had told them. ³³They were untying the colt when its owners came. The owners asked them, "Why are you untying the colt?"

³⁴They replied, "The Lord needs it."

³⁵Then the disciples brought it to Jesus. They threw their coats on the young donkey and put Jesus on it. ³⁶As he went along, people spread their coats on the road.

³⁷Jesus came near the place where the road goes down the Mount of Olives. There the whole crowd of disciples began to praise God with joy. In loud voices they praised him for all the miracles they had seen. They shouted,

³⁸"Blessed is the king who comes in the name of the
Lord!"   *(Psalm 118:26)*

"May there be peace and glory in the highest heaven!"

³⁹Some of the Pharisees in the crowd spoke to Jesus. "Teacher," they said, "tell your disciples to stop!"

⁴⁰"I tell you," he replied, "if they keep quiet, the stones will cry out."

⁴¹He approached Jerusalem. When he saw the city, he began to sob because of it. ⁴²He said, "I wish you had known on this day what would bring you peace! But now it is hidden from your eyes.

⁴³"The days will come when your enemies will arrive. They will build a wall of dirt up against your city. They will surround you and close you in on every side. ⁴⁴You didn't recognize the time when God would come to you. So your enemies will smash you to the ground. They will destroy you and all the people inside your walls. They will not leave one stone on top of another."

19:38 Blessed is the king who comes in the name of the Lord! May there be peace and glory in the highest heaven!

Jesus Clears Out the Temple

⁴⁵Then Jesus entered the temple area. He began chasing out those who were selling there. ⁴⁶He said, "It is written: 'My house will be a house of prayer.' *(Isaiah 56:7)* But you have made it a 'den for robbers.'" *(Jeremiah 7:11)*

⁴⁷Every day Jesus was teaching at the temple. But the chief priests and the teachers of the law were trying to kill him. So were the leaders among the people. ⁴⁸But they couldn't find any way to do it. All the people were paying close attention to his words.

The Authority of Jesus Is Questioned

20 One day Jesus was teaching the people in the temple courtyard. He was preaching the good news to them.

The chief priests and the teachers of the law came up to him. The elders came with them. ²"Tell us by what authority you are doing these things," they all said. "Who gave you this authority?"

³Jesus replied, "I will also ask you a question. Tell me, ⁴was John's baptism from heaven? Or did it come from human authority?"

⁵They talked to each other about it. They said, "If we say, 'From heaven,' he will ask, 'Why didn't you believe him?' ⁶But if we say, 'From human authority,' all the people will throw stones at us and kill us. They believe that John was a prophet."

⁷So they answered Jesus, "We don't know where John's baptism came from."

⁸Jesus said, "Then I won't tell you by what authority I am doing these things either."

The Story of the Renters

⁹Jesus went on to tell the people a story. "A man planted a vineyard," he said. "He rented it out to some farmers. Then he went away for a long time.

¹⁰"At harvest time he sent a servant to the renters. They were supposed to give him some of the fruit of the vineyard. But the renters beat the servant. Then they sent him away with nothing. ¹¹So the man sent another servant. They beat that one and treated him badly. They also sent him away with nothing. ¹²The man sent a third servant. The renters wounded him and threw him out.

¹³"Then the owner of the vineyard said, 'What should I do? I have a son, and I love him. I will send him. Maybe they will respect him.'

¹⁴"But when the renters saw the son, they talked the matter over. 'This is the one who will receive all the owner's property someday,' they said. 'Let's kill him. Then everything will be ours.' ¹⁵So they threw him out of the vineyard. And they killed him.

"What will the owner of the vineyard do to the renters? ¹⁶He will come and kill them. He will give the vineyard to others."

When the people heard this, they said, "We hope this never happens!"

¹⁷Jesus looked right at them and said, "Here is something I want you to explain the meaning of. It is written:

> "'The stone the builders did not accept
>   has become the most important stone of all.' *(Psalm 118:22)*

¹⁸Everyone who falls on that stone will be broken to pieces. But the stone will crush anyone it falls on."

¹⁹The teachers of the law and the chief priests looked for a way to arrest Jesus at once. They knew he had told that story against them. But they were afraid of the people.

Is It Right to Pay Taxes to Caesar?

²⁰The religious leaders sent spies to keep a close watch on Jesus. The spies pretended to be honest. They hoped they could trap Jesus with something he would say. Then they could hand him over to the power and authority of the governor.

²¹So the spies questioned Jesus. "Teacher," they said, "we know that you speak and teach what is right. We know you don't favor one person over another. You teach the way of God truthfully. ²²Is it right for us to pay taxes to Caesar or not?"

²³Jesus saw through their trickery. He said to them, ²⁴"Show me a silver coin. Whose picture and words are on it?"

²⁵"Caesar's," they replied.

He said to them, "Then give to Caesar what belongs to Caesar. And give to God what belongs to God."

²⁶They were not able to trap him with what he had said there

20:25 Give to Caesar what belongs to Caesar. And give to God what belongs to God.

in front of all the people. Amazed by his answer, they became silent.

Marriage When the Dead Rise

²⁷The Sadducees do not believe that people rise from the dead. Some of them came to Jesus with a question. ²⁸"Teacher," they said, "Moses wrote for us about a man's brother who dies. Suppose the brother leaves a wife but has no children. Then the man must get married to the widow. He must have children for his brother.

²⁹"There were seven brothers. The first one got married to a woman. He died without leaving any children. ³⁰The second one got married to her. ³¹And then the third one got married to her. One after another, the seven brothers got married to her. They all died. None left any children. ³²Finally, the woman died too. ³³Now then, when the dead rise, whose wife will she be? All seven were married to her."

³⁴Jesus replied, "The people of today get married. And their parents give them to get married. ³⁵But it will not be like that when the dead rise. Those who are considered worthy to take part in what happens at that time won't get married. And their parents won't give them to be married. ³⁶They can't die anymore. They are like the angels. They are God's children. They will be given a new form of life when the dead rise.

³⁷"Remember the story of Moses and the bush. Even Moses showed that the dead rise. He calls the Lord 'the God of Abraham, the God of Isaac, and the God of Jacob.' *(Exodus 3:6)* ³⁸He is not the God of the dead. He is the God of the living. In his eyes, everyone is alive."

³⁹Some of the teachers of the law replied, "You have spoken well, teacher!" ⁴⁰And no one dared to ask him any more questions.

Whose Son Is the Christ?

⁴¹Jesus said to them, "Why do they say that the Christ is the Son of David? ⁴²David himself says in the Book of Psalms,

> "'The Lord said to my Lord,
>   "Sit at my right hand
> ⁴³until I put your enemies
>   under your control."'   *(Psalm 110:1)*

⁴⁴David calls him 'Lord.' So how can he be David's son?"

⁴⁵All the people were listening. Jesus said to his disciples, ⁴⁶"Watch out for the teachers of the law. They like to walk around in long robes. They love to be greeted in the market places. They love to have the most important seats in the synagogues. They also love to have the places of honor at dinners. ⁴⁷They take over the houses of widows. They say long prayers to show off. God will punish those people very much."

The Widow's Offering

21 As Jesus looked up, he saw rich people putting their gifts into the temple offering boxes. ²He also saw a poor widow put in two very small copper coins.

³"What I'm about to tell you is true," Jesus said. "That poor widow has put in more than all the others. ⁴All of those other people gave out of their wealth. But even though she was poor, she put in everything. She had nothing left to live on."

Signs of the End

⁵Some of Jesus' disciples were talking about the temple. They spoke about how it was decorated with beautiful stones and with gifts that honored God. But Jesus asked, ⁶"Do you see all this? The time will come when not one stone will be left on top of another. Every stone will be thrown down."

⁷"Teacher," they asked, "when will these things happen? And what will be the sign that they are about to take place?"

⁸Jesus replied, "Keep watch! Be careful that you are not fooled. Many will come in my name. They will claim, 'I am he!' And they will say, 'The time is near!' Do not follow them. ⁹Do not be afraid when you hear about wars and about fighting against rulers. Those things must happen first. But the end will not come right away."

¹⁰Then Jesus said to them, "Nation will fight against nation. Kingdom will fight against kingdom. ¹¹In many places there will be powerful earthquakes. People will go hungry. There will be terrible sicknesses. Things will happen that will make people afraid. There will be great and miraculous signs from heaven.

¹²"But before all this, people will arrest you and treat you badly. They will hand you over to synagogues and prisons. You will be brought to kings and governors. All this will happen to you because of my name. ¹³In that way you will be witnesses to them. ¹⁴But make up your mind not to worry ahead of time about how to stand up for yourselves. ¹⁵I will give you words of wisdom.

None of your enemies will be able to withstand them or oppose them.

¹⁶"Even your parents, brothers, sisters, relatives and friends will hand you over to the authorities. They will put some of you to death. ¹⁷Everyone will hate you because of me. ¹⁸But not a hair on your head will be harmed. ¹⁹If you stand firm, you will gain life.

²⁰"A time is coming when you will see armies surround Jerusalem. Then you will know that it will soon be destroyed. ²¹Those who are in Judea should then escape to the mountains. Those in the city should get out. Those in the country should not enter the city. ²²This is the time when God will punish Jerusalem. Everything will come true, just as it has been written.

²³"How awful it will be in those days for pregnant women! How awful for nursing mothers! There will be terrible suffering in the land. There will be great anger against those people. ²⁴Some will be killed by the sword. Others will be taken as prisoners to all the nations. Jerusalem will be overrun by those who aren't Jews until the times of the non-Jews come to an end.

²⁵"There will be miraculous signs in the sun, moon and stars. The nations of the earth will be in terrible pain. They will be puzzled by the roaring and tossing of the sea. ²⁶Terror will make people faint. They will be worried about what is happening in the world. The sun, moon and stars will be shaken from their places.

²⁷"At that time people will see the Son of Man coming in a cloud. He will come with power and great glory. ²⁸When these things begin to take place, stand up. Lift up your heads. The time when you will be set free is very close."

²⁹Jesus told them a story. "Look at the fig tree and all the trees," he said. ³⁰"When you see leaves appear on the branches, you know that summer is near. ³¹In the same way, when you see these things happening, you will know that God's kingdom is near.

³²"What I'm about to tell you is true. The people living at that time will certainly not pass away until all these things have hap-

---

GREAT VERSE —TO— REMEMBER

21:33 Heaven and earth will pass away. But my words will never pass away.

pened. [33]Heaven and earth will pass away. But my words will never pass away.

[34]"Be careful. If you aren't, your hearts will be loaded down with wasteful living, drunkenness and the worries of life. Then that day will close on you like a trap. You will not be expecting it. [35]That day will come upon every person who lives on the whole earth.

[36]"Always keep watching. Pray that you will be able to escape all that is about to happen. Also, pray that you will not be judged guilty when the Son of Man comes."

[37]Each day Jesus taught at the temple. And each evening he went to spend the night on the hill called the Mount of Olives. [38]All the people came to the temple early in the morning. They wanted to hear Jesus speak.

Judas Agrees to Hand Jesus Over

22 The Feast of Unleavened Bread, called the Passover, was near. [2]The chief priests and the teachers of the law were looking for a way to get rid of Jesus. They were afraid of the people.

[3]Then Satan entered Judas, who was called Iscariot. Judas was one of the Twelve. [4]He went to the chief priests and the officers of the temple guard. He talked with them about how he could hand Jesus over to them. [5]They were delighted and agreed to give him money.

[6]Judas accepted their offer. He watched for the right time to hand Jesus over to them. He wanted to do it when no crowd was around.

The Last Supper

[7]Then the day of Unleavened Bread came. That was the time the Passover lamb had to be sacrificed. [8]Jesus sent Peter and John on ahead. "Go," he told them. "Prepare for us to eat the Passover meal."

[9]"Where do you want us to prepare for it?" they asked.

[10]Jesus replied, "When you enter the city, a man carrying a jar of water will meet you. Follow him to the house he enters. [11]Then say to the owner of the house, 'The Teacher asks: Where is the guest room? Where can I eat the Passover meal with my disciples?' [12]He will show you a large upstairs room with furniture in it. Prepare for us to eat there."

[13]Peter and John left. They found things just as Jesus had told them. So they prepared the Passover meal.

[14]When the hour came, Jesus and his apostles took their places at the table. [15]He said to them, "I have really looked forward to eating this Passover meal with you. I wanted to do this before I suffer. [16]I tell you, I will not eat the Passover meal again until it is celebrated in God's kingdom."

[17]After Jesus took the cup, he gave thanks. He said, "Take this cup and share it among yourselves. [18]I tell you, I will not drink from the fruit of the vine again until God's kingdom comes."

[19]Then Jesus took bread. He gave thanks and broke it. He handed it to them and said, "This is my body. It is given for you. Every time you eat it, do it in memory of me."

[20]In the same way, after the supper he took the cup. He said, "This cup is the new covenant in my blood. It is poured out for you. [21]But someone here is going to hand me over to my enemies. His hand is with mine on the table. [22]The Son of Man will go to his death, just as already decided. But how terrible it will be for the one who hands him over!"

[23]The apostles began to ask each other about this. They wondered which one of them would do it.

[24]They also started to argue. They disagreed about which of them was thought to be the most important person.

[25]Jesus said to them, "The kings of the nations hold power over their people. And those who order them around call themselves Protectors. [26]But you must not be like that. Instead, the most important among you should be like the youngest. The one who rules should be like the one who serves.

[27]"Who is more important? Is it the one at the table, or the one who serves? Isn't it the one who is at the table? But I am among you as one who serves. [28]You have stood by me during my troubles. [29]And I give you a kingdom, just as my Father gave me a kingdom. [30]Then you will eat and drink at my table in my kingdom. And you will sit on thrones, judging the 12 tribes of Israel.

GREAT VERSE —TO— REMEMBER

22:26 The most important among you should be like the youngest. The one who rules should be like the one who serves.

[31]"Simon, Simon! Satan has asked to sift you disciples like wheat. [32]But I have prayed for you, Simon. I have prayed that your faith will not fail. When you have turned back, help your brothers to be strong."

[33]But Simon replied, "Lord, I am ready to go with you to prison and to death."

[34]Jesus answered, "I tell you, Peter, you will say three times that you don't know me. And you will do it before the rooster crows today."

[35]Then Jesus asked them, "Did you need anything when I sent you without a purse, bag or sandals?"

"Nothing," they answered.

[36]He said to them, "But now if you have a purse, take it. And also take a bag. If you don't have a sword, sell your coat and buy one. [37]It is written: 'And he was counted among those who disobey the Law.' (Isaiah 53:12) I tell you that what is written about me must come true. Yes, it is already coming true."

[38]The disciples said, "See, Lord, here are two swords."

"That is enough," he replied.

Jesus Prays on the Mount of Olives

[39]Jesus went out as usual to the Mount of Olives. His disciples followed him. [40]When they reached the place, Jesus spoke. "Pray that you won't fall into sin when you are tempted," he said to them.

[41]Then he went a short distance away from them. There he got down on his knees and prayed. [42]He said, "Father, if you are willing, take this cup of suffering from me. But do what you want, not what I want."

[43]An angel from heaven appeared to Jesus and gave him strength. [44]Because he was very sad and troubled, he prayed even harder. His sweat was like drops of blood falling to the ground.

[45]After that, he got up from prayer and went back to the disciples. He found them sleeping. They were worn out because they were very sad.

[46]"Why are you sleeping?" he asked them. "Get up! Pray that you won't fall into sin when you are tempted."

Jesus Is Arrested

[47]While Jesus was still speaking, a crowd came up. The man named Judas was leading them. He was one of the Twelve. Judas approached Jesus to kiss him.

⁴⁸But Jesus asked him, "Judas, are you handing over the Son of Man with a kiss?"

⁴⁹Jesus' followers saw what was going to happen. So they said, "Lord, should we use our swords against them?" ⁵⁰One of them struck the servant of the high priest and cut off his right ear.

⁵¹But Jesus answered, "Stop this!" And he touched the man's ear and healed him.

⁵²Then Jesus spoke to the chief priests, the officers of the temple guard, and the elders. They had all come for him. "Am I leading a band of armed men against you?" he asked. "Do you have to come with swords and clubs? ⁵³Every day I was with you in the temple courtyard. And you didn't lay a hand on me. But this is your hour. This is when darkness rules."

Peter Says He Does Not Know Jesus

⁵⁴Then the men arrested Jesus and led him away. They took him into the high priest's house. Peter followed from far away. ⁵⁵They started a fire in the middle of the courtyard. Then they sat down together. Peter sat down with them.

⁵⁶A woman servant saw him sitting there in the firelight. She looked closely at him. Then she said, "This man was with Jesus."

⁵⁷But Peter said he had not been with him. "Woman, I don't know him," he said.

⁵⁸A little later someone else saw Peter. "You also are one of them," he said.

"Man, I am not!" Peter replied.

⁵⁹About an hour later, another person spoke up. "This fellow must have been with Jesus," he said. "He is from Galilee."

⁶⁰Peter replied, "Man, I don't know what you're talking about!"

Just as he was speaking, the rooster crowed. ⁶¹The Lord turned and looked right at Peter. Then Peter remembered what the Lord had spoken to him. "The rooster will crow today," Jesus had said. "Before it does, you will say three times that you don't know me." ⁶²Peter went outside. He broke down and sobbed.

The Guards Make Fun of Jesus

⁶³There were men guarding Jesus. They began laughing at him and beating him. ⁶⁴They blindfolded him. They said, "Prophesy! Who hit you?" ⁶⁵They also said many other things to make fun of him.

Jesus Is Brought to Pilate and Herod

⁶⁶At dawn, the elders of the people met together. These included the chief priests and the teachers of the law. Jesus was led to them. ⁶⁷"If you are the Christ," they said, "tell us."

Jesus answered, "If I tell you, you will not believe me. ⁶⁸And if I asked you, you would not answer. ⁶⁹But from now on, the Son of Man will be seated at the right hand of the mighty God."

⁷⁰They all asked, "Are you the Son of God then?"

He replied, "You are right in saying that I am."

⁷¹Then they said, "Why do we need any more witnesses? We have heard it from his own lips."

23 Then the whole group got up and led Jesus off to Pilate. ²They began to bring charges against Jesus. They said, "We have found this man misleading our people. He is against paying taxes to Caesar. And he claims to be Christ, a king."

³So Pilate asked Jesus, "Are you the king of the Jews?"

"Yes. It is just as you say," Jesus replied.

⁴Then Pilate spoke to the chief priests and the crowd. He announced, "I find no basis for a charge against this man."

⁵But they kept it up. They said, "His teaching stirs up the people all over Judea. He started in Galilee and has come all the way here."

⁶When Pilate heard this, he asked if the man was from Galilee. ⁷He learned that Jesus was from Herod's area of authority. So Pilate sent Jesus to Herod. At that time Herod was also in Jerusalem.

⁸When Herod saw Jesus, he was very pleased. He had been wanting to see Jesus for a long time. He had heard much about him. He hoped to see Jesus do a miracle.

⁹Herod asked him many questions, but Jesus gave him no answer. ¹⁰The chief priests and the teachers of the law were standing there. With loud shouts they were bringing charges against him.

¹¹Herod and his soldiers laughed at him and made fun of him. They dressed him in a beautiful robe. Then they sent him back to Pilate. ¹²That day Herod and Pilate became friends. Before this time they had been enemies.

¹³Pilate called together the chief priests, the rulers and the people. ¹⁴He said to them, "You brought me this man. You said he was turning the people against the authorities. I have questioned him in front of you. I have found no basis for your charges against him. ¹⁵Herod hasn't either. So he sent Jesus back to us. As

you can see, Jesus has done nothing that is worthy of death.
[16/17]So I will just have him whipped and let him go."

[18]With one voice the crowd cried out, "Kill this man! Give
Barabbas to us!" [19]Barabbas had been thrown into prison. He had
taken part in a struggle in the city against the authorities. He had
also committed murder.

[20]Pilate wanted to let Jesus go. So he made an appeal to the
crowd again. [21]But they kept shouting, "Crucify him! Crucify
him!"

[22]Pilate spoke to them for the third time. "Why?" he asked.
"What wrong has this man done? I have found no reason to have
him put to death. So I will just have him whipped and let
him go."

[23]But with loud shouts they kept calling for Jesus to be crucified.
The people's shouts won out.

[24]So Pilate decided to give them what they wanted. [25]He set free
the man they asked for. The man had been thrown in prison for
murder and for fighting against the authorities. Pilate gave Jesus
over to them so they could carry out their plans.

Jesus Is Nailed to a Cross

[26]As they led Jesus away, they took hold of Simon. Simon was
from Cyrene. He was on his way in from the country. They put
the cross on him. Then they made him carry it behind Jesus.

[27]A large number of people followed Jesus. Some were women
whose hearts were filled with sorrow. They cried loudly because
of him.

[28]Jesus turned and said to them, "Daughters of Jerusalem, do
not cry for me. Cry for yourselves and for your children. [29]The
time will come when you will say, 'Blessed are the women who
can't have children! Blessed are those who never gave birth or
nursed babies!' [30]It is written:

> "'They will say to the mountains, "Fall on us!"
> They will say to the hills, "Cover us!"'   *(Hosea 10:8)*

[31]People do these things when trees are green. So what will happen when trees are dry?"

[32]Two other men were also led out with Jesus to be killed. Both
of them had broken the law. [33]The soldiers brought them to the
place called The Skull. There they nailed Jesus to the cross. He
hung between the two criminals. One was on his right and one
was on his left.

³⁴Jesus said, "Father, forgive them. They don't know what they are doing." The soldiers divided up his clothes by casting lots.

³⁵The people stood there watching. The rulers even made fun of Jesus. They said, "He saved others. Let him save himself if he is the Christ of God, the Chosen One."

³⁶The soldiers also came up and poked fun at him. They offered him wine vinegar. ³⁷They said, "If you are the king of the Jews, save yourself."

³⁸A written sign had been placed above him. It read, THIS IS THE KING OF THE JEWS.

³⁹One of the criminals hanging there made fun of Jesus. He said, "Aren't you the Christ? Save yourself! Save us!"

⁴⁰But the other criminal scolded him. "Don't you have any respect for God?" he said. "Remember, you are under the same sentence of death. ⁴¹We are being punished fairly. We are getting just what our actions call for. But this man hasn't done anything wrong."

⁴²Then he said, "Jesus, remember me when you come into your kingdom."

⁴³Jesus answered him, "What I'm about to tell you is true. Today you will be with me in paradise."

Jesus Dies

⁴⁴It was now about noon. The whole land was covered with darkness until three o'clock. ⁴⁵The sun had stopped shining. The temple curtain was torn in two. ⁴⁶Jesus called out in a loud voice, "Father, into your hands I commit my very life." After he said this, he took his last breath.

⁴⁷The Roman commander saw what had happened. He praised God and said, "Jesus was surely a man who did what was right."

⁴⁸The people had gathered to watch that sight. When they saw what happened, they beat their chests and went away. ⁴⁹But all those who knew Jesus stood not very far away, watching those things. They included the women who had followed him from Galilee.

23:34 Jesus said, "Father, forgive them. They don't know what they are doing."

Jesus Is Buried

⁵⁰A man named Joseph was a member of the Council. He was a good and honest man. ⁵¹He had not agreed with what the leaders had decided and done. He was from Arimathea, a town in Judea. He was waiting for God's kingdom.

⁵²Joseph went to Pilate and asked for Jesus' body. ⁵³He took it down and wrapped it in linen cloth. Then he put it in a tomb cut in the rock. No one had ever been buried there. ⁵⁴It was Preparation Day. The Sabbath was about to begin.

⁵⁵The women who had come with Jesus from Galilee followed Joseph. They saw the tomb and how Jesus' body was placed in it. ⁵⁶Then they went home. There they prepared spices and perfumes. But they rested on the Sabbath day in order to obey the Law.

Jesus Rises From the Dead

24 It was very early in the morning on the first day of the week. The women took the spices they had prepared. Then they went to the tomb. ²They found the stone rolled away from it. ³When they entered the tomb, they did not find the body of the Lord Jesus. ⁴They were wondering about this.

Suddenly, two men in clothes as bright as lightning stood beside them. ⁵The women were terrified. They bowed down with their faces to the ground.

Then the men said to them, "Why do you look for the living among the dead? ⁶Jesus is not here! He has risen! Remember how he told you he would rise. It was while he was still with you in Galilee. ⁷He said, 'The Son of Man must be handed over to sinful people. He must be nailed to a cross. On the third day he will rise from the dead.'"

⁸Then the women remembered Jesus' words.

⁹They came back from the tomb. They told all these things to the Eleven and to all the others. ¹⁰Mary Magdalene, Joanna, Mary the mother of James, and the others with them were the ones who told the apostles. ¹¹But the apostles did not believe the women. Their words didn't make any sense to them.

¹²But Peter got up and ran to the tomb. He bent over and saw the strips of linen lying by themselves. Then he went away, wondering what had happened.

On the Road to Emmaus

¹³That same day two of Jesus' followers were going to a village

called Emmaus. It was about seven miles from Jerusalem. [14]They were talking with each other about everything that had happened.

[15]As they talked about those things, Jesus himself came up and walked along with them. [16]But they were kept from recognizing him.

[17]Jesus asked them, "What are you talking about as you walk along?"

They stood still, and their faces were sad. [18]One of them was named Cleopas. He said to Jesus, "You must be a visitor to Jerusalem. If you weren't, you would know the things that have happened there in the last few days."

[19]"What things?" Jesus asked.

"About Jesus of Nazareth," they replied. "He was a prophet. He was powerful in what he said and did in the eyes of God and all of the people. [20]The chief priests and our rulers handed Jesus over to be sentenced to death. They nailed him to a cross. [21]But we had hoped that he was the one who was going to set Israel free. Also, it is the third day since all this happened.

[22]"Some of our women amazed us too. Early this morning they went to the tomb. [23]But they didn't find his body. So they came and told us what they had seen. They saw angels, who said Jesus was alive. [24]Then some of our friends went to the tomb. They found it just as the women had said. But they did not see Jesus."

[25]Jesus said to them, "How foolish you are! How long it takes you to believe all that the prophets said! [26]Didn't the Christ have to suffer these things and then receive his glory?"

[27]Jesus explained to them what was said in all the Scriptures about himself. He began with Moses and all the Prophets.

[28]They approached the village where they were going. Jesus acted as if he were going farther. [29]But they tried hard to keep him from leaving. They said, "Stay with us. It is nearly evening. The day is almost over." So he went in to stay with them.

[30]He joined them at the table. Then he took bread and gave thanks. He broke it and began to give it to them. [31]Their eyes were opened, and they recognized him. But then he disappeared from their sight.

[32]They said to each other, "He talked with us on the road. He opened the Scriptures to us. Weren't our hearts burning inside us during that time?"

[33]They got up and returned at once to Jerusalem. There they found the Eleven and those with them. They were all gathered

together. ³⁴They were saying, "It's true! The Lord has risen! He has appeared to Simon!"

³⁵Then the two of them told what had happened to them on the way. They told how they had recognized Jesus when he broke the bread.

Jesus Appears to the Disciples

³⁶The disciples were still talking about this when Jesus himself suddenly stood among them. He said, "May peace be with you."

³⁷They were surprised and terrified. They thought they were seeing a ghost.

³⁸Jesus said to them, "Why are you troubled? Why do you have doubts in your minds? ³⁹Look at my hands and my feet. It is really I! Touch me and see. A ghost does not have a body or bones. But you can see that I do."

⁴⁰After he said that, he showed them his hands and feet. ⁴¹But they still did not believe it. They were amazed and filled with joy.

So Jesus asked them, "Do you have anything here to eat?"

⁴²They gave him a piece of cooked fish. ⁴³He took it and ate it in front of them.

⁴⁴Jesus said to them, "This is what I told you while I was still with you. Everything written about me must happen. Everything written about me in the Law of Moses, the Prophets and the Psalms must come true."

⁴⁵Then he opened their minds so they could understand the Scriptures. ⁴⁶He told them, "This is what is written. The Christ will suffer. He will rise from the dead on the third day. ⁴⁷His followers will preach in his name. They will tell others to turn away from their sins and be forgiven. All nations will hear it, beginning at Jerusalem. ⁴⁸You have seen these things with your own eyes.

⁴⁹"I am going to send you what my Father has promised. But for

---

24:49 I am going to send you what my Father has promised. But for now, stay in the city. Stay there until you have received power from heaven.

now, stay in the city. Stay there until you have received power from heaven."

Jesus Is Taken Up Into Heaven

⁵⁰Jesus led his disciples out to the area near Bethany. Then he lifted up his hands and blessed them. ⁵¹While he was blessing them, he left them. He was taken up into heaven.

⁵²Then they worshiped him. With great joy, they returned to Jerusalem. ⁵³Every day they went to the temple, praising God.

John

Why Was This Book Written? John was one of Jesus' first followers. John may have been one of John the Baptist's followers too. John wrote this Gospel. Jesus took John with him if something special was going to happen. Jesus loved John very much.

What Is This Book About? John wanted us to believe in Jesus and have eternal life. He taught us what Jesus said and did to prove he is God. John's stories showed Jesus' power when people were weak. John wrote about Jesus as a man too. Jesus was tired, hungry and sad at times, just like we are.

What Is in This Book?

The Word Became Human

1 In the beginning, the Word was already there. The Word was with God, and the Word was God. [2]He was with God in the beginning.

[3]All things were made through him. Nothing that has been made was made without him. [4]Life was in him, and that life was the light for all people. [5]The light shines in the darkness. But the darkness has not understood it.

[6]A man came who was sent from God. His name was John. [7]He came to give witness about that light. He gave witness so that all people could believe.

[8]John himself was not the light. He came only as a witness to the light. [9]The true light that gives light to everyone was coming into the world.

[10]The Word was in the world that was made through him. But the world did not recognize him. [11]He came to what was his own. But his own people did not accept him.

[12]Some people did accept him. They believed in his name. He gave them the right to become children of God. [13]To be a child of God has nothing to do with human parents. Children of God are not born because of human choice or because a husband wants them to be born. They are born because of what God does.

[14]The Word became a human being. He made his home with us. We have seen his glory. It is the glory of the One and Only.

He came from the Father. And he was full of grace and truth.

[15]John gives witness about him. He cries out and says, "This was the one I was talking about. I said, 'He who comes after me is more important than I am. He is more important because he was before me.'"

[16]We have all received one blessing after another. God's grace is not limited. [17]The law was given through Moses. Grace and truth came through Jesus Christ.

[18]No one has ever seen God. But God, the One and Only, is at the Father's side. He has shown us what God is like.

GREAT VERSE — TO — REMEMBER

1:1-2 In the beginning, the Word was already there. The Word was with God, and the Word was God. He was with God in the beginning.

John the Baptist Is Not the Christ

[19]The Jews of Jerusalem sent priests and Levites to ask John who he was. John gave witness to them. [20]He did not try to hide the truth. He spoke to them openly. He said, "I am not the Christ."

[21]They asked him, "Then who are you? Are you Elijah?"

He said, "I am not."

"Are you the Prophet we've been expecting?" they asked.

"No," he answered.

[22]They asked one last time, "Who are you? Give us an answer to take back to those who sent us. What do you say about yourself?"

[23]John replied, using the words of Isaiah the prophet. John said, "I am the voice of one calling in the desert, 'Make straight the way for the Lord.'" *(Isaiah 40:3)*

[24]Some Pharisees who had been sent [25]asked him, "If you are not the Christ, why are you baptizing people? Why, if you are not Elijah or the Prophet we've been expecting?"

[26]"I baptize with water," John replied. "But one is standing among you whom you do not know. [27]He is the one who comes after me. I am not good enough to untie his sandals."

[28]This all happened at Bethany on the other side of the Jordan River. That was where John was baptizing.

Jesus Is the Lamb of God

[29]The next day John saw Jesus coming toward him. John said, "Look! The Lamb of God! He takes away the sin of the world! [30]This is the one I was talking about. I said, 'A man who comes after me is more important than I am. That's because he was before me.' [31]I did not know him. But God wants to make it clear to Israel who this person is. That's the reason I came baptizing with water."

[32]Then John told them, "I saw the Holy Spirit come down from heaven like a dove. The Spirit remained on Jesus. [33]I would not have known him. But the one who sent me to baptize with water told me, 'You will see the Spirit come down and remain on someone. He is the one who will baptize with the Holy Spirit.' [34]I have seen it happen. I give witness that this is the Son of God."

Jesus Chooses the First Disciples

[35]The next day John was again with two of his disciples. [36]He saw Jesus walking by. John said, "Look! The Lamb of God!"

³⁷The two disciples heard him say this. So they followed Jesus.
³⁸Then Jesus turned around and saw them following. He asked, "What do you want?"

They said, "Rabbi, where are you staying?" *Rabbi* means Teacher.

³⁹"Come," he replied. "You will see."

So they went and saw where he was staying. They spent the rest of the day with him. It was about four o'clock in the afternoon.

⁴⁰Andrew was Simon Peter's brother. Andrew was one of the two disciples who heard what John had said. He had also followed Jesus. ⁴¹The first thing Andrew did was to find his brother Simon. He told him, "We have found the Messiah." Messiah means Christ. ⁴²And he brought Simon to Jesus.

Jesus looked at him and said, "You are Simon, son of John. You will be called Cephas." Cephas means Peter (or rock).

Jesus Chooses Philip and Nathanael

⁴³The next day Jesus decided to leave for Galilee. He found Philip and said to him, "Follow me."

⁴⁴Philip was from the town of Bethsaida. So were Andrew and Peter. ⁴⁵Philip found Nathanael and told him, "We have found the one that Moses wrote about in the Law. The prophets also wrote about him. He is Jesus of Nazareth, the son of Joseph."

⁴⁶"Nazareth! Can anything good come from there?" Nathanael asked.

"Come and see," said Philip.

⁴⁷Jesus saw Nathanael approaching. Here is what Jesus said about him. "He is a true Israelite. There is nothing false in him."

⁴⁸"How do you know me?" Nathanael asked.

Jesus answered, "I saw you while you were still under the fig tree. I saw you there before Philip called you."

⁴⁹Nathanael replied, "Rabbi, you are the Son of God. You are the King of Israel."

GREAT VERSE —TO— REMEMBER **1:41** The first thing Andrew did was to find his brother Simon. He told him, "We have found the Messiah."

⁵⁰Jesus said, "You believe because I told you I saw you under the fig tree. You will see greater things than that."

⁵¹Then he said to them, "What I'm about to tell you is true. You will see heaven open. You will see the angels of God going up and coming down on the Son of Man."

Jesus Changes Water Into Wine

2 On the third day there was a wedding. It took place at Cana in Galilee. Jesus' mother was there. ²Jesus and his disciples had also been invited to the wedding. ³When the wine was gone, Jesus' mother said to him, "They have no more wine."

⁴"Dear woman, why do you bring me into this?" Jesus replied. "My time has not yet come."

⁵His mother said to the servants, "Do what he tells you."

⁶Six stone water jars stood nearby. The Jews used water from that kind of jar for special washings to make themselves pure. Each jar could hold 20 to 30 gallons.

⁷Jesus said to the servants, "Fill the jars with water." So they filled them to the top.

⁸Then he told them, "Now dip some out. Take it to the person in charge of the dinner."

They did what he said. ⁹The person in charge tasted the water that had been turned into wine. He didn't realize where it had come from. But the servants who had brought the water knew.

Then the person in charge called the groom to one side. ¹⁰He said to him, "Everyone brings out the best wine first. They bring out the cheaper wine after the guests have had too much to drink. But you have saved the best till now."

¹¹That was the first of Jesus' miraculous signs. He did it at Cana in Galilee. Jesus showed his glory by doing it. And his disciples put their faith in him.

Jesus Clears Out the Temple

¹²After this, Jesus went down to Capernaum. His mother and brothers and disciples went with him. They all stayed there for a few days.

¹³It was almost time for the Jewish Passover Feast. So Jesus went up to Jerusalem. ¹⁴In the temple courtyard he found people who were selling cattle, sheep and doves. Others were sitting at tables exchanging money.

¹⁵So Jesus made a whip out of cords. He chased all the sheep and cattle from the temple area. He scattered the coins of the

people exchanging money. And he turned over their tables. ¹⁶He told those who were selling doves, "Get these out of here! How dare you turn my Father's house into a market!"

¹⁷His disciples remembered what had been written. It says, "My great love for your house will destroy me." *(Psalm 69:9)*

¹⁸Then the Jews asked him, "What miraculous sign can you show us? Can you prove your authority to do all of this?"

¹⁹Jesus answered them, "Destroy this temple. I will raise it up again in three days."

²⁰The Jews replied, "It has taken 46 years to build this temple. Are you going to raise it up in three days?"

²¹But the temple Jesus had spoken about was his body.

²²His disciples later remembered what he had said. That was after he had been raised from the dead. Then they believed the Scriptures. They also believed the words that Jesus had spoken.

²³Meanwhile, he was in Jerusalem at the Passover Feast. Many people saw the miraculous signs he was doing. And they believed in his name. ²⁴But Jesus did not fully trust them. He knew what people are like. ²⁵He didn't need others to tell him what people are like. He already knew what was in the human heart.

Jesus Teaches Nicodemus

3 There was a Pharisee named Nicodemus. He was one of the Jewish rulers. ²He came to Jesus at night and said, "Rabbi, we know you are a teacher who has come from God. We know that God is with you. If he weren't, you couldn't do the miraculous signs you are doing."

³Jesus replied, "What I'm about to tell you is true. No one can see God's kingdom without being born again."

⁴"How can I be born when I am old?" Nicodemus asked. "I can't go back inside my mother! I can't be born a second time!"

⁵Jesus answered, "What I'm about to tell you is true. No one can enter God's kingdom without being born through water and the Holy Spirit. ⁶People give birth to people. But the Spirit gives birth to spirit. ⁷You should not be surprised when I say, 'You must all be born again.'

⁸"The wind blows where it wants to. You hear its sound. But you can't tell where it comes from or where it is going. It is the same with everyone who is born through the Spirit."

⁹"How can this be?" Nicodemus asked.

¹⁰"You are Israel's teacher," said Jesus. "Don't you understand these things?

¹¹"What I'm about to tell you is true. We speak about what we know. We give witness to what we have seen. But still you people do not accept our witness. ¹²I have spoken to you about earthly things, and you do not believe. So how will you believe if I speak about heavenly things?

¹³"No one has ever gone into heaven except the One who came from heaven. He is the Son of Man. ¹⁴Moses lifted up the snake in the desert. The Son of Man must be lifted up also. ¹⁵Then everyone who believes in him can live with God forever.

¹⁶"God loved the world so much that he gave his one and only Son. Anyone who believes in him will not die but will have eternal life.

¹⁷"God did not send his Son into the world to judge the world. He sent his Son to save the world through him. ¹⁸Those who believe in him are not judged. But those who do not believe are judged already. They have not believed in the name of God's one and only Son.

¹⁹"Here is the judgment. Light has come into the world, but people loved darkness instead of light. They loved darkness because what they did was evil.

²⁰"All who do evil things hate the light. They will not come into the light. They are afraid that what they do will be seen. ²¹But those who live by the truth come into the light. They do this so that it will be easy to see that what they have done is with God's help."

John the Baptist Gives Witness About Jesus

²²After this, Jesus and his disciples went out into the countryside of Judea. There he spent some time with them. And he baptized people there.

²³John was also baptizing. He was at Aenon near Salim, where there was plenty of water. People were coming all the time to be baptized. ²⁴That was before John was put in prison.

3:16 God loved the world so much that he gave his one and only Son. Anyone who believes in him will not die but will have eternal life.

²⁵Some of John's disciples and a certain Jew began to argue. They argued about special washings to make people pure. ²⁶They came to John and said to him, "Rabbi, that man who was with you on the other side of the Jordan River is baptizing people. He is the one you gave witness about. Everyone is going to him."

²⁷John replied, "We can receive only what God gives us from heaven. ²⁸You yourselves are witnesses that I said, 'I am not the Christ. I was sent ahead of him.' ²⁹The bride belongs to the groom. The friend who helps the groom waits and listens for him. He is full of joy when he hears the groom's voice. That joy is mine, and it is now complete. ³⁰He must become more important. I must become less important.

³¹"The One who comes from above is above everything. The one who is from the earth belongs to the earth and speaks like someone from the earth. The One who comes from heaven is above everything. ³²He gives witness to what he has seen and heard. But no one accepts what he says. ³³The person who has accepted it has said, 'Yes. God is truthful.' ³⁴The One whom God has sent speaks God's words. God gives the Holy Spirit without limit.

³⁵"The Father loves the Son and has put everything into his hands. ³⁶Those who believe in the Son have eternal life. Those who say no to the Son will not have life. God's anger remains on them."

Jesus Talks With a Woman From Samaria

4 The Pharisees heard that Jesus was winning and baptizing more disciples than John. ²But in fact Jesus was not baptizing. His disciples were. ³When the Lord found out about all this, he left Judea. He went back to Galilee again.

⁴Jesus had to go through Samaria. ⁵He came to a town in Samaria called Sychar. It was near the piece of land Jacob had given his son Joseph. ⁶Jacob's well was there. Jesus was tired from the journey. So he sat down by the well. It was about noon.

⁷A woman from Samaria came to get some water. Jesus said to her, "Will you give me a drink?" ⁸His disciples had gone into the town to buy food.

⁹The Samaritan woman said to him, "You are a Jew. I am a Samaritan woman. How can you ask me for a drink?" She said this because Jews don't have anything to do with Samaritans.

¹⁰Jesus answered her, "You do not know what God's gift is. And you do not know who is asking you for a drink. If you did, you

would have asked him. He would have given you living water."

¹¹"Sir," the woman said, "you don't have anything to get water with. The well is deep. Where can you get this living water?

¹²"Our father Jacob gave us the well. He drank from it himself. So did his sons and his flocks and herds. Are you more important than he is?"

¹³Jesus answered, "All who drink this water will be thirsty again. ¹⁴But those who drink the water I give them will never thirst. In fact, the water I give them will become a spring of water in them. It will flow up into eternal life."

¹⁵The woman said to him, "Sir, give me this water. Then I will never be thirsty. And I won't have to keep coming here to get water."

¹⁶He told her, "Go. Get your husband and come back."

¹⁷"I have no husband," she replied.

Jesus said to her, "You are right when you say you have no husband. ¹⁸The fact is, you have had five husbands. And the man you have now is not your husband. What you have just said is very true."

¹⁹"Sir," the woman said, "I can see that you are a prophet. ²⁰Our people have worshiped on this mountain for a long time. But you Jews claim that the place where we must worship is in Jerusalem."

²¹Jesus said, "Believe me, woman. A time is coming when you will not worship the Father on this mountain or in Jerusalem. ²²You Samaritans worship what you do not know. We worship what we do know. Salvation comes from the Jews.

²³"But a new time is coming. In fact, it is already here. True worshipers will worship the Father in spirit and in truth. They are the kind of worshipers the Father is looking for.

²⁴"God is spirit. His worshipers must worship in spirit and in truth."

²⁵The woman said, "I know that Messiah is coming." (He is called Christ.) "When he comes, he will explain everything to us."

²⁶Then Jesus said, "I, the one speaking to you, am he."

GREAT VERSE —TO— REMEMBER   **4:24** God is spirit. His worshipers must worship in spirit and in truth.

The Disciples Join Jesus Again

²⁷Just then Jesus' disciples returned. They were surprised to find him talking with a woman. But no one asked, "What do you want?" No one asked, "Why are you talking with her?"

²⁸The woman left her water jar and went back to the town. She said to the people, ²⁹"Come. See a man who told me everything I've ever done. Could this be the Christ?"

³⁰The people came out of the town and made their way toward Jesus.

³¹His disciples were saying to him, "Rabbi, eat something!"

³²But he said to them, "I have food to eat that you know nothing about."

³³Then his disciples asked each other, "Did someone bring him food?"

³⁴Jesus said, "My food is to do what my Father sent me to do. My food is to finish his work.

³⁵"You say, 'Four months more, and then it will be harvest time.' But I tell you, open your eyes! Look at the fields! They are ripe for harvest right now. ³⁶Those who gather the crop are already getting paid. They are already harvesting the crop for eternal life. So those who plant and those who gather can now be glad together.

³⁷"Here is a true saying. 'One plants and another gathers.' ³⁸I sent you to gather what you have not worked for. Others have done the hard work. You have gathered the benefits of their work."

Many Samaritans Believe in Jesus

³⁹Many of the Samaritans from the town of Sychar believed in Jesus. They believed because of the woman's witness. She said, "He told me everything I've ever done."

⁴⁰Then the Samaritans came to him and tried to get him to stay with them. So he stayed two days. ⁴¹Because of his words, many more people became believers.

⁴²They said to the woman, "We no longer believe just because of what you said. We have now heard for ourselves. We know that this man really is the Savior of the world."

Jesus Heals the Official's Son

⁴³After the two days, Jesus left for Galilee. ⁴⁴He himself had pointed out that prophets are not respected in their own coun-

try. ⁴⁵When he arrived in Galilee, the people living there welcomed him. They had seen everything he had done in Jerusalem at the Passover Feast. That was because they had also been there.

⁴⁶Once more, Jesus visited Cana in Galilee. Cana is where he had turned the water into wine. A royal official was there. His son was sick in bed at Capernaum. ⁴⁷The official heard that Jesus had arrived in Galilee from Judea. So he went to Jesus and begged him to come and heal his son. The boy was close to death.

⁴⁸Jesus told him, "You people will never believe unless you see miraculous signs and wonders."

⁴⁹The royal official said, "Sir, come down before my child dies."

⁵⁰Jesus replied, "You may go. Your son will live."

The man believed what Jesus said, and so he left. ⁵¹While he was still on his way home, his servants met him. They gave him the news that his boy was living. ⁵²He asked what time his son got better. They said to him, "The fever left him yesterday afternoon at one o'clock."

⁵³Then the father realized what had happened. That was the exact time Jesus had said to him, "Your son will live." So he and all his family became believers.

⁵⁴This was the second miraculous sign that Jesus did after coming from Judea to Galilee.

Jesus Heals a Disabled Man

5 Some time later, Jesus went up to Jerusalem for a Jewish feast. ²In Jerusalem near the Sheep Gate is a pool. In the Aramaic language it is called Bethesda. It is surrounded by five rows of columns with a roof. ³/⁴Here a great number of disabled people used to lie down. Among them were the blind, those who could not walk, and those who could hardly move.

⁵One person who was there had been disabled for 38 years. ⁶Jesus saw him lying there. He knew that the man had been in that condition for a long time. So he asked him, "Do you want to get well?"

⁷"Sir," the disabled man replied, "I have no one to help me into the pool when the water is stirred. I try to get in, but someone else always goes down ahead of me."

⁸Then Jesus said to him, "Get up! Pick up your mat and walk."

⁹At once the man was healed. He picked up his mat and walked.

The day this happened was a Sabbath. ¹⁰So the Jews said to the man who had been healed, "It is the Sabbath. The law does not allow you to carry your mat."

¹¹But he replied, "The one who made me well said to me, 'Pick up your mat and walk.'"

¹²They asked him, "Who is this fellow? Who told you to pick it up and walk?"

¹³The one who was healed had no idea who it was. Jesus had slipped away into the crowd that was there.

¹⁴Later Jesus found him at the temple. Jesus said to him, "See, you are well again. Stop sinning, or something worse may happen to you." ¹⁵The man went away. He told the Jews it was Jesus who had made him well.

Life Because of the Son

¹⁶Jesus was doing these things on the Sabbath day. So the Jews began to oppose him.

¹⁷Jesus said to them, "My Father is always doing his work. He is working right up to this very day. I am working too."

¹⁸For this reason the Jews tried even harder to kill him. Jesus was not only breaking the Sabbath. He was even calling God his own Father. He was making himself equal with God.

¹⁹Jesus answered, "What I'm about to tell you is true. The Son can do nothing by himself. He can do only what he sees his Father doing. What the Father does, the Son also does. ²⁰This is because the Father loves the Son. He shows him everything he does. Yes, you will be amazed! The Father will show him even greater things than these.

²¹"The Father raises the dead and gives them life. In the same way, the Son gives life to anyone he wants to.

²²"Also, the Father does not judge anyone. He has given the Son the task of judging. ²³Then all people will honor the Son just as they honor the Father. Those who do not honor the Son do not honor the Father, who sent him.

²⁴"What I'm about to tell you is true. Those who hear my word

GREAT VERSE — TO — REMEMBER

5:24-25 Those who hear my word and believe him who sent me have eternal life. They will not be found guilty. They have crossed over from death to life.

and believe him who sent me have eternal life. They will not be found guilty. They have crossed over from death to life.

²⁵"What I'm about to tell you is true. A time is coming for me to give life. In fact, it has already begun. The dead will hear the voice of the Son of God. Those who hear it will live.

²⁶"The Father has life in himself. He has also allowed the Son to have life in himself. ²⁷And the Father has given him the authority to judge. This is because he is the Son of Man.

²⁸"Do not be amazed at this. A time is coming when all who are in the grave will hear his voice. ²⁹They will all come out of their graves. Those who have done good will rise and live again. Those who have done evil will rise and be found guilty.

³⁰"I can do nothing by myself. I judge only as I hear. And my judging is fair. I do not try to please myself. I try only to please the One who sent me.

Giving Witness About Jesus

³¹"If I give witness about myself, it doesn't count. ³²There is someone else who gives witness in my favor. And I know that his witness about me counts.

³³"You have sent people to John. He has given witness to the truth. ³⁴I do not accept human witness. I only talk about it so you can be saved. ³⁵John was a lamp that burned and gave light. For a while you chose to enjoy his light.

³⁶"The witness I have is more important than John's. I am doing the very work the Father gave me to finish. It gives witness that the Father has sent me.

³⁷"The Father who sent me has himself given witness about me. You have never heard his voice. You have never seen what he really looks like. ³⁸And his word does not live in you. This is because you do not believe the one he sent.

³⁹"You study the Scriptures carefully. You study them because you think they will give you eternal life. The Scriptures you study give witness about me. ⁴⁰But you refuse to come to me to have life.

⁴¹"I do not accept praise from people. ⁴²But I know you. I know that you do not have love for God in your hearts. ⁴³I have come in my Father's name, and you do not accept me. But if others come in their own name, you will accept them.

⁴⁴"You accept praise from one another. But you make no effort to receive the praise that comes from the only God. So how can you believe?

⁴⁵"Do not think I will bring charges against you in front of the Father. Moses is the one who does that. And he is the one you build your hopes on.

⁴⁶"Do you believe Moses? Then you should believe me. He wrote about me. ⁴⁷But you do not believe what he wrote. So how are you going to believe what I say?"

Jesus Feeds the Five Thousand

6 Some time after this, Jesus crossed over to the other side of the Sea of Galilee. It is also called the Sea of Tiberias. ²A large crowd of people followed him. They had seen the miraculous signs he had done on those who were sick.

³Then Jesus went up on a mountainside. There he sat down with his disciples. ⁴The Jewish Passover Feast was near.

⁵Jesus looked up and saw a large crowd coming toward him. So he said to Philip, "Where can we buy bread for these people to eat?" ⁶He asked this only to put Philip to the test. He already knew what he was going to do.

⁷Philip answered him, "Eight months' pay would not buy enough bread for each one to have a bite!"

⁸Another of his disciples spoke up. It was Andrew, Simon Peter's brother. ⁹He said, "Here is a boy with five small loaves of barley bread. He also has two small fish. But how far will that go in such a large crowd?"

¹⁰Jesus said, "Have the people sit down." There was plenty of grass in that place, and they sat down. The number of men among them was about 5,000.

¹¹Then Jesus took the loaves and gave thanks. He handed out the bread to those who were seated. He gave them as much as they wanted. And he did the same with the fish.

¹²When all of them had enough to eat, Jesus spoke to his disciples. "Gather the leftover pieces," he said. "Don't waste anything."

¹³So they gathered what was left over from the five barley loaves. They filled 12 baskets with the pieces left by those who had eaten.

¹⁴The people saw the miraculous sign that Jesus did. Then they began to say, "This must be the Prophet who is supposed to come into the world." ¹⁵But Jesus knew that they planned to come and force him to be their king. So he went away again to a mountain by himself.

Jesus Walks on the Water

[16]When evening came, Jesus' disciples went down to the lake. [17]There they got into a boat and headed across the lake toward Capernaum. By now it was dark. Jesus had not yet joined them.

[18]A strong wind was blowing, and the water became rough. [19]They rowed three or three and a half miles. Then they saw Jesus coming toward the boat. He was walking on the water. They were terrified.

[20]But he said to them, "It is I. Don't be afraid."

[21]Then they agreed to take him into the boat. Right away the boat reached the shore where they were heading.

[22]The next day the crowd that had stayed on the other side of the lake realized something. They saw that only one boat had been there. They knew that Jesus had not gotten into it with his disciples. And they knew that the disciples had gone away alone.

[23]Then some boats from Tiberias landed. It was near the place where the people had eaten the bread after the Lord gave thanks. [24]The crowd realized that Jesus and his disciples were not there. So they got into boats and went to Capernaum to look for Jesus.

Jesus Is the Bread of Life

[25]They found him on the other side of the lake. They asked him, "Rabbi, when did you get here?"

[26]Jesus answered, "What I'm about to tell you is true. You are not looking for me because you saw miraculous signs. You are looking for me because you ate the loaves until you were full. [27]Do not work for food that spoils. Work for food that lasts forever. That is the food the Son of Man will give you. God the Father has put his seal of approval on him."

[28]Then they asked him, "What does God want from us? What works does he want us to do?"

[29]Jesus answered, "God's work is to believe in the One he has sent."

[30]So they asked him, "What miraculous sign will you give us? What will you do so we can see it and believe you? [31]Long ago our people ate the manna in the desert. It is written in Scripture: 'He gave them bread from heaven to eat.'" *(Exodus 16:4; Nehemiah 9:15; Psalm 78:24,25)*

[32]Jesus said to them, "What I'm about to tell you is true. It is not Moses who has given you the bread from heaven. It is my Father who gives you the true bread from heaven. [33]The bread of God is the one who comes down from heaven. He gives life to the world."

³⁴"Sir," they said, "give us this bread from now on."

³⁵Then Jesus said, "I am the bread of life. No one who comes to me will ever go hungry. And no one who believes in me will ever be thirsty.

³⁶"But it is just as I told you. You have seen me, and you still do not believe. ³⁷Everyone the Father gives me will come to me. I will never send away anyone who comes to me.

³⁸"I have not come down from heaven to do what I want to do. I have come to do what the One who sent me wants me to do. ³⁹The One who sent me doesn't want me to lose anyone he has given me. He wants me to raise them up on the last day. ⁴⁰My father wants all who look to the Son and believe in him to have eternal life. I will raise them up on the last day."

⁴¹Then the Jews began to complain about Jesus. That was because he said, "I am the bread that came down from heaven." ⁴²They said, "Isn't this Jesus, the son of Joseph? Don't we know his father and mother? How can he now say, 'I came down from heaven'?"

⁴³"Stop complaining among yourselves," Jesus answered. ⁴⁴"People can't come to me unless the Father who sent me brings them. Then I will raise them up on the last day.

⁴⁵"It is written in the Prophets: 'They will all be taught by God.' *(Isaiah 54:13)* Everyone who listens to the Father and learns from him comes to me.

⁴⁶"No one has seen the Father except the One who has come from God. Only he has seen the Father. ⁴⁷What I'm about to tell you is true. Everyone who believes has life forever.

⁴⁸"I am the bread of life. ⁴⁹Long ago your people ate the manna in the desert, and they still died. ⁵⁰But here is the bread that comes down from heaven. People can eat it and not die. ⁵¹I am the living bread that came down from heaven. Everyone who eats some of this bread will live forever. The bread is my body. I will give it for the life of the world."

GREAT VERSE —TO— REMEMBER

6:35 Jesus said, "I am the bread of life. No one who comes to me will ever go hungry. And no one who believes in me will ever be thirsty."

⁵²Then the Jews began to argue sharply among themselves. They said, "How can this man give us his body to eat?"

⁵³Jesus said to them, "What I'm about to tell you is true. You must eat the Son of Man's body and drink his blood. If you don't, you have no life in you. ⁵⁴Those who eat my body and drink my blood have eternal life. I will raise them up on the last day.

⁵⁵"My body is real food. My blood is real drink. ⁵⁶Those who eat my body and drink my blood remain in me. And I remain in them.

⁵⁷"The living Father sent me, and I live because of him. In the same way, those who feed on me will live because of me. ⁵⁸This is the bread that came down from heaven. Long ago your people ate manna and died. But those who feed on this bread will live forever."

⁵⁹He said this while he was teaching in the synagogue in Capernaum.

Many Disciples Leave Jesus

⁶⁰Jesus' disciples heard this. Many of them said, "This is a hard teaching. Who can accept it?"

⁶¹Jesus was aware that his disciples were complaining about this. So he said to them, "Does this upset you? ⁶²What if you see the Son of Man go up to where he was before? ⁶³The Holy Spirit gives life. The body means nothing at all. The words I have spoken to you are spirit. They are also life. ⁶⁴But there are some of you who do not believe."

Jesus had known from the beginning which of them did not believe. And he had known who was going to hand him over to his enemies. ⁶⁵So he continued speaking. He said, "This is why I told you that people can't come to me unless the Father helps them."

⁶⁶From this time on, many of his disciples turned back. They no longer followed him.

GREAT VERSE —TO— REMEMBER   **6:68-69** Lord, who can we go to? You have the words of eternal life. We believe and know that you are the Holy One of God.

[67]"You don't want to leave also, do you?" Jesus asked the Twelve.

[68]Simon Peter answered him, "Lord, who can we go to? You have the words of eternal life. [69]We believe and know that you are the Holy One of God."

[70]Then Jesus replied, "Didn't I choose you, the 12 disciples? But one of you is a devil!" [71]He meant Judas, the son of Simon Iscariot. Judas was one of the Twelve. But later he was going to hand Jesus over to his enemies.

Jesus Goes to the Feast of Booths

7 After this, Jesus went around in Galilee. He stayed away from Judea on purpose. He knew that the Jews there were waiting to kill him.

[2]The Jewish Feast of Booths was near. [3]Jesus' brothers said to him, "You should leave here and go to Judea. Then your disciples will see the kinds of things you do. [4]No one who wants to be well known does things in secret. Since you are doing these things, show yourself to the world." [5]Even Jesus' own brothers did not believe in him.

[6]So Jesus told them, "The right time has not yet come for me. For you, any time is right. [7]The people of the world can't hate you. But they hate me. This is because I give witness that what they do is evil.

[8]"You go to the Feast. I am not yet going up to this Feast. For me, the right time has not yet come."

[9]After he said this, he stayed in Galilee.

[10]When his brothers had left for the Feast, he went also. But he went secretly, not openly. [11]At the Feast the Jews were watching for him. They were asking, "Where is he?"

[12]Many people in the crowd were whispering about him. Some said, "He is a good man."

Others replied, "No. He fools the people."

[13]But no one would say anything about him openly. They were afraid of the Jews.

Jesus Teaches at the Feast

[14]Jesus did nothing until halfway through the Feast. Then he went up to the temple courtyard and began to teach. [15]The Jews were amazed. They asked, "How did this man learn so much without studying?"

[16]Jesus answered, "What I teach is not my own. It comes from

him who sent me. [17]Those who choose to do what God wants them to do will find out whether my teaching comes from God or from me. [18]Those who speak on their own do it to get honor for themselves. But he who works for the honor of the one who sent him is truthful. There is nothing false about him.

[19]"Didn't Moses give you the law? But not one of you keeps the law. Why are you trying to kill me?"

[20]"You are controlled by demons," the crowd answered. "Who is trying to kill you?"

[21]Jesus said to them, "I did one miracle, and you are all amazed. [22]Moses gave you circumcision, and so you circumcise a child on the Sabbath day. But circumcision did not really come from Moses. It came from Abraham. [23]You circumcise a child on the Sabbath day. You think that if you do, you won't break the law of Moses. Then why are you angry with me? I healed a whole person on the Sabbath!

[24]"Stop judging only by what you see. Judge correctly."

Is Jesus the Christ?

[25]Then some of the people of Jerusalem began asking questions. They said, "Isn't this the man they are trying to kill? [26]Here he is! He is speaking openly. They aren't saying a word to him. Have the authorities really decided that he is the Christ? [27]But we know where this man is from. When the Christ comes, no one will know where he is from."

[28]Jesus was still teaching in the temple courtyard. He cried out, "Yes, you know me. And you know where I am from. I am not here on my own. He who sent me is true. You do not know him. [29]But I know him. I am from him, and he sent me."

[30]When he said this, they tried to arrest him. But no one laid a hand on him. His time had not yet come.

[31]Still, many people in the crowd put their faith in him. They said, "How will it be when the Christ comes? Will he do more miraculous signs than this man?"

[32]The Pharisees heard the crowd whispering things like this about him. Then the chief priests and the Pharisees sent temple guards to arrest him.

[33]Jesus said, "I am with you for only a short time. Then I will go to the One who sent me. [34]You will look for me, but you won't find me. You can't come where I am going."

[35]The Jews said to one another, "Where does this man plan to go? Does he think we can't find him? Will he go where our peo-

ple live scattered among the Greeks? Will he go there to teach the Greeks? [36]What did he mean when he said, 'You will look for me, but you won't find me'? And, 'You can't come where I am going'?"

[37]It was the last and most important day of the Feast. Jesus stood up and spoke in a loud voice. He said, "Let anyone who is thirsty come to me and drink. [38]Does anyone believe in me? Then, just as Scripture says, streams of living water will flow from inside the one who believes."

[39]When he said this, he meant the Holy Spirit. Those who believed in Jesus would receive the Spirit later. Up to that time, the Spirit had not been given. This was because Jesus had not yet received glory.

[40]When some of the people heard his words, they said, "This man must be the Prophet we've been expecting."

[41]Others said, "He is the Christ."

Still others asked, "How can the Christ come from Galilee? [42]Doesn't Scripture say that the Christ will come from David's family? Doesn't it say that he will come from Bethlehem, the town where David lived?"

[43]So the people did not agree about who Jesus was. [44]Some wanted to arrest him. But no one laid a hand on him.

The Jewish Leaders Do Not Believe

[45]Finally the temple guards went back to the chief priests and the Pharisees. They asked the guards, "Why didn't you bring him in?"

[46]"No one ever spoke the way this man does," the guards said.

[47]"You mean he has fooled you also?" the Pharisees replied. [48]"Have any of the rulers or Pharisees believed in him? [49]No! But this mob knows nothing about the law. There is a curse on them."

[50]Then Nicodemus, a Pharisee, spoke. He was the one who had gone to Jesus earlier. He asked, [51]"Does our law find people guilty without hearing them first? Doesn't it want to find out what they are doing?"

[52]They replied, "Are you from Galilee too? Look into it. You will find that a prophet does not come out of Galilee."

---

[53]Then each of them went home.

8 But Jesus went to the Mount of Olives. [2]At sunrise he arrived in the temple courtyard again. All the people gathered around him there. He sat down to teach them.

³The teachers of the law and the Pharisees brought in a woman. She had been caught in adultery. They made her stand in front of the group. ⁴They said to Jesus, "Teacher, this woman was caught having sex with a man who was not her husband. ⁵In the Law, Moses commanded us to kill such women by throwing stones at them. Now what do you say?" ⁶They were trying to trap Jesus with that question. They wanted to have a reason to bring charges against him.

But Jesus bent down and started to write on the ground with his finger.

⁷They kept asking him questions. So he stood up and said to them, "Has any one of you not sinned? Then you be the first to throw a stone at her."

⁸He bent down again and wrote on the ground.

⁹Those who heard began to go away. They left one at a time, the older ones first. Soon only Jesus was left. The woman was still standing there.

¹⁰Jesus stood up and asked her, "Woman, where are they? Hasn't anyone found you guilty?"

¹¹"No one, sir," she said.

"Then I don't find you guilty either," Jesus said. "Go now and leave your life of sin."

Jesus' Witness Is True

¹²Jesus spoke to the people again. He said, "I am the light of the world. Those who follow me will never walk in darkness. They will have the light that leads to life."

¹³The Pharisees argued with him. "Here you are," they said, "appearing as your own witness. But your witness does not count."

¹⁴Jesus answered, "Even if I give witness about myself, my witness does count. I know where I came from. And I know where I

GREAT VERSE —TO— REMEMBER

8:12 I am the light of the world. Those who follow me will never walk in darkness. They will have the light that leads to life.

am going. But you have no idea where I come from or where I am going. ¹⁵You judge by human standards. I don't judge anyone.

¹⁶"But if I do judge, what I decide is right. This is because I am not alone. I stand with the Father, who sent me. ¹⁷Your own Law says that the witness of two is what counts. ¹⁸I give witness about myself. My other witness is the Father, who sent me."

¹⁹Then they asked him, "Where is your father?"

"You do not know me or my Father," Jesus replied. "If you knew me, you would know my Father also."

²⁰He spoke these words while he was teaching in the temple area. He was near the place where the offerings were put. But no one arrested him. His time had not yet come.

²¹Once more Jesus spoke to them. "I am going away," he said. "You will look for me, and you will die in your sin. You can't come where I am going."

²²This made the Jews ask, "Will he kill himself? Is that why he says, 'You can't come where I am going'?"

²³But Jesus said, "You are from below. I am from above. You are from this world. I am not from this world. ²⁴I told you that you would die in your sins. Do you believe that I am the one I claim to be? If you don't, you will certainly die in your sins."

²⁵"Who are you?" they asked.

"Just what I have been claiming all along," Jesus replied. ²⁶"I have a lot to say that will judge you. But he who sent me can be trusted. And I tell the world what I have heard from him."

²⁷They did not understand that Jesus was telling them about his Father. ²⁸So Jesus said, "You will lift up the Son of Man. Then you will know that I am the one I claim to be. You will also know that I do nothing on my own. I speak just what the Father has taught me. ²⁹The one who sent me is with me. He has not left me alone, because I always do what pleases him."

³⁰Even while Jesus was speaking, many people put their faith in him.

The Children of Abraham

³¹Jesus spoke to the Jews who had believed him. "If you obey my teaching," he said, "you are really my disciples. ³²Then you will know the truth. And the truth will set you free."

³³They answered him, "We are Abraham's children. We have never been slaves of anyone. So how can you say that we will be set free?"

³⁴Jesus replied, "What I'm about to tell you is true. Everyone

who sins is a slave of sin. [35]A slave has no lasting place in the family. But a son belongs to the family forever. [36]So if the Son of Man sets you free, you will really be free.

[37]"I know you are Abraham's children. But you are ready to kill me. You have no room for my word. [38]I am telling you what I saw when I was with my Father. You do what you have heard from your father."

[39]"Abraham is our father," they answered.

Jesus said, "Are you Abraham's children? If you are, you will do the things Abraham did. [40]But you have decided to kill me. I am a man who has told you the truth I heard from God. Abraham didn't do the things you want to do. [41]You are doing the things your own father does."

"We are not children of people who weren't married to each other," they objected. "The only Father we have is God himself."

The Children of the Devil

[42]Jesus said to them, "If God were your Father, you would love me. I came from God, and now I am here. I have not come on my own. He sent me.

[43]"Why aren't my words clear to you? Because you can't really hear what I say. [44]You belong to your father, the devil. You want to obey your father's wishes.

"From the beginning, the devil was a murderer. He has never obeyed the truth. There is no truth in him. When he lies, he speaks his natural language. He does this because he is a liar. He is the father of lies.

[45]"But because I tell the truth, you don't believe me! [46]Can any of you prove I am guilty of sinning? Am I not telling the truth? Then why don't you believe me?

[47]"Those who belong to God hear what God says. The reason you don't hear is that you don't belong to God."

Jesus Makes Claims About Himself

[48]The Jews answered Jesus, "Aren't we right when we say you are a Samaritan? Aren't you controlled by a demon?"

[49]"I am not controlled by a demon," said Jesus. "I honor my Father. You do not honor me. [50]I am not seeking glory for myself. But there is one who seeks it. He is the judge. [51]What I'm about to tell you is true. Those who obey my word will never see death."

[52]Then the Jews cried out, "Now we know you are controlled

by a demon! Abraham died. So did the prophets. But you say that those who obey your word will never die. ⁵³Are you greater than our father Abraham? He died. So did the prophets. Who do you think you are?"

⁵⁴Jesus replied, "If I bring glory to myself, my glory means nothing. You claim that my Father is your God. He is the one who brings glory to me. ⁵⁵You do not know him. But I know him. If I said I did not, I would be a liar like you. But I do know him. And I obey his word.

⁵⁶"Your father Abraham was filled with joy at the thought of seeing my day. He saw it and was glad."

⁵⁷"You are not even 50 years old," the Jews said to Jesus. "And you have seen Abraham?"

⁵⁸"What I'm about to tell you is true," Jesus answered. "Before Abraham was born, I am!"

⁵⁹When he said this, they picked up stones to kill him. But Jesus hid himself. He slipped away from the temple area.

Jesus Heals a Man Born Blind

9 As Jesus went along, he saw a blind man. He had been blind since he was born. ²Jesus' disciples asked him, "Rabbi, who sinned? Was this man born blind because he sinned? Or did his parents sin?"

³"It isn't because this man sinned," said Jesus. "It isn't because his parents sinned. This happened so that God's work could be shown in his life. ⁴While it is still day, we must do the work of the One who sent me. Night is coming. Then no one can work. ⁵While I am in the world, I am the light of the world."

⁶After he said this, he spit on the ground. He made some mud with the spit. Then he put the mud on the man's eyes.

⁷"Go," he told him. "Wash in the Pool of Siloam." Siloam means Sent.

So the man went and washed. And he came home able to see.

⁸His neighbors and those who had earlier seen him begging asked questions. "Isn't this the same man who used to sit and beg?" they asked.

9:5 While I am in the world, I am the light of the world.

⁹Some claimed that he was.

Others said, "No. He only looks like him."

But the man who had been blind kept saying, "I am the man."

¹⁰"Then how were your eyes opened?" they asked.

¹¹He replied, "The man they call Jesus made some mud and put it on my eyes. He told me to go to Siloam and wash. So I went and washed. Then I could see."

¹²"Where is this man?" they asked him.

"I don't know," he said.

The Pharisees Want to Know What Happened

¹³They brought to the Pharisees the man who had been blind. ¹⁴The day Jesus made the mud and opened the man's eyes was a Sabbath. ¹⁵So the Pharisees also asked him how he was able to see.

"He put mud on my eyes," the man replied. "Then I washed. And now I can see."

¹⁶Some of the Pharisees said, "This man has not come from God. He does not keep the Sabbath day."

But others asked, "How can a sinner do such miraculous signs?"

So the Pharisees did not agree with each other.

¹⁷Finally they turned again to the blind man. "What do you have to say about him?" they asked. "It was your eyes he opened."

The man replied, "He is a prophet."

¹⁸The Jews still did not believe that the man had been blind and now could see. So they sent for his parents. ¹⁹"Is this your son?" they asked. "Is this the one you say was born blind? How is it that now he can see?"

²⁰"We know he is our son," the parents answered. "And we know he was born blind. ²¹But we don't know how he can now see. And we don't know who opened his eyes. Ask him. He is an adult. He can speak for himself."

²²His parents said this because they were afraid of the Jews. The Jews had already decided that anyone who said Jesus was the Christ would be put out of the synagogue. ²³That was why the man's parents said, "He is an adult. Ask him."

²⁴Again they called the man who had been blind to come to them. "Give glory to God by telling the truth!" they said. "We know that the man who healed you is a sinner."

²⁵He replied, "I don't know if he is a sinner or not. I do know one thing. I was blind, but now I can see!"

²⁶Then they asked him, "What did he do to you? How did he open your eyes?"

²⁷He answered, "I have already told you. But you didn't listen. Why do you want to hear it again? Do you want to become his disciples too?"

²⁸Then they began to attack him with their words. "You are this fellow's disciple!" they said. "We are disciples of Moses! ²⁹We know that God spoke to Moses. But we don't even know where this fellow comes from."

³⁰The man answered, "That is really surprising! You don't know where he comes from, and yet he opened my eyes. ³¹We know that God does not listen to sinners. He listens to godly people who do what he wants them to do. ³²Nobody has ever heard of anyone opening the eyes of a person born blind. ³³If this man had not come from God, he could do nothing."

³⁴Then the Pharisees replied, "When you were born, you were already deep in sin. How dare you talk like that to us!" And they threw him out.

The Blind Will See

³⁵Jesus heard that the Pharisees had thrown the man out. When he found him, he said, "Do you believe in the Son of Man?"

³⁶"Who is he, sir?" the man asked. "Tell me, so I can believe in him."

³⁷Jesus said, "You have now seen him. In fact, he is the one speaking with you."

³⁸Then the man said, "Lord, I believe." And he worshiped him.

³⁹Jesus said, "I have come into this world to judge it. I have come so that the blind will see and those who see will become blind."

⁴⁰Some Pharisees who were with him heard him say this. They asked, "What? Are we blind too?"

⁴¹Jesus said, "If you were blind, you would not be guilty of sin. But since you claim you can see, you remain guilty.

The Shepherd and the Flock

10 "What I'm about to tell you is true. What if someone does not enter the sheep pen through the gate but climbs in another way? That person is a thief and a robber. ²The one who enters through the gate is the shepherd of the sheep. ³The gatekeeper opens the gate for him. The sheep listen to his voice. He calls his own sheep by name and leads them out. ⁴When he has brought all of his own sheep out, he goes on ahead of them. His sheep follow him because they know his voice. ⁵But they will never follow a stranger. In fact, they will run away from him. They don't recognize a stranger's voice."

⁶Jesus used this story. But they did not understand what he was telling them.

⁷So Jesus said again, "What I'm about to tell you is true. I am the gate for the sheep. ⁸All who ever came before me were thieves and robbers. But the sheep did not listen to them. ⁹I am the gate. Those who enter through me will be saved. They will come in and go out. And they will find plenty of food. ¹⁰The thief comes only to steal and kill and destroy. I have come so they can have life. I want them to have it in the fullest possible way.

¹¹"I am the good shepherd. The good shepherd gives his life for the sheep. ¹²The hired man is not the shepherd who owns the sheep. So when the hired man sees the wolf coming, he leaves the sheep and runs away. Then the wolf attacks the flock and scatters it. ¹³The man runs away because he is a hired man. He does not care about the sheep.

¹⁴"I am the good shepherd. I know my sheep, and my sheep know me. ¹⁵They know me just as the Father knows me and I know the Father. And I give my life for the sheep.

¹⁶"I have other sheep that do not belong to this sheep pen. I must bring them too. They also will listen to my voice. Then there will be one flock and one shepherd.

¹⁷"The reason my Father loves me is that I give up my life. But I will take it back again. ¹⁸No one takes it from me. I give it up myself. I have the authority to give it up. And I have the authority to take it back again. I received this command from my Father."

¹⁹After Jesus spoke these words, the Jews again could not agree with each other. ²⁰Many of them said, "He is controlled by a demon. He has gone crazy! Why should we listen to him?"

²¹But others said, "A person controlled by a demon does not say things like this. Can a demon open the eyes of the blind?"

GREAT VERSE —TO— REMEMBER

10:27 My sheep listen to my voice. I know them, and they follow me.

The Jews Do Not Believe

²²Then came the Feast of Hanukkah at Jerusalem. It was winter. ²³Jesus was in the temple area walking in Solomon's Porch. ²⁴The Jews gathered around him. They said, "How long will you keep us waiting? If you are the Christ, tell us plainly."

²⁵Jesus answered, "I did tell you. But you do not believe. The kinds of things I do in my Father's name speak for me. ²⁶But you do not believe, because you are not my sheep.

²⁷"My sheep listen to my voice. I know them, and they follow me. ²⁸I give them eternal life, and they will never die. No one can steal them out of my hand. ²⁹My Father, who has given them to me, is greater than anyone. No one can steal them out of my Father's hand. ³⁰I and the Father are one."

³¹Again the Jews picked up stones to kill him.

³²But Jesus said to them, "I have shown you many miracles from the Father. Which one of these are you throwing stones at me for?"

³³"We are not throwing stones at you for any of these," replied the Jews. "We are stoning you for saying a very evil thing. You are only a human being. But you claim to be God."

³⁴Jesus answered them, "Isn't it written in your Law, 'I have said you are gods'? *(Psalm 82:6)* ³⁵We know that Scripture can't be broken. God's word came to some people, and he called them 'gods.' ³⁶If that is true, what about the One the Father set apart as his very own and sent into the world? Why do you charge me with saying a very evil thing? Is it because I said, 'I am God's Son'?

³⁷"Don't believe me unless I do what my Father does. ³⁸But what if I do it? Even if you don't believe me, believe the miracles. Then you will know and understand that the Father is in me and I am in the Father."

³⁹Again they tried to arrest him. But he escaped from them.

⁴⁰Then Jesus went back across the Jordan River. He went to the place where John had been baptizing in the early days. There he stayed. ⁴¹Many people came to him. They said, "John never did a miraculous sign. But everything he said about this man was true." ⁴²And in that place many believed in Jesus.

Lazarus Dies

11 A man named Lazarus was sick. He was from Bethany, the village where Mary and her sister Martha lived. ²Mary was the one who had poured perfume on the Lord. She had also wiped his feet with her hair. Her brother Lazarus was sick in bed.

³So the sisters sent a message to Jesus. "Lord," they told him, "the one you love is sick."

⁴When Jesus heard this, he said, "This sickness will not end in death. No, it is for God's glory. God's Son will receive glory because of it."

⁵Jesus loved Martha and her sister and Lazarus. ⁶But after he heard Lazarus was sick, he stayed where he was for two more days.

⁷Then he said to his disciples, "Let us go back to Judea."

⁸"But Rabbi," they said, "a short time ago the Jews tried to kill you with stones. Are you still going back there?"

⁹Jesus answered, "Aren't there 12 hours of daylight? Those who walk during the day will not stumble. They can see because of this world's light. ¹⁰But when they walk at night, they stumble. They have no light."

¹¹After he said this, Jesus went on speaking to them. "Our friend Lazarus has fallen asleep," he said. "But I am going there to wake him up."

¹²His disciples replied, "Lord, if he's sleeping, he will get better."

¹³Jesus had been speaking about the death of Lazarus. But his disciples thought he meant natural sleep.

¹⁴So then he told them plainly, "Lazarus is dead. ¹⁵For your benefit, I am glad I was not there. Now you will believe. But let us go to him."

¹⁶Then Thomas, who was called Didymus, spoke to the rest of the disciples. "Let us go also," he said. "Then we can die with him."

Jesus Comforts the Sisters

¹⁷When Jesus arrived, he found out that Lazarus had already been in the tomb for four days. ¹⁸Bethany was less than two miles from Jerusalem. ¹⁹Many Jews had come to Martha and Mary. They had come to comfort them, because their brother was dead.

²⁰When Martha heard that Jesus was coming, she went out to meet him. But Mary stayed at home.

²¹"Lord," Martha said to Jesus, "I wish you had been here! Then my brother would not have died. ²²But I know that even now God will give you anything you ask for."

²³Jesus said to her, "Your brother will rise again."

²⁴Martha answered, "I know he will rise again. This will happen at the resurrection on the last day."

²⁵Jesus said to her, "I am the resurrection and the life. Those

who believe in me will live, even if they die. ²⁶And those who live and believe in me will never die. Do you believe this?"

²⁷"Yes, Lord," she told him. "I believe that you are the Christ, the Son of God. I believe that you are the One who was supposed to come into the world."

²⁸After she said this, she went back home. She called her sister Mary to one side to talk to her. "The Teacher is here," Martha said. "He is asking for you."

²⁹When Mary heard this, she got up quickly and went to him. ³⁰Jesus had not yet entered the village. He was still at the place where Martha had met him. ³¹Some Jews had been comforting Mary in the house. They noticed how quickly she got up and went out. So they followed her. They thought she was going to the tomb to cry there.

³²Mary reached the place where Jesus was. When she saw him, she fell at his feet. She said, "Lord, I wish you had been here! Then my brother would not have died."

³³Jesus saw her crying. He saw that the Jews who had come along with her were crying also. His spirit became very sad, and he was troubled.

³⁴"Where have you put him?" he asked.

"Come and see, Lord," they replied.

³⁵Jesus sobbed.

³⁶Then the Jews said, "See how much he loved him!"

³⁷But some of them said, "He opened the eyes of the blind man. Couldn't he have kept this man from dying?"

Jesus Raises Lazarus From the Dead

³⁸Once more Jesus felt very sad. He came to the tomb. It was a cave with a stone in front of the entrance.

³⁹"Take away the stone," he said.

"But, Lord," said Martha, the sister of the dead man, "by this

GREAT VERSE —TO— REMEMBER

11:25 I am the resurrection and the life. Those who believe in me will live, even if they die. And those who live and believe in me will never die.

time there is a bad smell. Lazarus has been in the tomb for four days."

⁴⁰Then Jesus said, "Didn't I tell you that if you believed, you would see God's glory?"

⁴¹So they took away the stone.

Then Jesus looked up. He said, "Father, I thank you for hearing me. ⁴²I know that you always hear me. But I said this for the benefit of the people standing here. I said it so they will believe that you sent me."

⁴³Then Jesus called in a loud voice. He said, "Lazarus, come out!"

⁴⁴The dead man came out. His hands and feet were wrapped with strips of linen. A cloth was around his face.

Jesus said to them, "Take off the clothes he was buried in and let him go."

The Plan to Kill Jesus

⁴⁵Many of the Jews who had come to visit Mary saw what Jesus did. So they put their faith in him.

⁴⁶But some of them went to the Pharisees. They told the Pharisees what Jesus had done. ⁴⁷Then the chief priests and the Pharisees called a meeting of the Sanhedrin.

"What can we do?" they asked. "This man is doing many miraculous signs. ⁴⁸If we let him keep on doing this, everyone will believe in him. Then the Romans will come. They will take away our temple and our nation."

⁴⁹One of them spoke up. His name was Caiaphas. He was high priest at that time. He said, "You don't know anything at all! ⁵⁰You don't realize what is good for you. It is better if one person dies for the people than if the whole nation is destroyed."

⁵¹He did not say this on his own. But he was high priest at that time. So he told ahead of time that Jesus would die for the Jewish nation. ⁵²He also prophesied that Jesus would die for God's children scattered everywhere. He would die to bring them together and make them one.

⁵³So from that day on, the Jewish rulers planned to kill him.

⁵⁴Jesus no longer moved around openly among the Jews. Instead, he went away to an area near the desert. He went to a village called Ephraim. There he stayed with his disciples.

⁵⁵It was almost time for the Jewish Passover Feast. Many people went up from the country to Jerusalem. They went there for the special washing that would make them pure before the Passover

Feast. ⁵⁶They kept looking for Jesus as they stood in the temple area. They asked one another, "What do you think? Isn't he coming to the Feast at all?"

⁵⁷But the chief priests and the Pharisees had given orders. They commanded anyone who found out where Jesus was staying to report it. Then they could arrest him.

Mary Pours Perfume on Jesus

12 It was six days before the Passover Feast. Jesus arrived at Bethany, where Lazarus lived. Lazarus was the one Jesus had raised from the dead. ²A dinner was given at Bethany to honor Jesus. Martha served the food. Lazarus was among those at the table with Jesus.

³Then Mary took about a pint of pure nard. It was an expensive perfume. She poured it on Jesus' feet and wiped them with her hair. The house was filled with the sweet smell of the perfume.

⁴But Judas Iscariot didn't like what Mary did. He was one of Jesus' disciples. Later he was going to hand Jesus over to his enemies. Judas said, ⁵"Why wasn't this perfume sold? Why wasn't the money given to poor people? It was worth a year's pay."

⁶He didn't say this because he cared about the poor. He said it because he was a thief. Judas was in charge of the money bag. He used to help himself to what was in it.

⁷"Leave her alone," Jesus replied. "The perfume was meant for the day I am buried. ⁸You will always have the poor among you. But you won't always have me."

⁹Meanwhile a large crowd of Jews found out that Jesus was there, so they came. But they did not come only because of Jesus. They also came to see Lazarus. After all, Jesus had raised him from the dead.

¹⁰So the chief priests made plans to kill Lazarus too. ¹¹Because of Lazarus, many of the Jews were starting to follow Jesus. They were putting their faith in him.

Jesus Enters Jerusalem

¹²The next day the large crowd that had come for the Feast heard that Jesus was on his way to Jerusalem. ¹³So they took branches from palm trees and went out to meet him. They shouted,

"Hosanna!"

"Blessed is the one who comes in the name of the
Lord!"   *(Psalm 118:25,26)*

"Blessed is the King of Israel!"

¹⁴Jesus found a young donkey and sat on it. This is just as it is written in Scripture. It says,

> ¹⁵ "Do not be afraid, Daughter Zion.
>   See, your king is coming.
>   He is sitting on a donkey's colt."   (*Zechariah 9:9*)

¹⁶At first, Jesus' disciples did not understand all this. They realized it only after he had received glory. Then they realized that these things had been written about him. They realized that the people had done these things to him.

¹⁷A crowd had been with Jesus when he called Lazarus from the tomb and raised him from the dead. So they continued to tell everyone about what had happened. ¹⁸Many people went out to meet him. They had heard that he had done this miraculous sign.

¹⁹So the Pharisees said to one another, "This isn't getting us anywhere. Look how the whole world is following him!"

Jesus Tells About His Coming Death

²⁰There were some Greeks among the people who went up to worship during the Feast. ²¹They came to ask Philip for a favor. Philip was from Bethsaida in Galilee.

"Sir," they said, "we would like to see Jesus."

²²Philip went to tell Andrew. Then Andrew and Philip told Jesus.

²³Jesus replied, "The hour has come for the Son of Man to receive glory. ²⁴What I'm about to tell you is true. Unless a grain of wheat falls to the ground and dies, it remains only one seed. But if it dies, it produces many seeds.

²⁵"Those who love their life will lose it. But those who hate their life in this world will keep it and have eternal life. ²⁶Anyone who serves me must follow me. And where I am, my servant will also be. My Father will honor the one who serves me.

GREAT VERSE —TO— REMEMBER

12:25 Those who love their life will lose it. But those who hate their life in this world will keep it and have eternal life.

[27]"My heart is troubled. What should I say? 'Father, save me from this hour'? No. This is the very reason I came to this hour. [28]Father, bring glory to your name!"

Then a voice came from heaven. It said, "I have brought glory to my name. I will bring glory to it again."

[29]The crowd there heard the voice. Some said it was thunder. Others said an angel had spoken to Jesus.

[30]Jesus said, "This voice was for your benefit, not mine. [31]Now it is time for the world to be judged. Now the prince of this world will be thrown out. [32]But I am going to be lifted up from the earth. When I am, I will bring all people to myself." [33]He said this to show them how he was going to die.

[34]The crowd spoke up. "The Law tells us that the Christ will remain forever," they said. "So how can you say, 'The Son of Man must be lifted up'? Who is this 'Son of Man'?"

[35]Then Jesus told them, "You are going to have the light just a little while longer. Walk while you have the light. Do this before darkness catches up with you. Those who walk in the dark do not know where they are going. [36]While you have the light, put your trust in it. Then you can become children of light."

When he finished speaking, Jesus left and hid from them.

The Jews Still Do Not Believe

[37]Jesus had done all these miraculous signs in front of them. But they still would not believe in him. [38]This happened as Isaiah the prophet had said it would. He had said,

> "Lord, who has believed our message?
> To whom has the Lord shown his power?" *(Isaiah 53:1)*

[39]For this reason, they could not believe. As Isaiah says in another place,

> [40]"He has blinded their eyes.
> He has closed their minds.
> So they can't see with their eyes.
> They can't understand with their minds.
> They can't turn. If they could, I would heal them."
>
> *(Isaiah 6:10)*

[41]Isaiah said this because he saw Jesus' glory and spoke about him.

[42]At the same time, even among the leaders many believed in Jesus. But because of the Pharisees, they would not admit they believed. They were afraid they would be thrown out of the syn-

agogue. [43]They loved praise from people more than praise from God.

[44]Then Jesus cried out, "Those who believe in me do not believe in me only. They also believe in the One who sent me. [45]When they look at me, they see the One who sent me.

[46]"I have come into the world to be a light. No one who believes in me will stay in darkness.

[47]"I don't judge those who hear my words but do not obey them. I didn't come to judge the world. I came to save it. [48]But there is a judge for those who do not accept me and my words. The very words I have spoken will judge them on the last day.

[49]"I did not speak on my own. The Father who sent me commanded me what to say. He also told me how to say it. [50]I know that his command leads to eternal life. So everything I say is just what the Father has told me to say."

Jesus Washes His Disciples' Feet

13 It was just before the Passover Feast. Jesus knew that the time had come for him to leave this world. It was time for him to go to the Father. Jesus loved his disciples who were in the world. So he now showed them how much he really loved them.

[2]The evening meal was being served. The devil had already tempted Judas Iscariot, son of Simon. He had told Judas to hand Jesus over to his enemies. [3]Jesus knew that the Father had put everything under his power. He also knew he had come from God and was returning to God.

[4]So he got up from the meal and took off his outer clothes. He wrapped a towel around his waist. [5]After that, he poured water into a large bowl. Then he began to wash his disciples' feet. He dried them with the towel that was wrapped around him.

[6]He came to Simon Peter.

"Lord," Peter said to him, "are you going to wash my feet?"

[7]Jesus replied, "You don't realize now what I am doing. But later you will understand."

[8]"No," said Peter. "You will never wash my feet."

Jesus answered, "Unless I wash you, you can't share life with me."

[9]"Lord," Simon Peter replied, "not just my feet! Wash my hands and my head too!"

[10]Jesus answered, "Those who have had a bath need to wash only their feet. The rest of their body is clean. And you are clean. But not all of you are."

[11]Jesus knew who was going to hand him over to his enemies. That was why he said not every one was clean.

[12]When Jesus finished washing their feet, he put on his clothes. Then he returned to his place.

"Do you understand what I have done for you?" he asked them. [13]"You call me 'Teacher' and 'Lord.' You are right. That is what I am. [14]I, your Lord and Teacher, have washed your feet. So you also should wash one another's feet. [15]I have given you an example. You should do as I have done for you.

[16]"What I'm about to tell you is true. Servants are not more important than their masters. And messengers are not more important than those who send them. [17]Now you know these things. So you will be blessed if you do them.

Jesus Tells What Judas Will Do

[18]"I am not talking about all of you. I know those I have chosen. But this will happen so that Scripture will come true. It says, 'The one who shares my bread has deserted me.' *(Psalm 41:9)*

[19]"I am telling you now, before it happens. When it does happen, you will believe that I am he. [20]What I'm about to tell you is true. Anyone who accepts someone I send accepts me. And anyone who accepts me accepts the One who sent me."

[21]After he had said this, Jesus' spirit was troubled. Here is the witness he gave. "What I'm about to tell you is true," he said. "One of you is going to hand me over to my enemies."

[22]His disciples stared at one another. They had no idea which one of them he meant. [23]The disciple Jesus loved was next to him at the table. [24]Simon Peter motioned to that disciple. He said, "Ask Jesus which one he means."

[25]The disciple was leaning back against Jesus. He asked him, "Lord, who is it?"

[26]Jesus answered, "It is the one I will give this piece of bread to. I will give it to him after I have dipped it in the dish."

He dipped the piece of bread. Then he gave it to Judas Iscariot, son of Simon. [27]As soon as Judas took the bread, Satan entered into him.

"Do quickly what you are going to do," Jesus told him.

[28]But no one at the meal understood why Jesus said this to him. [29]Judas was in charge of the money. So some of the disciples thought Jesus was telling him to buy what was needed for the Feast. Others thought Jesus was talking about giving something to poor people.

³⁰As soon as Judas had taken the bread, he went out. And it was night.

Jesus Says That Peter Will Fail

³¹After Judas was gone, Jesus spoke. He said, "Now the Son of Man receives glory. And he brings glory to God. ³²If the Son brings glory to God, God himself will bring glory to the Son. God will do it at once.

³³"My children, I will be with you only a little longer. You will look for me. Just as I told the Jews, so I am telling you now. You can't come where I am going.

³⁴"I give you a new command. Love one another. You must love one another, just as I have loved you. ³⁵If you love one another, everyone will know you are my disciples."

³⁶Simon Peter asked him, "Lord, where are you going?"

Jesus replied, "Where I am going you can't follow now. But you will follow later."

³⁷"Lord," Peter asked, "why can't I follow you now? I will give my life for you."

³⁸Then Jesus answered, "Will you really give your life for me? What I'm about to tell you is true. Before the rooster crows, you will say three times that you don't know me!

Jesus Comforts His Disciples

14 "Do not let your hearts be troubled. Trust in God. Trust in me also.

²"There are many rooms in my Father's house. If this were not true, I would have told you. I am going there to prepare a place for you. ³If I go and do that, I will come back. And I will take you to be with me. Then you will also be where I am.

⁴"You know the way to the place where I am going."

GREAT VERSE —TO— REMEMBER

13:34 I give you a new command. Love one another. You must love one another, just as I have loved you. If you love one another, everyone will know you are my disciples.

Jesus Is the Way to the Father

⁵Thomas said to him, "Lord, we don't know where you are going. So how can we know the way?"

⁶Jesus answered, "I am the way and the truth and the life. No one comes to the Father except through me. ⁷If you really knew me, you would know my Father also. From now on, you do know him. And you have seen him."

⁸Philip said, "Lord, show us the Father. That will be enough for us."

⁹Jesus answered, "Don't you know me, Philip? I have been among you such a long time! Anyone who has seen me has seen the Father. So how can you say, 'Show us the Father'?

¹⁰"Don't you believe that I am in the Father? Don't you believe that the Father is in me? The words I say to you are not just my own. The Father lives in me. He is the One who is doing his work. ¹¹Believe me when I say I am in the Father. Also believe that the Father is in me. Or at least believe what the miracles show about me.

¹²"What I'm about to tell you is true. Those who have faith in me will do what I have been doing. In fact, they will do even greater things. That is because I am going to the Father.

¹³"And I will do anything you ask in my name. Then the Son will bring glory to the Father. ¹⁴You may ask me for anything in my name. I will do it.

The Father Will Send the Holy Spirit

¹⁵"If you love me, you will obey what I command. ¹⁶I will ask the Father. And he will give you another Friend to help you and to be with you forever. ¹⁷The Friend is the Spirit of truth. The world can't accept him. That is because the world does not see him or know him. But you know him. He lives with you, and he will be in you.

¹⁸"I will not leave you like children without parents. I will come to you.

GREAT VERSE —TO— REMEMBER

14:6 I am the way and the truth and the life. No one comes to the Father except through me.

¹⁹"Before long, the world will not see me anymore. But you will see me. Because I live, you will live also. ²⁰On that day you will realize that I am in my Father. You will know that you are in me, and I am in you.

²¹"Those who have my commands and obey them are the ones who love me. My Father will love those who love me. I too will love them. And I will show myself to them."

²²Then Judas spoke. "Lord," he said, "why do you plan to show yourself only to us? Why not also to the world?" The Judas who spoke those words was not Judas Iscariot.

²³Jesus replied, "Those who love me will obey my teaching. My Father will love them. We will come to them and make our home with them. ²⁴Those who do not love me will not obey my teaching. The words you hear me say are not my own. They belong to the Father who sent me.

²⁵"I have spoken all these things while I am still with you. ²⁶But the Father will send the Friend in my name to help you. The Friend is the Holy Spirit. He will teach you all things. He will remind you of everything I have said to you.

²⁷"I leave my peace with you. I give my peace to you. I do not give it to you as the world does. Do not let your hearts be troubled. And do not be afraid.

²⁸"You heard me say, 'I am going away. And I am coming back to you.' If you loved me, you would be glad I am going to the Father. The Father is greater than I am. ²⁹I have told you now before it happens. Then when it does happen, you will believe.

³⁰"I will not speak with you much longer. The prince of this world is coming. He has no power over me. ³¹But the world must learn that I love the Father. They must also learn that I do exactly what my Father has commanded me to do.

"Come now. Let us leave.

The Vine and the Branches

15 "I am the true vine. My Father is the gardener. ²He cuts off every branch joined to me that does not bear fruit. He trims every branch that does bear fruit. Then it will bear even more fruit.

³"You are already clean because of the word I have spoken to you. ⁴Remain joined to me, and I will remain joined to you. No branch can bear fruit by itself. It must remain joined to the vine. In the same way, you can't bear fruit unless you remain joined to me.

⁵"I am the vine. You are the branches. If you remain joined to me, and I to you, you will bear a lot of fruit. You can't do anything without me. ⁶If you do not remain joined to me, you are like a branch that is thrown away and dries up. Branches like those are picked up. They are thrown into the fire and burned.

⁷"If you remain joined to me and my words remain in you, ask for anything you wish. And it will be given to you. ⁸When you bear a lot of fruit, it brings glory to my Father. It shows that you are my disciples.

⁹"Just as the Father has loved me, I have loved you. Now remain in my love. ¹⁰If you obey my commands, you will remain in my love. In the same way, I have obeyed my Father's commands and remain in his love. ¹¹I have told you this so that my joy will be in you. I also want your joy to be complete.

¹²"Here is my command. Love each other, just as I have loved you. ¹³No one has greater love than the one who gives his life for his friends. ¹⁴You are my friends if you do what I command.

¹⁵"I do not call you servants anymore. Servants do not know their master's business. Instead, I have called you friends. I have told you everything I learned from my Father.

¹⁶"You did not choose me. Instead, I chose you. I appointed you to go and bear fruit. It is fruit that will last. Then the Father will give you anything you ask for in my name.

¹⁷"Here is my command. Love each other.

The World Hates the Disciples

¹⁸"Does the world hate you? Remember that it hated me first. ¹⁹If you belonged to the world, it would love you like one of its own. But you do not belong to the world. I have chosen you out of the world. That is why the world hates you.

²⁰"Remember the words I spoke to you. I said, 'Servants are not more important than their masters.' *(John 13:16)* If they hated me and tried to hurt me, they will do the same to you. If they obeyed my teaching, they will obey yours also. ²¹They will treat you like that

GREAT VERSE — TO — REMEMBER

15:13-14 No one has greater love than the one who gives his life for his friends. You are my friends if you do what I command.

because of my name. They do not know the One who sent me.

²²"If I had not come and spoken to them, they would not be guilty of sin. But now they have no excuse for their sin. ²³Those who hate me hate my Father also.

²⁴"I did miracles among them that no one else did. If I hadn't, they would not be guilty of sin. But now they have seen those miracles. And still they have hated both me and my Father. ²⁵This has happened so that what is written in their Law would come true. It says, 'They hated me without any reason.' *(Psalms 35:19; 69:4)*

²⁶"I will send the Friend to you from the Father. He is the Spirit of truth, who comes out from the Father. When the Friend comes to help you, he will give witness about me.

²⁷"You also must give witness. This is because you have been with me from the beginning.

16 "I have told you all of this so that you will not go down the wrong path. ²You will be thrown out of the synagogue. In fact, a time is coming when those who kill you will think they are doing God a favor. ³They will do things like that because they do not know the Father or me.

⁴"Why have I told you this? So that when the time comes, you will remember that I warned you. I didn't tell you this at first because I was with you.

What the Holy Spirit Will Do

⁵"Now I am going to the One who sent me. But none of you asks me, 'Where are you going?' ⁶Because I have said these things, you are filled with sadness.

⁷"But what I'm about to tell you is true. It is for your good that I am going away. Unless I go away, the Friend will not come to help you. But if I go, I will send him to you. ⁸When he comes, he will prove that the world's people are guilty. He will prove their guilt concerning sin and godliness and judgment.

⁹"The world is guilty as far as sin is concerned. That is because people do not believe in me. ¹⁰The world is guilty as far as godliness is concerned. That is because I am going to the Father, where you can't see me anymore. ¹¹The world is guilty as far as judgment is concerned. That is because the devil, the prince of this world, has already been judged.

¹²"I have much more to say to you. It is more than you can handle right now. ¹³But when the Spirit of truth comes, he will guide you into all truth. He will not speak on his own. He will speak

only what he hears. And he will tell you what is still going to happen.

¹⁴"He will bring me glory by receiving something from me and showing it to you. ¹⁵Everything that belongs to the Father is mine. That is why I said the Holy Spirit will receive something from me and show it to you.

¹⁶"In a little while, you will no longer see me. Then after a little while, you will see me."

The Disciples' Sadness Will Turn Into Joy

¹⁷Some of his disciples spoke to one another. They said, "What does he mean by saying, 'In a little while, you will no longer see me. Then after a little while, you will see me'? And what does he mean by saying, 'I am going to the Father'?" ¹⁸They kept asking, "What does he mean by 'a little while'? We don't understand what he is saying."

¹⁹Jesus saw that they wanted to ask him about those things. So he said to them, "Are you asking one another what I meant? Didn't you understand when I said, 'In a little while, you will no longer see me. Then after a little while, you will see me'? ²⁰What I'm about to tell you is true. You will cry and be full of sorrow while the world is full of joy. You will be sad, but your sadness will turn into joy.

²¹"A woman giving birth to a baby has pain. This is because her time to give birth has come. But when her baby is born, she forgets the pain. She forgets because she is so happy that a baby has been born into the world.

²²"That's the way it is with you. Now it's your time to be sad. But I will see you again. Then you will be full of joy. And no one will take your joy away.

²³"When that day comes, you will no longer ask me for anything. What I'm about to tell you is true. My Father will give you anything you ask for in my name. ²⁴Until now you have not asked for anything in my name. Ask, and you will receive what you ask for. Then your joy will be complete.

²⁵"I have not been speaking to you plainly. But a time is coming when I will speak clearly. Then I will tell you plainly about my Father. ²⁶When that day comes, you will ask for things in my name. I am not saying I will ask the Father instead of you asking him. ²⁷No, the Father himself loves you because you have loved me. He also loves you because you have believed that I came from God.

²⁸"I came from the Father and entered the world. Now I am leaving the world and going back to the Father."

²⁹Then Jesus' disciples said, "Now you are speaking plainly. You are not using words that aren't clear. ³⁰Now we can see that you know everything. You don't even need anyone to ask you questions. This makes us believe that you came from God."

³¹"At last you believe!" Jesus said. ³²"But a time is coming when you will be scattered and go to your own homes. In fact, that time is already here. You will leave me all alone. But I am not really alone. My Father is with me.

³³"I have told you these things, so that you can have peace because of me. In this world you will have trouble. But cheer up! I have won the battle over the world."

Jesus Prays for Himself

17 After Jesus said this, he looked toward heaven and prayed. He said,

"Father, the time has come. Bring glory to your Son. Then your Son will bring glory to you. ²You gave him authority over all people. He gives eternal life to all those you have given him.

³"And what is eternal life? It is knowing you, the only true God, and Jesus Christ, whom you have sent. ⁴I have brought you glory on earth. I have finished the work you gave me to do. ⁵So now, Father, give glory to me in heaven where your throne is. Give me the glory I had with you before the world began.

Jesus Prays for His Disciples

⁶"I have shown you to those you gave me out of the world. They were yours. You gave them to me. And they have obeyed your word. ⁷Now they know that everything you

GREAT VERSE —TO— REMEMBER

16:33 I have told you these things, so that you can have peace because of me. In this world you will have trouble. But cheer up! I have won the battle over the world.

have given me comes from you. ⁸I gave them the words you gave me. And they accepted them. They knew for certain that I came from you. They believed that you sent me.

⁹"I pray for them. I am not praying for the world. I am praying for those you have given me, because they are yours. ¹⁰All I have is yours, and all you have is mine. Glory has come to me because of them.

¹¹"I will not remain in the world any longer. But they are still in the world, and I am coming to you. Holy Father, keep them safe by the power of your name. It is the name you gave me. Keep them safe so they can be one, just as we are one.

¹²"While I was with them, I guarded them. I kept them safe through the name you gave me. None of them has been lost, except the one who was sentenced to be destroyed. It happened so that Scripture would come true.

¹³"I am coming to you now. But I say these things while I am still in the world. I say them so that those you gave me can have all my joy inside them. ¹⁴I have given them your word. The world has hated them. This is because they are not part of the world any more than I am. ¹⁵I do not pray that you will take them out of the world. I pray that you will keep them safe from the evil one.

¹⁶"They do not belong to the world, just as I do not belong to it. ¹⁷Use the truth to make them holy. Your word is truth. ¹⁸You sent me into the world. In the same way, I have sent them into the world. ¹⁹I make myself holy for them so that they too can be made holy in a true sense.

Jesus Prays for All Believers

²⁰"I do not pray only for them. I pray also for those who will believe in me because of their message. ²¹Father, I pray that all of them will be one, just as you are in me and I am in you. I want them also to be in us. Then the world will believe that you have sent me.

²²"I have given them the glory you gave me. I did this so they would be one, just as we are one. ²³I will be in them, just

17:17 Use the truth to make them holy. Your word is truth.

as you are in me. I want them to be brought together perfectly as one. This will let the world know that you sent me.
It will also show the world that you have loved those you
gave me, just as you have loved me.

²⁴"Father, I want those you have given me to be with me
where I am. I want them to see my glory, the glory you have
given me. You gave it to me because you loved me before the
world was created.

²⁵"Father, you are holy. The world does not know you, but
I know you. Those you have given me know you have sent
me. ²⁶I have shown you to them. And I will continue to show
you to them. Then the love you have for me will be in them.
I myself will be in them."

Jesus Is Arrested

18 When Jesus had finished praying, he left with his disciples. They crossed the Kidron Valley. On the other side
there was a grove of olive trees. Jesus and his disciples went
into it.

²Judas knew the place. He was going to hand Jesus over to his
enemies. Jesus had often met in that place with his disciples. ³So
Judas came to the grove. He was guiding a group of soldiers and
some officials. The chief priests and the Pharisees had sent them.
They were carrying torches, lanterns and weapons.

⁴Jesus knew everything that was going to happen to him. So he
went out and asked them, "Who is it that you want?"

⁵"Jesus of Nazareth," they replied.

"I am he," Jesus said.

Judas, who was going to hand Jesus over, was standing there
with them. ⁶When Jesus said, "I am he," they moved back. Then
they fell to the ground.

⁷He asked them again, "Who is it that you want?"

They said, "Jesus of Nazareth."

⁸"I told you I am he," Jesus answered. "If you are looking for
me, then let these men go." ⁹This happened so that the words
Jesus had spoken would come true. He had said, "I have not lost
anyone God has given me." *(John 6:39)*

¹⁰Simon Peter had a sword and pulled it out. He struck the high
priest's servant and cut off his right ear. The servant's name was
Malchus.

¹¹Jesus commanded Peter, "Put your sword away! Shouldn't I
drink the cup of suffering the Father has given me?"

Jesus Is Taken to Annas

¹²Then the group of soldiers, their leader and the Jewish officials arrested Jesus. They tied him up ¹³and brought him first to Annas. He was the father-in-law of Caiaphas, the high priest at that time. ¹⁴Caiaphas had advised the Jews that it would be good if one person died for the people.

Peter Says He Is Not Jesus' Disciple

¹⁵Simon Peter and another disciple were following Jesus. The high priest knew the other disciple. So that disciple went with Jesus into the high priest's courtyard. ¹⁶But Peter had to wait outside by the door.

The other disciple came back. He was the one the high priest knew. He spoke to the woman who was on duty there. Then he brought Peter in.

¹⁷The woman at the door spoke to Peter. "You are not one of Jesus' disciples, are you?" she asked him.

"I am not," he replied.

¹⁸It was cold. The servants and officials stood around a fire. They had made it to keep warm. Peter was also standing with them. He was warming himself.

The High Priest Questions Jesus

¹⁹Meanwhile, the high priest questioned Jesus. He asked him about his disciples and his teaching.

²⁰"I have spoken openly to the world," Jesus replied. "I always taught in synagogues or at the temple, where all the Jews come together. I didn't say anything in secret. ²¹Why question me? Ask the people who heard me. They certainly know what I said."

²²When Jesus said that, one of the officials nearby hit him in the face. "Is this any way to answer the high priest?" he asked.

²³"Have I said something wrong?" Jesus replied. "If I have, give witness to it. But if I spoke the truth, why did you hit me?"

²⁴While Jesus was still tied up, Annas sent him to Caiaphas, the high priest.

Peter Again Says He Is Not Jesus' Disciple

²⁵Simon Peter stood there. He was warming himself. Then someone asked him, "You aren't one of Jesus' disciples, are you?"

He said, "I am not."

²⁶One of the high priest's servants was a relative of the man

whose ear Peter had cut off. He said to Peter, "Didn't I see you with Jesus in the olive grove?"

²⁷Again Peter said no.

At that very moment a rooster began to crow.

Jesus Is Brought to Pilate

²⁸Then the Jews led Jesus from Caiaphas to the palace of the Roman governor. By now it was early morning. The Jews did not want to be made unclean. They wanted to be able to eat the Passover meal. So they did not enter the palace.

²⁹Pilate came out to them. He asked, "What charges are you bringing against this man?"

³⁰"He has committed crimes," they replied. "If he hadn't, we would not have handed him over to you."

³¹Pilate said, "Take him yourselves. Judge him by your own law."

"But we don't have the right to put anyone to death," the Jews complained. ³²This happened so that the words Jesus had spoken about how he was going to die would come true.

³³Then Pilate went back inside the palace. He ordered Jesus to be brought to him. Pilate asked him, "Are you the king of the Jews?"

³⁴"Is that your own idea?" Jesus asked. "Or did others talk to you about me?"

³⁵"Am I a Jew?" Pilate replied. "It was your people and your chief priests who handed you over to me. What have you done?"

³⁶Jesus said, "My kingdom is not part of this world. If it were, those who serve me would fight. They would try to keep the Jews from arresting me. My kingdom is from another place."

³⁷"So you are a king, then!" said Pilate.

Jesus answered, "You are right to say I am a king. In fact, that's the reason I was born. I came into the world to give witness to the truth. Everyone who is on the side of truth listens to me."

³⁸"What is truth?" Pilate asked.

Then Pilate went out again to the Jews. He said, "I find no basis for any charge against him. ³⁹But it is your practice for me to set one prisoner free for you at Passover time. Do you want me to set 'the king of the Jews' free?"

⁴⁰They shouted back, "No! Not him! Give us Barabbas!" Barabbas had taken part in an armed struggle against the country's rulers.

Jesus Is Sentenced to Be Crucified

19 Then Pilate took Jesus and had him whipped. ²The soldiers twisted thorns together to make a crown. They put it on his head. Then they put a purple robe on him. ³They went up to him again and again. They kept saying, "We honor you, king of the Jews!" And they hit him in the face.

⁴Once more Pilate came out. He said to the Jews, "Look, I am bringing Jesus out to you. I want to let you know that I find no basis for a charge against him."

⁵Jesus came out wearing the crown of thorns and the purple robe. Then Pilate said to them, "Here is the man!"

⁶As soon as the chief priests and their officials saw him, they shouted, "Crucify him! Crucify him!"

But Pilate answered, "You take him and crucify him. I myself find no basis for a charge against him."

⁷The Jews replied, "We have a law. That law says he must die. He claimed to be the Son of God."

⁸When Pilate heard that, he was even more afraid. ⁹He went back inside the palace. "Where do you come from?" he asked Jesus.

But Jesus did not answer him.

¹⁰"Do you refuse to speak to me?" Pilate said. "Don't you understand? I have the power to set you free or to nail you to a cross."

¹¹Jesus answered, "You were given power from heaven. If you weren't, you would have no power over me. So the one who handed me over to you is guilty of a greater sin."

¹²From then on, Pilate tried to set Jesus free. But the Jews kept shouting, "If you let this man go, you are not Caesar's friend! Anyone who claims to be a king is against Caesar!"

¹³When Pilate heard that, he brought Jesus out. Pilate sat down on the judge's seat. It was at a place called The Stone Pavement. In the Aramaic language it was called Gabbatha. ¹⁴It was about noon on Preparation Day of Passover Week.

"Here is your king," Pilate said to the Jews.

¹⁵But they shouted, "Kill him! Kill him! Crucify him!"

"Should I crucify your king?" Pilate asked.

"We have no king but Caesar," the chief priests answered.

¹⁶Finally, Pilate handed Jesus over to them to be nailed to a cross.

Jesus Is Nailed to a Cross

So the soldiers took charge of Jesus. ¹⁷He had to carry his own cross. He went out to a place called The Skull. In the Aramaic language it was called Golgotha. ¹⁸There they nailed Jesus to the cross. Two other men were crucified with him. One was on each side of him. Jesus was in the middle.

¹⁹Pilate had a notice prepared. It was fastened to the cross. It read, JESUS OF NAZARETH, THE KING OF THE JEWS. ²⁰Many of the Jews read the sign. The place where Jesus was crucified was near the city. The sign was written in the Aramaic, Latin and Greek languages.

²¹The chief priests of the Jews argued with Pilate. They said, "Do not write 'The King of the Jews.' Write that this man claimed to be king of the Jews."

²²Pilate answered, "I have written what I have written."

²³When the soldiers crucified Jesus, they took his clothes. They divided them into four parts. Each soldier got one part. Jesus' long, inner robe was left. It did not have any seams. It was made out of one piece of cloth from top to bottom.

²⁴"Let's not tear it," they said to one another. "Let's cast lots to see who will get it."

This happened so that Scripture would come true. It says,

> "They divided up my clothes among them.
> They cast lots for what I was wearing."   *(Psalm 22:18)*

So that is what the soldiers did.

²⁵Jesus' mother stood near his cross. So did his mother's sister, Mary the wife of Clopas, and Mary Magdalene.

²⁶Jesus saw his mother there. He also saw the disciple he loved standing nearby. Jesus said to his mother, "Dear woman, here is your son." ²⁷He said to the disciple, "Here is your mother." From that time on, the disciple took her into his home.

Jesus Dies

²⁸Later Jesus said, "I am thirsty." He knew that everything was now finished. He knew that what Scripture said must come true. ²⁹A jar of wine vinegar was there. So they soaked a sponge in it. They put the sponge on a stem of the hyssop plant. Then they lifted it up to Jesus' lips.

GREAT VERSE —TO— REMEMBER   **19:30** After Jesus drank he said, "It is finished." Then he bowed his head and died.

30After Jesus drank he said, "It is finished." Then he bowed his head and died.

31It was Preparation Day. The next day would be a special Sabbath. The Jews did not want the bodies left on the crosses during the Sabbath. So they asked Pilate to have the legs broken and the bodies taken down. 32The soldiers came and broke the legs of the first man who had been crucified with Jesus. Then they broke the legs of the other man.

33But when they came to Jesus, they saw that he was already dead. So they did not break his legs. 34Instead, one of the soldiers stuck his spear into Jesus' side. Right away, blood and water flowed out. 35The man who saw it has given witness. And his witness is true. He knows that he tells the truth. He gives witness so that you also can believe.

36These things happened in order that Scripture would come true. It says, "Not one of his bones will be broken." *(Exodus 12:46; Numbers 9:12; Psalm 34:20)* 37Scripture also says, "They will look on the one they have pierced." *(Zechariah 12:10)*

Jesus Is Buried

38Later Joseph asked Pilate for Jesus' body. Joseph was from the town of Arimathea. He was a follower of Jesus. But he followed Jesus secretly because he was afraid of the Jews. After Pilate gave him permission, Joseph came and took the body away.

39Nicodemus went with Joseph. He was the man who had earlier visited Jesus at night. Nicodemus brought some mixed spices, about 75 pounds. 40The two of them took Jesus' body. They wrapped it in strips of linen cloth, along with the spices. That was the way the Jews buried people.

41At the place where Jesus was crucified, there was a garden. A new tomb was there. No one had ever been put in it before. 42That day was the Jewish Preparation Day, and the tomb was nearby. So they placed Jesus there.

The Tomb Is Empty

20 Early on the first day of the week, Mary Magdalene went to the tomb. It was still dark. She saw that the stone had been moved away from the entrance. 2So she ran to Simon Peter and the other disciple, the one Jesus loved. She said, "They have taken the Lord out of the tomb! We don't know where they have put him!"

3So Peter and the other disciple started out for the tomb. 4Both of them were running. The other disciple ran faster than Peter. He reached the tomb first. ⁵He bent over and looked in at the strips of linen lying there. But he did not go in.

⁶Then Simon Peter, who was behind him, arrived. He went into the tomb. He saw the strips of linen lying there. ⁷He also saw the burial cloth that had been around Jesus' head. The cloth was folded up by itself. It was separate from the linen.

⁸The other disciple, who had reached the tomb first, also went inside. He saw and believed. ⁹They still did not understand from Scripture that Jesus had to rise from the dead.

Jesus Appears to Mary Magdalene

¹⁰Then the disciples went back to their homes. ¹¹But Mary stood outside the tomb crying. As she cried, she bent over to look into the tomb. ¹²She saw two angels dressed in white. They were seated where Jesus' body had been. One of them was where Jesus' head had been laid. The other sat where his feet had been placed.

¹³They asked her, "Woman, why are you crying?"

"They have taken my Lord away," she said. "I don't know where they have put him."

¹⁴Then she turned around and saw Jesus standing there. But she didn't realize that it was Jesus.

¹⁵"Woman," he said, "why are you crying? Who are you looking for?"

She thought he was the gardener. So she said, "Sir, did you carry him away? Tell me where you put him. Then I will go and get him."

¹⁶Jesus said to her, "Mary."

She turned toward him. Then she cried out in the Aramaic language, "Rabboni!" Rabboni means Teacher.

¹⁷Jesus said, "Do not hold on to me. I have not yet returned to the Father. Instead, go to those who believe in me. Tell them, 'I am returning to my Father and your Father, to my God and your God.'"

¹⁸Mary Magdalene went to the disciples with the news. She said, "I have seen the Lord!" And she told them that he had said these things to her.

Jesus Appears to His Disciples

¹⁹On the evening of that first day of the week, the disciples were together. They had locked the doors because they were afraid of the Jews.

Jesus came in and stood among them. He said, "May peace be with you!" ²⁰Then he showed them his hands and his side. The disciples were very happy when they saw the Lord.

²¹Again Jesus said, "May peace be with you! The Father has sent me. So now I am sending you." ²²He then breathed on them. He said, "Receive the Holy Spirit. ²³If you forgive anyone's sins, they are forgiven. If you do not forgive them, they are not forgiven."

Jesus Appears to Thomas

²⁴Thomas was one of the Twelve. He was called Didymus. He was not with the other disciples when Jesus came. ²⁵So they told him, "We have seen the Lord!"

But he said to them, "First I must see the nail marks in his hands. I must put my finger where the nails were. I must put my hand into his side. Only then will I believe what you say."

²⁶A week later, Jesus' disciples were in the house again. Thomas was with them. Even though the doors were locked, Jesus came in and stood among them.

He said, "May peace be with you!" ²⁷Then he said to Thomas, "Put your finger here. See my hands. Reach out your hand and put it into my side. Stop doubting and believe."

²⁸Thomas said to him, "My Lord and my God!"

²⁹Then Jesus told him, "Because you have seen me, you have believed. Blessed are those who have not seen me but still have believed."

³⁰Jesus did many other miraculous signs in front of his disciples. They are not written down in this book. ³¹But these are written down so that you may believe that Jesus is the Christ, the Son of God. If you believe this, you will have life because you belong to him.

Jesus Does a Miracle at the Sea

21 After this, Jesus appeared to his disciples again. It was by the Sea of Galilee. Here is what happened.

GREAT VERSE — TO — REMEMBER   **20:29** Because you have seen me, you have believed. Blessed are those who have not seen me but still have believed.

²Simon Peter and Thomas, who was called Didymus, were there together. Nathanael from Cana in Galilee and the sons of Zebedee were with them. So were two other disciples.

³"I'm going out to fish," Simon Peter told them. They said, "We'll go with you." So they went out and got into the boat. That night they didn't catch anything.

⁴Early in the morning, Jesus stood on the shore. But the disciples did not realize that it was Jesus.

⁵He called out to them, "Friends, don't you have any fish?"

"No," they answered.

⁶He said, "Throw your net on the right side of the boat. There you will find some fish."

When they did, they could not pull the net into the boat. There were too many fish in it.

⁷Then the disciple Jesus loved said to Peter, "It is the Lord!"

As soon as Simon Peter heard that, he put his coat on. He had taken it off earlier. Then he jumped into the water.

⁸The other disciples followed in the boat. They were towing the net full of fish. The shore was only about 100 yards away. ⁹When they landed, they saw a fire of burning coals. There were fish on it. There was also some bread.

¹⁰Jesus said to them, "Bring some of the fish you have just caught."

¹¹Simon Peter climbed into the boat. He dragged the net to shore. It was full of large fish. There were 153 of them. But even with that many fish the net was not torn.

¹²Jesus said to them, "Come and have breakfast."

None of the disciples dared to ask him, "Who are you?" They knew it was the Lord.

¹³Jesus came, took the bread and gave it to them. He did the same thing with the fish. ¹⁴This was the third time Jesus appeared to his disciples after he was raised from the dead.

Jesus Takes Peter Back

¹⁵When Jesus and the disciples had finished eating, Jesus spoke to Simon Peter. He said, "Simon, son of John, do you really love me more than these others do?"

"Yes, Lord," he said. "You know that I love you."

Jesus said, "Feed my lambs."

¹⁶Again Jesus said, "Simon, son of John, do you really love me?"

He answered, "Yes, Lord. You know that I love you."

Jesus said, "Take care of my sheep."

¹⁷Jesus spoke to him a third time. He said, "Simon, son of John, do you love me?"

Peter felt bad because Jesus asked him the third time, "Do you love me?" He said, "Lord, you know all things. You know that I love you."

Jesus said, "Feed my sheep. ¹⁸What I'm about to tell you is true. When you were younger, you dressed yourself. You went wherever you wanted to go. But when you are old, you will stretch out your hands. Someone else will dress you. Someone else will lead you where you do not want to go."

¹⁹Jesus said this to point out how Peter would die. His death would bring glory to God.

Then Jesus said to him, "Follow me!"

²⁰Peter turned around. He saw that the disciple Jesus loved was following them. This was the one who had leaned back against Jesus at the supper. He had said, "Lord, who is going to hand you over to your enemies?" ²¹When Peter saw that disciple, he asked, "Lord, what will happen to him?"

²²Jesus answered, "Suppose I want him to remain alive until I return. What does that matter to you? You must follow me."

²³Because of what Jesus said, a false report spread among the believers. The story was told that this disciple would not die. But Jesus did not say he would not die. He only said, "Suppose I want him to remain alive until I return. What does that matter to you?"

²⁴This is the disciple who gives witness to these things. He also wrote them down. We know that his witness is true.

²⁵Jesus also did many other things. What if every one of them were written down? I suppose that even the whole world would not have room for the books that would be written.

GREAT VERSE —TO— REMEMBER

21:25 Jesus also did many other things. What if every one of them were written down? I suppose that even the whole word would not have room for the books that would be written.

Acts

Why Was This Book Written? Luke wrote the book of Acts. He also wrote the book of Luke. Luke and Paul took many trips together. In the book of Acts, Luke wrote some stories about the trips. He wrote about the start of the Christian church too. He wanted us to know how the church grew.

What Is This Book About? The book of Acts tells us many things. It tells stories about Peter and Paul. It teaches us about the Holy Spirit. It teaches us about the church. The book of Acts tells us how people felt about the good news. It tells us what they did when they heard about Jesus.

What Is in This Book?

Jesus Is Taken Up Into Heaven

1 Theophilus, I wrote about Jesus in my earlier book. I wrote about all he did and taught [2]until the day he was taken up to heaven. Before Jesus left, he gave orders to the apostles he had chosen. He did this through the Holy Spirit. [3]After his suffering and death, he appeared to them. In many ways he proved that he was alive. He appeared to them over a period of 40 days. During that time he spoke about God's kingdom.

[4]One day Jesus was eating with them. He gave them a command. "Do not leave Jerusalem," he said. "Wait for the gift my Father promised. You have heard me talk about it. [5]John baptized with water. But in a few days you will be baptized with the Holy Spirit."

[6]When the apostles met together, they asked Jesus a question. "Lord," they said, "are you going to give the kingdom back to Israel now?"

[7]He said to them, "You should not be concerned about times or dates. The Father has set them by his own authority. [8]But you will receive power when the Holy Spirit comes on you. Then you will be my witnesses in Jerusalem. You will be my witnesses in all Judea and Samaria. And you will be my witnesses from one end of the earth to the other."

[9]After Jesus said this, he was taken up to heaven. They watched until a cloud hid him from their sight.

[10]While he was going up, they kept on looking at the sky. Suddenly two men dressed in white clothing stood beside them. [11]"Men of Galilee," they said, "why do you stand here looking at the sky? Jesus has been taken away from you into heaven. But he will come back in the same way you saw him go."

GREAT VERSE —TO— REMEMBER

1:8 But you will receive power when the Holy Spirit comes on you. Then you will be my witnesses in Jerusalem. You will be my witnesses in all Judea and Samaria. And you will be my witnesses from one end of the earth to the other.

Matthias Is Chosen to Take the Place of Judas

[12]The apostles returned to Jerusalem from the Mount of Olives. It is almost a mile from the city. [13]When they arrived, they went upstairs to the room where they were staying. Peter, John, James and Andrew were there. Philip, Thomas, Bartholomew and Matthew were there too. So were James, son of Alphaeus, Simon the Zealot, and Judas, son of James. [14]They all came together regularly to pray. The women joined them too. So did Jesus' mother Mary and his brothers.

[15]In those days Peter stood up among the believers. About 120 of them were there. [16]Peter said, "Brothers and sisters, a long time ago the Holy Spirit spoke through David's mouth about Judas. What he said in Scripture had to come true. Judas was the guide for the men who arrested Jesus. [17]But Judas was one of us. He shared with us in our work for God."

[18]Judas bought a field with the reward he got for the evil thing he had done. He fell down headfirst in the field. His body burst open. All his insides spilled out. [19]Everyone in Jerusalem heard about this. So they called that field Akeldama. In their language, Akeldama means The Field of Blood.

[20]Peter said, "Here is what is written in the book of Psalms. It says,

> "'May his home be deserted.
>   May no one live in it.'   *(Psalm 69:25)*

The Psalms also say,

> "'Let someone else take his place as leader.'   *(Psalm 109:8)*

[21]So we need to choose someone to take his place. It will have to be a person who was with us the whole time the Lord Jesus lived among us. [22]That time began when John was baptizing. It ended when Jesus was taken up from us. The one we choose must join us in giving witness that Jesus rose from the dead."

[23]So they suggested two men. One was Joseph, who was called Barsabbas. He was also called Justus. The other man was Matthias. [24]Then they prayed. "Lord," they said, "you know everyone's heart. Show us which of these two you have chosen. [25]Show us who should take the place of Judas as an apostle. He gave up being an apostle to go where he belongs." [26]Then they cast lots. Matthias was chosen. So he was added to the 11 apostles.

The Holy Spirit Comes at Pentecost

2 The day of Pentecost came. The believers all gathered in one place. ²Suddenly a sound came from heaven. It was like a strong wind blowing. It filled the whole house where they were sitting. ³They saw something that looked like tongues of fire. The flames separated and settled on each of them. ⁴All of them were filled with the Holy Spirit. They began to speak in languages they had not known before. The Spirit gave them the ability to do this.

⁵Godly Jews from every country in the world were staying in Jerusalem. ⁶A crowd came together when they heard the sound. They were bewildered because they each heard the believers speaking in their own language. ⁷The crowd was really amazed. They asked, "Aren't all these people from Galilee? ⁸Why, then, do we each hear them speaking in our own native language? ⁹We are Parthians, Medes and Elamites. We live in Mesopotamia, Judea and Cappadocia. We are from Pontus, Asia, ¹⁰Phrygia and Pamphylia. Others of us are from Egypt and the parts of Libya near Cyrene. Still others are visitors from Rome. ¹¹Some of the visitors are Jews. Others have accepted the Jewish faith. Also, Cretans and Arabs are here. We hear all these people speaking about God's wonders in our own languages!" ¹²They were amazed and bewildered. They asked one another, "What does this mean?"

¹³But some people in the crowd made fun of the believers. "They've had too much wine!" they said.

Peter Speaks to the Crowd

¹⁴Then Peter stood up with the Eleven. In a loud voice he spoke to the crowd. "My Jewish friends," he said, "let me explain this to you. All of you who live in Jerusalem, listen carefully to what I say. ¹⁵You think these people are drunk. But they aren't. It's only nine o'clock in the morning! ¹⁶No, here is what the prophet Joel meant. ¹⁷He said,

> "'In the last days, God says,
>   I will pour out my Holy Spirit on all people.
> Your sons and daughters will prophesy.
>   Your young men will see visions.
>   Your old men will have dreams.
> ¹⁸In those days I will pour out my Spirit
>   even on those who serve me, both men and women.
>   When I do, they will prophesy.

¹⁹ I will show wonders in the heavens above.
>   I will show miraculous signs on the earth below.
>   There will be blood and fire and clouds of smoke.
²⁰ The sun will become dark.
>   The moon will turn red like blood.
>   This will happen before the coming of the great and
>   glorious day of the Lord.
²¹ Everyone who calls
>   on the name of the Lord will be saved.'   *(Joel 2:28–32)*

²²"People of Israel, listen to this! Jesus of Nazareth was a man who had God's approval. God did miracles, wonders and signs among you through Jesus. You yourselves know this. ²³Long ago God planned that Jesus would be handed over to you. With the help of evil people, you put Jesus to death. You nailed him to the cross. ²⁴But God raised him from the dead. He set him free from the suffering of death. It wasn't possible for death to keep its hold on Jesus. ²⁵David spoke about him. He said,

> "'I know that the Lord is always with me.
>   He is at my right hand.
>   I will always be secure.
²⁶ So my heart is glad. Joy is on my tongue.
>   My body also will be full of hope.
²⁷ You will not leave me in the grave.
>   You will not let your Holy One rot away.
²⁸ You always show me the path that leads to life.
>   You will fill me with joy when I am with you.'

> *(Psalm 16:8–11)*

²⁹"Brothers and sisters, you can be sure that King David died. He was buried. His tomb is still here today. ³⁰But David was a prophet. He knew that God had made a promise to him. He had taken an oath that someone in David's family line would be king after him. ³¹David saw what was ahead. So he spoke about the Christ rising from the dead. He said that the Christ would not be left in the grave. His body wouldn't rot in the ground. ³²God has raised this same Jesus back to life. We are all witnesses of this. ³³Jesus has been given a place of honor at the right hand of God. He has received the Holy Spirit from the Father. This is what God had promised. It is Jesus who has poured out what you now see and hear. ³⁴David did not go up to heaven. But he said,

> "'The Lord said to my Lord,
>   "Sit at my right hand.

³⁵I will put your enemies
     under your control."'   *(Psalm 110:1)*

³⁶"So be sure of this, all you people of Israel. You nailed Jesus to the cross. But God has made him both Lord and Christ."

³⁷When the people heard this, their hearts were filled with shame. They said to Peter and the other apostles, "Brothers, what should we do?"

³⁸Peter replied, "All of you must turn away from your sins and be baptized in the name of Jesus Christ. Then your sins will be forgiven. You will receive the gift of the Holy Spirit. ³⁹The promise is for you and your children. It is also for all who are far away. It is for all whom the Lord our God will choose."

⁴⁰Peter said many other things to warn them. He begged them, "Save yourselves from these evil people." ⁴¹Those who accepted his message were baptized. About 3,000 people joined the believers that day.

The Believers Share Life Together

⁴²The believers studied what the apostles taught. They shared life together. They broke bread and ate together. And they prayed. ⁴³Everyone felt that God was near. The apostles did many wonders and miraculous signs. ⁴⁴All the believers were together. They shared everything they had. ⁴⁵They sold what they owned. They gave each other everything they needed. ⁴⁶Every day they met together in the temple courtyard. In their homes they broke bread and ate together. Their hearts were glad and honest and true. ⁴⁷They praised God. They were respected by all the people. Every day the Lord added to their group those who were being saved.

Peter Heals the Disabled Beggar

3 One day Peter and John were going up to the temple. It was three o'clock in the afternoon. It was the time for prayer. ²A

GREAT VERSE —TO— REMEMBER

2:38 All of you must turn away from your sins and be baptized in the name of Jesus Christ. Then your sins will be forgiven. You will receive the gift of the Holy Spirit.

man unable to walk was being carried to the temple gate called Beautiful. He had been that way since he was born. Every day someone put him near the gate. There he would beg from people going into the temple courtyards.

³He saw that Peter and John were about to enter. So he asked them for money. ⁴Peter looked straight at him, and so did John. Then Peter said, "Look at us!" ⁵So the man watched them closely. He expected to get something from them.

⁶Peter said, "I don't have any silver or gold. But I'll give you what I have. In the name of Jesus Christ of Nazareth, get up and walk." ⁷Then Peter took him by the right hand and helped him up. At once the man's feet and ankles became strong. ⁸He jumped to his feet and began to walk. He went with Peter and John into the temple courtyards. He walked and jumped and praised God. ⁹All the people saw him walking and praising God. ¹⁰They recognized him as the same man who used to sit and beg at the temple gate called Beautiful. They were filled with wonder. They were amazed at what had happened to him.

Peter Speaks to the Jews

¹¹The beggar was holding on to Peter and John. All the people were amazed. They came running to them at Solomon's Porch. ¹²When Peter saw this, he said, "People of Israel, why does this surprise you? Why do you stare at us? We haven't made this man walk by our own power or godliness. ¹³The God of our fathers, Abraham, Isaac and Jacob, has done this. He has brought glory to Jesus, who serves him. But you handed Jesus over to be killed. Pilate had decided to let him go. But you spoke against Jesus when he was in Pilate's court. ¹⁴You spoke against the Holy and Blameless One. You asked for a murderer to be set free instead. ¹⁵You killed the one who gives life. But God raised him from the dead. We are witnesses of this. ¹⁶This man whom you see and know was made strong because of faith in Jesus' name. Faith in Jesus has healed him completely. You can see it with your own eyes.

¹⁷"My friends, I know you didn't realize what you were doing. Neither did your leaders. ¹⁸But God had given a promise through all the prophets. And this is how he has made his promise come true. He said that his Christ would suffer. ¹⁹So turn away from your sins. Turn to God. Then your sins will be wiped away. The time will come when the Lord will make everything new. ²⁰He will send the Christ. Jesus has been appointed as the Christ for

you. [21]He must remain in heaven until the time when God makes everything new. He promised this long ago through his holy prophets. [22]Moses said, 'The Lord your God will raise up for you a prophet like me. He will be one of your own people. You must listen to everything he tells you. [23]Those who do not listen to him will be completely cut off from their people.' *(Deuteronomy 18:15,18,19)*

[24]"Samuel and all the prophets after him spoke about this. They said these days would come. [25]What the prophets said was meant for you. The covenant God made with your people long ago is yours also. He said to Abraham, 'All nations on earth will be blessed through your children.' *(Genesis 22:18; 26:4)* [26]God raised up Jesus, who serves him. God sent him first to you. He did it to bless you. He wanted to turn each of you from your evil ways."

Peter and John Are Taken to the Sanhedrin

4 Peter and John were speaking to the people. The priests, the captain of the temple guard, and the Sadducees came up to the apostles. [2]They were very upset by what the apostles were teaching the people. The apostles were saying that because Jesus rose from the dead, people can be raised from the dead. [3]So the temple authorities arrested Peter and John. It was already evening, so they put them in prison until the next day. [4]But many who heard the message believed. The number of believers grew to about 5,000.

[5]The next day the rulers, the elders and the teachers of the law met in Jerusalem. [6]Annas, the high priest, was there. So were Caiaphas, John, Alexander and others in the high priest's family. [7]They had Peter and John brought to them. They wanted to question them. "By what power did you do this?" they asked. "And through whose name?"

[8]Peter was filled with the Holy Spirit. He said to them, "Rulers and elders of the people! [9]Are you asking us to explain our actions today? Do you want to know why we were kind to a disabled man? Are you asking how he was healed? [10]Then listen to this, you and all the people of Israel! You nailed Jesus Christ of Nazareth to the cross. But God raised him from the dead. It is through Jesus' name that this man stands healed in front of you. [11]Scripture says that Jesus is

> "'the stone you builders did not accept.
>   But it has become the most important stone of all.'
>
> *(Psalm 118:22)*

[12]You can't be saved by believing in anyone else. God has given us no other name under heaven that will save us."

[13]The leaders saw how bold Peter and John were. They also realized that Peter and John were ordinary men with no training. This surprised the leaders. They realized that these men had been with Jesus. [14]The leaders could see the man who had been healed standing there with them. So there was nothing they could say. [15]They ordered Peter and John to leave the Sanhedrin. Then they talked things over. [16]"What can we do with these men?" they asked. "Everybody in Jerusalem knows they have done an outstanding miracle. We can't say it didn't happen. [17]We have to stop this thing. It must not spread any further among the people. We have to warn these men. They must never speak to anyone in Jesus' name again."

[18]Once again the leaders called in Peter and John. They commanded them not to speak or teach at all in Jesus' name. [19]But Peter and John replied, "Judge for yourselves. Which is right from God's point of view? Should we obey you? Or God? [20]There's nothing else we can do. We have to speak about the things we've seen and heard."

[21]The leaders warned them again. Then they let them go. They couldn't decide how to punish Peter and John. They knew that all the people were praising God for what had happened. [22]The man who had been healed by the miracle was over 40 years old.

The Believers Pray

[23]Peter and John were allowed to leave. They went back to their own people. They reported everything the chief priests and the elders had said to them. [24]When the believers heard this, they raised their voices together in prayer to God. "Lord and King," they said, "you made the heavens, the earth and the sea. You made everything in them. [25]Long ago you spoke by the Holy Spirit through the mouth of our father David, who served you. You said,

> "'Why are the nations angry?
>> Why do the people make useless plans?
> [26]The kings of the earth take their stand against the Lord.
>> The rulers of the earth gather together
>> against his Anointed King.'   *(Psalm 2:1,2)*

[27]"In fact, Herod and Pontius Pilate met together in this city with those who weren't Jews. They also met with the people of

Israel. All of them made plans against your holy servant Jesus. He is the one you anointed. [28]They did what your power and purpose had already decided should happen. [29]Now, Lord, consider the bad things they say they are going to do. Help us to be very bold when we speak your word. [30]Stretch out your hand to heal. Do miraculous signs and wonders through the name of your holy servant Jesus."

[31]After they prayed, the place where they were meeting was shaken. They were all filled with the Holy Spirit. They were bold when they spoke God's word.

The Believers Share What They Own

[32]All the believers were agreed in heart and mind. They didn't claim that anything they had was their own. They shared everything they owned. [33]With great power the apostles continued their teaching. They gave witness that the Lord Jesus had risen from the dead. And they were greatly blessed by God.

[34]There were no needy persons among them. From time to time, those who owned land or houses sold them. They brought the money from the sales. [35]They put it down at the apostles' feet. It was then given out to anyone who needed it.

[36]Joseph was a Levite from Cyprus. The apostles called him Barnabas. The name Barnabas means Son of Help. [37]Barnabas sold a field he owned. He brought the money from the sale. He put it down at the apostles' feet.

Ananias and Sapphira

5 A man named Ananias and his wife, Sapphira, also sold some land. [2]He kept part of the money for himself. Sapphira knew he had kept it. He brought the rest of it and put it down at the apostles' feet.

[3]Then Peter said, "Ananias, why did you let Satan fill your

GREAT VERSE —TO— REMEMBER

4:32 All the believers were agreed in heart and mind. They didn't claim that anything they had was their own. They shared everything they owned.

heart? He made you lie to the Holy Spirit. You have kept some of the money you received for the land. [4]Didn't the land belong to you before it was sold? After it was sold, you could have used the money as you wished. What made you think of doing such a thing? You haven't lied to just anyone. You've lied to God."

[5]When Ananias heard this, he fell down and died. All who heard what had happened were filled with fear. [6]Some young men came and wrapped up his body. They carried him out and buried him.

[7]About three hours later, the wife of Ananias came in. She didn't know what had happened. [8]Peter asked her, "Tell me. Is this the price you and Ananias sold the land for?"

"Yes," she said. "That's the price."

[9]Peter asked her, "How could you agree to test the Spirit of the Lord? Listen! You can hear the steps of the men who buried your husband. They are at the door. They will carry you out also."

[10]At that very moment she fell down at his feet and died. Then the young men came in. They saw that Sapphira was dead. So they carried her out and buried her beside her husband. [11]The whole church and all who heard about these things were filled with fear.

The Apostles Heal Many People

[12]The apostles did many miraculous signs and wonders among the people. All the believers used to meet together at Solomon's Porch. [13]No outsider dared to join them. But the people thought highly of them. [14]More and more men and women believed in the Lord. They joined the other believers. [15]So people brought those who were sick into the streets. They placed them on beds and mats. They hoped that at least Peter's shadow might fall on some of them as he walked by. [16]Crowds even gathered from the towns around Jerusalem. They brought their sick. They also brought those who were suffering because of evil spirits. All of them were healed.

An Angel Opens the Prison Doors

[17]The high priest and all his companions were Sadducees. They were very jealous of the apostles. [18]So they arrested them and put them in the public prison. [19]But during the night an angel of the Lord came. He opened the prison doors and brought the apostles out. [20]"Go! Stand in the temple courtyard," the angel said. "Tell the people all about this new life."

²¹Early the next day they did as they had been told. They entered the temple courtyard. There they began to teach the people.

The high priest and his companions arrived. They called the Sanhedrin together. The Sanhedrin was a gathering of all the elders of Israel. They sent for the apostles who were in prison. ²²The officers arrived at the prison. But they didn't find the apostles there. So they went back and reported it. ²³"We found the prison locked up tight," they said. "The guards were standing at the doors. But when we opened the doors, we didn't find anyone inside." ²⁴When the captain of the temple guard and the chief priests heard this report, they were bewildered. They wondered what would happen next.

²⁵Then someone came and said, "Look! The men you put in prison are standing in the temple courtyard. They are teaching the people." ²⁶So the captain went with his officers and brought the apostles back. But they didn't use force. They were afraid the people would kill them by throwing stones at them.

²⁷They brought the apostles to be judged by the Sanhedrin. The high priest questioned them. ²⁸"We gave you clear orders not to teach in Jesus' name," he said. "But you have filled Jerusalem with your teaching. You want to make us guilty of this man's death."

²⁹Peter and the other apostles replied, "We must obey God instead of people! ³⁰You had Jesus killed by nailing him to a cross. But the God of our people raised Jesus from the dead. ³¹Now Jesus is Prince and Savior. God has proved this by giving him a place of honor at his own right hand. He did it so that he could turn Israel away from their sins and forgive them. ³²We are witnesses of these things. And so is the Holy Spirit. God has given the Spirit to those who obey him."

³³When the leaders heard this, they became very angry. They wanted to put the apostles to death. ³⁴But a Pharisee named Gamaliel stood up in the Sanhedrin. He was a teacher of the law. He was honored by all the people. He ordered the men to be

GREAT VERSE —TO— REMEMBER

5:29 Peter and the other apostles replied, "We must obey God instead of people!"

taken outside for a little while. ³⁵Then he spoke to the Sanhedrin. "Men of Israel," he said, "think carefully about what you plan to do to these men. ³⁶Some time ago Theudas appeared. He claimed he was really somebody. About 400 people followed him. But he was killed. All his followers were scattered. So they accomplished nothing. ³⁷After this, Judas from Galilee came along. This was in the days when the Romans made a list of all the people. Judas led a gang of men against the Romans. He too was killed. All his followers were scattered. ³⁸So let me give you some advice. Leave these men alone! Let them go! If their plans and actions are only human, they will fail. ³⁹But if their plans come from God, you won't be able to stop these men. You will only find yourselves fighting against God."

⁴⁰His speech won the leaders over. They called the apostles in and had them whipped. The leaders ordered them not to speak in Jesus' name. Then they let the apostles go.

⁴¹The apostles were full of joy as they left the Sanhedrin. They considered it an honor to suffer shame for the name of Jesus. ⁴²Day after day, they kept teaching in the temple courtyards and from house to house. They never stopped telling the good news that Jesus is the Christ.

Seven Leaders Are Chosen

6 In those days the number of believers was growing. The Jews who followed Greek practices complained against the Jews who followed only Jewish practices. They said that the widows of men who followed Greek practices were not being taken care of. They weren't getting their fair share of food each day. ²So the Twelve gathered all the believers together. They said, "It wouldn't be right for us to give up teaching God's word in order to wait on tables. ³Brothers and sisters, choose seven of your men. They must be known as men who are wise and full of the Holy Spirit. We will turn this important work over to them. ⁴Then we can give our attention to prayer and to teaching the word."

⁵This plan pleased the whole group. They chose Stephen. He was full of faith and of the Holy Spirit. Philip, Procorus, Nicanor, Timon and Parmenas were chosen too. The group also chose Nicolas from Antioch. He had accepted the Jewish faith. ⁶The group brought them to the apostles. Then the apostles prayed and placed their hands on them.

⁷So God's word spread. The number of believers in Jerusalem

grew quickly. Also, a large number of priests began to obey Jesus' teachings.

Stephen Is Arrested

[8]Stephen was full of God's grace and power. He did great wonders and miraculous signs among the people. [9]But members of the group called the Synagogue of the Freedmen began to oppose him. Some of them were Jews from Cyrene and Alexandria. Others were Jews from Cilicia and Asia Minor. They all began to argue with Stephen. [10]But he was too wise for them. They couldn't stand up against the Holy Spirit who spoke through him.

[11]Then in secret they talked some men into lying about Stephen. They said, "We heard Stephen speak evil things against Moses. He also spoke evil things against God."

[12]So the people were stirred up. The elders and the teachers of the law were stirred up too. They arrested Stephen and brought him to the Sanhedrin. [13]They found people who were willing to tell lies. The false witnesses said, "This fellow never stops speaking against this holy place. He also speaks against the law. [14]We have heard him say that this Jesus of Nazareth will destroy this place. He says Jesus will change the practices that Moses handed down to us."

[15]All who were sitting in the Sanhedrin looked right at Stephen. They saw that his face was like the face of an angel.

Stephen Speaks to the Sanhedrin

7 Then the high priest questioned Stephen. "Is what these people are saying true?" he asked.

[2]"Brothers and fathers, listen to me!" Stephen replied. "The God of glory appeared to our father Abraham. At that time Abraham was still in Mesopotamia. He had not yet begun living in Haran. [3]'Leave your country and your people,' God said. 'Go to the land I will show you.' *(Genesis 12:1)*

[4]"So Abraham left the land of Babylonia. He settled in Haran. After his father died, God sent Abraham to this land where you are now living. [5]God didn't give him any property here. He didn't give him even a foot of land. But God made a promise to him and to all his family after him. He said they would possess the land. The promise was made even though at that time Abraham had no child.

[6]"Here is what God said to him. 'Your family after you will be

strangers in a country that is not their own. They will be slaves and will be treated badly for 400 years. ⁷But I will punish the nation that makes them slaves,' God said. 'After that, they will leave that country and worship me here.' *(Genesis 15:13,14)*

⁸"Then God made a covenant with Abraham. God told him that circumcision would show who the members of the covenant were. Abraham became Isaac's father. He circumcised Isaac eight days after he was born. Later, Isaac became Jacob's father. Jacob had 12 sons. They became the founders of the 12 tribes of Israel.

⁹"Jacob's sons were jealous of their brother Joseph. So they sold him as a slave. He was taken to Egypt. But God was with him. ¹⁰He saved Joseph from all his troubles. God made Joseph wise. He helped him to become the friend of Pharaoh, the king of Egypt. So Pharaoh made Joseph ruler over Egypt and his whole palace.

¹¹"There was not enough food for all Egypt and Canaan. This brought great suffering. Jacob and his sons couldn't find food. ¹²But Jacob heard that there was grain in Egypt. So he sent his sons on their first visit. ¹³On their second visit, Joseph told his brothers who he was. Pharaoh learned about Joseph's family.

¹⁴"After this, Joseph sent for his father Jacob and his whole family. The total number of people was 75. ¹⁵Then Jacob went down to Egypt. There he and his family died. ¹⁶Some of their bodies were brought back to Shechem. They were placed in a tomb Abraham had bought. He had purchased it from Hamor's sons at Shechem for a certain amount of money.

¹⁷"In Egypt the number of our people grew and grew. It was nearly time for God to make his promise to Abraham come true. ¹⁸Another king became ruler of Egypt. He knew nothing about Joseph. ¹⁹He was very evil and dishonest with our people. He beat them down. He forced them to throw out their newborn babies to die.

²⁰"At that time Moses was born. He was not an ordinary child. For three months he was taken care of by his family. ²¹Then he was placed outside. But Pharaoh's daughter took him home. She brought him up as her own son. ²²Moses was taught all the knowledge of the people of Egypt. He became a powerful speaker and a man of action.

²³"When Moses was 40 years old, he decided to visit the people of Israel. They were his own people. ²⁴He saw one of them being treated badly by a man of Egypt. So he went to help him. He got even by killing the man. ²⁵Moses thought his own people would

realize that God was using him to save them. But they didn't.

²⁶"The next day Moses saw two men of Israel fighting. He tried to make peace between them. 'Men, you are both of Israel,' he said. 'Why do you want to hurt each other?'

²⁷"But the man who was treating the other one badly pushed Moses to one side. He said, 'Who made you ruler and judge over us? ²⁸Do you want to kill me as you killed the Egyptian yesterday?' *(Exodus 2:14)* ²⁹When Moses heard this, he escaped to Midian. He lived there as a stranger. He became the father of two sons there.

³⁰"Forty years passed. Then an angel appeared to Moses in the flames of a burning bush. This happened in the desert near Mount Sinai. ³¹When Moses saw the bush, he was amazed. He went over for a closer look. There he heard the Lord's voice. ³²'I am the God of your fathers,' the Lord said. 'I am the God of Abraham, Isaac and Jacob.' *(Exodus 3:6)* Moses shook with fear. He didn't dare to look.

³³"Then the Lord said to him, 'Take off your sandals. The place you are standing on is holy ground. ³⁴I have seen my people beaten down in Egypt. I have heard their groans. I have come down to set them free. Now come. I will send you back to Egypt.'
(Exodus 3:5,7,8,10)

³⁵"This is the same Moses the two men of Israel would not accept. They had said, 'Who made you ruler and judge?' But God himself sent Moses to rule the people of Israel and set them free. He spoke to Moses through the angel who had appeared to him in the bush. ³⁶So Moses led them out of Egypt. He did wonders and miraculous signs in Egypt, at the Red Sea, and for 40 years in the desert.

³⁷"This is the same Moses who spoke to the people of Israel. 'God will send you a prophet,' he said. 'He will be like me. He will come from your own people.' *(Deuteronomy 18:15)* ³⁸Moses was with the Israelites in the desert. He was with the angel who spoke to him on Mount Sinai. Moses was with our people of long ago. He received living words to pass on to us.

³⁹"But our people refused to obey Moses. They would not accept him. In their hearts, they wished they were back in Egypt. ⁴⁰They told Aaron, 'Make us a god who will lead us. This fellow Moses led us out of Egypt. But we don't know what has happened to him!' *(Exodus 32:1)* ⁴¹That was the time they made a statue to be their god. It looked like a calf. They brought sacrifices to it. They were glad because of what they had made with their own hands. ⁴²But

God turned away from them. He left them to worship the sun, moon and stars. This agrees with what is written in the book of the prophets. There it says,

> "'People of Israel, did you bring me sacrifices and
>   offerings
>   for 40 years in the desert?
> [43] You lifted up the place where Molech was worshiped.
>   You lifted up the star of your god Rephan.
>   You made statues of them to worship.
> So I will send you away from your country.'   *(Amos 5:25–27)*
>   God sent them to Babylon and even farther.

[44]"Long ago our people had with them in the desert the holy tent where the tablets of the covenant were kept. Moses had made the holy tent as God had commanded him. It was made like the pattern he had seen. [45]Our people received the tent from God. They brought it with them when they took the land of Canaan. God drove out the nations that were in their way. At that time Joshua was Israel's leader.

"The tent remained in the land until David's time. [46]David was blessed by God. So David asked if he could build a house for the God of Jacob. [47]Instead, it was Solomon who built it for him.

[48]"But the Most High God does not live in houses made by human hands. As God says through the prophet,

> [49] "'Heaven is my throne.
>   The earth is under my control.
>   What kind of house will you build for me?
>
>   says the Lord.
>   Where will my resting place be?
> [50] Didn't my hand make all these things?'   *(Isaiah 66:1,2)*

[51]"You people! You won't obey! You are stubborn! You won't listen! You are just like your people of long ago! You always oppose the Holy Spirit! [52]Was there ever a prophet your people didn't try to hurt? They even killed those who told about the coming of the Blameless One. And now you have handed him over to his enemies. You have murdered him. [53]The law you received was brought by angels. But you haven't obeyed it."

Stephen Is Killed

[54]When the Sanhedrin heard this, they became very angry. They ground their teeth at Stephen. [55]But he was full of the Holy

Spirit. He looked up to heaven and saw God's glory. He saw Jesus standing at God's right hand. ⁵⁶"Look!" he said. "I see heaven open. The Son of Man is standing at God's right hand."

⁵⁷When the Sanhedrin heard this, they covered their ears. They yelled at the top of their voices. They all rushed at him. ⁵⁸They dragged him out of the city. They began to throw stones at him to kill him. The witnesses took off their coats. They placed them at the feet of a young man named Saul.

⁵⁹While the members of the Sanhedrin were throwing stones at Stephen, he prayed. "Lord Jesus, receive my spirit," he said. ⁶⁰Then he fell on his knees. He cried out, "Lord! Don't hold this sin against them!" When he had said this, he died.

8 Saul was there. He had agreed that Stephen should die.

The Church Is Scattered

On that day the church in Jerusalem began to be attacked and treated badly. All except the apostles were scattered throughout Judea and Samaria.

²Godly Jews buried Stephen. They sobbed and sobbed over him.

³But Saul began to destroy the church. He went from house to house. He dragged men and women away and put them in prison.

Philip Goes to Samaria

⁴The believers who had been scattered preached the word everywhere they went. ⁵Philip went down to a city in Samaria. There he preached about the Christ. ⁶The crowds listened to Philip. They saw the miraculous signs he did. They all paid close attention to what he said. ⁷Evil spirits screamed and came out of many people. Many who were disabled or who couldn't walk were healed. ⁸So there was great joy in that city.

GREAT VERSE — TO — REMEMBER

7:55 But [Stephen] was full of the Holy Spirit. He looked up to heaven and saw God's glory. He saw Jesus standing at God's right hand.

Simon the Evil Magician

⁹A man named Simon lived in the city. For quite a while he had practiced evil magic there. He amazed all the people of Samaria. He claimed to be someone great. ¹⁰All of the people listened to him, from the least important of them to the most important. They exclaimed, "This man is known as the Great Power of God!" ¹¹He had amazed them for a long time with his magic. So they followed him.

¹²But Philip preached the good news of God's kingdom. He preached the name of Jesus Christ. So men and women believed and were baptized. ¹³Simon himself believed and was baptized. He followed Philip everywhere. He was amazed by the great signs and miracles he saw.

¹⁴The apostles in Jerusalem heard that people in Samaria had accepted God's word. So they sent Peter and John to them. ¹⁵When they arrived there, they prayed that the believers would receive the Holy Spirit. ¹⁶The Holy Spirit had not yet come on any of them. They had only been baptized in the name of the Lord Jesus. ¹⁷Then Peter and John placed their hands on them. And they received the Holy Spirit.

¹⁸Simon watched as the apostles placed their hands on them. He saw that the Spirit was given to them. So he offered money to Peter and John. ¹⁹He said, "Give me this power too. Then everyone I place my hands on will receive the Holy Spirit."

²⁰Peter answered, "May your money be destroyed with you! Do you think you can buy God's gift with money? ²¹You have no part or share in this holy work. Your heart is not right with God. ²²Turn away from this evil sin of yours. Pray to the Lord. Perhaps he will forgive you for having such a thought in your heart. ²³I see that you are very bitter. You are a prisoner of sin."

²⁴Then Simon answered, "Pray to the Lord for me. Pray that nothing you have said will happen to me."

²⁵Peter and John gave witness and preached the Lord's word. Then they returned to Jerusalem. On the way they preached the good news in many villages in Samaria.

Philip and the Man From Ethiopia

²⁶An angel of the Lord spoke to Philip. "Go south to the desert road," he said. "It's the road that goes down from Jerusalem to Gaza." ²⁷So Philip started out. On his way he met an Ethiopian official. The man had an important position. He was in charge of all the wealth of Candace. She was the queen of Ethiopia. He had

gone to Jerusalem to worship. ²⁸On his way home he was sitting in his chariot. He was reading the book of Isaiah the prophet. ²⁹The Holy Spirit told Philip, "Go to that chariot. Stay near it."

³⁰So Philip ran up to the chariot. He heard the man reading Isaiah the prophet. "Do you understand what you're reading?" Philip asked.

³¹"How can I?" he said. "I need someone to explain it to me." So he invited Philip to come up and sit with him.

³²Here is the part of Scripture the official was reading. It says,

> "He was led like a sheep to be killed.
>> Just as lambs are silent while their wool is being cut
>>> off,
>> he did not open his mouth.
> ³³When he was treated badly, he was refused a fair trial.
>> Who can say anything about his children?
>> His life was cut off from the earth."   *(Isaiah 53:7,8)*

³⁴The official said to Philip, "Tell me, please. Who is the prophet talking about? Himself, or someone else?" ³⁵Then Philip began with that same part of Scripture. He told him the good news about Jesus.

³⁶/³⁷As they traveled along the road, they came to some water. The official said, "Look! Here is water! Why shouldn't I be baptized?" ³⁸He gave orders to stop the chariot. Then both Philip and the official went down into the water. Philip baptized him. ³⁹When they came up out of the water, the Spirit of the Lord suddenly took Philip away. The official did not see him again. He went on his way full of joy. ⁴⁰Philip was seen next at Azotus. From there he traveled all around. He preached the good news in all the towns. Finally he arrived in Caesarea.

Saul Becomes a Believer

9 Meanwhile, Saul continued to oppose the Lord's followers. He said they would be put to death. He went to the high priest. ²He asked the priest for letters to the synagogues in Damascus. He wanted to find men and women who belonged to the Way of Jesus. The letters would allow him to take them as prisoners to Jerusalem.

³On his journey, Saul approached Damascus. Suddenly a light from heaven flashed around him. ⁴He fell to the ground. He heard a voice speak to him. "Saul! Saul!" the voice said. "Why are you opposing me?"

⁵"Who are you, Lord?" Saul asked.

"I am Jesus," he replied. "I am the one you are opposing. ⁶Now get up and go into the city. There you will be told what you must do."

⁷The men traveling with Saul stood there. They weren't able to speak. They had heard the sound. But they didn't see anyone. ⁸Saul got up from the ground. He opened his eyes, but he couldn't see. So they led him by the hand into Damascus. ⁹For three days he was blind. He didn't eat or drink anything.

¹⁰In Damascus there was a believer named Ananias. The Lord called out to him in a vision. "Ananias!" he said.

"Yes, Lord," he answered.

¹¹The Lord told him, "Go to the house of Judas on Straight Street. Ask for a man from Tarsus named Saul. He is praying. ¹²In a vision he has seen a man named Ananias. The man has come and placed his hands on him. Now he will be able to see again."

¹³"Lord," Ananias answered, "I've heard many reports about this man. They say he has done great harm to God's people in Jerusalem. ¹⁴Now he has come here to arrest all those who worship you. The chief priests have given him authority to do this."

¹⁵But the Lord said to Ananias, "Go! I have chosen this man to work for me. He will carry my name to those who aren't Jews and to their kings. He will bring my name to the people of Israel. ¹⁶I will show him how much he must suffer for me."

¹⁷Then Ananias went to the house and entered it. He placed his hands on Saul. "Brother Saul," he said, "you saw the Lord Jesus. He appeared to you on the road as you were coming here. He has sent me so that you will be able to see again. You will be filled with the Holy Spirit."

¹⁸Right away something like scales fell from Saul's eyes. And he could see again. He got up and was baptized. ¹⁹After eating some food, he got his strength back.

Saul in Damascus and Jerusalem

Saul spent several days with the believers in Damascus. ²⁰At once he began to preach in the synagogues. He taught that Jesus is the Son of God. ²¹All who heard him were amazed. They asked, "Isn't he the man who caused great trouble in Jerusalem for those who worship Jesus? Hasn't he come here to take them as prisoners to the chief priests?" ²²But Saul grew more and more powerful. The Jews living in Damascus couldn't believe what was happening. Saul proved to them that Jesus is the Christ.

²³After many days, the Jews had a meeting. They planned to kill Saul. ²⁴But he learned about their plan. Day and night they watched the city gates closely in order to kill him. ²⁵But his followers helped him escape by night. They lowered him in a basket through an opening in the wall.

²⁶When Saul came to Jerusalem, he tried to join the believers. But they were all afraid of him. They didn't believe he was really one of Jesus' followers. ²⁷But Barnabas took him to the apostles. He told them about Saul's journey. He said that Saul had seen the Lord. He told how the Lord had spoken to Saul. Barnabas also said that Saul had preached without fear in Jesus' name in Damascus.

²⁸So Saul stayed with the believers. He moved about freely in Jerusalem. He spoke boldly in the Lord's name. ²⁹He talked and argued with Jews who followed Greek practices. But they tried to kill him. ³⁰The other believers heard about this. They took Saul down to Caesarea. From there they sent him off to Tarsus.

³¹Then the church throughout Judea, Galilee and Samaria enjoyed a time of peace. The Holy Spirit gave the church strength and boldness. So they grew in numbers. And they worshiped the Lord.

Peter Goes to Lydda and Joppa

³²As Peter traveled around the country, he went to visit God's people in Lydda. ³³There he found a disabled man named Aeneas. For eight years the man had spent most of his time in bed. ³⁴"Aeneas," Peter said to him, "Jesus Christ heals you. Get up! Take care of your mat!" So Aeneas got up right away. ³⁵Everyone who lived in Lydda and Sharon saw him. They turned to the Lord.

³⁶In Joppa there was a believer named Tabitha. Her name in the Greek language was Dorcas. She was always doing good and helping poor people.

³⁷About that time she became sick and died. Her body was

GREAT VERSE —TO— REMEMBER **9:31** The Holy Spirit gave the church strength and boldness. So they grew in numbers. And they worshiped the Lord.

washed and placed in a room upstairs. ³⁸Lydda was near Joppa. The believers heard that Peter was in Lydda. So they sent two men to him. They begged him, "Please come at once!"

³⁹Peter went with them. When he arrived, he was taken upstairs to the room. All the widows stood around him crying. They showed him the robes and other clothes Dorcas had made while she was still alive.

⁴⁰Peter sent them all out of the room. Then he got down on his knees and prayed. He turned toward the dead woman. He said, "Tabitha, get up." She opened her eyes. When she saw Peter, she sat up. ⁴¹He took her by the hand and helped her to her feet. Then he called the believers and the widows. He brought her to them. They saw that she was alive. ⁴²This became known all over Joppa. Many people believed in the Lord. ⁴³Peter stayed in Joppa for some time. He stayed with Simon, a man who worked with leather.

Cornelius Calls for Peter

10 A man named Cornelius lived in Caesarea. He was a Roman commander in the Italian Regiment. ²Cornelius and all his family were faithful and worshiped God. He gave freely to people who were in need. He prayed to God regularly. ³One day about three o'clock in the afternoon he had a vision. He saw an angel of God clearly. The angel came to him and said, "Cornelius!"

⁴Cornelius was afraid. He stared at the angel. "What is it, Lord?" he asked.

The angel answered, "Your prayers and gifts to poor people have come up like an offering to God. So he has remembered you. ⁵Now send men to Joppa. Have them bring back a man named Simon. He is also called Peter. ⁶He is staying with another Simon, a man who works with leather. His house is by the sea."

⁷The angel who spoke to him left. Then Cornelius called two of his servants. He also called a godly soldier who was one of his attendants. ⁸He told them everything that had happened. Then he sent them to Joppa.

Peter Has a Vision

⁹It was about noon the next day. The men were on their journey and were approaching the city. Peter went up on the roof to pray. ¹⁰He became hungry. He wanted something to eat. While the meal was being prepared, Peter had a vision. ¹¹He saw heaven

open up. There he saw something that looked like a large sheet. It was being let down to earth by its four corners. ¹²It had all kinds of four-footed animals in it. It also had reptiles of the earth and birds of the air. ¹³Then a voice told him, "Get up, Peter. Kill and eat."

¹⁴"No, Lord! I will not!" Peter replied. "I have never eaten anything that is not pure and 'clean.'"

¹⁵The voice spoke to him a second time. "Do not say anything is not pure that God has made 'clean,'" it said.

¹⁶This happened three times. Right away the sheet was taken back up to heaven.

¹⁷Peter was wondering what the vision meant. At that very moment the men sent by Cornelius found Simon's house. They stopped at the gate ¹⁸and called out. They asked if Simon Peter was staying there.

¹⁹Peter was still thinking about the vision. The Holy Spirit spoke to him. "Simon," he said, "three men are looking for you. ²⁰Get up and go downstairs. Don't let anything keep you from going with them. I have sent them."

²¹Peter went down and spoke to the men. "I'm the one you're looking for," he said. "Why have you come?"

²²The men replied, "We have come from Cornelius, the Roman commander. He is a good man who worships God. All the Jewish people respect him. A holy angel told him to invite you to his house. Cornelius wants to hear what you have to say." ²³Then Peter invited the men into the house to be his guests.

Peter Goes to the House of Cornelius

The next day Peter went with the three men. Some of the believers from Joppa went along. ²⁴The following day he arrived in Caesarea. Cornelius was expecting them. He had called together his relatives and close friends.

²⁵When Peter entered the house, Cornelius met him. As a sign of respect, he fell at Peter's feet. ²⁶But Peter made him get up. "Stand up," he said. "I am only a man myself."

²⁷Talking with Cornelius, Peter went inside. There he found a large group of people. ²⁸He said to them, "You know that it is against our law for a Jew to have anything to do with those who aren't Jews. But God has shown me that I should not say anyone is not pure and 'clean.' ²⁹So when you sent for me, I came without asking any questions. May I ask why you sent for me?"

³⁰Cornelius answered, "Four days ago at this very hour I was in

my house praying. It was three o'clock in the afternoon. Suddenly a man in shining clothes stood in front of me. ³¹He said, 'Cornelius, God has heard your prayer. He has remembered your gifts to poor people. ³²Send someone to Joppa to get Simon Peter. He is a guest in the home of another Simon, who works with leather. He lives by the sea.' ³³So I sent for you right away. It was good of you to come. Now we are all here. And God is here with us. We are ready to listen to everything the Lord has commanded you to tell us."

³⁴Then Peter began to speak. "I now realize how true it is that God treats everyone the same," he said. ³⁵"He accepts people from every nation. He accepts all who have respect for him and do what is right.

³⁶"You know the message God sent to the people of Israel. It is the good news of peace through Jesus Christ. He is Lord of all. ³⁷You know what has happened all through Judea. It started in Galilee after John preached about baptism. ³⁸You know how God anointed Jesus of Nazareth with the Holy Spirit and with power. Jesus went around doing good. He healed all who were under the devil's power. God was with him.

³⁹"We are witnesses of everything he did in the land of the Jews and in Jerusalem. They killed him by nailing him to a cross. ⁴⁰But on the third day God raised him from the dead. God allowed Jesus to be seen. ⁴¹But he wasn't seen by all the people. He was seen only by us. We are witnesses whom God had already chosen. We ate and drank with him after he rose from the dead.

⁴²"He commanded us to preach to the people. He told us to give witness that he is the one appointed by God to judge the living and the dead. ⁴³All the prophets give witness about him. They say that all who believe in him have their sins forgiven through his name."

⁴⁴While Peter was still saying these things, the Holy Spirit came

---

10:34-35 "I now realize how true it is that God treats everyone the same," [Peter] said. "He accepts people from every nation. He accepts all who have respect for him and do what is right."

on all who heard the message. ⁴⁵Some Jewish believers had come with Peter. They were amazed because the gift of the Holy Spirit had been poured out even on those who weren't Jews. ⁴⁶They heard them speaking in languages they had not known before. They also heard them praising God.

Then Peter said, ⁴⁷"Can anyone keep these people from being baptized with water? They have received the Holy Spirit just as we have." ⁴⁸So he ordered that they be baptized in the name of Jesus Christ. Then they asked Peter to stay with them for a few days.

Peter Explains His Actions

11 The apostles and the believers all through Judea heard that people who were not Jews had also received God's word. ²Peter went up to Jerusalem. There the Jewish believers found fault with him. ³They said, "You went into the house of those who aren't Jews. You ate with them."

⁴Peter explained everything to them. He told them exactly what had happened. ⁵"I was in the city of Joppa praying," he said. "There I had a vision. I saw something that looked like a large sheet. It was being let down from heaven by its four corners. It came down to where I was. ⁶I looked into it and saw four-footed animals of the earth. There were also wild animals, reptiles and birds. ⁷Then I heard a voice speaking to me. 'Get up, Peter,' the voice said. 'Kill and eat.'

⁸"I replied, 'No, Lord! I will not! Nothing that is not pure and "clean" has ever entered my mouth.'

⁹"A second time the voice spoke from heaven. 'Do not say anything is not pure that God has made "clean,"' the voice said. ¹⁰This happened three times. Then the sheet was pulled up into heaven.

¹¹"Just then three men stopped at the house where I was staying. They had been sent to me from Caesarea. ¹²The Holy Spirit told me not to let anything keep me from going with them. These six brothers here went with me. We entered the man's house. ¹³He told us how he had seen an angel appear in his house. The angel said, 'Send to Joppa for Simon Peter. ¹⁴He has a message to bring to you. You and your whole family will be saved through it.'

¹⁵"As I began to speak, the Holy Spirit came on them. He came just as he had come on us at the beginning. ¹⁶Then I remembered the Lord's words. 'John baptized with water,' he had said. 'But

you will be baptized with the Holy Spirit.' [17]God gave them the same gift he gave those of us who believed in the Lord Jesus Christ. So who was I to think that I could oppose God?"

[18]When they heard this, they didn't object anymore. They praised God. They said, "So then, God has allowed even those who aren't Jews to turn away from their sins and live."

Believers Are Called Christians for the First Time

[19]Some believers had been scattered by the suffering that came to them after Stephen's death. They traveled as far as Phoenicia, Cyprus and Antioch. But they told the message only to Jews. [20]Some believers from Cyprus and Cyrene went to Antioch. There they began to speak to Greeks also. They told them the good news about the Lord Jesus. [21]The Lord's power was with them. Large numbers of people believed and turned to the Lord.

[22]The church in Jerusalem heard about this. So they sent Barnabas to Antioch. [23]When he arrived and saw what the grace of God had done, he was glad. He told them all to remain true to the Lord with all their hearts. [24]Barnabas was a good man. He was full of the Holy Spirit and of faith. Large numbers of people came to know the Lord.

[25]Then Barnabas went to Tarsus to look for Saul. [26]He found him there. Then he brought him to Antioch. For a whole year Barnabas and Saul met with the church. They taught large numbers of people. At Antioch the believers were called Christians for the first time.

[27]In those days some prophets came down from Jerusalem to Antioch. [28]One of them was named Agabus. He stood up and spoke through the Spirit. He said there would not be nearly enough food anywhere in the Roman world. This happened while Claudius was the emperor. [29]The believers decided to provide help for the brothers and sisters living in Judea. All of them helped as much as they could. [30]They sent their gift to the elders through Barnabas and Saul.

GREAT VERSE — TO — REMEMBER

11:24 Barnabas was a good man. He was full of the Holy Spirit and of faith. Large numbers of people came to know the Lord.

An Angel Helps Peter Escape From Prison

12 About this time, King Herod arrested some people who belonged to the church. He planned to make them suffer greatly. ²He had James killed with a sword. James was John's brother. ³Herod saw that the death of James pleased the Jews. So he arrested Peter also. This happened during the Feast of Unleavened Bread. ⁴After Herod arrested Peter, he put him in prison. Peter was placed under guard. He was watched by four groups of four soldiers each. Herod planned to put Peter on public trial. It would take place after the Passover Feast.

⁵So Peter was kept in prison. But the church prayed hard to God for him.

⁶It was the night before Herod was going to bring him to trial. Peter was sleeping between two soldiers. Two chains held him there. Lookouts stood guard at the entrance. ⁷Suddenly an angel of the Lord appeared. A light shone in the prison cell. The angel struck Peter on his side. Peter woke up. "Quick!" the angel said. "Get up!" The chains fell off Peter's wrists.

⁸Then the angel said to him, "Put on your clothes and sandals." Peter did so. "Put on your coat," the angel told him. "Follow me." ⁹Peter followed him out of the prison. But he had no idea that what the angel was doing was really happening. He thought he was seeing a vision. ¹⁰They passed the first and second guards. Then they came to the iron gate leading to the city. It opened for them by itself. They went through it. They walked the length of one street. Suddenly the angel left Peter.

¹¹Then Peter realized what had happened. He said, "Now I know for sure that the Lord sent his angel. He set me free from Herod's power. He saved me from everything the Jewish people were hoping for."

¹²When Peter understood what had happened, he went to Mary's house. Mary was the mother of John Mark. Many people had gathered in her home. They were praying there. ¹³Peter knocked at the outer entrance. A servant named Rhoda came to answer the door. ¹⁴She recognized Peter's voice. She was so excited that she ran back without opening the door. "Peter is at the door!" she exclaimed.

¹⁵"You're out of your mind," they said to her. But she kept telling them it was true. So they said, "It must be his angel."

¹⁶Peter kept on knocking. When they opened the door and saw him, they were amazed. ¹⁷Peter motioned with his hand for them to be quiet. He explained how the Lord had brought him out of

prison. "Tell James and the others about this," he said. Then he went to another place.

[18]In the morning the soldiers were bewildered. They couldn't figure out what had happened to Peter. [19]So Herod had them look everywhere for Peter. But they didn't find him. Then Herod questioned the guards closely. He ordered that they be put to death.

Herod Dies

Herod went from Judea to Caesarea. He stayed there awhile. [20]He had been quarreling with the people of Tyre and Sidon. So they got together and asked for a meeting with him. This was because they depended on the king's country to supply them with food. They gained the support of Blastus and asked for peace. Blastus was a trusted personal servant of the king.

[21]The appointed day came. Herod was seated on his throne. He was wearing his royal robes. He made a speech to the people. [22]Then they shouted, "This is the voice of a god. It's not the voice of a man." [23]Right away an angel of the Lord struck Herod down. Herod had not given praise to God. So he was eaten by worms and died.

[24]But God's word continued to increase and spread.

[25]Barnabas and Saul finished their task. Then they returned from Jerusalem. They took John Mark with them.

Barnabas and Saul Are Sent Off

13 In the church at Antioch there were prophets and teachers. Among them were Barnabas, Simeon, and Lucius from Cyrene. Simeon was also called Niger. Another was Manaen. He had been brought up with Herod, the ruler of Galilee. Saul was among them too. [2]While they were worshiping the Lord and fasting, the Holy Spirit spoke. "Set apart Barnabas and Saul for me," he said. "I have appointed them to do special work." [3]The prophets and teachers fasted and prayed. They placed their hands on Barnabas and Saul. Then they sent them off.

Events on Cyprus

[4]Barnabus and Saul were sent on their way by the Holy Spirit. They went down to Seleucia. From there they sailed to Cyprus. [5]They arrived at Salamis. There they preached God's word in the Jewish synagogues. John was with them as their helper.

[6]They traveled all across the island until they came to Paphos. There they met a Jew named Bar-Jesus. He was an evil magician

and a false prophet. [7]He was an attendant of Sergius Paulus, the governor. Paulus was a man of understanding. He sent for Barnabas and Saul. He wanted to hear God's word.

[8]But Elymas, the evil magician, opposed them. The name Elymas means "magician." He tried to keep the governor from becoming a believer. [9]Saul was also known as Paul. He was filled with the Holy Spirit. He looked straight at Elymas. He said to him, [10]"You are a child of the devil! You are an enemy of everything that is right! You cheat people. You use all kinds of tricks. Won't you ever stop twisting the right ways of the Lord? [11]Now the Lord's hand is against you. You are going to go blind. You won't be able to see the light of the sun for a while."

Right away mist and darkness came over him. He tried to feel his way around. He wanted to find someone to lead him by the hand. [12]When the governor saw what had happened, he believed. He was amazed at what Paul was teaching about the Lord.

Paul Preaches in Pisidian Antioch

[13]From Paphos, Paul and his companions sailed to Perga in Pamphylia. There John left them and returned to Jerusalem. [14]From Perga they went on to Pisidian Antioch. On the Sabbath day they entered the synagogue and sat down. [15]The Law and the Prophets were read aloud. Then the synagogue rulers sent word to Paul and his companions. They said, "Brothers, do you have a message of hope for the people? If you do, please speak."

[16]Paul stood up and motioned with his hand. Then he said, "People of Israel, and you non-Jews who worship God, listen to me! [17]The God of Israel chose our people who lived long ago. He blessed them greatly while they were in Egypt. With his mighty power he led them out of that country. [18]He put up with them for about 40 years in the desert. [19]He destroyed seven nations in Canaan. Then he gave the land to his people as their rightful share. [20]All of this took about 450 years.

"After this, God gave them judges until the time of Samuel the prophet. [21]Then the people asked for a king. He gave them Saul, son of Kish. Saul was from the tribe of Benjamin. He ruled for 40 years. [22]God removed him and made David their king. Here is God's witness about him. 'David, son of Jesse, is a man dear to my heart,' he said. 'He will do everything I want him to do.'

[23]"From this man's family line God has brought to Israel the Savior Jesus. This is what he had promised. [24]Before Jesus came, John preached that we should turn away from our sins and be

baptized. He preached this to all Israel. ²⁵John was coming to the end of his work. 'Who do you think I am?' he said. 'I am not the one you are looking for. No, he is coming after me. I am not good enough to untie his sandals.'

²⁶"Listen, brothers and sisters, you children of Abraham! Listen, you non-Jews who worship God! This message of salvation has been sent to us. ²⁷The people of Jerusalem and their rulers did not recognize Jesus. By finding him guilty, they made the prophets' words come true. These are read every Sabbath day. ²⁸The people and their rulers had no reason at all for sentencing Jesus to death. But they asked Pilate to have him killed. ²⁹They did everything that had been written about Jesus. Then they took him down from the cross. They laid him in a tomb. ³⁰But God raised him from the dead. ³¹For many days he was seen by those who had traveled with him from Galilee to Jerusalem. Now they are his witnesses to our people.

³²"We are telling you the good news. What God promised our people long ago ³³he has done for us, their children. He has raised up Jesus. This is what is written in the second Psalm. It says,

"'You are my Son.
Today I have become your Father.'   *(Psalm 2:7)*

³⁴God raised Jesus from the dead. He will never rot in the grave. This is what is written in Scripture. It says,

"'Holy and sure blessings were promised to David.
I will give them to you.'   *(Isaiah 55:3)*

³⁵In another place it says,

"'You will not let your Holy One rot away.'   *(Psalm 16:10)*

³⁶"David carried out God's purpose while he lived. Then he died. He was buried with his people. His body rotted away. ³⁷But the One whom God raised from the dead did not rot away.

³⁸"My brothers and sisters, here is what I want you to know. I

GREAT VERSE —TO— REMEMBER

13:38-39 Your sins can be forgiven because of what Jesus has done. Through him everyone who believes is made right with God.

announce to you that your sins can be forgiven because of what Jesus has done. ³⁹Through him everyone who believes is made right with God. Moses' law could not make you right in God's eyes. ⁴⁰Be careful! Don't let what the prophets spoke about happen to you. They said,

⁴¹ "'Look, you who make fun of the truth!
     Wonder and die!
  I am going to do something in your days
     that you would never believe.
  You wouldn't believe it even if someone told you.'"

(Habakkuk 1:5)

⁴²Paul and Barnabas started to leave the synagogue. The people invited them to say more about these things on the next Sabbath day. ⁴³The people were told they could leave the service. Many Jews followed Paul and Barnabas. Many non-Jews who faithfully worshiped the God of the Jews did the same. Paul and Barnabas talked with them. They tried to get them to keep living in God's grace.

⁴⁴On the next Sabbath day, almost the whole city gathered to hear the word of the Lord. ⁴⁵When the Jews saw the crowds, they became very jealous. They said evil things against what Paul was saying.

⁴⁶Then Paul and Barnabas answered them boldly. "We had to speak God's word to you first," they said. "But you don't accept it. You don't think you are good enough for eternal life. So now we are turning to those who aren't Jews. ⁴⁷This is what the Lord has commanded us to do. He said,

"'I have made you a light for those who aren't Jews.
     You will bring salvation to the whole earth.'" *(Isaiah 49:6)*

⁴⁸When the non-Jews heard this, they were glad. They honored the word of the Lord. All who were appointed for eternal life believed.

⁴⁹The word of the Lord spread through the whole area. ⁵⁰But the Jews stirred up the important women who worshiped God. They also stirred up the men who were leaders in the city. They tried to get them to attack Paul and Barnabas. They threw them out of that area. ⁵¹Paul and Barnabas didn't like this. So they shook the dust from their feet. They went on to Iconium. ⁵²The believers were filled with joy and with the Holy Spirit.

Paul and Barnabas Preach in Iconium

14 At Iconium, Paul and Barnabas went into the Jewish synagogue as usual. They spoke there with great power. Large numbers of Jews and non-Jews became believers. ²But the Jews who refused to believe stirred up those who weren't Jews. They poisoned their minds against the two men and the new believers. ³So Paul and Barnabas spent a lot of time there. They spoke boldly for the Lord. He gave them the ability to do miraculous signs and wonders. In this way the Lord showed that they were telling the truth about his grace.

⁴The people of the city did not agree with each other. Some were on the side of the Jews. Others were on the side of the apostles. ⁵Jews and non-Jews alike planned to treat Paul and Barnabas badly. Their leaders agreed. They planned to kill them by throwing stones at them. ⁶But Paul and Barnabas found out about the plan. They escaped to the Lycaonian cities of Lystra and Derbe and to the surrounding area. ⁷There they continued to preach the good news.

Paul Preaches in Lystra

⁸In Lystra there sat a man who couldn't walk. He hadn't been able to use his feet since the day he was born. ⁹He listened as Paul spoke. Paul looked right at him. He saw that the man had faith to be healed. ¹⁰So he called out, "Stand up on your feet!" Then the man jumped up and began to walk.

¹¹The crowd saw what Paul had done. They shouted in the Lycaonian language. "The gods have come down to us in human form!" they exclaimed. ¹²They called Barnabas Zeus. Paul was the main speaker. So they called him Hermes. ¹³Just outside the city was the temple of the god Zeus. The priest of Zeus brought bulls and wreaths to the city gates. He and the crowd wanted to offer sacrifices to Paul and Barnabas.

¹⁴But the apostles Barnabas and Paul heard about this. So they tore their clothes. They rushed out into the crowd. They shouted, ¹⁵"Why are you people doing this? We are only human, just like

GREAT VERSE — TO — REMEMBER

14:15 We are bringing you good news. Turn away from these worthless things. Turn to the living God.

you. We are bringing you good news. Turn away from these worthless things. Turn to the living God. He is the one who made the heavens and the earth and the sea. He made everything in them. [16]In the past, he let all nations go their own way. [17]But he has given proof of what he is like. He has shown kindness by giving you rain from heaven. He gives you crops in their seasons. He provides you with plenty of food. He fills your hearts with joy." [18]Paul and Barnabas told them all these things. But they had trouble keeping the crowd from offering sacrifices to them.

[19]Then some Jews came from Antioch and Iconium. They won the crowd over to their side. They threw stones at Paul. They thought he was dead, so they dragged him out of the city. [20]The believers gathered around Paul. Then he got up and went back into the city. The next day he and Barnabas left for Derbe.

Paul and Barnabas Return to Antioch

[21]Paul and Barnabas preached the good news in the city of Derbe. They won large numbers of followers. Then they returned to Lystra, Iconium and Antioch. [22]There they helped the believers gain strength. They told them to remain true to what they had been taught. "We must go through many hard times to enter God's kingdom," they said. [23]Paul and Barnabas appointed elders for them in each church. The elders had trusted in the Lord. Paul and Barnabus prayed and fasted. They placed the elders in the Lord's care.

[24]After going through Pisidia, Paul and Barnabas came into Pamphylia. [25]They preached the word in Perga. Then they went down to Attalia.

[26]From Attalia they sailed back to Antioch. That was where they had been committed to God's grace. They had now completed the work God had given them to do. [27]When they arrived at Antioch, they gathered the church together. They reported all that God had done through them. They told how he had opened the way for non-Jews to believe. [28]And they stayed there a long time with the believers.

Church Leaders Meet in Jerusalem

15 Certain people came down from Judea to Antioch. Here is what they were teaching the believers. "Moses commanded you to be circumcised," they said. "If you aren't, you can't be saved." [2]But Paul and Barnabas didn't agree with this. They argued strongly with them. So Paul and Barnabas were appointed to go up to Jerusalem. Some other believers were chosen to go with them. They were supposed to see the apostles and elders about this question.

³The church sent them on their way. As they traveled through Phoenicia and Samaria, they told how those who weren't Jews had turned to God. This news made all the believers very glad. ⁴When they arrived in Jerusalem, the church welcomed them. The apostles and elders welcomed them too. Then Paul and Barnabas reported everything God had done through them.

⁵Some of the believers were Pharisees. They stood up and said, "Those who aren't Jews must be circumcised. They must obey the law of Moses."

⁶The apostles and elders met to consider this question. ⁷After they had talked it over, Peter got up and spoke to them. "Brothers," he said, "you know that some time ago God chose me to take the good news to those who aren't Jews. He wanted them to hear the good news and believe. ⁸God knows the human heart. By giving the Holy Spirit to non-Jews, he showed that he accepted them. He did the same for them as he had done for us. ⁹He showed that there is no difference between us and them. He made their hearts pure because of their faith.

¹⁰"Now then, why are you trying to test God? You test him when you put a heavy load on the believers' shoulders. Our people of long ago couldn't carry that load. We can't either. ¹¹No! We believe we are saved through the grace of our Lord Jesus. Those who aren't Jews are saved in the same way."

¹²Everyone became quiet as they listened to Barnabas and Paul. They were telling about the miraculous signs and wonders God had done through them among non-Jews. ¹³When they finished, James spoke up. "Brothers," he said, "listen to me. ¹⁴Simon Peter has explained to us how God first showed his concern for those who aren't Jews. He chose some of them to be his very own people. ¹⁵The prophets' words agree with this. It is written:

GREAT VERSE —TO— REMEMBER

15:11 We believe we are saved through the grace of our Lord Jesus. Those who aren't Jews are saved in the same way.

16 "'After this I will return
and rebuild David's fallen tent.
I will rebuild what was destroyed.
I will make it what it used to be.
17 Then the rest of the people can look to the Lord.
This means all the non-Jews who belong to me.
The Lord says this. He is the one who does these
things.' *(Amos 9:11,12)*
18 The Lord does things that have been known for a
long time.

19"Now here is my opinion. We should not make it hard for the
non-Jews who are turning to God. 20Here is what we should write
to them. They must not eat food polluted by being offered to
statues of gods. They must not commit sexual sins. They must
not eat the meat of animals that have been choked to death. And
they must not drink blood. 21These laws of Moses have been
preached in every city from the earliest times. They are read out
loud in the synagogues every Sabbath day."

A Letter Is Written to Non-Jewish Believers

22Then the apostles, the elders and the whole church decided
what to do. They would choose some of their own men. They
would send them to Antioch with Paul and Barnabas. So they
chose two leaders among the believers. Their names were Judas
Barsabbas and Silas. 23Here is the letter they sent with them.

The apostles and elders, your brothers, are writing this letter.

We are sending it to the non-Jewish believers in Antioch,
Syria and Cilicia.

Greetings.

24We have heard that some of our people came to you and
caused trouble. You were upset by what they said. But we had
given them no authority to go. 25So we all agreed to send our
dear friends Barnabas and Paul to you. We chose some others to go with them. 26Barnabas and Paul have put their lives
in danger for the name of our Lord Jesus Christ. 27So we are
sending Judas and Silas with them. What they say will agree
with this letter.

28It seemed good to the Holy Spirit and to us not to give
you a load that is too heavy. So here are a few basic rules.

²⁹Don't eat food that has been offered to statues of gods. Don't drink blood. Don't eat the meat of animals that have been choked to death. And don't commit sexual sins. You will do well to keep away from these things.

Farewell.

³⁰The men were sent down to Antioch. There they gathered the church together. They gave the letter to them. ³¹The people read it. They were glad for its message of hope. ³²Judas and Silas were prophets. They said many things to give strength and hope to the believers. ³³/³⁴Judas and Silas stayed there for some time. Then the believers sent them away with the blessing of peace. They sent them back to those who had sent them out.

³⁵Paul and Barnabas remained in Antioch. There they and many others taught and preached the word of the Lord.

Paul and Barnabas Do Not Agree

³⁶Some time later Paul spoke to Barnabas. "Let's go back to all the towns where we preached the word of the Lord," he said. "Let's visit the believers and see how they are doing." ³⁷Barnabas wanted to take John Mark with them. ³⁸But Paul didn't think it was wise to take him. Mark had deserted them in Pamphylia. He hadn't continued with them in their work. ³⁹Barnabas and Paul strongly disagreed with each other. So they went their separate ways. Barnabas took Mark and sailed for Cyprus. ⁴⁰But Paul chose Silas. The believers asked the Lord to give his grace to Paul and Silas as they went. ⁴¹Paul traveled through Syria and Cilicia. He gave strength to the churches there.

Timothy Joins Paul and Silas

16 Paul came to Derbe. Then he went on to Lystra. A believer named Timothy lived there. His mother was Jewish and a believer. His father was a Greek. ²The believers at Lystra and Iconium said good things about Timothy. ³Paul wanted to take him along on the journey. So he circumcised Timothy because of the Jews who lived in that area. They all knew that Timothy's father was a Greek. ⁴Paul and his companions traveled from town to town. They reported what the apostles and elders in Jerusalem had decided. The people were supposed to obey what was in the report. ⁵So the churches were made strong in the faith. The number of believers grew every day.

Paul's Vision of the Man From Macedonia

⁶Paul and his companions traveled all through the area of Phrygia and Galatia. The Holy Spirit had kept them from preaching the word in Asia Minor. ⁷They came to the border of Mysia. From there they tried to enter Bithynia. But the Spirit of Jesus would not let them. ⁸So they passed by Mysia. Then they went down to Troas.

⁹During the night Paul had a vision. He saw a man from Macedonia standing and begging him. "Come over to Macedonia!" the man said. "Help us!" ¹⁰After Paul had seen the vision, we got ready at once to leave for Macedonia. We decided that God had called us to preach the good news there.

Lydia Becomes a Believer

¹¹At Troas we got into a boat. We sailed straight for Samothrace. The next day we went on to Neapolis. ¹²From there we traveled to Philippi, a Roman colony. It is an important city in that part of Macedonia. We stayed there several days.

¹³On the Sabbath day we went outside the city gate. We walked down to the river. There we expected to find a place of prayer. We sat down and began to speak to the women who had gathered together. ¹⁴One of those listening was a woman named Lydia. She was from the city of Thyatira. Her business was selling purple cloth. She was a worshiper of God. The Lord opened her heart to accept Paul's message. ¹⁵She and her family were baptized. Then she invited us to her home. "Do you consider me a believer in the Lord?" she asked. "If you do, come and stay at my house." She succeeded in getting us to go home with her.

Paul and Silas Are Thrown Into Prison

¹⁶One day we were going to the place of prayer. On the way we were met by a female slave. She had a spirit that helped her to tell ahead of time what was going to happen. She earned a lot of money for her owners by telling fortunes. ¹⁷The woman followed Paul and the rest of us around. She shouted, "These men serve the Most High God. They are telling you how to be saved." ¹⁸She kept this up for many days. Finally Paul became upset. Turning around, he spoke to the spirit. "In the name of Jesus Christ," he said, "I command you to come out of her!" At that very moment the spirit left her.

¹⁹The female slave's owners realized that their hope of making

money was gone. So they grabbed Paul and Silas. They dragged them into the market place to face the authorities. ²⁰They brought them to the judges. "These men are Jews," her owners said. "They are making trouble in our city. ²¹They are suggesting practices that are against Roman law. These are practices we can't accept or take part in."

²²The crowd joined the attack against Paul and Silas. The judges ordered that Paul and Silas be stripped and beaten. ²³They were whipped without mercy. Then they were thrown into prison. The jailer was commanded to guard them carefully. ²⁴When he received his orders, he put Paul and Silas deep inside the prison. He fastened their feet so they couldn't get away.

²⁵About midnight Paul and Silas were praying. They were also singing hymns to God. The other prisoners were listening to them. ²⁶Suddenly there was a powerful earthquake. It shook the prison from top to bottom. All at once the prison doors flew open. Everybody's chains came loose.

²⁷The jailer woke up. He saw that the prison doors were open. He pulled out his sword and was going to kill himself. He thought the prisoners had escaped. ²⁸"Don't harm yourself!" Paul shouted. "We are all here!"

²⁹The jailer called out for some lights. He rushed in, shaking with fear. He fell down in front of Paul and Silas. ³⁰Then he brought them out. He asked, "Sirs, what must I do to be saved?"

³¹They replied, "Believe in the Lord Jesus. Then you and your family will be saved." ³²They spoke the word of the Lord to him. They also spoke to all the others in his house.

³³At that hour of the night, the jailer took Paul and Silas and washed their wounds. Right away he and his whole family were baptized. ³⁴The jailer brought them into his house. He set a meal in front of them. He and his whole family were filled with joy. They had become believers in God.

³⁵Early in the morning the judges sent their officers to the jailer. They ordered him, "Let those men go." ³⁶The jailer told Paul,

GREAT VERSE —TO— REMEMBER

16:30-31 "Sirs, what must I do to be saved?" They replied, "Believe in the Lord Jesus. Then you and your family will be saved."

"The judges have ordered me to set you and Silas free. You can leave now. Go in peace."

³⁷But Paul replied to the officers. "They beat us in public," he said. "We weren't given a trial. And we are Roman citizens! They threw us into prison. And now do they want to get rid of us quietly? No! Let them come themselves and personally lead us out."

³⁸The officers reported this to the judges. When the judges heard that Paul and Silas were Roman citizens, they became afraid. ³⁹So they came and said they were sorry. They led them out of the prison. Then they asked them to leave the city. ⁴⁰After Paul and Silas came out of the prison, they went to Lydia's house. There they met with the believers. They told them to be brave. Then they left.

Paul and Silas Arrive in Thessalonica

17 Paul and Silas passed through Amphipolis and Apollonia. They came to Thessalonica. A Jewish synagogue was there. ²Paul went into the synagogue as he usually did. For three Sabbath days in a row he talked about the Scriptures with the Jews. ³He explained and proved that the Christ had to suffer and rise from the dead. "This Jesus I am telling you about is the Christ!" he said. ⁴His words won some of the Jews over. They joined Paul and Silas. A large number of Greeks who worshiped God joined them too. So did quite a few important women.

⁵But the Jews were jealous. So they rounded up some evil fellows from the market place. Forming a crowd, they started all kinds of trouble in the city. The Jews rushed to Jason's house. They were looking for Paul and Silas. They wanted to bring them out to the crowd. ⁶But they couldn't find them. So they dragged Jason and some other believers to the city officials. "These men have caused trouble all over the world," they shouted. "Now they have come here. ⁷Jason has welcomed them into his house. They are all disobeying Caesar's commands. They say there is another king. He is called Jesus."

⁸When the crowd and the city officials heard this, they became very upset. ⁹They made Jason and the others give them money. They wanted to make sure they would return to the court. Then they let them go.

Paul and Silas Are Sent to Berea

¹⁰As soon as it was night, the believers sent Paul and Silas away to Berea. When they arrived, they went to the Jewish synagogue.

[11]The Bereans were very glad to receive Paul's message. They studied the Scriptures carefully every day. They wanted to see if what Paul said was true. So they were more noble than the Thessalonians. [12]Many of the Jews believed. A number of important Greek women also became believers. And so did many Greek men.

[13]The Jews in Thessalonica found out that Paul was preaching God's word in Berea. So they went there too. They stirred up the crowds and got them all worked up. [14]Right away the believers sent Paul to the coast. But Silas and Timothy stayed in Berea. [15]The men who went with Paul took him to Athens. Then they returned with orders that Silas and Timothy were supposed to join him as soon as they could.

Paul Preaches in Athens

[16]Paul was waiting for Silas and Timothy in Athens. He was very upset to see that the city was full of statues of gods. [17]So he went to the synagogue. There he talked with Jews and with Greeks who worshiped God. Each day he spoke with anyone who happened to be in the market place.

[18]A group of Epicurean and Stoic thinkers began to argue with him. Some of them asked, "What is this fellow chattering about?" Others said, "He seems to be telling us about gods we've never heard of." They said this because Paul was preaching the good news about Jesus. He was telling them that Jesus had risen from the dead.

[19]They took him to a meeting of the Areopagus. There they said to him, "What is this new teaching you're giving us? [20]You have some strange ideas. We've never heard them before. We want to know what they mean." [21]All the people of Athens spent their time talking about and listening to the latest ideas. People from other lands who lived there did the same.

[22]Then Paul stood up in the meeting of the Areopagus. He said, "People of Athens! I see that you are very religious in every way. [23]As I walked around, I looked carefully at the things you worship. I even found an altar with these words written on it: TO AN UNKNOWN GOD. Now I am going to tell you about this 'unknown god' that you worship.

[24]"He is the God who made the world. He also made everything in it. He is the Lord of heaven and earth. He doesn't live in temples built by hands. [25]He is not served by human hands. He doesn't need anything. He himself gives life and breath to all

people. He also gives them everything else they have. ²⁶From one man he made all the people of the world. Now they live all over the earth. He decided exactly when they should live. And he decided exactly where they should live. ²⁷God did this so that people would seek him. Then perhaps they would reach out for him and find him. They would find him even though he is not far from any of us. ²⁸'In him we live and move and exist.' As some of your own poets have also said, 'We are his children.'

²⁹"Yes, we are God's children. So we shouldn't think that God is made out of gold or silver or stone. He isn't a statue planned and made by clever people. ³⁰In the past, God didn't judge people for what they didn't know. But now he commands all people everywhere to turn away from their sins. ³¹He has set a day when he will judge the world fairly. He has appointed a man to be its judge. God has proved this to all people by raising that man from the dead."

³²When they heard Paul talk about the dead rising, some of them made fun of it. But others said, "We want to hear you speak about this again." ³³So Paul left the meeting of the Areopagus. ³⁴A few people became followers of Paul and believed in Jesus. Dionysius was one of them. He was a member of the Areopagus. A woman named Damaris also became a believer. And so did many others.

Paul Goes to Corinth

18 After this, Paul left Athens and went to Corinth. ²There he met a Jew named Aquila, who was a native of Pontus. Aquila had recently come from Italy with his wife Priscilla. The emperor Claudius had ordered all the Jews to leave Rome. Paul went to see Aquila and Priscilla. ³They were tentmakers, just as he was. So he stayed and worked with them. ⁴Every Sabbath day he went to the synagogue. He was trying to get both Jews and Greeks to believe in the Lord.

⁵Silas and Timothy came from Macedonia. Then Paul spent all

GREAT VERSE —TO— REMEMBER **17:24** He is the God who made the world. He also made everything in it. He is the Lord of heaven and earth.

his time preaching. He gave witness to the Jews that Jesus was the Christ. ⁶But the Jews opposed Paul. They treated him badly. He didn't like this. So he shook out his clothes. Then he said to them, "Anything that happens to you will be your own fault! Don't blame me for it! From now on I will go to people who are not Jews."

⁷Then Paul left the synagogue. He went next door to the house of Titius Justus, a man who worshiped God. ⁸Crispus was the synagogue ruler. He and his whole family came to believe in the Lord. Many others who lived in Corinth heard Paul. They too believed and were baptized.

⁹One night the Lord spoke to Paul in a vision. "Don't be afraid," he said. "Keep on speaking. Don't be silent. ¹⁰I am with you. No one will attack you and harm you. I have many people in this city." ¹¹So Paul stayed there for a year and a half. He taught them God's word.

¹²At that time Gallio was governor of Achaia. The Jews got together and attacked Paul. They brought him into court. ¹³"This man," they charged, "is trying to talk people into worshiping God in ways that are against the law."

¹⁴Paul was about to speak up for himself. But just then Gallio spoke to the Jews. "You Jews are not claiming that Paul has committed a crime, whether large or small," he said. "If you were, it would make sense for me to listen to you. ¹⁵But this is about your own law. It is a question of words and names. Settle the matter yourselves. I will not be a judge of such things." ¹⁶So he had them thrown out of the court. ¹⁷Then all the Jews turned against Sosthenes. He was the synagogue ruler. They beat him up in front of the court. But Gallio didn't care at all.

Priscilla and Aquila Teach Apollos

¹⁸Paul stayed in Corinth for some time. Then he left the believers and sailed for Syria. Priscilla and Aquila went with him. Before he sailed, he had his hair cut off at Cenchrea. He did this because he had made a promise to God. ¹⁹They arrived at Ephesus. There Paul said good-by to Priscilla and Aquila. He himself went into the synagogue and talked with the Jews. ²⁰The Jews asked him to spend more time with them. But he said no. ²¹As he left, he made them a promise. "If God wants me to," he said, "I will come back." Then he sailed from Ephesus. ²²When he landed at Caesarea, he went up to Jerusalem. There he greeted the church. He then went down to Antioch.

²³Paul spent some time in Antioch. Then he left and traveled all over Galatia and Phrygia. He gave strength to all the believers there.

²⁴At that time a Jew named Apollos came to Ephesus. He was an educated man from Alexandria. He knew the Scriptures very well. ²⁵Apollos had been taught the way of the Lord. He spoke with great power. He taught the truth about Jesus. But he only knew about John's baptism. ²⁶He began to speak boldly in the synagogue. Priscilla and Aquila heard him. So they invited him to their home. There they gave him a better understanding of the way of God.

²⁷Apollos wanted to go to Achaia. The brothers and sisters agreed with him. They wrote to the believers there. They asked them to welcome him. When he arrived, he was a great help to those who had become believers by God's grace. ²⁸He argued strongly against the Jews in public meetings. He proved from the Scriptures that Jesus was the Christ.

Paul Goes to Ephesus

19 While Apollos was at Corinth, Paul took the road to Ephesus. When he arrived, he found some believers there. ²He asked them, "Did you receive the Holy Spirit when you became believers?"

"No," they answered. "We haven't even heard that there is a Holy Spirit."

³So Paul asked, "Then what baptism did you receive?"

"John's baptism," they replied.

⁴Paul said, "John baptized people, calling them to turn away from their sins. He told them to believe in the one who was coming after him. Jesus is that one." ⁵After hearing this, they were baptized in the name of the Lord Jesus. ⁶Paul placed his hands on them. Then the Holy Spirit came on them. They spoke in languages they had not known before. They also prophesied. ⁷There were about 12 of them in all.

⁸Paul entered the synagogue. There he spoke boldly for three months. He tried to talk the people into accepting his teaching about God's kingdom. ⁹But some of them wouldn't listen. They refused to believe. In public they said evil things about the Way of Jesus. So Paul left them. He took the believers with him. Each day he talked with people in the lecture hall of Tyrannus. ¹⁰This went on for two years. So all the Jews and Greeks who lived in Asia Minor heard the word of the Lord.

¹¹God did amazing miracles through Paul. ¹²Even handkerchiefs and aprons that had touched him were taken to those who were sick. When this happened, their sicknesses were healed and evil spirits left them.

¹³Some Jews went around driving out evil spirits. They tried to use the name of the Lord Jesus to set free those who were controlled by demons. They said, "In Jesus' name I command you to come out. He is the Jesus that Paul is preaching about." ¹⁴Seven sons of Sceva were doing this. Sceva was a Jewish chief priest. ¹⁵One day the evil spirit answered them, "I know Jesus. And I know about Paul. But who are you?" ¹⁶Then the man who had the evil spirit jumped on Sceva's sons. He overpowered them all. He gave them a terrible beating. They ran out of the house naked and bleeding.

¹⁷The Jews and Greeks living in Ephesus heard about this. They were all overcome with fear. They held the name of the Lord Jesus in high honor. ¹⁸Many who believed now came and openly admitted the evil they had done. ¹⁹A number of those who had practiced evil magic brought their scrolls together. They set them on fire out in the open. They added up the value of the scrolls. They found that it would take more than two lifetimes to earn what the scrolls were worth.

²⁰The word of the Lord spread everywhere. It became more and more powerful.

²¹After all this had happened, Paul decided to go to Jerusalem. He went through Macedonia and Achaia. "After I have been to Jerusalem," he said, "I must visit Rome also." ²²He sent Timothy and Erastus, two of his helpers, to Macedonia. But he stayed a little longer in Asia Minor.

Trouble in Ephesus

²³At that time many people became very upset about the Way of Jesus. ²⁴There was a man named Demetrius who made things out of silver. He made silver models of the temple of the goddess Artemis. He brought in a lot of business for the other skilled workers. ²⁵One day he called them together. He also called others who were in the same kind of business. "Men," he said, "you know that we make good money from our work. ²⁶You have seen and heard what this fellow Paul is doing. He has talked to large numbers of people here in Ephesus. Almost everywhere in Asia Minor he has led people away from our gods. He says that the gods we make are not gods at all. ²⁷Our work is in danger of los-

ing its good name. People's faith in the temple of the great goddess Artemis will be weakened. Now she is worshiped through all of Asia Minor and the whole world. But soon she will be robbed of her greatness."

28When they heard this, they became very angry. They began shouting, "Great is Artemis of the Ephesians!" 29Soon people were making trouble in the whole city. They all rushed into the theater. They dragged Gaius and Aristarchus along with them. These two men had come with Paul from Macedonia. 30Paul wanted to appear in front of the crowd. But the believers wouldn't let him. 31Some of the officials in Asia Minor were friends of Paul. They sent him a message, begging him not to go into the theater.

32The crowd didn't know what was going on. Some were shouting one thing and some another. Most of the people didn't even know why they were there. 33The Jews pushed Alexander to the front. Some of the crowd tried to tell him what to say. But he motioned for them to be quiet. He wanted to speak up for himself in front of the people. 34But then they realized that he was a Jew. So they all shouted the same thing for about two hours. "Great is Artemis of the Ephesians!" they yelled.

35The city clerk quieted the crowd down. "People of Ephesus!" he said. "The whole world knows that the city of Ephesus guards the temple of the great Artemis. They know that Ephesus guards her statue, which fell from heaven. 36These facts can't be questioned. So calm down. Don't do anything foolish.

37"These men haven't robbed any temples. They haven't said evil things against our goddess. But you have brought them here anyhow. 38Demetrius and the other skilled workers may feel they have been wronged by someone. Let them bring charges. The courts are open. We have our governors. 39Is there anything else you want to bring up? Settle it in a court of law. 40As it is, today we are in danger of being charged with causing all this trouble. But there is no reason for it. We wouldn't be able to explain what has happened." 41After he said this, he sent the people away.

Paul Travels Through Macedonia and Greece

20 All the trouble came to an end. Then Paul sent for the believers. After cheering them up, he said good-by. He then left for Macedonia. 2He traveled through that area, speaking many words of hope to the people. Finally he arrived in Greece. 3There he stayed for three months. He was just about to sail for Syria. But the Jews were making plans against him. So he decided

to go back through Macedonia. ⁴Sopater, son of Pyrrhus, from Berea went with him. Aristarchus and Secundus from Thessalonica, Gaius from Derbe, and Timothy went too. Tychicus and Trophimus from Asia Minor also went with him. ⁵These men went on ahead. They waited for us at Troas. ⁶But we sailed from Philippi after the Feast of Unleavened Bread. Five days later we joined the others at Troas. We stayed there for seven days.

Eutychus Is Raised From the Dead

⁷On the first day of the week we met to break bread and eat together. Paul spoke to the people. He kept on talking until midnight because he planned to leave the next day. ⁸There were many lamps in the room upstairs where we were meeting. ⁹A young man named Eutychus was sitting in a window. He sank into a deep sleep as Paul talked on and on. Sound asleep, Eutychus fell from the third floor. When they picked him up from the ground, he was dead.

¹⁰Paul went down and threw himself on the young man. He put his arms around him. "Don't be alarmed," he told them. "He's alive!" ¹¹Then Paul went upstairs again. He broke bread and ate with them. He kept on talking until daylight. Then he left. ¹²The people took the young man home. They were greatly comforted because he was alive.

Paul Says Good-by to the Ephesian Elders

¹³We went on ahead to the ship. We sailed for Assos. There we were going to take Paul on board. He had planned it this way because he wanted to go there by land. ¹⁴So he met us at Assos. We took him on board and went on to Mitylene.

¹⁵The next day we sailed from there. We arrived near Kios. The day after that we crossed over to Samos. We arrived at Miletus the next day. ¹⁶Paul had decided to sail past Ephesus. He didn't want to spend time in Asia Minor. He was in a hurry to get to Jerusalem. If he could, he wanted to be there by the day of Pentecost.

¹⁷From Miletus, Paul sent for the elders of the church at Ephesus. ¹⁸When they arrived, he spoke to them. "You know how I lived the whole time I was with you," he said. "From the first day I came into Asia Minor, ¹⁹I was free of pride. I served the Lord with tears. I served him even though I was greatly tested by the evil plans of the Jews. ²⁰You know I haven't let anyone keep me from preaching anything that would be helpful to you. I have

taught you in public and from house to house. ²¹I have told both Jews and Greeks that they must turn away from their sins to God. They must have faith in our Lord Jesus.

²²"Now I am going to Jerusalem. The Holy Spirit compels me. I don't know what will happen to me there. ²³I only know that in every city the Spirit warns me. He tells me that I will face prison and suffering. ²⁴But my life means nothing to me. I only want to finish the race. I want to complete the work the Lord Jesus has given me. He wants me to give witness to others about the good news of God's grace.

²⁵"I have spent time with you preaching about the kingdom. I know that none of you will ever see me again. ²⁶So I tell you today that I am not guilty if anyone has not believed. ²⁷I haven't let anyone keep me from telling you everything God wants you to do.

²⁸"Keep watch over yourselves. Keep watch over all the believers. The Holy Spirit has made you leaders over them. Be shepherds of God's church. He bought it with his own blood.

²⁹"I know that after I leave, wild wolves will come in among you. They won't spare any of the sheep. ³⁰Even some of your own people will rise up and twist the truth. They want to get the believers to follow them. ³¹So be on your guard! Remember that for three years I never stopped warning you. Night and day I warned each of you with tears.

³²"Now I commit you to God's care. I commit you to the word of his grace. It can build you up. Then you will share in what God plans to give all his people. ³³I haven't longed for anyone's silver or gold or clothing. ³⁴You yourselves know that I have used my own hands to meet my needs. I have also met the needs of my companions. ³⁵In everything I did, I showed you that we must work hard and help the weak. We must remember the words of the Lord Jesus. He said, 'It is more blessed to give than to receive.'"

³⁶When Paul had said this, he got down on his knees with all of them and prayed. ³⁷They all cried as they hugged and kissed him. ³⁸What hurt them the most was that he had said they would never see his face again. Then they went with him to the ship.

GREAT VERSE —TO— REMEMBER

20:35 It is more blessed to give than to receive.

Paul Continues His Journey

21 After we had torn ourselves away from the Ephesian elders, we headed out to sea. We sailed straight to Cos. The next day we went to Rhodes. From there we continued on to Patara. ²We found a ship crossing over to Phoenicia. So we went on board and headed out to sea. ³We came near Cyprus and passed to the south of it. Then we sailed on to Syria. We landed at Tyre. There our ship was supposed to unload. ⁴We found the believers there and stayed with them for seven days. Led by the Holy Spirit, they tried to get Paul not to go on to Jerusalem. ⁵But when it was time to leave, we continued on our way. All the believers and their families went with us out of the city. There on the beach we got down on our knees to pray. ⁶We said good-by to each other. Then we went on board the ship. And they returned home.

⁷Continuing on from Tyre, we landed at Ptolemais. There we greeted the brothers and sisters. We stayed with them for a day. ⁸The next day we left and arrived at Caesarea. We stayed at the house of Philip the evangelist. He was one of the seven deacons. ⁹He had four unmarried daughters who prophesied.

¹⁰We stayed there several days. Then a prophet named Agabus came down from Judea. ¹¹He came over to us. Then he took Paul's belt and tied his own hands and feet with it. He said, "The Holy Spirit says, 'This is how the Jews of Jerusalem will tie up the owner of this belt. They will hand him over to people who are not Jews.'"

¹²When we heard this, we all begged Paul not to go up to Jerusalem. ¹³He asked, "Why are you crying? Why are you breaking my heart? I'm ready to be put in prison. In fact, I'm ready to die in Jerusalem for the Lord Jesus." ¹⁴We couldn't change his mind. So we gave up. We said, "May what the Lord wants to happen be done."

¹⁵After this, we got ready and went up to Jerusalem. ¹⁶Some of the believers from Caesarea went with us. They brought us to Mnason's home. We were supposed to stay there. Mnason was from Cyprus. He was one of the first believers.

Paul Arrives in Jerusalem

¹⁷When we arrived in Jerusalem, the brothers and sisters gave us a warm welcome. ¹⁸The next day Paul and the rest of us went to see James. All the elders were there. ¹⁹Paul greeted them. Then he

reported everything God had done among the non-Jews through his work.

²⁰When they heard this, they praised God. Then they spoke to Paul. "Brother," they said, "you see that thousands of Jews have become believers. All of them try very hard to obey the law. ²¹They have been told that you teach all the Jews who live among the non-Jews to turn away from Moses. They think that you teach them not to circumcise their children. They think that you teach them to give up our Jewish ways.

²²"What should we do? They will certainly hear that you have come. ²³So do what we tell you. There are four men with us who have made a promise to God. ²⁴Take them with you. Join them in the Jewish practice that makes people pure and clean. Pay their expenses so they can have their heads shaved. Then everybody will know that these reports about you are not true in any way. They will know that you yourself obey the law.

²⁵"We have already given written directions to the believers who are not Jews. They must not eat food that has been offered to statues of gods. They must not drink blood. They must not eat the meat of animals that have been choked to death. And they must not commit sexual sins."

²⁶The next day Paul took the men with him. They all made themselves pure and clean in the usual way. Then Paul went to the temple. There he reported the date when the days of cleansing would end. At that time the proper offering would be made for each of them.

Paul Is Arrested

²⁷The seven days of cleansing were almost over. Some Jews from Asia Minor saw Paul at the temple. They stirred up the whole crowd. They arrested Paul. ²⁸"People of Israel, help us!" they shouted. "This is the man who teaches everyone in all places against our people. He speaks against our law and against this

GREAT VERSE —TO— REMEMBER

21:19-20 Paul greeted them. Then he reported everything God had done among the non-Jews through his work. When they heard this, they praised God.

holy place. Besides, he has brought Greeks into the temple area. He has made this holy place unclean." ²⁹They said this because they had seen Trophimus the Ephesian in the city with Paul. They thought Paul had brought him into the temple area.

³⁰The whole city was stirred up. People came running from all directions. They grabbed Paul and dragged him out of the temple. Right away the temple gates were shut. ³¹The people were trying to kill Paul. But news reached the commander of the Roman troops. He heard that people were making trouble in the whole city of Jerusalem. ³²At once he took some officers and soldiers with him. They ran down to the crowd. The people causing the trouble saw the commander and his soldiers. So they stopped beating Paul.

³³The commander came up and arrested Paul. He ordered him to be held with two chains. Then he asked who Paul was and what he had done. ³⁴Some in the crowd shouted one thing, some another. But the commander couldn't get the facts because of all the noise. So he ordered that Paul be taken into the fort. ³⁵Paul reached the steps. But then the mob became so wild that he had to be carried by the soldiers. ³⁶The crowd that followed kept shouting, "Kill him!"

Paul Speaks to the Crowd

³⁷The soldiers were about to take Paul into the fort. Then he asked the commander, "May I say something to you?"

"Do you speak Greek?" he replied. ³⁸"Aren't you the Egyptian who turned some of our people against their leaders? Didn't you lead 4,000 terrorists out into the desert some time ago?"

³⁹Paul answered, "I am a Jew from Tarsus in Cilicia. I am a citizen of an important city. Please let me speak to the people."

⁴⁰The commander told him he could. So Paul stood on the steps and motioned to the crowd. When all of them were quiet, he **22** spoke to them in the Aramaic language. ¹"Brothers and fathers," Paul began, "listen to me now. I want to speak up for myself."

²When they heard that he was speaking to them in Aramaic, they became very quiet.

Then Paul said, ³"I am a Jew. I was born in Tarsus in Cilicia. But I grew up here in Jerusalem. I was well trained by Gamaliel in the law of our people. I wanted to serve God as much as any of you do today. ⁴I hurt the followers of the Way of Jesus. I sent many of them to their death. I arrested men and women. I threw them into prison. ⁵The high priest and the whole Council can give witness to this. I even had some official letters they had written to their friends in Damascus. So I went there to bring these people as prisoners to Jerusalem to be punished.

⁶"I had almost reached Damascus. About noon a bright light from heaven suddenly flashed around me. ⁷I fell to the ground and heard a voice speak to me. 'Saul! Saul!' it said. 'Why are you opposing me?'

⁸"'Who are you, Lord?' I asked.

"'I am Jesus of Nazareth,' he replied. 'I am the one you are opposing.'

⁹"The light was seen by my companions. But they didn't understand the voice of the one speaking to me.

¹⁰"'What should I do, Lord?' I asked.

"'Get up,' the Lord said. 'Go into Damascus. There you will be told everything you have been given to do.' ¹¹The brightness of the light had blinded me. So my companions led me by the hand into Damascus.

¹²"A man named Ananias came to see me. He was a godly Jew who obeyed the law. All the Jews living there respected him very much. ¹³He stood beside me and said, 'Brother Saul, receive your sight!' At that very moment I was able to see him.

¹⁴"Then he said, 'The God of our people has chosen you. He will tell you his plans for you. You are going to see the Blameless One. You are going to hear words from his mouth. ¹⁵Then you will give witness to all people about what you have seen and heard. ¹⁶So what are you waiting for? Get up and call on his name. Be baptized. Have your sins washed away.'

¹⁷"I returned to Jerusalem and was praying at the temple. Then it seemed to me that I was dreaming. ¹⁸I saw the Lord speaking to me. 'Quick!' he said. 'Leave Jerusalem at once. These people will not accept your witness about me.'

¹⁹"'Lord,' I replied, 'these people know what I used to do. I went from one synagogue to another and put believers in prison. I also beat them. ²⁰Stephen was a man who gave witness to others about you. I stood there when he was killed. I had agreed that he should die. I even guarded the coats of those who were killing him.'

²¹"Then the Lord said to me, 'Go. I will send you far away to people who are not Jews.'"

Paul the Roman Citizen

²²The crowd listened to Paul until he said this. Then they shouted, "Kill him! He's not fit to live!"

²³They shouted and threw off their coats. They threw dust into the air. ²⁴So the commanding officer ordered Paul to be taken into the fort. He gave orders for Paul to be whipped and questioned. He wanted to find out why the people were shouting at him like this. ²⁵A commander was standing there as they stretched Paul out to be whipped. Paul said to him, "Does the law allow you to whip a Roman citizen who hasn't even been found guilty?"

²⁶When the commander heard this, he went to the commanding officer and reported it. "What are you going to do?" the commander asked. "This man is a Roman citizen."

²⁷So the commanding officer went to Paul. "Tell me," he asked. "Are you a Roman citizen?"

"Yes, I am," Paul answered.

²⁸Then the officer said, "I had to pay a lot of money to become a citizen."

"But I was born a citizen," Paul replied.

²⁹Right away those who were about to question him left. Even the officer was alarmed. He realized that he had put Paul, a Roman citizen, in chains.

Paul Is Taken to the Sanhedrin

³⁰The commanding officer wanted to find out exactly what the Jews had against Paul. So the next day he let Paul out of prison. He ordered a meeting of the chief priests and all the Sanhedrin. Then he brought Paul and had him stand in front of them.

23 Paul looked straight at the Sanhedrin. "My brothers," he said, "I have always done my duty to God. To this very day I feel that I have done nothing wrong." ²Ananias the high priest heard this. So he ordered the men standing near Paul to hit him on the mouth. ³Then Paul said to him, "You pretender! God will hit you! You sit there and judge me by the law. But you yourself broke the law when you commanded them to hit me!"

⁴Those who were standing near Paul said, "How dare you talk like that to God's high priest!"

⁵Paul replied, "Brothers, I didn't realize he was the high priest. It is written: 'Do not speak evil about the ruler of your people.'"
(Exodus 22:28)

⁶Paul knew that some of them were Sadducees and the others Pharisees. So he called out in the Sanhedrin. "My brothers," he said, "I am a Pharisee. I am the son of a Pharisee. I believe that people will rise from the dead. That's why I am on trial."

⁷When he said this, the Pharisees and the Sadducees started to argue. They began to take sides. ⁸The Sadducees say that people will not rise from the dead. They don't believe there are angels or spirits either. But the Pharisees believe all these things.

⁹People were causing trouble and making a lot of noise. Some of the teachers of the law who were Pharisees stood up. They argued strongly. "We find nothing wrong with this man," they said. "What if a spirit or an angel has spoken to him?" ¹⁰The arguing got out of hand. The commanding officer was afraid that Paul would be torn to pieces by those who were arguing. So he ordered the soldiers to go down and take him away from them by force. They were supposed to bring him into the fort.

¹¹The next night the Lord stood near Paul. He said, "Be brave! You have given witness about me in Jerusalem. You must do the same in Rome."

The Plan to Kill Paul

¹²The next morning the Jews gathered secretly to make plans against Paul. They took an oath that they would not eat or drink anything until they had killed him. ¹³More than 40 men took part in this plan. ¹⁴They went to the chief priests and the elders. They said, "We have taken a strong oath. We have made a special promise to God. We will not eat anything until we have killed Paul. ¹⁵Now then, you and the Sanhedrin must make an appeal to the commanding officer. Ask him to bring Paul to you. Pretend you want more facts about his case. We are ready to kill him before he gets here."

¹⁶But Paul's nephew heard about this plan. So he went into the fort and told Paul.

¹⁷Then Paul called one of the commanders. He said to him, "Take this young man to the commanding officer. He has something to tell him." ¹⁸So the commander took Paul's nephew to the officer.

The commander said, "Paul, the prisoner, sent for me. He asked me to bring this young man to you. The young man has something to tell you."

¹⁹The commanding officer took the young man by the hand. He spoke to him in private. "What do you want to tell me?" the officer asked.

²⁰He said, "The Jews have agreed to ask you to bring Paul to the Sanhedrin tomorrow. They will pretend they want more facts

about him. ²¹Don't give in to them. More than 40 of them are waiting in hiding to attack him. They have taken an oath that they will not eat or drink anything until they have killed him. They are ready now. All they need is for you to bring Paul to the Sanhedrin."

²²The commanding officer let the young man go. But he gave him a warning. "Don't tell anyone you have reported this to me," he said.

Paul Is Taken to Caesarea

²³Then the commanding officer called for two of his commanders. He ordered them, "Gather a company of 200 soldiers, 70 horsemen and 200 men armed with spears. Get them ready to go to Caesarea at nine o'clock tonight. ²⁴Provide horses for Paul so that he may be taken safely to Governor Felix."

²⁵Here is the letter the officer wrote.

²⁶I, Claudius Lysias, am writing this letter.

I am sending it to His Excellency, Governor Felix.

Greetings.

²⁷The Jews grabbed Paul. They were about to kill him. But I came with my soldiers and saved him. I had learned that he is a Roman citizen. ²⁸I wanted to know why they were bringing charges against him. So I brought him to their Sanhedrin. ²⁹I found out that the charge against him was based on questions about their law. But there was no charge against him worthy of death or prison. ³⁰Then I was told about a plan against the man. So I sent him to you at once. I also ordered those bringing charges against him to tell you their case.

³¹The soldiers followed their orders. During the night they took Paul with them. They brought him as far as Antipatris. ³²The next day they let the horsemen go on with him. The soldiers returned to the fort. ³³The horsemen arrived in Caesarea. They gave the letter to the governor. Then they handed Paul over to him. ³⁴The governor read the letter. He asked Paul where he was from. He learned that Paul was from Cilicia. ³⁵So he said, "I will hear your case when those bringing charges against you get here." Then he ordered that Paul be kept under guard in Herod's palace.

Paul's Trial in Front of Felix

24 Five days later Ananias the high priest went down to Caesarea. Some elders and a lawyer named Tertullus went with him. They brought their charges against Paul to the governor. ²So Paul was called in. Tertullus began to bring the charges against Paul. He said to Felix, "We have enjoyed a long time of peace while you have been ruling. You are a wise leader. You have made this a better nation. ³Most excellent Felix, we gladly admit this everywhere and in every way. And we are very thankful. ⁴I don't want to bother you. But would you be kind enough to listen to us for a short time?

⁵"We have found that Paul is a troublemaker. He stirs up trouble among Jews all over the world. He is a leader of those who follow Jesus of Nazareth. ⁶/⁷He even tried to pollute our temple. So we arrested him. ⁸Question him yourself. Then you will learn the truth about all these charges we are bringing against him."

⁹The Jews said the same thing. They agreed that the charges were true.

¹⁰The governor motioned for Paul to speak. Paul said, "I know that you have been a judge over this nation for quite a few years. So I am glad to stand up for myself. ¹¹About 12 days ago I went up to Jerusalem to worship. You can easily check on this. ¹²Those bringing charges against me did not find me arguing with anyone at the temple. I wasn't stirring up a crowd in the synagogues or anywhere else in the city. ¹³They can't prove to you any of the charges they are making against me.

¹⁴"It is true that I worship the God of our people. I am a follower of the Way of Jesus. Those bringing charges against me call it a cult. I believe everything that agrees with the Law. I believe everything written in the Prophets. ¹⁵I have the same hope in God that these men have. I believe that both the godly and the ungodly will rise from the dead. ¹⁶So I always try not to do anything wrong in the eyes of God and people.

¹⁷"I was away for several years. Then I came to Jerusalem to bring my people gifts for those who were poor. I also came to offer sacrifices. ¹⁸They found me doing this in the temple court-

GREAT VERSE —TO— REMEMBER **24:14** I am a follower of the Way of Jesus.

yard. I had already been made pure and clean in the usual way. There was no crowd with me. I didn't stir up any trouble.

[19]"But there are some other Jews who should be here in front of you. They are from Asia Minor. They should bring charges if they have anything against me. [20]Let the Jews who are here tell you what crime I am guilty of. After all, I was put on trial by the Sanhedrin. [21]Perhaps they blame me for what I said when I was on trial. I shouted, 'I believe that people will rise from the dead. That is why I am on trial here today.'"

[22]Felix knew all about the Way of Jesus. So he put off the trial for the time being. "Lysias the commanding officer will come," he said. "Then I will decide your case." [23]He ordered the commander to keep Paul under guard. He told him to give Paul some freedom. He also told him to allow Paul's friends to take care of his needs.

[24]Several days later Felix came with his wife Drusilla. She was a Jew. Felix sent for Paul and listened to him speak about faith in Christ Jesus. [25]Paul talked about how to live right. He talked about how people should control themselves. He also talked about the time when God will judge everyone. Then Felix became afraid. "That's enough for now!" he said. "You may leave. When I find the time, I will send for you." [26]He was hoping that Paul would offer him some money to let him go. So he often sent for Paul and talked with him.

[27]Two years passed. Porcius Festus took the place of Felix. But Felix wanted to do the Jews a favor. So he left Paul in prison.

Paul's Trial in Front of Festus

25 Three days after Festus arrived, he went up from Caesarea to Jerusalem. [2]There the chief priests and Jewish leaders came to him and brought their charges against Paul. [3]They tried to get Festus to have Paul taken to Jerusalem. They asked for this as a favor. They were planning to hide and attack Paul along the way. They wanted to kill him. [4]Festus answered, "Paul is being held at Caesarea. Soon I'll be going there myself. [5]Let some of your leaders come with me. If the man has done anything wrong, they can bring charges against him there."

[6]Festus spent eight or ten days in Jerusalem with them. Then he went down to Caesarea. The next day he called the court together. He ordered Paul to be brought to him. [7]When Paul arrived, the Jews who had come down from Jerusalem stood around him. They brought many strong charges against him. But they couldn't prove them.

⁸Then Paul spoke up for himself. He said, "I've done nothing wrong against the law of the Jews or against the temple. I've done nothing wrong against Caesar."

⁹But Festus wanted to do the Jews a favor. So he said to Paul, "Are you willing to go up to Jerusalem? Are you willing to go on trial there? Are you willing to face these charges in my court?"

¹⁰Paul answered, "I'm already standing in Caesar's court. This is where I should go on trial. I haven't done anything wrong to the Jews. You yourself know that very well. ¹¹If I am guilty of anything worthy of death, I'm willing to die. But the charges brought against me by these Jews are not true. No one has the right to hand me over to them. I make my appeal to Caesar!"

¹²Festus talked it over with the members of his court. Then he said, "You have made an appeal to Caesar. To Caesar you will go!"

Festus Talks With King Agrippa

¹³A few days later King Agrippa and Bernice arrived in Caesarea. They came to pay a visit to Festus. ¹⁴They were spending many days there. So Festus talked with the king about Paul's case. He said, "There's a man here that Felix left as a prisoner. ¹⁵When I went to Jerusalem, the Jewish chief priests and the elders brought charges against the man. They wanted him to be found guilty.

¹⁶"I told them that this is not the way Romans do things. We don't judge people before they have faced those bringing charges against them. They must have a chance to speak up for themselves. ¹⁷When the Jews came back with me, I didn't waste any time. I called the court together the next day. I ordered the man to be brought in. ¹⁸Those bringing charges against him got up to speak. But they didn't charge him with any of the crimes I had expected. ¹⁹Instead, they argued with him about their own beliefs. They didn't agree about a dead man named Jesus. Paul claimed Jesus was alive.

²⁰"I had no idea how to look into such matters. So I asked Paul if he would be willing to go to Jerusalem. There he could be tried on these charges. ²¹But Paul made an appeal to have the Emperor decide his case. So I ordered him to be held until I could send him to Caesar."

²²Then Agrippa said to Festus, "I would like to hear this man myself."

Festus replied, "Tomorrow you will hear him."

Paul Speaks to Agrippa

²³The next day Agrippa and Bernice arrived. They acted like very important people. They entered the courtroom. The most important officers and the leading men of the city came with them. When Festus gave the command, Paul was brought in. ²⁴Festus said, "King Agrippa, and all who are here with us, take a good look at this man! Both in Jerusalem and here in Caesarea a large number of Jews have come to me about him. They keep shouting that he shouldn't live any longer. ²⁵I have found that he hasn't done anything worthy of death. But he made his appeal to the Emperor. So I decided to send him to Rome.

²⁶"I don't have anything certain to write about him to His Majesty. So I have brought him here today. Now all of you will be able to hear him. King Agrippa, it will also be very good for you to hear him. As a result of this hearing, I will have something to write. ²⁷It doesn't make sense to send a prisoner to Rome without listing the charges against him."

26 Agrippa said to Paul, "You may now speak for yourself."

So Paul motioned with his hand. Then he began to stand up for himself. ²"King Agrippa," he said, "I am happy to be able to stand here today. I will speak up for myself against all the charges brought by the Jews. ³I am very pleased that you are familiar with Jewish ways. You know the kinds of things they argue about. So I beg you to be patient as you listen to me.

⁴"The Jews all know how I have lived ever since I was a child. They know all about me from the beginning of my life. They know how I lived in my own country and in Jerusalem. ⁵They have known me for a long time. So if they wanted to, they could give witness that I lived by the rules of the Pharisees. Those rules are harder to obey than the rules of any other group in the Jewish faith.

⁶"Today I am on trial because of the hope I have. I believe in what God promised our people long ago. ⁷It is the promise that our 12 tribes are hoping to see come true. Because of this hope they serve God with a true and honest heart day and night. King Agrippa, it is also because of this hope that the Jews are bringing charges against me. ⁸Why should any of you think it is impossible for God to raise the dead?

⁹"I myself believed that I should do everything I could to oppose the name of Jesus of Nazareth. ¹⁰That's just what I was doing in Jerusalem. On the authority of the chief priests, I put

many of God's people in prison. I agreed that they should die. ¹¹I often went from one synagogue to another to have them punished. I tried to force them to speak evil things against Jesus. I hated them so much that I even went to cities in other lands to hurt them.

¹²"On one of these journeys I was on my way to Damascus. I had the authority and commission of the chief priests. ¹³About noon, King Agrippa, I was on the road. I saw a light coming from heaven. It was brighter than the sun. It was shining around me and my companions. ¹⁴We all fell to the ground. I heard a voice speak to me in the Aramaic language. 'Saul! Saul!' it said. 'Why are you opposing me? It is hard for you to go against what you know is right.'

¹⁵"Then I asked, 'Who are you, Lord?'

"'I am Jesus,' the Lord replied. 'I am the one you are opposing. ¹⁶Now get up. Stand on your feet. I have appeared to you to appoint you to serve me and be my witness. You will tell others that you have seen me today. You will also tell them that I will show myself to you again.

¹⁷"'I will save you from your own people and from those who aren't Jews. I am sending you to them ¹⁸to open their eyes. I want you to turn them from darkness to light. I want you to turn them from Satan's power to God. I want their sins to be forgiven. They will be forgiven when they believe in me. They will have their place among God's people.'

¹⁹"So then, King Agrippa, I obeyed the vision that appeared from heaven. ²⁰First I preached to people in Damascus. Then I preached in Jerusalem and in all Judea. I preached also to people who are not Jews. I told them to turn away from their sins to God. The way they live must prove that they have turned away from their sins. ²¹That's why the Jews grabbed me in the temple courtyard and tried to kill me.

²²"But God has helped me to this very day. So I stand here and give witness to both small and great. I have been saying nothing

GREAT VERSE —TO— REMEMBER

26:16 I have appeared to you to appoint you to serve me and be my witness. You will tell others that you have seen me today.

different from what the prophets and Moses said would happen.
²³They said the Christ would suffer. He would be the first to rise
from the dead. He would announce the light of life to his own
people and to those who aren't Jews."

²⁴While Paul was still speaking up for himself, Festus inter-
rupted. "You are out of your mind, Paul!" he shouted. "Your great
learning is driving you crazy!"

²⁵"I am not crazy, most excellent Festus," Paul replied. "What I
am saying is true and reasonable. ²⁶The king is familiar with these
things. So I can speak openly to him. I am certain he knows
everything that has been going on. After all, it was not done in
secret. ²⁷King Agrippa, do you believe the prophets? I know
you do."

²⁸Then Agrippa spoke to Paul. "Are you trying to talk me into
becoming a Christian?" he said. "Do you think you can do that
in such a short time?"

²⁹Paul replied, "I don't care if it takes a short time or a long
time. I pray to God for you and all who are listening to me today.
I pray that you may become like me, except for these chains."

³⁰The king stood up. The governor and Bernice and those sitting with them stood up too. ³¹They left the room and began to
talk with one another. "Why should this man die or be put in
prison?" they said. "He has done nothing worthy of that!"

³²Agrippa said to Festus, "This man could have been set free.
But he has made an appeal to Caesar."

Paul Sails for Rome

27 It was decided that we would sail for Italy. Paul and some
other prisoners were handed over to a Roman commander named Julius. He belonged to the Imperial Guard. ²We
boarded a ship from Adramyttium. It was about to sail for ports
along the coast of Asia Minor. We headed out to sea. Aristarchus
was with us. He was a Macedonian from Thessalonica.

³The next day we landed at Sidon. There Julius was kind to
Paul. He let Paul visit his friends so they could give him what he
needed. ⁴From there we headed out to sea again. We passed the
calmer side of Cyprus because the winds were against us.

⁵We sailed across the open sea off the coast of Cilicia and
Pamphylia. Then we landed at Myra in Lycia. ⁶There the commander found a ship from Alexandria sailing for Italy. He put us
on board. ⁷We moved along slowly for many days. We had trouble getting to Cnidus. The wind did not let us stay on course. So

we passed the calmer side of Crete, opposite Salmone. [8]It was not easy to sail along the coast. Then we came to a place called Fair Havens. It was near the town of Lasea.

[9]A lot of time had passed. Sailing had already become dangerous. By now it was after the Day of Atonement, a day of fasting. So Paul gave them a warning. [10]"Men," he said, "I can see that our trip is going to be dangerous. The ship and everything in it will be lost. Our own lives will be in danger also."

[11]But the commander didn't listen to what Paul said. Instead, he followed the advice of the pilot and the ship's owner. [12]The harbor wasn't a good place for ships to stay during winter. So most of the people decided we should sail on. They hoped we would reach Phoenix. They wanted to spend the winter there. Phoenix was a harbor in Crete. It faced both southwest and northwest.

The Storm

[13]A gentle south wind began to blow. They thought that this was what they had been waiting for. So they pulled up the anchor and sailed along the shore of Crete. [14]Before very long, a wind blew down from the island. It had the force of a hurricane. It was called a "northeaster."

[15]The ship was caught by the storm. We could not keep it sailing into the wind. So we gave up and were driven along. [16]We passed the calmer side of a small island called Cauda. We almost lost the lifeboat. [17]So the men lifted it on board. Then they tied ropes under the ship itself to hold it together. They were afraid it would get stuck on the sandbars of Syrtis. They lowered the sea anchor and let the ship be driven along.

[18]We took a very bad beating from the storm. The next day the crew began to throw the ship's contents overboard. [19]On the third day, they even threw the ship's gear overboard with their own hands. [20]The sun and stars didn't appear for many days. The storm was terrible. So we gave up all hope of being saved.

[21]The men had not eaten for a long time. Paul stood up in front of them. "Men," he said, "you should have taken my advice not to sail from Crete. Then you would have avoided this harm and loss.

[22]"Now I beg you to be brave. Not one of you will die. Only the ship will be destroyed. [23]I belong to God and serve him. Last night his angel stood beside me. [24]The angel said, 'Do not be afraid, Paul. You must go on trial in front of Caesar. God has

shown his grace by sparing the lives of all those sailing with you.'

²⁵"Men, continue to be brave. I have faith in God. It will happen just as he told me. ²⁶But we must run the ship onto the beach of some island."

The Ship Is Destroyed

²⁷On the 14th night we were still being driven across the Sea of Adria. About midnight the sailors had a feeling that they were approaching land. ²⁸They measured how deep the water was. They found that it was 120 feet deep. A short time later they measured the water again. This time it was 90 feet deep. ²⁹They were afraid we would crash against the rocks. So they dropped four anchors from the back of the ship. They prayed that daylight would come.

³⁰The sailors wanted to escape from the ship. So they let the lifeboat down into the sea. They pretended they were going to lower some anchors from the front of the ship. ³¹But Paul spoke to the commander and the soldiers. "These men must stay with the ship," he said. "If they don't, you can't be saved." ³²So the soldiers cut the ropes that held the lifeboat. They let it drift away.

³³Just before dawn Paul tried to get them all to eat. "For the last 14 days," he said, "you have wondered what would happen. You have gone without food. You haven't eaten anything. ³⁴Now I am asking you to eat some food. You need it to live. Not one of you will lose a single hair from your head."

³⁵After Paul said this, he took some bread and gave thanks to God. He did this where they all could see him. Then he broke it and began to eat. ³⁶All of them were filled with hope. So they ate some food. ³⁷There were 276 of us on board. ³⁸They ate as much as they wanted. They needed to make the ship lighter. So they threw the rest of the grain into the sea.

³⁹When daylight came, they saw a bay with a sandy beach. They didn't recognize the place. But they decided to run the ship onto the beach if they could. ⁴⁰So they cut the anchors loose and left them in the sea. At the same time, they untied the ropes that held the rudders. They lifted the sail at the front of the ship to the wind. Then they headed for the beach. ⁴¹But the ship hit a sandbar. So the front of it got stuck and wouldn't move. The back of the ship was broken to pieces by the pounding of the waves.

⁴²The soldiers planned to kill the prisoners. They wanted to keep them from swimming away and escaping. ⁴³But the commander wanted to save Paul's life. So he kept the soldiers from

carrying out their plan. He ordered those who could swim to jump overboard first and swim to land. ⁴⁴The rest were supposed to get there on boards or other pieces of the ship. That is how everyone reached land safely.

On Shore at Malta

28 When we were safe on shore, we found out that the island was called Malta. ²The people of the island were unusually kind. It was raining and cold. So they built a fire and welcomed all of us.

³Paul gathered some sticks and put them on the fire. A poisonous snake was driven out by the heat. It fastened itself on Paul's hand. ⁴The people of the island saw the snake hanging from his hand. They said to each other, "This man must be a murderer. He escaped from the sea. But Justice won't let him live." Justice was the name of a goddess.

⁵Paul shook the snake off into the fire. He was not harmed. ⁶The people expected him to swell up. They thought he would suddenly fall dead. They waited for a long time. But they didn't see anything unusual happen to him. So they changed their minds. They said he was a god.

⁷Publius owned property nearby. He was the chief official on the island. He welcomed us to his home. For three days he took care of us. He treated us with kindness. ⁸His father was sick in bed. The man suffered from fever and dysentery. So Paul went in to see him. Paul prayed for him. He placed his hands on him and healed him.

⁹Then the rest of the sick people on the island came. They too were healed. ¹⁰The people of the island honored us in many ways. When we were ready to sail, they gave us the supplies we needed.

Paul Arrives in Rome

¹¹After three months we headed out to sea. We sailed in a ship that had stayed at the island during the winter. It was a ship from Alexandria. On the front of it the figures of twin gods were carved. Their names were Castor and Pollux. ¹²We landed at Syracuse and stayed there for three days.

¹³From there we sailed to Rhegium. The next day the south wind came up. The day after that, we reached Puteoli. ¹⁴There we found some believers. They invited us to spend a week with them.

At last we came to Rome. ¹⁵The brothers and sisters there had heard we were coming. They traveled as far as the Forum of Appius and the Three Taverns to meet us. When Paul saw these people, he thanked God and was cheered up. ¹⁶When we got to Rome, Paul was allowed to live by himself. But a soldier guarded him.

Paul Preaches in Rome

¹⁷Three days later Paul called a meeting of the Jewish leaders. So they came. Paul said to them, "My brothers, I have done nothing against our people. I have also done nothing against what our people of long ago practiced. But I was arrested in Jerusalem. I was handed over to the Romans.

¹⁸"They questioned me. And they wanted to let me go. They saw I wasn't guilty of any crime worthy of death. ¹⁹But the Jews objected. So I had to make an appeal to Caesar.

"It wasn't that I had anything against my own people. ²⁰I share Israel's hope. That is why I am held with this chain. So I have asked to see you and talk with you."

²¹They replied, "We have not received any letters from Judea about you. None of our companions who came from there has reported or said anything bad about you. ²²But we want to hear what your ideas are. We know that people everywhere are talking against those who believe as you do."

²³They decided to meet Paul on a certain day. At that time even more people came to the place where he was staying. From morning until evening, he told them about God's kingdom and explained it to them. Using the Law of Moses and the Prophets, he tried to get them to believe in Jesus.

²⁴Some believed what he said. Others did not. ²⁵They didn't agree with each other. They began to leave after Paul had made a final statement. He said, "The Holy Spirit was right when he spoke to your people long ago. Through Isaiah the prophet the Spirit said,

²⁶" 'Go to your people. Say to them,
  "You will hear but never understand.
    You will see but never know what you are seeing."
²⁷These people's hearts have become stubborn.
    They can barely hear with their ears.
    They have closed their eyes.
  Otherwise they might see with their eyes.
    They might hear with their ears.

> They might understand with their hearts.
> They might turn, and then I would heal them.' *(Isaiah 6:9,10)*

28/29"Here is what I want you to know. God has sent his salvation to people who are not Jews. And they will listen!"

30For two whole years Paul stayed there in a house he rented. He welcomed all who came to see him. 31He preached boldly about God's kingdom. No one could keep him from teaching people about the Lord Jesus Christ.

Romans

Why Was This Book Written? The book of Romans is one of Paul's letters. Paul wrote this letter to his friends in Rome. He wanted them to know what he believed. Paul wrote the book at the end of his third missionary trip. Soon he would leave for Jerusalem.

What Is This Book About? Romans tells the good news about Jesus. Paul said that all people sin. He said that only Jesus does not sin. Paul said we must believe Jesus loves us. We must believe Jesus died for our sins. If we believe, God will forgive us. God will treat us as if we had never sinned.

What Is in This Book?

1 I, Paul, am writing this letter. I serve Christ Jesus. I have been appointed to be an apostle. God set me apart to tell others his good news. [2]He promised the good news long ago. He announced it through his prophets in the Holy Scriptures.

[3]The good news is about God's Son. As a human being, the Son of God belonged to King David's family line. [4]By the power of the Holy Spirit, he was appointed to be the mighty Son of God because he rose from the dead. He is Jesus Christ our Lord.

[5]I received God's grace because of what Jesus did so that I could bring glory to him. He made me an apostle to all those who aren't Jews. I must invite them to have faith in God and obey him. [6]You also are among those who are appointed to belong to Jesus Christ.

[7]I am sending this letter to all of you in Rome who are loved by God and appointed to be his people.

May God our Father and the Lord Jesus Christ give you grace and peace.

Paul Longs to Visit Rome

[8]First, I thank my God through Jesus Christ for all of you. People all over the world are talking about your faith. [9]I serve God with my whole heart. I preach the good news about his Son. God knows that I always remember you [10]in my prayers. I pray that now at last it may be God's plan to open the way for me to visit you.

[11]I long to see you. I want to make you strong by giving you a gift from the Holy Spirit. [12]I want us to cheer each other up by sharing our faith.

[13]Brothers and sisters, I want you to know that I planned many times to visit you. But until now I have been kept from coming. My work has produced results among others who are not Jews. In the same way, I want to see results among you.

[14]I have a duty both to Greeks and to non-Greeks. I have a duty both to wise people and to foolish people. [15]So I really want to preach the good news also to you who live in Rome.

[16]I am not ashamed of the good news. It is God's power. And it will save everyone who believes. It is meant first for the Jews. It is meant also for those who aren't Jews. [17]The good news shows how God makes people right with himself. From beginning to end, becoming right with God depends on a person's faith. It is written: "Those who are right with God will live by faith." (Habakkuk 2:4)

God's Anger Against Sinners

¹⁸God shows his anger from heaven. It is against all the godless and evil things people do. They are so evil that they say no to the truth. ¹⁹The truth about God is plain to them. God has made it plain.

²⁰Ever since the world was created it has been possible to see the qualities of God that are not seen. I'm talking about his eternal power and about the fact that he is God. Those things can be seen in what he has made. So people have no excuse for what they do.

²¹They knew God. But they didn't honor him as God. They didn't thank him. Their thinking became worthless. Their foolish hearts became dark. ²²They claimed to be wise. But they made fools of themselves. ²³They would rather have statues of gods than the glorious God who lives forever. Their statues of gods are made to look like people, birds, animals and reptiles.

²⁴So God let them go. He allowed them to do what their sinful hearts wanted to. He let them commit sexual sins. They polluted one another's bodies by what they did.

²⁵They chose a lie instead of God's truth. They worshiped and served created things. They didn't worship the Creator. But he must be praised forever. Amen.

²⁶So God let them go. They were filled with shameful longings. Their women committed sexual acts that were not natural. ²⁷In the same way, the men turned away from their natural love for women. They burned with sexual longing for each other. Men did shameful things with other men. They suffered in their bodies for all the twisted things they did.

²⁸They didn't think it was important to know God. So God let them go. He allowed them to have dirty minds. They did things they shouldn't do.

²⁹They are full of every kind of sin, evil and ungodliness. They

GREAT VERSE —TO— REMEMBER

1:17 The good news shows how God makes people right with himself. From beginning to end, getting right with God depends on a person's faith.

want more than they need. They commit murder. They want what belongs to other people. They fight and cheat. They hate others. They say mean things about other people. [30]They tell lies about them. They hate God. They are rude and proud. They brag. They think of new ways to do evil. They don't obey their parents. [31]They are foolish. They can't be trusted. They are not loving and kind.

[32]They know that God's commands are right. They know that those who do evil things should die. But they continue to do those very things. They also approve of others who do them.

God Judges Fairly

2 If you judge someone else, you have no excuse for it. When you judge another person, you are judging yourself. You do the same things you blame others for doing.

[2]We know that when God judges those who do evil things, he judges fairly. [3]Though you are only a human being, you judge others. But you yourself do the same things. So how do you think you will escape when God judges you?

[4]Do you make fun of God's great kindness and favor? Do you make fun of God when he is patient with you? Don't you realize that God's kindness is meant to turn you away from your sins?

[5]But you are stubborn. In your heart you are not sorry for your sins. You are storing up anger against yourself. The day of God's anger is coming. Then his way of judging fairly will be shown. [6]God "will give to all people in keeping with what they have done." *(Psalm 62:12; Proverbs 24:12)*

[7]God will give eternal life to those who keep on doing good. They want glory, honor, and life that never ends. [8]But there are others who only look out for themselves. They don't accept the truth. They go down an evil path. God will pour out his burning anger on them. [9]There will be trouble and suffering for everyone who does evil. That is meant first for the Jews. It is also meant for the non-Jews. [10]But there will be glory, honor and peace for everyone who does good. That is meant first for the Jews. It is also meant for the non-Jews. [11]God treats everyone the same.

2:6 God will give to all people in keeping with what they have done.

¹²Some people do not know God's law when they sin. They will not be judged by the law when they die. Others do know God's law when they sin. They will be judged by the law. ¹³Hearing the law does not make a person right with God. People are considered to be right with God only when they obey the law.

¹⁴Those who aren't Jews do not have the law. Sometimes they just naturally do what the law requires. They are a law for themselves. This is true even though they don't have the law. ¹⁵They show that what the law requires is written on their hearts. The way their minds judge them gives witness to that fact. Sometimes their thoughts find them guilty. At other times their thoughts find them not guilty.

¹⁶People will be judged on the day God appoints Jesus Christ to judge their secret thoughts. That's part of my good news.

The Jews and the Law

¹⁷Suppose you call yourself a Jew. You trust in the law. You brag that you are close to God. ¹⁸You know what God wants. You agree with what is best because the law teaches you. ¹⁹You are sure you can lead people who are blind. You are sure you are a light for those who are in the dark. ²⁰You claim to be able to teach foolish people. You can even teach babies. You think that in the law you have all knowledge and truth.

²¹You teach others. But you don't teach yourself! You preach against stealing. But you steal! ²²You say that people should not commit adultery. But you commit adultery! You hate statues of gods. But you rob temples! ²³You brag about the law. But when you break it, you rob God of his honor! ²⁴It is written: "Those who aren't Jews say evil things against God's name because of you." *(Isaiah 52:5; Ezekiel 36:22)*

²⁵Circumcision has value if you obey the law. But if you break the law, it is just as if you hadn't been circumcised. ²⁶Sometimes those who aren't circumcised do what the law requires. Won't God accept them as if they had been circumcised? ²⁷Many are not circumcised physically, but they obey the law. They will prove that you are guilty. You are breaking the law, even though you have the written law and are circumcised.

²⁸People are not Jews if they are Jews only on the outside. And circumcision is more than just something done to the outside of a person's body. ²⁹No, people are Jews only if they are Jews on the inside. And true circumcision means that the heart has been circumcised. It is done by the Holy Spirit. It is more than just

obeying the written Law. Then a person's praise will not come from others. It will come from God.

God Is Faithful

3 Is there any advantage in being a Jew? Is there any value in being circumcised? ²There is great value in every way! First of all, the Jews have been given the very words of God.

³What if some Jews did not believe? Will the fact that they don't have faith keep God from being faithful? ⁴Not at all! God is true, even though every human being is a liar. It is written:

> "You are right when you sentence me.
>   You are fair when you judge me." *(Psalm 51:4)*

⁵Doesn't the fact that we are wrong prove more clearly that God is right? Then what can we say? Can we say that God is not fair when he brings his anger down on us? As you can tell, I am just using human ways of thinking. ⁶God is certainly fair! If he weren't, how could he judge the world?

⁷Someone might argue, "When I lie, it becomes clearer that God is truthful. It makes his glory shine more brightly. Why then does he find me guilty of sin?"

⁸Why not say, "Let's do evil things so that good things will happen"? Some people actually lie by reporting that this is what we say. They are the ones who should be found guilty.

No One Is Right With God

⁹What should we say then? Are we Jews any better? Not at all! We have already claimed that Jews are sinners. The same is true of those who aren't Jews. ¹⁰It is written:

> "No one is right with God, no one at all.
> ¹¹   No one understands.
>   No one trusts in God.
> ¹²All of them have turned away.
>   They have all become worthless.
>   No one does anything good,
>   no one at all." *(Psalms 14:1–3; 53:1–3; Ecclesiastes 7:20)*
> ¹³"Their throats are like open graves.
>   With their tongues they tell lies." *(Psalm 5:9)*
> "The words from their lips are like the poison of a
>   snake." *(Psalm 140:3)*
> ¹⁴   "Their mouths are full of curses and bitterness."
>   *(Psalm 10:7)*

[15] "They run quickly to commit murder.
[16]   They leave a trail of failure and pain.
[17] They do not know the way of peace."   *(Isaiah 59:7,8)*
[18]   "They don't have any respect for God."   *(Psalm 36:1)*

[19] What the law says, it says to those who are ruled by the law. Its purpose is to shut every mouth and make the whole world accountable to God. [20] So it can't be said that anyone will be made right with God by obeying the law. Not at all! The law makes us more aware of our sin.

Becoming Right With God

[21] But now God has shown us how to become right with him. The Law and the Prophets give witness to this. It has nothing to do with obeying the law. [22] We are made right with God by putting our faith in Jesus Christ. That happens to all who believe. It is no different for the Jews than for anyone else. [23] Everyone has sinned. No one measures up to God's glory. [24] The free gift of God's grace makes all of us right with him. Christ Jesus paid the price to set us free. [25] God gave him as a sacrifice to pay for sins. So he forgives the sins of those who have faith in his blood.

God did all of that to prove that he is fair. Because of his mercy he did not punish people for the sins they had committed before Jesus died for them. [26] God did that to prove in our own time that he is fair. He proved that he is right. He also made right with himself those who believe in Jesus.

[27] So who can brag? No one! Are people saved by obeying the law? Not at all! They are saved because of their faith. [28] We firmly believe that people are made right with God because of their faith. They are not saved by obeying the law.

[29] Is God the God of Jews only? Isn't he also the God of those who aren't Jews? Yes, he is their God too. [30] There is only one God. When those who are circumcised believe in him, he makes them right with himself. When those who are not circumcised believe in him, he also makes them right with himself. [31] Does faith make the law useless? Not at all! We agree with the law.

GREAT VERSE —TO— REMEMBER

3:23 Everyone has sinned. No one measures up to God's glory.

Abraham's Faith Made Him Right With God

4 What should we say about those things? What did our father
Abraham discover about being right with God? [2]Did he
become right with God because of something he did? If so, he
could brag about it. But he couldn't brag to God. [3]What do we
find in Scripture? It says, "Abraham believed God. God accepted
Abraham's faith, and so his faith made him right with God." *(Genesis
15:6)*

[4]When people work, their pay is not considered a gift. It is
owed to them. [5]But things are different with God. He makes evil
people right with himself. If people trust in him, their faith is
accepted even though they do not work. Their faith makes them
right with God.

[6]King David says the same thing. He tells us how blessed some
people are. God makes those people right with himself. But they
don't have to do anything in return. David says,

[7]"Blessed are those
    whose lawless acts are forgiven.
    Blessed are those whose sins are taken away.
[8]Blessed are those
    whose sin the Lord never counts against them."

(Psalm 32:1,2)

[9]Is that blessing only for those who are circumcised? Or is it
also for those who are not circumcised? We have been saying that
God accepted Abraham's faith, and so his faith made him right
with God. [10]When did it happen? Was it after Abraham was circumcised, or before? It was before he was circumcised, not after!
[11]He was circumcised as a sign of the covenant God had made
with him. It showed that his faith had made him right with God
before he was circumcised.

So Abraham is the father of all believers who have not been circumcised. God accepts their faith. So their faith makes them right
with him. [12]Abraham is also the father of the circumcised who
believe. So just being circumcised is not enough. Those who are
circumcised must also follow the steps of our father Abraham.
He had faith before he was circumcised.

[13]Abraham and his family received a promise. God promised
that Abraham would receive the world. It would not come to him
because he obeyed the law. It would come because of his faith,
which made him right with God.

[14]Do those who obey the law receive the promise? If they do,

faith would have no value. God's promise would be worthless. [15]The law brings God's anger. Where there is no law, the law can't be broken.

[16]The promise is based on God's grace. The promise comes by faith. All of Abraham's children will certainly receive the promise. And it is not only for those who are ruled by the law. Those who have the same faith that Abraham had are also included. He is the father of us all. [17]It is written: "I have made you a father of many nations." *(Genesis 17:5)* God considers Abraham to be our father. The God that Abraham believed in gives life to the dead. Abraham's God also speaks of things that do not exist as if they do exist.

[18]When there was no reason for hope, Abraham believed because he had hope. He became the father of many nations, exactly as God had promised. God said, "That is how many children you will have." *(Genesis 15:5)*

[19]Without becoming weak in his faith, Abraham accepted the fact that he was past the time when he could have children. At that time he was about 100 years old. He also realized that Sarah was too old to have children. [20]But he kept believing in God's promise. He became strong in his faith. He gave glory to God. [21]He was absolutely sure that God had the power to do what he had promised. [22]That's why "God accepted Abraham because he believed. So his faith made him right with God." *(Genesis 15:6)*

[23]The words "God accepted Abraham's faith" were written not only for Abraham. [24]They were written also for us. We believe in the God who raised Jesus our Lord from the dead. So God will accept our faith and make us right with himself. [25]Jesus was handed over to die for our sins. He was raised to life in order to make us right with God.

Peace and Joy

5 We have been made right with God because of our faith. Now we have peace with him because of our Lord Jesus Christ. [2]Through faith in Jesus we have received God's grace. In that grace we stand. We are full of joy because we expect to share in God's glory.

[3]And that's not all. We are full of joy even when we suffer. We know that our suffering gives us the strength to go on. [4]The strength to go on produces character. Character produces hope. [5]And hope will never let us down. God has poured his love into

our hearts. He did it through the Holy Spirit, whom he has given to us.

⁶At just the right time Christ died for ungodly people. He died for us when we had no power of our own. ⁷It is unusual for anyone to die for a godly person. Maybe someone would be willing to die for a good person. ⁸But here is how God has shown his love for us. While we were still sinners, Christ died for us.

⁹The blood of Christ has made us right with God. So we are even more sure that Jesus will save us from God's anger. ¹⁰Once we were God's enemies. But we have been brought back to him because his Son has died for us. Now that God has brought us back, we are even more secure. We know that we will be saved because Christ lives.

¹¹And that is not all. We are full of joy in God because of our Lord Jesus Christ. Because of him, God has brought us back to himself.

Death Through Adam, Life Through Christ

¹²Sin entered the world because one man sinned. And death came because of sin. Everyone sinned, so death came to all people.

¹³Before the law was given, sin was in the world. But sin is not judged when there is no law. ¹⁴Death ruled from the time of Adam to the time of Moses. Death ruled even over those who did not sin as Adam did. He broke God's command. But he also became a pattern of the One who was going to come.

¹⁵God's gift is different from Adam's sin. Many people died because of the sin of that one man. But it was even more sure that God's grace would also come through one man. That man is Jesus Christ. God's gift of grace was more than enough for the whole world.

¹⁶The result of God's gift is different from the result of Adam's sin. God judged one sin. That brought guilt. But after many sins, God's gift made people right with him.

¹⁷One man sinned, and death ruled because of his sin. But we

GREAT VERSE — TO — REMEMBER

5:8 Here is how God has shown his love for us. While we were still sinners, Christ died for us.

are even more sure of what will happen because of what the one man, Jesus Christ, has done. Those who receive the rich supply of God's grace will rule with Christ in his kingdom. They have received God's gift and have been made right with him.

¹⁸One man's sin brought guilt to all people. So also one right act made all people right with God. And all who are right with God will live. ¹⁹Many people were made sinners because one man did not obey. But one man did obey. That is why many people will be made right with God.

²⁰The law was given so that sin would increase. But where sin increased, God's grace increased even more. ²¹Sin ruled because of death. So also grace rules in the lives of those who are right with God. The grace of God brings eternal life because of what Jesus Christ our Lord has done.

Living a New Life

6 What should we say then? Should we keep on sinning so that God's grace can increase? ²Not at all! As far as sin is concerned, we are dead. So how can we keep on sinning? ³All of us were baptized into Christ Jesus. Don't you know that we were baptized into his death? ⁴By being baptized, we were buried with Christ into his death. Christ has been raised from the dead by the Father's glory. And like Christ we also can live a new life.

⁵By being baptized, we have been joined with him in his death. We will certainly also be joined with him in his resurrection. ⁶We know that what we used to be was nailed to the cross with him. That happened so our sinful bodies would lose their power. We are no longer slaves of sin. ⁷Those who have died have been set free from sin.

⁸We died with Christ. So we believe that we will also live with him. ⁹We know that Christ was raised from the dead and will never die again. Death doesn't control him anymore. ¹⁰When he died, he died once and for all time as far as sin is concerned. Now that he lives, he lives as far as God is concerned.

¹¹In the same way, consider yourselves to be dead as far as sin is concerned. Now that you believe in Christ Jesus, consider yourselves to be alive as far as God is concerned.

¹²So don't let sin rule your body, which is going to die. Don't obey its evil longings. ¹³Don't give the parts of your body to serve sin. Don't let them be used to do evil. Instead, give yourselves to God. You have been brought from death to life. Give the parts of your body to him to do what is right.

¹⁴Sin will not be your master. Law does not rule you. God's grace has set you free.

Slaves to Right Living

¹⁵What should we say then? Should we sin because we are not ruled by law but by God's grace? Not at all!

¹⁶Don't you know that when you give yourselves to obey someone you become that person's slave? You can be slaves of sin. Then you will die. Or you can be slaves who obey God. Then you will live a godly life. ¹⁷You used to be slaves of sin. But thank God that with your whole heart you obeyed the teachings you were given! ¹⁸You have been set free from sin. You have become slaves to right living.

¹⁹Because you are human, you find this hard to understand. So I have said it in a way that will help you understand it. You used to give the parts of your body to be slaves to unclean living. You were becoming more and more evil. Now give your bodies to be slaves to right living. Then you will become holy.

²⁰Once you were slaves of sin. At that time right living did not control you. ²¹What benefit did you gain from doing the things you are now ashamed of? Those things lead to death!

²²You have been set free from sin. God has made you his slaves. The benefit you gain leads to holy living. And the end result is eternal life. ²³When you sin, the pay you get is death. But God gives you the gift of eternal life because of what Christ Jesus our Lord has done.

An Example From Marriage

7 Brothers and sisters, I am speaking to you who know the law. Don't you know that the law has authority over us only as long as we are alive? ²For example, by law a married woman is joined to her husband as long as he is living. But suppose her husband dies. Then the marriage law no longer applies to her.

GREAT VERSE – TO – REMEMBER

6:23 When you sin, the pay you get is death. But God gives you the gift of eternal life because of what Christ Jesus our Lord has done.

³But suppose that married woman gets married again while her husband is still alive. Then she is called a woman who commits adultery. But suppose her husband dies. Then she is free from that law. She is not guilty of adultery even if she marries another man.

⁴My brothers and sisters, when Christ died you also died as far as the law is concerned. Then it became possible for you to belong to him. He was raised from the dead. Now our lives can be useful to God. ⁵Our sinful nature used to control us. The law stirred up sinful longings in our bodies. So the things we did resulted in death.

⁶But now we have died to what used to control us. We have been set free from the law. Now we serve in the new way of the Holy Spirit. We no longer serve in the old way of the written law.

Struggling With Sin

⁷What should we say then? That the law is sin? Not at all! I wouldn't have known what sin was unless the law had told me. The law said, "Do not want what belongs to other people." *(Exodus 20:17; Deuteronomy 5:21)* If the law hadn't said that, I would not have known what it was like to want what belonged to others. ⁸But the commandment gave sin an opportunity. Sin caused me to want all kinds of things that belonged to others. No one can break a law that doesn't exist.

⁹Before I knew about the law, I was alive. But then the commandment came. Sin came to life, and I died. ¹⁰I found that the commandment that was supposed to bring life actually brought death. ¹¹When the commandment gave sin the opportunity, sin tricked me. It used the commandment to put me to death. ¹²So the law is holy. The commandment also is holy and right and good.

¹³Did what is good cause me to die? Not at all! Sin had to be recognized for what it really is. So it produced death in me through what was good. Because of the commandment, sin became totally sinful.

¹⁴We know that the law is holy. But I am not. I have been sold to be a slave of sin. ¹⁵I don't understand what I do. I don't do what I want to do. Instead, I do what I hate to do. ¹⁶I do what I don't want to do. So I agree that the law is good. ¹⁷As it is, I am no longer the one who does these things. It is sin living in me that does them.

¹⁸I know there is nothing good in my sinful nature. I want to do

what is good, but I can't. [19]I don't do the good things I want to do. I keep on doing the evil things I don't want to do. [20]I do what I don't want to do. But I am not really the one who is doing it. It is sin living in me.

[21]Here is the law I find working in me. When I want to do good, evil is right there with me. [22]Deep inside me I find joy in God's law. [23]But I see another law working in the parts of my body. It fights against the law of my mind. It makes me a prisoner of the law of sin. That law controls the parts of my body.

[24]What a terrible failure I am! Who will save me from this sin that brings death to my body? [25]I give thanks to God. He will do it through Jesus Christ our Lord.

So in my mind I am a slave to God's law. But in my sinful nature I am a slave to the law of sin.

The Holy Spirit Gives Life

8 Those who belong to Christ Jesus are no longer under God's sentence. [2]I am now controlled by the law of the Holy Spirit. That law gives me life because of what Christ Jesus has done. It has set me free from the law of sin that brings death.

[3]The written law was made weak by our sinful nature. But God did what the written law could not do. He made his Son to be like those who have a sinful nature. He sent him to be an offering for sin. In that way, he judged sin in his Son's human body. [4]Now we can do everything the law requires. Our sinful nature no longer controls the way we live. The Holy Spirit now controls the way we live.

[5]Don't live under the control of your sinful nature. If you do, you will think about what your sinful nature wants. Live under the control of the Holy Spirit. If you do, you will think about what the Spirit wants.

[6]The way a sinful person thinks leads to death. But the mind controlled by the Spirit brings life and peace. [7]The sinful mind is at war with God. It does not obey God's law. It can't. [8]Those who are controlled by their sinful nature can't please God.

[9]But your sinful nature does not control you. The Holy Spirit controls you. The Spirit of God lives in you. Anyone who does not have the Spirit of Christ does not belong to Christ.

[10]Christ lives in you. So your body is dead because of sin. But your spirit is alive because you have been made right with God. [11]The Spirit of the One who raised Jesus from the dead is living in you. So the God who raised Christ from the dead will also give

life to your bodies, which are going to die. He will do this by the power of his Spirit, who lives in you.

[12]Brothers and sisters, we have a duty. Our duty is not to live under the control of our sinful nature. [13]If you live under the control of your sinful nature, you will die. But by the power of the Holy Spirit you can put to death the sins your body commits. Then you will live.

[14]Those who are led by the Spirit of God are children of God. [15]You didn't receive a spirit that makes you a slave to fear once again. Instead you received the Holy Spirit, who makes you God's child. By the Spirit's power we call God *"Abba." Abba* means Father. [16]The Spirit himself joins with our spirits. Together they give witness that we are God's children.

[17]As his children, we will receive all that he has for us. We will share what Christ receives. But we must share in his sufferings if we want to share in his glory.

The Hope of Future Glory

[18]What we are suffering now is nothing compared with the glory that will be shown in us. [19]Everything God created looks forward to the time when his children will appear in their full and final glory. [20]The created world was bound to fail. But that was not the result of its own choice. It was planned that way by the One who made it. God planned [21]to set the created world free. He didn't want it to rot away completely. Instead, he wanted it to have the same glorious freedom that his children have.

[22]We know that all that God created has been groaning. It is in pain as if it were giving birth to a child. The created world continues to groan even now. [23]And that's not all. We have the Holy Spirit as the promise of future blessing. But we also groan inside ourselves as we look forward to the time when God will adopt us as full members of his family. Then he will give us everything he

8:28 We know that in all things God works for the good of those who love him. He appointed them to be saved in keeping with his purpose.

has for us. He will raise our bodies and give glory to them.

²⁴That's the hope we had when we were saved. But hope that can be seen is no hope at all. Who hopes for what is already there? ²⁵We hope for what we don't have yet. So we are patient as we wait for it.

²⁶In the same way, the Holy Spirit helps us when we are weak. We don't know what we should pray for. But the Spirit himself prays for us. He prays with groans too deep for words. ²⁷God, who looks into our hearts, knows the mind of the Spirit. And the Spirit prays for God's people, just as God wants him to pray.

We Will Win

²⁸We know that in all things God works for the good of those who love him. He appointed them to be saved in keeping with his purpose.

²⁹God planned that those he had chosen would become like his Son. In that way, Christ will be the first and most honored among many brothers and sisters. ³⁰And those God has planned for, he has also appointed to be saved. Those he has appointed, he has made right with himself. To those he has made right with himself, he has given his glory.

³¹What should we say then? Since God is on our side, who can be against us? ³²God did not spare his own Son. He gave him up for us all. Then won't he also freely give us everything else?

³³Who can bring any charge against God's chosen ones? God makes us right with himself. ³⁴Who can sentence us to death? Christ Jesus is at the right hand of God and is also praying for us. He died. More than that, he was raised to life.

³⁵Who can separate us from Christ's love? Can trouble or hard times or harm or hunger? Can nakedness or danger or war? ³⁶It is written:

> "Because of you, we face death all day long.
> We are considered as sheep to be killed." *(Psalm 44:22)*

³⁷No! In all these things we will do even more than win! We owe it all to Christ, who has loved us. ³⁸I am absolutely sure that not even death or life can separate us from God's love. Not even angels or demons, the present or the future, or any powers can do that. ³⁹Not even the highest places or the lowest, or anything else in all creation can do that. Nothing at all can ever separate us from God's love because of what Christ Jesus our Lord has done.

God's Free Choice

9 I speak the truth in Christ. I am not lying. My mind tells me that what I say is true. It is guided by the Holy Spirit. [2]My heart is full of sorrow. My sadness never ends. [3]I am so concerned about my people, who are members of my own race. I am ready to be cursed, if that would help them. I am even willing to be separated from Christ.

[4]They are the people of Israel. They have been adopted as God's children. God's glory belongs to them. So do the covenants. They received the law. They were taught to worship in the temple. They were given the promises. [5]The founders of our nation belong to them. Christ comes from their family line. He is God over all. May he always be praised! Amen.

[6]Their condition does not mean that God's word has failed. Not everyone in the family line of Israel really belongs to Israel. [7]Not everyone in Abraham's family line is really his child. Not at all! Scripture says, "Your family line will continue through Isaac." *(Genesis 21:12)* [8]In other words, God's children are not just Abraham's natural children. Instead, they are the children God promised to him. They are the ones considered to be Abraham's children. [9]God promised, "I will return at the appointed time. Sarah will have a son." *(Genesis 18:10,14)*

[10]And that's not all. Rebekah's children had the same father. He was our father Isaac. [11]Here is what happened. Rebekah's twins had not even been born. They hadn't done anything good or bad yet. So they show that God's purpose is based firmly on his free choice. [12]It was not because of anything they did but because of God's choice. So Rebekah was told, "The older son will serve the younger one." *(Genesis 25:23)* [13]It is written: "I chose Jacob instead of Esau." *(Malachi 1:2,3)*

[14]What should we say then? Is God unfair? Not at all! [15]He said to Moses,

> "I will have mercy on whom I have mercy.
> I will show love to those I love."   *(Exodus 33:19)*

[16]So it doesn't depend on what we want or do. It depends on God's mercy. [17]In Scripture, God says to Pharaoh, "I had a special reason for making you king. I decided to use you to show my power. I wanted my name to become known everywhere on earth." *(Exodus 9:16)* [18]So God does what he wants to do. He shows mercy to one person and makes another stubborn.

[19]One of you will say to me, "Then why does God still blame

us? Who can oppose what he wants to do?" ²⁰But who are you to talk back to God? Scripture says, "Can what is made say to the one who made it, 'Why did you make me like this?'" *(Isaiah 29:16; 45:9)* ²¹Isn't the potter free to make different kinds of pots out of the same lump of clay? Some are for special purposes. Others are for ordinary use.

²²What if God chose to show his great anger? What if he chose to make his power known? That is why he put up with people he was angry with. They had been made to be destroyed. ²³What if he did that to show the riches of his glory to others? Those are the people he shows his mercy to. He had prepared them to receive his glory. ²⁴We are those people. He has chosen us. We do not come only from the Jewish race. Many of us are not Jews. ²⁵God says in Hosea,

> "I will call those who are not my people 'my people.'
>   I will call the one who is not my loved one 'my loved
>   one.'" *(Hosea 2:23)*

²⁶He also says,

> "Once it was said to them,
>   'You are not my people.'
> In that very place they will be called 'children of the
>   living God.'" *(Hosea 1:10)*

²⁷Isaiah cries out concerning Israel. He says,

> "The number of people from Israel may be like the sand
>   by the sea.
> But only a few of them will be saved.
> ²⁸The Lord will carry out his sentence.
>   He will be quick to carry it out on earth, once and
>   for all." *(Isaiah 10:22,23)*

²⁹Earlier Isaiah had said,

> "The Lord who rules over all

9:25 I will call those who are not my people "my people." I will call the one who is not my loved one "my loved one."

left us children and grandchildren.
  If he hadn't, we would have become like Sodom.
  We would have been like Gomorrah."   *(Isaiah 1:9)*

Israel Does Not Believe

³⁰What should we say then? Those who aren't Jews did not look
for a way to be right with God. But they found it by having faith.
³¹Israel did look for a law that could make them right with God.
But they didn't find it. ³²Why not? Because they didn't look for
it by faith. They tried to get it by working for it. They tripped
over the stone that causes people to trip and fall. ³³It is written:

  "Look! In Zion I am laying a stone that causes people to
      trip.
  It is a rock that makes them fall.
  The one who trusts in him will never be put to shame."
                                          (Isaiah 8:14; 28:16)

10 Brothers and sisters, with all my heart I long for the people of Israel to be saved. I pray to God for them. ²I can
give witness about them that they really want to serve God. But
how they are trying to do it is not based on what they know.

³They didn't know how God makes people right with himself.
They tried to get right with God in their own way. They didn't do
it in God's way. ⁴Christ has completed the law. So now everyone
who believes can be right with God.

⁵Moses explained how the law could help a person live the
right kind of life. He said, "The one who does those things will
live by them." *(Leviticus 18:5)* ⁶But the way to live the right kind of life
by having faith is different. Scripture says, "Do not say in your
heart, 'Who will go up into heaven?'" *(Deuteronomy 30:12)* That means to
go up into heaven and bring Christ down. ⁷"And do not say,
'Who will go down into the grave?'" *(Deuteronomy 30:13)* That means to
bring Christ up from the dead.

⁸But what does it say? "The word is near you. It's in your mouth
and in your heart." *(Deuteronomy 30:14)* That means the word we are
preaching. You must put your faith in it. ⁹Say with your mouth,
"Jesus is Lord." Believe in your heart that God raised him from
the dead. Then you will be saved. ¹⁰With your heart you believe
and are made right with God. With your mouth you say that
Jesus is Lord. And so you are saved. ¹¹Scripture says, "The one
who trusts in him will never be put to shame." *(Isaiah 28:16)*

¹²There is no difference between those who are Jews and those

who are not. The same Lord is Lord of all. He richly blesses everyone who calls on him. [13]Scripture says, "Everyone who calls on the name of the Lord will be saved." *(Joel 2:32)*

[14]How can they call on him unless they believe in him? How can they believe in him unless they hear about him? How can they hear about him unless someone preaches to them? [15]And how can anyone preach without being sent? It is written: "How beautiful are the feet of those who bring good news!" *(Isaiah 52:7)*

[16]But not all the people of Israel accepted the good news. Isaiah says, "Lord, who has believed our message?" *(Isaiah 53:1)* [17]So faith comes from hearing the message. And the message that is heard is the word of Christ.

[18]But I ask: Didn't the people of Israel hear? Of course they did. It is written:

> "Their voice has gone out into the whole earth.
>   Their words have gone out from one end of the
>   world to the other." *(Psalm 19:4)*

[19]Again I ask: Didn't Israel understand? First, Moses says,

> "I will use people who are not a nation to make you
>   jealous.
> I will use a nation that has no understanding to
>   make you angry." *(Deuteronomy 32:21)*

[20]Then Isaiah boldly speaks about what God says. God said,

> "I was found by those who were not trying to find me.
> I made myself known to those who were not asking
>   for me." *(Isaiah 65:1)*

[21]But Isaiah also speaks about what God says concerning Israel. God said,

> "All day long I have held out my hands.

10:10 With your heart you believe and are made right with God. With your mouth you say that Jesus is Lord. And so you are saved.

> I have held them out to a stubborn people who do
> not obey me." *(Isaiah 65:2)*

God's Faithful People in Israel

11 So here is what I ask. Did God turn his back on his people? Not at all! I myself belong to Israel. I am one of Abraham's children. I am from the tribe of Benjamin. [2]God didn't turn his back on his people. After all, he chose them.

Don't you know what Scripture says about Elijah? He complained to God about Israel. [3]He said, "Lord, they have killed your prophets. They have torn down your altars. I'm the only one left. And they are trying to kill me." *(1Kings 19:10,14)*

[4]How did God answer him? God said, "I have kept 7,000 people for myself. They have not bowed down to Baal." *(1Kings 19:18)* [5]Some are also faithful today. They have been chosen by God's grace. [6]And if they are chosen by grace, it is no longer a matter of working for it. If it were, grace wouldn't be grace anymore.

[7]What should we say then? Israel did not receive what they wanted so badly. But those who were chosen did. God made the rest of them stubborn. [8]It is written:

> "God made it hard for them to understand.
> He gave them eyes that could not see.
> He gave them ears that could not hear.
> And they are still like that today." *(Deuteronomy 29:4; Isaiah 29:10)*

[9]David says,

> "Let their feast be a trap and a snare.
> Let it make Israel trip and fall. Let Israel get what's
> coming to them.
> [10]Let their eyes grow dark so they can't see.
> Let their backs be bent forever." *(Psalm 69:22,23)*

Two Kinds of Olive Branches

[11]Again, here is what I ask. They didn't trip and fall once and for all time, did they? Not at all! Because Israel sinned, those who aren't Jews can be saved. That will make Israel jealous of them. [12]Israel's sin brought riches to the world. Their loss brought riches to the non-Jews. What greater riches will come when all Israel turns to God!

[13]I am talking to you who are not Jews. I am the apostle to the non-Jews. So I think the work I do for God and others is very

important. [14]I hope somehow to stir up my own people to want what you have. Perhaps I can save some of them. [15]When they were not accepted, it became possible for the whole world to be brought back to God. So what will happen when they are accepted? It will be like life from the dead.

[16]The first handful of dough that is offered is holy. This makes all of the dough holy.

If the root is holy, so are the branches.

[17]Some of the natural branches have been broken off. You are a wild olive branch. But you have been joined to the tree with the other branches. Now you enjoy the life-giving sap of the olive tree root. [18]So don't think you are better than the other branches. Remember, you don't give life to the root. The root gives life to you.

[19]You will say, "Some branches were broken off so that I could be joined to the tree." [20]That's true. But they were broken off because they didn't believe. You stand only because you do believe. So don't be proud. Be afraid. [21]God didn't spare the natural branches. He won't spare you either.

[22]Think about how kind God is! Also think about how firm he is! He was hard on those who stopped following him. But he is kind to you. So you must continue to live in his kindness. If you don't, you also will be cut off.

[23]If the people of Israel do not continue in their unbelief, they will again be joined to the tree. God is able to join them to the tree again. [24]After all, weren't you cut from a wild olive tree? Weren't you joined to an olive tree that was taken care of? And wasn't that the opposite of how things should be done? How much more easily will the natural branches be joined to their own olive tree!

All Israel Will Be Saved

[25]Brothers and sisters, here is a mystery I want you to understand. It will keep you from being proud. Part of Israel has refused to obey God. That will continue until the full number of non-Jews has entered God's kingdom. [26]And so all Israel will be saved. It is written:

"The One who saves will come from Mount Zion.
　　He will remove sin from Jacob.
　[27]Here is my covenant with them.
　　I will take away their sins." *(Isaiah 59:20,21; 27:9; Jeremiah 31:33,34)*

²⁸As far as the good news is concerned, the people of Israel are enemies. That is for your good. But as far as God's choice is concerned, the people of Israel are loved. That is because of God's promises to the founders of our nation. ²⁹God does not take back his gifts. He does not change his mind about those he has chosen.

³⁰At one time you did not obey God. But now you have received mercy because Israel did not obey. ³¹In the same way, Israel has not been obeying God. But now they receive mercy because of God's mercy to you. ³²God has found everyone guilty of not obeying him. So now he can have mercy on everyone.

Praise to God

³³How very rich are God's wisdom and knowledge!
    How he judges is more than we can understand!
    Where he goes is more than we can know!
³⁴"Who can ever know what is in the Lord's mind?
    Or who can ever give him advice?"   *(Isaiah 40:13)*
³⁵"Have people ever given anything to God,
    so that God has to pay them back?"   *(Job 41:11)*
³⁶All things come from him.
  All things are directed by him.
  All things are for his good.
    May God be given the glory forever! Amen.

Living for God

12 Brothers and sisters, God has shown you his mercy. So I am asking you to offer up your bodies to him while you are still alive. Your bodies are a holy sacrifice that is pleasing to God. When you offer your bodies to God, you are worshiping him. ²Don't live any longer the way this world lives. Let your way of thinking be completely changed. Then you will be able to test what God wants for you. And you will agree that what he wants is right. His plan is good and pleasing and perfect.

³God's grace has been given to me. So here is what I say to every one of you. Don't think of yourself more highly than you should. Be reasonable when you think about yourself. Keep in mind the amount of faith God has given you. ⁴Each of us has one body with many parts. And the parts do not all have the same purpose. ⁵So also we are many persons. But in Christ we are one body. And each part of the body belongs to all the other parts.

⁶We all have gifts. They differ in keeping with the grace that God has given each of us. Do you have the gift of prophecy? Then use it in keeping with the faith you have. ⁷Is it your gift to serve? Then serve. Is it teaching? Then teach. ⁸Is it telling others how they should live? Then tell them. Is it giving to those who are in need? Then give freely. Is it being a leader? Then work hard at it. Is it showing mercy? Then do it cheerfully.

Love

⁹Love must be honest and true. Hate what is evil. Hold on to what is good. ¹⁰Love each other deeply. Honor others more than yourselves. ¹¹Never let the fire in your heart go out. Keep it alive. Serve the Lord. ¹²When you hope, be joyful. When you suffer, be patient. When you pray, be faithful. ¹³Share with God's people who are in need. Welcome others into your homes.

¹⁴Bless those who hurt you. Bless them, and do not call down curses on them. ¹⁵Be joyful with those who are joyful. Be sad with those who are sad. ¹⁶Agree with each other. Don't be proud. Be willing to be a friend of people who aren't considered important. Don't think that you are better than others.

¹⁷Don't pay back evil with evil. Be careful to do what everyone thinks is right. ¹⁸If possible, live in peace with everyone. Do that as much as you can.

¹⁹My friends, don't try to get even. Leave room for God to show his anger. It is written: "I am the One who judges people. I will pay them back," *(Deuteronomy 32:35)* says the Lord. ²⁰Do just the opposite. Scripture says,

"If your enemies are hungry, give them food to eat.

GREAT VERSE — TO — REMEMBER

12:2 Don't live any longer the way this world lives. Let your way of thinking be completely changed. Then you will be able to test what God wants for you. And you will agree that what he wants is right. His plan is good and pleasing and perfect.

If they are thirsty, give them something to drink.
By doing those things, you will pile up burning coals
on their heads."   *(Proverbs 25:21,22)*

²¹Don't let evil overcome you. Overcome evil by doing good.

Obey Those in Authority

13 All of you must be willing to obey completely those who rule over you. There are no authorities except the ones God has chosen. Those who now rule have been chosen by God. ²So when you oppose the authorities, you are opposing those whom God has appointed. Those who do that will be judged.

³If you do what is right, you won't need to be afraid of your rulers. But watch out if you do what is wrong! You don't want to be afraid of those in authority, do you? Then do what is right. The one in authority will praise you. ⁴He serves God and will do you good. But if you do wrong, watch out! The ruler doesn't carry a sword for no reason at all. He serves God. And God is carrying out his anger through him. The ruler punishes anyone who does wrong.

⁵You must obey the authorities. Then you will not be punished. You must also obey them because you know it is right.

⁶That's also why you pay taxes. The authorities serve God. Ruling takes up all their time. ⁷Give to everyone what you owe. Do you owe taxes? Then pay them. Do you owe anything else to the government? Then pay it. Do you owe respect? Then give it. Do you owe honor? Then show it.

Love, Because the Day Is Near

⁸Pay everything you owe. But you can never pay back all the love you owe each other. Those who love others have done everything the law requires. ⁹Here are some commandments to think about. "Do not commit adultery." "Do not commit murder." "Do not steal." "Do not want what belongs to others." *(Exodus 20:13–15,17; Deuteronomy 5:17–19,21)* These and other commandments are all included

---

GREAT VERSE —TO— REMEMBER

13:8 Pay everything you owe. But you can never pay back all the love you owe each other.

in one rule. Here's what it is. "Love your neighbor as you love yourself." *(Leviticus 19:18)* ¹⁰Love does not harm its neighbor. So love does everything the law requires.

¹¹When you do those things, keep in mind the times we are living in. The hour has come for you to wake up from your sleep. Our full salvation is closer now than it was when we first believed in Christ. ¹²The dark night of evil is nearly over. The day of Christ's return is almost here. So let us get rid of the works of darkness. Let us put on the armor of light.

¹³Let us act as we should, like people living in the daytime. Have nothing to do with wild parties. Don't get drunk. Don't take part in sexual sins or evil conduct. Don't fight with each other. Don't be jealous of anyone.

¹⁴Instead, put on the Lord Jesus Christ as your clothing. Don't think about how to satisfy what your sinful nature wants.

The Weak and the Strong

14 Accept those whose faith is weak. Don't judge them where you have differences of opinion. ²The faith of some people allows them to eat anything. But others eat only vegetables because their faith is weak. ³People who eat everything must not look down on those who do not. And people who don't eat everything must not judge those who do. God has accepted them. ⁴Who are you to judge someone else's servants? Whether they are faithful or not is their own master's concern. They will be faithful, because the Lord has the power to make them faithful.

⁵Some people consider one day to be more holy than another. Others think all days are the same. All people should be absolutely sure in their own minds. ⁶Those who think one day is special do it to honor the Lord. Those who eat meat do it to honor the Lord. They give thanks to God. Those who don't eat meat do it to honor the Lord. They also give thanks to God.

⁷We don't live for ourselves alone. And we don't die all by ourselves. ⁸If we live, we live to honor the Lord. If we die, we die to honor the Lord. So whether we live or die, we belong to the Lord.

⁹Christ died and came back to life. He did this to become the Lord of both the dead and the living. ¹⁰Now then, who are you to judge your brothers and sisters? Why do you look down on them? We will all stand in God's courtroom to be judged. ¹¹It is written:

"'You can be sure that I live,' says the Lord.

'And you can be just as sure that every knee will bow
down in front of me.
Every tongue will tell the truth to God.'" *(Isaiah 45:23)*

¹²So we will all have to explain to God the things we have done.

¹³Let us stop judging one another. Instead, make up your mind not to put anything in your brother or sister's way that would make them trip and fall.

¹⁴I am absolutely sure that no food is "unclean" in itself. I say this as one who belongs to the Lord Jesus. But you may consider something to be "unclean." If you do, it is "unclean" for you. ¹⁵Your brothers and sisters may be upset by what you eat. If they are, you are no longer acting as though you love them. So don't destroy them by what you eat. Christ died for them. ¹⁶Don't let something you consider good be spoken of as if it were evil.

¹⁷God's kingdom has nothing to do with eating or drinking. It is a matter of being right with God. It brings the peace and joy the Holy Spirit gives. ¹⁸Those who serve Christ in this way are pleasing to God. They are pleasing to people too.

¹⁹So let us do all we can to live in peace. And let us work hard to build each other up. ²⁰Don't destroy the work of God because of food. All food is "clean." But it is wrong for you to eat anything that causes someone else to trip and fall. ²¹Don't eat meat if it will cause your brothers and sisters to fall. Don't drink wine or do anything else that will make them fall.

²²No matter what you think about those things, keep it between yourself and God. Blessed are those who do not have to feel guilty for what they allow. ²³But those who have doubts are guilty if they eat. Their eating is not based on faith. Everything that is not based on faith is sin.

15 We who have strong faith should help the weak with their problems. We should not please only ourselves. ²We should all please our neighbors. Let us do what is good for them. Let us build them up.

³Even Christ did not please himself. It is written: "Those who

---

14:19 So let us do all we can to live in peace. And let us work hard to build each other up.

make fun of you have made fun of me also." *(Psalm 69:9)* ⁴Everything that was written in the past was written to teach us. The Scriptures give us strength to go on. They cheer us up and give us hope.

⁵Our God is a God who strengthens you and cheers you up. May he help you agree with each other as you follow Christ Jesus. ⁶Then you can give glory to God with one heart and voice. He is the God and Father of our Lord Jesus Christ.

⁷Christ has accepted you. So accept one another in order to bring praise to God. ⁸I tell you that Christ has become a servant of the Jews. He teaches us that God is true. He shows us that God will keep the promises he made to the founders of our nation. ⁹Jesus became a servant of the Jews so that people who are not Jews could give glory to God for his mercy. It is written:

> "I will praise you among those who aren't Jews.
> I will sing praises to you." *(2 Samuel 22:50; Psalm 18:49)*

¹⁰Again it says,

> "You non-Jews, be full of joy.
> Be joyful together with God's people." *(Deuteronomy 32:43)*

¹¹And again it says,

> "All you non-Jews, praise the Lord.
> All you nations, sing praises to him." *(Psalm 117:1)*

¹²And Isaiah says,

> "The Root of Jesse will grow up quickly.
> He will rule over the nations.
> Those who aren't Jews will put their hope in him."
>
> *(Isaiah 11:10)*

¹³May the God who gives hope fill you with great joy. May you have perfect peace as you trust in him. May the power of the Holy Spirit fill you with hope.

GREAT VERSE —TO— REMEMBER

15:7 Christ has accepted you. So accept one another in order to bring praise to God.

Paul Serves the Non-Jews

¹⁴My brothers and sisters, I am sure that you are full of goodness. What you know is complete. You are able to teach one another. ¹⁵I have written to you very boldly about some things. I wanted you to think about them again. The grace of God has allowed me ¹⁶to serve Christ Jesus among those who aren't Jews. My duty as a priest is to preach God's good news. Then the non-Jews will become an offering that pleases God. The Holy Spirit will make the offering holy.

¹⁷Because I belong to Christ Jesus, I can take pride in my work for God. ¹⁸I will not try to speak of anything except what Christ has done through me. He has been leading those who aren't Jews to obey God. He has been doing this by what I have said and done.

¹⁹He has given me power to do signs and miracles. He has given me the power of the Holy Spirit.

From Jerusalem all the way around to Illyricum I have finished preaching the good news about Christ. ²⁰I have always wanted to preach the good news where Christ was not known. I don't want to build on what someone else has started. ²¹It is written:

> "Those who were not told about him will understand.
> Those who have not heard will know what it all
> means." *(Isaiah 52:15)*

²²That's why I have often been kept from coming to you.

Paul Plans to Visit Rome

²³Now there is no more place for me to work in those areas. For many years I have been longing to see you. ²⁴So I plan to see you when I go to Spain. I hope to visit you while I am passing through. And I hope you will help me on my journey there. But first I want to enjoy being with you for a while.

²⁵Now I am on my way to Jerusalem to serve God's people there. ²⁶The believers in Macedonia and Achaia were pleased to take an offering for those who were poor among God's people in Jerusalem. ²⁷They were happy to do it. And of course they owe it to them. Those who aren't Jews have shared from the Jews' spiritual blessings. So the non-Jews should share their earthly blessings with the Jews.

²⁸I want to finish my task. I want to make sure that the poor in Jerusalem have received the offering. Then I will go to Spain. On

my way I will visit you. ²⁹I know that when I come to you, I will come with the full blessing of Christ.

³⁰Brothers and sisters, I am asking you through the authority of our Lord Jesus Christ to join me in my struggle by praying to God for me. Pray for me with the love the Holy Spirit provides. ³¹Pray that I will be saved from those in Judea who do not believe. Pray that my work in Jerusalem will be accepted by God's people there. ³²Then, as God has planned, I will come to you with joy. Together we will be renewed.

³³May the God who gives peace be with you all. Amen.

Personal Greetings

16 I would like you to welcome our sister Phoebe. She serves the church in Cenchrea. ²I ask you to receive her as one who belongs to the Lord. Receive her in the way God's people should. Give her any help she may need from you. She has been a great help to many people, including me.

³Greet Priscilla and Aquila. They work together with me in serving Christ Jesus. ⁴They have put their lives in danger for me. I am thankful for them. So are all the non-Jewish churches.

⁵Greet also the church that meets in the house of Priscilla and Aquila.

Greet my dear friend Epenetus. He was the first person in Asia Minor to become a believer in Christ.

⁶Greet Mary. She worked very hard for you.

⁷Greet Andronicus and Junias, my relatives. They have been in prison with me. They are leaders among the apostles. They became believers in Christ before I did.

⁸Greet Ampliatus. I love him as a brother in the Lord.

⁹Greet Urbanus. He works together with me in serving Christ. And greet my dear friend Stachys.

¹⁰Greet Apelles. Even though he was put to the test, he remained faithful as one who belonged to Christ.

Greet those who live in the house of Aristobulus.

¹¹Greet Herodion, my relative.

Greet the believers who live in the house of Narcissus.

¹²Greet Tryphena and Tryphosa. Those women work hard for the Lord.

Greet my dear friend Persis. She is another woman who has worked very hard for the Lord.

¹³ Greet Rufus. He is a choice believer in the Lord. And greet his mother. She has been like a mother to me too.

¹⁴ Greet Asyncritus, Phlegon and Hermes. Greet Patrobas, Hermas and the believers with them.

¹⁵ Greet Philologus, Julia, Nereus and his sister. Greet Olympas and all of God's people with them.

¹⁶ Greet one another with a holy kiss.

All the churches of Christ send their greetings.

¹⁷I am warning you, brothers and sisters, to watch out for those who try to keep you from staying together. They want to trip you up. They teach you things opposite to what you have learned. Stay away from them. ¹⁸People like that are not serving Christ our Lord. They are serving only themselves. With smooth talk and with words they don't mean they fool people who don't know any better.

¹⁹Everyone has heard that you obey God. So you have filled me with joy. I want you to be wise about what is good. And I want you to have nothing to do with what is evil.

²⁰The God who gives peace will soon crush Satan under your feet.

May the grace of our Lord Jesus be with you.

²¹Timothy works together with me. He sends his greetings to you. So do Lucius, Jason and Sosipater, my relatives.

²²I, Tertius, wrote down this letter. I greet you as a believer in the Lord.

²³/²⁴Gaius sends you his greetings. He has welcomed me and the whole church here into his house.

Erastus is the director of public works here in the city. He sends you his greetings. Our brother Quartus also greets you.

²⁵May God receive glory. He is able to strengthen your faith because of the good news I preach. It is the message about Jesus Christ. It is in keeping with the mystery that was hidden for a very long time. ²⁶The mystery has now been made known through the writings of the prophets. The eternal God commanded that it be made known. He wanted all nations to believe and obey him. ²⁷May the only wise God receive glory forever through Jesus Christ. Amen.

1 Corinthians

Why Was This Book Written? Paul wrote this letter at the start of his third missionary trip. He was in Ephesus. He heard sad news about his friends in Corinth. They were fighting with each other in church. Paul wrote to teach them how to behave.

What Is This Book About? Most people in Corinth did not believe in God. Paul wrote this letter to teach the Christians in Corinth what was right and wrong. This letter has many important parts. It teaches us about love and the Lord's Supper. It tells about Jesus rising from the dead too.

What Is in This Book?

1 I, Paul, am writing this letter. I have been chosen to be an apostle of Christ Jesus just as God planned. Our brother Sosthenes joins me in writing.

²We are sending this letter to you, the members of God's church in Corinth. You have been made holy because you belong to Christ Jesus. God has chosen you to be his holy people. He has done the same for all those everywhere who pray to our Lord Jesus Christ. Jesus is their Lord and ours.

³May God our Father and the Lord Jesus Christ give you grace and peace.

Paul Gives Thanks

⁴I always thank God for you. I thank him because of the grace he has given to you who belong to Christ Jesus. ⁵You have been blessed in every way because of him. All your teaching of the truth is better. Your understanding of it is more complete. ⁶Our witness about Christ has been proved to be true in you.

⁷There is no gift of the Holy Spirit that you don't have. You are full of hope as you wait for our Lord Jesus Christ to come again. ⁸He will keep you strong to the very end. Then you will be without blame on the day our Lord Jesus Christ returns.

⁹God is faithful. He has chosen you to share life with his Son, Jesus Christ our Lord.

Taking Sides in the Church

¹⁰Brothers and sisters, I ask all of you to agree with one another. I make my appeal in the name of our Lord Jesus Christ. Then you won't take sides. You will be in complete agreement in all that you think.

¹¹My brothers and sisters, some people who live in Chloe's house have told me you are arguing with each other. ¹²Here is what I mean. One of you says, "I follow Paul." Another says, "I

GREAT VERSE —TO— REMEMBER

1:8 [The Holy Spirit] will keep you strong to the very end. Then you will be without blame on the day our Lord Jesus Christ returns.

follow Apollos." Another says, "I follow Peter." And still another says, "I follow Christ."

¹³Does Christ take sides? Did Paul die on the cross for you? Were you baptized in the name of Paul? ¹⁴I'm thankful that I didn't baptize any of you except Crispus and Gaius. ¹⁵No one can say that you were baptized in my name.

¹⁶It's true that I also baptized those who live in the house of Stephanas. Besides that, I don't remember if I baptized anyone else.

¹⁷Christ did not send me to baptize. He sent me to preach the good news. He commanded me not to use the kind of wisdom that people commonly use. That would take all the power away from the cross of Christ.

Christ Is God's Power and Wisdom

¹⁸The message of the cross seems foolish to those who are lost and dying. But it is God's power to us who are being saved. ¹⁹It is written:

"I will destroy the wisdom of those who are wise.
I will do away with the cleverness of those who think
they are so smart."   *(Isaiah 29:14)*

²⁰Where is the wise person? Where is the educated person? Where are the great thinkers of this world? Hasn't God made the wisdom of the world foolish? ²¹God wisely planned that the world would not know him through its own wisdom. It pleased God to use the foolish things we preach to save those who believe.

²²Jews require miraculous signs. Greeks look for wisdom. ²³But we preach about Christ and his death on the cross. That is very hard for Jews to accept. And everyone else thinks it's foolish.

²⁴But there are those God has chosen, both Jews and others. To them Christ is God's power and God's wisdom. ²⁵The foolish things of God are wiser than human wisdom. The weakness of God is stronger than human strength.

²⁶Brothers and sisters, think of what you were when God chose you. Not many of you were considered wise by human standards. Not many of you were powerful. Not many of you belonged to important families.

²⁷But God chose the foolish things of the world to shame the wise. He chose the weak things of the world to shame the strong. ²⁸God chose the things of this world that are common and looked

down on. He chose what is not considered to be important to do away with what is considered to be important. ²⁹So no one can brag to God.

³⁰Because of what God has done, you belong to Christ Jesus. He has become God's wisdom for us. He makes us right with God. He makes us holy and sets us free. ³¹It is written: "Those who brag should brag about what the Lord has done." *(Jeremiah 9:24)*

2 Brothers and sisters, when I came to you I didn't come with fancy words or great wisdom. I preached to you the truth about God's love. ²I made up my mind to pay attention to only one thing while I was with you. That one thing was Jesus Christ and his death on the cross.

³When I came to you, I was weak and afraid and trembling all over. ⁴I didn't preach my message with clever and compelling words. As I preached, the Holy Spirit showed his power. ⁵That was so you would believe not because of human wisdom but because of God's power.

Wisdom From the Holy Spirit

⁶The words we speak to those who have grown in the faith are wise. Our words are different from the words of the wise people or rulers of this world. People like that aren't going anywhere. ⁷No, we speak about God's secret wisdom. His wisdom has been hidden. But before time began, God planned that his wisdom would bring us heavenly glory.

⁸None of the rulers of this world understood God's wisdom. If they had, they would not have nailed the Lord of glory to the cross. ⁹It is written:

> "No eye has seen,
>   no ear has heard,
> no mind has known
>   what God has prepared for those who love him."
>
> *(Isaiah 64:4)*

GREAT VERSE —TO— REMEMBER

2:9 No eye has seen, no ear has heard, no mind has known what God has prepared for those who love him.

[10]But God has shown it to us through his Spirit.

The Spirit understands all things. He understands even the deep things of God. [11]Who can know the thoughts of another person? Only a person's own spirit can know them. In the same way, only the Spirit of God knows God's thoughts.

[12]We have not received the spirit of the world. We have received the Spirit who is from God. The Spirit helps us understand what God has freely given us.

[13]That is what we speak about. We don't use words taught to us by people. We use words taught to us by the Holy Spirit. We use the words of the Spirit to teach the truths of the Spirit.

[14]Some people don't have the Holy Spirit. They don't accept the things that come from the Spirit of God. Things like that are foolish to them. They can't understand them. In fact, such things can't be understood without the Spirit's help.

[15]Those who have the Spirit can judge all things. But no one can judge those who have the Spirit. It is written:

> [16]"Who can ever know what is in the Lord's mind?
> Can anyone ever teach him?"   *(Isaiah 40:13)*

But we have the mind of Christ.

Taking Sides in the Church

3 Brothers and sisters, I couldn't speak to you as if you were guided by the Holy Spirit. I had to speak to you as if you were following the ways of the world. You aren't growing as Christ wants you to. You are still like babies. [2]The words I spoke to you were like milk, not like solid food. You weren't ready for solid food yet. And you still aren't ready for it.

[3]You are still following the ways of the world. Some of you are jealous. Some of you argue. So aren't you following the ways of the world? Aren't you acting like ordinary human beings? [4]One of you says, "I follow Paul." Another says, "I follow Apollos." Aren't you acting like ordinary human beings?

[5]After all, what is Apollos? And what is Paul? We are only people who serve. We helped you to believe. The Lord has given each of us our own work to do. [6]I planted the seed. Apollos watered it. But God made it grow.

[7]So the one who plants is not important. The one who waters is not important. It is God who makes things grow. He is the One who is important. [8]The one who plants and the one who waters have the same purpose. The Lord will give each of us a reward for

our work. [9]We work together with God. You are like God's field. You are like his building.

[10]God has given me the grace to lay a foundation as a master builder. Now someone else is building on it. But each one should build carefully. [11]No one can lay any other foundation than the one that has already been laid. That foundation is Jesus Christ.

[12]A person may build on it using gold, silver, jewels, wood, hay or straw. [13]But each person's work will be shown for what it is. On judgment day it will be brought to light. It will be put through fire. The fire will test how good everyone's work is. [14]If the building doesn't burn up, God will give the builder a reward for his work. [15]If the building burns up, the builder will lose everything. The builder will be saved, but only like one escaping through the flames.

[16]Don't you know that you yourselves are God's temple? God's Spirit lives in you. [17]If anyone destroys God's temple, God will destroy that person. God's temple is holy. And you are that temple.

[18]Don't fool yourselves. Suppose some of you think you are wise by the standards of the world. Then you should become a "fool" so that you can become wise.

[19]The wisdom of this world is foolish in God's eyes. It is written: "God catches the wise in their own tricks." *(Job 5:13)* [20]It is also written: "The Lord knows that the thoughts of the wise don't amount to anything." *(Psalm 94:11)*

[21]So no more bragging about human beings! All things are yours. [22]That means Paul or Apollos or Peter or the world or life or death or the present or the future. All are yours. [23]You are joined to Christ and belong to him. And Christ is joined to God.

Apostles of Christ

4 Here is how you should think of us. We serve Christ. We are trusted with God's secret truth. [2]Those who have been given a trust must prove that they are faithful.

[3]I care very little if I am judged by you or by any human court. I don't even judge myself. [4]I don't feel I have done anything wrong. But that doesn't mean I'm not guilty. The Lord judges me.

[5]So don't judge anything before the appointed time. Wait until the Lord returns. He will bring to light what is hidden in the dark. He will show the real reasons why people do what they do. At that time each person will receive praise from God.

⁶Brothers and sisters, I have used myself and Apollos as examples to help you. You can learn from us the meaning of the saying, "Don't go beyond what is written." Then you won't be proud that you follow one person instead of another.

⁷Who makes you different from anyone else? What do you have that you did not receive? And if you did receive it, why do you brag as though you did not?

⁸You already have everything you want, don't you? Have you already become rich? Have you begun to rule as kings? And did you do that without us? I wish that you really had begun to rule. Then we could rule with you!

⁹It seems to me that God has put us apostles on display at the end of a parade. We are like people sentenced to die in front of a crowd. We have been made a show for the whole creation to see. Angels and people are staring at us.

¹⁰We are fools for Christ. But you are so wise in Christ! We are weak. But you are so strong! You are honored. But we are looked down on! ¹¹Up to this very hour we are hungry and thirsty. We are dressed in rags. We are being treated badly. We have no homes. ¹²We work hard with our own hands. When others call down a curse on us, we bless them. When we are attacked, we put up with it. ¹³When others say bad things about us, we answer kindly. Up to this moment we have become the world's garbage. We are everybody's trash.

¹⁴I am not writing this to shame you. You are my dear children, and I want to warn you. ¹⁵You may have 10,000 believers in Christ watching over you. But you don't have many fathers. I became your father by serving Christ Jesus and telling you the good news. ¹⁶So I'm asking you to follow my example.

¹⁷That's the reason I'm sending Timothy to you. He is like a son to me, and I love him. He is faithful in serving the Lord. He will

GREAT VERSE — TO — REMEMBER

3:13 Each person's work will be shown for what it is. On judgment day it will be brought to light. It will be put through fire. The fire will test how good everyone's work is.

remind you of my way of life in serving Christ Jesus. And that agrees with what I teach everywhere in every church.

¹⁸Some of you have become proud. You act as if I weren't coming to you. ¹⁹But I will come very soon, if that's what the Lord wants. Then I will find out how those proud people are talking. I will also find out what power they have. ²⁰The kingdom of God is not a matter of talk. It is a matter of power.

²¹Which do you want? Should I come to you with a whip? Or should I come in love and with a gentle spirit?

Throw the Evil Person Out!

5 It is actually reported that there is sexual sin among you. I'm told that a man is living with his father's wife and is having sex with her. Even people who do not know God don't commit that sin. ²And you are proud! Shouldn't you be filled with sadness instead? Shouldn't you have put the man who did that out of your church?

³Even though I am not right there with you, I am with you in spirit. And I have already judged the one who did that, just as if I were there.

⁴When you come together in the name of our Lord Jesus, I will be with you in spirit. The power of our Lord Jesus will also be with you. ⁵When you come together like that, hand that man over to Satan. Then his sinful nature will be destroyed. His spirit will be saved on the day the Lord returns.

⁶Your bragging is not good. It is like yeast. Don't you know that just a little yeast works its way through the whole batch of dough? ⁷Get rid of the old yeast. Be like a new batch of dough without yeast. That is what you really are, because Christ has been offered up for us. He is our Passover lamb.

⁸So let us keep the Feast, but not with the old yeast. I'm talking about yeast that is full of hatred and evil. Let us keep the Feast with bread made without yeast. Let us do it with bread that is honest and true.

⁹I wrote a letter to you to tell you to stay away from people who commit sexual sins. ¹⁰I didn't mean the people of this world who sin that way or who always want more and more. I didn't mean those who cheat or who worship statues of gods. In that case you would have to leave this world!

¹¹But here is what I am writing to you. You must stay away from any who claim to be believers but who do those things. Stay away from those who commit sexual sins or who always want more

and more. Stay away from those who worship statues of gods or who tell lies about others. Stay away from those who get drunk or who cheat. Don't even eat with people like that.

¹²Is it my business to judge those outside the church? Aren't you supposed to judge those inside the church? ¹³God will judge those outside. Scripture says, "Get rid of that evil person!" *(Deuteronomy 17:7; 19:19; 21:21; 22:21,24; 24:7)*

Do Not Take Believers to Court

6 Suppose one of you wants to bring a charge against another believer. Should you take it to the ungodly to be judged? Why not take it to God's people?

²Don't you know that God's people will judge the world? And if you are going to judge the world, aren't you able to judge small cases? ³Don't you know that we will judge angels? Then we should be able to judge the things of this life even more!

⁴So if you want to press charges in matters like that, appoint as judges members of the church who aren't very important! ⁵I say this to shame you. Is it possible that no one among you is wise enough to judge matters between believers? ⁶Instead, one believer goes to court against another. And this happens in front of unbelievers!

⁷The very fact that you take another believer to court means you have lost the battle already. Why not be treated wrongly? Why not be cheated? ⁸Instead, you yourselves cheat and do wrong. And you do it to your brothers and sisters.

⁹Don't you know that evil people will not receive God's kingdom? Don't be fooled. Those who commit sexual sins will not receive the kingdom. Neither will those who worship statues of gods or commit adultery. Neither will men who are prostitutes or homosexuals. ¹⁰Neither will thieves or those who always want more and more. Neither will those who are often drunk or tell lies or cheat. People who live like that will not receive God's kingdom.

¹¹Some of you used to do those things. But your sins were washed away. You were made holy. You were made right with God. All of that was done in the name of the Lord Jesus Christ and by the Spirit of our God.

Sexual Sins

¹²Some of you say, "Everything is permitted for me." But not everything is good for me. Again some of you say, "Everything is

permitted for me." But I will not be controlled by anything. [13]Some of you say, "Food is for the stomach. And the stomach is for food." But God will destroy both of them.

The body is not meant for sexual sins. The body is meant for the Lord. And the Lord is meant for the body. [14]By his power God raised the Lord from the dead. He will also raise us up.

[15]Don't you know that your bodies belong to the body of Christ? Should I take what belongs to Christ and join it to a prostitute? Never! [16]Don't you know that when you join yourself to a prostitute, you become one with her in body? Scripture says, "The two will become one." *(Genesis 2:24)* [17]But anyone who is joined to the Lord becomes one with him in spirit.

[18]Keep far away from sexual sins. All the other sins people commit are outside their bodies. But sexual sins are sins against one's own body.

[19]Don't you know that your bodies are temples of the Holy Spirit? The Spirit is in you. You have received him from God. You do not belong to yourselves. [20]Christ has paid the price for you. So use your bodies in a way that honors God.

Marriage

7 Now I want to deal with the things you wrote me about. Some of you say, "It is good for a man not to have sex with a woman." [2]But since there is so much sexual sin, each man should have his own wife. And each woman should have her own husband. [3]A husband should satisfy his wife's sexual needs. And a wife should satisfy her husband's sexual needs.

[4]The wife's body does not belong only to her. It also belongs to her husband. In the same way, the husband's body does not belong only to him. It also belongs to his wife. [5]You shouldn't stop giving yourselves to each other except when you both agree to do so. And that should be only to give yourselves time to pray

GREAT VERSE — TO — REMEMBER

6:19 Don't you know that your bodies are temples of the Holy Spirit? The Spirit is in you. You have received him from God. You do not belong to yourselves.

for a while. Then you should come together again. In that way, Satan will not tempt you when you can't control yourselves.

[6]I say those things to you as my advice, not as a command. [7]I wish all of you were like me. But you each have your own gift from God. One has this gift. Another has that.

[8]I speak to those who are not married. I also speak to widows. It is good for you to stay single like me. [9]But if you can't control yourselves, you should get married. It is better to get married than to burn with sexual longing.

[10]I give a command to those who are married. It is a direct command from the Lord, not from me. A wife must not leave her husband. [11]But if she does, she must not get married again. Or she can go back to her husband. And a husband must not divorce his wife.

[12]I also have something to say to everyone else. It is from me, not a direct command from the Lord. Suppose a brother has a wife who is not a believer. If she is willing to live with him, he must not divorce her. [13]And suppose a woman has a husband who is not a believer. If he is willing to live with her, she must not divorce him. [14]The unbelieving husband has been made holy through his wife. The unbelieving wife has been made holy through her believing husband. If that were not the case, your children would not be pure and clean. But as it is, they are holy.

[15]If the unbelievers leave, let them go. In that case, a believing man or woman does not have to stay married. God wants us to live in peace. [16]Wife, how do you know if you can save your husband? Husband, how do you know if you can save your wife?

[17]But each of you should remain in the place in life that the Lord has given you. Stay as you were when God chose you. That's the rule all the churches must follow.

[18]Was a man already circumcised when God chose him? Then he should not become uncircumcised. Was he uncircumcised when God chose him? Then he should not be circumcised. [19]Being circumcised means nothing. Being uncircumcised means nothing. Doing what God commands is what counts.

[20]Each of you should stay as you were when God chose you.

[21]Were you a slave when God chose you? Don't let it trouble you. But if you can get your master to set you free, do it. [22]Those who were slaves when the Lord chose them are now the Lord's free people. Those who were free when God chose them are now slaves of Christ. [23]Christ has paid the price for you. Don't become slaves of human beings.

²⁴Brothers and sisters, you are accountable to God. So all of you should stay as you were when God chose you.

²⁵Now I want to say something about virgins. I have no direct command from the Lord. But I give my opinion. Because of the Lord's mercy, I give it as one who can be trusted.

²⁶Times are hard for you right now. So I think it's good for you to stay as you are. ²⁷Are you married? Then don't get a divorce. Are you single? Then don't look for a wife. ²⁸But if you get married, you have not sinned. And if a virgin gets married, she has not sinned. But those who get married will have many troubles in this life. I want to save you from that.

²⁹Brothers and sisters, what I mean is that the time is short. From now on, those who have a husband or wife should live as if they did not. ³⁰Those who are sad should live as if they were not. Those who are happy should live as if they were not. Those who buy something should live as if it were not theirs to keep. ³¹Those who use the things of the world should not become all wrapped up in them. The world as it now exists is passing away.

³²I don't want you to have anything to worry about. A single man is concerned about the Lord's matters. He wants to know how he can please the Lord. ³³But a married man is concerned about the matters of this world. He wants to know how he can please his wife. ³⁴His concerns pull him in two directions.

A single woman or a virgin is concerned about the Lord's matters. She wants to serve the Lord with both body and spirit. But a married woman is concerned about the matters of this world. She wants to know how she can please her husband.

³⁵I'm saying those things for your own good. I'm not trying to hold you back. I want you to be free to live in a way that is right. I want you to give yourselves completely to the Lord.

³⁶Suppose a man thinks he is not acting properly toward the virgin he has promised to marry. Suppose she is getting old, and he feels that he should marry her. He should do as he wants. He is not sinning. They should get married.

³⁷But suppose the man has decided not to marry the virgin. And suppose he has no compelling need to get married and can control himself. If he has made up his mind not to get married, he also does the right thing.

³⁸So then, the man who marries the virgin does the right thing. But the man who doesn't marry her does an even better thing.

³⁹A woman has to stay married to her husband as long as he lives. If he dies, she is free to marry anyone she wants to. But the

one she marries must belong to the Lord. [40]In my opinion, she is happier if she stays single. And I also think that I am led by the Spirit of God in saying that.

Food Offered to Statues of Gods

8 Now I want to deal with food offered to statues of gods. We know that we all have knowledge. Knowledge makes people proud. But love builds them up. [2]Those who think they know something still don't know as they should. [3]But those who love God are known by God.

[4]So then, here is what I say about eating food that is offered to statues of gods. We know that a god made by human hands is really nothing at all in the world. We know there is only one God. [5]There may be so-called gods either in heaven or on earth. In fact, there are many "gods" and many "lords." [6]But for us there is only one God. He is the Father. All things came from him, and we live for him. And there is only one Lord. He is Jesus Christ. All things came because of him, and we live because of him.

[7]But not everyone knows that. Some people still think that statues of gods are real gods. When they eat food that was offered to statues of gods, they think of it as food that was offered to real gods. And because they have a weak sense of what is right and wrong, they feel guilty. [8]But food doesn't bring us close to God. We are no worse if we don't eat. We are no better if we do eat.

[9]But be careful how you use your freedom. Be sure it doesn't trip up someone who is weaker than you.

[10]Suppose you who have that knowledge are eating in a temple of one of those gods. And suppose someone who has a weak sense of what is right and wrong sees you. Won't that person become bold and eat what has been offered to statues of gods? [11]If so, then your knowledge destroys that weak brother or sister for whom Christ died.

[12]When you sin against other believers in that way, you harm their weak sense of what is right and wrong. By doing that you sin against Christ.

GREAT VERSE — TO — REMEMBER

8:6 For us there is only one God. He is the Father. All things came from him, and we live for him.

¹³So what should I do if what I eat causes my brothers and sisters to fall into sin? I will never eat meat again. In that way, I will not cause them to fall.

The Rights of an Apostle

9 Am I not free? Am I not an apostle? Haven't I seen Jesus our Lord? Aren't you the result of my work for the Lord? ²Even though others may not think of me as an apostle, I am certainly one to you! You are the proof that I am the Lord's apostle. ³That is what I say to stand up for myself when people judge me.

⁴Don't we have the right to eat and drink? ⁵Don't we have the right to take a believing wife with us when we travel? The other apostles do. The Lord's brothers do. Peter does. ⁶Or are Barnabas and I the only ones who have to work for a living?

⁷Who serves as a soldier but doesn't get paid? Who plants a vineyard but doesn't eat any of its grapes? Who takes care of a flock but doesn't drink any of the milk? ⁸Do I say that from only a human point of view? The Law says the same thing.

⁹Here is what is written in the Law of Moses. "Do not stop an ox from eating while it helps separate the grain from the straw." *(Deuteronomy 25:4)* Is it oxen that God is concerned about? ¹⁰Doesn't he say that for us? Yes, it was written for us. When farmers plow and when they separate the grain, they should do it because they hope to share in the crop.

¹¹We have planted spiritual seed among you. Is it too much to ask that we receive from you some of the things we need? ¹²Others have the right to receive help from you. Don't we have even more right to do so?

But we didn't use that right. No, we have put up with everything. We didn't want to keep the good news of Christ from spreading.

¹³Don't you know that those who work in the temple get their food from the temple? Don't you know that those who serve at the altar eat from what is offered on the altar? ¹⁴In the same way, those who preach the good news should receive their living from their work. That is what the Lord has commanded.

¹⁵But I haven't used any of those rights. And I'm not writing because I hope you will do things like that for me. I would rather die than have anyone take away my pride in my work. ¹⁶But when I preach the good news, I can't brag. I have to preach it. How terrible it will be for me if I do not preach the good news! ¹⁷If I preach because I want to, I get a reward. If I preach because

I have to, I'm only doing my duty. ¹⁸Then what reward do I get? Here is what it is. I am able to preach the good news free of charge. And I can do it without making use of my rights when I preach it.

¹⁹I am free. I don't belong to anyone. But I make myself a slave to everyone. I do it to win as many as I can to Christ.

²⁰To the Jews I became like a Jew. That was to win the Jews. To those under the law I became like one who was under the law, even though I myself am not under the law. That was to win those under the law. ²¹To those who don't have the law I became like one who doesn't have the law. I am not free from God's law. I am under Christ's law. Now I can win those who don't have the law. ²²To those who are weak I became weak. That was to win the weak.

I have become all things to all people so that in all possible ways I might save some. ²³I do all of that because of the good news. And I want to share in its blessings.

²⁴In a race all the runners run. But only one gets the prize. You know that, don't you? So run in a way that will get you the prize. ²⁵All who take part in the games train hard. They do it to get a crown that will not last. But we do it to get a crown that will last forever.

²⁶So I do not run like someone who doesn't run toward the finish line. I do not fight like a boxer who hits nothing but air. ²⁷No, I train my body and bring it under control. Then after I have preached to others, I myself will not break the rules and fail to win the prize.

Warnings From Israel's History

10 Brothers and sisters, here is what I want you to know about our people who lived long ago. They were all led by the cloud. They all walked through the Red Sea. ²They were all baptized into Moses in the cloud and in the sea. ³They all ate the same supernatural food. ⁴They all drank the same supernatural water. They drank from the supernatural rock that went with them. That rock was Christ.

⁵But God was not pleased with most of them. Their bodies were scattered all over the desert.

⁶Now those things happened as examples for us. They are supposed to keep us from longing for evil things, as the people of Israel did.

⁷So don't worship statues of gods, as some of them did. It is

written: "The people sat down to eat and drink. Then they got up to dance wildly in front of their god." *(Exodus 32:6)* ⁸We should not commit sexual sins, as some of them did. In one day 23,000 of them died. ⁹We should not put the Lord to the test, as some of them did. They were killed by snakes. ¹⁰Don't tell your leaders how unhappy you are with them. That's what some of the people of Israel did. And they were killed by the destroying angel.

¹¹Those things happened to them as examples for us. They were written down to warn us who are living at the time when God's work is being completed. ¹²So be careful. When you think you are standing firm, you might fall.

¹³You are tempted in the same way all other human beings are. God is faithful. He will not let you be tempted any more than you can take. But when you are tempted, God will give you a way out so that you can stand up under it.

Sharing in the Body and Blood of Christ

¹⁴My dear friends, run away from statues of gods. Don't worship them. ¹⁵I'm talking to people who are reasonable. Judge for yourselves what I say.

¹⁶When we give thanks for the cup at the Lord's Supper, aren't we sharing in the blood of Christ? When we break the bread, aren't we sharing in the body of Christ? ¹⁷Just as there is one loaf, so we who are many are one body. We all eat from the one loaf.

¹⁸Think about the people of Israel. Don't those who eat the offerings share in the altar? ¹⁹Do I mean that what is offered to a statue of a god is anything? Do I mean that a statue of a god is anything? ²⁰No! But what is offered by those who worship statues of gods is really offered to demons. It is not offered to God. I don't want you to be sharing with demons.

²¹You can't drink the cup of the Lord and the cup of demons too. You can't have a part in both the Lord's table and the table

GREAT VERSE —TO— REMEMBER

10:13 God is faithful. He will not let you be tempted any more than you can take. But when you are tempted, God will give you a way out.

of demons. ²²Are we trying to make the Lord jealous? Are we stronger than he is?

The Believer's Freedom

²³You say, "Everything is permitted." But not everything is good for us. Again you say, "Everything is permitted." But not everything builds us up. ²⁴We should not look out for our own interests. Instead, we should look out for the interests of others.

²⁵Eat anything that is sold in the meat market. Don't ask if it's right or wrong. ²⁶Scripture says, "The earth belongs to the Lord. And so does everything in it." *(Psalm 24:1)*

²⁷Suppose an unbeliever invites you to a meal and you want to go. Then eat anything that is put in front of you. Don't ask if it's right or wrong.

²⁸But suppose someone says to you, "This food has been offered to a statue of a god." Then don't eat it. Keep in mind the good of the one who told you. And don't eat because of a sense of what is right and wrong. ²⁹I'm talking about the other person's sense of what is right and wrong, not yours.

Why should my freedom be judged by what someone else thinks? ³⁰Suppose I give thanks when I eat. Then why should I be blamed for eating food I thank God for?

³¹So eat and drink and do everything else for the glory of God. ³²Don't do anything that causes another person to trip and fall. It doesn't matter if that person is a Jew or a Greek or a member of God's church.

³³Follow my example. I try to please everyone in every way. I'm not looking out for what is good for me. I'm looking out for the interests of others. I do it so that they might be saved.

11 Follow my example, just as I follow the example of Christ.

Proper Worship

²I praise you for being faithful in remembering me. I also praise

---

10:31 So eat and drink and do everything else for the glory of God.

you for staying true to all my teachings, just as I gave them to you.

³Now I want you to know that the head of every man is Christ. The head of the woman is the man. And the head of Christ is God. ⁴Every man who prays or prophesies with his head covered brings shame on his head. ⁵And every woman who prays or prophesies with her head uncovered brings shame on her head. It is just as if her head were shaved.

⁶What if a woman does not cover her head? She should have her hair cut off. But it is shameful for her to cut her hair or shave it off. So she should cover her head.

⁷A man should not cover his head. He is the likeness and glory of God. But the woman is the glory of the man. ⁸The man did not come from the woman. The woman came from the man.

⁹Also, the man was not created for the woman. The woman was created for the man. ¹⁰That's why a woman should have her head covered. It shows that she is under authority. She should also cover her head because of the angels.

¹¹But here is how things are for those who belong to the Lord. The woman is not independent of the man. And the man is not independent of the woman. ¹²The woman came from the man, and the man is born from the woman. But everything comes from God.

¹³You be the judge. Is it proper for a woman to pray to God without covering her head? ¹⁴Suppose a man has long hair. Doesn't the very nature of things teach you that it is shameful? ¹⁵And suppose a woman has long hair. Doesn't the very nature of things teach you that it is her glory? Long hair is given to her as a covering.

¹⁶If anyone wants to argue about that, we don't have any other practice. And God's churches don't either.

The Lord's Supper

¹⁷In the following matters, I don't praise you. Your meetings do more harm than good.

¹⁸First, here is what people are telling me. When you come together as a church, you take sides. And in some ways I believe it. ¹⁹No doubt you need to take sides in order to show which of you God agrees with!

²⁰When you come together, it is not the Lord's Supper you eat. ²¹As you eat, each of you goes ahead without waiting for anyone else. One remains hungry and another gets drunk. ²²Don't you

have homes to eat and drink in? Or do you think so little of God's church that you shame those in it who have nothing? What should I say to you? Should I praise you for that? Certainly not!

²³I passed on to you what I received from the Lord. On the night the Lord Jesus was handed over to his enemies, he took bread. ²⁴When he had given thanks, he broke it. He said, "This is my body. It is given for you. Every time you eat it, do it in memory of me." ²⁵In the same way, after supper he took the cup. He said, "This cup is the new covenant in my blood. Every time you drink it, do it in memory of me."

²⁶When you eat the bread and drink the cup, you are announcing the Lord's death until he comes again.

²⁷So do not eat the bread or drink the cup of the Lord in a way that isn't worthy of him. If you do, you will be guilty of sinning against the body and blood of the Lord.

²⁸We should take a careful look at ourselves before we eat the bread and drink from the cup. ²⁹Those who eat and drink must recognize the body of the Lord. If they don't, God will judge them for it. ³⁰That is why many of you are weak and sick. That is why a number of you have died.

³¹We should judge ourselves. Then we would not be found guilty. ³²When the Lord judges us, he corrects us. Then we will not be judged along with the rest of the world.

³³My brothers and sisters, when you come together to eat, wait for each other. ³⁴Those who are hungry should eat at home. Then when you come together, you will not be judged.

When I come, I will give you more directions.

Gifts of the Holy Spirit

12 Brothers and sisters, I want you to know about the gifts of the Holy Spirit.

²You know that at one time you were unbelievers. You were somehow drawn away to worship statues of gods that couldn't even speak. ³So I tell you that no one who is speaking with the help of God's Spirit says, "May Jesus be cursed." And without the help of the Holy Spirit no one can say, "Jesus is Lord."

⁴There are different kinds of gifts. But they are all given by the same Spirit. ⁵There are different ways to serve. But they all come from the same Lord. ⁶There are different ways to work. But the same God makes it possible for all of us to have all those different things.

⁷The Holy Spirit is given to each of us in a special way. That is

for the good of all. ⁸To some people the Spirit gives the message of wisdom. To others the same Spirit gives the message of knowledge. ⁹To others the same Spirit gives faith. To others that one Spirit gives gifts of healing. ¹⁰To others he gives the power to do miracles. To others he gives the ability to prophesy. To others he gives the ability to tell the spirits apart. To others he gives the ability to speak in different kinds of languages they had not known before. And to still others he gives the ability to explain what was said in those languages.

¹¹All of the gifts are produced by one and the same Spirit. He gives them to each person, just as he decides.

One Body but Many Parts

¹²There is one body. But it has many parts. Even though it has many parts, they make up one body. It is the same with Christ. ¹³We were all baptized by one Holy Spirit into one body. It didn't matter whether we were Jews or Greeks, slaves or free people. We were all given the same Spirit to drink.

¹⁴The body is not made up of just one part. It has many parts. ¹⁵Suppose the foot says, "I am not a hand. So I don't belong to the body." It is still part of the body. ¹⁶And suppose the ear says, "I am not an eye. So I don't belong to the body." It is still part of the body.

¹⁷If the whole body were an eye, how could it hear? If the whole body were an ear, how could it smell? ¹⁸God has placed each part in the body just as he wanted it to be. ¹⁹If all the parts were the same, how could there be a body? ²⁰As it is, there are many parts. But there is only one body.

²¹The eye can't say to the hand, "I don't need you!" The head can't say to the feet, "I don't need you!" ²²In fact, it is just the opposite. The parts of the body that seem to be weaker are the ones we can't do without. ²³The parts that we think are less

---

GREAT VERSE —TO— REMEMBER

12:4-5 There are different kinds of gifts. But they are all given by the same Spirit. There are different ways to serve. But they all come from the same Lord.

important we treat with special honor. The private parts aren't shown. But they are treated with special care. ²⁴The parts that can be shown don't need special care.

But God has joined together all the parts of the body. And he has given more honor to the parts that didn't have any. ²⁵In that way, the parts of the body will not take sides. All of them will take care of each other. ²⁶If one part suffers, every part suffers with it. If one part is honored, every part shares in its joy.

²⁷You are the body of Christ. Each one of you is a part of it. ²⁸First, God has appointed apostles in the church. Second, he has appointed prophets. Third, he has appointed teachers. Then he has appointed people who do miracles and those who have gifts of healing. He also appointed those able to help others, those able to direct things, and those who can speak in different kinds of languages they had not known before.

²⁹Is everyone an apostle? Is everyone a prophet? Is everyone a teacher? Do all work miracles? ³⁰Do all have gifts of healing? Do all speak in languages they had not known before? Do all explain what is said in those languages? ³¹But above all, you should want the more important gifts.

Love

And now I will show you the best way of all.

13 Suppose I speak in the languages of human beings and of angels. If I don't have love, I am only a loud gong or a noisy cymbal. ²Suppose I have the gift of prophecy. Suppose I can understand all the secret things of God and know everything about him. And suppose I have enough faith to move mountains. If I don't have love, I am nothing at all. ³Suppose I give everything I have to poor people. And suppose I give my body to be burned. If I don't have love, I get nothing at all.

⁴Love is patient. Love is kind. It does not want what belongs to others. It does not brag. It is not proud. ⁵It is not rude. It does

GREAT VERSE — TO — REMEMBER

13:4, 7-8 Love is patient. Love is kind ... It always protects. It always trusts. It always hopes. It never gives up. Love never fails.

not look out for its own interests. It does not easily become angry. It does not keep track of other people's wrongs.

⁶Love is not happy with evil. But it is full of joy when the truth is spoken. ⁷It always protects. It always trusts. It always hopes. It never gives up.

⁸Love never fails. But prophecy will pass away. Speaking in languages that had not been known before will end. And knowledge will pass away.

⁹What we know now is not complete. What we prophesy now is not perfect. ¹⁰But when what is perfect comes, the things that are not perfect will pass away.

¹¹When I was a child, I talked like a child. I thought like a child. I had the understanding of a child. When I became an adult, I put childish ways behind me.

¹²Now we see only a dim likeness of things. It is as if we were seeing them in a mirror. But someday we will see clearly. We will see face to face. What I know now is not complete. But someday I will know completely, just as God knows me completely.

¹³And now these three remain: faith, hope and love. But the greatest of these is love.

The Gifts the Holy Spirit Gives

14 Follow the way of love. You should also want the gifts the Holy Spirit gives. Most of all, you should want the gift of prophecy.

²Those who speak in languages they had not known before do not speak to people. They speak only to God. In fact, no one understands them. What they say with their spirits remains a mystery. ³But those who prophesy speak to people. They say things to make others stronger, to give them hope and to comfort them. ⁴Those who speak in other languages build themselves up. But those who prophesy build up the church.

⁵I would like all of you to speak in other languages. But I would rather have you prophesy. Those who prophesy are more helpful than those who speak in other languages. But that is not the case

GREAT VERSE —TO— REMEMBER

13:13 And now these three remain: faith, hope and love. But the greatest of these is love.

if those who speak in other languages explain what they have said. Then the whole church can be built up.

⁶Brothers and sisters, suppose I were to come to you and speak in other languages. What good would I be to you? None! I would need to come with new truth or knowledge, or a prophecy or a teaching.

⁷Here are some examples. Certain objects make sounds. Take a flute or a harp. No one will know what the tune is unless different notes are played. ⁸Also, if the trumpet call isn't clear, who will get ready for battle?

⁹It's the same with you. You must speak words that people understand. If you don't, no one will know what you are saying. You will just be speaking into the air.

¹⁰It is true that there are all kinds of languages in the world. And they all have meaning. ¹¹But if I don't understand what someone is saying, I am a stranger to that person. And that person is a stranger to me.

¹²It's the same with you. You want to have gifts of the Spirit. So try to do your best in using gifts that build up the church.

¹³For that reason, those who speak in languages they had not known before should pray that they can explain what they say. ¹⁴If I pray in another language, my spirit prays. But my mind does not pray. ¹⁵So what should I do? I will pray with my spirit. But I will also pray with my mind. I will sing with my spirit. But I will also sing with my mind.

¹⁶Suppose you are praising God with your spirit. And suppose there are visitors among you who don't understand what's going on. How can they say "Amen" when you give thanks? They don't know what you are saying. ¹⁷You might be giving thanks well enough. But the others are not being built up.

¹⁸I thank God that I speak in other languages more than all of you do. ¹⁹But in the church I would rather speak five words that people can understand than 10,000 words in another language. Then I would be teaching others.

²⁰Brothers and sisters, stop thinking like children. Be like babies as far as evil is concerned. But be grown up in your thinking. ²¹In the Law it is written:

> "Through people who speak unfamiliar languages
>   and through the lips of strangers
>   I will speak to these people.
>   But even then they will not listen to me." *(Isaiah 28:11,12)*

That is what the Lord says.

²²So speaking in other languages is a sign for those who don't believe. It is not a sign for those who do believe. But prophecy is for believers. It is not for those who don't believe.

²³Suppose the whole church comes together and everyone speaks in other languages. And suppose visitors or unbelievers come in. Won't they say you are out of your minds? ²⁴But suppose unbelievers or visitors come in while everyone is prophesying. Then they will be shown by all who speak that they are sinners. They will be judged by all. ²⁵The secrets of their hearts will be brought out into the open. They will fall down and worship God. They will exclaim, "God is really here among you!"

Proper Worship

²⁶Brothers and sisters, what should we say then? When you come together, every one of you brings something. You bring a hymn or a teaching or a word from God. You bring a message in another language or explain what was said. All of those things must be done to make the church strong.

²⁷No more than two or three people should speak in another language. And they should speak one at a time. Then someone must explain what was said. ²⁸If there is no one to explain, the speakers should keep quiet in the church. They can speak to themselves and to God.

²⁹Only two or three prophets are supposed to speak. Others should decide if what is being said is true. ³⁰What if a message from God comes to someone else who is sitting there? Then the one who is speaking should stop.

³¹Those who prophesy can all take turns. In that way, everyone can be taught and be given hope. ³²Those who prophesy should control their speaking. ³³God is not a God of disorder. He is a God of peace.

As in all the churches of God's people, ³⁴women should remain silent in the meetings. They are not allowed to speak. They must follow the lead of those who are in authority, as the Law says. ³⁵If they have a question about something, they should ask their own husbands at home. It is shameful for women to speak in church meetings.

³⁶Did the word of God begin with you? Or are you the only people it has reached? ³⁷Suppose some think they are prophets or have gifts of the Holy Spirit. They should agree that what I am writing to you is the Lord's command. ³⁸Anyone who does not recognize that will not be recognized.

³⁹Brothers and sisters, you should want to prophesy. And don't stop people from speaking in languages they had not known before. ⁴⁰But everything should be done in a proper and orderly way.

Paul Explains the Good News

15 Brothers and sisters, I want to remind you of the good news I preached to you. You received it and have put your faith in it. ²Because you believed the good news, you are saved. But you must hold firmly to the message I preached to you. If you don't, you have believed it for nothing.

³What I received I passed on to you. And it is the most important of all. Here is what it is. Christ died for our sins, just as Scripture said he would. ⁴He was buried. He was raised from the dead on the third day, just as Scripture said he would be. ⁵He appeared to Peter.

Then he appeared to the Twelve. ⁶After that, he appeared to more than 500 believers at the same time. Most of them are still living. But some have died. ⁷He appeared to James. Then he appeared to all the apostles. ⁸Last of all, he also appeared to me. I was like someone who wasn't born at the right time or in a normal way.

⁹I am the least important of the apostles. I'm not even fit to be called an apostle. I tried to destroy God's church. ¹⁰But because of God's grace I am what I am. And his grace was not wasted on me. No, I have worked harder than all the other apostles. But I didn't do the work. God's grace was with me.

¹¹So whether it was I or the other apostles who preached to you, that is what we preach. And that is what you believed.

Believers Will Rise From the Dead

¹²We have preached that Christ has been raised from the dead. So how can some of you say that no one rises from the dead? ¹³If no one rises from the dead, then not even Christ has been raised. ¹⁴And if Christ has not been raised, what we preach doesn't mean anything. Your faith doesn't mean anything either. ¹⁵More than that, we would be lying about God. We have given witness that God raised Christ from the dead. But he did not raise him if the dead are not raised.

¹⁶If the dead are not raised, then Christ has not been raised either. ¹⁷And if Christ has not been raised, your faith doesn't

mean anything. Your sins have not been forgiven. ¹⁸Those who have died believing in Christ are also lost.

¹⁹Do we have hope in Christ only for this life? Then people should pity us more than anyone else.

²⁰But Christ really has been raised from the dead. He is the first of all those who will rise.

²¹Death came because of what a man did. Rising from the dead also comes because of what a man did. ²²Because of Adam, all people die. So because of Christ, all will be made alive.

²³But here is the order of events. Christ is the first of those who rise from the dead. When he comes back, those who belong to him will be raised. ²⁴Then the end will come. Christ will destroy all rule, authority and power. He will hand over the kingdom to God the Father.

²⁵Christ must rule until he has put all his enemies under his control. ²⁶The last enemy that will be destroyed is death. ²⁷Scripture says that God "has put everything under his control." *(Psalm 8:6)* It says that "everything" has been put under him. But it is clear that this does not include God himself, who puts everything under Christ. ²⁸When he has done that, the Son also will be under God's rule. God puts everything under the Son. In that way, God will be all in all.

²⁹Suppose no one rises from the dead. Then what will people do who are baptized for the dead? Suppose the dead are not raised at all. Then why are people baptized for them? ³⁰And why would we put ourselves in danger every hour?

³¹I die every day. I really mean that, brothers and sisters. Here is something you can be sure of. I take pride in what Christ Jesus our Lord has done for you through my work. ³²Did I fight wild animals in Ephesus for only human reasons? Then what have I gotten for it? If the dead are not raised,

> "Let us eat and drink,
>   because tomorrow we will die." *(Isaiah 22:13)*

³³Don't let anyone fool you. "Bad companions make a good

GREAT VERSE —TO— REMEMBER **15:22** Because of Adam, all people die. So because of Christ, all will be made alive.

person bad." ³⁴You should come back to your senses and stop sinning. Some of you don't know anything about God. I say this to make you ashamed.

The Body That Rises From the Dead

³⁵But someone might ask, "How are the dead raised? What kind of body will they have?" ³⁶How foolish! What you plant doesn't come to life unless it dies. ³⁷When you plant something, it isn't a completely grown plant that you put in the ground. You only plant a seed. Maybe it's wheat or something else. ³⁸But God gives the seed a body just as he has planned. And to each kind of seed he gives its own body.

³⁹All earthly creatures are not the same. People have one kind of body. Animals have another. Birds have another kind. Fish have still another.

⁴⁰There are also heavenly bodies as well as earthly bodies. Heavenly bodies have one kind of glory. Earthly bodies have another. ⁴¹The sun has one kind of glory. The moon has another kind. The stars have still another. And one star's glory is different from that of another star.

⁴²It will be like that with bodies that are raised from the dead. The body that is planted does not last forever. The body that is raised from the dead lasts forever. ⁴³It is planted without honor. But it is raised in glory. It is planted in weakness. But it is raised in power. ⁴⁴It is planted as an earthly body. But it is raised as a spiritual body.

Just as there is an earthly body, there is also a spiritual body. ⁴⁵It is written: "The first Adam became a living person." *(Genesis 2:7)* The last Adam became a spirit that gives life. ⁴⁶What is spiritual did not come first. What is earthly came first. What is spiritual came after that. ⁴⁷The first man came from the dust of the earth. The second man came from heaven.

⁴⁸Those who belong to the earth are like the one who came from the earth. And those who are spiritual are like the one who came from heaven. ⁴⁹We are like the earthly man. And we will be like the man from heaven.

⁵⁰Brothers and sisters, here is what I'm telling you. Bodies made of flesh and blood can't share in the kingdom of God. And what dies can't share in what never dies.

⁵¹Listen! I am telling you a mystery. We will not all die. But we will all be changed. ⁵²That will happen in a flash, as quickly as you can wink an eye. It will happen when the last trumpet

sounds. The trumpet will sound, and the dead will be raised to live forever. And we will be changed.

[53]Our natural bodies don't last forever. They must be dressed with what does last forever. What dies must be dressed with what does not die. [54]In fact, that is going to happen. What does not last will be dressed with what lasts forever. What dies will be dressed with what does not die. Then what is written will come true. It says, "Death has been swallowed up. It has lost the battle." *(Isaiah 25:8)*

[55] "Death, where is the battle you thought you were
          winning?
      Death, where is your sting?"   *(Hosea 13:14)*

[56]The sting of death is sin. And the power of sin is the law. [57]But let us give thanks to God! He wins the battle for us because of what our Lord Jesus Christ has done.

[58]My dear brothers and sisters, stand firm. Don't let anything move you. Always give yourselves completely to the work of the Lord. Because you belong to the Lord, you know that your work is not worthless.

The Offering for God's People

16 Now I want to deal with the offering of money for God's people.

Do what I told the churches in Galatia to do. [2]On the first day of every week, each of you should put some money away. The amount should be in keeping with how much money you make. Save the money so that you won't have to take up an offering when I come. [3]When I arrive, I will send some people with your gift to Jerusalem. They will be people you consider to be good. And I will give them letters that explain who they are. [4]If it seems good for me to go also, they will go with me.

What Paul Asks for Himself

[5]After I go through Macedonia, I will come to you. I will only be passing through Macedonia. [6]But I might stay with you for a while. I might even spend the winter. Then you can help me on my journey everywhere I go.

[7]I don't want to see you now while I am just passing through. I hope to spend some time with you, if the Lord allows it. [8]But I will stay at Ephesus until the day of Pentecost. [9]A door has

opened wide for me to do some good work here. There are many people who oppose me.

¹⁰Timothy might come to you. Make sure he has nothing to worry about while he is with you. He is doing the work of the Lord, just as I am. ¹¹No one should refuse to accept him. Send him safely on his way so he can return to me. I'm expecting him to come back along with the others.

¹²I want to say something about our brother Apollos. I tried my best to get him to go to you with the others. But he didn't want to go right now. He will go when he can.

¹³Be on your guard. Stand firm in the faith. Be brave. Be strong. ¹⁴Be loving in everything you do.

¹⁵You know that the first believers in Achaia were from the family of Stephanas. They have spent all their time serving God's people. Brothers and sisters, I am asking you ¹⁶to follow the lead of people like them. Follow everyone who joins in the task and works hard at it.

¹⁷I was glad when Stephanas, Fortunatus and Achaicus arrived. They have supplied me with what you couldn't give me. ¹⁸They renewed my spirit, and yours also. People like that are worthy of honor.

Final Greetings

¹⁹The churches in Asia Minor send you greetings. Aquila and Priscilla greet you warmly because of the Lord's love. So does the church that meets in their house. ²⁰All the brothers and sisters here send you greetings. Greet one another with a holy kiss.

²¹I, Paul, am writing this greeting with my own hand.

²²If anyone does not love the Lord, let a curse be on that person! Come, Lord!

²³May the grace of the Lord Jesus be with you.

²⁴I give my love to all of you who belong to Christ Jesus. Amen.

GREAT VERSE —TO— REMEMBER

16:13-14 Be on your guard. Stand firm in the faith. Be brave. Be strong. Be loving in everything you do.

2 Corinthians

Why Was This Book Written? Paul's first letter to his friends in Corinth taught them what was right and wrong. Some people were angry about that letter. They would not change the way they lived. Other people felt sorry. They wrote to Paul and said they were sorry. They would change.

What Is This Book About? Paul wrote this letter in two parts. He wrote the first part for his friends who changed and lived the way God wanted. He wrote the second part to angry people in the church. They said untrue things about Paul and God. Paul wanted them to know the truth.

What Is in This Book?

1 I, Paul, am writing this letter. I am an apostle of Christ Jesus just as God planned. Timothy our brother joins me in writing.

We are sending this letter to you, the members of God's church in Corinth. It is also for all of God's people everywhere in Achaia.

²May God our Father and the Lord Jesus Christ give you grace and peace.

God Gives Comfort

³Give praise to the God and Father of our Lord Jesus Christ! He is the Father who gives tender love. All comfort comes from him. ⁴He comforts us in all our troubles. Now we can comfort others when they are in trouble. We ourselves have received comfort from God. ⁵We share the sufferings of Christ. We also share his comfort.

⁶If we are having trouble, it is so that you will be comforted and renewed. If we are comforted, it is so that you will be comforted. Then you will be able to put up with the same suffering we have gone through. ⁷Our hope for you remains firm. We know that you suffer just as we do. In the same way, God comforts you just as he comforts us.

⁸Brothers and sisters, we want you to know about the hard times we suffered in Asia Minor. We were having a lot of trouble. It was far more than we could stand. We even thought we were going to die. ⁹In fact, in our hearts we felt as if we were under the sentence of death.

But that happened so that we would not depend on ourselves but on God. He raises the dead to life. ¹⁰God has saved us from deadly dangers. And he will continue to do it. We have put our hope in him. He will continue to save us.

¹¹You must help us by praying for us. Then many people will give thanks because of what will happen to us. They will thank God for his kindness to us in answer to the prayers of many.

GREAT VERSE —TO— REMEMBER

1:3 Give praise to the God and Father of our Lord Jesus Christ! He is the Father who gives tender love. All comfort comes from him.

Paul Changes His Plans

[12]Here is what we take pride in. Our sense of what is right and wrong gives witness that we have acted in God's holy and honest ways. That is how we live in the world. We live that way most of all when we are dealing with you. Our way of living is not wise in the eyes of the world. But it is in keeping with God's grace.

[13]We are writing only what you can read and understand. And here is what I hope. [14]Up to this point you have understood some of the things we have said. But now I hope that someday you will be able to take pride in us, just as we will take pride in you on the day the Lord Jesus returns. When you are able to do that, you will understand us completely.

[15]I was sure of those things. So I planned to visit you first. Here is how I thought you would be helped twice. [16]I planned to visit you on my way to Macedonia. I would have come back to you from there. Then you would have sent me on my way to Judea.

[17]When I planned all of that, did I do it without much thought? No. I don't make my plans the way the world makes theirs. In the same breath the world says, "Yes! Yes!" and "No! No!"

[18]But just as sure as God is faithful, our message to you is not "Yes" and "No." [19]Silas, Timothy and I preached to you about the Son of God, Jesus Christ. Our message did not say "Yes" and "No" at the same time. The message of Christ has always been "Yes."

[20]God has made a great many promises. They are all "Yes" because of what Christ has done. So through Christ we say "Amen." We want God to receive glory.

[21]He makes both us and you stand firm because we belong to Christ. He anointed us. [22]He put his Spirit in our hearts and marked us as his own. We can now be sure that he will give us everything he promised us.

[23]I call God as my witness. I wanted to spare you. So I didn't return to Corinth. [24]Your faith is not under our control. You stand firm in your own faith. But we work together with you for your joy.

GREAT VERSE —TO— REMEMBER   **2:14** Give thanks to God! He always leads us in the winners' parade because we belong to Christ.

2 So I made up my mind that I would not make another painful visit to you. ²If I make you sad, who is going to make me glad? Only you, the one I made sad.

³I wrote what I did for a special reason. When I came, I didn't want to be troubled by those who should make me glad. I was sure that all of you would share my joy. ⁴I was very troubled when I wrote to you. My heart was sad. My eyes were full of tears. I didn't want to make you sad. I wanted to let you know that I love you very deeply.

Forgive Those Who Make You Sad

⁵Suppose someone has made us sad. In some ways, he hasn't made me sad so much as he has made all of you sad. But I don't want to put this too strongly. ⁶He has been punished because most of you decided he should be. That is enough for him.

⁷Now you should forgive him and comfort him. Then he won't be sad more than he can stand. ⁸So I'm asking you to tell him again that you still love him.

⁹I wrote to you for a special reason. I wanted to see if you could stand the test. I wanted to see if you could obey everything that was asked of you.

¹⁰Anyone you forgive I also forgive. Was there anything to forgive? If so, I have forgiven it for your benefit, knowing that Christ is watching. ¹¹We don't want Satan to outsmart us. We know how he does his evil work.

Serving Under the New Covenant

¹²I went to Troas to preach the good news about Christ. There I found that the Lord had opened a door of opportunity for me. ¹³But I still had no peace of mind. I couldn't find my brother Titus there. So I said good-by to the believers at Troas and went on to Macedonia.

¹⁴Give thanks to God! He always leads us in the winners' parade because we belong to Christ. Through us, God spreads the knowledge of Christ everywhere like perfume. ¹⁵God considers us to be the sweet smell that Christ is spreading among people who are being saved and people who are dying. ¹⁶To the one, we are the smell of death. To the other, we are the perfume of life. Who is able to do that work?

¹⁷Unlike many people, we aren't selling God's word to make money. In fact, it is just the opposite. Because of Christ we speak honestly before God. We speak like people God has sent.

3 Are we beginning to praise ourselves again? Some people need letters that speak well of them. Do we need those kinds of letters, either to you or from you?

²You yourselves are our letter. You are written on our hearts. Everyone knows you and reads you. ³You make it clear that you are a letter from Christ. You are the result of our work for God. You are a letter written not with ink but with the Spirit of the living God. You are a letter written not on tablets made out of stone but on human hearts.

⁴Through Christ, we can be sure of this because of our faith in God's power. ⁵In ourselves we are not able to claim anything for ourselves. The power to do what we do comes from God. ⁶He has given us the power to serve under a new covenant. The covenant is not based on the written Law of Moses. It comes from the Holy Spirit. The written Law kills, but the Spirit gives life.

The Glory of the New Covenant

⁷The Law was written in letters on stone. Even though it was a way of serving God, it led to death. But even that way of serving God came with glory. And even though the glory was fading, the people of Israel couldn't look at Moses' face very long.

⁸Since all of that is true, won't the work of the Holy Spirit be even more glorious? ⁹The Law that sentences people to death is glorious. How much more glorious is the work of the Spirit! His work makes people right with God.

¹⁰The glory of the old covenant is nothing compared with the far greater glory of the new. ¹¹The glory of the old is fading away. How much greater is the glory of the new! It will last forever.

¹²Since we have that kind of hope, we are very bold. ¹³We are not like Moses. He used to cover his face with a veil. That was to keep the people of Israel from looking at his face while the brightness was fading away.

¹⁴But their minds were made stubborn. To this very day, the same veil remains when the old covenant is read. The veil has not been removed. Only faith in Christ can take it away. ¹⁵To this very day, when the Law of Moses is read, a veil covers the minds of those who hear it.

¹⁶But when anyone turns to the Lord, the veil is taken away. ¹⁷Now the Lord is the Holy Spirit. And where the Spirit of the Lord is, freedom is also there.

¹⁸Our faces are not covered with a veil. We all display the Lord's glory. We are being changed to become more like him so that we

have more and more glory. And the glory comes from the Lord, who is the Holy Spirit.

A Treasure in Clay Jars

4 So because of God's mercy, we have work to do. He has given it to us. And we don't give up. ²Instead, we have given up doing secret and shameful things. We don't twist God's word. In fact, we do just the opposite. We present the truth plainly. In the sight of God, we make our appeal to everyone's sense of what is right and wrong.

³Suppose our good news is covered with a veil. Then it is veiled to those who are dying. ⁴The god of this world has blinded the minds of those who don't believe. They can't see the light of the good news of Christ's glory. He is the likeness of God.

⁵We do not preach about ourselves. We preach about Jesus Christ. We say that he is Lord. And we serve you because of him.

⁶God said, "Let light shine out of darkness." *(Genesis 1:3)* He made his light shine in our hearts. It shows us the light of God's glory in the face of Christ.

⁷Treasure is kept in clay jars. In the same way, we have the treasure of the good news in these earthly bodies of ours. That shows that the mighty power of the good news comes from God. It doesn't come from us.

⁸We are pushed hard from all sides. But we are not beaten down. We are bewildered. But that doesn't make us lose hope. ⁹Others make us suffer. But God does not desert us. We are knocked down. But we are not knocked out. ¹⁰We always carry around the death of Jesus in our bodies. In that way, the life of Jesus can be shown in our bodies.

¹¹We who are alive are always in danger of death because we are serving Jesus. So his life can be shown in our earthly bodies. ¹²Death is at work in us. But life is at work in you.

¹³It is written: "I believed, and so I have spoken." *(Psalm 116:10)* With that same spirit of faith we also believe. And we also speak.

¹⁴We know that God raised the Lord Jesus from the dead. And

GREAT VERSE — TO — REMEMBER   **4:8-9** We are pushed hard from all sides. But we are not beaten down ... God does not desert us.

he will also raise us up with Jesus. He will bring us with you to God in heaven. [15]All of that is for your benefit. God's grace is reaching more and more people. So they will become more and more thankful. They will give glory to God.

[16]We don't give up. Our bodies are becoming weaker and weaker. But our spirits are being renewed day by day. [17]Our troubles are small. They last only for a short time. But they are earning for us a glory that will last forever. It is greater than all our troubles.

[18]So we don't spend all our time looking at what we can see. Instead, we look at what we can't see. What can be seen lasts only a short time. But what can't be seen will last forever.

Our Home in Heaven

5 We know that the earthly tent we live in will be destroyed. But we have a building made by God. It is a house in heaven that lasts forever. Human hands did not build it.

[2]During our time on earth we groan. We long to put on our house in heaven as if it were clothing. [3]Then we will not be naked.

[4]While we live in this tent of ours, we groan under our heavy load. We don't want to be naked. We want to be dressed with our house in heaven. What must die will be swallowed up by life.

[5]God has made us for that very purpose. He has given us the Holy Spirit as a down payment. The Spirit makes us sure of what is still to come.

[6]So here is what we can always be certain about. As long as we are at home in our bodies, we are away from the Lord. [7]We live by believing, not by seeing. [8]We are certain about that. We would rather be away from our bodies and at home with the Lord. [9]So we try our best to please him. We want to please him whether we are at home in our bodies or away from them.

[10]We must all stand in front of Christ to be judged. We will be judged for the good things and the bad things we do while we

---

5:17 Anyone who believes in Christ is a new creation. The old is gone! The new has come!

are in our bodies. Then all of us will receive what we are supposed to get.

Christ Brings Us Back to God

¹¹We know what it means to have respect for the Lord. So we try to help other people to understand it.

What we are is plain to God. I hope it is also plain to your way of thinking. ¹²We are not trying to make an appeal to you again. But we are giving you a chance to take pride in us. Then you can answer those who take pride in how people look rather than in what is really in their hearts.

¹³Are we out of our minds? That is because we want to serve God. Does what we say make sense? That is because we want to serve you.

¹⁴Christ's love controls us. We are sure that one person died for everyone. And so everyone died. ¹⁵Christ died for everyone. He died so that those who live should not live for themselves anymore. They should live for Christ. He died for them and was raised again.

¹⁶So from now on we don't look at anyone the way the world does. At one time we looked at Christ in that way. But we don't anymore.

¹⁷Anyone who believes in Christ is a new creation. The old is gone! The new has come! ¹⁸It is all from God. He brought us back to himself through Christ's death on the cross. And he has given us the task of bringing others back to him through Christ.

¹⁹God was bringing the world back to himself through Christ. He did not hold people's sins against them. God has trusted us with the message that people may be brought back to him. ²⁰So we are Christ's official messengers. It is as if God were making his appeal through us. Here is what Christ wants us to beg you to do. Come back to God!

²¹Christ didn't have any sin. But God made him become sin for us. So we can be made right with God because of what Christ has done for us.

6 We work together with God. So we are asking you not to receive God's grace and then do nothing with it. ²He says,

> "When I showed you my favor, I heard you.
> On the day I saved you, I helped you."   *(Isaiah 49:8)*

I tell you, now is the time God shows his favor. Now is the day he saves.

Paul's Sufferings

³We don't put anything in anyone's way. So no one can find fault with our work for God. ⁴Instead, we make it clear that we serve God in every way. We serve him by holding steady. We stand firm in all kinds of trouble, hard times and suffering.

⁵We don't give up when we are beaten or put in prison. When people stir up trouble in the streets, we continue to serve God. We work hard for him. We go without sleep and food. ⁶We remain pure. We understand completely what it means to serve God. We are patient and kind. We serve him in the power of the Holy Spirit. We serve him with true love. ⁷We speak the truth. We serve in the power of God. We hold the weapons of godliness in the right hand and in the left. ⁸We serve God in times of glory and shame. We serve him whether the news about us is bad or good. We are true to our calling.

But people treat us as if we were pretenders. ⁹We are known, but people treat us as if we were unknown. We are dying, but we continue to live. We are beaten, but we are not killed. ¹⁰We are sad, but we are always full of joy. We are poor, but we make many people rich. We have nothing, but we own everything.

¹¹Believers at Corinth, we have spoken freely to you. We have opened our hearts wide to you. ¹²We are not holding back our love from you. But you are holding back your love from us. ¹³I speak to you as if you were my children. It is only fair that you open your hearts wide to us also.

Do Not Be Joined to Unbelievers

¹⁴Do not be joined to unbelievers. What do right and wrong have in common? Can light and darkness be friends? ¹⁵How can Christ and Satan agree? What does a believer have in common with an unbeliever? ¹⁶How can the temple of the true God and the statues of other gods agree?

We are the temple of the living God. God has said, "I will live with them. I will walk among them. I will be their God. And they will be my people." *(Leviticus 26:12; Jeremiah 32:38; Ezekiel 37:27)*

¹⁷"So come out from among them
   and be separate,

                                        says the Lord.
   Do not touch anything that is not pure and clean.
      Then I will receive you." *(Isaiah 52:11; Ezekiel 20:34,41)*
¹⁸"I will be your Father.

> You will be my sons and daughters,
>   says the Lord who rules over all." *(2 Samuel 7:14; 7:8)*

7 Dear friends, we have these promises from God. So let us make ourselves pure from everything that pollutes our bodies and spirits. Let us be completely holy. We want to honor God.

Paul's Joy

²Make room for us in your hearts. We haven't done anything wrong to anyone. We haven't caused anyone to sin. We haven't taken advantage of anyone.

³I don't say this to judge you. I have told you before that you have an important place in our hearts. We would live or die with you. ⁴I have great faith in you. I am very proud of you. I am very happy. Even with all our troubles, my joy has no limit.

⁵When I came to Macedonia, my body wasn't able to rest. I was attacked no matter where I went. I had battles on the outside and fears on the inside.

⁶But God comforts those who are sad. He comforted me when Titus came. ⁷I was comforted not only when he came but also by the comfort you had given him. He told me how much you longed for me. He told me about your deep sadness and concern for me. That made my joy greater than ever.

⁸Even if my letter made you sad, I'm not sorry I sent it. At first I was sorry. I see that my letter hurt you, but only for a little while. ⁹Now I am happy. I'm not happy because you were made sad. I'm happy because your sadness led you to turn away from your sins. You became sad just as God wanted you to. So you were not hurt in any way by us.

¹⁰Godly sadness causes us to turn away from our sins and be saved. And we are certainly not sorry about that! But worldly sadness brings death.

¹¹Look at what that godly sadness has produced in you. You are

---

GREAT VERSE —TO— REMEMBER

6:16 We are the temple of the living God. God has said, "I will live with them. I will walk among them. I will be their God. And they will be my people."

working hard to clear yourselves. You are angry and alarmed. You are longing to see me. You are concerned. You are ready to make sure that the right thing is done. In every way you have proved that you are not guilty in that matter.

[12]So even though I wrote to you, it wasn't because of the one who did the wrong. It wasn't because of the one who was hurt. Instead, I wrote you so that in the sight of God you could see for yourselves how faithful you are to us. [13]All of that cheers us up.

We were also very glad to see how happy Titus was. You have all renewed his spirit. [14]I had bragged about you to him. And you have not let me down. Everything we said to you was true. In the same way, our bragging about you to Titus has also turned out to be true. [15]His love for you is even greater when he remembers that you all obeyed his teaching. You received him with fear and trembling. [16]I am glad I can have complete faith in you.

Giving Freely to Others

8 Brothers and sisters, we want you to know about the grace that God has given to the churches in Macedonia. [2]They have suffered a great deal. But their joy was more than full. Even though they were very poor, they gave very freely.

[3]I give witness that they gave as much as they could. In fact, they gave even more than they could. Completely on their own, [4]they begged us for the chance to share in serving God's people in that way. [5]They did more than we expected. First they gave themselves to the Lord. Then they gave themselves to us in keeping with what God wanted.

[6]Titus had already started collecting money from you. So we asked him to get you to finish making your kind gift.

[7]You do well in everything else. You do well in faith and in speaking. You do well in knowledge and in complete commitment. And you do well in your love for us. So make sure that you also do well in the grace of giving to others.

[8]I am not commanding you to do it. But I want to put you to the test. I want to find out if you really love God. I want to compare your love with that of others.

[9]You know the grace shown by our Lord Jesus Christ. Even though he was rich, he became poor to help you. Because he became poor, you can become rich.

[10]Here is my advice about what is best for you in that matter. Last year you were the first to give. You were also the first to want to give. [11]So finish the work. Then your longing to do it will be

matched by your finishing it. Give on the basis of what you have.
¹²Do you really want to give? Then the gift is received in keeping with what you have, not with what you don't have.

¹³We don't want others to have it easy at your expense. We want things to be equal. ¹⁴Right now you have plenty in order to take care of what they need. Then they will have plenty to take care of what you need. That will make things equal. ¹⁵It is written: "Those who gathered a lot didn't have too much. And those who gathered a little had enough." *(Exodus 16:18)*

Paul Sends Titus to Corinth

¹⁶God put into the heart of Titus the same concern I have for you. I am thankful to God for this. ¹⁷Titus welcomed our appeal. He is also excited about coming to you. It was his own idea.

¹⁸Along with Titus, we are sending another brother. All the churches praise him for his service in telling the good news. ¹⁹He was also chosen by the churches to go with us as we bring the offering. We are in charge of it. We want to honor the Lord himself. We want to show how ready we are to help.

²⁰We want to keep anyone from blaming us for how we take care of that large gift. ²¹We are trying hard to do what is right in the Lord's eyes and in the eyes of people.

²²We are also sending another one of our brothers with them. He has often proved to us in many ways that he is very committed. He is now even more committed because he has great faith in you.

²³Titus is my helper. He and I work together among you. Our brothers are messengers from the churches. They honor Christ. ²⁴So show them that you really love them. Show them why we are proud of you. Then the churches can see it.

9 I don't need to write to you about giving to God's people. ²I know how much you want to help. I have been bragging about it to the people in Macedonia. I have been telling them that since last year you who live in Achaia were ready to give. You are so excited that it has stirred up most of them to take action.

³But I am sending the brothers. Then our bragging about you in this matter will have a good reason. You will be ready, just as I said you would be.

⁴Suppose people from Macedonia come with me and find out that you are not prepared. Then we, as well as you, would be ashamed of being so certain.

⁵So I thought I should try to get the brothers to visit you ahead of time. They will finish the plans for the large gift you had promised. Then it will be ready as a gift that is freely given. It will not be given by force.

Planting Many Seeds

⁶Here is something to remember. The one who plants only a little will gather only a little. And the one who plants a lot will gather a lot. ⁷You should each give what you have decided in your heart to give. You shouldn't give if you don't want to. You shouldn't give because you are forced to. God loves a cheerful giver.

⁸And God is able to shower all kinds of blessings on you. In all things and at all times you will have everything you need. You will do more and more good works. ⁹It is written:

"They have spread their gifts around to poor people.
   Their good works continue forever."   *(Psalm 112:9)*

¹⁰God supplies seed to the planter. He supplies bread for food. God will also supply and increase the amount of your seed. He will increase the results of your good works. ¹¹You will be made rich in every way. Then you can always give freely. We will take your many gifts to the people who need them. And they will give thanks to God.

¹²Your gifts meet the needs of God's people. And that's not all. Your gifts also cause many people to thank God.

¹³You have shown yourselves to be worthy by what you have given. So people will praise God because you obey him. That proves that you really believe the good news about Christ. They will also praise God because you share freely with them and with everyone else. ¹⁴Their hearts will be filled with longing for you when they pray for you. God has given you grace that is better than anything.

¹⁵Let us give thanks to God for his gift. It is so great that no one can tell how wonderful it really is!

GREAT VERSE —TO— REMEMBER   **9:7** You should each give what you have decided in your heart to give ... God loves a cheerful giver.

Paul Speaks Up for Himself

10 Christ is gentle and free of pride. So I make my appeal to you. I, Paul, am the one you call shy when I am face to face with you. But when I am away from you, you call me bold. [2]I beg you that when I come I won't have to be as bold as I expect to be toward some people. They think that I live the way the people of this world live.

[3]I do live in the world. But I don't fight my battles the way the people of the world do. [4]The weapons I fight with are not the weapons the world uses. In fact, it is just the opposite. My weapons have the power of God to destroy the camps of the enemy.

[5]I destroy every claim and every reason that keeps people from knowing God. I keep every thought under control in order to make it obey Christ. [6]Until you have obeyed completely, I will be ready to punish you every time you don't obey.

[7]You are looking only at what appears on the surface of things. Suppose you are sure you belong to Christ. Then you should consider again that I belong to Christ just as much as you do.

[8]Do I brag too much about the authority the Lord gave me? If I do, it's because I want to build you up, not pull you down. And I'm not ashamed of that kind of bragging.

[9]Don't think that I'm trying to scare you with my letters. [10]Some say, "His letters sound important. They are powerful. But in person he doesn't seem like much. And what he says doesn't amount to anything." [11]People like that have a lot to learn. What I say in my letters when I'm away from you, I will do in my actions when I'm with you.

[12]I don't dare to compare myself with those who praise themselves. I'm not that kind of person. They measure themselves by themselves. They compare themselves with themselves. When they do that, they are not wise.

[13]But I won't brag more than I should. Instead, I will brag only about what I have done in the area God has given me. It is an area that reaches all the way to you. [14]I am not going too far in my bragging. I would be going too far if I hadn't come to where you live. But I did get there with the good news about Christ.

[15]And I won't brag about work done by others. If I did, I would be bragging more than I should. As your faith continues to grow, I hope that my work among you will greatly increase. [16]Then I will be able to preach the good news in the areas beyond you. I

don't want to brag about work already done in someone else's territory.

[17]But, "Those who brag should brag about what the Lord has done." *(Jeremiah 9:24)* [18]Those who praise themselves are not accepted. Those the Lord praises are accepted.

Paul and Those Who Pretend to Be Apostles

11 I hope you will put up with a little of my foolish bragging. But you are already doing that.

[2]My jealousy for you comes from God himself. I promised to give you to only one husband. That husband is Christ. I wanted to be able to give you to him as if you were a pure virgin. [3]But Eve was tricked by the snake's clever lies. And I'm afraid that in the same way your minds will somehow be led down the wrong path. They will be led away from your true and pure love for Christ.

[4]Suppose someone comes to you and preaches about a Jesus different from the Jesus we preached about. Or suppose you receive a spirit different from the one you received before. Or suppose you receive a message of good news different from the one you accepted earlier. You put up with those kinds of things easily enough.

[5]But I don't think I'm in any way less important than those "super-apostles." [6]I may not be a trained speaker. But I do have knowledge. I've made that very clear to you in every way.

[7]When I preached God's good news to you free of charge, I put myself down in order to lift you up. Was that a sin? [8]Did I rob other churches when I received help from them so that I could serve you? [9]When I was with you and needed something, I didn't cause you any expense. The believers who came from Macedonia gave me what I needed. I haven't caused you any expense at all. And I won't ever do it.

[10]I'm sure that the truth of Christ is in me. And I'm just as sure that nobody in Achaia will keep me from bragging. [11]Why? Because I don't love you? No! God knows I do! [12]And I will keep on doing what I'm doing. That will stop those who claim they have things to brag about. They think they have a chance to be considered equal with us.

[13]People like that are false apostles. They work hard to trick others. They only pretend to be apostles of Christ.

[14]That comes as no surprise. Even Satan himself pretends to be an angel of light. [15]So it doesn't surprise us that those who serve

Satan pretend to be serving God. They will finally get exactly what they should.

Paul Brags About His Sufferings

[16]I will say it again. Don't let anyone think I'm a fool. But if you do, receive me just as you would receive a fool. Then I can do a little bragging.

[17]When I brag about myself like this, I'm not talking the way the Lord would. I'm talking like a fool. [18]Many are bragging the way the people of the world do. So I will brag like that too.

[19]You are so wise! You gladly put up with fools! [20]In fact, you even put up with anyone who makes you a slave or uses you. You put up with those who take advantage of you. You put up with those who claim to be better than you. You put up with those who slap you in the face.

[21]I'm ashamed to have to say that I was too weak for that!

What anyone else dares to brag about, I also dare to brag about. I'm speaking like a fool! [22]Are they Hebrews? So am I. Do they belong to the people of Israel? So do I. Are they Abraham's children? So am I. [23]Are they serving Christ? I am serving him even more. I'm out of my mind to talk like this!

I have worked much harder. I have been in prison more often. I have suffered terrible beatings. Again and again I almost died. [24]Five times the Jews gave me 39 strokes with a whip. [25]Three times I was beaten with sticks. Once they tried to kill me by throwing stones at me. Three times I was shipwrecked. I spent a night and a day in the open sea.

[26]I have had to keep on the move. I have been in danger from rivers. I have been in danger from robbers. I have been in danger from people from my own country. I have been in danger from those who aren't Jews. I have been in danger in the city, in the country, and at sea. I have been in danger from people who pretended they were believers.

[27]I have worked very hard. Often I have gone without sleep. I have been hungry and thirsty. Often I have gone without food. I have been cold and naked.

[28]Besides everything else, every day I am concerned about all the churches. It is a very heavy load. [29]If anyone is weak, I feel weak. If anyone is led into sin, I burn on the inside.

[30]If I have to brag, I will brag about the things that show how weak I am. [31]I am not lying. The God and Father of the Lord Jesus knows this. May God be praised forever. [32]In Damascus the gov-

ernor who served under King Aretas had their city guarded. He wanted to arrest me. ³³But I was lowered in a basket from a window in the wall. So I slipped through the governor's hands.

Paul's Vision and His Painful Problem

12 We can't gain anything by bragging. But I have to do it anyway. I am going to tell you what I've seen. I want to talk about what the Lord has shown me.

²I know a believer in Christ who was taken up to the third heaven 14 years ago. I don't know if his body was taken up or not. Only God knows. ³I don't know if that man was in his body or out of it. Only God knows. But I do know that ⁴he was taken up to paradise. He heard things that couldn't be put into words. They were things that people aren't allowed to talk about.

⁵I will brag about a man like that. But I won't brag about myself. I will brag only about how weak I am.

⁶Suppose I decide to brag. That would not make me a fool, because I would be telling the truth. But I don't do it. Then no one will think more of me than he should because of what I do or say.

⁷I could have become proud of myself because of the amazing and wonderful things God has shown me. So I was given a problem that caused pain in my body. It is a messenger from Satan to make me suffer. ⁸Three times I begged the Lord to take it away from me. ⁹But he said to me, "My grace is all you need. My power is strongest when you are weak."

So I am very happy to brag about how weak I am. Then Christ's power can rest on me. ¹⁰Because of how I suffered for Christ, I'm glad that I am weak. I am glad in hard times. I am glad when people say mean things about me. I am glad when things are difficult. And I am glad when people make me suffer. When I am weak, I am strong.

Paul's Concern for the People of Corinth

¹¹I have made a fool of myself. But you made me do it. You

GREAT VERSE —TO— REMEMBER

12:9 But he said to me, "My grace is all you need. My power is strongest when you are weak."

should have praised me. Even though I am nothing, I am in no way less important than the "super-apostles." ¹²You can recognize apostles by the signs, wonders and miracles they do. Those things were faithfully done among you no matter what happened.

¹³How were you less important than the other churches? The only difference was that I didn't cause you any expense. Forgive me for that wrong!

¹⁴Now I am ready to visit you for the third time. I won't cause you any expense. I don't want what you have. What I really want is you. After all, children shouldn't have to save up for their parents. Parents should save up for their children. ¹⁵So I will be very happy to spend everything I have for you. I will even spend myself. If I love you more, will you love me less?

¹⁶In any case, I haven't caused you any expense. But I'm such a tricky fellow! I have caught you by tricking you!

¹⁷Did I take advantage of you through any of the people I sent to you? ¹⁸I asked Titus to go to you. And I sent our brother with him. Titus didn't take advantage of you, did he? Didn't I act in the same spirit? Didn't I follow the same path?

¹⁹All this time, have you been thinking that I've been speaking up for myself? No, I've been speaking with God as my witness. I've been speaking like a believer in Christ. Dear friends, everything I do is to help you become stronger.

²⁰I'm afraid that when I come I won't find you as I want you to be. I'm afraid that you won't find me as you want me to be. I'm afraid there will be arguing, jealousy and fits of anger. I'm afraid you will separate into your own little groups. Then you will tell lies about each other. You will talk about each other. I'm afraid you will be proud and cause trouble.

²¹I'm afraid that when I come again my God will put me to shame in front of you. Then I will be sad about many who sinned earlier and have not turned away from it. They have not turned away from uncleanness, sexual sins and wild living. They have done all those things.

Final Warnings

13 This will be my third visit to you. Scripture says, "Every matter must be proved by the words of two or three witnesses." *(Deuteronomy 19:15)* ²I already warned you during my second visit. I now say it again while I'm away. When I return, I won't spare those who sinned earlier. I won't spare any of the others either.

³You are asking me to prove that Christ is speaking through me. He is not weak in dealing with you. He is powerful among you. ⁴It is true that Christ was nailed to the cross because he was weak. But he lives by God's power. In the same way, I share his weakness. But by God's power I will live with him to serve you.

⁵Take a good look at yourselves to see if you are really believers. Test yourselves. Don't you realize that Christ Jesus is in you? Unless, of course, you fail the test! ⁶I hope you will discover that I haven't failed the test.

⁷I pray to God that you won't do anything wrong. I don't pray so that people will see that I have passed the test. Instead, I pray so that you will do what is right, even if it seems I have failed. ⁸I can't do anything to stop the truth. I can only work for the truth.

⁹I'm glad when I am weak but you are strong. I pray that you will become perfect. ¹⁰That's why I write these things before I come to you. Then when I do come, I won't have to be hard on you when I use my authority.

The Lord gave me the authority to build you up. He didn't give it to me to tear you down.

Final Greetings

¹¹Finally, brothers and sisters, good-by. Try to be perfect. Pay attention to what I'm saying. Agree with one another. Live in peace. And the God who gives love and peace will be with you.

¹²Greet one another with a holy kiss. ¹³All of God's people send their greetings.

¹⁴May the grace shown by the Lord Jesus Christ, and the love that God has given us, and the sharing of life brought about by the Holy Spirit be with you all.

GREAT VERSE — TO — REMEMBER

13:11 Agree with one another. Live in peace. And the God who gives love and peace will be with you.

Galatians

Why Was This Book Written? Galatia was a part of the world we now call Turkey. Paul wrote this letter to some churches there. They were being taught by false teachers. These teachers taught wrong things about Paul and God's rules for Christians. They said Paul did not teach the truth.

What Is This Book About? In this letter Paul talked about false teachers. He said Christians must believe God's words. He wrote that we cannot be saved by only doing what the Jewish law says. He taught that we are saved when we believe in Jesus Christ.

What Is in This Book?

1 I, Paul, am writing this letter. I am an apostle. People have not sent me. No human authority has sent me. I have been sent by Jesus Christ and by God the Father. God raised Jesus from the dead. ²All the brothers and sisters who are with me join me in writing.

We are sending this letter to you, the members of the churches in Galatia.

³May God our Father and the Lord Jesus Christ give you grace and peace. ⁴Jesus gave his life for our sins. He set us free from this evil world. That was what our God and Father wanted. ⁵Give glory to God for ever and ever. Amen.

There Is No Other Good News

⁶I am amazed. You are so quickly deserting the One who chose you because of the grace that Christ has provided. You are turning to a different "good news." ⁷What you are accepting is really not the good news at all.

It seems that some people have gotten you all mixed up. They are trying to twist the good news about Christ.

⁸But suppose even we should preach a different "good news." Suppose even an angel from heaven should preach it. I'm talking about a different one than the good news we gave you. Let that person be judged by God forever. ⁹I have already said it. Now I will say it again. Anyone who preaches a "good news" that is different from the one you accepted should be judged by God forever.

¹⁰Am I now trying to get people to think well of me? Or do I want God to think well of me? Am I trying to please people? If I were, I would not be serving Christ.

Paul Was Appointed by God

¹¹Brothers and sisters, here is what I want you to know. The good news I preached is not something a human being made up. ¹²No one gave it to me. No one taught it to me. Instead, I received it from Jesus Christ. He showed it to me.

¹³You have heard of my earlier way of life as a Jew. With all my strength I attacked the church of God. I tried to destroy it. ¹⁴I was moving ahead in my Jewish way of life. I went beyond many Jews who were my own age. I held firmly to the teachings passed down by my people.

¹⁵But God set me apart from the time I was born. He showed me

his grace by appointing me. He was pleased [16]to show his Son in my life. He wanted me to preach about Jesus among those who aren't Jews.

When God appointed me, I didn't talk to anyone. [17]I didn't go up to Jerusalem to see those who were apostles before I was. Instead, I went at once into Arabia. Later I returned to Damascus.

[18]Then after three years I went up to Jerusalem. I went there to get to know Peter. I stayed with him for 15 days. [19]I didn't see any of the other apostles. I only saw James, the Lord's brother. [20]Here is what you can be sure of. And God gives witness to it. What I am writing you is not a lie.

[21]Later I went to Syria and Cilicia. [22]The members of Christ's churches in Judea did not know me in a personal way. [23]They only heard others say, "The man who used to attack us has changed. He is now preaching the faith he once tried to destroy." [24]And they praised God because of me.

Paul Is Accepted by the Apostles

2 Fourteen years later I went up again to Jerusalem. This time I went with Barnabas. I took Titus along also. [2]I went because God showed me what he wanted me to do. I told the people there the good news that I preach among those who aren't Jews. But I spoke in private to those who seemed to be leaders. I was afraid that I was running or had run my race for nothing.

[3]Titus was with me. He was a Greek. But even he was not forced to be circumcised.

[4]That matter came up because some who pretended to be believers had slipped in among us. They wanted to find out about the freedom we have because we belong to Christ Jesus. They wanted to make us slaves again.

[5]We didn't give in to them for a moment. We wanted the truth of the good news to remain with you.

[6]Some people in Jerusalem seemed to be important. It makes no difference to me what they were. God does not judge by what he sees on the outside. Those people added nothing to my message.

[7]In fact, it was just the opposite. They saw that I had been trusted with the task of preaching the good news just as Peter had been. My task was to preach to the non-Jews. Peter's task was to preach to the Jews. [8]God was working through Peter as an apostle to the Jews. He was also working through me as an apostle to the non-Jews.

⁹James, Peter and John are considered to be pillars in the church. They recognized the special grace that was given to me. So they shook my hand and the hand of Barnabas. They wanted to show they accepted us. They agreed that we should go to the non-Jews. They would go to the Jews. ¹⁰They asked only one thing. They wanted us to continue to remember poor people. That was what I really wanted to do anyway.

Paul Opposes Peter

¹¹When Peter came to Antioch, I told him to his face that I was against what he was doing. He was clearly wrong. ¹²He used to eat with those who weren't Jews. But certain people came from the group that was led by James. When they arrived, Peter began to draw back. He separated himself from the non-Jews. He was afraid of the circumcision group.

¹³Peter's actions were not honest. The other Jews joined him. Even Barnabas was led down the wrong path.

¹⁴I saw what they were doing. It was not in line with the truth of the good news. So I spoke to Peter in front of them all. "You are a Jew," I said. "But you live like one who is not. So why do you force non-Jews to follow Jewish ways?"

God's Grace and Our Faith

¹⁵We are Jews by birth. We are not "non-Jewish sinners." ¹⁶We know that people are not made right with God by obeying the law. It is by believing in Jesus Christ. So we too have put our faith in Christ Jesus. That is so we can be made right with God by believing in Christ, not by obeying the law. No one can be made right with God by obeying the law.

¹⁷We are trying to be made right with God through Christ. But it is clear that we are sinners. So does that mean that Christ causes us to sin? Certainly not! ¹⁸Suppose I build again what I had destroyed. Then I prove that I break the law.

¹⁹Because of the law, I died as far as the law is concerned. I died so that I might live for God. ²⁰I have been crucified with Christ.

2:20 I have been crucified with Christ. I don't live any longer. Christ lives in me.

I don't live any longer. Christ lives in me. My faith in the Son of God helps me to live my life in my body. He loved me. He gave himself for me.

²¹I do not get rid of the grace of God. What if a person could become right with God by obeying the law? Then Christ died for nothing!

Faith or Obeying the Law

3 You foolish people of Galatia! Who has put you under an evil spell? When I preached, I clearly showed you that Jesus Christ had been nailed to the cross.

²I would like to learn just one thing from you. Did you receive the Holy Spirit by obeying the law? Or did you receive the Spirit by believing what you heard? ³Are you so foolish? You began with the Holy Spirit. Are you now trying to complete God's work in you by your own strength?

⁴Have you suffered so much for nothing? And was it really for nothing? ⁵Why does God give you his Spirit? Why does he work miracles among you? Is it because you do what the law says? Or is it because you believe what you have heard?

⁶Think about Abraham. Scripture says, "Abraham believed God. God accepted Abraham because he believed. So his faith made him right with God." *(Genesis 15:6)* ⁷So you see, those who have faith are children of Abraham.

⁸Long ago, Scripture knew that God would make non-Jews right with himself by believing in him. He announced the good news ahead of time to Abraham. He said, "All nations will be blessed through you." *(Genesis 12:3; 18:18; 22:18)* ⁹So those who have faith are blessed along with Abraham. He was the man of faith.

¹⁰All who depend on obeying the law are under a curse. It is written: "May those who don't continue to do everything that is written in the Book of the Law be under God's curse." *(Deuteronomy 27:26)* ¹¹We know that no one is made right with God by keeping

3:11 We know that no one is made right with God by keeping the law. Scripture says, "Those who are right with God will live by faith."

the law. Scripture says, "Those who are right with God will live by faith." *(Habakkuk 2:4)*

¹²The law is not based on faith. In fact, it is just the opposite. It teaches that "the one who does those things will live by them." *(Leviticus 18:5)*

¹³Christ set us free from the curse of the law. He did it by becoming a curse for us. It is written: "May everyone who is hung on a pole be under God's curse." *(Deuteronomy 21:23)* ¹⁴Christ Jesus set us free so that the blessing given to Abraham would come to non-Jews through Christ. He did it so that we might receive the promise of the Holy Spirit by believing in Christ.

The Law and the Promise

¹⁵Brothers and sisters, let me give you an example from everyday life. No one can get rid of an official agreement between people. No one can add to it. It can't be changed after it has been made. It is the same with God's covenant. ¹⁶The promises were given to Abraham. They were also given to his seed. Scripture does not say, "and to seeds." That means many people. It says, "and to your seed." *(Genesis 12:7; 13:15; 24:7)* That means one person. And that one person is Christ.

¹⁷Here is what I mean. The law came 430 years after the promise. But the law does not get rid of God's covenant and promise. The covenant had already been made by God. So the law does not do away with the promise.

¹⁸The great gift that God has for us does not depend on the law. If it did, it would no longer depend on a promise. But God gave it to Abraham as a free gift through a promise.

¹⁹Then what was the purpose of the law? It was added because of human sin. And it was supposed to control us until the promised Seed had come. The law was put into effect through angels by a go-between. ²⁰A go-between does not take sides. God didn't use a go-between when he made his promise to Abraham. But the same God was at work in both the Law and the promise.

²¹So is the law opposed to God's promises? Certainly not! What if a law had been given that could give life? Then people could become right with God by obeying the law. ²²But Scripture announces that the whole world is a prisoner because of sin. It does so in order that what was promised might be given to those who believe. The promise comes through faith in Jesus Christ.

²³Before faith in Christ came, we were held prisoners by the law. We were locked up until faith was made known. ²⁴So the law was

put in charge until Christ came. He came so that we might be made right with God by believing in Christ.

²⁵But now faith in Christ has come. So we are no longer under the control of the law.

Children of God

²⁶You are all children of God by believing in Christ Jesus. ²⁷All of you who were baptized into Christ have put on Christ as if he were your clothes. ²⁸There is no Jew or Greek. There is no slave or free person. There is no male or female. Because you belong to Christ Jesus, you are all one.

²⁹You who belong to Christ are Abraham's seed. You will receive what God has promised.

4 Here is what I have been saying. As long as your own children are young, they are no different from slaves in your house. They are no different, even though they own all of the property. ²They are under the care of guardians and those who manage the property. They are under their care until the time when their fathers give them the property. ³It is the same with us. When we were children, we were slaves to the basic things the people of the world believe.

⁴But then the right time came. God sent his Son. A woman gave birth to him. He was born under the authority of the law. ⁵He came to set free those who were under the law. He wanted us to be adopted as children with all the rights children have.

⁶Because you are his children, God sent the Spirit of his Son into our hearts. He is the Holy Spirit. By his power we call God "Abba." *Abba* means Father.

⁷So you aren't slaves any longer. You are God's children. Because you are his children, he gives you what he promised to give his people.

Paul's Concern for the Believers in Galatia

⁸At one time you didn't know God. You were slaves to gods that are really not gods at all. ⁹But now you know God. Even better, God knows you. So why are you turning back to those weak and worthless beliefs? Do you want to be slaves to them all over again?

¹⁰You are observing special days and months and seasons and years! ¹¹I am afraid for you. I am afraid that somehow I have wasted my efforts on you.

Paul's Appeal to the Believers

[12]I make my appeal to you, brothers and sisters. I'm asking you to become like me. After all, I became like you. You didn't do anything wrong to me.

[13]As you know, it was because I was sick that I first preached the good news to you. [14]My sickness was hard on you. But you didn't put me off. You didn't make fun of me. Instead, you welcomed me as if I were an angel of God. You welcomed me as if I were Christ Jesus himself.

[15]What has happened to all of your joy? If you could have torn out your own eyes and given them to me, you would have. I can give witness to that. [16]Have I become your enemy now by telling you the truth?

[17]Those people are trying hard to win you over. But it is not for your good. They want to take you away from us. They want you to commit yourselves to them. [18]It is fine to be committed to something, if the purpose is good. And you shouldn't be committed only when I am with you. You should always be committed.

[19]My dear children, I am in pain for you. Once again I have pain like a woman giving birth. And my pain will continue until Christ makes you like himself.

[20]I wish I could be with you now. I wish I could change my tone of voice. As it is, you bewilder me.

Hagar and Sarah

[21]You who want to be under the authority of the law, tell me something. Don't you know what the law says? [22]It is written that Abraham had two sons. The slave woman gave birth to one of them. The free woman gave birth to the other one. [23]Abraham's son by the slave woman was born in the usual way. But his son by the free woman was born because of God's promise.

[24]Those things can be taken as examples. The two women stand for two covenants. One covenant comes from Mount Sinai. It gives birth to children who are going to be slaves. It is Hagar. [25]Hagar stands for Mount Sinai in Arabia. She stands for the present city of Jerusalem. That's because she and her children are slaves.

[26]But the Jerusalem that is above is free. She is our mother. [27]It is written:

"Be glad, woman,
  you who have no children.
Start shouting,
  you who have no labor pains.
The woman who is all alone has more children
  than the woman who has a husband." *(Isaiah 54:1)*

²⁸Brothers and sisters, you are children because of God's promise just as Isaac was. ²⁹At that time, the son born in the usual way tried to hurt the son born by the power of the Holy Spirit. It is the same now.

³⁰But what does Scripture say? "Get rid of the slave woman. Get rid of her son. The slave woman's son will never have a share of the family's property with the free woman's son." *(Genesis 21:10)*

³¹Brothers and sisters, we are not the slave woman's children. We are the free woman's children.

Christ Sets Us Free

5 Christ has set us free. He wants us to enjoy freedom. So stand firm. Don't let the chains of slavery hold you again.

²Here is what I, Paul, say to you. Don't let yourselves be circumcised. If you do, Christ won't be of any value to you. ³I say it again. Every man who lets himself be circumcised must obey the whole law.

⁴Some of you are trying to be made right with God by obeying the law. You have been separated from Christ. You have fallen away from God's grace.

⁵But we expect to be made completely holy because of our faith in Christ. Through the Holy Spirit we wait in hope. ⁶Circumcision and uncircumcision aren't worth anything to those who believe in Christ Jesus. The only thing that really counts is faith that shows itself through love.

⁷You were running a good race. Who cut in on you and kept you from obeying the truth? ⁸The One who chooses you does not keep you from obeying the truth. ⁹You should know that "just a little yeast works its way through the whole batch of dough."

GREAT VERSE —TO— REMEMBER

5:5 We expect to be made completely holy because of our faith in Christ.

¹⁰The Lord makes me certain that you will not think in any other way. The one who has gotten you all mixed up will pay the price. It doesn't matter who that may be.

¹¹Brothers and sisters, I am not still preaching that people must be circumcised. If I were, why am I still being opposed? If that were what I preach, then the cross wouldn't upset anyone.

¹²So then, what about troublemakers who try to get others to be circumcised? I wish they would go the whole way! I wish they would cut off everything that marks them as men!

Chosen to Be Free

¹³My brothers and sisters, you were chosen to be free. But don't use your freedom as an excuse to live in sin. Instead, serve one another in love. ¹⁴The whole law can be found in a single command. "Love your neighbor as you love yourself." *(Leviticus 19:18)*

¹⁵You must not keep on biting each other. You must not keep eating each other up. Watch out! You might destroy each other.

Living by the Holy Spirit's Power

¹⁶So I say, live by the Holy Spirit's power. Then you will not do what your sinful nature wants you to do.

¹⁷The sinful nature does not want what the Spirit delights in. And the Spirit does not want what the sinful nature delights in. The two are at war with each other. That's what makes you do what you don't want to do. ¹⁸But if you are led by the Spirit, you are not under the authority of the law.

¹⁹What the sinful nature does is clear. It enjoys sexual sins, impure acts and wild living. ²⁰It worships statues of gods. It also worships evil powers. It is full of hatred and fighting. It is full of jealousy and fits of anger. It is interested only in getting ahead. It stirs up trouble. It separates people into their own little groups. ²¹It wants what others have. It gets drunk and takes part in wild

---

GREAT VERSE — TO — REMEMBER

5:22-23 The fruit the Holy Spirit produces is love, joy and peace. It is being patient, kind, and good. It is being faithful and gentle and having control of oneself.

parties. It does many things of that kind. I warn you now as I did before. People who live like that will not receive God's kingdom.

²²But the fruit the Holy Spirit produces is love, joy and peace. It is being patient, kind, and good. It is being faithful ²³and gentle and having control of oneself. There is no law against things of that kind.

²⁴Those who belong to Christ Jesus have nailed their sinful nature to his cross. They don't want what their sinful nature loves and longs for.

²⁵Since we live by the Spirit, let us march in step with the Spirit. ²⁶Let us not become proud. Let us not make each other angry. Let us not want what belongs to others.

Do Good to Everyone

6 Brothers and sisters, what if someone is caught in a sin? Then you who are guided by the Spirit should correct that person. Do it in a gentle way. But be careful. You could be tempted too. ²Carry each other's heavy loads. If you do, you will give the law of Christ its full meaning.

³If you think you are somebody when you are nobody, you are fooling yourselves. ⁴Each of you should put your own actions to the test. Then you could take pride in yourself. You wouldn't be comparing yourself to somebody else. ⁵Each of you should carry your own load.

⁶Those who are taught the word must share all good things with their teacher.

⁷Don't be fooled. You can't outsmart God. People gather a crop from what they plant. ⁸Some plant to please their sinful nature. From that nature they will harvest death. Others plant to please the Holy Spirit. From the Spirit they will harvest eternal life.

⁹Let us not become tired of doing good. At the right time we will gather a crop if we don't give up. ¹⁰So when we can do good to everyone, let us do it. Let us make a special point of doing good to those who belong to the family of believers.

The Creation of a New Nature

¹¹Look at the big letters I'm using as I write to you with my own hand!

¹²Some people want others to think well of them. They are trying to force you to be circumcised. They do it for only one reason. They don't want to suffer by being connected with the cross of Christ. ¹³Even those who are circumcised don't obey the law. But

they want you to be circumcised. Then they can brag about what
has been done to your body.

¹⁴I never want to brag about anything except the cross of our
Lord Jesus Christ. Through that cross the ways of the world have
been crucified as far as I am concerned. And I have been crucified
as far as the ways of the world are concerned.

¹⁵Circumcision and uncircumcision don't mean anything.
What really counts is the creation of a new nature.

¹⁶May peace and mercy be given to all who follow this rule.
May peace and mercy be given to the Israel that belongs to God.

¹⁷Finally, let no one cause trouble for me. My body has marks
that show I belong to Jesus.

¹⁸Brothers and sisters, may the grace of our Lord Jesus Christ be
with your spirit. Amen.

Ephesians

Why Was This Book Written? Paul wrote this letter from Rome. He was in prison. He wrote to his friends in Ephesus. Ephesus was a big city. There were many churches in the city. There were many churches nearby too. This letter was passed around to all of them.

What Is This Book About? Paul wrote this letter about the church. He wrote that we are all one family in Jesus. He said we must love each other. Paul also wrote that Christians must fight the devil. We are like soldiers, but we do not use guns or swords. We must believe in Jesus and his words.

What Is in This Book?

1 I, Paul, am writing this letter. I am an apostle of Christ Jesus just as God planned.

I am sending this letter to you, God's people in Ephesus. Because you belong to Christ Jesus, you are faithful.

²May God our Father and the Lord Jesus Christ give you grace and peace.

God Gives Spiritual Blessings

³Give praise to the God and Father of our Lord Jesus Christ. He has blessed us with every spiritual blessing. Those blessings come from the heavenly world. They belong to us because we belong to Christ.

⁴God chose us to belong to Christ before the world was created. He chose us to be holy and without blame in his eyes. He loved us. ⁵So he decided long ago to adopt us as his children. He did it because of what Jesus Christ has done. It pleased God to do it. ⁶All those things bring praise to his glorious grace. God freely gave us his grace because of the One he loves.

⁷We have been set free because of what Christ has done. Through his blood our sins have been forgiven. We have been set free because God's grace is so rich. ⁸He poured his grace on us by giving us great wisdom and understanding.

⁹He showed us the mystery of his plan. It was in keeping with what he wanted to do. It was what he had planned through Christ. ¹⁰It will all come about when history has been completed. God will then bring together all things in heaven and on earth under one ruler. The ruler is Christ.

¹¹We were also chosen to belong to him. God decided to choose us long ago in keeping with his plan. He works out everything to fit his plan and purpose. ¹²We were the first to put our hope in Christ. We were chosen to bring praise to his glory.

¹³You also became believers in Christ. That happened when you heard the message of truth. It was the good news about how you

GREAT VERSE —TO— REMEMBER

1:4 God chose us to belong to Christ before the world was created. He chose us to be holy and without blame in his eyes. He loved us.

could be saved. When you believed, he marked you with a seal. The seal is the Holy Spirit that he promised.

[14]The Spirit marks us as God's own. We can now be sure that someday we will receive all that God has promised. That will happen after God sets all of his people completely free. All of those things will bring praise to his glory.

Paul Prays and Gives Thanks

[15]I have heard about your faith in the Lord Jesus. I have also heard about your love for all of God's people. That is why [16]I have not stopped thanking God for you. I always remember you in my prayers.

[17]I pray to the God of our Lord Jesus Christ. God is the glorious Father. I keep asking him to give you the wisdom and understanding that come from the Holy Spirit. I want you to know God better.

[18]I also pray that your mind might see more clearly. Then you will know the hope God has chosen you to receive. You will know that the things God's people will receive are rich and glorious. [19]And you will know his great power. It can't be compared with anything else. It is at work for us who believe. It is like the mighty strength [20]God showed when he raised Christ from the dead.

He seated him at his right hand in his heavenly kingdom. [21]There Christ sits far above all who rule and have authority. He also sits far above all powers and kings. He is above every title that can be given in this world and in the world to come.

[22]God placed all things under Christ's rule. He appointed him to be ruler over everything for the church. [23]The church is Christ's body. It is filled by Christ. He fills everything in every way.

God Has Given Us New Life Through Christ

2 You were living in your sins and lawless ways. But in fact you were dead. [2]You used to live as sinners when you followed the ways of this world. You served the one who rules over the spiritual forces of evil. He is the spirit who is now at work in those who don't obey God.

[3]At one time we all lived among them. We tried to satisfy what our sinful nature wanted to do. We followed its longings and thoughts. God was angry with us and everyone else because of the kind of people we were.

[4]But God loves us deeply. He is full of mercy. [5]So he gave us new

life because of what Christ has done. He gave us life even when we were dead in sin. God's grace has saved you.

⁶God raised us up with Christ. He has seated us with him in his heavenly kingdom because we belong to Christ Jesus. ⁷He has done it to show the riches of his grace for all time to come. His grace can't be compared with anything else. He has shown it by being kind to us because of what Christ Jesus has done.

⁸God's grace has saved you because of your faith in Christ. Your salvation doesn't come from anything you do. It is God's gift. ⁹It is not based on anything you have done. No one can brag about earning it.

¹⁰God made us. He created us to belong to Christ Jesus. Now we can do good things. Long ago God prepared them for us to do.

God's New Family

¹¹You who are not Jews by birth, here is what I want you to remember. You are called "uncircumcised" by those who call themselves "circumcised." But they have only been circumcised in their bodies by human hands.

¹²Before you believed in Christ, you were separated from him. You were not considered to be citizens of Israel. You were not included in what the covenants promised. You were without hope and without God in the world. ¹³At one time you were far away from God. But now you belong to Christ Jesus. He spilled his blood for you. That has brought you near to God.

¹⁴Christ himself is our peace. He has made Jews and non-Jews into one group of people. He has destroyed the hatred that was like a wall between us. ¹⁵Through his body on the cross, Christ put an end to the law with all its commands and rules. He wanted to create one new group of people out of the two. He wanted to make peace between them.

¹⁶He planned to bring both of them as one body back to God because of the cross. Christ put their hatred to death on that cross.

2:8 God's grace has saved you because of your faith in Christ. Your salvation doesn't come from anything you do. It is God's gift.

¹⁷He came and preached peace to you who were far away. He also preached peace to those who were near. ¹⁸Through Christ we both come to the Father by the power of one Holy Spirit.

¹⁹So you are no longer strangers and outsiders. You are citizens together with God's people. You are members of God's family.

²⁰You are a building that is built on the apostles and prophets. They are the foundation. Christ Jesus himself is the most important stone in the building. ²¹The whole building is held together by him. It rises to become a holy temple because it belongs to the Lord.

²²And because you belong to him, you too are being built together. You are being made into a house where God lives through his Spirit.

Paul Is the Messenger to Non-Jews

3 I, Paul, am a prisoner because of Christ Jesus. I am in prison because of my work among you who are not Jews.

²I am sure you have heard that God appointed me to share his grace with you. ³I'm talking about the mystery God showed me. I have already written a little about it. ⁴By reading it you will be able to understand what I know about the mystery of Christ.

⁵The mystery was not made known to people of other times. But now the Holy Spirit has made it known to God's holy apostles and prophets.

⁶Here is the mystery. Because of the good news, God's promises are for non-Jews as well as for Jews. Both groups are parts of one body. They share in the promise. It belongs to them because they belong to Christ Jesus.

⁷I now serve the good news because God gave me his grace. His power is at work in me. ⁸I am by far the least important of all of God's people. But he gave me the grace to preach to the non-Jews about the wonderful riches that Christ gives.

⁹God told me to make clear to everyone how the mystery came about. In times past it was kept hidden in the mind of God, who created all things. ¹⁰He wanted the rulers and authorities in the

GREAT VERSE —TO— REMEMBER   **2:19** You are no longer strangers and outsiders ... You are members of God's family.

heavenly world to come to know his great wisdom. The church would make it known to them.

[11]That was God's plan from the beginning. He has worked it out through Christ Jesus our Lord. [12]Through him and through faith in him we can approach God. We can come to him freely. We can come without fear.

[13]So here is what I'm asking you to do. Don't lose hope because I am suffering for you. It will lead to the time when God will give you his glory.

Paul Prays for God's People

[14]I bow in prayer to the Father because of my work among you. [15]From the Father his whole family in heaven and on earth gets its name.

[16]I pray that he will use his glorious riches to make you strong. May his Holy Spirit give you his power deep down inside you. [17]Then Christ will live in your hearts because you believe in him.

And I pray that your love will have deep roots. I pray that it will have a strong foundation. [18]May you have power with all God's people to understand Christ's love. May you know how wide and long and high and deep it is. [19]And may you know his love, even though it can't be known completely. Then you will be filled with everything God has for you.

[20]God is able to do far more than we could ever ask for or imagine. He does everything by his power that is working in us. [21]Give him glory in the church and in Christ Jesus. Give him glory through all time and for ever and ever. Amen.

The Body of Christ Is One

4 I am a prisoner because of the Lord. So I am asking you to live a life worthy of what God chose you for.

[2]Don't be proud at all. Be completely gentle. Be patient. Put up with one another in love. [3]The Holy Spirit makes you one in every way. So try your best to remain as one. Let peace keep you together.

GREAT VERSE —TO— REMEMBER

4:2 Don't be proud at all. Be completely gentle. Be patient. Put up with one another in love.

⁴There is one body. There is one Spirit. You were appointed to one hope when you were chosen. ⁵There is one Lord. There is one faith and one baptism. ⁶There is one God and Father of all. He is over everything. He is through everything. He is in everything.

⁷But each one of us has received a gift of grace, just as Christ wanted us to have it. ⁸That is why Scripture says,

> "When he went up to his place on high,
>> he led a line of prisoners.
> He gave gifts to people." *(Psalm 68:18)*

⁹What does "he went up" mean? It can only mean that he also came down to the lower, earthly places. ¹⁰The One who came down is the same as the One who went up higher than all the heavens. He did it in order to fill all of creation. ¹¹He is the One who gave some the gift to be apostles. He gave some the gift to be prophets. He gave some the gift of preaching the good news. And he gave some the gift to be pastors and teachers. ¹²He did it so that they might prepare God's people to serve. If they do, the body of Christ will be built up.

¹³That will continue until we all become one in the faith and in the knowledge of God's Son. Then we will be grown up in the faith. We will receive everything that Christ has for us.

¹⁴We will no longer be babies in the faith. We won't be like ships tossed around by the waves. We won't be blown here and there by every new teaching. We won't be blown around by the cleverness and tricks of people who try to hide their evil plans. ¹⁵Instead, we will speak the truth in love. We will grow up into Christ in every way.

He is the Head. ¹⁶He makes the whole body grow and build itself up in love. Under the control of Christ, each part of the body does its work. It supports the other parts. In that way, the body is joined and held together.

Living as Children of Light

¹⁷Here is what I'm telling you. I am speaking for the Lord as I warn you. You must no longer live like those who aren't Jews. Their thoughts don't have any purpose. ¹⁸They can't understand the truth. They are separated from the life of God. That is because they don't know him. And they don't know him because their hearts are stubborn.

¹⁹They have lost all feeling for what is right. They have given themselves over to the evil pleasures of their bodies. They take

part in every kind of unclean act. And they always long for more.

²⁰But that is not what you have learned about Christ. ²¹I'm sure you heard of him. I'm sure you were taught by him. What you learned was the truth about Jesus.

²²You were taught not to live the way you used to. You must get rid of your old way of life. That's because it is polluted by longing for things that lead you down the wrong path.

²³You were taught to be made new in your thinking. ²⁴You were taught to start living a new life. It is created to be truly good and holy, just as God is.

²⁵So each of you must get rid of your lying. Speak the truth to your neighbor. We are all parts of one body.

²⁶Scripture says, "When you are angry, do not sin." *(Psalm 4:4)* Do not let the sun go down while you are still angry. ²⁷Don't give the devil a chance.

²⁸Those who have been stealing must never steal again. Instead, they must work. They must do something useful with their own hands. Then they will have something to give to people in need.

²⁹Don't let any evil talk come out of your mouths. Say only what will help to build others up and meet their needs. Then what you say will help those who listen.

³⁰Do not make God's Holy Spirit sad. He marked you with a seal for the day when God will set you completely free.

³¹Get rid of all hard feelings, anger and rage. Stop all fighting and lying. Put away every form of hatred. ³²Be kind and tender to one another. Forgive each other, just as God forgave you because of what Christ has done.

5 You are the children that God dearly loves. So be just like him. ²Lead a life of love, just as Christ did. He loved us. He gave himself up for us. He was a sweet-smelling offering and sacrifice to God.

³There should not be even a hint of sexual sin among you. Don't do anything unclean. And do not always want more and more. Things like that are not what God's holy people should do.

⁴There must not be any unclean speech or foolish talk or dirty

---

GREAT VERSE — TO — REMEMBER

4:32 Be kind and tender to one another. Forgive each other, just as God forgave you.

jokes. All of them are out of place. Instead, you should give thanks.

⁵Here is what you can be sure of. Those who give themselves over to sexual sins are lost. So are people whose lives are not pure. The same is true of those who always want more and more. People who do those things might as well worship statues of gods. No one who does them will receive a share in the kingdom of Christ and of God.

⁶Don't let anyone fool you with words that don't mean anything. Because of things like that, God is angry with those who don't obey. ⁷So don't go along with people like that.

⁸At one time you were in the dark. But now you are in the light because of what the Lord has done. Live like children of the light. ⁹The light produces what is completely good, right and true. ¹⁰Find out what pleases the Lord.

¹¹Have nothing to do with the acts of darkness. They don't produce anything good. Show what they are really like. ¹²It is shameful even to talk about what people who don't obey do in secret.

¹³But everything the light shines on can be seen. ¹⁴Light makes everything clear. That is why it is said,

> "Wake up, sleeper.
>   Rise from the dead.
> Then Christ will shine on you."

¹⁵So be very careful how you live. Do not live like people who aren't wise. Live like people who are wise. ¹⁶Make the most of every opportunity. The days are evil. ¹⁷So don't be foolish. Instead, understand what the Lord wants.

¹⁸Don't fill yourself up with wine. Getting drunk will lead to wild living. Instead, be filled with the Holy Spirit.

¹⁹Speak to each other with psalms, hymns and spiritual songs. Sing and make music in your heart to the Lord. ²⁰Always give thanks to God the Father for everything. Give thanks to him in the name of our Lord Jesus Christ.

²¹Follow the lead of one another because of your respect for Christ.

Wives and Husbands

²²Wives, follow the lead of your husbands as you follow the Lord. ²³The husband is the head of the wife, just as Christ is the head of the church. The church is Christ's body. He is its Savior.

²⁴The church follows the lead of Christ. In the same way, wives should follow the lead of their husbands in everything.

²⁵Husbands, love your wives. Love them just as Christ loved the church. He gave himself up for her. ²⁶He did it to make her holy. He made her clean by washing her with water and the word. ²⁷He did it to bring her to himself as a brightly shining church. He wants a church that has no stain or wrinkle or any other flaw. He wants a church that is holy and without blame.

²⁸In the same way, husbands should love their wives. They should love them as they love their own bodies. Any man who loves his wife loves himself. ²⁹After all, people have never hated their own bodies. Instead, they feed and care for their bodies. And that is what Christ does for the church. ³⁰We are parts of his body.

³¹Scripture says, "That's why a man will leave his father and mother and be joined to his wife. The two will become one." *(Genesis 2:24)* ³²That is a deep mystery. But I'm talking about Christ and the church.

³³A husband also must love his wife. He must love her just as he loves himself. And a wife must respect her husband.

Children and Parents

6 Children, obey your parents as believers in the Lord. Obey them because it's the right thing to do. ²Scripture says, "Honor your father and mother." That is the first commandment that has a promise. ³"Then things will go well with you. You will live a long time on the earth." *(Deuteronomy 5:16)*

⁴Fathers, don't make your children angry. Instead, train them and teach them the ways of the Lord as you raise them.

Slaves and Masters

⁵Slaves, obey your masters here on earth. Respect them and honor them with a heart that is true. Obey them just as you would obey Christ. ⁶Don't obey them only to please them when they are watching. Do it because you are slaves of Christ. Be sure your heart does what God wants.

⁷Serve your masters with all your heart. Work as if you were not serving people but the Lord. ⁸You know that the Lord will give you a reward. He will give to each of you in keeping with the good you do. It doesn't matter whether you are slaves or free.

⁹Masters, treat your slaves in the same way. When you warn them, don't be too hard on them. You know that the One who

is their Master and yours is in heaven. And he treats everyone the same.

God's Armor

[10]Finally, let the Lord make you strong. Depend on his mighty power. [11]Put on all of God's armor. Then you can stand firm against the devil's evil plans. [12]Our fight is not against human beings. It is against the rulers, the authorities and the powers of this dark world. It is against the spiritual forces of evil in the heavenly world.

[13]So put on all of God's armor. Evil days will come. But you will be able to stand up to anything. And after you have done everything you can, you will still be standing.

[14]So stand firm. Put the belt of truth around your waist. Put the armor of godliness on your chest. [15]Wear on your feet what will prepare you to tell the good news of peace. [16]Also, pick up the shield of faith. With it you can put out all of the flaming arrows of the evil one. [17]Put on the helmet of salvation. And take the sword of the Holy Spirit. The sword is God's word.

[18]At all times, pray by the power of the Spirit. Pray all kinds of prayers. Be watchful, so that you can pray. Always keep on praying for all of God's people.

[19]Pray also for me. Pray that when I open my mouth, the right words will be given to me. Then I can be bold as I tell the mystery of the good news. [20]Because of the good news, I am being held by chains as the Lord's messenger. So pray that I will be bold as I preach the good news. That's what I should do.

Final Greetings

[21]Tychicus is a dear brother. He is faithful in serving the Lord. He will tell you everything about me. Then you will know how I am and what I am doing. [22]That's why I am sending him to you.

6:18 Pray by the power of the Spirit. Pray all kinds of prayers. Be watchful, so that you can pray. Always keep on praying for all of God's people.

I want you to know how we are. And I want him to cheer you up.

[23]May God the Father and the Lord Jesus Christ give peace to the brothers and sisters. May they also give them love and faith.

[24]May grace be given to everyone who loves our Lord Jesus Christ with a love that will never die.

Philippians

Why Was This Book Written? Paul wrote this letter from Rome. He wrote to his friends in Philippi. They had sent Paul a gift. A man named Epaphroditus brought it to Paul. Epaphroditus became sick while visiting Paul. Paul wrote this letter to tell them that Epaphroditus was feeling better. He thanked his friends for the gift.

What Is This Book About? Paul wrote this letter from prison. It is full of happy things. Paul knew his friends at Philippi loved him. They helped him when they could. He was happy that he could work for the Lord. It did not matter that he was in prison. He could still tell people about Jesus.

What Is in This Book?

1 We, Paul and Timothy, are writing this letter. We serve Christ Jesus.

We are sending this letter to you, all of God's people in Philippi. You belong to Christ Jesus. We are also sending this letter to your leaders and deacons.

²May God our Father and the Lord Jesus Christ give you grace and peace.

Paul Prays and Gives Thanks

³I thank my God every time I remember you. ⁴In all my prayers for all of you, I always pray with joy. ⁵I am happy because you have joined me in spreading the good news. You have done so from the first day until now.

⁶I am sure that the One who began a good work in you will carry it on until it is completed. That will be on the day Christ Jesus returns.

⁷It is right for me to feel this way about all of you. I love you with all my heart. I may be held by chains, or I may be standing up for the truth of the good news. Either way, all of you share in God's grace together with me. ⁸God can give witness that I long for all of you. I love you with the love that Christ Jesus gives.

⁹I pray that your love will grow more and more. And let it be based on knowledge and understanding. ¹⁰Then you will be able to know what is best. You will be pure and without blame until the day Christ returns. ¹¹You will be filled with the fruit of right living produced by Jesus Christ. All of those things bring glory and praise to God.

Paul Honors Christ in Prison

¹²Brothers and sisters, here is what I want you to know. What has happened to me has really helped to spread the good news. ¹³One thing has become clear. I am being held by chains because

---

1:6 I am sure that the One who began a good work in you will carry it on until it is completed.

of my stand for Christ. All of the palace guards and everyone else know it.

[14]Because I am being held by chains, most of the believers in the Lord have become bolder. They now speak God's word more boldly and without fear.

[15]It's true that some preach about Christ because they are jealous. But others preach about Christ to help me in my work. [16]The last group acts out of love. They know I have been put here to stand up for the good news. [17]But the others preach about Christ only to get ahead. They are not honest and true. They think they can stir up trouble for me while I am being held by chains.

[18]But what does it matter? Here is the important thing. Whether for reasons that are right or wrong, Christ is being preached about. That makes me very glad.

And I will continue to be glad. [19]I know that you are praying for me. I also know that the Spirit of Jesus Christ will help me. So no matter what happens, I'm sure I will still be saved.

[20]I completely expect and hope that I won't be ashamed in any way. I'm sure I will be brave enough. Now as always Christ will be lifted high through my body. He will be lifted up whether I live or die.

[21]For me, life finds all of its meaning in Christ. Death also has its benefits.

[22]Suppose I go on living in my body. Then I will be able to carry on my work. It will bear a lot of fruit. But what should I choose? I don't know. [23]I can't decide between the two. I long to leave this world and be with Christ. That is better by far.

[24]But it is more important for you that I stay alive. [25]I'm sure of that. So I know I will remain with you. And I will continue with all of you to help you grow and be joyful in what you have been taught. [26]I'm sure I will be with you again. Then your joy in Christ Jesus will be greater than ever because of me.

[27]No matter what happens, live in a way that brings honor to the good news about Christ. Then I will know that you stand firm with one purpose. I may come and see you or only hear about you. But I will know that you work together as one person. And I will know that you work to spread the teachings of the good news.

[28]So don't be afraid in any way of those who oppose you. That will show them that they will be destroyed and that you will be saved. That's what God will do.

²⁹Here is what he has given you to do for Christ. You must not only believe in him. You must also suffer for him.

³⁰You are going through the same struggle you saw me go through. As you have heard, I am still struggling.

Thinking Like Christ

2 Are you cheerful because you belong to Christ? Does his love comfort you? Is the Holy Spirit your companion? Has Christ been gentle and loving toward you? ²Then make my joy complete by agreeing with each other. Have the same love. Be one in spirit and purpose.

³Don't do anything only to get ahead. Don't do it because you are proud. Instead, be free of pride. Think of others as better than yourselves.

⁴None of you should look out just for your own good. You should also look out for the good of others.

⁵You should think in the same way Christ Jesus does.

⁶In his very nature he was God.
But he did not think that being equal with God was
something he should hold on to.
⁷Instead, he made himself nothing.
He took on the very nature of a servant.
He was made in human form.
⁸He appeared as a human being.
He came down to the lowest level.
He obeyed God completely, even though it led to his
death.
In fact, he died on a cross.
⁹So God lifted him up to the highest place.
He gave him the name that is above every name.
¹⁰When the name of Jesus is spoken, everyone's knee will
bow to worship him.

2:3 Don't do anything only to get ahead. Don't do it because you are proud. Instead, be free of pride. Think of others as better than yourselves.

Every knee in heaven and on earth and under the
earth will bow to worship him.
¹¹Everyone's mouth will say that Jesus Christ is Lord.
And God the Father will receive the glory.

Living Like Christ

¹²My dear friends, you have always obeyed God. You obeyed
while I was with you. And you have obeyed even more while I
am not with you. So continue to work out your own salvation.
Do it with fear and trembling. ¹³God is working in you. He wants
your plans and your acts to be in keeping with his good purpose.

¹⁴Do everything without finding fault or arguing. ¹⁵Then you
will be pure and without blame. You will be children of God
without fault in a sinful and evil world. Among the people of the
world you shine like stars in the heavens. ¹⁶You shine as you hold
out to them the word of life. So I can brag about you on the day
Christ returns. I can be happy that I didn't run or work for
nothing.

¹⁷But my life might even be poured out like a drink offering on
your sacrifices. I'm talking about the way you serve because you
believe. Even so, I am glad. I am joyful with all of you. ¹⁸So you
too should be glad and joyful with me.

Timothy and Epaphroditus

¹⁹I hope to send Timothy to you soon if the Lord Jesus allows
it. Then I will be cheered up when I receive news about you. ²⁰I
have no one else like Timothy. He truly cares about how you are
doing.

²¹All the others are looking out for their own interests. They are
not looking out for the interests of Jesus Christ. ²²But you know
that Timothy has proved himself. He has served with me like a
son with his father in spreading the good news.

²³So I hope to send him as soon as I see how things go with me.
²⁴And I'm sure I myself will come soon if the Lord allows it.

²⁵But I think it's necessary to send Epaphroditus back to you. He

GREAT VERSE —TO— REMEMBER

2:14-15 Do everything without
finding fault or arguing. Then you
will be pure and without blame.

is my brother in the Lord. He is a worker and a soldier of Christ together with me. He is also your messenger. You sent him to take care of my needs. ²⁶He longs for all of you. He is troubled because you heard he was sick.

²⁷He was very sick. In fact, he almost died. But God had mercy on him. He also had mercy on me. God spared me sadness after sadness. ²⁸So I want even more to send him to you. Then when you see him again, you will be glad. And I won't worry so much.

²⁹Welcome him as a brother in the Lord with great joy. Honor people like him. ³⁰He almost died for the work of Christ. He put his life in danger to make up for the help you couldn't give me.

Do Not Trust Human Nature

3 Finally, my brothers and sisters, be joyful because you belong to the Lord. It is no trouble for me to write about some important matters to you again. If you know about them, you will have a safe path to follow.

²Watch out for those dogs. They do evil things. When they circumcise, it is nothing more than a useless cutting of the body.

³But we have been truly circumcised. We worship God by the power of his Spirit. We brag about what Christ Jesus has done. We don't put our trust in our weak human nature.

⁴I have many reasons to trust in my human nature. Others may think they have reasons to trust in theirs. But I have even more. ⁵I was circumcised on the eighth day. I am part of the people of Israel. I am from the tribe of Benjamin. I am a pure Hebrew. As far as the law is concerned, I am a Pharisee. ⁶As far as being committed is concerned, I opposed and attacked the church. As far as keeping the Law is concerned, I kept it perfectly.

⁷I thought things like that were for my benefit. But now I consider them to be nothing because of Christ. ⁸Even more, I consider everything to be nothing compared to knowing Christ Jesus my Lord. To know him is the best thing of all. Because of him I have lost everything. But I consider all of it to be garbage so I can get to know Christ. ⁹I want to be joined to him.

For me, being right with God does not come from the law. It

3:1 Be joyful because you belong to the Lord.

comes because I believe in Christ. It comes from God. It is received by faith.

[10]I want to know Christ better. I want to know the power that raised him from the dead. I want to share in his sufferings. I want to become like him by sharing in his death. [11]Then by God's grace I will rise from the dead.

Moving on Toward the Goal

[12]I have not yet received all of those things. I have not yet been made perfect. But I move on to take hold of what Christ Jesus took hold of me for.

[13]Brothers and sisters, I don't consider that I have taken hold of it yet. But here is the one thing I do. I forget what is behind me. I push hard toward what is ahead of me. [14]I move on toward the goal to win the prize. God has appointed me to win it. The heavenly prize is Christ Jesus himself.

[15]All of us who are grown up in the faith should see things that way. Maybe you think differently about something. But God will make it clear to you. [16]Only let us live up to what we have already reached.

[17]Brothers and sisters, join with others in following my example. Pay close attention to those who live in keeping with the pattern we gave you.

[18]I have told you those things many times before. Now I say it again with tears in my eyes. Many people live like enemies of the cross of Christ. [19]The only thing they have coming to them is death. Their stomach is their god. They brag about what they should be ashamed of. They think only about earthly things.

[20]But we are citizens of heaven. And we can hardly wait for a Savior from there. He is the Lord Jesus Christ. [21]He has the power to bring everything under his control. By his power he will change our earthly bodies. They will become like his glorious body.

4 My brothers and sisters, that is how you should stand firm in the Lord's strength. I love you and long for you. Dear friends, you are my joy and my crown.

Do What Is Best

[2]Here is what I'm asking Euodia and Syntyche to do. I want them to agree with each other because they belong to the Lord.

[3]My true companion, here is what I ask you to do. Help those women. They have served at my side. They have helped me

spread the good news. So have Clement and the rest of those who have worked together with me. Their names are all written in the book of life.

⁴Always be joyful because you belong to the Lord. I will say it again. Be joyful. ⁵Let everyone know how gentle you are. The Lord is coming soon.

⁶Don't worry about anything. Instead, tell God about everything. Ask and pray. Give thanks to him. ⁷Then God's peace will watch over your hearts and your minds because you belong to Christ Jesus. God's peace can never be completely understood.

⁸Finally, my brothers and sisters, always think about what is true. Think about what is noble, right and pure. Think about what is lovely and worthy of respect. If anything is excellent or worthy of praise, think about those kinds of things. ⁹Do what you have learned or received or heard from me. Follow my example.

The God who gives peace will be with you.

Paul Gives Thanks for Help Received

¹⁰At last you are concerned about me again. That makes me very happy. We belong to the Lord. I know that you have been concerned. But you had no chance to show it.

¹¹I'm not saying that because I need anything. I have learned to be content no matter what happens to me. ¹²I know what it's like not to have what I need. I also know what it's like to have more than I need. I have learned the secret of being content no matter what happens. I am content whether I am well fed or hungry. I am content whether I have more than enough or not enough. ¹³I can do everything by the power of Christ. He gives me strength.

¹⁴But it was good of you to share in my troubles. ¹⁵And you believers at Philippi know what happened when I left Macedonia. Not one church helped me in the matter of giving

GREAT VERSE —TO— REMEMBER

4:8 Always think about what is true. Think about what is noble, right and pure ... If anything is excellent or worthy of praise, think about those kinds of things.

and receiving. You were the only one that did. That was in the early days when you first heard the good news. [16]Even when I was in Thessalonica, you sent me help when I needed it. You did it again and again.

[17]I'm not looking for a gift. I'm looking for what is best for you. [18]I have received my full pay, and even more than that. I have everything I need. That's because Epaphroditus brought me the gifts you sent. They are a sweet-smelling offering. They are a gift that God accepts. He is pleased with it.

[19]My God will meet all your needs. He will meet them in keeping with his wonderful riches that come to you because you belong to Christ Jesus.

[20]Give glory to our God and Father for ever and ever. Amen.

Final Greetings

[21]Greet all of God's people. They belong to Christ Jesus. The brothers and sisters who are with me send greetings. [22]All of God's people here send you greetings. Most of all, those who live in the palace of Caesar send you greetings.

[23]May the grace of the Lord Jesus Christ be with your spirit. Amen.

Colossians

Why Was This Book Written? Paul wrote this letter from a Roman prison. Paul wrote this letter because of false teachers at Colosse. They said Jesus was not God. They said people had to follow special rules. They said they must worship angels too.

What Is This Book About? Paul wrote the book of Colossians to tell believers the truth. The false teachers were wrong. Paul taught that Jesus is God. Paul said that believing in Jesus and his death saves us from our sins. We are free from people's rules if we believe in Jesus.

What Is in This Book?

1 I, Paul, am writing this letter. I am an apostle of Christ Jesus just as God planned. Our brother Timothy joins me in writing.

²We are sending this letter to you, our brothers and sisters in Colosse. You belong to Christ. You are holy and faithful.

May God our Father give you grace and peace.

Paul Prays and Gives Thanks

³We always thank God, the Father of our Lord Jesus Christ, when we pray for you. ⁴We thank him because we have heard about your faith in Christ Jesus. We have also heard that you love all of God's people.

⁵Your faith and love are based on the hope you have. What you hope for is stored up for you in heaven. You have already heard about it. You were told about it when the message of truth was given to you. I'm talking about the good news ⁶that has come to you.

All over the world the good news is bearing fruit and growing. It has been doing that among you since the day you heard it. That is when you understood God's grace in all its truth.

⁷You learned the good news from Epaphras. He is dear to us. He serves Christ together with us. He faithfully works for Christ and for us among you. ⁸He also told us about your love that comes from the Holy Spirit.

⁹That's why we have not stopped praying for you. We have been praying for you since the day we heard about you. We have been asking God to fill you with the knowledge of what he wants. We pray that he will give you spiritual wisdom and understanding.

¹⁰We pray that you will lead a life that is worthy of the Lord. We pray that you will please him in every way. So we want you to bear fruit in every good thing you do. We want you to grow to know God better. ¹¹We want you to be very strong, in keeping with his glorious power. We want you to be patient. Never give up. Be joyful ¹²as you give thanks to the Father.

He has made you fit to share with all his people. You will all receive a share in the kingdom of light.

¹³He has saved us from the kingdom of darkness. He has brought us into the kingdom of the Son he loves. ¹⁴Because of what the Son has done, we have been set free. Because of him, all of our sins have been forgiven.

Christ Is Far Above Everything

[15]Christ is the exact likeness of God, who can't be seen. He is first, and he is over all of creation. [16]All things were created by him. He created everything in heaven and on earth. He created everything that can be seen and everything that can't be seen. He created kings, powers, rulers and authorities. Everything was created by him and for him. [17]Before anything was created, he was already there. He holds everything together.

[18]And he is the head of the body, which is the church. He is the beginning. He is the first to be raised from the dead. That happened so that he would be far above everything. [19]God was pleased to have his whole nature living in Christ. [20]God was pleased to bring all things back to himself because of what Christ has done. That includes all things on earth and in heaven. God made peace through Christ's blood, through his death on the cross.

[21]At one time you were separated from God. You were enemies in your minds because of your evil ways. [22]But because Christ died, God has brought you back to himself. Christ's death has made you holy in God's sight. So now you don't have any flaw. You are free from blame.

[23]But you must keep your faith steady and firm. Don't move away from the hope that the good news holds out to you. It is the good news that you heard. It has been preached to every creature under heaven. I, Paul, now serve the good news.

Paul's Work for the Church

[24]I am happy because of what was suffered for you. And in my body I fill up my share in Christ's sufferings. I do it for his body, which is the church. [25]I serve the church. God appointed me to bring all of his word to you.

[26]That word contains the mystery that has been hidden for many ages. But now it has been made known to God's people. [27]God has chosen to make known to them the glorious riches of that mystery. He has made it known among those who aren't

GREAT VERSE — TO — REMEMBER

1:15 Christ is the exact likeness of God, who can't be seen. He is first, and he is over all of creation.

Jews. And here is what it is. Christ is in you. He is your hope of glory.

²⁸We preach about him. With all the wisdom we have, we warn and teach everyone. When we bring them to God, we want them to be perfect as people who belong to Christ.

²⁹That's what I'm working for. I work hard with all of Christ's strength. His strength works powerfully in me.

2 I want you to know how hard I am working for you. I'm concerned for those who are in Laodicea. I'm also concerned for everyone who has not met me in person. ²I want their hearts to be made cheerful and strong. I want them to be joined together in love. Then their understanding will be rich and complete. They will know the mystery of God. That mystery is Christ.

³All the treasures of wisdom and knowledge are hidden in him.

⁴But I don't want anyone to fool you with fast talk that only sounds good. ⁵So even though I am away from you in body, I am with you in spirit. I am glad to see that you are doing everything in good order. And I am happy that your faith in Christ is so strong.

Freedom From Human Rules

⁶You received Christ Jesus as Lord. So keep on living in him. ⁷Have your roots in him. Build yourselves up in him. Grow strong in what you believe, just as you were taught. Be more thankful than ever before.

⁸Make sure no one captures you. They will try to capture you by using false reasoning that has no meaning. Their ideas depend on human teachings. They also depend on the basic things the people of this world believe. They don't depend on Christ.

⁹God's whole nature is living in Christ in human form. ¹⁰Because you belong to Christ, you have everything you need. He is the ruler over every power and authority.

¹¹When you received Christ, you were also circumcised by putting away your sinful nature. Human hands didn't circumcise you. Christ did.

2:6-7 You received Christ Jesus as Lord. So keep on living in him. Have your roots in him.

¹²When you were baptized, you were buried together with him. You were raised to life together with him by believing in God's power. God raised Jesus from the dead.

¹³At one time you were dead in your sins. Your sinful nature was not circumcised. But God gave you new life together with Christ. He forgave us all of our sins.

¹⁴He wiped out the written Law with its rules. The Law was against us. It opposed us. He took it away and nailed it to the cross. ¹⁵He took away the weapons of the powers and authorities. He made a public show of them. He won the battle over them by dying on the cross.

¹⁶So don't let anyone judge you because of what you eat or drink. Don't let anyone judge you about holy days. I'm talking about special feasts and New Moons and Sabbath days. ¹⁷They are only a shadow of the things that were going to come. But what is real is found in Christ.

¹⁸Some people enjoy pretending they aren't proud. They worship angels. But don't let people like that hold you back from winning the prize. They tell you every little thing about what they have seen. Their minds are not guided by the Holy Spirit. So they are proud of their useless ideas.

¹⁹They aren't connected to the Head. But the whole body grows from the Head. The muscles and tendons hold the body together. And God causes it to grow.

²⁰The people of the world believe certain basic things. You died with Christ as far as things like that are concerned. So why do you act as if you still belong to the world? Here are the rules you follow. ²¹"Do not handle! Do not taste! Do not touch!" ²²Rules like that are all going to die out as time goes by. They are only based on human rules and teachings.

²³It is true that those rules seem wise. Because of them, people give themselves over to their own kind of worship. They pretend they aren't proud. They treat their bodies very badly. But rules like that don't help. They don't stop people from chasing after sinful pleasures.

GREAT VERSE —TO— REMEMBER

3:2 Think about things that are in heaven. Don't think about things that are on earth.

Rules for Holy Living

3 You have been raised up with Christ. So think about things that are in heaven. That is where Christ is. He is sitting at God's right hand. ²Think about things that are in heaven. Don't think about things that are on earth.

³You died. Now your life is hidden with Christ in God. ⁴Christ is your life. When he appears again, you also will appear with him in heaven's glory.

⁵So put to death anything that belongs to your earthly nature. Get rid of your sexual sins and unclean acts. Don't let your feelings get out of control. Remove from your life all evil longings. Stop always wanting more and more. You might as well be worshiping statues of gods. ⁶God's anger is going to come because of those things. ⁷That's the way you lived at one time in your life.

⁸But now here are the kinds of things you must get rid of. You must put away anger, rage, hate and lies. Let no dirty words come out of your mouths. ⁹Don't lie to each other.

You have gotten rid of your old way of life and its habits. ¹⁰You have started living a new life. It is being made new so that what you know has the Creator's likeness.

¹¹Here there is no Greek or Jew. There is no difference between those who are circumcised and those who are not. There is no rude outsider, or even a Scythian. There is no slave or free person. But Christ is everything. And he is in everything.

¹²You are God's chosen people. You are holy and dearly loved. So put on tender mercy and kindness as if they were your clothes. Don't be proud. Be gentle and patient. ¹³Put up with each other. Forgive the things you are holding against one another. Forgive, just as the Lord forgave you.

¹⁴And over all of those good things put on love. Love holds them all together perfectly as if they were one.

¹⁵Let the peace that Christ gives rule in your hearts. As parts of one body, you were appointed to live in peace. And be thankful.

¹⁶Let Christ's word live in you like a rich treasure. Teach and correct each other wisely. Sing psalms, hymns and spiritual songs. Sing with thanks in your hearts to God. ¹⁷Do everything you say or do in the name of the Lord Jesus. Always give thanks to God the Father through Christ.

Rules for Christian Families

¹⁸Wives, follow the lead of your husbands. That's what the Lord wants you to do.

¹⁹Husbands, love your wives. Don't be mean to them.
²⁰Children, obey your parents in everything. That pleases the Lord.
²¹Fathers, don't make your children bitter. If you do, they will lose hope.
²²Slaves, obey your earthly masters in everything. Don't do it just to please them when they are watching you. Obey them with an honest heart. Do it out of respect for the Lord.
²³Work at everything you do with all your heart. Work as if you were working for the Lord, not for human masters. ²⁴Work because you know that you will finally receive as a reward what the Lord wants you to have. You are serving the Lord Christ.
²⁵Those who do wrong will be paid back for what they do. God treats everyone the same.

4 Masters, give your slaves what is right and fair. Do it because you know that you also have a Master in heaven.

More Directions

²Spend a lot of time in prayer. Always be watchful and thankful.
³Pray for us too. Pray that God will open a door for our message. Then we can preach the mystery of Christ. Because I preached it, I am being held by chains. ⁴Pray that I will preach it clearly, as I should.
⁵Be wise in the way you act toward outsiders. Make the most of every opportunity. ⁶Let the words you speak always be full of grace. Season them with salt. Then you will know how to answer everyone.

Final Greetings

⁷Tychicus will tell you all the news about me. He is a dear brother. He is a faithful worker. He serves the Lord together with us. ⁸I am sending him to you for one reason. I want you to know what is happening here. I want him to cheer you up and make your hearts strong.

4:5-6 Make the most of every opportunity. Let the words you speak always be full of grace.

⁹He is coming with Onesimus, our faithful and dear brother. He is one of you. They will tell you everything that is happening here.

¹⁰Aristarchus is in prison with me. He sends you his greetings. So does Mark, the cousin of Barnabas. You have been given directions about him. If he comes to you, welcome him. ¹¹Jesus, who is called Justus, also sends greetings. They are the only Jews who work together with me for God's kingdom. They have been a comfort to me.

¹²Epaphras sends greetings. He is one of you. He serves Christ Jesus. He is always praying hard for you. He prays that you will stand firm in holding to all that God has in mind for us. He prays that you will continue to grow in your knowledge of what God wants you to do. He also prays that you will be completely sure about it. ¹³I am happy to tell you that he is working very hard for you. He is also working hard for everyone in Laodicea and Hierapolis.

¹⁴Our dear friend Luke, the doctor, sends greetings. So does Demas.

¹⁵Give my greetings to the brothers and sisters in Laodicea. Also give my greetings to Nympha and the church that meets in her house.

¹⁶After this letter has been read to you, send it on. Be sure that it is also read to the church in Laodicea. And be sure that you read the letter from Laodicea.

¹⁷Tell Archippus, "Be sure that you complete the work the Lord gave you to do."

¹⁸I, Paul, am writing this greeting with my own hand. Remember that I am being held by chains. May grace be with you.

1 Thessalonians

Why Was This Book Written? Paul visited Thessalonica on his second missionary trip. He started a church there. He stayed there for only three weeks. Some Jews became angry at Paul's teaching. Paul had to leave. He wrote this letter to cheer up the friends he left behind. He wanted to teach them more about Jesus.

What Is This Book About? Many Christians in Thessalonica were put in prison. They were beaten too. Paul said that they must not give up faith in Jesus. Paul also taught that Jesus would come again sometime. When Jesus does return all Christians will go to live with him. We must work hard until then.

What Is in This Book?

1 I, Paul, am writing this letter. Silas and Timothy join me in writing.

We are sending this letter to you, the members of the church in Thessalonica. You belong to God the Father and the Lord Jesus Christ.

May grace and peace be given to you.

Paul Gives Thanks

²We always thank God for all of you. We pray for you. ³We never forget you when we pray to our God and Father. Your work is produced by your faith. Your service is the result of your love. Your strength to continue comes from your hope in our Lord Jesus Christ.

⁴Brothers and sisters, you are loved by God. We know that he has chosen you. ⁵Our good news didn't come to you only in words. It came with power. It came with the Holy Spirit's help. He gave us complete faith in what we were preaching. You know how we lived among you for your good.

⁶We and the Lord were your examples. You followed us. You suffered terribly. Even so, you welcomed our message with the joy the Holy Spirit gives. ⁷So you became a model to all the believers in the lands of Macedonia and Achaia.

⁸The Lord's message rang out from you. That was true not only in Macedonia and Achaia. Your faith in God has also become known everywhere. So we don't have to say anything about it. ⁹The believers themselves report the kind of welcome you gave us. They tell about how you turned away from statues of gods to serve the living and true God. ¹⁰They tell about how you are waiting for his Son to come from heaven.

God raised him from the dead. He is Jesus. He saves us from God's anger, and his anger is sure to come.

Paul's Work for God in Thessalonica

2 Brothers and sisters, you know that our visit to you was not a failure. ²You know what happened earlier in the city of

1:3 Your work is produced by your faith. Your service is the result of your love.

Philippi. We suffered, and people treated us badly there. But God gave us the boldness to tell you his good news. We preached to you even though people opposed us strongly.

³The appeal we make is based on truth. It comes from a pure heart. We are not trying to trick you. ⁴In fact, it is just the opposite. God has accepted us to preach. He has trusted us with the good news. We aren't trying to please people. We want to please God. He puts our hearts to the test.

⁵As you know, we never praised you if we didn't mean it. We didn't put on a mask to cover up any sinful longing. God is our witness that this is true. ⁶We were not expecting people to praise us. We were not looking for praise from you or anyone else.

As Christ's apostles, we could have caused you some expense. ⁷But we were gentle among you. We were like a mother caring for her little children. ⁸We loved you so much that we were happy to share with you God's good news. We were also happy to share our lives with you. You had become very special to us.

⁹Brothers and sisters, I am sure you remember how hard we worked. We labored night and day while we preached to you God's good news. We didn't want to cause you any expense.

¹⁰You are witnesses of how we lived among you believers. God is also a witness that we were holy and godly and without blame. ¹¹You know that we treated each of you as a father treats his own children.

¹²We gave you hope and strength. We comforted you. We really wanted you to live in a way that is worthy of God. He chooses you to enter his glorious kingdom.

¹³We never stop thanking God for the way you received his word. You heard it from us. But you didn't accept it as a human word. You accepted it for what it really is. It is God's word. It is at work in you who believe.

¹⁴Brothers and sisters, you became like the members of God's churches in Judea. They are believers in Christ Jesus, just as you are. People in your own country made you suffer. You went through the same things the church members in Judea suffered from the Jews.

¹⁵The Jews who killed the Lord Jesus and the prophets also forced us to leave. They do not please God. They are enemies of everyone. ¹⁶They try to keep us from speaking to those who aren't Jews. The Jews don't want them to be saved. In that way, the Jews always increase their sins to the limit. God's anger has come on them at last.

Paul Longs to See the Believers in Thessalonica

¹⁷Brothers and sisters, we were torn away from you for a short time. We were no longer with you in person, but we kept you in our thoughts. We really longed to see you. So we tried very hard to do so. ¹⁸We wanted to come to you. Again and again I, Paul, wanted to come. But Satan stopped us.

¹⁹What is our hope? What is our joy? When our Lord Jesus returns, what is the crown we will delight in? Isn't it you? ²⁰Yes, you are our glory and our joy.

3 We couldn't wait any longer. So we thought it was best to be left by ourselves in Athens. ²We sent our brother Timothy to give you strength and hope in your faith. He works together with God in spreading the good news about Christ. ³We sent him so that no one would be upset by times of testing.

You know very well that we have to go through them. ⁴In fact, when we were with you, we kept telling you that our enemies would make us suffer. As you know very well, it has turned out that way.

⁵That's the reason I sent someone to find out about your faith. I couldn't wait any longer. I was afraid that Satan might have tempted you in some way. Then our efforts would have been useless.

Timothy Brings a Good Report

⁶But Timothy has come to us from you just now. He has brought good news about your faith and love. He has told us that you always have happy memories of us. He has also said that you long to see us, just as we long to see you.

⁷Brothers and sisters, in all our trouble and suffering your faith cheered us up. ⁸Now we really live, because you are standing firm in the Lord.

⁹How can we thank God enough for you because of all the joy that comes only from our God? ¹⁰Night and day we pray very hard that we will see you again. We want to give you what is missing in your faith.

¹¹Now may our God and Father himself and our Lord Jesus open up a way for us to come to you. ¹²May the Lord make your love grow. May it be like a rising flood. May your love for one another increase. May it also increase for everyone else. May it be just like our love for you. ¹³May the Lord give you strength in your hearts. Then you will be holy and without blame in the

sight of our God and Father. May that be true when our Lord Jesus comes with all his holy ones.

Living in a Way That Pleases God

4 Finally, brothers and sisters, we taught you how to live in a way that pleases God. In fact, that is how you are living. In the name of the Lord Jesus we ask and beg you to do it more and more.

²You know the directions we gave you. They were given by the authority of the Lord Jesus.

³God wants you to be made holy. He wants you to stay away from sexual sins. ⁴He wants all of you to learn to control your own bodies. You must live in a way that is holy. You must live with honor. ⁵Don't long to commit sexual sins like those who don't know God. ⁶None of you should sin against a brother or sister by doing that. You should not take advantage of them. The Lord will punish everyone who commits those kinds of sins. We have already told you and warned you about that. ⁷God chose us to live pure lives. He wants us to be holy.

⁸So if you refuse to accept my teaching, you turn your back on God, not on people. God gives you his Holy Spirit.

⁹We don't need to write to you about love among believers. God himself has taught you to love each other. ¹⁰In fact, you do love all the brothers and sisters all around Macedonia. But we are asking you to love each other more and more.

¹¹Do everything you can to live a quiet life. Mind your own business. Work with your hands, just as we told you to. ¹²Then unbelievers will have respect for your everyday life. And you won't have to depend on anyone.

The Lord Is Coming

¹³Brothers and sisters, we want you to know what happens to those who die. We don't want you to be sad, as other people are. They don't have any hope.

4:11 Do everything you can to live a quiet life. Mind your own business. Work with your hands, just as we told you to.

¹⁴We believe that Jesus died and rose again. When he returns, many who believe in him will have died already. We believe that God will bring them back with Jesus.

¹⁵That agrees with what the Lord has said. When the Lord comes, many of us will still be alive. We tell you that we will certainly not go up before those who have died.

¹⁶The Lord himself will come down from heaven. We will hear a loud command. We will hear the voice of the leader of the angels. We will hear a blast from God's trumpet. Many who believe in Christ will have died already. They will rise first. ¹⁷After that, we who are still alive and are left will be caught up together with them. We will be taken up in the clouds. We will meet the Lord in the air. And we will be with him forever.

¹⁸So cheer each other up with these words of comfort.

5 Brothers and sisters, we don't have to write to you about times and dates. ²You know very well that the day of the Lord will come like a thief in the night. ³People will be saying that everything is peaceful and safe. Then suddenly they will be destroyed. It will happen like birth pains coming on a pregnant woman. None of the people will escape.

⁴Brothers and sisters, you are not in darkness. So that day should not surprise you as a thief would. ⁵All of you are children of the light. You are children of the day. We don't belong to the night. We don't belong to the darkness.

⁶So let us not be like the others. They are asleep. Instead, let us be wide awake and in full control of ourselves.

⁷Those who sleep, sleep at night. Those who get drunk, get drunk at night. ⁸But we belong to the day. So let us control ourselves. Let us put the armor of faith and love on our chest. Let us put on the hope of salvation like a helmet.

⁹God didn't choose us to receive his anger. He chose us to receive salvation because of what our Lord Jesus Christ has done.

¹⁰Jesus died for us. Some will be alive when he comes. Others will be dead. Either way, we will live together with him. ¹¹So cheer each other up with the hope you have. Build each other up. In fact, that's what you are doing.

Final Directions

¹²Brothers and sisters, we ask you to have respect for the godly leaders who work hard among you. They have authority over you. They correct you. ¹³Have a lot of respect for them. Love them because of what they do. Live in peace with each other.

¹⁴Brothers and sisters, we are asking you to warn those who don't want to work. Cheer up those who are shy. Help those who are weak. Put up with everyone. ¹⁵Make sure that nobody pays back one wrong act with another. Always try to be kind to each other and to everyone else.

¹⁶Always be joyful. ¹⁷Never stop praying. ¹⁸Give thanks no matter what happens. God wants you to thank him because you believe in Christ Jesus.

¹⁹Don't put out the Holy Spirit's fire. ²⁰Don't treat prophecies as if they amount to nothing. ²¹Put everything to the test. Hold on to what is good. ²²Stay away from every kind of evil.

²³God is the God who gives peace. May he make you holy through and through. May your whole spirit, soul and body be kept free from blame. May you be without blame from now until our Lord Jesus Christ comes. ²⁴The One who has chosen you is faithful. He will do all these things.

²⁵Brothers and sisters, pray for us. ²⁶Greet all the believers with a holy kiss. ²⁷While the Lord is watching, here is what I command you. Have this letter read to all the believers.

²⁸May the grace of our Lord Jesus Christ be with you.

GREAT VERSE —TO— REMEMBER   **5:16-18** Always be joyful. Never stop praying. Give thanks no matter what happens.

2 Thessalonians

Why Was This Book Written? Paul wrote this letter to the Thessalonians soon after he wrote the first one. They had not done what Paul wanted them to do. They felt Jesus was coming back very soon. They had stopped working. Paul wrote to them again. He told them to keep working and not be lazy.

What Is This Book About? The first letter to the Thessalonians was a happy letter. This letter was not. Paul was not happy with the people. Paul told them to work hard until Jesus came back. He told them what the second coming would be like. Paul called it "the day of the Lord."

What Is in This Book?

1 I, Paul, am writing this letter. Silas and Timothy join me in writing.

We are sending this letter to you, the members of the church in Thessalonica. You belong to God our Father and the Lord Jesus Christ.

²May God the Father and the Lord Jesus Christ give you grace and peace.

Paul Prays and Gives Thanks

³Brothers and sisters, we should always thank God for you. That is only right, because your faith is growing more and more. The love you all have for each other is increasing. ⁴So among God's churches we brag about the fact that you don't give up easily. We brag about your faith in all the suffering and testing you are going through.

⁵All of this proves that when God judges, he is fair. So you will be considered worthy to enter God's kingdom. You are suffering for his kingdom.

⁶God is fair. He will pay back trouble to those who give you trouble. ⁷He will help you who are troubled. And he will also help us.

All of those things will happen when the Lord Jesus appears from heaven. He will come in blazing fire. He will come with the angels who are given the power to do what God wants. ⁸He will punish those who don't know God. He will punish those who don't obey the good news about our Lord Jesus. ⁹They will be destroyed forever. They will be shut out of heaven. They will never see the glory of the Lord's power.

¹⁰All of those things will happen when he comes. On that day his glory will be seen in his holy people. Everyone who has believed will be amazed when they see him. That includes you, because you believed the witness we gave you.

¹¹Keeping this in mind, we never stop praying for you. Our God has chosen you. We pray that he will consider you worthy of his

GREAT VERSE —TO— REMEMBER

1:11 Our God has chosen you. We pray that he will consider you worthy of his choice.

choice. We pray that by his power he will make every good thing you have planned come true. We pray that he will make perfect all that you have done by faith. [12]We pray this so that the name of our Lord Jesus will receive glory through what you have done. We also pray that you will receive glory through what he has done. We pray all these things in keeping with the grace of our God and the Lord Jesus Christ.

The Man of Sin

2 Brothers and sisters, we want to ask you something. It has to do with the coming of our Lord Jesus Christ. It concerns the time when we will go to be with him.

[2]What if you receive a prophecy, report or letter that is supposed to have come from us? What if it says that the day of the Lord has already come? If it does, we ask you not to become easily upset or alarmed.

[3]Don't let anyone trick you in any way. That day will not come until people rise up against God. It will not come until the man of sin appears. He is a marked man. He is sentenced to be destroyed. [4]He will oppose everything that is called God. He will oppose everything that is worshiped. He will give himself power over everything. He will set himself up in God's temple. He will announce that he himself is God.

[5]Don't you remember? When I was with you, I used to tell you those things.

[6]Now you know what is holding the man of sin back. He is held back so that he can make his appearance at the right time. [7]The secret power of sin is already at work. But the one who now holds that power back will keep doing it until he is taken out of the way.

[8]Then the man of sin will appear. The Lord Jesus will overthrow him with the breath of his mouth. The glorious brightness of Jesus' coming will destroy the man of sin.

[9]The coming of the man of sin will be Satan's work. His work will be seen in all kinds of fake miracles, signs and wonders. [10]It will be seen in every kind of evil that fools people who are dying. They are dying because they refuse to love the truth. The truth would save them.

[11]So God will fool them completely. Then they will believe the lie. [12]Many will not believe the truth. They will take pleasure in evil. They will be judged.

Stand Firm

¹³Brothers and sisters, we should always thank God for you. The Lord loves you. God chose you from the beginning. He wanted you to be saved. Salvation comes through the Holy Spirit's work. He makes people holy. It also comes through believing the truth. ¹⁴He chose you to be saved by accepting the good news that we preach. And you will share in the glory of our Lord Jesus Christ.

¹⁵Brothers and sisters, stand firm. Hold on to what we taught you. We passed our teachings on to you by what we preached and wrote.

¹⁶Our Lord Jesus Christ and God our Father loved us. By his grace God gave us comfort that will last forever. The hope he gave us is good.

May our Lord Jesus Christ and God our Father ¹⁷comfort your hearts. May they make you strong in every good thing you do and say.

Paul Asks for Prayer

3 Finally, brothers and sisters, pray for us. Pray that the Lord's message will spread quickly. Pray that others will honor it just as you did. ²And pray that we will be saved from sinful and evil people. Not everyone is a believer.

³But the Lord is faithful. He will strengthen you. He will guard you from the evil one.

⁴We trust in the Lord. So we are sure that you are doing the things we tell you to do. And we are sure that you will keep on doing them.

⁵May the Lord fill your hearts with God's love. May Christ give you the strength to go on.

Paul Warns Those Who Do Not Want to Work

⁶Brothers and sisters, here is a command we give you in the name of the Lord Jesus Christ. Keep away from every believer

3:3 But the Lord is faithful. He will strengthen you. He will guard you from the evil one.

who doesn't want to work. Keep away from those who don't live up to the teaching you received from us.

⁷You know how you should follow our example. We worked when we were with you. ⁸We didn't eat anyone's food without paying for it. In fact, it was just the opposite. We worked night and day. We worked very hard so that we wouldn't cause any expense to any of you.

⁹We worked, even though we have the right to receive help from you. We did it in order to be a model for you to follow. ¹⁰Even when we were with you, we gave you a rule. We said, "Anyone who will not work will not eat."

¹¹We hear that some people among you don't want to work. They aren't really busy. Instead, they are bothering others. ¹²We belong to the Lord Jesus Christ. So we strongly command people like that to settle down. They have to earn the food they eat.

¹³Brothers and sisters, don't ever get tired of doing the right thing.

¹⁴Keep an eye on those who don't obey the directions in our letter. Watch them closely. Have nothing to do with them. Then they will feel ashamed. ¹⁵But don't think of them as enemies. Instead, warn them as brothers and sisters.

Final Greetings

¹⁶May the Lord who gives peace give you peace at all times and in every way. May the Lord be with all of you.

¹⁷I, Paul, write this greeting in my own handwriting. That's how I prove that I am the author of all my letters. I always do it that way.

¹⁸May the grace of our Lord Jesus Christ be with you all.

1 Timothy

Why Was This Book Written? Timothy was Paul's young friend. He went on trips with Paul and helped him. Timothy left Paul to lead a church in Ephesus. Paul wrote this letter to him while he was there.

What Is This Book About? Timothy was a young man. He was the church leader. It was an important job. Paul's letter told Timothy how people in a church should act. Paul also wrote about the church leaders. He told how they should act too.

What Is in This Book?

1 I, Paul, am writing this letter. I am an apostle of Christ Jesus, just as God our Savior commanded. Christ Jesus also commanded it. We have put our hope in him.

²Timothy, I am sending you this letter. You are my true son in the faith.

May God the Father and Christ Jesus our Lord give you grace, mercy and peace.

Paul Warns Against Certain Teachers of the Law

³Stay there in Ephesus. That is what I told you to do when I went into Macedonia. I want you to command certain people not to teach things that aren't true. ⁴Command them not to spend their time on stories that aren't completely true. They must not waste time on family histories that never end. Things like that cause people to argue instead of doing God's work. His work is done by faith.

⁵Love is the purpose of my command. Love comes from a pure heart. It comes from a good sense of what is right and wrong. It comes from faith that is honest and true.

⁶Some have wandered away from those teachings. They would rather talk about things that have no meaning. ⁷They want to be teachers of the law. And they are very sure about that law. But they don't know what they are talking about.

⁸We know that the law is good if it is used properly. ⁹We also know that the law isn't made for godly people. It is made for those who break the law. It is for those who refuse to obey. It is for ungodly and sinful people. It is for those who aren't holy and who don't believe. It is for those who kill their fathers or mothers. It is for murderers.

¹⁰It is for those who commit adultery. It is for those who have a twisted view of sex. It is for people who buy and sell slaves. It is for liars. It is for those who give witness to things that aren't true. And it is for anything else that is the opposite of true teaching.

¹¹True teaching agrees with the glorious good news of the blessed God. He trusted me with that good news.

The Lord Pours Out His Grace on Paul

¹²I am thankful to Christ Jesus our Lord. He has given me strength. I thank him that he considered me faithful. And I thank him for appointing me to serve him.

¹³I used to speak evil things against Jesus. I tried to hurt his followers. I really pushed them around. But God showed me mercy anyway. I did those things without knowing any better. I wasn't a believer.

¹⁴Our Lord poured out more and more of his grace on me. Along with it came faith and love from Christ Jesus.

¹⁵Here is a saying that you can trust. It should be accepted completely. Christ Jesus came into the world to save sinners.

And I am the worst sinner of all. ¹⁶But for that very reason, God showed me mercy. And I am the worst of sinners. He showed me mercy so that Christ Jesus could show that he is very patient. Jesus was an example for those who would come to believe in him. Then they would receive eternal life.

¹⁷The eternal King will never die. He can't be seen. He is the only God. Give him honor and glory for ever and ever. Amen.

¹⁸My son Timothy, I give you these teachings. They are in keeping with the prophecies that were once made about you. By following them, you can fight the good fight. ¹⁹Then you will hold on to faith. You will hold on to a good sense of what is right and wrong.

Some have not accepted these teachings. By doing that, they have destroyed their faith. They are like a ship that has sunk. ²⁰Hymenaeus and Alexander are among them. I have handed them over to Satan. That will teach them not to speak evil things against God.

Directions for Worship

2 First, I want all of you to pray for everyone. Ask God to bless them. Give thanks for them.

²Pray for kings. Pray for all who are in authority. Pray that we will live peaceful and quiet lives. And pray that we will be godly and holy.

³That is good. It pleases God our Savior. ⁴He wants everyone to be saved. He wants them to come to know the truth.

GREAT VERSE — TO — REMEMBER

1:15 Here is a saying that you can trust. It should be accepted completely. Christ Jesus came into the world to save sinners.

⁵There is only one God. And there is only one go-between for God and human beings. He is the man Christ Jesus. ⁶He gave himself to pay for the sins of everyone. That was a witness given by God at just the right time.

⁷I was appointed to be a messenger and an apostle to preach the good news. I am telling the truth. I'm not lying. God appointed me to be a teacher of the true faith to those who aren't Jews.

⁸I want people everywhere to pray. I want them to lift up holy hands. I don't want them to be angry when they pray. I don't want them to argue.

⁹I also want women to dress simply. They should wear clothes that are right and proper. They shouldn't braid their hair. They shouldn't wear gold or pearls. They shouldn't spend too much on clothes. ¹⁰Instead, they should put on good works as if they were their clothes. That is proper for women who claim to worship God.

¹¹When a woman is learning, she should be quiet. She should follow the leaders in every way. ¹²I do not let women teach. I do not let them have authority over men. They must be quiet.

¹³Adam was made first. Then Eve was made. ¹⁴Adam was not the one who was tricked. The woman was tricked and became a sinner. ¹⁵Will women be saved by having children? Only if they keep on believing, loving, and leading a holy life in a proper way.

Leaders and Deacons

3 Here is a saying you can trust. If anyone wants to be a leader in the church, he wants to do a good work for God and people.

²A leader must be free from blame. He must be faithful to his wife. In anything he does, he must not go too far. He must control himself. He must be worthy of respect. He must welcome people into his home. He must be able to teach. ³He must not get drunk. He must not push people around. He must be gentle. He must not be a person who likes to argue. He must not love money.

⁴He must manage his own family well. He must make sure that his children obey him and show him proper respect. ⁵Suppose someone doesn't know how to manage his own family. Then how can he take care of God's church?

⁶The leader must not be a new believer. If he is, he might become proud. Then he would be judged just like the devil.

⁷The leader must also be respected by those who are outside the church. Then he will not be put to shame. He will not fall into the devil's trap.

⁸Deacons also must be worthy of respect. They must be honest and true. They must not drink too much wine. They must not try to get money by cheating people. ⁹They must hold on to the deep truths of the faith. Even their own minds tell them to do that. ¹⁰First they must be tested. Then let them serve as deacons if there is nothing against them.

¹¹In the same way, their wives must be worthy of respect. They must not say things that harm others. In anything they do, they must not go too far. They must be worthy of trust in everything.

¹²A deacon must be faithful to his wife. He must manage his children and family well. ¹³Those who have served well earn the full respect of others. They also become more sure of their faith in Christ Jesus.

¹⁴I hope I can come to you soon. But now I am writing these directions to you. ¹⁵Then if I have to put off my visit, you will know how you should act in God's family. The family of God is the church of the living God. It is the pillar and foundation of the truth.

¹⁶There is no doubt that godliness is a great mystery.

Jesus appeared in a body.
The Holy Spirit proved that he was the Son of God.
He was seen by angels.
He was preached among the nations.
People in the world believed in him.
He was taken up to heaven in glory.

Directions for Timothy

4 The Holy Spirit clearly says that in the last days some people will leave the faith. They will follow spirits that will fool them. They will believe things that demons will teach them.

²Teachings like those come from liars who pretend to be what they are not. Their sense of what is right and wrong has been burned as if with a hot iron. ³They do not allow people to get married. They order them not to eat certain foods. But God created those foods. So people who believe and know the truth should receive them and give thanks for them.

⁴Everything God created is good. You shouldn't turn anything down. Instead, you should thank God for it. ⁵The word of God and prayer make it holy.

⁶Point these things out to the brothers and sisters. Then you will serve Christ Jesus well. You were brought up in the truths of the faith. You received good teaching. You followed it.

⁷Don't have anything to do with godless stories and silly tales. Instead, train yourself to be godly. ⁸Training the body has some value. But being godly has value in every way. It promises help for the life you are now living and the life to come.

⁹Here is a saying you can trust. You can accept it completely. ¹⁰We work hard for it. Here is the saying. We have put our hope in the living God. He is the Savior of all people. Most of all he is the Savior of those who believe.

¹¹Command those things. Teach them. ¹²Don't let anyone look down on you because you are young. Set an example for the believers in what you say and in how you live. Also set an example in how you love and in what you believe. Show the believers how to be pure.

¹³Until I come, spend your time reading Scripture out loud to one another. Spend your time preaching and teaching. ¹⁴Don't fail to use the gift the Holy Spirit gave you. He gave it to you through a message from God. It was given when the elders placed their hands on you.

¹⁵Keep on doing those things. Give them your complete attention. Then everyone will see how you are coming along. ¹⁶Be careful of how you live and what you believe. Never give up. Then you will save yourself and those who hear you.

Advice About Widows, Elders and Slaves

5 Don't tell an older man off. Make an appeal to him as if he were your father. Treat younger men as if they were your brothers. ²Treat older women as if they were your mothers. Treat younger women as if they were your sisters. Be completely pure in the way you treat them.

³Take care of the widows who really need help. ⁴But suppose a

GREAT VERSE — TO — REMEMBER

4:12 Don't let anyone look down on you because you are young. Set an example for the believers in what you say and in how you live.

widow has children or grandchildren. They should first learn to put their faith into practice. They should care for their own family. In that way they will pay back their parents and grandparents. That pleases God.

⁵The widow who really needs help and is left all alone puts her hope in God. Night and day she keeps on praying. Night and day she asks God for help. ⁶But the widow who lives for pleasure is dead even while she is still living.

⁷Give those directions to the people also. Then no one can be blamed. ⁸You should provide for your relatives. Most of all, you should take care of your own family. If you don't, you have left the faith. You are worse than those who don't believe.

⁹No widow should be put on the list of widows unless she is more than 60 years old. She must also have been faithful to her husband. ¹⁰She must be well known for the good things she does. That includes bringing up children. It includes inviting guests into her home. It includes washing the feet of God's people. It includes helping those who are in trouble. A widow should spend her time doing all kinds of good things.

¹¹Don't put younger widows on that kind of list. They might want pleasure more than they want Christ. Then they would want to get married again. ¹²If they do that, they will be judged. They have broken their first promise.

¹³Besides, they get into the habit of having nothing to do. They go around from house to house. They waste time. They talk about others. They bother people. They say things they shouldn't say.

¹⁴So here is the advice I give to younger widows. Get married. Have children. Take care of your own homes. Don't give the enemy the chance to tell lies about you. ¹⁵In fact, some have already turned away to follow Satan.

¹⁶Suppose a woman is a believer and has widows in her family. She should help them. She shouldn't let the church pay the expenses. Then the church can help the widows who really need it.

¹⁷The elders who do the church's work well are worth twice as much honor. That is true in a special way of elders who preach and teach. ¹⁸Scripture says, "Do not stop the ox from eating while it helps separate the grain from the straw." *(Deuteronomy 25:4)* Scripture also says, "Workers are worthy of their pay." *(Luke 10:7)*

¹⁹Don't believe a charge against an elder unless two or three witnesses bring it. ²⁰Elders who sin should be corrected in front of the other believers. That will be a warning to the others.

²¹I command you to follow those directions. I command you in the sight of God and Christ Jesus and the chosen angels. Treat everyone the same. Don't favor one person over another.

²²Don't be too quick to place your hands on others to set them apart to serve God. Don't take part in the sins of others. Keep yourself pure.

²³Stop drinking only water. If your stomach is upset, drink a little wine. It can also help the other sicknesses you often have.

²⁴The sins of some people are easy to see. They are already being judged. Others will be judged later. ²⁵In the same way, good works are easy to see. But even good works that are hard to see can't stay hidden.

6 All who are forced to serve as slaves should consider their masters worthy of full respect. Then people will not speak evil things against God's name and against what we teach.

²Some slaves have masters who are believers. They shouldn't show less respect for their masters just because they are believers. Instead, they should serve them even better. That's because those who benefit from their service are believers. They are loved by them.

Teach the slaves those things. Try hard to get them to do them.

Love for Money

³Suppose some people teach ideas that are false. They don't agree with the true teaching of our Lord Jesus Christ. They don't agree with godly teaching. ⁴People like that are proud. They don't understand anything. They like to argue more than they should. They can't agree about what words mean.

All of that results in wanting what others have. It causes fighting, harmful talk, and evil distrust. ⁵It stirs up trouble all the time among people whose minds are twisted by sin. The truth they once had has been taken away from them. They think they can get rich by being godly.

⁶You gain a lot when you live a godly life. But you must be happy with what you have. ⁷We didn't bring anything into the world. We can't take anything out of it. ⁸If we have food and clothing, we will be happy with that.

⁹People who want to get rich are tempted. They fall into a trap. They are tripped up by wanting many foolish and harmful things. Those who live like that are dragged down by what they do. They are destroyed and die.

¹⁰Love for money causes all kinds of evil. Some people want to

get rich. They have wandered away from the faith. They have wounded themselves with many sorrows.

Paul Gives a Command to Timothy

[11]But you are a man of God. Run away from all of those things. Try hard to do what is right and godly. Have faith, love and gentleness. Hold on to what you believe. [12]Fight the good fight along with all other believers. Take hold of eternal life. You were chosen for it when you openly told others what you believe. Many witnesses heard you.

[13]God gives life to everything. Christ Jesus told the truth when he gave witness to Pontius Pilate. In the sight of God and Christ, I give you a command. [14]Obey it until our Lord Jesus Christ appears. Obey it completely. Then no one can find fault with it or you.

[15]God will bring Jesus back at a time that pleases him. God is the blessed and only Ruler. He is the greatest King of all. He is the most powerful Lord of all. [16]God is the only one who can't die. He lives in light that no one can get close to. No one has seen him. No one can see him.

Give honor and power to him forever. Amen.

[17]Command people who are rich in this world not to be proud. Tell them not to put their hope in riches. Wealth is so uncertain. Command those who are rich to put their hope in God. He richly provides us with everything to enjoy.

[18]Command the rich to do what is good. Tell them to be rich in doing good things. They must give freely. They must be willing to share. [19]In that way they will put riches away for themselves. It will provide a firm basis for the next life. Then they will take hold of the life that really is life.

[20]Timothy, guard what God has trusted you with. Turn away from godless chatter. Stay away from opposing ideas that are falsely called knowledge. [21]Some people believe them. By doing that they have wandered away from the faith.

May God's grace be with you.

GREAT VERSE —TO— REMEMBER **6:12** Fight the good fight along with all other believers. Take hold of eternal life.

2 Timothy

Why Was This Book Written? Paul wrote this second letter to Timothy. Paul was in prison in Rome again. He knew he was going to die soon. He wrote this letter to cheer Timothy up. Paul told him to share the good news with others after Paul died.

What Is This Book About? Paul wrote this letter to give Timothy some advice. He gave him commands to help lead the church. He told Timothy to teach the truth. Paul wanted Timothy to be faithful to Jesus.

What Is in This Book?

1 I, Paul, am writing this letter. I am an apostle of Christ Jesus just as God planned. He sent me to tell about the promise of life that is found in Christ Jesus.

²Timothy, I am sending you this letter. You are my dear son.

May God the Father and Christ Jesus our Lord give you grace, mercy and peace.

Paul Tells Timothy to Be Faithful

³I serve God, knowing that what I have done is right. That is how our people served him long ago. Night and day I thank God for you. Night and day I always remember you in my prayers.

⁴I remember your tears. I long to see you so that I can be filled with joy. ⁵I remember your honest and true faith. It was alive first in your grandmother Lois and in your mother Eunice. And I am certain that it is now alive in you also.

⁶That is why I remind you to help God's gift grow, just as a small spark grows into a fire. God put his gift in you when I placed my hands on you.

⁷God didn't give us a spirit that makes us weak and fearful. He gave us a spirit that gives us power and love. It helps us control ourselves.

⁸So don't be ashamed to give witness about our Lord. And don't be ashamed of me, his prisoner. Instead, join with me as I suffer for the good news. God's power will help us do that.

⁹God has saved us. He has chosen us to live a holy life. It wasn't because of anything we have done. It was because of his own purpose and grace. Through Christ Jesus, God gave us that grace even before time began. ¹⁰It has now been made known through the coming of our Savior, Christ Jesus. He has destroyed death. Because of the good news, he has brought life out into the light. That life never dies.

¹¹I was appointed to announce the good news. I was appointed to be an apostle and a teacher. ¹²That's why I'm suffering the way

GREAT VERSE —TO— REMEMBER

1:7 God didn't give us a spirit that makes us weak and fearful. He gave us a spirit that gives us power and love.

I am. But I'm not ashamed. I know the One I have believed in. I am sure he is able to take care of what I have given him. I can trust him with it until the day he returns as judge.

¹³Follow what you heard from me as the pattern of true teaching. Follow it with faith and love because you belong to Christ Jesus. ¹⁴Guard the truth of the good news that you were trusted with. Guard it with the help of the Holy Spirit who lives in us.

¹⁵You know that all the believers in Asia Minor have deserted me. They include Phygelus and Hermogenes.

¹⁶May the Lord show mercy to all who live in the house of Onesiphorus. He often cheered me up. He was not ashamed that I was being held by chains. ¹⁷In fact, it was just the opposite. When he was in Rome, he looked everywhere for me. At last he found me.

¹⁸May Onesiphorus find mercy from the Lord on the day Jesus returns as judge. You know very well how many ways Onesiphorus helped me in Ephesus.

2 My son, be strong in the grace that is found in Christ Jesus. ²You have heard me teach in front of many witnesses. Pass on to people you can trust the things you've heard me say. Then they will be able to teach others also. ³Like a good soldier of Christ Jesus, share in the hard times with us.

⁴Those who serve as soldiers do not take part in things that don't have anything to do with the army. They want to please their commanding officer. ⁵In the same way, those who take part in a sport don't receive the winner's crown unless they play by the rules. ⁶The farmer who works hard should be the first to receive a share of the crops.

⁷Think about what I'm saying. The Lord will help you understand what all of it means.

⁸Remember Jesus Christ. He came from David's family line. He was raised from the dead. That is my good news. ⁹I am suffering for it. I have even been put in chains like someone who has committed a crime. But God's word is not held back by chains.

¹⁰So I put up with everything for the good of God's chosen people. Then they also can be saved. Christ Jesus saves them. He gives them glory that will last forever.

¹¹Here is a saying you can trust.

If we died with him,
we will also live with him.
¹²If we don't give up,
we will also rule with him.

If we say we don't know him,
    he will also say he doesn't know us.
¹³Even if we are not faithful,
    he will remain faithful.
    He must be true to himself.

A Worker Who Pleases God

¹⁴Keep reminding the believers of those things. While God is watching, warn them not to argue about words. That doesn't have any value. It only destroys those who listen.

¹⁵Do your best to be a person who pleases God. Be a worker who doesn't need to be ashamed. Teach the message of truth correctly.

¹⁶Stay away from godless chatter. Those who take part in it will become more and more ungodly. ¹⁷Their teaching will spread like a deadly sickness.

Hymenaeus and Philetus are two of those teachers. ¹⁸They have wandered away from the truth. They say that the time when people will rise from the dead has already come. They destroy the faith of some people.

¹⁹But God's solid foundation stands firm. Here is the message written on it. "The Lord knows who his own people are." *(Numbers 16:5)* Also, "All who say they believe in the Lord must turn away from evil."

²⁰In a large house there are things made out of gold and silver. But there are also things made out of wood and clay. Some have honorable purposes. Others do not. ²¹Suppose people stay away from what is not honorable. Then the Master will be able to use them for honorable purposes. They will be made holy. They will be ready to do any good work.

²²Run away from the evil things that young people long for. Try hard to do what is right. Have faith, love and peace. Do these things together with those who call on the Lord from a pure heart. ²³Don't have anything to do with arguing. It is dumb and foolish. You know it only leads to fights.

²⁴Those who serve the Lord must not fight. Instead, they must

GREAT VERSE —TO— REMEMBER

2:15 Do your best to be a person who pleases God. Be a worker who doesn't need to be ashamed.

be kind to everyone. They must be able to teach. They must not hold anything against anyone. [25]They must gently teach those who oppose them.

Maybe God will give a change of heart to those who are against you. That will lead them to know the truth. [26]Maybe they will come to their senses. Maybe they will escape the devil's trap. He has taken them prisoner to do what he wanted.

Terrible Times in the Last Days

3 Here is what I want you to know. There will be terrible times in the last days. [2]People will love themselves. They will love money. They will brag and be proud. They will tear others down. They will not obey their parents. They won't be thankful or holy. [3]They won't love others. They won't forgive others. They will tell lies about people. They will be out of control. They will be wild. They will hate what is good.

[4]They will turn against their friends. They will act without thinking. They will think they are better than others. They will love what pleases them instead of loving God. [5]They will act as if they were serving God. But what they do will show that they have turned their backs on God's power. Have nothing to do with those people.

[6]They are the kind who worm their way into the homes of silly women. They get control over them. Women like that are loaded down with sins. They give in to all kinds of evil longings. [7]They are always learning. But they never come to know the truth.

[8]Jannes and Jambres opposed Moses. In the same way, the teachers I'm talking about oppose the truth. Their minds are twisted. As far as the faith is concerned, God doesn't accept them. [9]They won't get very far. Just like Jannes and Jambres, their foolish ways will be clear to everyone.

Paul Gives a Command to Timothy

[10]But you know all about my teaching. You know how I live and what I live for. You know about my faith and love. You know how patient I am. You know I haven't given up. [11]You know that I was treated badly. You know that I suffered greatly. You know what kinds of things happened to me in Antioch, Iconium and Lystra. You know how badly I have been treated. But the Lord saved me from all of my troubles.

[12]In fact, everyone who wants to live a godly life in Christ Jesus will be treated badly. [13]Evil people and pretenders will go from

bad to worse. They will fool others, and others will fool them.

[14]But I want you to continue to follow what you have learned. Don't give up what you are sure of. You know the people you learned it from. [15]You have known the Holy Scriptures ever since you were a little child. They are able to teach you how to be saved by believing in Christ Jesus.

[16]God has breathed life into all of Scripture. It is useful for teaching us what is true. It is useful for correcting our mistakes. It is useful for making our lives whole again. It is useful for training us to do what is right. [17]By using Scripture, God's people can be completely prepared to do every good thing.

4 I give you a command in the sight of God and Christ Jesus. Christ will judge the living and the dead. Because he and his kingdom are coming, here is the command I give you. [2]Preach the word. Be ready to serve God in good times and bad. Correct people's mistakes. Warn them. Cheer them up with words of hope. Be very patient as you do these things. Teach them carefully.

[3]The time will come when people won't put up with true teaching. Instead, they will try to satisfy their own longings. They will gather a large number of teachers around them. The teachers will say what the people want to hear. [4]The people will turn their ears away from the truth. They will turn to stories that aren't completely true.

[5]But I want you to keep your head no matter what happens. Don't give up when times are hard. Work to spread the good news. Do everything God has given you to do.

[6]I am already being poured out like a drink offering. The time has come for me to leave.

[7]I have fought the good fight. I have finished the race. I have kept the faith. [8]Now there is a crown waiting for me. It is given to those who are right with God. The Lord, who judges fairly, will give it to me on the day he returns. He will not give it only

GREAT VERSE —TO— REMEMBER

3:16-17 God has breathed life into all of Scripture ... By using Scripture, God's people can be completely prepared to do every good thing.

to me. He will also give it to all those who are longing for him to return.

Personal Words

[9]Do your best to come to me quickly.

[10]Demas has deserted me. He has gone to Thessalonica. He left me because he loved this world. Crescens has gone to Galatia. Titus has gone to Dalmatia. [11]Only Luke is with me. Get Mark and bring him with you. He helps me in my work for the Lord. [12]I sent Tychicus to Ephesus.

[13]When you come, bring my coat. I left it with Carpus at Troas. Also bring my scrolls. Most of all, bring the ones made out of animal skins.

[14]Remember Alexander, the one who works with metal? He did me a great deal of harm. The Lord will pay him back for what he has done. [15]You too should watch out for him. He strongly opposed our message.

[16]The first time I was put on trial, no one came to help me. Everyone deserted me. I hope they will be forgiven for it.

[17]The Lord stood at my side. He gave me the strength to preach the whole message. Then all those who weren't Jews heard it. I was saved from the lion's mouth. [18]The Lord will save me from every evil attack. He will bring me safely to his heavenly kingdom.

Give him glory for ever and ever. Amen.

Final Greetings

[19]Greet Priscilla and Aquila. Greet those who live in the house of Onesiphorus.

[20]Erastus stayed in Corinth. I left Trophimus sick in Miletus.

[21]Do your best to get here before winter.

Eubulus greets you. So do Pudens, Linus, Claudia and all the brothers and sisters.

[22]May the Lord be with your spirit. May God's grace be with you.

Titus

Why Was This Book Written? Paul wrote this short letter to a man named Titus. Titus was a Christian friend and helper of Paul. Titus had gone on some trips with Paul. Titus was the leader of the church on the island of Crete.

What Is This Book About? This letter is like the two letters Paul wrote to Timothy. Paul wanted Titus to know how to lead the church. He told him how the church should act. Paul also told Titus what a leader should do. He gave Titus some good advice.

What Is in This Book?

1 I, Paul, am writing this letter. I serve God. I am an apostle of Jesus Christ. God sent me to help his chosen people believe in Christ. I have been sent to help them understand the truth that leads to godly living. ²Faith and understanding rest on the hope of eternal life. Before time began, God promised to give that life. And he does not lie. ³At just the right time he made his word plain. He did it through the preaching that he trusted me with. God our Savior has commanded all those things.

⁴Titus, I am sending you this letter. You are my true son in the faith we share.

May God the Father and Christ Jesus our Savior give you grace and peace.

The Work of Titus on Crete

⁵I left you on the island of Crete. There were some things that hadn't been finished. You needed to sort them out. You also had to appoint elders in every town. I told you how to do it.
⁶An elder must be without blame. He must be faithful to his wife. His children must be believers. They must not give anyone a reason to say that they are wild and don't obey.
⁷A church leader is trusted with God's work. That's why he must be without blame. He must not look after only his own interests. He must not get angry easily. He must not get drunk. He must not push people around. He must not try to get money by cheating people.
⁸Instead, he must welcome people into his home. He must love what is good. He must control his mind and feelings. He must do what is right. He must be holy. He must control what his body longs for. ⁹The message as it has been taught can be trusted. He must hold firmly to it. Then he will be able to use true teaching to comfort others and build them up. He will be able to prove that people who oppose it are wrong.
¹⁰Many people refuse to obey God. All they do is talk a lot. They try to fool others. No one does these things more than the circumcision group. ¹¹They must be stopped. They are destroying entire families. They are teaching things they shouldn't. They do it to get money by cheating people.
¹²Even one of their own prophets has said, "People from Crete are always liars. They are evil beasts. They don't want to work. They live only to eat." ¹³What I have just said is true. So give them a strong warning. Then they will understand the faith correctly.

¹⁴They will pay no attention to Jewish stories that aren't completely true. They won't listen to the commands of those who turn away from the truth.

¹⁵To people who are pure, all things are pure. But to those who have twisted minds and don't believe, nothing is pure. In fact, their minds and their sense of what is right and wrong are twisted. ¹⁶They claim to know God. But their actions show they don't know him. They are hated by God. They refuse to obey him. They aren't fit to do anything good.

Teaching God's People

2 What you teach must agree with true teaching.
²Tell the older men that in anything they do, they must not go too far. They must be worthy of respect. They must control themselves. They must have true faith. They must love others. They must not give up.

³In the same way, teach the older women to lead a holy life. They must not tell lies about others. They must not let wine control them. Instead, they must teach what is good. ⁴Then they can train the younger women to love their husbands and children.

⁵The younger women must control themselves. They must be pure. They must take good care of their homes. They must be kind. They must follow the lead of their husbands. Then no one will be able to speak evil things against God's word.

⁶In the same way, help the young men to control themselves. ⁷Do what is good. Set an example for them in everything. When you teach, be honest and serious. ⁸No one can question the truth. So teach what is true. Then those who oppose you will be ashamed. That's because they will have nothing bad to say about us.

⁹Teach slaves to obey their masters in everything they do. Tell them to try to please their masters. They must not talk back to them. ¹⁰They must not steal from them. Instead, they must show

---

GREAT VERSE — TO — REMEMBER

2:11-12 God's saving grace has appeared to all people. It teaches us to say no to godless ways and sinful longings.

that they can be trusted completely. Then they will make the teaching about God our Savior appealing in every way.

[11]God's saving grace has appeared to all people. [12]It teaches us to say no to godless ways and sinful longings. We must control ourselves. We must do what is right. We must lead godly lives in today's world. [13]That's how we should live as we wait for the blessed hope God has given us.

We are waiting for Jesus Christ to appear in all his glory. He is our great God and Savior. [14]He gave himself for us. By doing that, he set us free from all evil. He wanted to make us pure. He wanted us to be his very own people. He wanted us to long to do what is good.

[15]Those are the things you should teach. Cheer people up and give them hope. Correct them with full authority. Don't let anyone look down on you.

Do What Is Good

3 Remind God's people to obey rulers and authorities. Remind them to be ready to do what is good. [2]Tell them not to speak evil things against anyone. Remind them to live in peace. They must consider the needs of others. They must be kind and gentle toward all people.

[3]At one time we too acted like fools. We didn't obey God. We were tricked. We were controlled by all kinds of longings and pleasures. We were full of evil. We wanted what belongs to others. People hated us, and we hated one another.

[4]But the kindness and love of God our Savior appeared. [5]He saved us. It wasn't because of the good things we had done. It was because of his mercy. He saved us by washing away our sins. We were born again. The Holy Spirit gave us new life.

[6]God poured out the Spirit on us freely because of what Jesus Christ our Savior has done. [7]His grace made us right with God. So now we have received the hope of eternal life as God's children.

3:1 Remind God's people to obey rulers and authorities. Remind them to be ready to do what is good.

⁸You can trust that saying. Those things are important. Treat them that way. Then those who have trusted in God will be careful to commit themselves to doing what is good. Those things are excellent. They are for the good of everyone.

⁹But keep away from foolish disagreements. Don't argue about family histories. Don't make trouble. Don't fight about what the law teaches. Don't argue about things like that. It doesn't do any good. It doesn't help anyone.

¹⁰Warn people who try to get believers to take sides and separate into their own little groups. Warn them more than once. After that, have nothing to do with them. ¹¹You can be sure that people like that are twisted and sinful. Their own actions judge them.

Final Words

¹²I will send Artemas or Tychicus to you. Then do your best to come to me at Nicopolis. I've decided to spend the winter there.

¹³Do everything you can to help Zenas the lawyer and Apollos. Send them on their way. See that they have everything they need.

¹⁴Our people must learn to commit themselves to doing what is good. Then they will be able to provide for the daily needs of others. If they do that, their lives won't turn out to be useless.

¹⁵Everyone who is with me sends you greetings. Greet those who love us in the faith.

May God's grace be with you all.

Philemon

Why Was This Book Written? Paul wrote this letter to Philemon. Philemon was a leader in the church at Colosse. He was also a friend of Paul's. Philemon's slave had taken some money and run away. The slave's name was Onesimus. Onesimus met Paul and became a Christian.

What Is This Book About? Paul gave this letter to Onesimus. He told him to go back to Philemon with this letter. In the letter Paul asked Philemon to forgive Onesimus. He asked him to treat Onesimus like a brother. Paul said he would pay back the money Onesimus stole. He wanted Philemon to set Onesimus free.

What Is in This Book?

[1]I, Paul, am writing this letter. I am a prisoner because of Christ Jesus. Our brother Timothy joins me in writing.

Philemon, we are sending you this letter. You are our dear friend. You work together with us. [2]We are also sending it to our sister Apphia and to Archippus. He is a soldier of Christ together with us. And we are sending it to the church that meets in your home.

[3]May God our Father and the Lord Jesus Christ give you grace and peace.

Paul Prays and Gives Thanks

[4]I always thank my God when I remember you in my prayers. [5]That's because I hear about your faith in the Lord Jesus. I hear about your love for all of God's people. [6]I pray that you will be active in sharing what you believe. Then you will completely understand every good thing we have in Christ.

[7]Your love has given me great joy. It has cheered me up. My brother, you have renewed the hearts of God's people.

Paul Makes an Appeal for Onesimus

[8]Because of the authority Christ has given me, I could be bold. I could order you to do what you should do anyway. [9]But I make my appeal to you on the basis of our love for each other.

I, Paul, am an old man. I am now also a prisoner because of Christ Jesus. [10]I make an appeal to you for my son Onesimus. He became a son to me while I was being held by chains. [11]Before that, he was useless to you. But now he has become useful to you and to me.

[12]I'm sending Onesimus back to you. My very heart goes with him. [13]I would have liked to keep him with me. Then he could have taken your place in helping me while I'm being held by

---

GREAT VERSE —TO— REMEMBER

6 I pray that you will be active in sharing what you believe. Then you will completely understand every good thing we have in Christ.

chains because of the good news. [14]But I didn't want to do anything unless you agreed. Any favor you do must be done because you want to do it, not because you have to.

[15]Onesimus was separated from you for a little while. Maybe that was so you could have him back for good. [16]You could have him back not as a slave. Instead, he would be better than a slave. He would be a dear brother. He is very dear to me. But he is even more dear to you, both as a man and as a brother in the Lord.

[17]Do you think of me as a believer who works together with you? Then welcome Onesimus as you would welcome me. [18]Has he done anything wrong to you? Does he owe you anything? Then charge it to me. [19]I'll pay it back. I, Paul, am writing this with my own hand. I won't even mention that you owe me your very life.

[20]My brother, I wish I could receive some benefit from you because we both belong to the Lord. Renew my heart. We know that Christ is the one who really renews it. [21]I'm sure you will obey. So I'm writing to you. I know you will do even more than I ask.

[22]There is one more thing. Have a guest room ready for me. I hope I can return to all of you in answer to your prayers.

[23]Epaphras sends you greetings. Together with me, he is a prisoner because of Christ Jesus. [24]Mark, Aristarchus, Demas and Luke work together with me. They also send you greetings.

[25]May the grace of the Lord Jesus Christ be with your spirit.

Hebrews

Why Was This Book Written? The book of Hebrews was written when the church was new. People were sent to prison for believing in Jesus. Some were killed for their faith. Some Jewish Christians were scared. They thought about giving up their faith in Jesus. It was hard to be a Christian.

What Is This Book About? This book was written to cheer up Jewish Christians. It said believing in Jesus was good. The book of Hebrews tells of many people who believed in God. They are our examples. We must believe and trust God too.

What Is in This Book?

The Son Is Greater Than the Angels

1 In the past, God spoke to our people through the prophets. He spoke at many times. He spoke in different ways. ²But in these last days, he has spoken to us through his Son. He is the one whom God appointed to receive all things. God made everything through him. ³The Son is the gleaming brightness of God's glory. He is the exact likeness of God's being. He uses his powerful word to hold all things together. He provided the way for people to be made pure from sin. Then he sat down at the right hand of the King, the Majesty in heaven. ⁴So he became higher than the angels. The name he received is more excellent than theirs.

⁵God never said to any of the angels,

> "You are my Son.
> Today I have become your Father."   *(Psalm 2:7)*

Or,

> "I will be his Father.
> And he will be my Son."   *(2 Samuel 7:14; 1Chronicles 17:13)*

⁶God's first and only Son is over all things. When God brings him into the world, he says,

> "Let all of God's angels worship him."   *(Deuteronomy 32:43)*

⁷Here is something else God says about the angels.

> "God makes his angels to be like winds.
> He makes those who serve him to be like flashes of
> lightning."   *(Psalm 104:4)*

⁸But here is what he says about the Son.

> "You are God. Your throne will last for ever and ever.
> Your kingdom will be ruled by what is right.
> ⁹You have loved what is right and hated what is evil.
> So your God has placed you above your companions.

1:3 The Son is the gleaming brightness of God's glory. He is the exact likeness of God's being.

He has filled you with joy by pouring the sacred oil on
your head." *(Psalm 45:6,7)*

[10]He also says,

"Lord, in the beginning you made the earth secure. You
placed it on its foundations.
The heavens are the work of your hands.
[11]They will pass away. But you remain.
They will all wear out like a piece of clothing.
[12]You will roll them up like a robe.
They will be changed as a person changes clothes.
But you remain the same.
Your years will never end." *(Psalm 102:25–27)*

[13]God never said to an angel,

"Sit at my right hand
until I put your enemies
under your control." *(Psalm 110:1)*

[14]All angels are spirits who serve. God sends them to serve those
who will receive salvation.

A Warning to Pay Attention

2 So we must pay more careful attention to what we have
heard. Then we will not drift away from it. [2]Even the message God spoke through angels had to be obeyed. Every time
people broke the Law, they were punished. Every time they didn't
obey, they were punished. [3]Then how will we escape if we don't
pay attention to God's great salvation?

The Lord first announced that salvation. Those who heard him
gave us the message about it. [4]God gave witness to it through
signs and wonders. He gave witness through different kinds of
miracles. He also gave witness through the gifts of the Holy Spirit.
He gave them out as it pleased him.

Jesus Was Made Like His Brothers and Sisters

[5]God has not put angels in charge of the world that is going to

GREAT
VERSE
— TO —
REMEMBER

2:1 So we must pay more careful
attention to what we have heard.

come. We are talking about that world. ⁶There is a place where someone has given witness to it. He said,

> "What is a human being that you think about him?
> What is the son of man that you care for him?
> ⁷You made him a little lower than the angels.
> You placed on him a crown of glory and honor.
> ⁸   You have put everything under his control."
>
> *(Psalm 8:4–6)*

So God has put everything under him. Everything is under his control.

We do not now see everything under his control. ⁹But we do see Jesus already given a crown of glory and honor. He was made a little lower than the angels. He suffered death. By the grace of God, he tasted death for everyone. That is why he was given his crown.

¹⁰God has made everything. He has acted in exactly the right way. He is bringing his many sons and daughters to share in his glory. To do so, he has made the One who saved them perfect because of his sufferings.

¹¹The One who makes people holy and the people he makes holy belong to the same family. So Jesus is not ashamed to call them his brothers and sisters. ¹²He says,

> "I will announce your name to my brothers and sisters.
> I will sing your praises among those who worship
>   you."   *(Psalm 22:22)*

¹³Again he says,

> "I will put my trust in him."   *(Isaiah 8:17)*

And again he says,

> "Here I am. Here are the children God has given me."
>
> *(Isaiah 8:18)*

¹⁴Those children have bodies made out of flesh and blood. So Jesus became human like them in order to die for them. By doing that, he could destroy the one who rules over the kingdom of death. I'm talking about the devil. ¹⁵Jesus could set people free who were afraid of death. All their lives they were held as slaves by that fear.

¹⁶It is certainly Abraham's children that he helps. He doesn't help angels. ¹⁷So he had to be made like his brothers and sisters in every way. Then he could serve God as a kind and faithful high

priest. And then he could pay for the sins of the people by dying for them.

[18]He himself suffered when he was tempted. Now he is able to help others who are being tempted.

Jesus Is Greater Than Moses

3 Holy brothers and sisters, God chose you to be his people. So keep thinking about Jesus. He is our apostle. He is our high priest. We believe in him.

[2]Moses was faithful in everything he did in the house of God. In the same way, Jesus was faithful to the One who appointed him.

[3]The person who builds a house has greater honor than the house itself. In the same way, Jesus has been found worthy of greater honor than Moses. [4]Every house is built by someone. But God is the builder of everything.

[5]Moses was faithful as one who serves in the house of God. He gave witness to what God would say in days to come. [6]But Christ is faithful as a son over God's house. We are his house if we continue to come boldly to God. We must also hold on to the hope we take pride in.

A Warning Against Unbelief

[7]The Holy Spirit says,

> "Listen to his voice today.
> [8]　If you hear it, don't be stubborn.
> You were stubborn when you opposed me.
> 　You did that when you were put to the test in the
> 　　desert.
> [9]There your people of long ago put me to the test.
> 　For 40 years they saw what I did.
> [10]That is why I was angry with them.
> 　I said, 'Their hearts are always going down the wrong
> 　　path.

GREAT VERSE —TO— REMEMBER

3:12 Make sure that none of you has a sinful heart. Do not let an unbelieving heart turn you away from the living God.

They have not known my ways.'
   [11]So in my anger I took an oath.
   I said, 'They will never enjoy the rest I planned for
      them.'"   *(Psalm 95:7–11)*

[12]Brothers and sisters, make sure that none of you has a sinful heart. Do not let an unbelieving heart turn you away from the living God. [13]But build one another up every day. Do it as long as there is still time. Then none of you will become stubborn. You won't be fooled by sin's tricks.

[14]We belong to Christ if we hold firmly to the faith we had at first. But we must hold to it until the end. [15]It has just been said,

   "Listen to his voice today.
      If you hear it, don't be stubborn.
   You were stubborn when you opposed me."   *(Psalm 95:7,8)*

[16]Who were those who heard and refused to obey? Weren't they all the people Moses led out of Egypt? [17]Who was God angry with for 40 years? Wasn't it with those who sinned? They died in the desert. [18]What people did God promise with an oath that they would never enjoy the rest I planned for them? Wasn't it those who didn't obey?

[19]So we see that they weren't able to enter. That's because they didn't believe.

God's People Enter His Sabbath Rest

4 God's promise of enjoying his rest still stands. So let us be careful that none of you fails to receive it.

[2]The good news was preached to our people of long ago. It has also been preached to us. The message they heard didn't have any value for them. They didn't combine it with faith. [3]Now we who have believed enjoy that rest. God said,

   "In my anger I took an oath.
   I said, 'They will never enjoy the rest I planned for
      them.'"   *(Psalm 95:11)*

Ever since God created the world, his work has been finished.

[4]Somewhere he spoke about the seventh day. He said, "On the seventh day God rested from all his work." *(Genesis 2:2)* [5]In the part of Scripture I talked about earlier God said, "They will never enjoy the rest I planned for them." *(Psalm 95:11)*

[6]It is still true that some will enter that rest. But those who had

the good news preached to them earlier didn't go in. That was because they didn't obey.

⁷So God again chose a certain day. He named it Today. He did that when he spoke through David a long time later. As it was said earlier,

> "Listen to his voice today.
> If you hear it, don't be stubborn." *(Psalm 95:7,8)*

⁸Suppose Joshua had given them rest. If he had, God would not have spoken later about another day. ⁹So there is still a Sabbath rest for God's people.

¹⁰God rested from his work. Those who enjoy God's rest also rest from their work. ¹¹So let us make every effort to enjoy that rest. Then no one will fall into sin by following the example of those who didn't obey God.

¹²The word of God is living and active. It is sharper than any sword that has two edges. It cuts deep enough to separate soul from spirit. It can separate joints from bones. It judges the thoughts and purposes of the heart. ¹³Nothing God created is hidden from him. His eyes see everything. He will hold us accountable for everything we do.

Jesus Is the Great High Priest

¹⁴We have a great high priest. He has gone up into the heavens. He is Jesus the Son of God. So let us hold firmly to what we say we believe.

¹⁵We have a high priest who can feel it when we are weak and hurting. We have a high priest who has been tempted in every way, just as we are. But he did not sin. ¹⁶So let us boldly approach the throne of grace. Then we will receive mercy. We will find grace to help us when we need it.

5 Every high priest is chosen from among men. He is appointed to act for them in everything that has to do with God. He offers gifts and sacrifices for their sins. ²He is able to deal gently with those who have gone down the wrong path without

GREAT VERSE —TO— REMEMBER   **4:14** We have a great high priest. He has gone up into the heavens. He is Jesus the Son of God.

knowing it. He can do that because he himself is weak. [3]That's why he has to offer sacrifices for his own sins. He must also do it for the sins of the people.

[4]No one can take that honor for himself. He must be appointed by God, just as Aaron was.

[5]Even Christ did not take the glory of becoming a high priest for himself. God said to him,

> "You are my Son.
> Today I have become your Father." *(Psalm 2:7)*

[6]In another place he said,

> "You are a priest forever,
> just like Melchizedek." *(Psalm 110:4)*

[7]Jesus prayed while he lived on earth. He made his appeal with loud cries and tears. He prayed to the One who could save him from death. God heard him because he truly honored God.

[8]Jesus was God's Son. But by suffering he learned what it means to obey. [9]In that way he was made perfect. Eternal salvation comes from him. He saves all those who obey him.

[10]God appointed him to be the high priest, just like Melchizedek.

A Warning Against Falling Away

[11]We have a lot to say about that. But it is hard to explain it to you. You learn too slowly. [12]By this time you should be teachers. But in fact, you need someone to teach you all over again. You need even the simple truths of God's word. You need milk, not solid food.

[13]Anyone who lives on milk is still a baby. That person does not want to learn about living a godly life. [14]Solid food is for those who are grown up. They have trained themselves with a lot of practice. They can tell the difference between good and evil.

6 So let us leave the simple teachings about Christ. Let us grow up as believers. Let us not start all over again with the basic teachings. They taught us that we need to turn away from doing things that lead to death. They taught us that we must have faith in God. [2]They taught us about different kinds of baptism. They taught us about placing hands on people. They taught us that people will rise from the dead. They taught us that God will judge everyone. And they taught us that what he decides will last forever.

³If God permits, we will go beyond those teachings and grow up.

⁴What if some people fall away from the faith? It won't be possible to bring them back. It is true that they have seen the light. They have tasted the heavenly gift. They have shared in the Holy Spirit. ⁵They have tasted the good things of God's word. They have tasted the powers of the age to come. ⁶But they have fallen away from the faith. So it won't be possible to bring them back. They won't be able to turn away from their sins. They are losing everything. That's because they are nailing the Son of God to the cross all over again. They are bringing shame on him in front of everyone.

⁷Some land drinks the rain that falls on it. It produces a crop that is useful to those who farm the land. That land receives God's blessing. ⁸But other land produces only thorns and weeds. That land isn't worth anything. It is in danger of coming under God's curse. In the end, it will be burned.

⁹Dear friends, we have to say these things. But we are sure of better things in your case. We are talking about the things that go along with being saved.

¹⁰God is fair. He will not forget what you have done. He will remember the love you have shown him. You showed it when you helped his people. And you show it when you keep on helping them.

¹¹We want each of you to be faithful to the very end. We want you to be sure of what you hope for. ¹²We don't want you to slow down. Instead, be like those who have faith and are patient. They will receive what God promised.

God Keeps His Promise

¹³When God made his promise to Abraham, he took an oath to keep it. But there was no one greater than himself to take an oath by. So he took his oath by making an appeal to himself.

GREAT VERSE — TO — REMEMBER

6:10 God is fair. He will not forget what you have done. He will remember the love you have shown him. You showed it when you helped his people.

¹⁴He said, "I will certainly bless you. I will give you many children." *(Genesis 22:17)* ¹⁵Abraham was patient while he waited. Then he received what God promised him.

¹⁶People take oaths by someone greater than themselves. An oath makes a promise certain. It puts an end to all arguing. ¹⁷So God took an oath when he made his promise. He wanted to make it very clear that his purpose does not change. He wanted those who would receive what was promised to know that.

¹⁸God took an oath so we would have good reason not to give up. We have run away from everything else to take hold of the hope offered to us in God's promise. So God gave his promise and his oath. Those two things can't change. He couldn't lie about them.

¹⁹Our hope is certain. It is something for the soul to hold on to. It is strong and secure. It goes all the way into the Most Holy Room behind the curtain. ²⁰That is where Jesus has gone. He went there to open the way ahead of us. He has become a high priest forever, just like Melchizedek.

Melchizedek the Priest

7 Melchizedek was the king of Salem. He was the priest of God Most High. He met Abraham, who was returning from winning a battle over some kings. Melchizedek blessed him. ²Abraham gave him a tenth of everything.

First, the name Melchizedek means "king of what is right." Also, "king of Salem" means "king of peace." ³Melchizedek has no father or mother. He has no family line. His days have no beginning. His life has no end. He remains a priest forever, just like the Son of God.

⁴Think how great Melchizedek was. Even our father Abraham gave him a tenth of what he had captured. ⁵Now the law lays down a rule for the sons of Levi who become priests. They must collect a tenth from the people. They must collect it even from those who belong to the family line of Abraham.

⁶Melchizedek did not trace his family line from Levi. But he collected a tenth from Abraham. Melchizedek blessed the one who had received the promises. ⁷Without a doubt, the more important person blesses the less important one. ⁸In the one case, the tenth is collected by people who die. But in the other case, it is collected by the one who is said to be living.

⁹Levi collects the tenth. But we might say that Levi paid the

tenth through Abraham. [10]That's because when Melchizedek met Abraham, Levi was still in Abraham's body.

Jesus Is Like Melchizedek

[11]Suppose the Levites who were priests could have made people perfect. The law was given to the people so they could become perfect through the priests. Then why was there still a need for another priest to come? And why did he need to be like Melchizedek? Why wasn't he from Aaron's family line?

[12]A change of priests requires a change of law. [13]Those things are said about one who is from a different tribe. No one from that tribe has ever served at the altar. [14]It is clear that our Lord came from the family line of Judah. Moses said nothing about priests who were from that tribe.

[15]But suppose another priest like Melchizedek appears. Then what we have said is even more clear. [16]He has not become a priest because of a rule about his family line. He has become a priest because of his powerful life. His life can never be destroyed. [17]Scripture says,

> "You are a priest forever,
>   just like Melchizedek."   *(Psalm 110:4)*

[18]The old rule is done away with. It was weak and useless. [19]The law didn't make anything perfect. Now a better hope has been given to us. That hope brings us near to God.

[20]The change of priests was made with an oath. Others became priests without any oath. [21]But Jesus became a priest with an oath. God said to him,

> "The Lord has taken an oath and made a promise.
>   He will not change his mind. He has said,
>   'You are a priest forever.'"   *(Psalm 110:4)*

[22]Because of that oath, Jesus makes the promise of a better covenant certain.

[23]There were many priests in Levi's family line. Death kept them from continuing in office. [24]But Jesus lives forever. So he always holds the office of priest. [25]People now come to God through him. And he is able to save them completely and for all time. Jesus lives forever. He prays for them.

[26]A high priest like that meets our need. He is holy, pure and without blame. He isn't like other people. He does not sin. He is lifted high above the heavens.

²⁷He isn't like the other high priests. They need to offer sacrifices day after day. First they bring offerings for their own sins. Then they do it for the sins of the people. But Jesus gave one sacrifice for the sins of the people. He gave it once and for all time. He did it by offering himself.

²⁸The law appoints men who are weak to be high priests. But God's oath came after the law. The oath appointed the Son. He has been made perfect forever.

The High Priest of a New Covenant

8 Here is the point of what we are saying. We have a high priest like that. He sat down at the right hand of the throne of the King, the Majesty in heaven. ²He serves in the sacred tent. The Lord set up the true holy tent. People did not set it up.

³Every high priest is appointed to offer gifts and sacrifices. So that priest also had to have something to offer.

⁴What if he were on earth? Then he would not be a priest. There are already priests who offer the gifts required by the law. ⁵They serve at a sacred tent. But it is only a copy and shadow of what is in heaven. That's why God warned Moses when he was about to build the holy tent. God said, "Be sure to make everything just like the pattern I showed you on the mountain." *(Exodus 25:40)*

⁶Jesus has been given a greater work to do for God. He is the go-between for the new covenant. That covenant is better than the old one. It is based on better promises.

⁷Suppose nothing had been wrong with that first covenant. Then no one would have looked for another covenant. ⁸But God found fault with the people. He said,

"A new day is coming, says the Lord.
    I will make a new covenant
with the house of Israel.
    I will also make it with the house of Judah.
⁹It will not be like the covenant
    I made with their people of long ago.
That was when I took them by the hand.
    I led them out of Egypt.
My new covenant will be different because they didn't
    remain faithful to my old covenant.
So I turned away from them,
                                    says the Lord.

¹⁰This is the covenant I will make with Israel
> after that time, says the Lord.
I will put my laws in their minds.
> I will write my laws on their hearts.
I will be their God.
> And they will be my people.
¹¹They will not teach a neighbor anymore.
> And they will not teach a friend anymore.
They will not say, 'Know the Lord.'
They will all know me.
> From the least important of them to the most
> > important
everyone will know me.
¹²I will forgive their evil ways.
> I will not remember their sins anymore." *(Jeremiah 31:31–34)*

¹³God called that covenant "new." So he has made the first one out of date. And what is out of date and getting older will soon disappear.

Worship in the Holy Tent on Earth

9 The first covenant had rules for worship. It also had a sacred tent on earth.

²A holy tent was set up. The lampstand was in the first room. So were the table and the holy bread. That was called the Holy Room. ³Behind the second curtain was a room called the Most Holy Room. ⁴It had the golden altar for incense. It also had the wooden chest called the ark of the covenant. The ark was covered with gold. It held the gold jar of manna. It held Aaron's wooden staff that had budded. It also held the stone tablets. The words of the covenant were written on them.

⁵The cherubim were above the ark. God showed his glory there. The cherubim spread their wings over the place where sin was paid for. But we can't deal with those things more completely now.

⁶That's how everything was arranged in the holy tent. The priests entered it at regular times. They went into the outer room to do their work for God and others. ⁷But only the high priest went into the inner room. He went in only once a year. He never entered without taking blood with him. He offered the blood for himself. He also offered it for the sins the people had committed because they didn't know any better.

[8]Here is what the Holy Spirit was showing us. He was telling us that God had not yet clearly shown the way into the Most Holy Room. It would not be clearly shown as long as the first holy tent was still standing.

[9]That's an example for the present time. It shows us that the gifts and sacrifices they offered were not enough. They were not able to remove the worshiper's feelings of guilt. [10]They deal only with food and drink and different kinds of special washings. They are rules that deal with things outside our bodies. People had to obey them only until the new covenant came.

The Blood of Christ

[11]Christ came to be the high priest of the good things that are already here. When he came, he went through the greater and more perfect holy tent. The tent was not made by people. In other words, it is not a part of this creation.

[12]He did not enter by spilling the blood of goats and calves. He entered the Most Holy Room by spilling his own blood. He did it once and for all time. He paid the price to set us free from sin forever.

[13]The blood of goats and bulls is sprinkled on people. So are the ashes of a young cow. They are sprinkled on people the Law called unclean. The people are sprinkled to make them holy. That makes them clean on the outside.

[14]But Christ offered himself to God without any flaw. He did this through the power of the eternal Holy Spirit. So how much more will his blood wash from our minds our feelings of guilt for committing sin! Sin always leads to death. But now we can serve the living God.

[15]That's why Christ is the go-between of a new covenant. Now those God calls to himself will receive the eternal gift he promised. They will receive it now that Christ has died to save

GREAT VERSE — TO — REMEMBER

9:14 But Christ offered himself to God without any flaw ... So how much more will his blood wash from our minds our feelings of guilt for committing sin!

them. He died to set them free from the sins they committed under the first covenant.

¹⁶What happens in the case of a will? It is necessary to prove that the person who made the will has died. ¹⁷A will is in effect only when somebody has died. It never takes effect while the one who made it is still living. ¹⁸That's why even the first covenant was not put into effect without the spilling of blood.

¹⁹Moses first announced every commandment of the law to all the people. Then he took the blood of calves. He also took water, bright red wool and branches of a hyssop plant. He sprinkled the scroll. He also sprinkled all of the people. ²⁰He said, "This is the blood of the covenant God has commanded you to keep." *(Exodus 24:8)* ²¹In the same way, he sprinkled the holy tent with blood. He also sprinkled everything that was used in worship there.

²²In fact, the law requires that nearly everything be made clean with blood. Without the spilling of blood, no one can be forgiven.

²³So the copies of the heavenly things had to be made pure with those sacrifices. But the heavenly things themselves had to be made pure with better sacrifices.

²⁴Christ did not enter a sacred tent made by people. That tent was only a copy of the true one. He entered heaven itself. He did it to stand in front of God for us. He is there right now.

²⁵The high priest enters the Most Holy Room every year. He enters with blood that is not his own. But Christ did not enter heaven to offer himself again and again. ²⁶If he had, he would have had to suffer many times since the world was created. But now he has appeared once and for all time. He has come at the end of the ages to do away with sin. He has done that by offering himself.

²⁷People have to die once. After that, God will judge them. ²⁸In the same way, Christ was offered up once. He took away the sins of many people.

He will also come a second time. At that time he will not suffer for sin. Instead, he will come to bring salvation to those who are waiting for him.

Christ's Sacrifice Is Once and for All Time

10 The law is only a shadow of the good things that are coming. It is not the real things themselves. The same sacrifices have to be offered over and over again. They must be offered year after year. That's why the law can never make perfect those who come near to worship. ²If it could, wouldn't the sacrifices have stopped being offered? The worshipers would have been made clean once and for all time. They would not have felt guilty for their sins anymore.

³But those offerings remind people of their sins every year. ⁴It isn't possible for the blood of bulls and goats to take away sins.

⁵So when Christ came into the world, he said,

> "You didn't want sacrifices and offerings.
>   Instead, you prepared a body for me.
>   ⁶You weren't pleased
>   with burnt offerings and sin offerings.
>   ⁷Then I said, 'Here I am. It is written about me in the
>   scroll.
>   God, I have come to do what you want.'"   *(Psalm 40:6–8)*

⁸First Christ said, "You didn't want sacrifices and offerings. You didn't want burnt offerings and sin offerings. You weren't pleased with them." He said that even though the law required people to bring them. ⁹Then he said, "Here I am. I have come to do what you want." He did away with the first. He did it to put the second in place.

¹⁰We have been made holy by what God wanted. We have been made holy because Jesus Christ offered his body once and for all time.

¹¹Day after day every priest stands and does his special duties. He offers the same sacrifices again and again. But they can never take away sins.

¹²Jesus our priest offered one sacrifice for sins for all time. Then he sat down at the right hand of God. ¹³Since that time, he waits for his enemies to be put under his control. ¹⁴By that one sacrifice he has made perfect forever those who are being made holy.

¹⁵The Holy Spirit also gives witness to us about this. First he says,

> ¹⁶"This is the covenant I will make with them
>   after that time, says the Lord.
>   I will put my laws in their hearts.
>   I will write my laws on their minds."   *(Jeremiah 31:33)*

¹⁷Then he adds,

> "I will not remember their sins anymore.
>   I will not remember the evil things they have done."
>
>   *(Jeremiah 31:34)*

¹⁸Where those have been forgiven, there is no longer any offering for sin.

A Warning to Remain Faithful

¹⁹Brothers and sisters, we are not afraid to enter the Most Holy Room. We enter boldly because of the blood of Jesus. ²⁰His way is new because he lives. It has been opened for us through the curtain. I'm talking about his body.

²¹We also have a great priest over the house of God. ²²So let us come near to God with an honest and true heart. Let us come near with a faith that is sure and strong. Our hearts have been sprinkled. Our minds have been cleansed from a sense of guilt. Our bodies have been washed with pure water.

²³Let us hold firmly to the hope we claim to have. The One who promised is faithful.

²⁴Let us consider how we can stir up one another to love. Let us help one another to do good works. ²⁵Let us not give up meeting together. Some are in the habit of doing this. Instead, let us cheer each other up with words of hope. Let us do it all the more as you see the day coming when Christ will return.

²⁶What if we keep sinning on purpose? What if we do it even after we know the truth? Then there is no offering for our sins. ²⁷All we can do is to wait in fear for God to judge. His blazing fire will burn up his enemies.

²⁸Anyone who did not obey the law of Moses died without mercy if there were two or three witnesses. ²⁹What should be done to those who have hated the Son of God? What should be done to those who have said no to him? What should be done to those who have treated as an unholy thing the blood of the covenant that makes them holy? What should be done to those who have made fun of the Holy Spirit who brings God's grace? Don't you think people like that should be punished more than anyone else?

³⁰We know the One who said, "I am the One who judges peo-

GREAT VERSE — TO — REMEMBER

10:24 Let us consider how we can stir up one another to love. Let us help one another to do good works.

ple. I will pay them back." *(Deuteronomy 32:35)* Scripture also says, "The Lord will judge his people." *(Deuteronomy 32:36; Psalm 135:14)*

³¹It is a terrible thing to fall into the hands of the living God.

³²Remember those earlier days after you received the light. At that time you stood firm in a great struggle. You did it even in the face of suffering.

³³Sometimes you were made fun of in front of others. You were treated badly. At other times you stood side by side with people who were being treated like that. ³⁴You suffered together with people in prison. When your property was taken from you, you accepted it with joy. You knew that God had given you better and more lasting things.

³⁵So don't throw away your bold faith. It will bring you rich rewards. ³⁶You need to be faithful. Then you will do what God wants. You will receive what he has promised. ³⁷In just a very little while,

> "The one who is coming will come. He will not wait.
> ³⁸   The one who is in the right will live by faith.
>   If he pulls back,
>   I will not be pleased with him."   *(Habakkuk 2:3,4)*

³⁹But we aren't people who pull back and are destroyed. We are people who believe and are saved.

Living by Faith

11 Faith is being sure of what we hope for. It is being certain of what we do not see. ²That is what the people of long ago were praised for.

³We have faith. So we understand that everything was made when God commanded it. That's why we believe that what we see was not made out of what could be seen.

⁴Abel had faith. So he offered to God a better sacrifice than Cain did. Because of his faith Abel was praised as a godly man. God said good things about his offerings. Because of his faith Abel still speaks. He speaks even though he is dead.

GREAT VERSE —TO— REMEMBER   **11:1** Faith is being sure of what we hope for. It is being certain of what we do not see.

⁵Enoch had faith. So he was taken from this life. He didn't die. He just couldn't be found. God had taken him away. Before God took him, Enoch was praised as one who pleased God.

⁶Without faith it isn't possible to please God. Those who come to God must believe that he exists. And they must believe that he rewards those who look to him.

⁷Noah had faith. So he built an ark to save his family. He built it because of his great respect for God. God had warned him about things that could not yet be seen. Because of his faith he showed the world that it was guilty. Because of his faith he was considered right with God.

⁸Abraham had faith. So he obeyed God. God called him to go to a place he would later receive as his own. So he went. He did it even though he didn't know where he was going. ⁹Because of his faith he made his home in the land God had promised him. He was like an outsider in a strange country. He lived there in tents. So did Isaac and Jacob. They received the same promise he did. ¹⁰Abraham was looking forward to the city that has foundations. He was waiting for the city that God planned and built.

¹¹Abraham had faith. So God made it possible for him to become a father. He became a father even though he was too old. Sarah also was too old to have children. But Abraham believed that the One who made the promise was faithful. ¹²Abraham was past the time when he could have children. But many children came from that one man. They were as many as the stars in the sky. They were as many as the sand on the seashore. No one could count them.

¹³All those people were still living by faith when they died. They didn't receive the things God had promised. They only saw them and welcomed them from a long way off. They openly said that they were outsiders and strangers on earth.

¹⁴People who say things like that show that they are looking for a country of their own. ¹⁵What if they had been thinking of the country they had left? Then they could have returned to it. ¹⁶Instead, they longed for a better country. They wanted one in heaven.

So God is pleased when they call him their God. In fact, he has prepared a city for them.

¹⁷Abraham had faith. So he offered Isaac as a sacrifice. That happened when God put him to the test. Abraham had received the promises. But he was about to offer his one and only son. ¹⁸God had said to him, "Your family line will continue through Isaac."

(Genesis 21:12) Even so, Abraham was going to offer him up. [19]Abraham believed that God could raise the dead. In a way, he did receive Isaac back from death.

[20]Isaac had faith. So he blessed Jacob and Esau. He told them what was ahead for them.

[21]Jacob had faith. So he blessed each of Joseph's sons. He blessed them when he was dying. Because of his faith he worshiped God as he leaned on the top of his wooden staff.

[22]Joseph had faith. So he spoke to the people of Israel about their leaving Egypt. He gave directions about his bones. He did that toward the end of his life.

[23]Moses' parents had faith. So they hid him for three months after he was born. They saw he was a special child. They were not afraid of the king's command.

[24]Moses had faith. So he refused to be called the son of Pharaoh's daughter. That happened after he had grown up. [25]He chose to be treated badly together with the people of God. He chose that instead of enjoying sin's pleasures for a short time. [26]He suffered shame because of Christ. He thought it had great value. He considered it better than the riches of Egypt. He was looking ahead to God's reward.

[27]Because of his faith he left Egypt. It wasn't because he was afraid of the king's anger. He didn't let anything stop him. He saw the One who can't be seen.

[28]Because of his faith he was the first to keep the Passover Feast. He commanded the people of Israel to sprinkle blood on their doorways. He did it so that the destroying angel would not touch their oldest sons.

[29]The people had faith. So they passed through the Red Sea. They went through it as if it were dry land. The Egyptians tried to do it also. But they drowned.

[30]The people had faith. So the walls of Jericho fell down. It happened after they had marched around the city for seven days.

[31]Rahab, the prostitute, had faith. So she welcomed the spies. That's why she wasn't killed with those who didn't obey God.

[32]What more can I say? I don't have time to tell about all the others. I don't have time to talk about Gideon, Barak, Samson and Jephthah. I don't have time to tell about David, Samuel and the prophets. [33]Because of their faith they took over kingdoms. They ruled fairly. They received the blessings God had promised. They shut the mouths of lions. [34]They put out great fires. They escaped being killed by the sword. Their weakness was turned to

strength. They became powerful in battle. They beat back armies from other countries.

[35]Women received their dead back. The dead were raised to life again. Others were made to suffer greatly. But they refused to be set free. They did that so that after death they would be raised to a better life.

[36]Some were laughed at. Some were whipped. Still others were held by chains. They were put in prison. [37]Some were killed with stones. They were sawed in two. They were put to death by the sword. They went around wearing the skins of sheep and goats. They were poor. They were attacked. They were treated badly. [38]The world was not worthy of them. They wandered in deserts and mountains. They lived in caves. They lived in holes in the ground.

[39]All of those people were praised because they had faith. But none of them received what God had promised. [40]God had planned something better for us. So they would only be made perfect together with us.

12 A huge cloud of witnesses is all around us. So let us throw off everything that stands in our way. Let us throw off any sin that holds on to us so tightly. Let us keep on running the race marked out for us.

[2]Let us keep looking to Jesus. He is the author of faith. He also makes it perfect. He paid no attention to the shame of the cross. He suffered there because of the joy he was looking forward to. Then he sat down at the right hand of the throne of God.

[3]He put up with attacks from sinners. So think about him. Then you won't get tired. You won't lose hope.

God Trains His Children

[4]You struggle against sin. But you have not yet fought to the point of spilling your blood. [5]You have forgotten that word of hope. It speaks to you as children. It says,

GREAT VERSE —TO— REMEMBER

12:1-2 Let us throw off any sin that holds on to us so tightly. Let us keep on running the race marked out for us. Let us keep looking to Jesus.

> "My child, think of the Lord's training as important.
> Do not lose hope when he corrects you.
> ⁶The Lord trains those he loves.
> He punishes everyone he accepts as a child."

(Proverbs 3:11,12)

⁷Put up with hard times. God uses them to train you. He is treating you as children. What children are not trained by their parents? ⁸God trains all of his children. But what if he doesn't train you? Then you are like children of people who weren't married to each other. You are not truly God's children.

⁹Besides, we have all had human parents who trained us. We respected them for it. How much more should we be trained by the Father of our spirits and live!

¹⁰Our parents trained us for a little while. They did what they thought was best. But God trains us for our good. He wants us to share in his holiness.

¹¹No training seems pleasant at the time. In fact, it seems painful. But later on it produces a harvest of godliness and peace. It does that for those who have been trained by it.

¹²So lift your sagging arms. Strengthen your weak knees. ¹³"Make level paths for your feet to walk on." *(Proverbs 4:26)* Then those who have trouble walking won't be disabled. Instead, they will be healed.

A Warning Against Saying No to God

¹⁴Try your best to live in peace with everyone. Try to be holy. Without holiness no one will see the Lord.

¹⁵Be sure that no one misses God's grace. See to it that a bitter plant doesn't grow up. If it does, it will cause trouble. And it will pollute many people. ¹⁶See to it that no one commits sexual sins.

See to it that no one is godless like Esau. He sold the rights to what he would receive as the oldest son. He sold them for a single meal. ¹⁷As you know, after that he wanted to receive his father's blessing. But he was turned away. With tears he tried to get the blessing. But he couldn't get his father to change his mind.

¹⁸You haven't come to a mountain that can be touched. You haven't come to a mountain that is burning with fire. You haven't come to darkness, gloom and storm. ¹⁹You haven't come to a blast from God's trumpet. You haven't come to a voice speaking to you. When people heard that voice long ago, they begged it not to say anything more to them. ²⁰What God commanded was too

much for them. He said, "If even an animal touches the mountain, it must be killed with stones." *(Exodus 19:12,13)* ²¹The sight was
terrifying. Moses said, "I am trembling with fear." *(Deuteronomy 9:19)*

²²But you have come to Mount Zion. You have come to the
Jerusalem in heaven. It is the city of the living God. You have
come to a joyful gathering of angels. There are thousands and
thousands of them. ²³You have come to the church of God's people. God's first and only Son is over all things. God's people share
in what belongs to his Son. Their names are written in heaven.
You have come to God. He is the judge of all people.

You have come to the spirits of godly people who have been
made perfect. ²⁴You have come to Jesus. He is the go-between of
a new covenant. You have come to the sprinkled blood. It
promises better things than the blood of Abel.

²⁵Be sure that you don't say no to the One who speaks. People
did not escape when they said no to the One who warned them
on earth. And what if we turn away from the One who warns us
from heaven? How much less will we escape!

²⁶At that time his voice shook the earth. But now he has
promised, "Once more I will shake the earth. I will also shake the
heavens." *(Haggai 2:6)* ²⁷The words "once more" point out that what
can be shaken can be taken away. I'm talking about created
things. Then what can't be shaken will remain.

²⁸We are receiving a kingdom that can't be shaken. So let us be
thankful. Then we can worship God in a way that pleases him.
We will worship him with deep respect and wonder. ²⁹Our "God
is like a fire that burns everything up." *(Deuteronomy 4:24)*

Final Words

13 Keep on loving each other as brothers and sisters. ²Don't
forget to welcome strangers. By doing that, some people
have welcomed angels without knowing it.

³Remember those in prison as if you were in prison with them.
And remember those who are treated badly as if you yourselves
were suffering.

⁴All of you should honor marriage. You should keep the marriage bed pure. God will judge the person who commits adultery.
He will judge everyone who commits sexual sins.

⁵Don't be controlled by love for money. Be happy with what
you have. God has said,

"I will never leave you.

I will never desert you." *(Deuteronomy 31:6)*

⁶So we can say boldly,

"The Lord helps me. I will not be afraid.
What can people do to me?"   *(Psalm 118:6,7)*

⁷Remember your leaders. They spoke God's word to you. Think about the results of their way of life. Copy their faith.

⁸Jesus Christ is the same yesterday and today and forever.

⁹Don't be carried away by all kinds of strange teachings. It is good that God's grace makes our hearts strong. Don't depend on foods the Law requires. They have no value for the people who eat them. ¹⁰Some worship at the holy tent. But we have an altar that they have no right to eat from.

¹¹The high priest carries the blood of animals into the Most Holy Room. He brings their blood as a sin offering. But the bodies are burned outside the camp. ¹²Jesus also suffered outside the city gate. He suffered to make the people holy by spilling his own blood.

¹³So let us go to him outside the camp. Let us be willing to suffer the shame he suffered. ¹⁴Here we do not have a city that lasts. But we are looking for the city that is going to come.

¹⁵So let us never stop offering to God our praise through Jesus. Let us offer it as the fruit of lips that say they believe in him.

¹⁶Don't forget to do good. Don't forget to share with others. God is pleased with those kinds of offerings.

¹⁷Obey your leaders. Put yourselves under their authority. They keep watch over you. They know they are accountable to God for everything they do. Obey them so that their work will be a joy. If you make their work a heavy load, it won't do you any good.

¹⁸Pray for us. We feel sure we have done what is right. We long to live as we should in every way.

¹⁹I beg you to pray that I may return to you soon.

²⁰Our Lord Jesus is the great Shepherd of the sheep. The God who gives peace brought him back from the dead. He did it

GREAT VERSE —TO— REMEMBER   **13:8** Jesus Christ is the same yesterday and today and forever.

because of the blood of the eternal covenant. May God [21]supply you with everything good. Then you can do what he wants. May he do in us what is pleasing to him. We can do it only with the help of Jesus Christ. Give him glory for ever and ever. Amen.

[22]Brothers and sisters, I beg you to accept my word. It tells you to be faithful. I have written you only a short letter.

[23]I want you to know that our brother Timothy has been set free. If he arrives soon, I will come with him to see you.

[24]Greet all of your leaders. Greet all of God's people. The believers from Italy send you their greetings.

[25]May grace be with you all.

James

Why Was This Book Written? James wrote this letter. James was Jesus' brother. Jesus' brothers did not believe in him before he died. They became Christians after he rose from the dead. James lived in Jerusalem. He was a church leader there.

What Is This Book About? James taught people how to live as Christians. He said we must tell others that we believe in Jesus. He said we must also show our faith to others by what we do. If we only talk like Christians our faith is no good. We must act like Christians too.

What Is in This Book?

1 I, James, am writing this letter. I serve God and the Lord Jesus Christ.

I am sending this letter to you, the 12 tribes that are scattered among the nations.

Greetings.

Facing All Kinds of Trouble

²My brothers and sisters, you will face all kinds of trouble. When you do, think of it as pure joy. ³Your faith will be put to the test. You know that when that happens it will produce in you the strength to continue. ⁴The strength to keep going must be allowed to finish its work. Then you will be all you should be. You will have everything you need.

⁵If any of you need wisdom, ask God for it. He will give it to you. God gives freely to everyone. He doesn't find fault.

⁶But when you ask, you must believe. You must not doubt. People who doubt are like waves of the sea. The wind blows and tosses them around. ⁷People like that shouldn't expect to receive anything from the Lord. ⁸They can't make up their minds. They can never decide what to do.

⁹Believers who find themselves in a low position in life should be proud that God has given them a high position. ¹⁰But those who are rich should take pride in their low position. That's because they will fade away like wild flowers.

¹¹The sun rises. Its burning heat dries up the plants. Their blossoms fall. Their beauty is destroyed. In the same way, rich people will fade away even as they go about their business.

¹²Blessed are those who keep on going when times are hard. After they have come through them, they will receive a crown. The crown is life itself. God has promised it to those who love him.

¹³When you are tempted, you shouldn't say, "God is tempting me." God can't be tempted by evil. And he doesn't tempt anyone.

¹⁴But your own evil longings tempt you. They lead you on and drag you away. ¹⁵When they are allowed to grow, they give birth to sin. When sin has grown up, it gives birth to death.

¹⁶My dear brothers and sisters, don't let anyone fool you. ¹⁷Every good and perfect gift is from God. It comes down from the Father. He created the heavenly lights. He does not change like shadows that move.

¹⁸God chose to give us new birth through the message of truth. He wanted us to be the first and best of everything he created.

Listen to the Word and Do What It Says

¹⁹My dear brothers and sisters, pay attention to what I say. Everyone should be quick to listen. But they should be slow to speak. They should be slow to get angry. ²⁰Human anger doesn't produce the kind of life God wants.

²¹So get rid of everything that is dirty and sinful. Get rid of the evil that is all around us. Don't be too proud to accept the word that is planted in you. It can save you.

²²Don't just listen to the word. You fool yourselves if you do that. You must do what it says.

²³Suppose you listen to the word but don't do what it says. Then you are like people who look at their faces in a mirror. ²⁴After looking at themselves, they leave. Right away they forget what they look like.

²⁵But suppose you take a good look at the perfect law that gives freedom. You keep looking at it. You don't forget what you've heard, but you do what the law says. Then you will be blessed in what you do.

²⁶Suppose you think your beliefs are right because of how you live. But you don't control what you say. Then you are fooling yourselves. Your beliefs are not worth anything at all.

²⁷Here are the kinds of beliefs that God our Father accepts as pure and without fault. When widows and children who have no parents are in trouble, take care of them. And keep yourselves from being polluted by the world.

Treat Everyone the Same

2 My brothers and sisters, you are believers in our glorious Lord Jesus Christ. So treat everyone the same.

²Suppose someone comes into your meeting wearing a gold ring and fine clothes. And suppose a poor person in worn-out clothes also comes in. ³Would you show special attention to the

1:17 Every good and perfect gift is from God. It comes down from the Father.

one who is wearing fine clothes? Would you say, "Here's a good seat for you"? Would you say to the poor person, "You stand there"? Or "Sit on the floor by my feet"? ⁴If you would, aren't you treating some people better than others? Aren't you like judges who have evil thoughts?

⁵My dear brothers and sisters, listen to me. Hasn't God chosen those who are poor in the world's eyes to be rich in faith? Hasn't he chosen them to receive the kingdom? Hasn't he promised it to those who love him?

⁶But you have put down poor people. Aren't rich people taking advantage of you? Aren't they dragging you into court? ⁷Aren't they speaking evil things against the worthy name of Jesus? Remember, you belong to him.

⁸The royal law is found in Scripture. It says, "Love your neighbor as you love yourself." *(Leviticus 19:18)* If you really keep that law, you are doing what is right. ⁹But you sin if you don't treat everyone the same. The law judges you because you have broken it.

¹⁰Suppose you keep the whole law but trip over just one part of it. Then you are guilty of breaking all of it. ¹¹God said, "Do not commit adultery." *(Exodus 20:14; Deuteronomy 5:18)* He also said, "Do not commit murder." *(Exodus 20:13; Deuteronomy 5:17)* Suppose you don't commit adultery but do commit murder. Then you have broken the law.

¹²Speak and act like people who are going to be judged by the law that gives freedom. ¹³Those who have not shown mercy will not receive mercy when they are judged. To show mercy is better than to judge.

Show Your Faith by What You Do

¹⁴My brothers and sisters, what good is it if people claim they have faith but don't act like it? Can that kind of faith save them? ¹⁵Suppose a brother or sister has no clothes or food. ¹⁶Suppose one of you says, "Go. I hope everything turns out fine for you. Keep warm. Eat well." And you do nothing about what they

GREAT VERSE —TO— REMEMBER

2:14,17 What good is it if people claim they have faith but don't act like it? ... It is the same with faith. If it doesn't cause us to do something, it's dead.

really need. Then what good have you done?

¹⁷It is the same with faith. If it doesn't cause us to do something, it's dead.

¹⁸But someone will say, "You have faith. I do good works."

Show me your faith that doesn't do good works. And I will show you my faith by what I do. ¹⁹You believe there is one God. Good! Even the demons believe that. And they tremble!

²⁰You foolish person! Do you want proof that faith without good works is useless? ²¹Our father Abraham offered his son Isaac on the altar. Wasn't he considered to be right with God because of what he did? ²²So you see that what he believed and what he did were working together. What he did made his faith complete.

²³That is what Scripture means where it says, "Abraham believed God. God accepted Abraham because he believed. So his faith made him right with God." *(Genesis 15:6)* And that's not all. God called Abraham his friend. ²⁴So you see that people are made right with God by what they do. It doesn't happen only because of what they believe.

²⁵Didn't God make even Rahab the prostitute right with him? That's because of what she did. She gave the spies a place to stay. Then she sent them off in a different direction.

²⁶The body without the spirit is dead. In the same way, faith without good works is dead.

Control What You Say

3 My brothers and sisters, most of you shouldn't want to be teachers. You know that those of us who teach will be held more accountable.

²All of us get tripped up in many ways. Suppose you are never wrong in what you say. Then you are perfect. You are able to keep your whole body under control.

³We put a bit in the mouth of a horse to make it obey us. We can control the whole animal with it. ⁴And how about ships? They are very big. They are driven along by strong winds. But they are steered by a very small rudder. It makes them go where the captain wants to go.

⁵In the same way, the tongue is a small part of the body. But it brags a lot. Think about how a small spark can set a big forest on fire.

⁶The tongue also is a fire. The tongue is the most evil part of the body. It pollutes the whole person. It sets a person's whole way of life on fire. And the tongue is set on fire by hell.

⁷People have controlled all kinds of animals, birds, reptiles and creatures of the sea. They still control them. ⁸But no one can control the tongue. It is an evil thing that never rests. It is full of deadly poison.

⁹With our tongues we praise our Lord and Father. With our tongues we call down curses on people. We do it even though they have been created to be like God. ¹⁰Praise and cursing come out of the same mouth. My brothers and sisters, it shouldn't be that way.

¹¹Can fresh water and salt water flow out of the same spring? ¹²My brothers and sisters, can a fig tree bear olives? Can a grapevine bear figs? Of course not. And a saltwater spring can't produce fresh water either.

Two Kinds of Wisdom

¹³Are any of you wise and understanding? You should show it by living a good life. Wise people aren't proud when they do good works.

¹⁴But suppose your hearts are jealous and bitter. Suppose you are concerned only about getting ahead. Don't brag about it. Don't say no to the truth. ¹⁵Wisdom like that doesn't come down from heaven. It belongs to the earth. It doesn't come from the Holy Spirit. It comes from the devil.

¹⁶Are you jealous? Are you concerned only about getting ahead? Then your life will be a mess. You will be doing all kinds of evil things.

¹⁷But the wisdom that comes from heaven is pure. That's the most important thing about it. And that's not all. It also loves peace. It thinks about others. It obeys. It is full of mercy and good fruit. It is fair. It doesn't pretend to be what it is not.

¹⁸Those who make peace should plant peace like a seed. If they do, it will produce a crop of right living.

Obey God

4 Why do you fight and argue among yourselves? Isn't it because of your sinful longings? They fight inside you.

²You want something, but you can't get it. You kill and want what others have. But you can't have what you want. You argue and fight. You don't have what you want, because you don't ask God. ³When you do ask for something, you don't receive it. Why? Because you ask for the wrong reason. You want to spend your money on your sinful pleasures.

⁴You are not faithful to God. Don't you know that to be a friend of the world is to hate God? Anyone who chooses to be a friend of the world becomes an enemy of God. ⁵Don't you know what Scripture says? The spirit that God caused to live in us wants us to belong only to God. Don't you think Scripture has a reason for saying that? ⁶God continues to give us more grace. That's why Scripture says,

"God opposes those who are proud.
But he gives grace to those who are not." *(Proverbs 3:34)*

⁷So obey God. Stand up to the devil. He will run away from you. ⁸Come near to God, and he will come near to you. Wash your hands, you sinners. Make your hearts pure, you who can't make up your minds.

⁹Be full of sorrow. Cry and sob. Change your laughter to crying. Change your joy to sadness. ¹⁰Bow down to the Lord. He will lift you up.

¹¹My brothers and sisters, don't speak against one another. Anyone who speaks against another believer speaks against the law. And anyone who judges another believer judges the law. When you judge the law, you are not keeping it. Instead, you are acting as if you were its judge.

¹²There is only one Lawgiver and Judge. He is the One who is able to save life or destroy it. But who are you to judge your neighbor?

Bragging About Tomorrow

¹³Now listen, you who say, "Today or tomorrow we will go to this or that city. We will spend a year there. We will buy and sell and make money." ¹⁴You don't even know what will happen tomorrow. What is your life? It is a mist that appears for a little while. Then it disappears. ¹⁵Instead, you should say, "If it pleases the Lord, we will live and do this or that."

GREAT VERSE —TO— REMEMBER

4:7-8 So obey God. Stand up to the devil. He will run away from you. Come near to God, and he will come near to you.

[16]As it is, you are proud. You brag about it. That kind of bragging is evil. [17]So when you know the good things you should do and don't do them, you sin.

A Warning to Rich People

5 You rich people, listen to me. Cry and sob, because you will soon be suffering.

[2]Your riches have rotted. Moths have eaten your clothes. [3]Your gold and silver have lost their brightness. Their dullness will give witness against you. Your wanting more and more will eat your body like fire. You have stored up riches in these last days.

[4]You have even failed to pay the workers who mowed your fields. Their pay is crying out against you. The cries of those who gathered the harvest have reached the ears of the Lord who rules over all.

[5]You have lived an easy life on earth. You have given yourselves everything you wanted. You have made yourselves fat like cattle that will soon be butchered. [6]You have judged and murdered people who aren't guilty. And they weren't even opposing you.

Be Patient When You Suffer

[7]Brothers and sisters, be patient until the Lord comes. See how the farmer waits for the land to produce its rich crop. See how patient he is for the fall and spring rains. [8]You too must be patient. You must stand firm. The Lord will soon come back.

[9]Brothers and sisters, don't find fault with one another. If you do, you will be judged. And the Judge is standing at the door!

[10]Brothers and sisters, think about the prophets who spoke in the name of the Lord. They are an example of how to be patient when you suffer. [11]As you know, we think that people who don't give up are blessed. You have heard that Job was patient. And you have seen what the Lord finally did for him. The Lord is full of tender mercy and loving concern.

[12]My brothers and sisters, don't take an oath when you make a promise. Don't call on heaven or earth or anything else to back up what you say. Let your "Yes" be yes. And let your "No" be no. If you don't, you will be judged.

The Prayer of Faith

[13]Are any of you in trouble? Then you should pray. Are any of you happy? Then sing songs of praise.

¹⁴Are any of you sick? Then send for the elders of the church to pray over you. Ask them to anoint you with oil in the name of the Lord. ¹⁵The prayer offered by those who have faith will make you well. The Lord will heal you. If you have sinned, you will be forgiven.

¹⁶So admit to one another that you have sinned. Pray for one another so that you might be healed. The prayer of a godly person is powerful. It makes things happen.

¹⁷Elijah was just like us. He prayed hard that it wouldn't rain. And it didn't rain on the land for three and a half years. ¹⁸Then he prayed again. That time it rained. And the earth produced its crops.

¹⁹My brothers and sisters, suppose one of you wanders away from the truth and someone brings you back. ²⁰Then here is what I want you to remember. Those who turn sinners from going down the wrong path will save them from death. God will erase many sins by forgiving them.

5:13 Are any of you in trouble? Then you should pray. Are any of you happy? Then sing songs of praise.

1 Peter

Why Was This Book Written? **P**eter was one of Jesus' twelve disciples. He wrote this letter. He wrote to the Christians who lived in north Asia. They were being hurt for believing in Jesus. Some were put in prison too. Peter wrote to cheer them up.

What Is This Book About? **P**eter wanted the people to be brave. He reminded them Jesus had been hurt too. Jesus was brave. He trusted God. Peter said Jesus had died for them. They were special to God. We must trust God too. We must live the way God wants us to live.

What Is in This Book?

1 I, Peter, am writing this letter. I am an apostle of Jesus Christ.

I am sending this letter to you, God's chosen people. You are strangers in the world. You are scattered all over Pontus, Galatia, Cappadocia, Asia and Bithynia. ²You have been chosen in keeping with what God the Father had planned. That happened through the Spirit's work to make you pure and holy. God chose you so that you might obey Jesus Christ. He wanted you to be made clean by the blood of Christ.

May more and more grace and peace be given to you.

Peter Praises God for a Hope That Is Alive

³Give praise to the God and Father of our Lord Jesus Christ. In his great mercy he has given us a new birth and a hope that is alive. It is alive because Jesus Christ rose from the dead. ⁴He has given us new birth so that we might share in what belongs to him. It is a gift that can never be destroyed. It can never spoil or even fade away. It is kept in heaven for you. ⁵Through faith you are kept safe by God's power. Your salvation is going to be completed. It is ready to be shown to you in the last days.

⁶Because you know this, you have great joy. You have joy even though you may have had to suffer for a little while. You may have had to suffer sadness in all kinds of trouble.

⁷Your troubles have come in order to prove that your faith is real. It is worth more than gold. Gold can pass away even though fire has made it pure. Your faith is meant to bring praise, honor and glory to God. That will happen when Jesus Christ returns.

⁸Even though you have not seen him, you love him. Though you do not see him now, you believe in him. You are filled with a glorious joy that can't be put into words. ⁹You are receiving the salvation of your souls. It is the result of your faith.

¹⁰The prophets searched very hard and with great care to find out about that salvation. They spoke about the grace that was going to come to you. ¹¹They wanted to find out when that salvation would come. The Spirit of Christ in them was telling them about the sufferings of Christ that were going to come. He was

---

1:7 Your troubles have come in order to prove that your faith is real. It is worth more than gold.

also telling them about the glory that would follow.

¹²It was made known to the prophets that they were not serving themselves. Instead, they were serving you when they spoke about the things that you have now heard. Those who have preached the good news to you have told you those things. They have done it with the help of the Holy Spirit sent from heaven. Even angels long to look into those things.

Be Holy

¹³So prepare your minds for action. Control yourselves. Put your hope completely in the grace that will be given to you when Jesus Christ returns.

¹⁴You should obey. You shouldn't give in to evil longings. They controlled your life when you didn't know any better. ¹⁵The one who chose you is holy. So you should be holy in all that you do. ¹⁶It is written: "Be holy, because I am holy." *(Leviticus 11:44,45; 19:2)*

¹⁷You call on a Father who judges each person's work without favoring one over another. So live your lives as strangers here. Have the highest respect for God.

¹⁸The blood of Christ set you free from an empty way of life. That way of life was handed down to you by your own people long ago. You know that you were not bought with things that can pass away, like silver or gold. ¹⁹Instead, you were bought by the priceless blood of Christ. He is a perfect lamb. He doesn't have any flaws at all. ²⁰He was chosen before God created the world. But he came into the world in these last days for you.

²¹Because of what Christ has done, you believe in God. It was God who raised him from the dead. And it was God who gave him glory. So your faith and hope are in God.

²²You have made yourselves pure by obeying the truth. So you have an honest and true love for your brothers and sisters. Love each other deeply, from the heart.

²³You have been born again by means of the living word of God. His word lasts forever. You were not born again from a seed that will die. You were born from a seed that can't die. ²⁴It is written:

> "All people are like grass.
>   All of their glory is like the flowers in the field.
> The grass dries up. The flowers fall to the ground.

²⁵   But the word of the Lord stands forever." *(Isaiah 40:6–8)*

And that word was preached to you.

2 So get rid of every kind of evil. Stop telling lies. Don't pretend to be something you are not. Stop wanting what others have. Don't speak against each other.

²Like babies that were just born, you should long for the pure milk of God's word. It will help you grow up as believers. ³You can do it now that you have tasted how good the Lord is.

The Living Stone and a Chosen People

⁴Christ is the living Stone. People did not accept him. But God chose him. God places the highest value on him.

⁵You also are like living stones. As you come to him you are being built into a house for worship. There you will be holy priests. You will offer spiritual sacrifices. God will accept them because of what Jesus Christ has done.

⁶In Scripture it says,

> "Look! I am placing a stone in Zion.
>> It is a chosen and very valuable stone.
>> It is the most important stone in the building.
> The one who trusts in him
>> will never be put to shame."   *(Isaiah 28:16)*

⁷The stone is very valuable to you who believe. But to people who do not believe,

> "The stone the builders did not accept
>> has become the most important stone of all."
>   *(Psalm 118:22)*

⁸And,

> "It is a stone that causes people to trip.
>> It is a rock that makes them fall."   *(Isaiah 8:14)*

They trip and fall because they do not obey the message. That is also what God planned for them.

2:9 God chose you to be his people. You are royal priests. You are a holy nation. You are a people who belong to God.

⁹But God chose you to be his people. You are royal priests. You are a holy nation. You are a people who belong to God. All of this is so that you can sing his praises. He brought you out of darkness into his wonderful light. ¹⁰Once you were not a people. But now you are the people of God. Once you had not received mercy. But now you have received mercy.

¹¹Dear friends, you are outsiders and strangers in this world. So I'm asking you not to give in to your sinful longings. They fight against your soul. ¹²People who don't believe might say you are doing wrong. But lead good lives among them. Then they will see your good works. And they will give glory to God on the day he comes to judge.

Obey Your Rulers and Masters

¹³Follow the lead of every human authority. Do it because the Lord wants you to. Obey the king. He is the highest authority. ¹⁴Obey the governors. The king sends them to punish those who do wrong. He also sends them to praise those who do right. ¹⁵By doing good you will put a stop to the talk of foolish people. They don't know what they are saying. God wants you to stop them.

¹⁶Live like free people. But don't use your freedom to cover up evil. Live like people who serve God. ¹⁷Show proper respect to everyone. Love the community of believers. Have respect for God. Honor the king.

¹⁸Slaves, obey your masters with all the respect you should give them. Obey not only those who are good and kind. Obey also those who are not kind. ¹⁹Suppose a person suffers pain unfairly because he wants to obey God. That is worthy of praise. ²⁰But suppose you receive a beating for doing wrong, and you put up with it. Will anyone honor you for that? Of course not. But suppose you suffer for doing good, and you put up with it. God will praise you for that.

²¹Christ suffered for you. He left you an example. He expects you to follow in his steps. You too were chosen to suffer. ²²Scripture says,

> "He didn't commit any sin.
> No lies ever came out of his mouth." *(Isaiah 53:9)*

²³People shouted at him and made fun of him. But he didn't do the same back to them. He suffered. But he didn't say that bad things would happen to them. Instead, he trusted in the One who judges fairly.

²⁴He himself carried our sins in his body on the cross. He did it so that we would die as far as sins are concerned. Then we would lead godly lives. His wounds have made you whole.

²⁵You were like sheep who were wandering away. But now you have returned to the Shepherd. He is the Leader of your souls.

Wives and Husbands

3 Wives, follow the lead of your husbands. Suppose some of them don't believe God's word. Then let them be won to Christ without words by seeing how their wives behave. ²Let them see how pure you are. Let them see that your lives are full of respect for God.

³Braiding your hair doesn't make you beautiful. Wearing gold jewelry or fine clothes doesn't make you beautiful. ⁴Instead, your beauty comes from inside you. It is the beauty of a gentle and quiet spirit. Beauty like that doesn't fade away. God places great value on it.

⁵This is how the holy women of the past used to make themselves beautiful. They put their hope in God. And they followed the lead of their own husbands.

⁶Sarah was like that. She obeyed Abraham. She called him her master. Do you want to be like her? Then do what is right. And don't give in to fear.

⁷Husbands, take good care of your wives. They are weaker than you. So treat them with respect. Honor them as those who will share with you the gracious gift of life. Then nothing will stand in the way of your prayers.

Suffering for Doing Good

⁸Finally, I want all of you to live together in peace. Be understanding. Love one another like members of the same family. Be kind and tender. Don't be proud. ⁹Don't pay back evil with evil. Don't pay back unkind words with unkind words. Instead, pay

---

3:9 Don't pay back evil with evil. Don't pay back unkind words with unkind words. Instead, pay them back with kind words.

them back with kind words. That's what you have been chosen to do. You can receive a blessing by doing it.

¹⁰Scripture says,

"Do you want to love life
    and see good days?
Then keep your tongues from speaking evil.
    Keep your lips from telling lies.
¹¹Turn away from evil, and do good.
    Look for peace, and go after it.
¹²The Lord's eyes look with favor on those who are godly.
    His ears are open to their prayers.
But the Lord doesn't look with favor on those who do
    evil." *(Psalm 34:12–16)*

¹³Who is going to hurt you if you really want to do good? ¹⁴But suppose you suffer for doing what is right. Then you will be blessed. Scripture also says, "Don't fear what others fear. Don't be afraid." *(Isaiah 8:12)*

¹⁵But make sure in your hearts that Christ is Lord. Always be ready to give an answer to anyone who asks you about the hope you have. Be ready to give the reason for it. But do it gently and with respect.

¹⁶Live so that you don't have to feel you've done anything wrong. Some people may say evil things about your good conduct as believers in Christ. If they do, they will be put to shame for speaking like that about you. ¹⁷It is better to suffer for doing good than for doing evil if that's what God wants.

¹⁸Christ died for sins once and for all time. The One who did what is right died for those who don't do right. He died to bring you to God. His body was put to death. But the Holy Spirit brought him back to life.

¹⁹By means of the Spirit, Christ went and preached to the spirits in prison. ²⁰Long ago they did not obey. God was patient while Noah was building the ark. He waited, but only a few people went into the ark. A total of eight were saved by means of water.

GREAT VERSE —TO— REMEMBER **4:8** Love one another deeply. Love erases many sins by forgiving them.

²¹The water of the flood is a picture of the baptism that now saves you also. The baptism I'm talking about has nothing to do with removing dirt from your body. Instead, it promises God that you will keep a clear sense of what is right and wrong.

Jesus Christ has saved you by rising from the dead. ²²He has gone into heaven. He is at God's right hand. Angels, authorities and powers are under his control.

Living for God

4 Christ suffered in his body. So get ready as a soldier does. Prepare yourselves to think in the same way Christ did. Do it because those who have suffered in their bodies are finished with sin. ²As a result, they don't live the rest of their lives on earth controlled by evil human longings. Instead, they live to do what God wants.

³You have spent enough time in the past doing what ungodly people choose to do. You lived a wild life. You longed for evil things. You got drunk. You went to wild parties. You worshiped statues of gods. The Lord hates that.

⁴Ungodly people think that it's strange when you no longer join them in what they do. They want you to rush into the same flood of wasteful living. So they say bad things about you.

⁵But they will have to explain their actions to God. He is ready to judge the living and the dead. ⁶That's why the good news was preached even to people who are now dead. Human judges said they were guilty as far as their bodies were concerned. But God set their spirits free to live as he wanted them to.

⁷The end of all things is near. So keep a clear mind. Control yourselves. Then you can pray. ⁸Most of all, love one another deeply. Love erases many sins by forgiving them. ⁹Welcome others into your homes without complaining.

¹⁰God's gifts of grace come in many forms. Each of you has received a gift in order to serve others. You should use it faithfully. ¹¹If you speak, you should do it like one speaking God's very words. If you serve, you should do it with the strength God provides. Then in all things God will be praised through Jesus Christ.

Give him the glory and the power for ever and ever. Amen.

Suffering for Being a Christian

¹²Dear friends, don't be surprised by the painful suffering you are going through. Don't feel as if something strange were happening to you. ¹³Be joyful that you are taking part in Christ's

sufferings. Then you will be filled with joy when Christ returns in glory.

[14]Suppose people make fun of you because you believe in Christ. Then you are blessed, because God's Spirit rests on you. He is the Spirit of glory. [15]Suppose you suffer. Then it shouldn't be because you are a murderer or a thief. It shouldn't be because you do evil things. It shouldn't be because you poke your nose into other people's business. [16]But suppose you suffer for being a Christian. Then don't be ashamed. Instead, praise God because you are known by that name.

[17]It is time for people to be judged. It will begin with the family of God. And since it begins with us, what will happen to people who don't obey God's good news? [18]Scripture says,

> "Suppose it is hard for godly people to be saved.
> Then what will happen to ungodly people and
> sinners?" *(Proverbs 11:31)*

[19]Some people will suffer because God has planned it that way. They should commit themselves to their faithful Creator. And they should continue to do good.

To Elders and Young Men

5 I'm speaking to the elders among you. I was a witness of Christ's sufferings. And I will also share in the glory that is going to come. I'm making my appeal to you as one who is an elder together with you. [2]Be shepherds of God's flock, the believers who are under your care. Serve as their leaders. Don't serve them because you have to. Instead, do it because you want to. That's what God wants you to do. Don't do it because you want to get more and more money. Do it because you really want to serve.

[3]Don't act as if you were a ruler over those who are under your care. Instead, be examples to the flock. [4]The Chief Shepherd will come again. Then you will receive the crown of glory. It is a crown that will never fade away.

[5]Young men, follow the lead of those who are older. All of you, put on a spirit that is free of pride toward each other as if it were your clothes. Scripture says,

> "God opposes those who are proud.
> But he gives grace to those who are not." *(Proverbs 3:34)*

[6]So don't be proud. Put yourselves under God's mighty hand.

Then he will honor you at the right time. ⁷Turn all your worries over to him. He cares about you.

⁸Control yourselves. Be on your guard. Your enemy the devil is like a roaring lion. He prowls around looking for someone to chew up and swallow. ⁹Stand up to him. Stand firm in what you believe. All over the world you know that your brothers and sisters are going through the same kind of suffering.

¹⁰God always gives you all the grace you need. So you will only have to suffer for a little while. Then God himself will build you up again. He will make you strong and steady. And he has chosen you to share in his eternal glory because you belong to Christ.

¹¹Give him the power for ever and ever. Amen.

Final Greetings

¹²I consider Silas to be a faithful brother. With his help I have written you this short letter. I have written it to cheer you up. And I have written to give witness about the true grace of God. Stand firm in it.

¹³The members of the church in Babylon send you their greetings. They were chosen together with you. Mark, my son in the faith, also sends you his greetings. ¹⁴Greet each other with a friendly kiss.

May God give peace to all of you who believe in Christ.

5:7 Turn all your worries over to him. He cares about you.

2 Peter

Why Was This Book Written? This is Peter's second letter to Christians in Asia. He had told them to be brave when they were in prison. Now they were in trouble again. False teachers gave them bad advice. Peter wanted them to know the truth.

What Is This Book About? Peter wanted the Christians to have faith. He told them much about God. He told them how God wanted them to act. Peter wanted them to live a holy life. Peter said God would get rid of the false teachers. He also said Jesus would come again.

What Is in This Book?

1 I, Simon Peter, am writing this letter. I serve Jesus Christ. I am his apostle.

I am sending this letter to you who have received a faith as valuable as ours. You received it because our God and Savior Jesus Christ does what is right and fair for everyone.

²May more and more grace and peace be given to you. May they come to you as you learn more about God and about Jesus our Lord.

Be Sure That God Has Chosen You

³God's power has given us everything we need to lead a godly life. All of that has come to us because we know the One who chose us. He chose us because of his own glory and goodness.

⁴He has also given us his very great and valuable promises. He did it so you could share in his nature. He also did it so you could escape from the evil in the world. That evil is caused by sinful longings.

⁵So you should try very hard to add goodness to your faith. To goodness, add knowledge. ⁶To knowledge, add the ability to control yourselves. To the ability to control yourselves, add the strength to keep going. To the strength to keep going, add godliness. ⁷To godliness, add kindness to believers. And to kindness to believers, add love.

⁸You should possess more and more of those good points. They will make you useful and fruitful as you get to know our Lord Jesus Christ better.

⁹But what if some of you do not have those good points? Then you can't see very well. You are blind. You have forgotten that your past sins have been washed away.

¹⁰My brothers and sisters, be very sure that God has appointed you to be saved. Be sure that he has chosen you. If you do everything I have just said, you will never trip and fall. ¹¹You will receive a rich welcome into the kingdom that lasts forever. It is the kingdom of our Lord and Savior Jesus Christ.

GREAT VERSE —TO— REMEMBER **1:3** God's power has given us everything we need to lead a godly life.

Prophecy Comes From God

[12]So I will always remind you of these things. I'll do it even though you know them. I'll do it even though you now have deep roots in the truth. [13]I think it is right for me to remind you. It is right as long as I live in this tent. I'm talking about my body.

[14]I know my tent will soon be removed. Our Lord Jesus Christ has made that clear to me. [15]I hope that you will always be able to remember these things after I'm gone. I will try very hard to see that you do.

[16]We told you about the time our Lord Jesus Christ came with power. But we didn't make up stories when we told you about it. With our own eyes we saw him in all his majesty. [17]God the Father gave him honor and glory. The voice of the Majestic Glory came to him. It said, "This is my Son, and I love him. I am very pleased with him." (Matthew 17:5; Mark 9:7; Luke 9:35) [18]We ourselves heard the voice that came from heaven. We were with him on the sacred mountain.

[19]The word of the prophets is made more certain. We have that word. You must pay attention to it. It is like a light shining in a dark place. It will shine until the day Jesus comes. Then the Morning Star will rise in your hearts.

[20]Above all, here is what you must understand. No prophecy in Scripture ever came from a prophet's own understanding. [21]It never came simply because people wanted it to. Instead, the Holy Spirit guided the prophets as they spoke. So prophecy comes from God.

False Teachers Will Be Destroyed

2 But there were also false prophets among the people. In the same way there will be false teachers among you. In secret they will bring in teachings that will destroy you. They will even turn against the Lord and Master who died to save them. His death paid for their sins. They will quickly destroy themselves. [2]Many people will follow their shameful ways. They will give the way of truth a bad name.

[3]Those teachers are never satisfied. They want to get something out of you. So they make up stories to take advantage of you. They have been under a sentence of death for a long time. The One who will destroy them has not been sleeping.

[4]God did not spare angels when they sinned. Instead, he sent them to hell. He put them in dark prisons. He will keep them

there until he judges them. ⁵God did not spare the world's ungodly people long ago. He brought the flood on them. But Noah preached about the right way to live. God kept him safe. He also saved seven others. ⁶God judged the cities of Sodom and Gomorrah. He burned them to ashes. He made them an example of what is going to happen to ungodly people.

⁷God saved Lot. He was a man who did what was right. He was shocked by the dirty, sinful lives of people who didn't obey God's laws. ⁸That good man lived among them day after day. He saw and heard the evil things they were doing. They were breaking God's laws. And his godly spirit was deeply troubled.

⁹So the Lord knows how to keep godly people safe in times of testing. He also knows how to keep ungodly people under guard until the day they will be judged. In the meantime, he continues to punish them. ¹⁰Most of all, this is true of people who follow the evil longings of their sinful natures. They hate to be under authority.

Those false prophets are bold and proud. They aren't afraid to speak evil things against heavenly beings. ¹¹Angels are stronger and more powerful than those people. But even angels don't bring to the Lord evil charges against heavenly beings.

¹²Those people speak evil about things they don't understand. They are like wild animals. They do what comes naturally to them. They are born only to be caught and destroyed. Just like animals, they too will die.

¹³They will be paid back with harm for the harm they have done. Their idea of pleasure is to have wild parties in the middle of the day. They are like spots and stains. They enjoy their sinful pleasures while they eat with you. ¹⁴They stare at women who are not their wives. They want to have sex with them. They never stop sinning. They trap those who are not firm in their faith. They have mastered the art of getting what they want. God has placed them under his curse.

¹⁵They have left God's way. They have wandered off. They follow the way of Balaam, son of Beor. He loved to get paid for doing his evil work. ¹⁶But a donkey corrected him for the wrong he did. Animals don't speak. But the donkey spoke with a human voice. It tried to stop the prophet from doing a very dumb thing.

¹⁷Those false prophets are like springs without water. They are like mists driven by a storm. The blackest darkness is reserved for them.

¹⁸They speak empty, bragging words. They make their appeal

to the earthly longings of people's sinful nature. They tempt new believers who are just escaping from the company of sinful people. [19]They promise to give freedom to the new believers. But they themselves are slaves to sinful living. People are slaves to anything that controls them.

[20]They may have escaped the sin of the world. They may have come to know our Lord and Savior Jesus Christ. But what if they are once again caught up in sin? And what if it has become their master? Then they are worse off at the end than they were at the beginning.

[21]What if they had not known the way of godliness? That would have been better than to have known it and then to have turned their backs on it. The way of godliness is the sacred command that was passed on to them.

[22]What the proverbs say about them is true. "A dog returns to where it has thrown up." *(Proverbs 26:11)* And, "A pig that is washed goes back to rolling in the mud."

The Day of the Lord

3 Dear friends, this is now my second letter to you. I have written both of them as reminders. I want to stir you up to think in a way that is pure. [2]I want you to remember the words the holy prophets spoke in the past. Remember the command our Lord and Savior gave through your apostles.

[3]First of all, here is what you must understand. In the last days people will make fun of the truth. They will laugh at it. They will follow their own evil longings. [4]They will say, "Where is this 'return' he promised? Everything goes on in the same way it has since our people of long ago died. In fact, it has continued that way since God first created everything."

[5]Long ago, God's word brought the heavens into being. His word separated the earth from the waters. And the waters surrounded it. But those people forget things like that on purpose. [6]The waters also flooded the world of that time. It was destroyed.

[7]By God's word the heavens and earth of today are being reserved for fire. They are being kept for the day when God will judge. Then ungodly people will be destroyed.

[8]Dear friends, here is one thing you must not forget. With the Lord a day is like a thousand years. And a thousand years are like a day. [9]The Lord is not slow to keep his promise. He is not slow in the way some people understand it. He is patient with you.

He doesn't want anyone to be destroyed. Instead, he wants all people to turn away from their sins.

¹⁰But the day of the Lord will come like a thief. The heavens will disappear with a roar. Fire will destroy everything in them. God will judge the earth and everything in it.

¹¹So everything will be destroyed. And what kind of people should you be? You should lead holy and godly lives. ¹²Live like that as you look forward to the day of God. It will make the day come more quickly. On that day fire will destroy the heavens. Its heat will melt everything in them.

¹³But we are looking forward to a new heaven and a new earth. Godliness will make its home there. All of this is in keeping with God's promise.

¹⁴Dear friends, I know you are looking forward to that. So try your best to be found pure and without blame. Be at peace with God. ¹⁵Remember that while our Lord is waiting patiently to return, people are being saved.

Our dear brother Paul also wrote to you about that. God made him wise to write as he did. ¹⁶He writes the same way in all his letters. He speaks about what I have just told you. His letters include some things that are hard to understand. People who don't know better and aren't firm in the faith twist what he says. They twist the other Scriptures too. So they will be destroyed.

¹⁷Dear friends, you already know that. So be on your guard. Then you won't be led down the wrong path by the mistakes of people who don't obey the law. You won't fall from your safe position.

¹⁸Grow in the grace of our Lord and Savior Jesus Christ. Get to know him better.

Give him glory both now and forever. Amen.

GREAT VERSE — TO — REMEMBER

3:9 The Lord ... is patient with you. He doesn't want anyone to be destroyed. Instead, he wants all people to turn away from their sins.

1 John

Why Was This Book Written? John wrote this letter. He also wrote the next two letters. He wrote the Gospel called John too. This letter warned about false teachers. The false teachers said Jesus was not God. They said Jesus was not Christ. John wanted to tell the truth.

What Is This Book About? John said we must know that Jesus is God. We must also know that Jesus was a man. John said we must do what God says. We must love each other. If we do these things then we are God's children.

What Is in This Book?

The Word of Life

1 Here is what we announce to everyone about the Word of life. He was already here from the beginning. We have heard him. We have seen him with our eyes. We have looked at him. Our hands have touched him. ²That life has appeared. We have seen him. We give witness about him. And we announce to you that same eternal life. He was already with the Father. He has appeared to us.

³We announce to you what we have seen and heard. We do it so you can share life together with us. And we share life with the Father and with his Son, Jesus Christ. ⁴We are writing this to make our joy complete.

Walking in the Light

⁵Here is the message we have heard from him and announce to you. God is light. There is no darkness in him at all.

⁶Suppose we say that we share life with God but still walk in the darkness. Then we are lying. We are not living by the truth. ⁷But suppose we walk in the light, just as he is in the light. Then we share life with one another. And the blood of Jesus, his Son, makes us pure from all sin.

⁸Suppose we claim we are without sin. Then we are fooling ourselves. The truth is not in us. ⁹But God is faithful and fair. If we admit that we have sinned, he will forgive us our sins. He will forgive every wrong thing we have done. He will make us pure. ¹⁰If we say we have not sinned, we are calling God a liar. His word has no place in our lives.

2 My dear children, I'm writing this to you so that you will not sin. But suppose someone does sin. Then we have one who speaks to the Father for us. He stands up for us. He is Jesus Christ, the Blameless One. ²He gave his life to pay for our sins.

GREAT VERSE —TO— REMEMBER

1:9 God is faithful and fair. If we admit that we have sinned, he will forgive us our sins. He will forgive every wrong thing we have done. He will make us pure.

But he not only paid for our sins. He also paid for the sins of the whole world.

³We know that we have come to know God if we obey his commands.

⁴Suppose someone says, "I know him." But suppose that person does not do what God commands. Then that person is a liar and is not telling the truth. ⁵But if anyone obeys God's word, then God's love is truly made complete in that person. Here is how we know we belong to him. ⁶Those who claim to belong to him must live just as Jesus did.

⁷Dear friends, I'm not writing you a new command. Instead, I'm writing one you have heard before. You have had it since the beginning.

⁸But I am writing what amounts to a new command. Its truth was shown in how Jesus lived. It is also shown in how you live. The darkness is passing away. The true light is already shining.

⁹Suppose people claim to be in the light but hate a brother or sister. Then they are still in the darkness.

¹⁰Those who love their brothers and sisters are living in the light. There is nothing in them to make them fall into sin. ¹¹But those who hate a brother or sister are in the darkness. They walk around in the darkness. They don't know where they are going. The darkness has made them blind.

> ¹²Dear children, I'm writing to you
>   because your sins have been forgiven.
>   They have been forgiven because of what Jesus has
>   done.
> ¹³Fathers, I'm writing to you
>   because you have known the One who is from the
>   beginning.
>   Young people, I'm writing to you
>   because you have won the battle over the evil one.
>
>   Dear children, I'm writing to you
>   because you have known the Father.
> ¹⁴Fathers, I'm writing to you
>   because you have known the One who is from the
>   beginning.
>   Young people, I'm writing to you
>   because you are strong.
>   God's word lives in you.
>   You have won the battle over the evil one.

Do Not Love the World

¹⁵Do not love the world or anything in it. If you love the world, love for the Father is not in you.

¹⁶Here is what people who belong to this world do. They try to satisfy what their sinful natures want to do. They long for what their sinful eyes look at. They brag about what they have and what they do. All of this comes from the world. It doesn't come from the Father.

¹⁷The world and its evil longings are passing away. But those who do what God wants them to do live forever.

A Warning About the Enemies of Christ

¹⁸Dear children, we are living in the last days. You have heard that the great enemy of Christ is coming. But even now many enemies of Christ have already come. That's how we know that these are the last days.

¹⁹The enemies left our group. They didn't really belong to us. If they had belonged to us, they would have remained with us. But by leaving they showed that none of them belonged to us.

²⁰You have received the Spirit from the Holy One. And all of you know the truth. ²¹I'm not writing to you because you don't know the truth but because you do know it. I'm writing to you because no lie comes from the truth.

²²Who is the liar? The person who says that Jesus is not the Christ. People who say that are the enemies of Christ. They say no to the Father and the Son. ²³Those who say no to the Son don't belong to the Father. But anyone who says yes to the Son belongs to the Father also.

²⁴Make sure that you don't forget what you have heard from the beginning. Then you will remain joined to the Son and to the Father. ²⁵That's what God has promised us. We have eternal life.

²⁶I'm writing these things to warn you about those who are trying to lead you down the wrong path.

²⁷But you have received the Holy Spirit from God. He continues to live in you. So you don't need anyone to teach you. God's Spirit teaches you about everything. What he says is true. He doesn't lie. Remain joined to Christ, just as you have been taught by the Spirit.

Children of God

²⁸Dear children, remain joined to Christ. Then when he comes,

we can be bold. We will not be ashamed to meet him when he comes.

²⁹You know that God is right and always does what is right. And you know that everyone who does what is right has been born again because of what God has done.

3 How great is the love the Father has given us so freely! Now we can be called children of God. And that's what we really are! The world doesn't know us because it didn't know him.

²Dear friends, now we are children of God. He still hasn't let us know what we will be. But we know that when Christ appears, we will be like him. We will see him as he really is. ³He is pure. All who hope to be like him make themselves pure.

⁴Everyone who sins breaks the law. In fact, breaking the law is sin. ⁵But you know that Christ came to take our sins away. And there is no sin in him. ⁶No one who remains joined to him keeps on sinning. No one who keeps on sinning has seen him or known him.

⁷Dear children, don't let anyone lead you down the wrong path. Those who do what is right are holy, just as Christ is holy. ⁸Those who do what is sinful belong to the devil. They are just like him. He has been sinning from the beginning. But the Son of God came to destroy the devil's work.

⁹Those who are born again because of what God has done will not keep on sinning. God's very nature remains in them. They can't go on sinning. They have been born again because of what God has done.

¹⁰Here is how you can tell the difference between the children of God and the children of the devil. Those who don't do what is right do not belong to God. Those who don't love their brothers and sisters do not belong to him either.

Love One Another

¹¹From the beginning we have heard that we should love one another. ¹²Don't be like Cain. He belonged to the evil one. He murdered his brother. And why did he murder him? Because the

GREAT VERSE —TO— REMEMBER

3:1 How great is the love the Father has given us so freely! Now we can be called children of God.

things Cain had done were wrong. But the things his brother had done were right.

¹³My brothers and sisters, don't be surprised if the world hates you. ¹⁴We know that we have left our old dead condition and entered into new life. We know it because we love our brothers and sisters. Those who do not are still living in their old condition.

¹⁵Those who hate their brothers and sisters are murderers. And you know that murderers do not have eternal life in their hearts.

¹⁶We know what love is because Jesus Christ gave his life for us. So we should give our lives for our brothers and sisters.

¹⁷Suppose you see a brother or sister in need and are able to help them. If you don't take pity on them, how can the love of God be in you?

¹⁸Dear children, don't just talk about love. Put your love into action. Then it will truly be love. ¹⁹That's how we know that we hold to the truth. And that's how we put our hearts at rest, knowing that God is watching. ²⁰Our hearts may judge us. But God is greater than our hearts. He knows everything.

²¹Dear friends, if our hearts do not judge us, we can be bold with God. ²²And he will give us anything we ask. That's because we obey his commands. We do what pleases him.

²³God has commanded us to believe in the name of his Son, Jesus Christ. He has also commanded us to love one another. ²⁴Those who obey his commands remain joined to him. And he remains joined to them.

How do we know that God lives in us? We know it because of the Holy Spirit he gave us.

Put the Spirits to the Test

4 Dear friends, do not believe every spirit. Put the spirits to the test to see if they belong to God. Many false prophets have gone out into the world.

²How can you recognize the Spirit of God? Every spirit that agrees that Jesus Christ came in a human body belongs to God. ³But every spirit that doesn't agree with this does not belong to God. It is the spirit of the great enemy of Christ. You have heard that the enemy is coming. Even now he is already in the world.

⁴Dear children, you belong to God. You have not accepted the teachings of the false prophets. That's because the One who is in you is more powerful than the one who is in the world.

⁵False prophets belong to the world. So they speak from the

world's point of view. The world listens to them. ⁶We belong to God. And those who know God listen to us. But those who don't belong to God don't listen to us. That's how we can tell the difference between the Spirit of truth and the spirit of lies.

We Love Because God Loved Us

⁷Dear friends, let us love one another, because love comes from God. Everyone who loves has been born again because of what God has done. That person knows God. ⁸Anyone who does not love does not know God, because God is love.

⁹How did God show his love for us? He sent his one and only Son into the world. He sent him so we could receive life through him.

¹⁰What is love? It is not that we loved God. It is that he loved us and sent his Son to give his life to pay for our sins.

¹¹Dear friends, since God loved us that much, we should also love one another. ¹²No one has ever seen God. But if we love one another, God lives in us. His love is made complete in us.

¹³We know that we belong to him and he belongs to us. He has given us his Holy Spirit.

¹⁴The Father has sent his Son to be the Savior of the world. We have seen it. We give witness to it. ¹⁵God lives in those who agree that Jesus is the Son of God. They remain joined to God. ¹⁶So we know that God loves us. We depend on it.

God is love. Those who lead a life of love show that they are joined to God. And God is joined to them.

¹⁷So love is made complete among us. We will be bold on the day God judges us. That's because in this world we love as Jesus did.

¹⁸There is no fear in love. Instead, perfect love drives fear away. Fear has to do with being punished. The one who fears does not have perfect love.

¹⁹We love because he loved us first. ²⁰Those who say they love

GREAT VERSE —TO— REMEMBER

4:7 Let us love one another, because love comes from God. Everyone who loves has been born again because of what God has done.

God but in fact hate a brother or sister are liars. They don't love a brother or sister, whom they have seen. So they can't love God, whom they have not seen. ²¹Here is the command God has given us. Those who love God must also love their brothers and sisters.

Faith in the Son of God

5 Everyone who believes that Jesus is the Christ is born again because of what God has done. And everyone who loves the Father loves his children as well.

²How do we know that we love God's children? We know it when we love God and obey his commands. ³Here is what it means to love God. It means that we obey his commands. And his commands are not hard to obey. ⁴That's because everyone who is a child of God has won the battle over the world. Our faith has won the battle for us.

⁵Who is it that has won the battle over the world? Only the person who believes that Jesus is the Son of God.

⁶Jesus Christ is the one who was baptized in water and died on the cross. He wasn't just baptized in water. He also died on the cross. The Holy Spirit has given a truthful witness about him. That's because the Spirit is the truth.

⁷There are three that give witness about Jesus. ⁸They are the Holy Spirit, the baptism of Jesus and his death. And the three of them agree.

⁹We accept the witness of people. But the witness of God is more important because it is God who gives it. He has given witness about his Son.

¹⁰Those who believe in the Son of God have accepted that witness in their hearts. Those who do not believe God's witness are calling him a liar. That's because they have not believed his witness about his Son.

¹¹Here is God's witness. He has given us eternal life. That life is found in his Son. ¹²Those who belong to the Son have life. Those who do not belong to the Son of God do not have life.

Final Words

¹³I'm writing these things to you who believe in the name of the Son of God. I'm doing it so you will know that you have eternal life.

¹⁴There is one thing we can be sure of when we come to God in prayer. If we ask anything in keeping with what he wants, he

hears us. ¹⁵If we know that God hears what we ask for, we know that we have it.

¹⁶Suppose you see your brother or sister commit a sin. But that sin is not the kind that leads to death. Then you should pray for them. And God will give life to them. I'm talking about someone whose sin does not lead to death. But there is a sin that does lead to death. I'm not saying that you should pray about that. ¹⁷Every wrong thing we do is sin. But there are sins that do not lead to death.

¹⁸We know that those who are children of God do not keep on sinning. The Son of God keeps them safe. The evil one can't harm them. ¹⁹We know that we are children of God. We know that the whole world is under the control of the evil one.

²⁰We also know that the Son of God has come. He has given us understanding. Now we can know the One who is true. And we belong to the One who is true. We also belong to his Son, Jesus Christ. He is the true God. He is eternal life.

²¹Dear children, keep away from statues of gods.

5:14 There is one thing we can be sure of when we come to God in prayer. If we ask anything in keeping with what he wants, he hears us.

2 John

Why Was This Book Written? John wrote many letters. He wrote this letter for a special lady and her family. We do not know who the lady was. John may have been writing to a church too.

What Is This Book About? John said some important things. He said Christians should love each other. He said we must do what God says. If we love God we will do what he says. We will love each other. John also wrote about false teachers. He said they were dangerous.

What Is in This Book?

¹I, the elder, am writing this letter.

I am sending it to the chosen lady and her children. I love all of you because of the truth. I'm not the only one who loves you. So does everyone who knows the truth. ²I love you because of the truth that is alive in us. That truth will be with us forever.

³God the Father and Jesus Christ his Son will give you grace, mercy and peace. Those blessings will be with us because we love the truth.

⁴It has given me great joy to find some of your children living by the truth. That's just what the Father commanded us to do. ⁵Dear lady, I'm not writing you a new command. I'm writing a command we've had from the beginning. I'm asking that we love one another. ⁶The way we show our love is to obey God's commands. He commands you to lead a life of love. That's what you have heard from the beginning.

⁷Many people who try to fool others have gone out into the world. They don't agree that Jesus Christ came in a human body. People like that try to trick others. They are enemies of Christ. ⁸Watch out that you don't lose what you have worked for. Make sure that you get your complete reward.

⁹Some people run ahead of others. They don't follow the teaching of Christ. People like that don't belong to God. But those who follow the teaching of Christ belong to the Father and the Son. ¹⁰Suppose some people come to you and don't teach these truths. Then don't take them into your house. Don't welcome them. ¹¹Anyone who welcomes them shares in their evil work.

¹²I have a lot to write to you. But I don't want to use paper and ink. Instead, I hope I can visit you. Then I can talk with you face to face. That will make our joy complete.

¹³The children of your chosen sister send their greetings.

GREAT VERSE —TO— REMEMBER

6 The way we show our love is to obey God's commands. He commands you to lead a life of love. That's what you have heard from the beginning.

3 John

Why Was This Book Written? This letter was written to Gaius. John wrote this letter. Gaius was John's friend. He was a leader in the church. Another man in the church was not acting like a friend. His name was Diotrephes. He did not like John's teaching.

What Is This Book About? John wrote to say thank you to Gaius. Gaius had been helpful. John also wrote to scold Diotrephes. Diotrephes had not been helpful. John said he would come to visit soon. He would talk to the men. He said he would fix the problem between them when he came.

What Is in This Book?

¹I, the elder, am writing this letter.

I am sending it to you, my dear friend Gaius. I love you because of the truth.

²Dear friend, I know that your spiritual life is going well. I pray that you also may enjoy good health. And I pray that everything else may go well with you.
³Some believers came to me and told me that you are faithful to the truth. They told me that you continue to live by it. That gave me great joy. ⁴I have no greater joy than to hear that my children are living by the truth.
⁵Dear friend, you are faithful in what you are doing for the believers. You are faithful even though they are strangers to you. ⁶They have told the church about your love. Please help them by sending them on their way in a manner that honors God.
⁷They started on their journey to serve Jesus Christ. They didn't receive any help from those who aren't believers. ⁸So we should welcome people like them. We should work together with them for the truth.
⁹I wrote to the church. But Diotrephes won't have anything to do with us. He loves to be the first in everything. ¹⁰So if I come, I will point out what he is doing. He is saying evil things about us to others. Even that doesn't satisfy him. He refuses to welcome other believers. He also keeps others from welcoming them. In fact, he throws them out of the church.
¹¹Dear friend, don't be like those who do evil. Be like those who do good. Anyone who does what is good belongs to God. Anyone who does what is evil hasn't really seen or known God.
¹²Everyone says good things about Demetrius. He lives in keeping with the truth. We also say good things about him. And you know that our witness is true.

GREAT VERSE —TO— REMEMBER

11 Don't be like those who do evil. Be like those who do good. Anyone who does what is good belongs to God. Anyone who does what is evil hasn't really seen or known God.

¹³I have a lot to write to you. But I don't want to write with pen and ink. ¹⁴I hope I can see you soon. Then we can talk face to face.

May you have peace. The friends here send their greetings. Greet the friends there by name.

Jude

Why Was This Book Written?

James and Jesus had a brother. His name was Jude. Jude wrote this short letter. He wrote to warn Christians about false teachers. Peter had written about false teachers too. Jude wanted to tell the truth. He wanted to cheer people up.

What Is This Book About?

The false teachers said that Jesus was not God. They said people could live sinful lives. Jude said God would punish the false teachers. He would destroy them.

What Is in This Book?

¹I, Jude, am writing this letter. I serve Jesus Christ. I am a brother of James.

I am sending this letter to you who have been chosen by God. You are loved by God the Father. You are kept safe by Jesus Christ.

²May more and more mercy, peace, and love be given to you.

A Warning Against Ungodly Teachers

³Dear friends, I really wanted to write to you about the salvation we share. But now I feel I should write and ask you to stand up for the faith. God's people were trusted with it once and for all time.

⁴Certain people have slipped in among you in secret. Long ago it was written that they would be judged. They are godless people. They use the grace of our God as an excuse for sexual sins. They say no to Jesus Christ. He is our only Lord and King.

⁵I want to remind you about some things you already know. The Lord saved his people. He brought them out of Egypt. But later he destroyed those who did not believe. ⁶Some of the angels didn't stay where they belonged. They didn't keep their positions of authority. The Lord has kept those angels in darkness. They are held by chains that last forever. On judgment day, God will judge them.

⁷The people of Sodom and Gomorrah and the towns around them also did evil things. They gave themselves over to sexual sins. They committed sins of the worst possible kind. They are an example of those who are punished with fire. The fire never goes out.

⁸In the very same way, those dreamers pollute their own bodies. They don't accept authority. They speak evil things against heavenly beings. ⁹But not even Michael did that. He was the leader of the angels. He argued with the devil about the body of Moses. But he didn't dare to speak evil things against the devil. Instead, he said, "May the Lord stop you!"

¹⁰But those people speak evil things against what they don't understand. They are like wild animals. They can't think for themselves. They do what comes naturally to them. Those are the very things that destroy them.

¹¹How terrible it will be for them! They followed the way of Cain. They rushed ahead and made the same mistake as Balaam did. They did it because they loved money. They are like Korah. He turned against his leaders. Those people will certainly be destroyed, just as Korah was.

¹²They are like stains at the meals you share. They eat too much. They have no shame. They are shepherds who feed only themselves. They are like clouds without rain. They are blown along by the wind. They are like trees in the fall. Since they have no fruit, they are pulled up. So they die twice.

¹³They are like wild waves of the sea. Their shame rises up like foam. They are like falling stars. God has reserved a place of very black darkness for them. He will keep them there forever.

¹⁴Enoch was the seventh man in the family line of Adam. He gave a prophecy about those people. He said, "Look! The Lord is coming with thousands and thousands of his holy ones. ¹⁵He is coming to judge everyone. He is coming to sentence all ungodly people. He will judge them for all the ungodly acts they have done. They have done them in ungodly ways. He will sentence ungodly sinners for all the bad things they have said about him."

¹⁶Those people complain. They find fault with others. They follow their own evil longings. They brag about themselves. They praise others to help themselves.

Remain in God's Love

¹⁷Dear friends, remember what the apostles of our Lord Jesus Christ said was going to happen. ¹⁸They told you, "In the last days, some people will make fun of the truth. They will follow their own ungodly longings." ¹⁹They are the people who separate you from one another. They do only what comes naturally. They are not led by the Holy Spirit.

²⁰Dear friends, build yourselves up in your most holy faith. Let the Holy Spirit guide and help you when you pray. ²¹The mercy of our Lord Jesus Christ will bring you eternal life. As you wait for his mercy, remain in God's love.

²²Show mercy to those who doubt. ²³Pull others out of the fire. Save them. To others, show mercy mixed with fear. Hate even the clothes that are stained by the sins of those who wear them.

GREAT VERSE —TO— REMEMBER

20 Dear friends, build yourselves up in your most holy faith. Let the Holy Spirit guide and help you when you pray.

Praise to God

²⁴Give praise to the One who is able to keep you from falling into sin. He will bring you into his heavenly glory without any fault. He will bring you there with great joy. ²⁵Give praise to the only God. He is our Savior. Glory, majesty, power and authority belong to him. Give praise to him through Jesus Christ our Lord. Give praise to the One who was before all time, who now is, and who will be forever. Amen.

Revelation

Why Was This Book Written? John wrote the book of Revelation. The Roman rulers wanted to punish John. They made him live all by himself. They put him on an island. His family lived in the city. Jesus gave John a dream. It was about the future. John wrote about the dream in the book of Revelation.

What Is This Book About? It was hard to be a Christian. John wanted Christians to trust God. He said God takes care of everything on earth. John's dream showed that Jesus is our judge. Jesus will punish all evil. Jesus will take Christians to heaven. Jesus has more power than people.

What Is in This Book?

1 This is the revelation that God gave to Jesus Christ. Jesus shows those who serve God what will happen soon. God made it known by sending his angel to his servant John. ²John gives witness to everything he saw. The things he gives witness to are God's word and what Jesus Christ has said.

³Blessed is the one who reads the words of this prophecy. Blessed are those who hear it and think everything it says is important. The time when these things will come true is near.

Greetings

⁴I, John, am writing this letter.

I am sending it to the seven churches in Asia Minor.

May grace and peace come to you from the One who is, and who was, and who will come. May grace and peace come to you from the seven spirits who are in front of God's throne. ⁵May grace and peace come to you from Jesus Christ. What Jesus gives witness to can always be trusted. He was the first to rise from the dead. He rules over the kings of the earth.

Give glory and power to the One who loves us! He has set us free from our sins by pouring out his blood for us. ⁶He has made us members of his royal family. He has made us priests who serve his God and Father. Give him glory and power for ever and ever! Amen.

⁷Look! He is coming with the clouds!
  Every eye will see him.
Even those who pierced him will see him.
  All the nations of the earth will be sad because of
    him.
  This will really happen! Amen.

⁸"I am the Alpha and the Omega, the First and the Last," says

1:8 "I am the Alpha and the Omega, the First and the Last," says the Lord God. "I am the One who is, and who was, and who will come. I am the Mighty One."

the Lord God. "I am the One who is, and who was, and who will come. I am the Mighty One."

One Who Looks Like a Son of Man

[9]I, John, am a believer like you. I am a friend who suffers like you. As members of Jesus' royal family, we can put up with anything that happens to us.

I was on the island of Patmos because I taught God's word and what Jesus said. [10]The Holy Spirit took complete control of me on the Lord's Day. I heard a loud voice behind me that sounded like a trumpet. [11]The voice said, "Write on a scroll what you see. Send it to these seven churches: Ephesus, Smyrna, Pergamum, Thyatira, Sardis, Philadelphia and Laodicea."

[12]I turned around to see who was speaking to me. When I turned, I saw seven golden lampstands. [13]In the middle of them was someone who looked "like a son of man." *(Daniel 7:13)*

He was dressed in a long robe with a gold strip of cloth around his chest. [14]The hair on his head was white like wool, as white as snow. His eyes were like a blazing fire. [15]His feet were like bronze metal glowing in a furnace. His voice sounded like rushing waters. [16]He held seven stars in his right hand. Out of his mouth came a sharp, two-edged sword. His face was like the sun shining in all its brightness.

[17]When I saw him, I fell at his feet as if I were dead.

Then he put his right hand on me and said, "Do not be afraid. I am the First and the Last. [18]I am the Living One. I was dead. But look! I am alive for ever and ever! And I hold the keys to Death and Hell.

[19]"So write down what you have seen. Write about what is happening now and what will happen later. [20]Here is what the mystery of the seven stars you saw in my right hand means. They are the angels of the seven churches. And the seven golden lampstands you saw stand for the seven churches.

The Letter to the Church in Ephesus

2 "Here is what I command you to write to the church in Ephesus.

Here are the words of the One who holds the seven stars in his right hand. He also walks among the seven golden lampstands. [2]He says: I know what you are doing. You work long and hard. I know you can't put up with those who are evil.

You have tested those who claim to be apostles but are not. You have found out that they are liars. ³You have been faithful and have put up with a lot of trouble because of me. You have not given up.

⁴But here is something I hold against you. You don't have as much love as you had at first. ⁵Remember how far you have fallen! Turn away from your sins. Do the things you did at first. If you don't, I will come to you and remove your lampstand from its place.

⁶But you do have this in your favor. You hate the way the Nicolaitans act. I hate it too.

⁷Everyone who has ears should listen to what the Holy Spirit says to the churches. I will allow those who overcome to eat from the tree of life in God's paradise.

The Letter to the Church in Smyrna

⁸"Here is what I command you to write to the church in Smyrna.

Here are the words of the One who is the First and the Last. He is the One who died and came to life again. ⁹He says: I know that you suffer and are poor. But you are rich! Some people say they are Jews but are not. I know that their words are evil. Their worship is satanic.

¹⁰Don't be afraid of what you are going to suffer. I tell you, the devil will put some of you in prison to test you. You will be treated badly for ten days. Be faithful, even if it means you must die. Then I will give you a crown. The crown is life itself.

¹¹Everyone who has ears should listen to what the Holy Spirit says to the churches. Those who overcome will not be hurt at all by the second death.

The Letter to the Church in Pergamum

¹²"Here is what I command you to write to the church in Pergamum.

Here are the words of the One who has the sharp, two-edged sword. ¹³He says: I know that you live where Satan has his throne. But you remain true to me. You did not give up your faith in me, even in the days of Antipas, my faithful witness. He was put to death in your city, where Satan lives.

¹⁴But I have a few things against you. You have people there who follow the teaching of Balaam. He taught Balak to lead

the people of Israel into sin. So they ate food that had been offered to statues of gods. And they committed sexual sins. [15]You also have people who follow the teaching of the Nicolaitans.

[16]So turn away from your sins! If you don't, I will come to you soon. I will fight against those people with the sword that comes out of my mouth.

[17]Everyone who has ears should listen to what the Holy Spirit says to the churches. I will give hidden manna to those who overcome. I will also give each of them a white stone with a new name written on it. Only the one who receives that name will know it.

The Letter to the Church in Thyatira

[18]"Here is what I command you to write to the church in Thyatira.

Here are the words of the Son of God. He is the One whose eyes are like blazing fire. His feet are like polished bronze metal. [19]He says: I know what you are doing. I know your love and your faith. I know how well you have served. I know you don't give up easily. In fact, you are doing more now than you did at first.

[20]But here is what I have against you. You put up with that woman Jezebel. She calls herself a prophet. With her teaching, she has led my servants into sexual sin. She has tricked them into eating food offered to statues of gods.

[21]I have given her time to turn away from her sinful ways. But she doesn't want to. [22]She sinned on a bed. So I will make her suffer on a bed. And those who commit adultery with her will suffer greatly. Their only way out is to turn away from what she taught them to do. [23]I will strike her children dead. Then all the churches will know that I am the One who searches hearts and minds. I will pay each of you back for what you have done.

[24]I won't bother the rest of you in Thyatira. You don't follow the teaching of Jezebel. You haven't learned what some people call Satan's deep secrets. [25]Just hold on to what you have until I come.

[26]I will give authority over the nations to all who overcome and who carry out my plans to the end. [27]It is written:

'He will rule them with an iron rod.

He will break them to pieces like clay pots.' *(Psalm 2:9)*

I have received this authority from my Father. [28]I will also give the morning star to all who overcome.

[29]Everyone who has ears should listen to what the Holy Spirit says to the churches.

The Letter to the Church in Sardis

3 "Here is what I command you to write to the church in Sardis.

Here are the words of the One who holds the seven spirits of God. He has the seven stars in his hand. He says: I know what you are doing. People think you are alive, but you are dead. [2]Wake up! Strengthen what is left, or it will die. You have not done all that my God wants you to do.

[3]So remember what you have been taught and have heard. Obey it. Turn away from your sins. If you don't wake up, I will come like a thief. You won't know when I will come to you.

[4]But you have a few people in Sardis who have kept their clothes clean. They will walk with me, dressed in white, because they are worthy. [5]Those who overcome will also be dressed in white. I will never erase their names from the book of life. I will speak of them by name to my Father and his angels.

[6]Everyone who has ears should listen to what the Holy Spirit says to the churches.

The Letter to the Church in Philadelphia

[7]"Here is what I command you to write to the church in Philadelphia.

Here are the words of the One who is holy and true. He holds the key of David. No one can shut what he opens. And no one can open what he shuts. [8]He says: I know what you are doing. Look! I have put an open door in front of you. No one can shut it. I know that you don't have much strength. But you have obeyed my word. You have not said no to me.

[9]Some people claim they are Jews but are not. They are liars. Their worship is from Satan. I will make them come and fall down at your feet. I will make them say in public that I love you.

¹⁰You have kept my command to put up with anything that happens. So I will keep you from the time of suffering that is going to come to the whole world. It will test those who live on the earth.

¹¹I am coming soon. Hold on to what you have. Then no one will take away your crown.

¹²I will see to it that those who overcome will be pillars in the temple of my God. They will never leave it again. I will write the name of my God on them. I will write the name of the city of my God on them. This is the new Jerusalem, which is coming down out of heaven from my God. I will also write my new name on them.

¹³Everyone who has ears should listen to what the Holy Spirit says to the churches.

The Letter to the Church in Laodicea

¹⁴"Here is what I command you to write to the church in Laodicea.

Here are the words of the One who is the Amen. What he gives witness to is faithful and true. He rules over what God has created. ¹⁵He says: I know what you are doing. I know you aren't cold or hot. I wish you were either one or the other! ¹⁶But you are lukewarm. You aren't hot or cold. So I am going to spit you out of my mouth.

¹⁷You say, 'I am rich. I've become wealthy and don't need a thing.' But you don't realize how pitiful and miserable you have become. You are poor, blind and naked.

¹⁸I advise you to buy from me gold made pure by fire. Then you will become rich. Buy from me white clothes to wear. Then you will be able to cover your shameful nakedness. And buy from me healing lotion to put on your eyes. Then you will be able to see.

¹⁹I correct and train those I love. So be sincere, and turn away from your sins.

²⁰Here I am! I stand at the door and knock. If any of you

3:20 Here I am! I stand at the door and knock. If any of you hear my voice and open the door, I will come in.

hear my voice and open the door, I will come in and eat with you. And you will eat with me.

²¹I will give those who overcome the right to sit with me on my throne. In the same way, I overcame. Then I sat down with my Father on his throne.

²²Everyone who has ears should listen to what the Holy Spirit says to the churches."

The Throne in Heaven

4 After this I looked, and there in front of me was a door standing open in heaven. I heard the voice I had heard before. It sounded like a trumpet. The voice said, "Come up here. I will show you what must happen after this."

²At once the Holy Spirit took complete control of me. There in front of me was a throne in heaven with someone sitting on it. ³The One who sat there shone like jewels. Around the throne was a rainbow that looked like an emerald.

⁴Twenty-four other thrones surrounded that throne. Twenty-four elders were sitting on them. The elders were dressed in white. They had gold crowns on their heads.

⁵From the throne came flashes of lightning, rumblings and thunder. Seven lamps were blazing in front of the throne. These stand for the seven spirits of God. ⁶There was something that looked like a sea of glass in front of the throne. It was as clear as crystal.

In the inner circle, around the throne, were four living creatures. They were covered with eyes, in front and in back. ⁷The first creature looked like a lion. The second looked like an ox. The third had a human face. The fourth looked like a flying eagle. ⁸Each of the four living creatures had six wings. Each creature was covered all over with eyes, even under the wings. Day and night, they never stop saying,

"Holy, holy, holy
is the Lord God who rules over all.
He was, and he is, and he will come."

4:8 Holy, holy, holy is the Lord God who rules over all. He was, and he is, and he will come.

⁹The living creatures give glory, honor and thanks to the One who sits on the throne and who lives for ever and ever. ¹⁰At the same time, the 24 elders fall down and worship the One who sits on the throne and who lives for ever and ever. They lay their crowns in front of the throne. They say,

> ¹¹ "You are worthy, our Lord and God!
> You are worthy to receive glory and honor and power.
> You are worthy because you created all things.
> They were created and they exist.
> That is the way you planned it."

The Scroll and the Lamb

5 Then I saw a scroll in the right hand of the One sitting on the throne. The scroll had writing on both sides. It was sealed with seven seals.

²I saw a mighty angel calling out in a loud voice, "Who is worthy to break the seals and open the scroll?" ³But no one in heaven or on earth or under the earth could open the scroll. No one could even look inside it.

⁴I cried and cried because no one was found who was worthy to open the scroll or look inside.

⁵Then one of the elders said to me, "Do not cry! The Lion of the tribe of Judah has won the battle. He is the Root of David. He is able to break the seven seals and open the scroll."

⁶Then I saw a Lamb that looked as if he had been put to death. He stood in the center of the area around the throne. The Lamb was surrounded by the four living creatures and the elders. He had seven horns and seven eyes. The eyes stand for the seven spirits of God, which are sent out into all the earth.

⁷The Lamb came and took the scroll from the right hand of the One sitting on the throne. ⁸Then the four living creatures and the 24 elders fell down in front of the Lamb. Each one had a harp. They were holding golden bowls full of incense, which stand for the prayers of God's people.

⁹Here is the new song they sang.

> "You are worthy to take the scroll
> and break open its seals.
> You are worthy because you were put to death.
> With your blood you bought people for God.

They come from every tribe, language, people and
nation.
¹⁰You have made them members of a royal family.
You have made them priests to serve our God.
They will rule on the earth."

¹¹Then I looked and heard the voice of millions and millions of
angels. They surrounded the throne. They surrounded the living
creatures and the elders. ¹²In a loud voice they sang,

"The Lamb, who was put to death, is worthy!
He is worthy to receive power and wealth and wisdom
and strength!
He is worthy to receive honor and glory and praise!"

¹³All creatures in heaven, on earth, under the earth, and on the
sea, and all that is in them, were singing. I heard them say,

"May praise and honor for ever and ever
be given to the One who sits on the throne and to
the Lamb!
Give them glory and power
for ever and ever!"

¹⁴The four living creatures said, "Amen." And the elders fell
down and worshiped.

The Seals

6 I watched as the Lamb broke open the first of the seven seals.
Then I heard one of the four living creatures say in a voice
that sounded like thunder, "Come!" ²I looked, and there in front
of me was a white horse! Its rider held a bow in his hands. He
was given a crown. He rode out like a hero on his way to victory.
³The Lamb broke open the second seal. Then I heard the second

---

5:13 May praise and honor for
ever and ever be given to the One
who sits on the throne and to the
Lamb! Give them glory and power
for ever and ever!

living creature say, "Come!" ⁴Another horse came out. It was flaming red. Its rider was given power to take peace from the earth and to make people kill each other. He was given a large sword.

⁵The Lamb broke open the third seal. Then I heard the third living creature say, "Come!" I looked, and there in front of me was a black horse! Its rider was holding a pair of scales in his hand. ⁶Next, I heard what sounded like a voice coming from among the four living creatures. It said, "A quart of wheat for a day's pay. And three quarts of barley for a day's pay. But don't spoil the olive oil and the wine!"

⁷The Lamb broke open the fourth seal. Then I heard the voice of the fourth living creature say, "Come!" ⁸I looked, and there in front of me was a pale horse! Its rider's name was Death. Following close behind him was Hell. They were given power over a fourth of the earth. They were given power to kill people with the sword, hunger and sickness. They could also use the earth's wild animals to kill.

⁹He broke open the fifth seal. I saw souls under the altar. They were the souls of people who were killed because of God's word and their faithful witness. ¹⁰They called out in a loud voice. "How long, Lord and King, holy and true?" they asked. "How long will you wait to judge those who live on the earth? How long will it be until you pay them back for killing us?"

¹¹Then each of them was given a white robe. "Wait a little longer," they were told. "There are still more of your believing brothers and sisters who must be killed."

¹²I watched as he broke open the sixth seal. There was a powerful earthquake. The sun turned black like black clothes that were made from the hair of a goat. The whole moon turned as red as blood. ¹³The stars in the sky fell to earth. They dropped like ripe figs from a tree shaken by a strong wind. ¹⁴The sky rolled back like a scroll. Every mountain and island was moved out of its place.

¹⁵Everyone hid in caves and among the rocks of the mountains. This included the kings of the earth, the princes and the generals, rich people and powerful people. It also included every slave and everyone who was free. ¹⁶They called out to the mountains and rocks, "Fall on us! Hide us from the face of the One who sits on the throne! Hide us from the anger of the Lamb! ¹⁷The great day of their anger has come. Who can live through it?"

144,000 Are Sealed

7 After this I saw four angels. They were standing at the four corners of the earth. They were holding back the four winds of the earth. This kept the winds from blowing on the land or on the sea or on any tree.

²Then I saw another angel coming up from the east. He had the seal of the living God. He called out in a loud voice to the four angels who had been allowed to harm the land and the sea. ³"Do not harm the land or the sea or the trees," he said. "Wait until we mark with a seal the foreheads of those who serve our God."

⁴Then I heard how many people were sealed. There were 144,000 from all the tribes of Israel.

> ⁵From the tribe of Judah, 12,000 were sealed.
> From the tribe of Reuben, 12,000.
> From the tribe of Gad, 12,000.
> ⁶From the tribe of Asher, 12,000.
> From the tribe of Naphtali, 12,000.
> From the tribe of Manasseh, 12,000.
> ⁷From the tribe of Simeon, 12,000.
> From the tribe of Levi, 12,000.
> From the tribe of Issachar, 12,000.
> ⁸From the tribe of Zebulun, 12,000.
> From the tribe of Joseph, 12,000.
> From the tribe of Benjamin, 12,000.

The Huge Crowd Wearing White Robes

⁹After this I looked, and there in front of me was a huge crowd of people. They stood in front of the throne and in front of the Lamb. There were so many that no one could count them. They came from every nation, tribe, people and language. They were wearing white robes. In their hands they were holding palm branches. ¹⁰They cried out in a loud voice,

> "Salvation belongs to our God,
> who sits on the throne.

7:10 Salvation belongs to our God, who sits on the throne. Salvation also belongs to the Lamb.

Salvation also belongs to the Lamb."

[11]All the angels were standing around the throne. They were standing around the elders and the four living creatures. They fell down on their faces in front of the throne and worshiped God. [12]They said,

"Amen!
May praise and glory
and wisdom be given to our God for ever and ever.
Give him thanks and honor and power and strength.
Amen!"

[13]Then one of the elders spoke to me. "Who are these people dressed in white robes?" he asked. "Where did they come from?"
[14]I answered, "Sir, you know."
He said, "They are the ones who have come out of the time of terrible suffering. They washed their robes and made them white in the blood of the Lamb. [15]So

"they are in front of the throne of God.
They serve him day and night in his temple.
The One who sits on the throne will spread his tent
over them.
[16]Never again will they be hungry.
Never again will they be thirsty.
The sun will not beat down on them.
The heat of the desert will not harm them.
[17]The Lamb, who is at the center of the area around the
throne, will be their shepherd.
He will lead them to springs of living water.
And God will wipe away every tear from their eyes."

The Seventh Seal and the Gold Cup

8 The Lamb opened the seventh seal. Then there was silence in heaven for about half an hour.
[2]I saw the seven angels who stand in front of God. Seven trumpets were given to them.
[3]Another angel came and stood at the altar. He had a shallow gold cup for burning incense. He was given a lot of incense to offer on the golden altar in front of the throne. With the incense he offered the prayers of all God's people. [4]The smoke of the incense together with the prayers of God's people rose up from the angel's hand. It went up in front of God.

⁵Then the angel took the cup and filled it with fire from the altar. He threw it down on the earth. There were rumblings and thunder, flashes of lightning, and an earthquake.

The Trumpets

⁶Then the seven angels who had the seven trumpets got ready to blow them.

⁷The first angel blew his trumpet. Hail and fire mixed with blood were thrown down on the earth. A third of the earth was burned up. A third of the trees were burned up. All the green grass was burned up.

⁸The second angel blew his trumpet. Something that looked like a huge mountain on fire was thrown into the sea. A third of the sea turned into blood. ⁹A third of the living creatures in the sea died. A third of the ships were destroyed.

¹⁰The third angel blew his trumpet. Then a great star fell from the sky. It looked like a blazing torch. It fell on a third of the rivers and on the springs of water. ¹¹The name of the star is Wormwood. A third of the water turned bitter. Many people died from it.

¹²The fourth angel blew his trumpet. Then a third of the sun was struck. A third of the moon was struck. A third of the stars were struck. So a third of each of them turned dark. Then a third of the day had no light. The same thing happened to a third of the night.

¹³As I watched, I heard an eagle that was flying high in the air. It called out in a loud voice, "How terrible! How terrible it will be for those living on the earth! How terrible! They will suffer as soon as the next three angels blow their trumpets!"

9 The fifth angel blew his trumpet. Then I saw a star that had fallen from the sky to the earth. The star was given the key to the tunnel leading down into the Abyss. ²When the star opened the Abyss, smoke rose up from it like the smoke from a huge furnace. The sun and sky were darkened by the smoke from the Abyss.

³Out of the smoke came locusts. They settled down on the earth. They were given power like the power of scorpions of the earth. ⁴They were told not to harm the grass of the earth or any plant or tree. They were supposed to harm only the people who didn't have God's seal on their foreheads. ⁵They were not allowed to kill them. But they could hurt them over and over for five

months. The pain the people suffered was like the sting of a scorpion when it strikes someone.

⁶In those days, people will look for a way to die but won't find it. They will want to die, but death will escape them.

⁷The locusts looked like horses ready for battle. On their heads they wore something like crowns of gold. Their faces looked like human faces. ⁸Their hair was like women's hair. Their teeth were like lions' teeth. ⁹Their chests were covered with something that looked like armor made out of iron. The sound of their wings was like the thundering of many horses and chariots rushing into battle. ¹⁰They had tails and stings like scorpions. And in their tails they had power to hurt people over and over for five months.

¹¹Their king was the angel of the Abyss. In the Hebrew language his name is Abaddon. In Greek it is Apollyon.

¹²The first terrible judgment is past. Two others are still coming.

¹³The sixth angel blew his trumpet. Then I heard a voice coming from the corners of the golden altar that stands in front of God. ¹⁴The voice spoke to the sixth angel who had the trumpet. It said, "Set the four angels free who are held at the great river Euphrates."

¹⁵The four angels had been ready for this very hour and day and month and year. They were set free to kill a third of all people. ¹⁶The number of troops on horseback was 200,000,000. I heard how many there were.

¹⁷The horses and riders I saw in my vision had armor on their chests. It was flaming red, dark blue, and yellow like sulfur. The heads of the horses looked like lions' heads. Out of their mouths came fire, smoke and sulfur. ¹⁸A third of all people were killed by the three plagues of fire, smoke and sulfur that came out of the horses' mouths. ¹⁹The power of the horses was in their mouths and in their tails. The tails were like snakes whose heads could bite.

²⁰The people who were not killed by these plagues still did not turn away from what they had been doing. They did not stop worshiping demons. They kept worshiping statues of gods made out of gold, silver, bronze, stone and wood, which can't see or hear or walk. ²¹The people also did not turn away from their murders, witchcraft, sexual sins and stealing.

The Angel and the Little Scroll

10 Then I saw another mighty angel coming down from heaven. He was wearing a cloud like a robe. There was a rainbow above his head. His face was like the sun. His legs were like pillars of fire. ²He was holding a little scroll. It was lying open in his hand. The angel put his right foot on the sea and his left foot on the land. ³Then he gave a loud shout like the roar of a lion. When he shouted, the voices of the seven thunders spoke.

⁴When they had spoken, I was getting ready to write. But I heard a voice from heaven say, "Seal up what the seven thunders have said. Do not write it down."

⁵Then the angel I had seen standing on the sea and on the land raised his right hand to heaven. ⁶He made a promise in the name of the One who lives for ever and ever. He took an oath in the name of the One who created the sky, earth and sea and all that is in them. He said, "There will be no more waiting! ⁷But in the days when the seventh angel is ready to blow his trumpet, the last part of God's plan will be carried out. God told all this to the prophets who served him long ago."

⁸Then the voice I had heard from heaven spoke to me again. It said, "Go and take the scroll from the angel standing on the sea and on the land. It is lying open in his hand."

⁹So I went to the angel and asked him to give me the little scroll. He said to me, "Take it and eat it. It will become sour in your stomach. But in your mouth it will taste as sweet as honey." ¹⁰I took the little scroll from the angel's hand and ate it. In my mouth it tasted as sweet as honey. But when I had eaten it, it became sour in my stomach. ¹¹Then I was told, "You must prophesy again about many peoples, nations, languages and kings."

The Two Witnesses

11 I was given a long stick that looked like a measuring rod. I was told, "Go and measure the temple of God and the altar. Count the worshipers who are there. ²But do not measure the outer courtyard. It has been given to those who aren't Jews. They will overrun the holy city for 42 months.

³"I will give power to my two witnesses. They will prophesy for 1,260 days. They will be dressed in black clothes to show how sad they are."

⁴The witnesses are the two olive trees and the two lampstands that stand in front of the Lord of the earth. ⁵If anyone tries to harm them, fire comes from their mouths and eats up their enemies. This is how anyone who wants to harm them must die.

⁶These witnesses have power to close up the sky. Then it will

not rain while they are prophesying. They also have power to turn the waters into blood. And they can strike the earth with every kind of plague as often as they want to.

⁷When they have finished giving their witness, the beast that comes up from the Abyss will attack them. He will overpower them and kill them. ⁸Their bodies will lie in the street of the great city where their Lord was nailed to the cross. The city is sometimes pictured as Sodom, or as Egypt.

⁹For three and a half days, people from every tribe, language and nation will stare at their bodies. They will refuse to bury them. ¹⁰Those who live on the earth will be happy about this and will celebrate. They will send each other gifts, because these two prophets had made them suffer.

¹¹But after the three and a half days, a breath of life from God entered the two witnesses. They stood up. Terror struck those who saw them.

¹²Then the two witnesses heard a loud voice from heaven. It said to them, "Come up here." They went up to heaven in a cloud. Their enemies watched it happen.

¹³At that very hour there was a powerful earthquake. A tenth of the city crumbled and fell. In the earthquake, 7,000 people were killed. Those who lived through it were terrified. They gave glory to the God of heaven.

¹⁴The second terrible judgment has passed. The third is coming soon.

The Seventh Trumpet

¹⁵The seventh angel blew his trumpet. There were loud voices in heaven. They said,

"The kingdom of the world has become the kingdom of
       our Lord and of his Christ.
   He will rule for ever and ever."

¹⁶The 24 elders were sitting on their thrones in front of God. They fell on their faces and worshiped God. ¹⁷They said,

"Lord God who rules over all, we give thanks to you.
   You are the One who is and who was.
We give you thanks because you have taken your great
       power
   and have begun to rule.
¹⁸The nations were angry,
   and the time for your anger has come.

The time has come to judge the dead.
It is time to reward your servants the prophets
and your own people and those who honor you.
There is a reward for all your people,
both great and small.
It is time to destroy
those who destroy the earth."

¹⁹Then God's temple in heaven was opened. Inside it the wooden chest called the ark of his covenant could be seen. There were flashes of lightning, rumblings and thunder, an earthquake and a great hailstorm.

The Woman and the Dragon

12 A great and miraculous sign appeared in heaven. It was a woman wearing the sun like clothes. The moon was under her feet. On her head she wore a crown of 12 stars. ²She was pregnant. She cried out in pain because she was about to have a baby.

³Then another sign appeared in heaven. It was a huge red dragon. He had seven heads and ten horns. On his seven heads he wore seven crowns. ⁴His tail swept a third of the stars out of the sky. It threw them down to earth.

The dragon stood in front of the woman who was about to have a baby. He wanted to eat her child the moment it was born.

⁵She gave birth to a son. He will rule all the nations with an iron rod. Her child was taken up to God and to his throne.

⁶The woman escaped into the desert where God had a place prepared for her. There she would be taken care of for 1,260 days.

⁷There was war in heaven. Michael and his angels fought against the dragon. And the dragon and his angels fought back. ⁸But the dragon wasn't strong enough. He and his angels lost their place in heaven.

⁹The great dragon was thrown down to the earth, and his angels with him. The dragon is that old serpent called the devil, or Satan. He leads the whole world down the wrong path.

11:17 Lord God who rules over all, we give thanks to you. You are the One who is and who was.

¹⁰Then I heard a loud voice in heaven. It said,

"Now the salvation and the power and the kingdom of
    our God have come.
The authority of his Christ has come.
Satan, who brings charges against our brothers and
        sisters,
    has been thrown down.
He brings charges against them before our God day
    and night.
    ¹¹They overcame him
    because the Lamb gave his life's blood for them.
They overcame him
    by giving witness about Jesus to others.
They were willing to risk their lives,
    even if it led to death.
    ¹²So be joyful, you heavens!
    Be glad, all you who live there!
But how terrible it will be for the earth and the sea!
    The devil has come down to you.
He is very angry.
He knows his time is short."

¹³The dragon saw that he had been thrown down to the earth.
So he chased the woman who had given birth to the boy.
¹⁴The woman was given the two wings of a great eagle so that
she could fly away. She could fly to the place prepared for her in
the desert. There she would be taken care of for three and a half
years. She would be out of the serpent's reach.

¹⁵Then the serpent spit water like a river out of his mouth. He
wanted to catch her and sweep her away in the flood. ¹⁶But the
earth helped the woman. It opened its mouth and swallowed the
river that the dragon had spit out.

¹⁷The dragon was very angry with the woman. He went off to
make war against the rest of her children. They obey God's com-
13 mands and hold firmly to what Jesus has said. ¹The
dragon stood on the seashore.

The Beast out of the Sea

I saw a beast coming out of the sea. He had ten horns and seven
heads. There were ten crowns on his horns. On each head was an
evil name that was displeasing to God.

²The beast I saw looked like a leopard. But he had feet like a

bear and a mouth like a lion. The dragon gave the beast his power, his throne, and great authority. ³One of the beast's heads seemed to have had a deadly wound. But the wound had been healed. The whole world was amazed and followed the beast.

⁴People worshiped the dragon, because he had given authority to the beast. They also worshiped the beast. They asked, "Who is like the beast? Who can make war against him?"

⁵The beast was given a mouth to brag and speak evil things against God. The beast was allowed to use his authority for 42 months. ⁶He opened his mouth to speak evil things against God. He told lies about God's character and about the place where God lives and about those who live in heaven with him. ⁷He was allowed to make war against God's people and to overcome them. He was given authority over every tribe, people, language and nation.

⁸All who live on earth whose names have not been written in the book of life will worship the beast. The book of life belongs to the Lamb whose death was planned before the world was created.

⁹Everyone who has an ear should listen.

¹⁰Those who are to be captured
   will be captured.
Those who are to be killed with a sword
   will be killed with a sword.

So God's people must be patient and faithful.

The Beast out of the Earth

¹¹Then I saw another beast. This one came out of the earth. He had two horns like a lamb. But he spoke like a dragon. ¹²He had all the authority of the first beast. He did what that beast wanted. He made the earth and all who live on it worship the first beast. The first beast was the one whose deadly wound had been healed.

¹³The second beast did great and miraculous signs. He even made fire come from heaven. It came down to earth where everyone could see it. ¹⁴He did the signs the first beast wanted him to do. In that way the second beast tricked those who live on the earth. He ordered them to set up a statue to honor the first beast. The first beast was the one who had been wounded by the sword and still lived.

¹⁵The second beast was allowed to give breath to the statue so

it could speak. He was allowed to kill all who refused to worship the statue. ¹⁶He also forced everyone to receive a mark on the right hand or on the forehead. People great or small, rich or poor, free or slave had to receive the mark. ¹⁷They could not buy or sell anything unless they had the mark. The mark is the name of the beast or the number of his name.

¹⁸Here is a problem that you have to be wise to figure out. If you can, figure out what the beast's number means. It is a human number. The number is 666.

The Lamb and the 144,000

14 I looked, and there in front of me was the Lamb. He was standing on Mount Zion. With him were 144,000 people. Written on their foreheads were his name and his Father's name.

²I heard a sound from heaven. It was like the roar of rushing waters and loud thunder. The sound I heard was like the music of harps being played.

³Then everyone sang a new song in front of the throne. They sang it in front of the four living creatures and the elders. No one could learn the song except the 144,000. They had been set free from the evil of the earth.

⁴They had not committed sexual sins with women. They had kept themselves pure. They follow the Lamb wherever he goes. They were purchased from among people as a first offering to God and the Lamb. ⁵Their mouths told no lies. They are without blame.

The Three Angels

⁶I saw another angel. He was flying high in the air. He came to tell everyone on earth the good news that will always be true. He told it to every nation, tribe, language and people. ⁷In a loud voice he said, "Have respect for God. Give him glory. The hour has come for God to judge. Worship him who made the heavens and the earth. Worship him who made the sea and the springs of water."

⁸A second angel followed him. He said, "Fallen! Babylon the Great has fallen! The city of Babylon made all the nations drink the strong wine of her terrible sins."

⁹A third angel followed them. He said in a loud voice, "Watch out, all you who worship the beast and his statue! Watch out, all you who have his mark on your forehead or your hand! ¹⁰You, too, will drink the wine of God's great anger. His wine has been

poured full strength into the cup of his anger. You will be burned with flaming sulfur. The holy angels and the Lamb will see it happen. ¹¹The smoke of your terrible suffering will rise for ever and ever. Day and night, there is no rest for you who worship the beast and his statue. There is no rest for you who receive the mark of his name."

¹²God's people need to be very patient. They are the ones who obey God's commands. They remain faithful to Jesus.

¹³Then I heard a voice from heaven. "Write this," it said. "Blessed are the dead who die as believers in the Lord from now on."

"Yes," says the Holy Spirit. "They will rest from their labor. What they have done will not be forgotten."

The Harvest of the Earth

¹⁴I looked, and there in front of me was a white cloud. Sitting on the cloud was One who looked "like a son of man." *(Daniel 7:13)* He wore a gold crown on his head. In his hand was a sharp, curved blade for cutting grain.

¹⁵Then another angel came out of the temple. He called in a loud voice to the one sitting on the cloud. "Take your blade," he said. "Cut the grain. The time has come. The earth is ready to be harvested."

¹⁶So the one sitting on the cloud swung his blade over the earth. And the earth was harvested.

¹⁷Another angel came out of the temple in heaven. He too had a sharp, curved blade. ¹⁸Still another angel came from the altar. He was in charge of the fire on the altar. He called out in a loud voice to the angel who had the sharp blade. "Take your blade," he said, "and gather the bunches of grapes from the earth's vine. Its grapes are ripe."

¹⁹So the angel swung his blade over the earth. He gathered its grapes. Then he threw them into a huge winepress. The winepress stands for God's anger.

GREAT VERSE — TO — REMEMBER

14:13 Blessed are the dead who die as believers in the Lord from now on ... They will rest from their labor.

²⁰In the winepress outside the city, the grapes were stomped on. Blood flowed out of the pit. It spread over the land for about 180 miles. It rose as high as the horses' heads.

Seven Angels With Seven Plagues

15 I saw in heaven another great and miraculous sign. Seven angels were about to bring the seven last plagues. The plagues would complete God's anger.

²Then I saw something that looked like a sea of glass mixed with fire. Standing beside the sea were those who had won the battle over the beast. They had also overcome his statue and the number of his name. They held harps given to them by God.

³They sang the song of Moses, who served God, and the song of the Lamb. They sang,

"Lord God who rules over all,
    everything you do is great and wonderful.
King of the ages,
    your ways are true and fair.
⁴Lord, who will not have respect for you?
    Who will not bring glory to your name?
You alone are holy.
All nations will come
    and worship you.
They see that the things you do are right."

⁵After this I looked, and the temple was opened in heaven. The temple is the holy tent where the tablets of the covenant were kept.

⁶Out of the temple came the seven angels who were bringing the seven plagues. They were dressed in clean, shining linen. They wore gold strips of cloth around their chests.

⁷Then one of the four living creatures gave seven golden bowls to the seven angels. The bowls were filled with the anger of God, who lives for ever and ever. ⁸The temple was filled with smoke that came from the glory and power of God. No one could enter the temple until the seven plagues of the seven angels were completed.

The Seven Bowls of God's Anger

16 Then I heard a loud voice from the temple speaking to the seven angels. "Go," it said. "Pour out the seven bowls of God's anger on the earth."

²The first angel went and poured out his bowl on the land. Ugly and painful sores broke out on the people who had the mark of the beast and worshiped his statue.

³The second angel poured out his bowl on the sea. It turned into blood like the blood of a dead person. Every living thing in the sea died.

⁴The third angel poured out his bowl on the rivers and on the springs of water. They became blood.

⁵Then I heard the angel who was in charge of the waters. He said,

> "The way you judge is fair.
>   You are the Holy One.
>   You are the One who is and who was.
> ⁶The beast's worshipers have poured out the life's blood
>   of your people and your prophets.
> So you have given those worshipers blood to drink.
>   That's exactly what they should get."

⁷Then I heard the altar reply,

> "Lord God who rules over all,
>   the way you judge is true and fair."

⁸The fourth angel poured out his bowl on the sun. The sun was allowed to burn people with fire. ⁹They were burned by the blazing heat. So they spoke evil things against the name of God, who controlled these plagues. But they refused to turn away from their sins. They did not give glory to God.

¹⁰The fifth angel poured out his bowl on the throne of the beast. The kingdom of the beast became very dark. People bit their tongues because they were suffering so much. ¹¹They spoke evil things against the God of heaven because of their pains and their sores. But they refused to turn away from the sins they had committed.

¹²The sixth angel poured out his bowl on the great river Euphrates. Its water dried up to prepare the way for the kings from the East.

¹³Then I saw three evil spirits that looked like frogs. They came out of the mouths of the dragon, the beast and the false prophet. ¹⁴They are spirits of demons performing miraculous signs. They go out to gather the kings of the whole world for battle. That battle will take place on the great day of the God who rules over all.

¹⁵"Look! I am coming like a thief! Blessed are those who stay

awake and keep their clothes with them. They will not be caught naked. They will not be put to shame."

[16]Then the evil spirits gathered the kings together. The place where the kings met is called Armageddon in the Hebrew language.

[17]The seventh angel poured out his bowl into the air. Out of the temple came a loud voice from the throne. It said, "It is done!"

[18]Then there came flashes of lightning, rumblings, thunder and a powerful earthquake. There has never been an earthquake as terrible as this since people have lived on earth. [19]The great city split into three parts. The cities of the nations crumbled and fell. God remembered Babylon the Great. He gave her the cup filled with the wine of his terrible anger.

[20]Every island ran away. The mountains could not be found. [21]Huge hailstones of about 100 pounds each fell from the sky. The hail crushed people. They spoke evil things against God because the plague of hail was so terrible.

The Woman and the Beast

17 One of the seven angels who had the seven bowls came to me. He said, "Come. I will show you how the great prostitute will be punished. She is the one who sits on many waters. [2]The kings of the earth took part in her evil ways. The people living on earth were drunk with the wine of her terrible sins."

[3]Then the angel carried me away in a vision. The Holy Spirit took me into a desert. There I saw a woman sitting on a bright red beast. It was covered with names that say evil things that are displeasing to God. It had seven heads and ten horns.

[4]The woman was dressed in purple and bright red. She was gleaming with gold, jewels and pearls. In her hand she held a golden cup filled with things that God hates. It was filled with her terrible, dirty sins. [5]This name was written on her forehead:

MYSTERY

BABYLON THE GREAT

THE MOTHER OF PROSTITUTES

THE MOTHER OF EVERYTHING ON EARTH THAT GOD HATES.

[6]I saw that the woman was drunk with the blood of God's people. They are the ones who gave witness to Jesus.

When I saw her, I was very amazed.

[7]Then the angel said to me, "Why are you amazed? I will

explain to you the mystery of the woman and of the beast she rides on. The beast is the one who has the seven heads and ten horns. [8]The beast that you saw used to exist. But now he does not. He will come up out of the Abyss. He will be destroyed. Some of the people who live on the earth will be amazed when they see the beast. Their names have not been written in the book of life from the time the world was created. They will be amazed because even though the beast used to exist and now does not, he will come again.

[9]"Here is a problem that you have to be wise to understand. The seven heads are seven hills that the woman sits on. [10]They are also seven kings. Five have fallen, one is ruling, and the other has still not come. When he does come, he must remain for a little while.

[11]"The beast who used to exist, and now does not, is an eighth king. He belongs to the other seven. He will be destroyed.

[12]"The ten horns you saw are ten kings. They have not yet received a kingdom. But for one hour they will receive authority to rule together with the beast. [13]They have only one purpose. So they give their power and authority to the beast. [14]They will make war against the Lamb. But the Lamb will overcome them because he is the most powerful Lord of all and the greatest King of all. His appointed, chosen and faithful followers will be with him."

[15]Then the angel spoke to me. "You saw the waters the prostitute sits on," he said. "They stand for all the nations of the world, no matter what their race or language is. [16]The beast and the ten horns you saw will hate the prostitute. They will destroy her and leave her naked. They will eat her flesh and burn her with fire. [17]God has put it into their hearts to carry out his purpose. So they agreed to give the beast their power to rule. They will give him that power until God's words come true.

[18]"The woman you saw stands for the great city that rules over the kings of the earth."

Babylon Falls

18 After these things I saw another angel coming down from heaven. He had great authority. His glory filled the earth with light. [2]With a mighty voice he shouted,

"Fallen! Babylon the Great has fallen!
    She has become a place where demons live.
    She has become a den for every evil spirit.

She has become a nest for every 'unclean' and hated
bird.
3 All the nations have drunk
the strong wine of her terrible sins.
The kings of the earth took part in her evil ways.
The traders of the world grew rich from her great
wealth."

4 Then I heard another voice from heaven. It said,

"Come out of her, my people.
Then you will not take part in her sins.
You will not suffer from any of her plagues.
5 Her sins are piled up to heaven.
God has remembered her crimes.
6 Do to her as she has done to others.
Pay her back double for what she has done.
Mix her a double dose of what she has mixed for
others.
7 Give her as much pain and suffering
as the glory and wealth she gave herself.
She brags to herself,
'I rule like a queen. I am not a widow.
I will never be sad.'
8 But she will be plagued by death, sadness and hunger.
In a single day they will all catch up with her.
She will be burned up by fire.
The Lord God who judges her is mighty.

9 "The kings of the earth who committed terrible sins with her
will sob. They will be sad because they used to share her riches.
They will see the smoke rising as she burns. 10 They will be terrified by her suffering. Standing far away, they will exclaim,

"'How terrible! How terrible it is for you, great city!
How terrible for you, Babylon, city of power!
In just one hour you have been destroyed!'

11 "The traders of the world will cry and be sad over her. No one
buys what they sell anymore. 12 Here is what they had for sale:

gold, silver, jewels, pearls.
Fine linen, purple, silk, bright red cloth.
Every kind of expensive wood.

All sorts of articles made out of ivory, valuable wood,
> bronze, iron and marble.
¹³Cinnamon, spice, incense, myrrh, frankincense.
Wine, olive oil, fine flour, wheat.
Cattle, sheep, horses, carriages, human slaves.

¹⁴"The merchants will say, 'The pleasure you longed for has left you. All your riches and glory have disappeared forever.' ¹⁵The traders who sold these things and became rich because of her will stand far away. Her suffering will terrify them. They will cry and be sad. ¹⁶They will cry out,

> "'How terrible! How terrible it is for you, great city,
> dressed in fine linen, purple and bright red!
> How terrible for you, great city, gleaming with gold,
> jewels and pearls!
> ¹⁷In just one hour your great wealth has been destroyed!'

"Every sea captain and all who travel by ship will stand far away. So will the sailors and all who earn their living from the sea. ¹⁸They will see the smoke rising as Babylon burns. They will ask, 'Was there ever a city like this great city?' ¹⁹They will throw dust on their heads. They will cry and be sad. They will cry out,

> "'How terrible! How terrible it is for you, great city!
> All who had ships on the sea
> became rich because of her wealth!
> In just one hour she has been destroyed!
> ²⁰Heaven, be glad for this!
> God's people, be glad! Apostles and prophets, be
> glad!
> God has judged her for the way she treated you.'"

²¹Then a mighty angel picked up a huge rock. It was the size of a large millstone. He threw it into the sea. Then he said,

> "That is how
> the great city of Babylon will be thrown down.
> Never again will it be found.
> ²²The songs of musicians will never be heard in you
> again.
> Gone will be the music of harp, flute and trumpet.
> No worker of any kind
> will ever be found in you again.
> The sound of a millstone

will never be heard in you again.
²³The light of a lamp
　　will never shine in you again.
The voices of brides and grooms
　　will never be heard in you again.
Your traders were among the world's most important
　　　　people.
By your magic spell all the nations were led down
　　the wrong path.
²⁴You were guilty of the murder of prophets and God's
　　　　people.
You were guilty of the blood of all who have been
　　killed on the earth."

Hallelujah!

19 After these things I heard a roar in heaven. It sounded
like a huge crowd shouting,

"Hallelujah!
Salvation and glory and power belong to our God.
²　The way he judges is true and fair.
He has judged the great prostitute.
　　She polluted the earth with her terrible sins.
God has paid her back for killing those who served
　　him."

³Again they shouted,

"Hallelujah!
The smoke from her fire goes up for ever and ever."

⁴The 24 elders and the four living creatures bowed down. They
worshiped God, who was sitting on the throne. They cried out,

"Amen! Hallelujah!"

⁵Then a voice came from the throne. It said,

GREAT VERSE —TO— REMEMBER

19:5 Praise our God, all you who serve him! Praise God, all you who have respect for him, both great and small!

"Praise our God,
all you who serve him!
Praise God, all you who have respect for him,
both great and small!"

⁶Then I heard the noise of a huge crowd. It sounded like the roar of rushing waters and like loud thunder. The people were shouting,

"Hallelujah!
Our Lord God is the King who rules over all.
⁷Let us be joyful and glad!
Let us give him glory!
It is time for the Lamb's wedding.
His bride has made herself ready.
⁸Fine linen, bright and clean,
was given to her to wear."

Fine linen stands for the right things that God's people do.

⁹Here is what the angel told me to write. "Blessed are those who are invited to the wedding supper of the Lamb!" Then he added, "These are the true words of God."
¹⁰When I heard this, I fell at his feet to worship him.
But he said to me, "Don't do that! I serve God, just as you do. I am God's servant, just like other believers who hold firmly to what Jesus has taught. Worship God! What Jesus taught is the very heart of prophecy."

The Rider on the White Horse

¹¹I saw heaven standing open. There in front of me was a white horse. Its rider is called Faithful and True. When he judges or makes war, he is always fair. ¹²His eyes are like blazing fire. On his head are many crowns. A name is written on him that only he knows. ¹³He is dressed in a robe dipped in blood. His name is The Word of God.
¹⁴The armies of heaven were following him, riding on white horses. They were dressed in fine linen, white and clean.
¹⁵Out of the rider's mouth comes a sharp sword. He will strike down the nations with it. Scripture says, "He will rule them with an iron rod." *(Psalm 2:9)* He stomps on the grapes of God's winepress. The winepress stands for the terrible anger of the God who rules over all.

¹⁶On the robe of the rider and on his thigh he has this name written:

GREATEST KING OF ALL AND THE MOST POWERFUL LORD OF ALL.

¹⁷I saw an angel standing in the sun. He cried in a loud voice to all the birds flying high in the air, "Come! Gather together for the great supper of God. ¹⁸Come and eat the dead bodies of kings, generals, and other mighty people. Eat the bodies of horses and their riders. Eat the bodies of all people, free and slave, great and small."

¹⁹Then I saw the beast and the kings of the earth with their armies. They had gathered together to make war against the rider on the horse and his army.

²⁰But the beast and the false prophet were captured. The false prophet had done miraculous signs for the beast. In this way the false prophet had tricked those who had received the mark of the beast and had worshiped his statue. The beast and the false prophet were thrown alive into the lake of fire that burns with sulfur. ²¹The rest of them were killed with the sword that came out of the rider's mouth. All the birds stuffed themselves with the dead bodies.

The Thousand Years

20 I saw an angel coming down out of heaven. He had the key to the Abyss. In his hand he held a heavy chain.

²He grabbed the dragon, that old serpent. The serpent is also called the devil, or Satan. The angel put him in chains for 1,000 years. ³Then he threw him into the Abyss. He locked it and sealed him in. This was to keep Satan from fooling the nations anymore until the 1,000 years were ended. After that, he must be set free for a short time.

⁴I saw thrones. Those who had been given authority to judge were sitting on them. I also saw the souls of those whose heads had been cut off because they had given witness for Jesus and because of God's word. They had not worshiped the beast or his statue. They had not received his mark on their foreheads or hands. They came to life and ruled with Christ for 1,000 years.

⁵This is the first resurrection. The rest of the dead did not come to life until the 1,000 years were ended.

⁶Blessed and holy are those who take part in the first resurrection. The second death has no power over them. They will be priests of God and of Christ. They will rule with him for 1,000 years.

Satan Is Judged

⁷When the 1,000 years are over, Satan will be set free from his prison. ⁸He will go out to fool the nations. He will gather them from the four corners of the earth. He will bring Gog and Magog together for battle.

Their troops are as many as the grains of sand on the seashore. ⁹They marched across the whole earth. They surrounded the place where God's people were camped. It was the city he loves. But fire came down from heaven and burned them up.

¹⁰The devil, who fooled them, was thrown into the lake of burning sulfur. That is where the beast and the false prophet had been thrown. They will all suffer day and night for ever and ever.

The Dead Are Judged

¹¹I saw a great white throne and the One who was sitting on it. When the earth and sky saw his face, they ran away. There was no place for them.

¹²I saw the dead, great and small, standing in front of the throne. Books were opened. Then another book was opened. It was the book of life. The dead were judged by what they had done. The things they had done were written in the books. ¹³The sea gave up the dead that were in it. And Death and Hell gave up their dead. The dead were judged by what they had done.

¹⁴Then Death and Hell were thrown into the lake of fire. The lake of fire is the second death. ¹⁵Anyone whose name was not written in the book of life was thrown into the lake of fire.

The New Jerusalem

21 I saw a new heaven and a new earth. The first heaven and the first earth were completely gone. There was no longer any sea.

²I saw the Holy City, the new Jerusalem. It was coming down

GREAT VERSE —TO— REMEMBER

21:1-2 I saw a new heaven and a new earth. The first heaven and the first earth were completely gone...I saw the Holy City, the new Jerusalem.

out of heaven from God. It was prepared like a bride beautifully dressed for her husband.

³I heard a loud voice from the throne. It said, "Now God makes his home with human beings. He will live with them. They will be his people. And God himself will be with them and be their God. ⁴He will wipe away every tear from their eyes. There will be no more death or sadness. There will be no more crying or pain. Things are no longer the way they used to be."

⁵He who was sitting on the throne said, "I am making everything new!" Then he said, "Write this down. You can trust these words. They are true."

⁶He said to me, "It is done. I am the Alpha and the Omega, the First and the Last. I am the Beginning and the End. Anyone who is thirsty may drink from the spring of the water of life. It doesn't cost anything! ⁷Those who overcome will receive all this from me. I will be their God, and they will be my children.

⁸"But others will have their place in the lake of fire that burns with sulfur. Those who are afraid and those who do not believe will be there. Murderers and those who pollute themselves will join them. Those who commit sexual sins and those who practice witchcraft will go there. Those who worship statues of gods and all who tell lies will be there too. It is the second death."

⁹One of the seven angels who had the seven bowls came and spoke to me. The bowls were filled with the seven last plagues. The angel said, "Come. I will show you the bride, the wife of the Lamb."

¹⁰Then he carried me away in a vision. The Spirit took me to a huge, high mountain. He showed me Jerusalem, the Holy City. It was coming down out of heaven from God. ¹¹It shone with the glory of God. It gleamed like a very valuable jewel. It was like a jasper, as clear as crystal.

¹²The city had a huge, high wall with 12 gates. Twelve angels were at the gates, one at each of them. On the gates were written the names of the 12 tribes of Israel. ¹³There were three gates on the east and three on the north. There were three gates on the south and three on the west. ¹⁴The wall of the city had 12 foundations. Written on them were the names of the 12 apostles of the Lamb.

¹⁵The angel who talked with me had a gold measuring rod. He used it to measure the city, its gates and its walls.

¹⁶The city was laid out like a square. It was as long as it was wide. The angel measured the city with the rod. It was 1,400 miles long. It was as wide and high as it was long.

[17]He measured the wall of the city. It was 200 feet thick. The angel did the measuring as a human being would. [18]The wall was made out of jasper. The city was made out of pure gold, as pure as glass.

[19]The foundations of the city walls were decorated with every kind of jewel. The first foundation was made out of jasper. The second was made out of sapphire. The third was made out of chalcedony. The fourth was made out of emerald. [20]The fifth was made out of sardonyx. The sixth was made out of carnelian. The seventh was made out of chrysolite. The eighth was made out of beryl. The ninth was made out of topaz. The tenth was made out of chrysoprase. The eleventh was made out of jacinth. The twelfth was made out of amethyst.

[21]The 12 gates were made from 12 pearls. Each gate was made out of a single pearl. The main street of the city was made out of pure gold, as clear as glass.

[22]I didn't see a temple in the city. This was because the Lamb and the Lord God who rules over all are its temple. [23]The city does not need the sun or moon to shine on it. God's glory is its light, and the Lamb is its lamp.

[24]The nations will walk by the light of the city. The kings of the world will bring their glory into it. [25]Its gates will never be shut, because there will be no night there. [26]The glory and honor of the nations will be brought into it.

[27]Only what is pure will enter it. No one who fools others or does shameful things will enter it. Only those whose names are written in the Lamb's book of life will enter the city.

The River of Life

22 Then the angel showed me the river of the water of life. It was as clear as crystal. It flowed from the throne of God and of the Lamb. [2]It flowed down the middle of the city's main street.

On each side of the river stood the tree of life, bearing 12 crops of fruit. Its fruit was ripe every month. The leaves of the tree bring healing to the nations.

[3]There will no longer be any curse. The throne of God and of the Lamb will be in the city. God's servants will serve him. [4]They will see his face. His name will be on their foreheads.

[5]There will be no more night. They will not need the light of a lamp or the light of the sun. The Lord God will give them light. They will rule for ever and ever.

⁶The angel said to me, "You can trust these words. They are true. The Lord is the God of the spirits of the prophets. He sent his angel to show those who serve him the things that must soon take place."

Jesus Is Coming

⁷"Look! I am coming soon! Blessed are those who obey the words of the prophecy in this book."

⁸I, John, am the one who heard and saw these things.

After I had heard and seen them, I fell down to worship at the feet of the angel. He is the one who had been showing me these things.

⁹But he said to me, "Don't do that! I serve God, just as you do. I am God's servant, just like the other prophets and all who obey the words of this book. Worship God!"

¹⁰Then he told me, "Do not seal up the words of the prophecy in this book. These things are about to happen. ¹¹Let those who do wrong keep on doing wrong. Let those who are evil continue to be evil. Let those who do what is right keep on doing what is right. And let those who are holy continue to be holy."

¹²"Look! I am coming soon! I bring my rewards with me. I will reward each of you for what you have done. ¹³I am the Alpha and the Omega. I am the First and the Last. I am the Beginning and the End.

¹⁴"Blessed are those who wash their robes. They will have the right to come to the tree of life. They will be allowed to go through the gates into the city.

¹⁵"Outside the city are the dogs and those who practice witchcraft. Outside are also those who commit sexual sins and murder. Those who worship statues of gods, and everyone who loves and does what is false, are outside too.

¹⁶"I, Jesus, have sent my angel to give you this witness for the

22:7 Look! I am coming soon! Blessed are those who obey the words of the prophecy in this book.

churches. I am the Root and the Son of David. I am the bright Morning Star."

[17]The Holy Spirit and the bride say, "Come!" Let those who hear say, "Come!" Anyone who is thirsty should come. Anyone who wants to take the free gift of the water of life should do so.

[18]I am warning everyone who hears the words of the prophecy of this book. If you add anything to them, God will add to you the plagues told about in this book. [19]If you take any words away from this book of prophecy, God will take away from you your share in the tree of life. He will also take away your place in the Holy City. This book tells about these things.

[20]He who gives witness to these things says, "Yes. I am coming soon."

Amen. Come, Lord Jesus!

[21]May the grace of the Lord Jesus be with God's people. Amen.

NEW TESTAMENT TIMES

Many years ago there were trails that came into the land of Israel. They came from the east and from the north. Other trails came from Egypt in the south.

Traders used these trails to travel from one place to another. They traveled mostly by camel. They bought and sold goods along the way. The trails went *through* Israel. But they also *met* in Israel. It was almost like Israel was the center of the world.

In a way, Israel *was* the center of the world. Jesus was born there. All of the things that happened in Bible times seemed to say, "Israel is a special land."

Places of Worship

The beautiful temple stood in the city of Jerusalem. It was the center of worship for the Jews. Herod rebuilt the temple not long before Jesus was born. The temple was on a hill. Its shining white marble walls could be seen all over the city. Large stone gates opened on all four sides. Jesus called this temple his Father's house (John 2:16).

Each Jewish town also had a smaller meeting place. These were called "synagogues." The leader of the synogogue studied the Old Testament and the Jewish laws. He then could teach the people.

On the inside synagogues looked much like some of our churches. The people sat on benches. The leader stood on a stage. A special box held the scrolls of the books of the Bible.

On the Sabbath day the people came to the synagogue to worship. The leader read a verse to call the people to worship. Then there were readings of thanksgiving and praise. Someone would lead in prayer. After that, the leader might ask someone to read from the Bible. Any member who was able to teach could give the sermon. The service was closed with a blessing.

The Laws of God

God gave the Jews the Ten Commandments and many other laws at Mount Sinai. Many Jews thought that trying to keep the law was the only way to please God. They began to add many of their own laws to God's laws. They began to see themselves as very good people.

Jesus told the Jews that they were going in the wrong direction. They were so busy doing many little things that they were forgetting big things that were more important. They were forgetting to love others. They were forgetting to take care of the poor. They were forgetting to love God.

The Sabbath Day

God gave the people of Israel the Sabbath as a day of rest. On the seventh day of every week they rested from their work. They offered special sacrifices.

The scribes and Pharisees later added hundreds of laws about how people should keep the Sabbath day holy. Then the people forgot that God gave the Sabbath day to be a special day. Instead they just worried about obeying all the rules.

On the Sabbath day people could not travel very far. They

could not carry anything from one place to another. They were not supposed to spit on the ground. If they did they might be plowing a little row in the dirt. And that would be work! If a hen laid an egg on the Sabbath, they were not supposed to eat that egg. The hen had worked on the Sabbath to lay it.

When Jesus and his disciples picked some grain and ate it on the Sabbath, the Pharisees said they were working. When Jesus healed sick people on the Sabbath, the Pharisees said he was breaking the law. They got angry and wanted to kill him.

Religious Groups

The most important religious groups in New Testament times were the Pharisees and the Sadducees. The Sadducees were rich and powerful men. The high priest, the chief priests and rich businessmen all belonged to the Sadducees. The Sadducees were against any new group that tried to change Jewish life. That's why they were against Jesus and his disciples. The Sadducees also turned away from many of the teachings of the Pharisees. They did not believe that people would rise from the dead. They did not believe in angels or demons. They did not keep all the laws of the Pharisees. They only kept the law of Moses.

The Pharisees added hundreds of laws to the law God gave Moses. They were mostly interested in keeping all these laws. Many of the Pharisees forgot God's other laws. They were proud of how good they were, but they did not love other people. However, there were also Pharisees who truly loved God and others and tried to do what was right.

Seventy of the most important Pharisees and Sadducees made up the Jewish high court. This court was called the Sanhedrin. The high priest led the court. The Romans let this court decide what to do when someone had broken a Jewish law. But this court did not have the power to put anyone to death. If the Sanhedrin thought someone should die, they had to bring the person to the Roman courts.

The Roman Empire

Rome had begun to grow larger and stronger before Christ was born. Wars were fought and many new lands were added to the Roman Empire. This empire was very large. It included Spain and Germany, North Africa, Asia Minor, Syria and Israel.

Many good things happened because of Roman rule. There was peace between all of the different countries in the empire. The Romans also set up good government everywhere. They built roads for safe and easy travel. Many of the people were able to speak and understand the same language–Greek.

The Romans did not know that all these things would make it easier for the gospel to spread to many lands. They did not know that God had prepared the way for Jesus and the spread of the good news. Later Jesus' disciples traveled more easily to far-away lands because there was peace and because there were good roads. They could bring the gospel in the Greek language to many people in many areas.

Tax Collectors

The Jews hated the Romans. They believed the Romans had no right to rule over them. They believed the Romans had no right to take their money for taxes. They didn't like the soldiers who lived in their country. The Jews also hated the Romans because they tried to change the Jewish way of life. The Romans wanted everyone to act like Romans. The Jews were looking for the Messiah. They thought he would become their king and would free them from the Romans.

The Jews hated tax collectors even more than the Romans. Many tax collectors were Jews who were working for Rome. Many tax collectors were not honest. They took more money than they were supposed to take. They were cheating their own people to help the enemy.

Jesus often talked and ate with tax collectors. Matthew was a tax collector. So was Zacchaeus. Both became followers of Jesus.

Everyday Life

Life in New Testament times was much different from life today. It was a simple life. Most people did not have any extras. In fact, they often had just enough to live. The people worked hard, and children had to share in the work.

The people built their houses of mud bricks that were hardened by laying them out in the sun. Sometimes the front part of the house had no roof over it. This part was like a small yard. Behind it was a living room with small bedrooms at the back. The floor of the house was of hard and smooth clay. Builders made the roof of heavy wooden beams with boards laid across them. They covered the boards with a mixture of mud and straw. This flat roof was a good place to work or to sit. Sometimes people slept on the roof on hot nights. Usually a ladder or sometimes steps led up to the roof.

Most people had very little furniture–just some wooden stools, a low wooden table and some sleeping mats. There was a place for fire and sometimes a small clay oven for baking bread. There was no chimney, so the smoke had to find its way out of the small high window openings. Some houses had wooden doors. Others had doorways covered with grass mats or cloth.

Food

The people ate foods like milk and cheese, grapes, figs, olives, honey and barley cakes, eggs, chicken, fish, goat meat, beans, cucumbers and onions.

The first meal of the day was usually bread and cheese. Sometimes a family would eat a light meal at noon. Again, bread was the main part. The people had their large meal of the day in the evening. They usually ate bread and fish, fruit and vegetables. The common people often ate meat only on very special days.

Clothing

The clothing of New Testament times was simple. Besides underclothing, the people wore robes with a belt tied around the waist. Over the robe they often wore a cape. Children usually had shorter, knee-length clothing. They sometimes wore a kind of pull-over shirt. Women decorated their clothing with brightly colored weaving and sewing.

The people wore sandals without socks. Their feet were often dusty from walking on their dirt streets and roads. They washed their feet often.

Work

The people did many different kinds of work. Some were farmers and builders and makers of pottery. Others were bakers and doctors and teachers. There were watchmen who guarded the cities. There were workers in leather and workers in metal. Jesus' father was a carpenter. Jesus also knew about herding sheep. Peter and James and John were fishermen. Matthew was a tax collector. There were scribes who wrote letters and copied the laws and the books of the Bible.

Women had to work hard in their homes. The first thing they would do in the morning was make the bread for the day. They would grind the grain into flour, then make dough into loaves of bread and bake them. The women also had to carry water from the well and get wood for the fire. They made all the clothes for the family, spinning and weaving their own cloth out of flax and wool.

Parents expected their children to help with the work. Girls helped their mothers with all the household work. Boys helped their fathers in their work and were expected to follow the same trade as their fathers.

Schools

Parents taught their children Bible verses when they were still very young. They learned verses from the law and stories from the Old Testament.

When boys were five or six years old, they went to school. The leader of the synagogue taught them. For the first four years, they studied mostly the first five books of the Bible. By then they knew the laws of God very well. They also learned how to read and write Hebrew. For the next several years they studied other books of the Bible and other Jewish writings.

When a Jewish boy reached the age of twelve or thirteen, he was considered to be a man. The boy and his family and friends celebrated with a special ceremony and often a party. Most boys left school at this age.

Conclusion

The time of the New Testament was the best time for Jesus to come. The people were looking and waiting for him. The safe roads made it much easier for early Christians to travel to spread the good news of the Savior. The common language made it much easier for them to tell others about Jesus. People were eager to hear about him. God had everything planned and ready.

DICTIONARY

A

Abyss
The deep pit where Satan and evil spirits will be held in chains.

adultery
1. Having sex with someone who is not the person's husband or wife. 2. Not being faithful or true to God.

altar
A table or raised place where a sacrifice was offered to God.

Amen
A Hebrew word that means *it is true* or *let it be true.*

angel
A spirit who is God's helper and tells people God's words.

anoint
To pour olive oil on people's heads so God will heal them.

anointed
To be set apart as God's special servant.

apostle
1. One of the twelve men who were with Jesus and who later taught others about him.
2. Someone who teaches others about God.

Aramaic
The language many people spoke in Jesus' time.

ark of the covenant
A large gold chest in which the tablets of the covenant were kept.

armor
Special clothing people wore to keep them safe in battle.

B

Baal
The name of the main Canaanite god.

Babylon
1. The capital city of Babylonia.
2. A word that stands for any powerful, sinful city.

baptize
To sprinkle, pour or cover a person with water as a sign that sin is washed away.

Beelzebub
Another name for Satan.

blessed

1. Made happy. 2. Helped by God.

C

cast lots

Something done to find out what God wants. It is like drawing straws to see who will go first.

chariot

A two-wheeled cart pulled by war horses.

cherubim

Heavenly creatures who serve God.

chief priest

See *priest*.

Christ

A Greek word that means *the Anointed One*. It means the same thing as the Hebrew word *Messiah*.

circumcision

Cutting off the loose fold of skin at the end of the male sex organ.

"clean"

Something that God accepts.

commandment

A law that God gives.

Council

The most important Jewish court of law in Jesus' time.

covenant

A treaty between two persons or groups in which promises are made.

crucify

To put people to death by nailing them to crosses.

curse

A prayer or spoken command for evil or harm to come on someone.

D

deacon

A leader of the church who serves other people.

demon

An evil spirit.

devil

See *Satan*.

disciples

Followers who believe and do what their teacher says.

divorce

The legal way for a man and woman to put an end to their marriage.

dysentery

A sickness that produces watery bowel movements.

E

elders

The leaders of a church, town or nation who make decisions.

eternal
Forever. Without beginning or end.

evil spirit
One of the devil's helpers.

F

fast
To go for a time without eating, sometimes also without drinking.

Feast of Booths
A feast when the Israelites celebrated the harvest of their crops. They lived in tents for eight days.

Feast of Dedication
See *Feast of Hanukkah*.

Feast of Hanukkah
A feast when the Jews celebrated the time when the temple was made pure and set apart for God again.

Feast of Passover
See *Passover*.

Feast of Unleavened Bread
A time to remember when God set the Israelites free from Egypt. It was celebrated along with the Feast of Passover.

fig
A sweet fruit that grows on trees in warm countries near the sea.

G

glory
Praise. Honor. Greatness.

God
The creator and ruler of the world. The One who saves his people.

grace
God's kindness to human beings. It is given without being earned.

H

hallelujah
A Hebrew word that means *praise the Lord*.

Hanukkah
See *Feast of Hanukkah*.

harvest
Gathering a crop when it is ready.

heaven
1. God's home. 2. The sky.

Hebrew
1. Another name for a person in the family line of Abraham. 2. The language spoken by the people of Israel.

Herod
The first name of five men who ruled over Israel for the Roman emperor.

high priest
The one in charge of everything

and everybody at the holy tent and the temple.

holy

Set apart for God. Clean. Pure.

Holy Spirit

God's Spirit who lives in the hearts of believers and works in their lives.

holy tent

The place the people of Israel used for worship when they were wandering in the desert after leaving Egypt. Years later Solomon built the first temple for worship.

homosexual

Someone who has sex with another person of the same sex.

hosanna

A Hebrew word that means *please save us now* and later came to be used in praising God.

hymn

A song of praise to God.

hyssop

A plant that was used to sprinkle water or blood to make something clean and pure.

I

incense

Spices that give a pleasing smell when they are burned.

Israel

1. The new name God gave to Jacob. 2. The nation that came from the family line of Jacob. 3. The northern tribes that separated from Judah to serve their own king.

J

Jesus

The Greek form of the Hebrew name Joshua, which means *the Lord saves.*

Jews

What the people of Israel were called beginning late in the 6th century B.C.

judge

1. To decide if something is good or bad. 2. A person who decides what is right and wrong in matters of law.

K

kingdom

An area or group of people ruled by a king.

L

law

Rules about what is right and wrong.

Law

The first five books of the Bible.

Levites

Men from the tribe of Levi who took care of the holy tent or the temple.

locust
A type of grasshopper that destroys crops.

Lord
A title for God or Christ.

lots
See *cast lots*.

M

manger
A food box for animals.

manna
Special food from heaven that God gave to the people of Israel in the desert.

mercy
More kindness and forgiveness than people are worthy to receive.

millstone
A heavy rock used to crush grain to make flour.

miracle
Something very special and wonderful that only God can do.

miraculous signs
Things that are very wonderful and special that only God can do and that point us to him.

O

oath
A special promise made in the sight of God.

offering
Something given to God as a part of worship.

oxen
Large cattle that are used on the farm because of their size and great strength.

P

Passover
A feast that was celebrated every year to remember the time when God set the people of Israel free from Egypt. God "passed over" their homes if they were marked with blood on the doorways.

Pentecost
A feast that was celebrated fifty days after Passover. On the day of Pentecost the Holy Spirit came to live in Christians.

pharaoh
The title of any ruler of early Egypt.

Pharisees
A group of Jews who were very careful to follow God's laws and their own rules about God's laws.

pillar
A tall, upright post that was used to help hold a building up.

pierce
To poke through with a sharp instrument.

plague
1. Any sickness that kills many people. 2. Anything that causes a lot of suffering or loss.

pregnant
Carrying a baby inside a woman's body until the baby is born.

Preparation Day
The day before the Sabbath day. Used to get ready for it.

priest
A person who served in the holy tent or the temple. He gave his own as well as other people's offerings and prayers to God.

prophecy
A message God gives to his people through his messenger.

prophesy
1. To give a message from God. 2. To tell what the future will be.

prophet
A person who receives messages from God and tells them to other people.

prostitutes
People who get paid to let others have sex with them.

proverbs
Wise sayings.

psalms
Poems or songs of praise or prayer.

R

Rabbi
A teacher of Jewish law.

Raca
An insult that means someone is foolish.

resurrection
Coming back to life after being dead.

right hand
The place of honor, power and authority.

S

Sabbath
The seventh day of the week. The day of rest and worship.

sacred
Set apart for God. Holy.

sacrifice
1. To give something to God as an offering. 2. Something that is given to God as an offering.

Sadducees
A group of Jewish leaders who followed only the first five books of the Bible. They did not believe anyone could come back from the dead.

salvation
Being set free from the guilt of

sin. Being saved from the power of evil.

Sanhedrin
The most important Jewish court of law in Jesus' time.

Satan
God's most powerful enemy, also called the devil.

saved
Set free from danger or sin.

Savior
The One who sets us free from our sins.

Scripture
God's written Word. Also called the Bible.

scroll
A long sheet of paper or animal skin for writing. It was rolled up on two sticks for storage.

seal
1. An object like a ring with a drawing or pattern cut into it.
2. A mark made by pressing this object into clay, wax or paper.

shepherd
A person who takes care of sheep.

sinner
A person who does things God does not like.

Son of Man
A name Jesus gave to himself to show he is God's anointed prophet, priest and king.

soul
A person's entire spiritual being.

spiritual
Having to do with matters that are connected with God and the Bible.

staff
A stick a shepherd uses to lean on and to take care of sheep.

synagogue
A Jewish place of worship and teaching.

T

tassels
Hanging groups of thread that are tied together at one end. Usually sewn to the edge of a rug or piece of clothing.

temple
A building where people worship.

tempt
To try to get someone to do something wrong.

threshing floor
The place where heads of grain are beaten or stepped on to separate the grain from the stem.

tomb
A place to bury dead bodies. It

was usually a cave with a big stone door.

Twelve, the

The men Jesus chose as his first disciples. See also *disciples*.

U

"unclean"

Something that God does not accept.

unleavened bread

A flat bread made without yeast.

V

vineyard

A place where grapes grow.

virgin

A woman who has never had sex with a man.

vision

Something that God puts in a person's mind. Something like a dream, but the person is usually awake.

W

widow

A woman whose husband has died.

winepress

A place where juice is pressed out of grapes.

wisdom

Understanding that comes from God. Wise thinking.

YZ

yeast

Something added to dough to make bread rise.

Zealot

A Jewish person who wanted to fight and get rid of the Roman rulers.

Zion

1. The city of Jerusalem. 2. The hill on which King David's house and the temple once stood.

WHO'S WHO
IN THE
NEW
TESTAMENT

Agrippa

A Roman ruler who wanted to hear for himself what the famous prisoner Paul had to say.

You can read about Agrippa in Acts 25:22—26:32.

Ananias

God sent Ananias to Saul after Saul was stopped by Jesus on the road to Damascus.

You can read about Ananias in Acts 9:10-19.

Ananias and Sapphira

Ananias and Sapphira lied to Peter about land they had sold.

You can read about Ananias and Sapphira in Acts 5:1-10.

Andrew

Andrew took his brother Simon Peter to see Jesus. Andrew became a disciple of Jesus.

You can read about Andrew in John 1:40-42.

Anna

Anna was a prophetess who had waited a long time for Jesus to come. She was there when Jesus was presented at the temple as a baby.

You can read about Anna in Luke 2:36-38.

Apollos

Apollos was a Jew from Alexandria who came to Ephesus and preached the good news boldly and powerfully.

You can read about Apollos in Acts 18:24-28.

Aquila

See *Priscilla and Aquila*.

Barnabas

Barnabas was a member of the early church. He traveled many miles—alone and with Paul—to tell others about Jesus.

You can read about Barnabas in Acts 13:1-3.

Barsabbas

Barsabbas and Matthias were the possible replacements for Judas Iscariot. Matthias was chosen.

You can read about Barsabbas in Acts 1:21-26.

Bartholomew

Bartholomew was one of the twelve disciples who followed Jesus.

You can read about Bartholomew in Matthew 10:1-4 and in Acts 1:13.

Caiaphas

Caiaphas was the high priest when Jesus was arrested, tried and killed.

You can read about Caiaphas in John 18:12-14.

Cornelius

Cornelius was the first non-Jew to whom Peter brought the message of Jesus' love.

The story of Cornelius can be found in Acts 10.

Demetrius

Demetrius lived in Ephesus and made silver statues of the goddess Artemis. He was worried about his business when Paul began to preach in his city and people believed in Jesus.

You can read about Demetrius in Acts 19:23-41.

Dorcas

See *Tabitha*.

Elizabeth

Elizabeth was an old woman when she had a son, John the Baptist.

When John grew up, told the people that Jesus was coming.

You can read about Elizabeth in Luke 1:5-25,57-66.

Eutychus

Eutychus fell out of a window when he fell asleep listening to a long message by Paul.

You can read the story of Eutychus in Acts 20:7-12.

Felix

Felix was a Roman ruler in Judea. He told Paul he was interested in the gospel, but he never believed.

You can read about Felix in Acts 24.

Festus

Festus followed Felix as the Roman ruler in Judea. He thought Paul's great learning was driving Paul crazy.

You can read about Festus in Acts 25:1-12; 26:24.

Herodias

Herodias was Herod's sister-in-law. Herodias told her daughter to trick Herod into killing John the Baptist.

You can read about Herodias in Matthew 14:1-12.

Herod

Several Herods ruled over Israel for the Roman emperor. One Herod tried to kill the baby Jesus and another killed John the Baptist.

You can read about these rulers in Matthew 2:3-16 and 14:1-12.

James

James and his brother John, sons of Zebedee, were disciples of Jesus.

You can read a story about James and John in Matthew 20:20-28.

James

James, the son of Alphaeus, was another of Jesus' twelve disciples.

You can read about James in Matthew 10:1-4.

James

James was a half-brother of Jesus and was a leader in the early church. He wrote the book of James.

You can read about James in Acts 21:17-19 and in the book of James.

Jesus

Jesus is the main person in the New Testament. He lived and died in order to bring salvation to the people of the world.

You can read the story of Jesus' birth in Luke 2:1-20.
You can read the story of Jesus' baptism in Matthew 3:13-17.
You can read the story of Jesus' death in Mark 15:33-41.
You can read the story of Jesus' resurrection in Matthew 28.

John

John, the brother of James, was known as the disciple whom Jesus loved. John wrote the book of John, the three letters of John and the book of Revelation.

You can read a story about John in Acts 4:1–23.

John the Baptist

John the Baptist was sent by God to tell the people that Jesus the Savior was coming.

You can read about John the Baptist in Luke 3:1-20.

Joseph

Joseph married Mary, Jesus' mother, after he was visited by an angel messenger from God.

You can read about Joseph in Matthew 1:18-25.

Joseph of Arimathea

Joseph of Arimathea asked Pilate for Jesus' body. Joseph buried Jesus in a new tomb.

You can read about Joseph of Arimathea in John 19:38-42.

Judas Iscariot

Judas Iscariot was one of Jesus' twelve disciples. He handed Jesus over to be killed for thirty pieces of silver.

You can read about Judas Iscariot in Matthew 26:14-16,47-54.

Jude

Jude was probably the same person as Judas, the brother of James and Jesus.

You can read about Jude in the book of Jude.

Lazarus

Lazarus was the brother of Mary and Martha. When Lazarus got sick and died, Jesus raised him back to life.

You can read about this event in John 11:1-44.

Levi

See *Matthew*.

Luke

Luke was a doctor who traveled with Paul. He talked to many people about Jesus and wrote down what they said in the book of Luke. He also wrote the book of Acts.

Luke is mentioned by Paul in Colossians 4:14.

Lydia

Lydia made and sold purple cloth in the city of Philippi. She became a believer when Paul came and told her the story of Jesus.

You can read about Lydia in Acts 16:11-15.

Mark

Mark, also called John, went along with Paul and Barnabas on their first trip to tell others about Jesus. Mark wrote the book of Mark, telling in a simple way the story of Jesus.

You can read about Mark in Acts 13:4-5.

Martha

See *Mary and Martha*.

Mary

An angel came to tell Mary that she had been chosen by God to be the mother of Jesus.

You can read about Mary in Luke 1:26-45.

Mary and Martha

Mary and Martha opened their home to Jesus when he came to Bethany. Their brother was Lazarus.

You can read about Mary and Martha in Luke 10:38-42.

Mary Magdalene

Mary Magdalene was the first of Jesus' followers to learn that he had risen from the dead.

You can read about Mary Magdalene in John 20:10-18.

Matthew

Matthew, also called Levi, was a tax collector. Jesus called him to be a disciple.

You can read about Matthew in Mark 2:13-14.

Matthias

Matthias was chosen to replace Judas as one of the twelve apostles after Jesus had gone back to heaven.

You can read about Matthias in Acts 1:15-26.

Nicodemus

Nicodemus came at night to talk to Jesus. Jesus told him how he could be born again.

You can read about Nicodemus in John 3:1-21.

Onesimus

Onesimus was a runaway slave who became a friend and helper of Paul. Paul wrote a letter to Philemon about him.

You can read about Onesimus in the book of Philemon.

Paul

Paul, who was earlier called Saul, was attacking the followers of Jesus. Jesus spoke to him on the road to Damascus, and from then on Paul told many others about Jesus. He wrote many of the books of the New Testament.

You can read about Paul in Acts 9:1-18.

Peter

Peter was one of Jesus' disciples. His name had been Simon, but Jesus called him Peter, which means the "Rock." Peter is mentioned often in all the gospels and in Acts. He wrote the books of 1 & 2 Peter.

You can read a story about Peter in Matthew 14:22-33.

Philip

Philip was one of Jesus' twelve disciples.

You can read about Philip in John 1:43-48.

Philip

Another Philip served as a deacon in the early church. He told a man from Ethiopia the good news about Jesus.

You can read about this Philip in Acts 8:26-40.

Philemon

Paul wrote to ask Philemon to take back a runaway slave, Onesimus.

You can read about Philemon in the book of Philemon.

Pontius Pilate

Pontius Pilate did not want to be in charge of Jesus' death. He let a mob take Jesus away to be killed.

You can read about Pontius Pilate in Matthew 27:11-26.

Priscilla and Aquila

Priscilla and Aquila were tentmakers. Paul worked and lived with them while he was in Corinth.

You can read about Priscilla and Aquila in Acts 18:1-4,18–26.

Saul

See *Paul.*

Silas

Silas traveled with Paul and helped him on some of his trips to spread the good news of Jesus.

You can read about Silas in Acts 15:22,36-41.

Simeon

Simeon was a very old man who had waited a long time for Jesus to be born. When Jesus was brought to the temple as a baby, Simeon held him and praised God.

You can read about Simeon in Luke 2:25-35.

Simon

See *Peter*.

Simon

Simon was a man from the city of Cyrene in Africa. He was forced to carry Jesus' cross to Golgotha.

You can read about Simon in Matthew 27:32.

Simon

This Simon practiced magic in the city of Samaria. He tried to buy the ability to do miracles from Philip.

You can read about Simon in Acts 8:9-25.

Simon the Zealot

Simon the Zealot was one of the twelve disciples of Jesus.

You can read about Simon the Zealot in Luke 6:12-16.

Stephen

Stephen would not say he didn't believe in Jesus. He was the first believer to be killed for his faith in Jesus.

You can read about Stephen in Acts 7:54-60.

Tabitha

Tabith lived in Joppa. She helped the poor people. She died and was raised from death by Peter.

You can read about Tabitha in Acts 9:36-43.

Thaddaeus

Thaddaeus was one of Jesus' twelve disciples.

You can read about Thaddaeus in Mark 3:13-19.

Thomas

Thomas was a disciple of Jesus. He would not believe at first that Jesus had risen from the dead.

You can read about Thomas in John 20:24-29.

Timothy

Timothy was a young but experienced leader in the early church. He often went with the apostle Paul on trips.

You can read about Timothy in 1 and 2 Timothy.

Titus

Titus was a friend and helper of Paul.

You can read about Titus in the book of Titus.

Zacchaeus

Zacchaeus was a very short man. He climbed a tree in order to see Jesus in a crowd. Jesus stopped and spoke to him.

You can read about Zacchaeus in Luke 19:1-10.

Zechariah

Zechariah could not speak after he was told he was to be the father of John the Baptist.

You can read about Zechariah story in Luke 1:5-25.